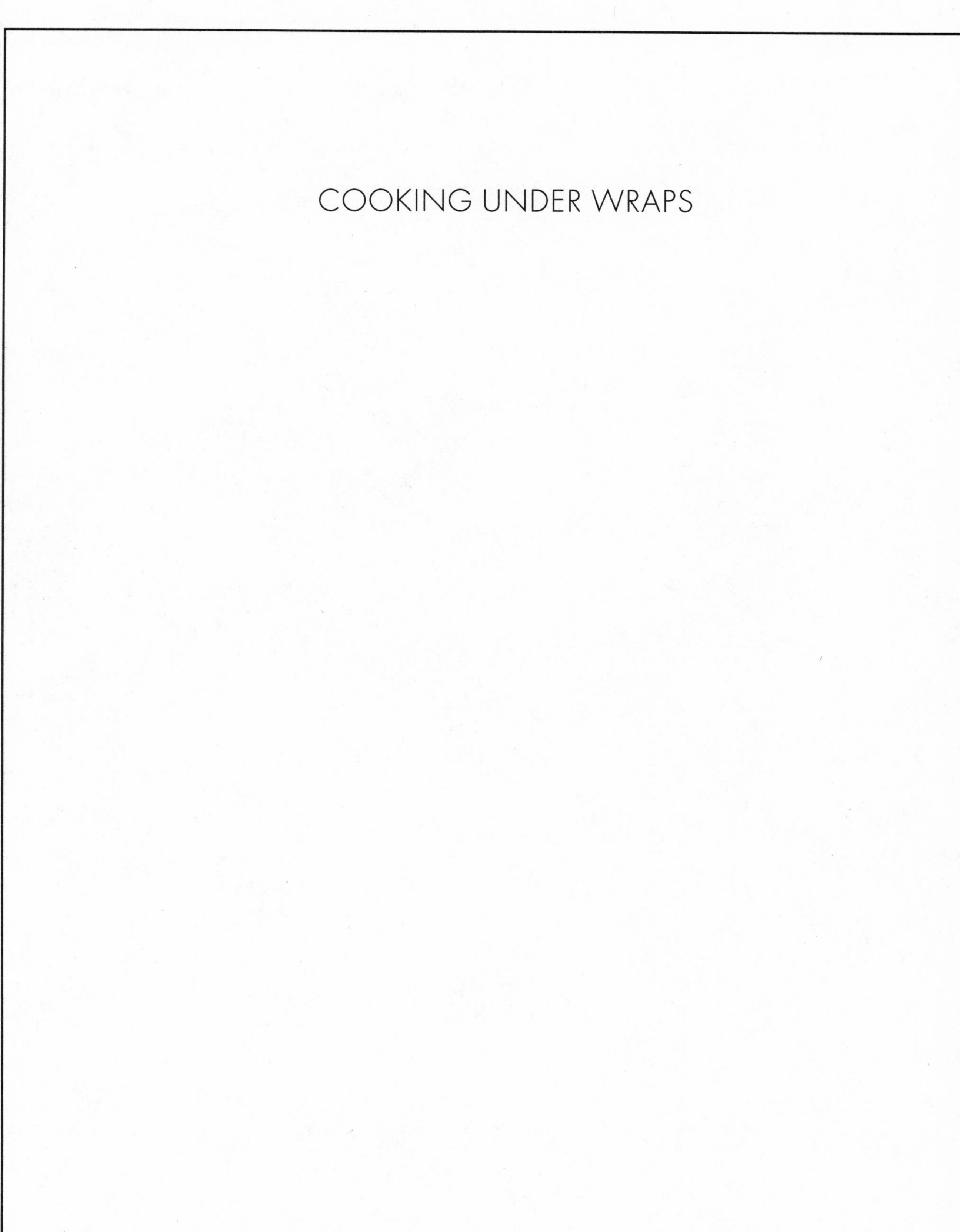
COOKING UNDER WRAPS

ALSO BY NICOLE ROUTHIER

The Foods of Vietnam
(1989)

COOKING
under wraps

NICOLE ROUTHIER

PHOTOGRAPHS BY MARTIN JACOBS

WILLIAM MORROW AND COMPANY, INC.
NEW YORK

It is the policy of William Morrow and Company, Inc., and its imprints and affiliates, recognizing the importance of preserving what has been written, to print the books we publish on acid-free paper, and we exert our best efforts to that end.

Library of Congress Cataloging-in-Publication Data

Routhier, Nicole.
Cooking under wraps / Nicole Routhier.
p. cm.
Includes index.
ISBN 0-688-10867-9
1. Cookery, International. I. Title.
TX725.A1R67 1993
641.59—dc20 92-26605
CIP

Printed in the United States of America

First Edition

1 2 3 4 5 6 7 8 9 10

BOOK DESIGN BY CHERYL CARRINGTON

This book is lovingly dedicated
to the memory of the best Jewish grandmother
a young Vietnamese girl ever had

PREFACE

I grew up in Southeast Asia, where eating food wrapped in noodles, rice paper, and lettuce was a common part of family meals. When we moved to Europe, many dishes struck a familiar note: French crêpes, German dumplings, Italian ravioli—all impressed me as Western versions of specialties I had grown up with.

Later, when we were all living in the international village of S.H.A.P.E. (Supreme Headquarters of Allied Powers in Europe) near Brussels, my mother and the other officers' wives took turns hosting potluck parties in their homes. Each of the women was encouraged to bring a dish representative of her ethnic background. As we dined on specialties like Mexican tacos, Korean beef dumplings (mandu), German potato dumplings (kartoffelnudeln), and Greek stuffed grape leaves (dolmades), we traded stories about our homelands. Through this culinary and cultural exchange, I discovered that wrapping foods is a universal practice. That was the beginning of my fascination with the variety of forms and flavors that wrapped foods can take.

My enduring passion for this style of cooking convinced me that it was a subject worthy of an entire book. The dishes that appear here include some of my earliest childhood favorites along with others that were discovered through my travels or that have been suggested by friends. Developing the recipes for this book and getting a sense of how wrapped foods are prepared and eaten in each part of the world has been an exciting way to educate my palate. I particularly enjoy finding the threads of continuity that link recipes or cooking techniques across different cultures.

As I explored the intricacies of the subject, I realized that volumes could be written on it. The aim of this book is not to provide an encyclopedic view of foods under wraps. Instead, in selecting the recipes for this book, I have chosen favorite dishes to show both the traditional ways wrapped foods are enjoyed in different cultures and how contemporary concepts can be borrowed to extend their appeal. Many recipes represent my experimentation with new combinations of ingredients and cooking techniques that range far beyond national and cultural frontiers. My hope is that, based on the examples in this book, you too will use your imagination to create new combinations. With wrapped foods, the possibilities are inexhaustible.

In America, there is an increasingly receptive audience willing to explore and experiment with the cuisines that are part of our international heritage. In that respect, this cookbook is a celebration and an homage to all the varied groups that make up the great melting pot of this country. I would like this book to endure as a reference as well as a collection of well-loved recipes. Most important of all, I hope that *Cooking Under Wraps* offers you, your family, and your friends as much pleasure as possible at the table.

Nicole Routhier
New York City

ACKNOWLEDGMENTS

In completing this book, I've been most fortunate to be associated with many talented and supportive people whose help was immeasurable.

I am sincerely grateful to Maria Guarnaschelli, my editor, whose acute editing and challenging comments made me work and think a little harder. She left no stone unturned and offered invaluable help and advice in making this book the best that it could be. Thank you, Maria, for your dedication.

I wish to thank the following people for their masterly team effort in the production and design of this book: Deborah Weiss Geline and Judith Sutton, copyeditors; Bob Aulicino, art director; Cheryl Carrington, book and jacket designer; Harvey Hoffman, Karen Lumley, and Nick Mazzella, production department; and Chas Edwards, Maria's able assistant.

Thanks, too, to Denise Landis and Maureen Haviland, whose enthusiastic testing and detailed comments contributed to ensuring the accuracy of my recipes.

I owe much to my friend and favorite photographer Martin Jacobs for skillfully translating my vision of cooking under wraps into inspiring, simply delicious pictures. The talented team that provided the framework for the pictures—Linda Johnson, prop-stylist, and William Smith, food-stylist—also greatly contributed to displaying the sensuality of the food. I must also thank Judy-Ann Milagrano for helping me in the kitchen.

My gratitude goes to Laura Hartman Maestro whose artful line drawings make the recipes' techniques easy to follow.

A heartfelt thanks to Judith Weber, my literary agent, and to Lisa and Lou Ekus, supportive friends and able publicists, for encouraging and advising me throughout this project. No friend or writer could be blessed with more.

I am indebted to Jean-George Vongerichten, Flo Braker, and Jessica Harris for graciously sharing their recipes.

My husband, Anthony Laudin, deserves special praise for introducing me to the world of computers, for his willingness to taste just about anything, for his fine critical comments, and for all his invaluable help and support. In addition, I'm very proud to acknowledge his talented work in photographing the technical steps, which served as the base for the illustrator's line drawings in this book.

CONTENTS

INTRODUCTION

Now that nouvelle cuisine is outmoded, more and more cooks are reacquainting themselves with informal and homey foods. This return to basics derives from a growing interest in fundamental techniques and tastes. As part of this transition, the traditional art of encasing food in wrappers such as noodles, edible leaves, vegetables, or pastry doughs is enjoying a big surge in popularity.

Most cultures include wrapped food in their culinary repertoires. A simple pancake folded around a filling can become a Norwegian lefse, Russian blintz, French crêpe, Mexican burrito, or Chinese mu-shu. Vegetable wrappers can range from Mediterranean stuffed grape leaves to Eastern European stuffed cabbage to Japanese rolled seaweed. Because of this universality, international foods such as sushi, spring rolls, calzones, dumplings, and strudels have become favorites all over America. The reason for their popularity is obvious. They are easy-to-eat, fun foods that combine the pleasure of eating something with your hands with the surprise of what is hidden inside the wrapper. The delight in eating wrapped foods is also often undeniably tied to their unique, sensuous shapes: round buns, cylindrical tubes, puffy pillows, or half-moon pockets.

This style of food preparation surely originated in ancient times as a practical way to cook and serve food in the same container. At some time after the first deliberate use of fire, cooking was discovered. Archaeologists suggest that roasting over a spit must have been the first method used, before pottery was developed. They also believe that the practice of spit-roasting taught hungry hunters in the Neolithic era that cut-up meat cooks faster than one whole piece. Since small pieces of meat could not be cooked directly on a fire, primitive people may have used large leaves to wrap up the morsels, thus creating a natural container in which to cook, with the leaves acting as a protection from the flames.

Research shows that as early as 4000 B.C., and possibly earlier, pit cooking was practiced in New Guinea, the Ukraine, and some parts of the Near East. Anthropologists believe that pit cooking was developed so that large amounts of foods could be cooked at one time, to feed many members of a tribe. A makeshift oven was dug in the ground and lined with a bed of hot stones or burning embers. Various types of foods, such as fish, beans, corn, and starchy roots, were wrapped in banana leaves, corn husks, or other leaves indigenous to an area. The wrapped foods were placed in the pit and then covered with another layer of hot stones. The intense heat from the rocks caused the moisture in the leaves to steam the foods inside. This special "wet" cooking method assured even, thorough cooking and yielded moist and flavorful foods.

Archaeology has traced the origins of bread to a doughy paste made with ground grains and water. Prehistoric man originally gathered and ate wild grains as he found them. Later, however, he began to grind the grains and mix them with water. By heating the dough on stones in open fires, he learned to make a flat cake. The grainy paste could easily be carried, either ready-mixed or requiring only the addition of a little water. Thus, flatbreads may have been the first convenience food in history. As a good case in point, the Bible tells us that the Israelites carried unleavened dough with them in their hasty departure from Egypt.

It is easy to imagine that these early breads may also have served as wrappers around stewlike concoctions or pieces of cooked meats. Today's Mexican tortilla and Indian chapati, the Chinese po ping, and the American pancake are all direct descendants of those early unleavened flatbreads.

The Egyptians became the world's first master bakers. Breads remained unleavened until about 2000 B.C. The delicious discovery of leavened bread probably occurred by accident in the Nile Valley when some yeasty microorganism drifted into a batch of unattended fresh dough and a perceptive baker noticed the slow-rising phenomenon. Mystified, he may have watched it for hours until it stopped increasing in size and then popped it into that recently invented gadget, an oven. What emerged after baking was a lighter and tastier bread than ever before.

The Egyptians also found that kneading the dough results in a fluffier bread and that enriching the dough with herbs, honey, eggs, or oils enhances flavor and texture. Hieroglyphics, and even preserved loaves, have been found in the tombs of the pharoahs that show that the dough was often molded into intricate shapes before baking. Ever since, bakers around the world have continued to develop a never-ending variety of breads and cakes as well as new doughs, such as phyllo, brioche, and puff pastry. Simultaneously, over the course of time dough wrappers evolved as containers to transform food into portable meals—turnovers, pies, stuffed buns, and sandwiches.

One of Asia's major contributions to the culinary world was the noodle. It is thought that as early as 1500 B.C. noodles were already a staple food in China. By 100 B.C., trade caravans had spread their use, so that broad noodles were a regular part of the diet in Asia, ancient Rome, Greece, and Persia. By the thirteenth century, even before Marco Polo's expeditions, noodles were a staple in parts of Italy, the Middle East, and North Africa.

In the seventh century, fried and steamed dumplings of meat encased in noodle dough were popular street snacks in China and Japan. These and other sophisticated noodle dishes were an important part of Asian cuisine. The Mongols and Tartars who swept across Asia into Europe may have helped introduce or popularize them in Eastern Europe, Russia, and Italy. Today, of course, Italian cuisine is famous for savory fillings wrapped in dough, as in cannelloni, ravioli, and tortellini.

In many ways, today's favorite wrapped dishes from around the world have ancient origins. However, while the traditional methods are still at the base, modern cooks are creating new favorites by using updated ingredients and techniques to broaden the range of flavors and textures. In contemporary cooking, a vast range of imaginative ingredients can be used to provide tasty receptacles for savory or sweet fillings. For example, the use of leaves as containers has led to dishes wrapped in vegetables such as potatoes, zucchini, or eggplant. This practice was even elevated to cult status during the 1970s by advocates of nouvelle cuisine and cuisine minceur.

The recipes in this book include many traditional favorites from around the world. Showing how to make these favorites was only one of my goals. I also wanted to use dishes that people are familiar with as a starting point to explore how their tastes and techniques can be extended to create new dishes.

Deciding how to organize the book wasn't an easy task. The diversity of wrappers and the variety of techniques, shapes, and sizes of the different dishes made it difficult to follow a traditional approach, with separate sections for appetizers, main courses, and desserts or chapters for meat, fish, vegetables, and so forth. In the end, it seemed most natural to arrange the chapters based on the classification of the wrappers. Most important, this made it easier to provide a unified explanation of why certain doughs or other wrappers are related to each other, why they are unique, and how they work.

In your journey through the recipes in this book, I hope you will become as passionate about cooking under wraps as I am. As you discover the great variety among these treasured foods, the one similarity you are apt to find is that you like them all as I do. Along the way, I also hope that their mystery will be dispelled.

leaf and vegetable wrappers

Cooking foods wrapped in leaves and other vegetable products is one of the most ancient styles of food preparation. Early cooks must have discovered that a leaf wrapper has benefits other than just holding the food while in the fire: It provides moisture so the filling doesn't dry out during cooking, it makes a compact and colorful food package, and it enhances the food with a light, clean, and fresh taste. The added bonus with this style of cooking is that many of the wrappers can be eaten as well, something that obviously cannot be duplicated with aluminum foil or parchment paper.

Leaf and vegetable wrappers have many virtues for today's health-conscious diners. Naturally delicate, they are best suited for wrapping fish, seafood, and other items that cook quickly and that lend themselves to low-fat methods such as baking, steaming, simmering, and grilling. Also, since these wrappers contribute moisture and flavors to the dish, little extra fat or oil is needed.

Leaf wrappers are common in tropical and subtropical countries where corn and bananas play a prominent role in the people's diet. There are few foodstuffs that have as many uses as these two staples. Nothing is wasted, and even the leaves and husks make their way into food preparation.

The ubiquitous tamales of South America perhaps best represent this style of cooking. Tamales are savory or sweet preparations of corn dough filled with meat, seafood, or vegetables that are wrapped in corn husks or banana leaves and then steamed or simmered. Tamales are usually prepared in individual portions, but I find it easier and sometimes more appealing to make a single large dish, like Chicken Tamale Pie with Mole Sauce (page 36).

Southeast Asia produces its own version of the tamale. Rice dough filled with a sweet or savory filling is wrapped in banana, bamboo, or lotus leaves and steamed or grilled. Try Sweet Banana and Black Bean Pudding (page 39) for dessert and sample the intriguing tastes of this uncommonly delicious preparation. Traveling back across the Pacific, the filling and the wrapper may vary but the methods of preparation and cooking stay the same. Baked Bluefish, Hawaiian Style (page 30), in which the fish is cooked inside a ti leaf, is a perfect example.

The thing I love most about serving dishes like Lobster and Scallops Grilled in Corn Husks (page 32) is the feeling that a treasure hunt is about to begin when the package is presented at the table. As it is opened and the steaming aromas are released, curiosity and excitement are heightened, enhancing the pleasure of the dining experience.

Other edible leaves as well are commonly used as wrappers. Most people are undoubtedly familiar with foods presented in cabbage and grape leaves. A favorite in Eastern European cuisine, where it has developed quite an honorable status, is the cabbage roll, usually filled with ground meat. As a good example, I have included in this chapter the one traditional recipe I would not dare to improvise on, My Grandmother's Stuffed Cabbage Rolls (page 20).

Stuffed grape leaves are a culinary standard in Mediterranean cooking. The most famous are Greek dolmades, made with a meat or rice filling and simmered until tender. I think grape leaves are too good and too versatile to be limited to one kind of preparation. You can wrap them around a fillet of fish, as in Red Snapper Fillets in Grape Leaves (page 10), thin slices of meat, as in Beef Grilled in Grape Leaves, Vietnamese Style (page 8), or even pieces of cheese. When grilled, grape leaves become interestingly crackly and flavorful.

Asian people have long had a passion for wrapping one thing inside another and then eating it out of hand. A fresh lettuce leaf is frequently used as the outer wrapper, as in Sweet Potato Shrimp Cakes in Lettuce Cups (page 14). Anyone who has eaten rolled sushi will be familiar with the paper-thin sheets of dried seaweed called *nori*. A marine vegetable, nori is a unique wrapper used in many Japanese-style dishes to impart a fresh, saline taste to food. Shrimp Beignets in Seaweed (page 22) is one delicious example.

Ever since the introduction of "nouvelle cuisine," vegetable leaves such as lettuce, spinach, and Swiss chard have become the undisputed wrappers of choice to replace traditional items like bacon and caul fat, because of their nonfat qualities. In the process of experimentation, many firm vegetables as well, like eggplant, potatoes, and zucchini, have been transformed into wrappers by slicing them into paper-thin sheets. Oysters and Black Bean Lettuce Bundles (page 12) and Crisp Potato Ravioli (page 26) exemplify this style of creative cooking.

I can't possibly include all the glorious ways to use leaf and vegetable wrappers, but I do hope the recipes in this chapter will inspire you to experiment on your own.

HOW TO USE LEAF WRAPPERS

BANANA LEAVES In traditional Asian and Latin American cooking, fresh banana leaves are used as containers and as a wrap for food to be steamed, boiled, or grilled. The smell of steamed banana leaves is sweet and food cooked inside takes on a light, fragrant taste. It is traditional to serve the food in the leaf, but the leaf is not eaten. Frozen banana leaves are available in one-pound packages in Asian and Latin American markets all year round. The leaves, which are about three feet long, have been cut in half lengthwise and the central rib removed. To use, soak the folded stack of frozen leaves in hot water until they are thawed and can be easily separated without tearing. Using scissors, cut the leaves to the required size. Gently wipe the leaves with a damp cloth, being careful to go in the same direction as the veins to avoid tearing. Wrap any leftover leaves and refreeze.

CORN HUSKS To use fresh corn husks when they are in season, carefully remove the husks by cutting through them with a sharp knife at the point where the husks are attached to the cob. Gently peel off the husks one at a time, selecting the larger, more perfect ones for wrappers. To store, layer the leaves in stacks of ten. Roll up each stack loosely, seal in a storage bag, and freeze for up to six months. To use, run the rolls of husks under warm water until they are thawed and can be easily separated without tearing. Any leftover husks can be refrozen.

Dried corn husks (*hojas de maiz*), taken from large ears of field corn, are traditionally used to prepare tamales. Nearly all Mexican groceries and some South American markets carry them in eight-ounce or one-pound packages. An excellent brand is Mojave, imported from Mexico. Choose the widest and longest husks and make sure they are not bug-eaten or ripped.

To dry your own corn husks, place fresh husks on paper in direct sunlight and let them dry naturally over a period of several days until they become creamy yellow, stiff, and brittle. Carefully wrap the dried husks in a plastic bag and store in a dark, dry place for up to a year.

To use dried corn husks, soak them in boiling water for about thirty minutes. Carefully transfer the husks to a colander to drain and pat them dry with a cloth or paper towel.

DRIED SEAWEED SHEETS (NORI) *Nori* is a generic Japanese term for marine algae. It also refers to the paper-thin square sheets of pressed dried algae (Asakusa nori) that are essential for wrapping sushi and many other Japanese specialties. When purchasing nori, choose the variety labeled "yaki-nori," which is Asakusa nori that has been pretoasted. They come ten sheets to a package and are available in Asian markets, some supermarkets, and most health food stores. After opening, wrap the unused sheets in an airtight plastic bag along with the moisture-absorbing granules with which they were originally packed. Stored in a cool, dry spot, they will keep for up to a year. To use, work with only one sheet at a time. Keep the package of the remaining sheets covered with a damp kitchen towel while you work to prevent them from curling. Moisten each nori sheet by dabbing it with a wet cloth or sponge to make it pliable before wrapping the food.

GRAPE LEAVES If you are lucky enough to have access to fresh grape leaves, use them by all means. The best time to pick them is during the month of June, when grape leaves are at their most tender.

Select young, tender grape leaves from the ends of the vines. Trim the stems and wash the leaves thoroughly in cold water. Then bring a large pot of salted water to a boil, add the leaves in batches, and blanch them for about three minutes. Use a slotted spoon to remove them from the pot and place them in a large bowl of cold water. When all the leaves have been blanched, drain them well, then proceed with the recipe.

To store blanched grape leaves, layer the leaves, dull side up, in stacks of about twenty. Place each stack on a sheet of plastic wrap and roll the leaves and plastic wrap into a cylinder, squeezing out any excess water as you proceed. Place the rolls in a plastic bag and freeze for up to several months. To use, place the rolls in warm water until the leaves are thawed and can be easily separated without tearing. Leftover grape leaves can be refrozen.

For those of us who are less fortunate, there are bottled or canned grape leaves in brine. They can be purchased in sixteen-ounce jars in Middle Eastern markets and many supermarkets. Each jar contains about forty to fifty leaves. Two excellent brands are Krinos, imported from Greece, and Orlando, from California.

Since the leaves are packed very tightly, remove them very carefully from the jar to prevent tearing. Once opened, store the leaves in the same jar or any other nonmetal container with their original brine, and they will keep in the refrigerator indefinitely. Before using, be sure to soak the leaves for at least thirty minutes in cold water and then rinse them well to remove the briny taste.

TIPS ON LEAF AND VEGETABLE WRAPPERS

- Fresh leafy vegetables such as spinach, Swiss chard, and lettuce should be washed several times in cold water to remove all traces of dirt and sand. Remove the greens from the water, rather than the water from the greens. This allows the grit and dirt to settle to the bottom of the sink or container, not back onto the greens.
- To retain the bright green color of vegetable leaves, blanch them very briefly in boiling salted water, then quickly remove them to a bowl of ice water to instantly stop the cooking process. (This technique is called "shocking.") Blanching makes the leaves more pliable for wrapping around pieces of food. Do not overcook the leaves, which would destroy their flavor and cause them to have a yellowish, unappetizing appearance.
- To remove the outer leaves from a head of cabbage, first core the cabbage, then boil the whole cabbage head for about five minutes. As the outer leaves become limp, use a fork to remove them one by one, being careful not to tear them.
- Wrapping food individually in single leaves can be time-consuming, but if you get organized, it won't take too long. Before you assemble the dish, have the filling ready and a large surface to work on. To assemble, lay out as many

leaves as will fit on the countertop, with the wider sides of the leaves toward you. Place some filling toward the wide end of each leaf, fold over the sides, and then roll up. Place the stuffed leaves seam side down on a baking pan. Repeat until all of the leaves are used.

- Grape leaves wrapped around small pieces of cheese such as goat cheese, Fontina, Jack, or smoked mozzarella and grilled make excellent hors d'oeuvres.

— *planning ahead* —

The cooked dolmades can be prepared up to 3 days ahead. Let them cool completely, then cover and refrigerate. Let come to room temperature or reheat before serving.

Vegetarian Grape Leaves, Mediterranean Style

Grape leaves are widely used throughout the Middle East as food wrappers. In Greece, grape leaves stuffed with ground beef or lamb and dill-flavored rice are called dolmades and are served with an egg and lemon sauce called avgolemono. The Turkish version of the dish usually contains rice, a bit of meat, and some raisins and nuts. The Lebanese flavor the filling with mint and serve the stuffed leaves with a yogurt dip.

This recipe contains a little bit of everything except meat. After the dolmades are assembled, they are simmered in a lemon-flavored broth, which gives them a delightful tang. Serve these piquant rolls at room temperature as hors d'oeuvres or warm with Avgolemono Sauce (page 71) as a first course.

YIELD: 20 dolmades for hors d'oeuvres, or enough for 4 to 5 first-course servings

HERBED RICE FILLING

2 tablespoons olive oil
1 medium onion, finely chopped
1 tablespoon minced garlic
½ cup long-grain rice
2 tablespoons pine nuts, toasted (see Cook's Notes)
¼ cup chopped fresh dill
¼ cup chopped fresh mint leaves
½ teaspoon salt
⅓ cup chicken broth, homemade (page 368) or store-bought
Freshly ground black pepper to taste

20 large grape leaves, rinsed well and patted dry
1 tablespoon fresh lemon juice
¼ cup olive oil
1¼ cups chicken broth, homemade (page 368) or store-bought

PREPARE THE FILLING: Heat the olive oil in a skillet over moderately low heat. Add the onion and garlic and cook until soft, about 2 minutes. Add the rice and cook, stirring, for 1 minute. Add the pine nuts, herbs, salt, and the broth. Cook, stirring frequently, until the liquid is absorbed, about 3 minutes. Season with black pepper. Remove the pan from the heat and allow to cool. (The rice will only be partially cooked; it will be cooked to completion in subsequent steps.)

ASSEMBLE THE DOLMADES: Snip off the stems from the grape leaves. Place the leaves smooth side down on a flat surface with the stem ends toward you. Place 1 scant tablespoon of the filling near the stem end of each leaf. Fold the sides of the leaf over the filling, then fold over the bottom of the leaf and roll up (not too tightly) to make a neat, compact package.

COOK THE DOLMADES: In a pan or skillet just large enough to hold the dolmades in a single layer, arrange the rolls seam side down and close together. Combine the lemon juice, olive oil, and broth in a small bowl. Pour the liquid over the dolmades. If necessary, add a little water so that the rolls are just barely covered with liquid. Put a plate, upside down, over the dolmades to keep them from coming apart. Place the pan over high heat and bring to a boil. Reduce the heat to low, cover the pan, and simmer until the dolmades are very tender when pierced with a fork, about 30 minutes. Remove the pan from the heat, uncover, and allow to cool.

Serve the dolmades warm or at room temperature.

— *cook's notes* —

You may substitute slivered almonds for the pine nuts.

To toast pine nuts or slivered almonds, spread them out in a pie pan and toast in a preheated 350°F oven until golden brown, about 6 to 8 minutes.

To reheat the dolmades, arrange them in a single layer in a baking pan. Add enough water to cover the bottom of the pan and cover the pan with foil. Place in a preheated 350°F oven and bake until the dolmades are heated through, about 15 to 20 minutes.

— *planning ahead* —

Both the assembled rolls and the dipping sauce can be prepared a day ahead, covered, and refrigerated. Bring to room temperature before cooking and serving.

The bamboo skewers must be soaked in water for 30 minutes before use.

Beef Grilled in Grape Leaves, Viëtnamese Style

This recipe for grilled beef in grape leaves is an updated version of a Vietnamese favorite called Bo La Lot. La lot, or Piper lolot, is an Asian aromatic with large, shiny, heart-shaped leaves that bear a striking resemblance to grape leaves. The leaves are usually wrapped around slices of marinated beef or ground meat mixtures. The popularity of this dish is sometimes attributed to the presence of a mild narcotic in the leaves. Fortunately, the pleasures of eating Bo La Lot are not diminished by substituting grape leaves for this rare plant. These grilled little bundles are fabulous and still addictive when served with a spicy sweet-and-sour dipping sauce.

YIELD: 20 rolls, enough for 4 first-course servings

SPECIAL EQUIPMENT: 4 presoaked bamboo skewers

DIPPING SAUCE

¼ cup rice vinegar
¼ cup fish sauce (see Cook's Notes)
¼ cup hot water
2 tablespoons sugar
2 tablespoons fresh lime juice
1 teaspoon minced garlic
2 small fresh hot red chiles (such as jalapeño or serrano), seeded and chopped

SCALLION OIL

¼ cup peanut oil
2 scallions, finely sliced

GRILLED BEEF FILLING

1 pound rump roast or beef sirloin (in 1 piece)
2 tablespoons minced garlic
2 tablespoons light soy sauce
2 teaspoons five-spice powder (page 9)
1 teaspoon sugar
¼ cup peanut oil
¼ cup unsalted dry-roasted peanuts, coarsely ground
Freshly ground black pepper to taste

20 large grape leaves, rinsed well and patted dry

PREPARE THE DIPPING SAUCE: Combine all the sauce ingredients in a blender or food processor and purée. Pour the sauce into a small bowl, cover, and set aside.

PREPARE THE SCALLION OIL: Place the oil in a small saucepan over moderately high heat. Heat until the oil is hot but not smoking, about 300°F. Remove the pan from the heat and add the sliced scallions. Let steep at room temperature until the oil is completely cool.

PREPARE THE FILLING: Cut the beef crosswise against the grain into thin 2- by 1-inch slices. Combine the garlic, soy sauce, five-spice powder, sugar, oil, ground nuts, and pepper in a small mixing bowl. Add the meat and mix with your hands until the meat slices are well coated with the spices. Cover and let sit at room temperature for about 30 minutes to allow the flavors to meld.

ASSEMBLE THE STUFFED GRAPE LEAVES: Snip off the stems from the grape leaves. Place the leaves smooth side down on a flat surface with the stem ends toward you. Place 5 or 6 pieces of meat near the stem end of each leaf. Fold the sides of the leaf over the meat, then fold over the bottom of the leaf and roll up to make a neat, compact package.

Prepare a moderately hot fire in a charcoal grill, or preheat the broiler.

Thread 5 rolls onto each skewer. Brush both sides of the rolls with the scallion oil. Reserve the remaining oil.

Grill or broil the rolls until the leaves are crisp and brown, about 5 to 6 minutes, turning the rolls occasionally.

TO SERVE: Unskewer the beef rolls onto dinner plates. Drizzle some scallion oil over the rolls and pass the dipping sauce on the side.

Chinese five-spice powder is a fragrant and powerful mixture of spices for poultry, fish, and meat. If you cannot locate it in a specialty or Asian food shop, you can make it from scratch.

CHINESE FIVE-SPICE POWDER

2 teaspoons Szechuan peppercorns
2 tablespoons fennel seeds
2 tablespoons aniseed
2 star anise
1 1-inch cinnamon stick
½ teaspoon whole cloves

Grind the spices to a very fine powder in a spice grinder or blender. Sift through a fine-meshed sieve. (There should be about 2 tablespoons.) Store the mix in an airtight jar. It will keep for weeks at room temperature. Use it only sparingly; a little goes a long way.

cook's notes

When buying fish sauce, look for the Squid or Tiparos brand. Once opened, fish sauce lasts, covered, up to a year at room temperature. Fish sauce is available in Asian markets and in some well-stocked supermarkets.

You can serve these beef rolls as hors d'oeuvres. Wrap only 2 or 3 slices of beef in each grape leaf and grill the rolls for 3 to 4 minutes.

Slices of squab meat or chicken breast can replace the beef.

— planning ahead —

The wrapped fillets can be prepared up to 4 hours ahead, covered, and refrigerated.

Red Snapper Fillets Grilled in Grape Leaves

The grape leaf wrapping in this dish keeps the fish succulent and adds flavor, creating a clean, pure taste. It tastes even better grilled over charcoal. For a complete meal, throw chunks of vegetables such as bell pepper, squash, onion, and eggplant on the grill while you grill the fish. For a simpler meal, season individual fillets with salt and pepper to taste, wrap in grape leaves, and grill. Serve with Tomato Sauce (page 66).

YIELD: 4 main-course servings

MARINADE

¼ cup olive oil
2 tablespoons fresh lime juice
½ teaspoon salt
Freshly ground black pepper to taste

4 4-ounce skinless fillets of red snapper

HERB AND BREAD CRUMB TOPPING

2 tablespoons finely chopped fresh parsley
2 tablespoons finely chopped fresh thyme leaves
¼ cup dried bread crumbs
¼ cup minced shallots
1 tablespoon minced garlic

20 large grape leaves, rinsed well and patted dry
Olive oil, for brushing
4 lime wedges, for garnish

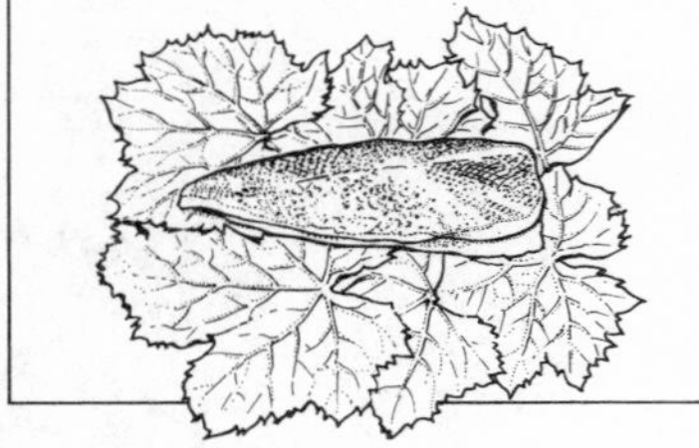

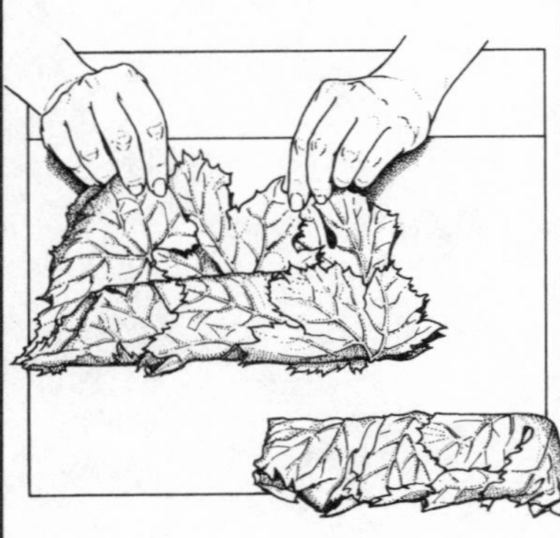

PREPARE THE MARINADE: Combine all the marinade ingredients in a small bowl.

Place the fish in a shallow dish and rub some of the marinade over both sides of the fish fillets. Set the fillets aside and reserve the remaining marinade.

PREPARE THE TOPPING: Add the parsley, thyme, bread crumbs, shallots, and garlic to the reserved marinade and mix with a wooden spoon to combine.

Cover 2 of the fillets with the herb topping. Pat the mixture in place with your hand to make the topping adhere to the fish. Place the remaining 2 fillets on top of the first 2 to form two pairs.

Prepare a moderately hot fire in a grill or preheat the broiler.

WRAP THE FILLETS: Snip off the stems from the grape leaves. On a work surface, overlap 10 of the grape leaves, smooth side down, to form a rectangular sheet of about 9 by 15 inches, or large enough to envelop a fillet pair. Place one pair lengthwise down the center of the sheet and fold the four sides over to completely enclose the fish. There is no need to tie the wrapped fillets with string; the leaves adhere to themselves naturally. Wrap the second fillet pair in the same fashion.

COOK THE FILLETS: Lightly brush the wrapped fillets with olive oil. Grill or broil until the leaves are crisp and brown, about 6 minutes. Don't worry if the leaves burn a little; they will still taste delicious. Use a wide metal spatula to turn the fillets over and continue to cook for 6 minutes longer. To check for doneness, make a small slit through the fish with a paring knife. When properly cooked, the fish should be flaky and look opaque. If the fish is still slightly undercooked, continue grilling or broiling for 1 minute longer on each side.

TO SERVE: Cut each bundle in half on the diagonal and place on four warm dinner plates. Garnish with the lime wedges.

VARIATION

BACON-WRAPPED FILLETS OF FISH: On a work surface, overlap 5 thin strips of bacon to form a sheet, with a short edge near you. Position one fillet pair diagonally across the center of the bacon sheet. Fold the sides of the bacon sheet over to completely enclose the fish. Tuck the excess bacon under the fish. Transfer to a baking sheet, seam side down. Wrap the second pair of fillets with 5 more strips of bacon and cook as instructed above.

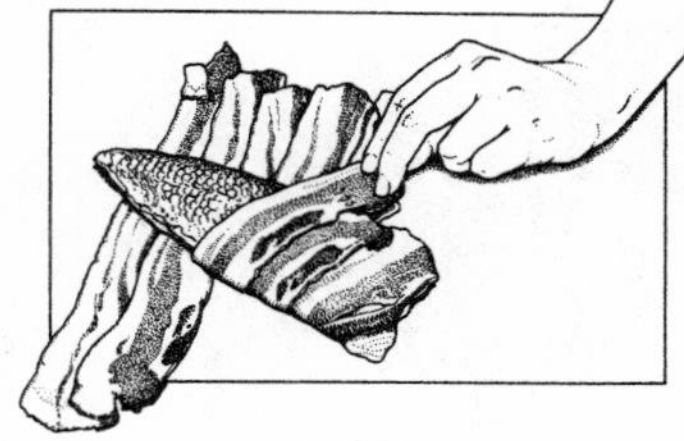

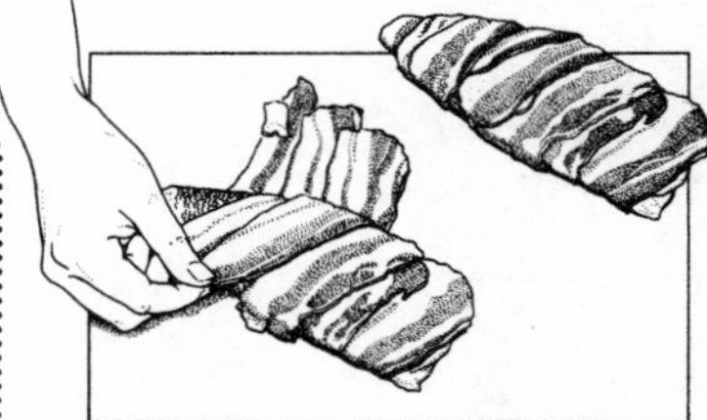

— *planning ahead* —

Both the dressing and the oyster bundles can be prepared up to 4 hours in advance, covered, and

Oysters and Black Bean Lettuce Bundles

This dish proves that good things come in small packages. It's a beautiful, simple, and very refreshing appetizer that is well suited for hot weather dining. Tender lettuce leaves are filled with cider-poached oysters that have been marinated in a mixture of vinegar, herbs, fermented black beans, and tomatoes. The little bundles look both lovely and intriguing on the plate, and when popped into the mouth, they melt away.

YIELD: 12 bundles for hors d'oeuvres, or enough for 4 appetizer servings

BLACK BEAN DRESSING

1 tablespoon plus 1 teaspoon red wine vinegar
2 teaspoons apple cider
2 tablespoons fermented black beans, rinsed well, drained, and coarsely chopped (see Cook's Notes)
1 tablespoon minced shallots
½ teaspoon finely grated fresh ginger
2 teaspoons minced garlic
⅓ cup olive oil
½ cup finely diced freshly tomatoes
2 tablespoons chopped fresh coriander leaves

1 cup apple cider
12 shucked oysters, drained
Salt and freshly ground black pepper to taste

12 Boston lettuce leaves (use the tender inner leaves)
12 fresh chives

PREPARE THE DRESSING: In a small mixing bowl, combine all of the dressing ingredients. Mix well with a wooden spoon, cover, and set aside.

POACH THE OYSTERS: Bring the cider to a boil in a small saucepan, then immediately remove from the heat. Add the oysters, cover, and let them steep until the cider cools to room temperature.

Drain the oysters and discard the poaching liquid. Pat the oysters dry with paper towels and add them to the dressing. Gently mix with a wooden spoon to combine, and season with salt and pepper. Cover and let marinate in the refrigerator for at least 30 minutes.

Meanwhile, BLANCH THE LETTUCE LEAVES: Place a bowl of ice water next to the sink. Bring 3 quarts of salted water to a boil in a large pot over high heat. Carefully add the lettuce leaves, pushing them down into the water with a slotted spoon, and cook until just wilted, about 5 seconds. Carefully drain the leaves in a colander set in the sink, then transfer them to the bowl of cold water. Let them soak until they are bright green and cold, about 5 minutes. Remove the leaves and drain them on kitchen towels. Pat them dry. With a small sharp knife, pare down the stems on the outer sides until they are as thin as the leaves.

ASSEMBLE THE BUNDLES: Place an oyster along with about 1 teaspoon of the dressing in the center of a lettuce leaf. Fold the sides of the leaf up and over the filling to form a little bundle. Tie the bundle, using a whole chive as string. Wrap the remaining oysters in the same fashion.

Place the wrapped oysters on a platter, cover with plastic wrap, and refrigerate until ready to serve. Reserve the remaining dressing.

TO SERVE: Spoon some of the reserved dressing onto chilled appetizer plates and place 3 oyster bundles on each plate. Or pass the bundles around as hors d'oeuvres, along with the marinade for dipping.

— cook's notes —

Fermented black beans, which are whole soy beans preserved in salt and ginger, are often used in Chinese stir-fries and braised dishes. They are sold in plastic bags at Asian markets.

When in season, small Swiss chard leaves or beet leaves may be blanched and used instead of lettuce.

If fresh chives are not available, substitute blanched scallion leaves.

— planning ahead —

The cakes can be made a day ahead, cooled, covered, and refrigerated (see Cook's Notes). The dipping sauce can be prepared a day ahead and refrigerated. Bring to room temperature before serving. The lettuce cups can be washed, dried, stacked in order of size, and wrapped in a plastic bag, and refrigerated overnight.

Sweet Potato Shrimp Cakes in Lettuce Cups

These tempting Vietnamese shrimp and potato cakes are full of contrast. Wrapped up with mint in chilled, bright green lettuce leaves and dipped into a spicy, sweet, and tangy sauce, they become irresistible. Cool and hot, sweet and spicy, crisp and tender, all these elements coalesce in this truly special appetizer. This is an excellent dish for a potluck party.

YIELD: 16 cakes, enough for 4 to 5 first-course servings

DIPPING SAUCE

¼ cup rice vinegar
¼ cup fish sauce (see Cook's Notes)
¼ cup hot water
2 tablespoons sugar
2 tablespoons fresh lime juice
1 teaspoon minced garlic
2 small fresh hot red chiles (such as jalapeño or serrano), seeded and chopped
½ cup finely shredded carrot

16 perfect lettuce leaves, preferably Boston (use the tender inner leaves)
1 bunch of fresh mint

SHRIMP AND SWEET POTATO CAKES

1 sweet potato (about ½ pound), peeled
½ teaspoon salt
8 raw medium shrimp (about ¼ pound)
¼ cup cornstarch
2 large eggs, lightly beaten
1 scallion, chopped
1 small onion, minced (about ¼ cup)
½ teaspoon minced garlic
2 teaspoons fish sauce
1 teaspoon sugar
2 teaspoons curry powder, preferably Madras brand
Freshly ground black pepper to taste

⅔ cup vegetable oil, for frying

PREPARE THE DIPPING SAUCE: Combine all the sauce ingredients except the shredded carrot in a blender or food processor and purée. Pour the sauce into a small bowl. Stir in the shredded carrot, cover, and set aside.

PREPARE THE LETTUCE CUPS AND MINT: Wash the lettuce leaves in cold water and pat them dry. Stack the lettuce cups in order of size so they fit into each other and wrap them with damp paper towels. Snip off the stems from the mint, wash the leaves, and pat them dry. Seal the lettuce and mint in plastic bags and refrigerate.

PREPARE THE SWEET POTATO: In a food processor fitted with a medium shredding disk, shred the sweet potato. Place it in a colander set in the sink, sprinkle on the salt, and mix well with your hands. Let the potato stand until it is very soft and wet, about 15 minutes.

Meanwhile, PREPARE THE SHRIMP: Shell and devein the shrimp, then cut them into ½-inch pieces. Using the back of a chef's knife or cleaver, mash the shrimp, but do not reduce to a paste; you should have some chunky bits remaining. Place the shrimp in a medium mixing bowl.

Squeeze the sweet potato dry with your hands and add it to the shrimp. Add the cornstarch and mix well with a wooden spoon. Add the remaining pancake ingredients, and mix well to combine. The mixture should just hold together.

Preheat the oven to 250°F.

COOK THE SHRIMP AND POTATO CAKES: Divide the oil between two 9-inch skillets set over moderate heat. Cook only 4 or 5 cakes at a time in each pan; do not crowd the pans or the cakes will steam rather than fry. Drop the potato and shrimp mixture by tablespoonfuls into the hot oil. Press down with the back of a spoon to form cakes about 2½ inches in diameter. The cakes should not be too thick. Cook until they are crisp and golden brown on the bottom, about 1½ minutes. Turn the cakes with tongs and cook on the other side until brown and crispy, about 1½ minutes. If the cakes begin to brown too fast, lower the heat so they cook through without burning. Remove the cakes to paper towels to drain. Keep them warm in the oven while you fry the remaining cakes.

TO SERVE: Arrange the cakes on a warm platter. Arrange the lettuce and mint on a platter. Divide the dipping sauce among small saucers or bowls. Invite each guest to place a cake on a lettuce leaf, then add a few sprigs of mint and some shredded carrot from the sauce. Wrap the lettuce around the filling to form a bundle and dip into the sauce before eating out of hand.

cook's notes

When buying fish sauce, look for the Squid or Tiparos brand. Once opened, fish sauce lasts up to a year at room temperature. Fish sauce is available in Asian markets and in some well-stocked supermarkets.

If the cakes have been refrigerated, reheat them in a 350°F oven until they are heated through, about 10 to 15 minutes.

If extra crunch is desired, use well-chilled iceberg lettuce leaves taken from near the heart.

— *planning ahead* —

The sauce can be prepared a day ahead, covered, and refrigerated. The wrapped fillets can be prepared up to 4 hours ahead, covered, and refrigerated. Bring them to room temperature before cooking.

Stuffed Fillet of Sea Bass Roasted in Swiss Chard

When Swiss chard is in season, from early summer until Thanksgiving, I like to wrap the bright red and green leaves with their delicious sweet, beetlike taste around fillets of fish. (I save the stems for sautéing or adding to soups.) In this particular dish, a crabmeat filling is sandwiched between two fillets of sea bass and wrapped in Swiss chard leaves. The wrapped fillets are quickly seared in a skillet and then transferred to the oven to roast. A simple and truly wonderful basil vinaigrette perfectly complements the subtle flavor of the fish.

Keep the accompaniments for this dish simple. Bread and green salad are perfect.

YIELD: 4 main-course servings

BASIL VINAIGRETTE

¼ cup loosely packed fresh basil leaves
⅔ cup extra-virgin olive oil
2 tablespoons balsamic vinegar
1 tablespoon light soy sauce
¼ teaspoon sugar
2 tablespoons boiling water
Salt and freshly ground black pepper to taste

CRABMEAT FILLING

4 dried shiitake mushrooms (see Cook's Notes)
1 tablespoon olive oil
½ cup chopped shallots
8 ounces fresh lump crabmeat, well picked over
2 teaspoons minced garlic
2 tablespoons chopped fresh chives or scallions
Salt and freshly ground black pepper to taste

8 large Swiss chard leaves
4 6-ounce fillets of sea bass
Salt and freshly ground black pepper to taste
1 tablespoon olive oil

PREPARE THE BASIL VINAIGRETTE: Place the basil, olive oil, vinegar, soy sauce, and sugar in a blender, and process until puréed. With the motor on, add the boiling water, and process for 5 seconds. Season with salt and pepper to taste. Cover and set aside.

Place the dried mushrooms in a small bowl and cover with boiling water. Soak the mushrooms until softened, about 30 minutes. Drain, discarding the liquid, and squeeze the mushrooms dry. Cut off and discard the stems. Finely chop the caps and set aside.

MAKE THE FILLING: Heat 1 tablespoon of the oil in a skillet over moderately high heat. Add the shallots and sauté until soft, about 3 minutes. Add the crabmeat, garlic, and chopped mushrooms, and sauté until the garlic is fragrant and the crabmeat heated through, about 1 minute. Remove the pan from the heat. Add the chives and season with salt and pepper. Set aside to cool.

BLANCH THE SWISS CHARD: Place a bowl of ice water next to the sink. Bring 3 quarts of salted water to a boil in a large pot over high heat. Carefully add the chard leaves, pushing them down into the water with a slotted spoon, and cook until just wilted, about 5 seconds. Carefully drain the leaves in a colander set in the sink, then transfer them to the bowl of cold water. Let them soak until they are cold, about 5 minutes. Remove the leaves and drain them on clean kitchen towels. Pat them dry. With a small sharp knife, pare down the thick ribs on the back until they are as thin as the leaves. Set aside.

Preheat the oven to 400°F.

ASSEMBLE THE FILLETS: Season the fillets with salt and pepper. Cover 2 of the fillets with the filling. Pat the mixture in place to make it adhere to the fish. Place the remaining 2 fillets on top to form two pairs. Cut each fillet pair crosswise in half. Crisscross 2 of the Swiss chard leaves. Place a fillet pair half in the center of the leaves. Fold the four sides of the leaves over the fish to completely enclose it. Repeat with the remaining fish and chard to make 3 more packets.

COOK THE FILLETS: Heat the oil in a large ovenproof skillet set over high heat. Add the wrapped fillets and sear on each side for 30 seconds. Place the skillet in the oven and roast the fish for 12 to 15 minutes.

Transfer the roasted fillets to preheated dinner plates, drizzle on some basil vinaigrette, and serve at once.

— cook's notes —

Dried shiitake mushrooms, also known as Chinese black mushrooms, are available in many well-stocked supermarkets and in Asian markets. They can be also ordered by mail from American Spoon Foods, P.O. Box 566, Petoskey, MI 49770 (616-347-9030); or from Hans Johansson, 44 West 74th Street, New York, NY 10023 (212-787-6496).

If Swiss chard is unavailable, substitute blanched iceberg or romaine lettuce leaves.

The sea bass can be replaced by most any firm white-fleshed fish, such as pompano, porgies, striped bass, sole, sea trout, or coho.

— *planning ahead* —

The molded rice salads can be prepared a day ahead, covered, and refrigerated. Bring to room temperature before serving.

Molded Rice Salad Provençale

Whenever I prepare this dish, memories of my teen years in Provence come back to me. I vividly remember my mother whipping up a delicious and refreshing rice salad on hot summer days when she didn't feel like cooking. That salad was the basis for this dish. Cooked rice and corn are splashed with a mustard vinaigrette while they are still warm, ready to soak up the dressing's aroma. Artichoke hearts, tomatoes, olives, capers, anchovies, tuna fish, and fresh basil are tossed with the rice to add flavor and texture. For an elegant and colorful presentation, I enjoy packing the salad in a mold that has been lined with blanched Swiss chard leaves. The result is as good as any rice dish possibly can be.

YIELD: 4 light lunch or dinner servings

SPECIAL EQUIPMENT: Four 8-ounce ramekins or soufflé dishes

MUSTARD DRESSING

2 teaspoons minced garlic
1 tablespoon Dijon mustard
2 tablespoons red wine vinegar
½ teaspoon sugar
¼ cup olive oil
¼ cup vegetable oil
Salt and freshly ground black pepper to taste

RICE SALAD

½ cup long-grain rice
½ cup fresh or frozen corn kernels
½ cup finely diced green bell pepper
½ cup coarsely chopped marinated artichoke hearts
1 cup finely diced fresh tomatoes
⅓ cup finely diced red onion
⅓ cup chopped black olives
2 tablespoons capers, drained
4 canned anchovy fillets, drained and coarsely chopped
1 6½-ounce can tuna packed in oil, drained
2 tablespoons chopped fresh chives or scallions
2 tablespoons chopped fresh parsley
¼ cup shredded fresh basil leaves

8 large Swiss chard leaves

MAKE THE DRESSING: Place the garlic, mustard, vinegar, and sugar in a medium bowl. Slowly whisk in the olive oil, then the vegetable oil until slightly thickened and emulsified. Season with salt and pepper. Cover and set aside.

MAKE THE RICE SALAD: Place the rice in a medium saucepan, add salted water to cover, and bring to a boil over high heat. Lower the heat to moderately high and gently boil for 10 minutes. Add the corn and cook until the rice is tender and the corn just cooked through, 3 to 4 more minutes. Drain the rice and corn in a fine-mesh sieve set in the sink, rinse under cold running water, and drain well. Transfer the rice and corn to a large bowl and add the remaining salad ingredients. Add ½ cup of the dressing and toss to mix. Cover and set aside. Reserve the remaining dressing.

BLANCH THE SWISS CHARD: Place a bowl of ice water next to the sink. Bring 3 quarts of salted water to a boil in a large pot over high heat. Carefully add the chard leaves, pushing them down into the water with a slotted spoon, and cook until just wilted, about 5 seconds. Carefully drain the leaves in a colander set in the sink, then transfer them to the bowl of cold water. Let them soak until they are cold, about 5 minutes. Remove the leaves and drain them on clean kitchen towels. Pat them dry. With a small sharp knife, pare down the thick ribs on the back until they are as thin as the leaves.

ASSEMBLE THE RICE SALADS: Crisscross 2 of the Swiss chard leaves across the bottom of each ramekin, with the ends extending over the sides of the mold. Fill each mold with 1 cup of the rice salad. Fold the overhanging leaves across the top to completely enclose the filling.

TO SERVE: Invert the ramekins onto chilled dinner plates to unmold the rice salads. Spoon some of the reserved dressing around each salad.

— *planning ahead* —

The tomato sauce may be prepared a day in advance. The cabbage rolls can be assembled up to 4 hours ahead, covered, and refrigerated.

The cooked stuffed cabbage will keep in the refrigerator for up to 3 days. In fact, this dish is even better when reheated and served the next day.

My Grandmother's Stuffed Cabbage Rolls

I have a weakness for stuffed cabbage. My husband's grandmother knew exactly how to turn this to her advantage. When she wanted me to visit her, she would make some and call me. This guaranteed my showing up at her apartment without any encouragement. What I like most about my grandmother's stuffed cabbage is the harmony of sweet raisins and brown sugar with a robust, slightly acidic, tomato sauce. To me, stuffed cabbage and grandmothers go together. They both are comforting in ways that cannot be easily described.

YIELD: 10 large cabbage rolls, enough for 5 main-course servings

TOMATO SAUCE

2 tablespoons light olive oil
1 cup chopped onions
2 teaspoons minced garlic
1 28-ounce can peeled tomatoes in juice
1 cup canned tomato sauce
⅓ cup packed brown sugar
Salt and freshly ground black pepper to taste

1 2-pound green cabbage

GROUND BEEF FILLING

1¼ pounds ground beef round
½ cup minced onion
1 teaspoon minced garlic
2 large eggs, lightly beaten
3 tablespoons ketchup
¼ cup chopped fresh dill
½ teaspoon salt
¼ teaspoon freshly ground black pepper
4 slices white bread, crusts removed

⅓ cup raisins
2 tablespoons fresh lemon juice
Salt and freshly ground black pepper to taste

PREPARE THE TOMATO SAUCE: Heat the oil in a 4-quart soup pot over moderately low heat. Add the onions and garlic and cook, stirring frequently with a wooden spoon, until soft and lightly browned, about 10 minutes. Break up the tomatoes with your hands and add them to the pot along with their juice, the canned tomato sauce, and the brown sugar. Season with salt and pepper and stir to blend. Reduce the heat to low, cover the pot, and simmer gently for about 45 minutes.

Meanwhile, PREPARE THE CABBAGE: Fill a large deep pot with 5 quarts of salted water and bring to a boil over moderately high heat. Cut the core out of the cabbage and discard. Place the cabbage, cored end up, in the boiling water and cook for about 5 to 6 minutes. As the large outer leaves become limp, use a fork to peel them off one by one, being careful not to tear them. Carefully drain the cabbage leaves and the heart in a colander set in the sink. Refresh under cold running water.

Choose the 10 best-shaped, largest leaves. Trim the ribs on the underside so that they are the same thickness as the leaves and can be easily bent. Finely shred the cabbage heart and any remaining leaves. You should have about 1 to 1½ cups; add the shredded cabbage to the tomato sauce.

PREPARE THE FILLING: Place the meat, onion, garlic, eggs, ketchup, dill, salt, and pepper in a large mixing bowl. Dip the bread slices in water to soften, then squeeze to remove excess water. Add the bread to the bowl. Blend all the ingredients thoroughly with your hands.

ASSEMBLE THE CABBAGE ROLLS: Place a cabbage leaf smooth side up, with the stem toward you, on a work surface. Place about ⅓ cup of the filling near the stem end of the leaf. Mold the filling into a log shape across the leaf with your hands. Fold the sides of the leaf over the filling, then fold over the bottom end of the leaf and roll up to make a neat, compact package. There is no need to tie the roll with string; the leaf will adhere to itself naturally. Assemble the remaining rolls in the same fashion.

COOK THE CABBAGE ROLLS: After the tomato sauce has cooked for 45 minutes, place the cabbage rolls seam side down, in a single layer, in the sauce. Add the raisins and lemon juice to the sauce. Cover the pot and continue cooking over low heat until the cabbage rolls are very tender, about 1 hour. Taste the sauce and adjust the seasoning with salt and pepper if necessary.

TO SERVE: Place 2 cabbage rolls in each of four warm pasta bowls. Ladle the sauce over the rolls. Serve with fresh bread to sop up all the goodness of the tomato sauce.

cook's notes

I prefer using green cabbage because it will hold the filling much better than Savoy cabbage.

— *planning ahead* —

The nori packages can be assembled up to 4 hours ahead, covered with plastic wrap, and refrigerated until ready to cook.

Shrimp Beignets in Seaweed

I love the briny taste of seaweeds and am always looking for different ways to use them. These delicious bite-sized fritters of shrimp and crackly nori seaweed are the result of one such experiment. They take no time to prepare and will disappear in a blink! An added bonus is that they are just as good cold as they are hot, so they are perfect for cold buffets or take-along snacks. Try serving them with the Soy Dipping Sauce on page 24.

YIELD: 14 triangles for hors d'oeuvres, or enough for 4 to 6 appetizer servings

SHRIMP FILLING

8 ounces raw medium shrimp
2 ounces ground pork
8 fresh or canned water chestnuts, peeled and chopped
½ egg white, lightly beaten
½ teaspoon sugar
¼ teaspoon salt
1½ teaspoons grated fresh ginger
1½ teaspoons dry sherry or vermouth
1½ teaspoons cornstarch
1 teaspoon light soy sauce
1 teaspoon Oriental sesame oil
2 tablespoons chopped scallions
Freshly ground black pepper to taste

FOR ASSEMBLY

4 sheets (7 by 8 inches) yaki-nori (toasted dried seaweed)
14 medium raw shrimp, peeled but tail section left on, deveined
Peanut oil, for frying

PREPARE THE FILLING: Shell, devein, and rinse the shrimp. Pat the shrimp dry and dice them coarsely. In a medium bowl, combine the shrimp with the remaining filling ingredients. Cover and set aside for about 30 minutes to allow the flavors to meld.

Work with 1 sheet of the nori at a time, keeping the remaining sheets in the package covered with a damp kitchen towel to prevent them from drying out.

ASSEMBLE THE BEIGNETS: Cut a sheet of nori along the diagonal into 4 triangles. Work with only one triangle at a time, keeping the remaining pieces covered with a damp kitchen towel to prevent them from curling.

Place a triangle of nori on a work surface with the longest edge toward you. Moisten the nori by dabbing it with a wet cloth or sponge. Place 1 teaspoon of the filling centered at the bottom of the nori. Top the filling with a whole shrimp, leaving the tail extending over the bottom edge of the nori. Top the shrimp with an additional 1 teaspoon filling. Mold the filling into a triangular shape around the body of the shrimp, with the tail extending through the point. Fold the bottom corners of the nori over the filling, overlapping them and tightly enclosing the filling. Fold the packet over onto the top part of the nori, forming a triangular packet with the shrimp tail extending out the top. Gently press the nori to seal the packet, tucking any loose edges under the triangle. Cover the beignet with a kitchen towel while you assemble the remaining beignets in the same manner.

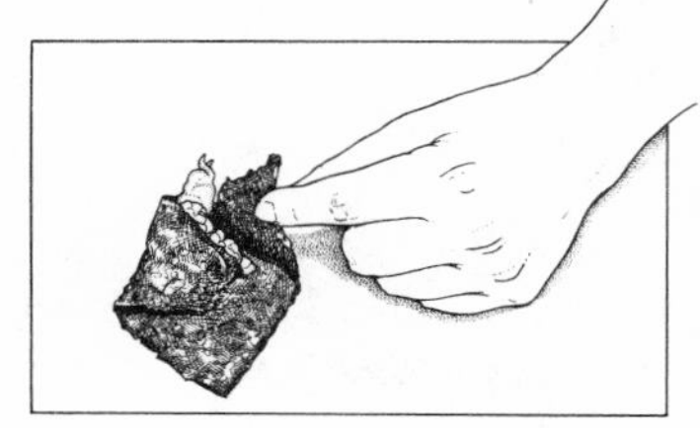

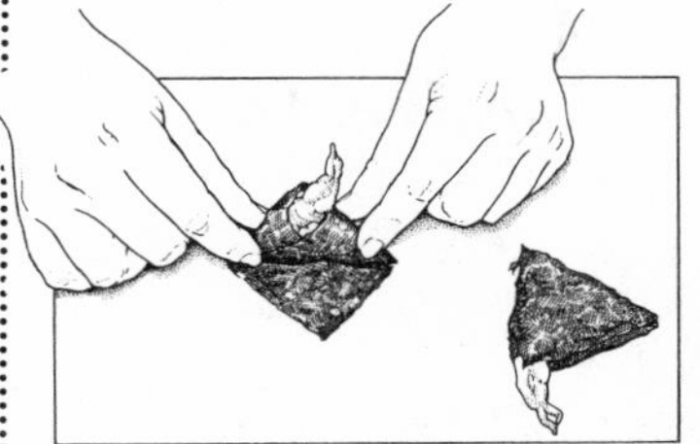

FRY THE BEIGNETS: In a deep heavy saucepan or an electric fryer, slowly heat 1½ to 2 inches of oil to 350°F. Slide in a few beignets at a time and fry until crisp and golden brown on both sides, about 2 minutes total. Use a slotted spoon to transfer the beignets to paper towels to drain.

Serve the beignets warm, with Soy Dipping Sauce if desired.

— *planning ahead* —

The sushi rolls can be prepared up to 2 days ahead, individually wrapped in plastic wrap and refrigerated. Bring to room temperature before serving.

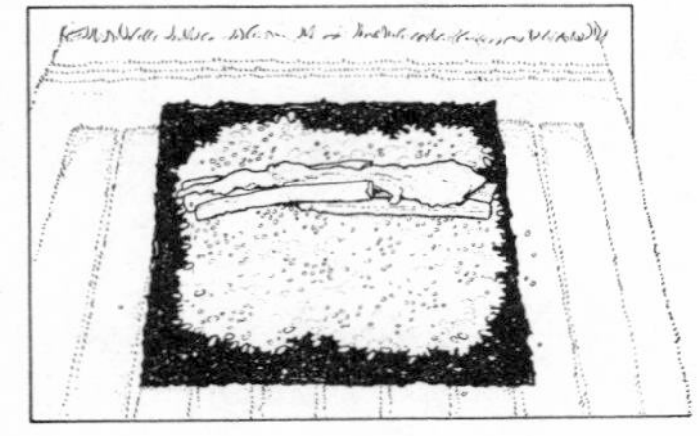

Smoked Salmon Sushi Rolls

This is my favorite recipe for sushi, the popular Japanese hand-rolled fish and seaweed morsels. I must admit I am not very adventurous when it comes to eating sushi made with raw fish. In this simple and clean-tasting roll, seasoned sweet rice, wasabi (Japanese horseradish), fresh vegetable strips, and smoked salmon are wrapped in seaweed, which is then cut into bite-size pieces for an artful presentation.

There are many ways of wrapping sushi but the technique used in this recipe is one of the most common. Although a rectangular bamboo mat called a ***makisushi*** is usually used to roll up the filled seaweed sheet, I find that a kitchen towel will do nicely.

Sushi is traditionally served with a small saucer of light soy sauce flavored with wasabi (Japanese horseradish) on the side. For these rolls, I prefer a soy sauce well seasoned with sesame and chili oils.

YIELD: 6 rolls, enough for 6 light first-course servings or 36 hors d'oeuvres

SOY DIPPING SAUCE

¼ cup light soy sauce
¼ cup rice vinegar
2 teaspoons sugar
1 tablespoon chopped scallion
2 teaspoons finely shredded fresh ginger
½ teaspoon Oriental sesame oil
½ teaspoon chili oil

SUSHI RICE

2 cups short-grain rice
⅓ cup rice vinegar or distilled white vinegar
2 tablespoons mirin (sweet sake) or sherry
3 tablespoons sugar
1½ teaspoons salt

FOR ASSEMBLY

6 sheets (7 by 8 inches) yaki-nori (toasted dried seaweed)
1 tablespoon wasabi (see Cook's Notes)
¼ cup toasted sesame seeds (see Cook's Notes)
12 thin 3½-inch-long strips red bell pepper
12 thin 3½-inch-long strips carrot
12 3½-inch-long peeled strips cucumber
12 thin wedges avocado
6 slices smoked salmon (about 6 ounces)
Red pickled ginger (beni-shoga), for garnish (see Cook's Notes) (optional)

PREPARE THE DIPPING SAUCE: Combine the soy sauce, vinegar, and ¼ cup water in a small saucepan and bring to a boil. Remove the saucepan from the heat, stir in the remaining sauce ingredients, and let the mixture stand for 10 minutes to blend the flavors. Cover and set aside.

MAKE THE SUSHI RICE: Combine the rice with 2 cups water in a large heavy-bottomed saucepan, and bring to a boil over high heat. Briefly stir with a wooden spoon, reduce the heat to low, cover, and cook until all the water has been absorbed and the rice is tender, about 20 minutes. Transfer the hot rice to a large mixing bowl. Combine the vinegar, mirin, sugar, and salt in a small bowl, and stir until the sugar and salt are dissolved. Gradually add the vinegar mixture to the rice, mixing well by "slicing" (use a slashing, rather than circular, motion) across the rice with a rice paddle or flat wooden spoon. Cover the bowl with a damp cloth and let cool to room temperature.

Work with 1 sheet of the nori at a time, keeping the remaining sheets in the package covered with a damp kitchen towel, to prevent curling.

ASSEMBLE THE ROLLS: Place a nori sheet on a bamboo rolling mat or on a damp kitchen towel, with a longer side toward you. Moisten the nori by dabbing it with a wet cloth or sponge. Moisten your hands in warm water, then spread one sixth of the rice over all but the top 2 inches of the seaweed sheet. Spread ½ teaspoon of wasabi across the middle of the rice, then sprinkle 2 teaspoons of the toasted sesame seeds over all. Arrange 2 strips of each vegetable and 2 avocado wedges in a line across the bottom of the rice. Fold 1 slice of the salmon in half lengthwise and place on top. Using the mat or towel as an aid, roll the bottom of the sushi up and over, forming a tight cylinder. Continue rolling up to the top 2 inches of bare seaweed. If the top is a little dry, moisten with water before rolling over it to seal the sushi. Place the completed roll on a platter and cover with plastic wrap. Repeat with the remaining ingredients to make 5 more rolls.

TO SERVE: With a slightly moistened, very sharp knife, trim the ends off the sushi rolls and discard. Carefully cut each roll into 1-inch rounds. Serve with the Soy Dipping Sauce and pickled ginger.

— *cook's notes* —

Wasabi tastes like horseradish but is more piquant. It lends a very strong, sharp flavor to raw fish dishes such as sushi and sashimi. It is available in Japanese groceries and many supermarkets in paste and powdered form. The ready-to-use paste, packaged in a tube, keeps in the refrigerator for months. The green powder, which comes in small cans, must be mixed with a little water to form a paste. Use about 1½ teaspoons water per tablespoon of wasabi powder.

Red pickled ginger (beni-shoga) is a popular garnish and condiment for many Japanese dishes. It's typically served with sushi but you can also serve it with cold meat or fish. It comes thinly sliced in small jars, available in Japanese groceries. After opening the jar, store it in the refrigerator covered and in its original liquid, and it will keep for many months.

Mirin, yaki-nori, wasabi, rice vinegar, and makisushi are available in special sushi-making kits at Japanese markets and some supermarkets.

To toast sesame seeds, place them in a dry skillet over moderate heat and cook, stirring constantly, until golden brown, about 3 minutes. Cool before using.

— *planning ahead* —

The uncooked potato ravioli can be assembled a day ahead, covered with plastic wrap, and refrigerated overnight or frozen for up to a week.

Crisp Potato Ravioli

Crispy outside and tender inside, these upscale potato chips will make an impression at any cocktail hour. A dollop of mashed potatoes flavored with cheese and fresh chives is sandwiched between two paper-thin slices of potato, which are pinched closed around the edges. Depending on personal preference, they can be deep-fried, or brushed with melted butter and baked in a very hot oven. Either way, they are deliciously addictive. They taste even better when dipped in sour cream. Eat them right after they are cooked as they don't reheat well. Like most small treats, these potato ravioli are a bit time-consuming but relatively easy to make. You may want to prepare lots of these for your next cocktail party!

YIELD: About 48 ravioli for hors d'oeuvres

3 large baking potatoes (about 1½ pounds)
1 tablespoon unsalted butter
1 tablespoon sour cream
¼ cup grated Gruyère cheese or smoked cheese (such as Gouda or Bruder Basil)
1 tablespoon chopped fresh chives
Salt and freshly ground black pepper to taste
½ teaspoon salt
Juice of 1 lemon

FOR ASSEMBLY

1 tablespoon all-purpose flour mixed with 1 tablespoon cold water to form a paste
4 tablespoons unsalted butter, melted
Vegetable oil, for deep-frying
Sour cream, for dipping (optional)

Peel the potatoes. Place them in a bowl and cover them with cold water to prevent discoloration.

MAKE THE FILLING: Quarter one of the potatoes and place it in a small saucepan. Cover the potato with cold water and bring to a boil over high heat. Reduce the heat to moderate and cook until the potato is fork-tender but not mushy, about 15 minutes. Drain. Transfer the potato to a small mixing bowl. Add the butter and mash the potato thoroughly, until no lumps remain, using a potato masher. Mix in the sour cream, cheese, and fresh chives. Season with salt and pepper. Cover and refrigerate.

PREPARE THE POTATO SLICES: Use a vegetable peeler, a mandoline, or a good kitchen slicer to cut the remaining potatoes crosswise into paper-thin rounds. Place the potato slices in a colander and sprinkle with the salt and lemon juice. Gently toss the slices with your hands to coat them evenly. Set the colander in the sink until the potatoes become very soft and pliable, about 10 minutes. Pat the slices dry with paper towels.

ASSEMBLE THE POTATO RAVIOLI: Lay several potato slices on a work surface. Place ½ teaspoon of the filling in the center of each, leaving about a ¼-inch border all around. Brush a little flour paste around the edges. Top each potato slice with another potato slice about the same size, and press around the filling to seal the slices together. Brush both sides of the potato ravioli with melted butter and place them on a baking sheet. Don't be concerned if the potatoes have started to brown around the edges. The melted butter will act as a protective coating and prevent them from discoloring further. Assemble the remaining potato ravioli in the same fashion. Cover and refrigerate for at least 30 minutes, or overnight, for the flour paste to seal the potatoes.

TO FRY THE POTATO RAVIOLI: In a deep heavy saucepan or an electric fryer, slowly heat 2 to 3 inches of oil to 350°F. Fry the potatoes in small batches until lightly golden, about 2 minutes. Using a slotted spoon, transfer the ravioli to paper towels to drain. (At this point the potatoes will not be quite crisp.) Raise the oil temperature to 360°F. Return the ravioli to the hot oil and cook until they are very crisp and golden brown, about 1 minute. Remove the potatoes and drain on paper towels.

TO BAKE THE POTATO RAVIOLI: Preheat the oven to 400°F. Place the sheet of ravioli in the oven and bake until the tops are golden brown and crisp, about 12 minutes. Turn them over and bake 12 minutes longer. Baked potato ravioli will look flatter than fried ones but will taste just as good.

Serve the potato ravioli hot, with sour cream on the side if desired.

— cook's notes —

If the potato ravioli have been frozen, thaw them before frying. Or bake them unthawed for about 15 minutes on each side.

If you want to make these delicious treats in large quantities for entertaining but don't have the time to seal them one by one, here's a different way of presenting these hors d'oeuvres; if prepared this way, you will need about twice as much filling to top the potato slices. Arrange the softened potato slices on a large buttered baking sheet. Brush the slices with melted butter, then place them in a preheated 400°F oven and bake until just light golden and crisp, about 5 minutes. Remove the baking sheet from the oven. Use a pastry bag to pipe about 1 teaspoon of filling onto the center of each slice. Return the baking sheet into the oven and bake until the potato filling is just heated through, about 3 minutes.

Mashed goat cheese or very finely ground cooked meat seasoned with thyme, sage, basil, or curry powder may replace the potato filling.

— planning ahead —

The wrapped pork chops can be prepared up to 4 hours ahead, covered, and refrigerated. Bring to room temperature before cooking.

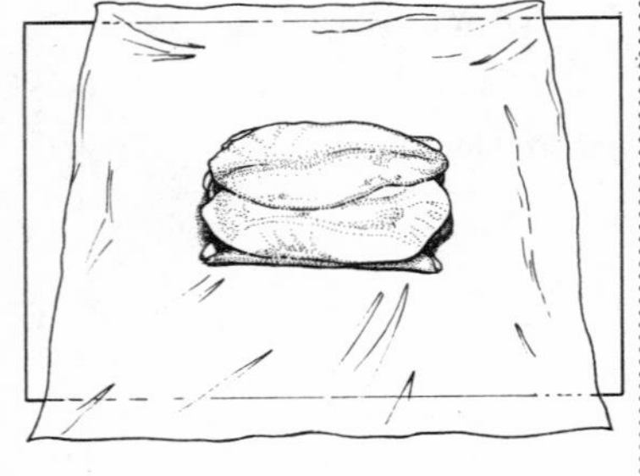

Potato-Wrapped Pork Chops with Mustard Cream Sauce

I think pork is one of the most flavorful and succulent meats there is. Today's lean-bred pork also makes it a healthy alternative to red meat. At home, I am always looking for new ways to prepare pork chops beyond simply broiling or braising them. This recipe was inspired by the wave of potato-wrapped fish dishes that suddenly appeared in many fancy restaurants.

In place of the fish, boneless center-cut pork loin chops are stuffed with garlic and mushrooms, then wrapped in paper-thin slices of potato and broiled. An easy-to-prepare creamy sauce with Dijon mustard and baked garlic perfectly complements the crunchiness of the potato and the assertive flavors of the stuffed pork. This elegant dish will please both your family and your most discriminating guests.

YIELD: 4 main-course servings

16 garlic cloves (unpeeled)
1 tablespoon olive oil

2 tablespoons unsalted butter
4 ounces fresh shiitake or wild mushrooms, stems removed and caps cut into strips (see Cook's Notes)
Dash of cognac
Salt and freshly ground black pepper to taste

4 6-ounce boneless center-cut pork loin chops
1 tablespoon chopped fresh thyme leaves
2 large Idaho potatoes (about 1½ pounds; see Cook's Notes)
Juice of 1 lemon
½ teaspoon salt
5 tablespoons unsalted butter, melted

MUSTARD CREAM SAUCE

½ cup sour cream
½ cup heavy cream
2 teaspoons fresh lemon juice
2 teaspoon Dijon mustard
¼ cup chicken broth
Salt and freshly ground black pepper to taste
Dash of Tabasco

Preheat the oven to 350°F.

BAKE THE GARLIC: Place the garlic cloves on a piece of foil and drizzle with the oil. Fold the edges of the foil over the garlic and twist the edges of the packet shut. Bake until the garlic is soft, about 30 minutes. Remove the packet from the oven and let cool. Carefully open the packet, reserving the oil. Peel the garlic cloves and set aside.

SAUTÉ THE MUSHROOMS: Melt the butter in a large skillet over moderate heat. Add the mushrooms and sauté until they are limp, about 2 to 3 minutes. Remove the pan from the heat, add the cognac, and tilt the pan toward the flame to ignite it (or use a match if cooking on an electric stove). Shake the mushrooms in the pan until the flames die out. Season with salt and pepper. Set aside and allow to cool.

PREPARE THE CHOPS: Using a sharp paring knife, cut a deep pocket into one side of each pork chop. Lightly sprinkle the chops inside and out with salt and pepper. Insert 2 cloves of baked garlic inside each pocket, then stuff with 1 tablespoon of the sautéed mushrooms. Gently press on the chops to seal the pockets.

Lightly butter a large nonstick skillet and place it over moderately high heat. Add the chops and brown on each side for about 1 minute. Transfer to a plate to cool. Reserve the pan with the drippings for the sauce. Rub both sides of the chops with the thyme.

PREPARE THE POTATOES: Peel the potatoes. Use a mandoline or a vegetable peeler to cut the potatoes into long paper-thin slices. Place the potato slices in a colander and sprinkle on the lemon juice and salt. Gently toss the slices with your hands to coat them evenly. Set the colander in the sink until the potatoes become very soft and pliable, about 10 minutes. Pat the slices dry with paper towel.

Generously butter a baking sheet.

WRAP THE CHOPS: Brush a large sheet of wax paper with melted butter. On the buttered paper, shingle about one quarter of the potato slices horizontally to form a 5- by 9-inch sheet. Gently brush the sheet of potatoes with melted butter. Center a chop across the potato sheet. Lift the bottom edge of the wax paper and fold it over to cover the chop with the potatoes and lightly press the wax paper to make the potatoes adhere to the chop. Peel back the wax paper. Lift the top edge of the wax paper and fold it over to cover the chop with the potatoes; lightly press down to make them adhere. Brush the potatoes with melted butter. Don't be concerned if the potatoes have started to brown around the edges. The melted butter will act as a protective coating and prevent them from discoloring further. Insert a wide spatula under the chop and transfer it to the prepared baking sheet.

Wrap the remaining chops in the same fashion. Cover and refrigerate for at least 30 minutes for the butter to seal the potatoes.

continued

— cook's notes —

Fresh shiitake mushrooms are available in many well-stocked supermarkets. Some markets call them Black Forest mushrooms.

It is very important that you choose the largest potatoes available to prepare this dish. They should measure approximately 5 inches long by 2½ inches wide and weigh at least 8 ounces each.

The potato wrapping can be used on boneless and skinless fish steaks such as salmon, swordfish, or tuna weighing about 6 ounces each. Season the fish with salt and pepper to taste, then brush lightly with melted butter or olive oil. Wrap each fish steak in potato slices the same way as for the pork chops. Simply broil the fillets until the potato skin is golden and crisp and the fish flakes easily when pierced with a fork, about 5 minutes on each side.

Preheat the oven broiler.

MAKE THE SAUCE: Add the remaining 8 cloves baked garlic and the reserved oil to the pan of drippings. Use the back of a wooden spoon to mash the cloves into a paste. Mix in the sour cream, heavy cream, lemon juice, mustard, and chicken broth. Bring the mixture to a boil over moderately high heat, scraping the bottom of the pan to release any browned bits. Reduce the heat to moderately low and simmer until the sauce is lightly thickened and coats the back of a spoon, about 2 minutes. Remove the pan from the heat. Season the sauce with salt, pepper, and Tabasco, and cover the pan to keep the sauce warm.

COOK THE PORK CHOPS: Place the chops under the broiler 6 inches from the heat source and broil until the potatoes are browned and crisp, about 4 minutes. Using a wide spatula, turn the chops over and broil for 3 more minutes. Reduce the oven temperature to 400°F and bake for 15 minutes, brushing the chops occasionally with the butter that accumulates on the baking sheet.

TO SERVE: Spoon the mustard cream sauce onto warm dinner plates, and place the chops on top.

— *planning ahead* —

The fish packages can be assembled up to 4 hours ahead and refrigerated. Bring to room temperature before baking.

In true Hawaiian tradition, laulaus (fish packages) are always served at a luau, the feast for happy occasions. Laulaus are steamed in a pit oven along with the requisite pig and other foods. Fortunately, the pleasures of serving laulaus can be transferred into your kitchen with this simplest and most delicious of preparations. Serve with steamed white rice, preferably an aromatic variety such as jasmine or basmati.

YIELD: 2 main-course servings

GINGER SAUCE

1 2-ounce piece fresh ginger
2 teaspoons oyster sauce
1 teaspoon fresh lime juice
1 teaspoon light soy sauce
1 teaspoon Oriental sesame oil
1 teaspoon dry sherry

4 ti leaves (see Cook's Notes)
Vegetable oil
2 8-ounce fillets of bluefish (about ¾ inch thick)
Freshly ground black pepper to taste
4 thin slices lime
6 scallions, trimmed and cut into slivers
Fresh coriander sprigs
Sesame oil, for sprinkling (optional)

MAKE THE SAUCE: Crush the ginger with a mallet or a rolling pin to break the fibers. Squeeze the ginger with your hand, letting the juice drip into a small bowl. You should have about 2 teaspoons of ginger juice. Stir in the oyster sauce, lime juice, soy sauce, sesame oil, and sherry. Set the sauce aside.

Preheat the oven to 425°F.

ASSEMBLE THE LAULAUS: Pare down the thick rib on the underside of the ti leaves. Lightly brush the top of the leaves with oil. For each packet, crisscross 2 leaves. Arrange a fish fillet in the center of each cross, and pour half of the sauce over the fillet. Season the fish with pepper, and top with 2 lime slices, half of the scallions, and some coriander sprigs. Fold the arms of the crosses over to enclose the fillets. Secure the packets with toothpicks or tie with kitchen string. Set the packets on a baking pan.

Bake the packets for 12 to 15 minutes, or until an instant-read thermometer inserted through the fish packet reads 120°F to 125°F. Do not overcook.

Remove the packets from the oven and place them on serving plates. Let each diner open a packet at the table and, if desired, sprinkle about ½ teaspoon of sesame oil over the fish before eating.

— cook's notes —

Abundant in Hawaii and Polynesia, fresh ti leaves are used much like banana leaves. On the mainland, they can be obtained at some florists. Be sure to peel the stiff stem from the underside of the leaf before using to wrap food. If ti leaves are unavailable, substitute banana leaves, cooking parchment, or foil.

Carp, tilefish, catfish, or striped bass fillets may be prepared in the same manner. Adjust the cooking time according to the thickness of the fish.

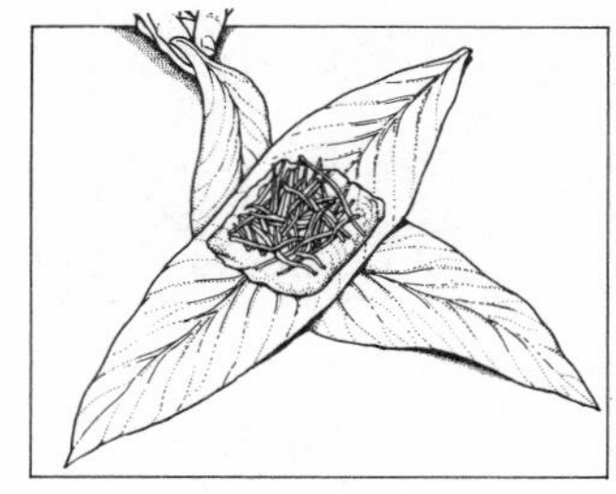

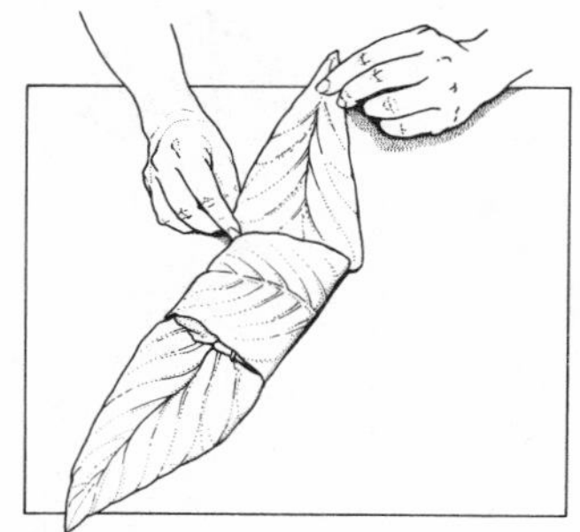

— planning ahead —

Both the vinaigrette and assembled seafood packets may be prepared up to 4 hours in advance, covered, and refrigerated, leaving just a quick grilling for the last minute.

Lobster and Scallops Grilled in Corn Husks

No dish says "backyard cooking" like this lively preparation for lobster and scallops. Husks from fresh corn in season form the wrappers for this easy-to-make yet scrumptious entrée, which is served with a piquant tomato, basil, and lime vinaigrette. The wonderful bouquet that is released from the corn husks as they are grilled is an appetizing bonus. This great summer dish is elegant, deliciously refreshing, and one of my favorites.

YIELD: 8 first-course or 4 light entrée servings

2 live Maine lobsters (1 to 1½ pounds each)
8 large fresh sea scallops (1½ to 2 inches in diameter, about 1 pound)
4 large fresh ears corn in the husk
2 tablespoons olive oil
Salt and freshly ground black pepper to taste

TOMATO VINAIGRETTE

⅔ cup olive oil
¼ cup fresh lime juice
2 tablespoons plus 2 teaspoons light soy sauce
3 tablespoons finely chopped shallots
1 teaspoon sugar
2 large ripe tomatoes, peeled, seeded, and coarsely chopped
2 small fresh hot chile peppers or 1 jalapeño pepper, seeded and minced
2 tablespoons finely shredded fresh basil leaves (about 20 leaves)
Salt and freshly ground black pepper to taste

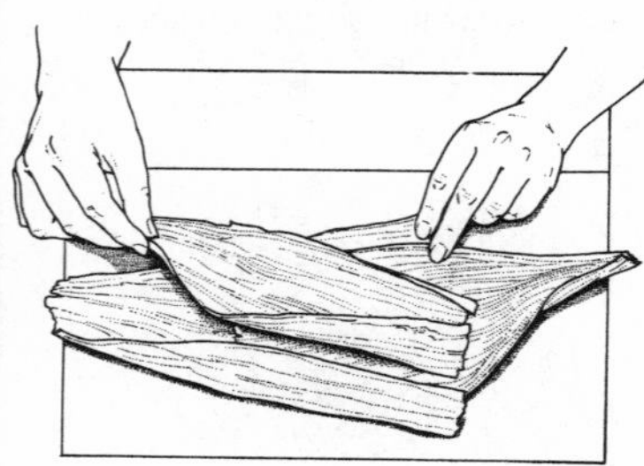

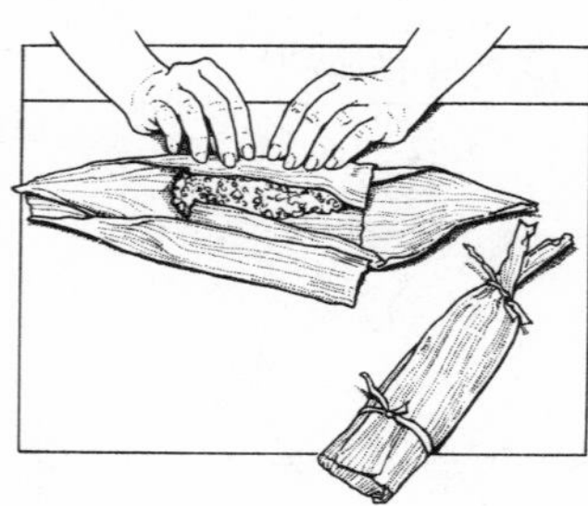

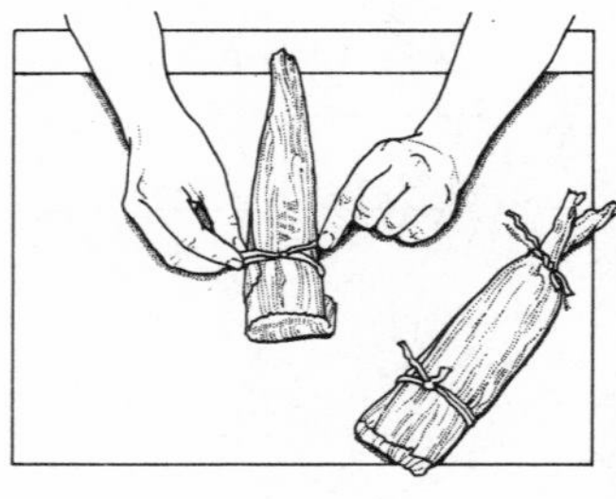

PARBOIL THE LOBSTERS: In a large pot, bring 4 quarts of salted water to a rolling boil over high heat. With tongs, lower the lobsters headfirst into the pot. Bring the water back to a boil and cook the lobsters for 2 minutes. Drain the lobsters in a colander set in the sink and let cool. (The lobster meat is not fully cooked at this point.)

REMOVE THE MEAT FROM THE LOBSTERS: Using kitchen gloves to protect your hands, twist the claws off the lobsters. Gently crack the claw shells with a hammer or the back of a heavy cleaver, being careful not to damage the meat. Remove the meat with a cocktail fork; the meat should come out in a single piece. Cut the claw meat lengthwise in half.

Gently detach the lobster tails from the heads. Use scissors to cut lengthwise through the back of each tail, being careful not to damage the meat. Spread the shell open and remove the tail meat in a single piece. With a small knife or toothpick, remove and discard the long, thin intestinal tract running the length of the tail meat. Cut the tail meat into ½-inch-thick medallions. You should have about 16 medallions.

Place all the lobster meat on a platter, cover, and refrigerate. Discard the lobster heads and shells or freeze them to make a lobster sauce or bisque.

PREPARE THE SCALLOPS: Rinse the scallops and pat dry. Remove and discard the little muscles on the sides of the scallops. Cut each scallop in half horizontally.

Combine the lobster meat with the scallops and divide the seafood mixture into 8 portions of one half lobster claw, 2 medallions of tail meat, and 2 scallop slices each. Cover and refrigerate.

PREPARE THE CORN HUSKS: Carefully remove the husks from each ear of corn. Select the 24 widest husks and set aside. Cut 2 additional husks lengthwise into 8 thin strips each and set aside for tying the corn husk packages. Reserve the corn for another use, or cook to serve as an accompaniment to this entrée.

ASSEMBLE THE SEAFOOD PACKETS: Place 2 corn husks concave side up on a work surface, overlapping them at the wider ends by 2 inches. Center a third husk on top of the other 2 for reinforcement. Pack one portion of the seafood mixture in a log shape down the center of the corn husks. Drizzle ½ teaspoon of the olive oil over the shellfish and season lightly with salt and pepper. Fold the sides of the corn husks up and over the filling to cover it completely. Tie at either end with a corn husk strip to secure the filling, forming a cigar-shaped packet.

Repeat the assembly with the remaining corn husks and seafood filling to make 7 more packets. Place the packets on a large platter and refrigerate until ready to cook.

PREPARE THE VINAIGRETTE: In a small bowl, whisk together the olive oil, lime juice, soy sauce, shallots, and sugar. Add the chopped tomatoes, chile peppers, and basil, and stir with a wooden spoon to combine. Season with salt and pepper if necessary. Cover and let stand at room temperature for at least 30 minutes for the flavors to meld.

Prepare a moderately hot fire in an outdoor grill.

COOK THE PACKETS: Lightly brush the corn husk packets with the remaining 2 teaspoons olive oil and arrange them on the grill. Cover the barbecue, leaving the vent partially open, and cook for about 6 minutes on each side. Do not overcook, or the seafood will be tough.

TO SERVE: Cut the packets open and present the seafood in the wrappers. Spoon some of the vinaigrette over the seafood before eating.

— cook's notes —

Live lobsters should be cooked as soon as they come from the market. If you cannot cook the lobsters you buy immediately, rinse them under cold water and drain. Transfer to a large pan, cover with a moistened towel, and refrigerate until cooking time. Rinse again and cut off the rubber bands restraining the claws with scissors just before cooking.

If cooking and picking the lobsters is too much of a hassle for you, just buy ½ pound cooked lobster meat from your local fish store.

If you don't have a grill, cook the packets for 6 minutes on each side in a dry skillet or on a griddle, set over medium heat and covered with a lid or a large inverted stainless steel bowl.

— *planning ahead* —

The seafood sausages can be assembled a day ahead, covered, and refrigerated until ready to cook.

Seafood Sausages Steamed in Corn Husks

At first glance, these look like cigar-shaped tamales, but when you open them up, the corn husk packets reveal sausages of seafood! The husks take the place of sausage casings, providing a simple and handsome way to enclose a seafood mousse. Unlike casings, corn husks require no special equipment for stuffing. Just wrap the damp, pliable husks around the filling and tie the ends, then steam the sausages until firm. Served with a mustard sauce, this tasty and spectacular dish is ideal for a party.

YIELD: 6 sausages, enough for 6 main-course servings

SPECIAL EQUIPMENT: A metal steamer

SEAFOOD MOUSSE

½ pound sea scallops
4 ounces raw shelled shrimp
1 medium carrot, peeled and cut into ¼-inch dice (about ½ cup)
1 teaspoon ground ginger
1½ teaspoons salt, or more to taste
¼ teaspoon freshly ground white pepper, or more to taste
¼ teaspoon freshly grated nutmeg
½ pound skinless salmon fillet, rinsed well, patted dry, cut into ½-inch pieces, and chilled
1 large egg
½ cup heavy cream, well chilled
1 10-ounce package frozen chopped spinach, thawed and squeezed dry
Salt and freshly ground black pepper to taste
19 large dried corn husks, soaked in boiling water for 30 minutes to soften
3 tablespoons unsalted butter, melted

MUSTARD SAUCE

1 cup sour cream
½ cup bottled clam juice, plus additional if necessary
¼ cup Dijon mustard
2 tablespoons unsalted butter
Salt and freshly ground white pepper to taste

PREPARE THE SCALLOPS AND SHRIMP: Rinse the scallops and pat dry. Remove and discard the little muscles on the sides of the scallops. Cut the scallops into ½-inch pieces and place in a small bowl. Peel and devein the shrimp and cut into ½-inch pieces. Add to the scallops, cover, and refrigerate.

BLANCH THE CARROT: Bring 2 cups of salted water to a boil in a small saucepan over moderate heat. Add the carrot and cook until just tender, about

2 minutes. Drain in a colander set in the sink and refresh under cold running water. Set aside.

PREPARE THE SEAFOOD MOUSSE: In a small bowl, combine the ground ginger, salt, white pepper, and nutmeg. Set aside. Purée the salmon in a food processor until very smooth, about 20 seconds. Add the egg and the spice mixture and process until well mixed. Scrape down the sides of the bowl with a rubber spatula. With the motor running, slowly add the cream through the feed tube and blend until very smooth, about 45 seconds. Transfer the salmon purée to a large mixing bowl and fold in the scallops, shrimp, carrot, and spinach. Test the mousse for seasoning by sautéing a tiny bit of the mixture until it is cooked through. If it seems underseasoned, adjust to taste. Cover and refrigerate.

ASSEMBLE THE SEAFOOD SAUSAGES: Drain and pat dry the corn husks. Tear 1 of the husks lengthwise into 12 strips about ¼-inch wide. These strips will be used to tie the seafood packets.

Place 2 large corn husks concave side up on a work surface, overlapping the ends by 5 inches. Center a third husk on top of the other 2 for reinforcement. Lightly brush the husks with melted butter. Pack one sixth (about ½ cup) of the seafood mousse in a log shape along one long edge of the corn husk sheet, leaving about 5 inches at either side exposed. Roll the filling and husks up into a compact cylinder; the filling will expand during steaming, so do not wrap it too tightly. Fold one end of the husks under the packet and secure it by tying with a strip of corn husk. Use another strip to tie the other end of the husks into a tail.

Repeat the assembly to make 5 more seafood sausages.

STEAM THE SEAFOOD SAUSAGES: Fill the bottom of the steamer pot with 1 to 2 inches of water. Bring to a boil over moderate heat. Place the seafood packets on the steamer rack over the boiling water, tightly cover, and steam until the filling is firm, about 15 to 20 minutes.

Meanwhile, MAKE THE SAUCE: Combine the sour cream, clam juice, mustard, and butter in a medium saucepan. Heat over low heat just until the sour cream and butter melt, stirring frequently; be sure that it doesn't boil or it will curdle. The sauce should just coat the back of a spoon. If the sauce is too thick, thin with a little clam juice. Remove the sauce from the heat and season with salt and pepper if necessary.

TO SERVE: Place each corn husk packet on a warm dinner plate. Cut the ties from the flat ends and peel back the husks to reveal the seafood sausages. Spoon the mustard sauce around the packets and serve.

— cook's notes —

If dried corn husks are unavailable, wrap the seafood sausages in lightly buttered parchment paper and bake in a preheated 400°F oven until the packets are puffed and browned, about 15 to 20 minutes.

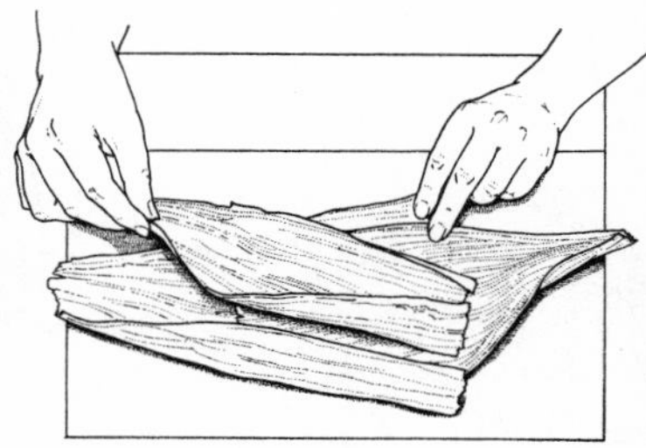

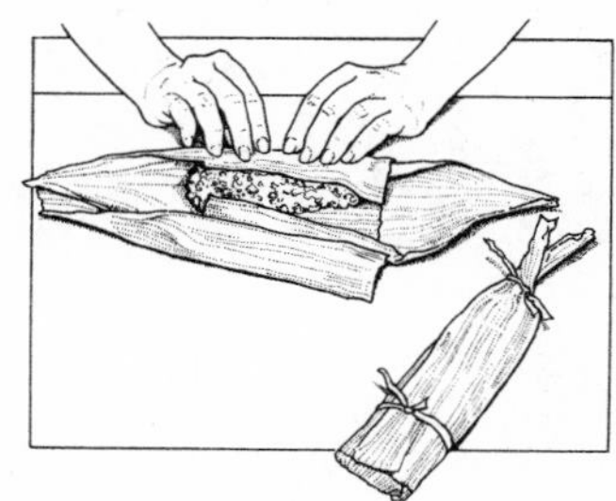

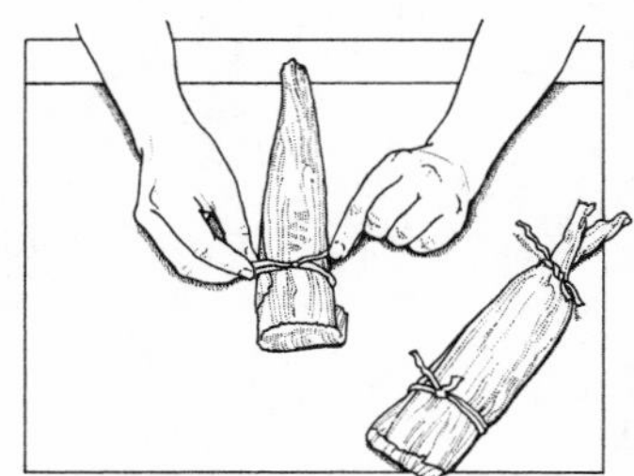

— *planning ahead* —

Both the mole sauce and chicken filling can be made a day ahead, covered, and refrigerated. The uncooked tamale pie can be assembled a day ahead and refrigerated. Both the unbaked tamale pie and the mole sauce actually improve in flavor on standing for a day.

Chicken Tamale Pie with Mole Sauce

Tamales are traditional South American preparations in which a cornmeal dough is spread on corn husks or banana leaves, covered with any of a number of different fillings, rolled and shaped like a fat cylinder, and then steamed or simmered. When unwrapped at the table, the tamale reveals a fragrant and steaming hot cake so tender that it practically collapses under the touch of a fork. The key to making a dough that is feathery light is to beat in enough shortening and broth to trap some air, causing the dough to expand as the tamales cook.

I have tried many kinds of tamales but this one for roast chicken and mole sauce is my favorite because it offers a unique depth of flavors and textures and is less complex than most to prepare. To save time, I make a single pie by encasing the tamale dough and chicken filling in banana leaves, which infuse a subtly sweet fragrance to the dish. Since tamale dough is usually quite powdery and bland, I like to boost its flavors by adding coarsely ground fresh corn kernels and spices such as cumin and chili powder.

YIELD: 6 main-course servings

SPECIAL EQUIPMENT: A 10-inch square baking dish or 9-inch pie pan; a large shallow baking pan large enough to hold the baking dish or pie pan

TAMALE DOUGH

⅔ cups chicken broth, homemade (page 000) or store-bought
2 teaspoons sugar
2 teaspoons ground cumin
2 teaspoons chili powder
1 teaspoon salt
½ cup masa harina (see Cook's Notes)
¾ cup yellow cornmeal
1½ cups fresh or frozen corn kernels
1 cup plus 2 tablespoons solid vegetable shortening

CHICKEN FILLING

1 teaspoon minced garlic
½ teaspoon cumin
½ teaspoon salt, or more to taste
Freshly ground black pepper to taste
1 tablespoon plus 1 teaspoon olive oil
2 large boneless skinless chicken breast halves (about 1 pound)

MOLE SAUCE

4 dried ancho chiles, soaked in boiling water for 30 minutes to soften (see Cook's Notes)
2 medium ripe tomatoes
2 large garlic cloves, peeled
1 teaspoon dried oregano leaves
1 teaspoon ground cumin
1 teaspoon chili powder
1 teaspoon ground coriander
¼ teaspoon salt, or more to taste
½ teaspoon cayenne pepper
¼ teaspoon freshly ground black pepper, or more to taste
1½ cups chicken broth, homemade (page 368) or store-bought, plus additional if necessary
1 ounce semisweet chocolate, coarsely chopped
1 teaspoon sugar, or more to taste

1 scallion, thinly sliced
3 large banana leaves (10 by 20 inches each)

Combine the chicken broth, sugar, cumin, chili, and salt in a small saucepan and bring to a boil over moderately high heat. Remove the pan from the heat and stir with a wooden spoon until the sugar and salt are dissolved. Set aside.

PREPARE THE TAMALE DOUGH: Mix together the masa harina and cornmeal in a bowl. Set aside. Coarsely chop the corn in a food processor. Remove to a small bowl and set aside. Add the shortening to the bowl of the food processor and process until light and fluffy, about 15 seconds. Add the cornmeal mixture and blend until smooth, scraping down the sides of the bowl occasionally with a rubber spatula. With the motor running, gradually add the seasoned chicken broth through the feed tube and process until well mixed. Remove the dough to a bowl and mix in the chopped corn. Cover and refrigerate.

PREPARE THE CHICKEN: In a mortar using a pestle, pound the garlic, cumin, salt, and pepper to a paste. Blend in 1 teaspoon of the olive oil. Rub the paste all over the chicken breasts. Heat the remaining 1 tablespoon olive oil in a medium skillet over moderate heat. Add the chicken and brown on each side for 1 minute. Cover the skillet, reduce the heat to low, and cook for 5 minutes. Turn the chicken over, cover, and cook just until tender, about 5 minutes longer. Remove the chicken pieces to a plate and set aside to cool. Reserve the skillet with the drippings for the sauce.

PREPARE THE MOLE SAUCE: Remove and discard the seeds from the ancho chiles. Coarsely chop the chiles, and place them in the bowl of a food processor or in a blender. Spear the tomatoes with a fork and roast them over an open flame, turning to cook all sides, until the skins begin to blacken, about 2 minutes.

continued

— *cook's notes* —

Masa harina is fresh corn dough that has been dried and ground to a powder. I use Quaker Oats Masa Harina, which is available in many supermarkets. If you have access to Mexican groceries, look for the Maseca brand. After opening, wrap the container tightly and store it in a dry area. It will keep for at least a year.

Chile ancho (literally, "wide peppers") is the name for a dried poblano chile with wrinkled almost black skin. Ancho chiles are available in Mexican groceries. An average ancho weighs about half an ounce. A purée of soaked ancho chiles will be brownish red with a mild, rich, almost sweet taste and an underlying hint of bitterness.

If banana leaves are unavailable but you can get ahold of fresh corn husks, by all means use them to line the baking dish. Use parchment paper as the last resort.

Leftover tamale pie can be wrapped in foil and refrigerated. To reheat, place the foil-covered pie in a preheated 400°F oven for 15 to 20 minutes, until heated through.

Alternatively, cut the tomatoes in half, place them skin side up under a preheated broiler, and broil until the skin is blackened. Rub the skin off the tomatoes. Coarsely chop the tomatoes, and add to the food processor. Spear the garlic cloves on a fork and roast them over the flame until fragrant, soft, and lightly charred, about 45 seconds. Add the garlic to the food processor, along with the oregano, cumin, chili powder, ground coriander, salt, cayenne, and black pepper. Purée the mixture until smooth. Add it to the drippings in the skillet, and stir in the chicken broth.

Place the pan over moderately low heat, bring to a simmer, and gently cook, stirring frequently with a wooden spoon and scraping the bottom of the pan to release the browned bits, until the sauce is well flavored and slightly reduced, about 15 minutes. Add the chocolate and sugar, and stir until the chocolate is just melted. Remove the pan from the heat and allow to cool.

Add any juices that have collected on the plate of chicken to the mole sauce. Taste the sauce and add more sugar, salt, and/or pepper if necessary for a well-balanced taste. The sauce should have the consistency of heavy cream. If it's too thick, thin it with a little chicken broth.

PREPARE THE CHICKEN FILLING: Cut the chicken into ½-inch cubes, and place the chicken pieces in a medium bowl. Add the scallion and ½ cup of the mole sauce, and stir with a wooden spoon to combine. Taste the filling and add salt and pepper if necessary. Cover the remaining sauce and set aside.

Preheat the oven to 400°F. Adjust an oven rack to the center shelf.

ASSEMBLE THE TAMALE PIE: Cover the bottom of the baking dish or pie pan with 2 crossed banana leaves, leaving a generous overhang around the edges of the pan. Spread half of the tamale dough evenly over the leaves. Spread the chicken filling evenly over the dough. Cover the filling with the remainder of the tamale dough. Trim the third banana leaf to a 10-inch square (or 9-inch round) and place it over the filling. Fold the overhanging leaves over, so that the filling is completely covered, then cover the top of the pie with foil. Set the pie inside the larger baking pan and pour enough boiling water into the larger pan to reach halfway up the sides of the tamale pie dish.

Place the baking pan in the oven and bake for 1 hour, or until the tamale pie is steaming hot and very tender. As the water evaporates, add more boiling water to maintain the water level in the pan. Remove the pie from the larger pan and allow to cool slightly on a rack.

Reheat the reserved mole sauce.

TO SERVE: Remove the foil and open out the leaves to expose the tamale pie. Cut the pie into squares or wedges and place on warm dinner plates. Spoon some mole sauce around each serving.

Sweet Banana and Black Bean Pudding

As a child growing up in Laos, I loved to sneak out to a little roadside food stand to snack on sticky rice flavored with coconut and stuffed with bananas or sweet beans. Made almost like a tamale, this creamy and fruity puddinglike dessert of sweet rice, banana, and black beans is wrapped in banana leaves, then steamed or grilled over charcoal. It is at its best served at room temperature.

— *planning ahead* —

The cooked puddings can be refrigerated overnight. Bring to room temperature before serving.

YIELD: 8 dessert servings

SPECIAL EQUIPMENT: A metal steamer

½ cup dried black beans
1½ cups short-grain sweet rice or sticky rice (see Cook's Notes)
1½ cups plus 2 tablespoons canned unsweetened coconut milk (see Cook's Notes)
1 teaspoon vanilla extract
⅓ cup sugar
¼ teaspoon salt
9 banana leaves, 10 by 12 inches each
2 ripe bananas, peeled, halved lengthwise, and then halved crosswise
Toasted sesame seeds, for garnish (optional)

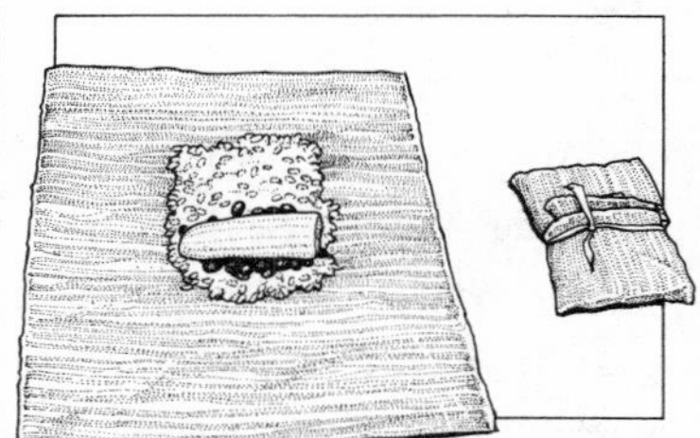

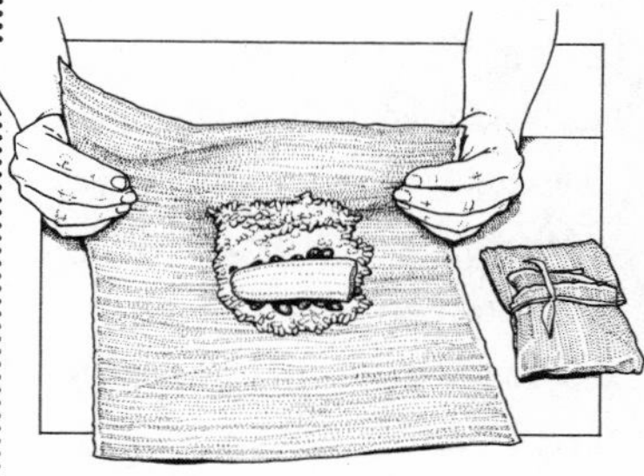

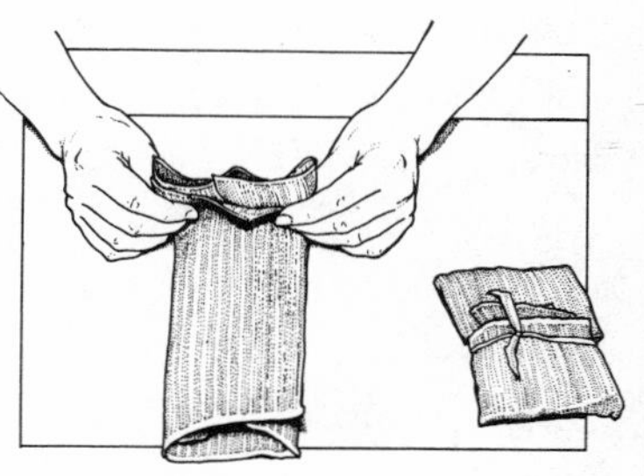

Place the beans and rice in separate bowls, cover with hot tap water, and soak for 2 hours, or overnight. Drain.

PREPARE THE BLACK BEANS: Place the beans in a saucepan, cover with 2 cups cold water, and bring to a boil over moderate heat. Reduce the heat to low and cook until tender, about 40 minutes, adding more water if necessary to keep the beans covered. Drain into a colander set in the sink, rinse with cold water, and drain well. Place the beans in a mixing bowl. Using a potato masher or fork, mash the beans with 2 tablespoons of the coconut milk. Set aside.

PREPARE THE SWEET RICE: In a medium saucepan, combine the remaining 1½ cups coconut milk, the vanilla, sugar, and salt and bring to a boil over moderate heat. Add the rice, reduce the heat to moderately low, and cook, stirring constantly, until the milk is absorbed and the rice is just half cooked, about 8 minutes. Remove and allow to cool.

WRAP THE PUDDINGS: Tear 1 of the banana leaves into 8 strips about ¼ inch wide. These strips will be used to tie the packets of pudding. Place another banana leaf on a work surface with the central vein running from bottom to top. Place about ⅓ cup of the rice mixture in the center of the leaf. Using the back of a wet spoon or spatula, spread the rice to form a 4- by 6-inch rectangle, with a short side toward you. Spread 1 heaping tablespoon of the mashed beans over the top half of the rice rectangle. Place a piece of banana across the beans. Lift the bottom of the banana leaf up and over so that the bottom half of the rice rectangle is covering the beans and banana. Fold the top edge over to secure the filling, then fold the sides over, overlapping them slightly. Secure by tying a strip of banana leaf around the package. Repeat the assembly to make 7 more packages.

STEAM THE PUDDINGS: Fill the bottom of the steamer pot with 1 to 2 inches of water, and bring to a boil over moderate heat. Place the packets on the steamer rack over the boiling water. Tightly cover and steam until the rice is tender, about 25 minutes.

Remove the packets, allow to cool, and serve. Let your guests open up the banana leaves at the table and enjoy. Sprinkle the puddings with toasted sesame seeds if desired.

— cook's notes —

Sweet rice, also called sticky rice, is available at Asian markets. There are two types of sweet rice: the Chinese and Japanese short-grained (moki) type and the longer-grained Thai variety, which I prefer. The cooked rice has a soft, sticky texture with a slightly sweet flavor.

Do not confuse coconut milk with coconut cream. Excellent canned unsweetened coconut milk is available in Asian markets and some supermarkets. After opening, it can be refrigerated for up to 1 week. For longer storage, freeze it in ice cube trays, then store the cubes in plastic bags. Before using, heat the frozen coconut milk until completely melted. Four cubes equal about ½ cup. You may substitute heavy cream for the coconut milk, but the taste will be slightly altered.

If banana leaves are unavailable, substitute fresh or dried corn husks, ti leaves, aluminum foil, or parchment paper. If using foil, first wrap the filling in plastic, or the foil will give a metallic taste to the puddings.

As an alternative to steaming, place the packets on a grill above low coals and cook, turning occasionally, for 25 minutes. Remove the packets and allow to cool.

If fresh mango is in season, try it in place of the mashed black beans and banana.

Dunkanoo

This recipe was kindly offered to me by Jessica Harris, expert on African and Caribbean cooking and author of *Sky Juice and Flying Fish: Traditional Caribbean Cooking* (Fireside Books, 1991). This dish has its origins in Ghana, West Africa, where it is known as *dokono.* It moved to the New World via West African slaves and was adapted by Jamaican cooks, who called it *dunkanoo.* It is a sweet concoction of grated corn mixed with sugar, coconut milk, raisins, and spices, such as cinnamon and ginger. Individual portions are wrapped in banana leaves and steamed. If you enjoy steamed puddings, this exotic and sublime-tasting dessert is for you.

— *planning ahead* —

The uncooked dunkanoo packets can be refrigerated for up to a day before steaming. Steamed dunkanoo can be refrigerated for up to a day before serving.

YIELD: 6 dessert servings

SPECIAL EQUIPMENT: A metal steamer

SWEET CORN FILLING

3 large ears fresh corn, preferably white, husked
¼ cup raisins
3 tablespoons quick-cooking tapioca (see Cook's Notes)
⅓ cup unsweetened coconut milk (see Cook's Notes)
¼ cup light brown sugar
1½ teaspoons ground cinnamon
½ teaspoon ground ginger
1 tablespoon dark rum

7 10-inch square banana leaves

MAKE THE FILLING: Working over a large bowl, cut the corn kernels from the cobs by running a sharp knife from the top of the ear straight down to the stem. Leave about ⅛ inch of pulp on the cob to avoid the tough cob fibers. After removing the kernels, scrape the back of the knife down the cob to extract all the remaining meat and "milk." You should have about 3 cups corn kernels.

Place the corn kernels and their liquid in the bowl of a food processor fitted with the metal blade and pulse to obtain a coarse purée. Do not overprocess; the mixture will be too runny. Transfer the purée to a medium bowl. Add the remaining filling ingredients and mix well with a fork.

WRAP THE DUNKANOO: Tear 1 of the banana leaves into 12 strips about ¼ inch wide. These strips will be used to tie the dunkanoo. Place another banana leaf on a work surface with the central vein running from top to bottom. Place one sixth of the filling mixture (about ⅓ cup) in the center of the leaf. Using the back of a spoon or spatula, spread the mixture to form a 3- by 5-inch rectangle, with a long side toward you. Fold first the top, then the bottom of the leaf over the filling. Fold the sides of the leaf over, overlapping them slightly, and secure the package by tying a strip of banana leaf around each end. Assemble the remaining dunkanoos in the same manner.

STEAM THE DUNKANOO: Fill the bottom of the steamer pot with 1 to 2 inches of water, and bring to a boil over moderate heat. Place the dunkanoo packets on the steamer rack over the boiling water. Tightly cover and steam until the corn is tender and the tapioca cooked through, about 30 minutes. Remove the packets, and allow to cool to room temperature.

TO SERVE: Let your guests open up the banana leaves at the table and enjoy.

— cook's notes —

Quick-cooking granulated tapioca, also called instant tapioca, is available in specialty food stores and in many supermarkets.

Do not confuse coconut milk with coconut cream. Excellent canned unsweetened coconut milk is available in Asian markets and some supermarkets. After opening, it can be refrigerated for up to 1 week. For longer storage, freeze it in ice cube trays, then store the cubes in plastic bags. Before using, heat the frozen coconut milk until completely melted. Four cubes equal about ½ cup. You may substitute heavy cream for the coconut milk, but the taste will be slightly altered.

If banana leaves are unavailable, substitute fresh or dried corn husks, ti leaves, aluminum foil, or parchment paper. If using foil, first wrap the filling in plastic, or the foil will give a metallic taste to the dunkanoos.

phyllo

P*hyllo,* also spelled *filo,* is the Greek word for "leaf." It also refers to tissue-thin pastry leaves made from flour and water mixed with a little egg and olive oil. In the Middle East and Greece, phyllo is used much as puff pastry is in France to create a delicate, flaky, multilayered crust, for exquisite pies, strudels, and turnovers. These pastries can be made with savory fillings for hors d'oeuvres, appetizers, or entrées or with sweet confections for dessert.

To create the characteristic crisp, flaky, golden crust of baked phyllo, melted butter is lightly brushed over the leaves, sheet by sheet, as the leaves are folded or stacked to form layers. Often, bread crumbs or ground nuts are sprinkled between the sheets to ensure the separation and flakiness of the layers and to absorb any excess moisture from the filling.

Because phyllo yields a light-textured and flavorful pastry with just a small amount of fat, more and more cooks, including myself, are experimenting with it in this health-conscious age as an alternative to puff pastry or short doughs. Although the recipes call for melted butter to be brushed over the phyllo, you can substitute: For example, olive oil, peanut oil, or a blend of canola and sesame oil could be used, but they will of course change the flavor of the finished dish. If you are concerned with calories or cholesterol, feel free to use margarine or your favorite oil spray. But be aware that only butter will give phyllo that appetizing uniformly golden look.

The popularity of phyllo is deservedly beginning to expand out from the Middle Eastern and Mediterranean cuisines onto the world stage. Phyllo is so versatile that it can be wrapped around almost any cooked filling and assembled in any number of shapes. The triangular form is the classic shape for traditional turnovers such as Greek Spanakopetes (page 52) and Flaky Tunisian Triangles (page 56). This shape is also ideal for desserts like the Lemony Rhubarb Turnovers (page 82).

Phyllo is also great for strudel rolls, like Austrian Apfelstrudel (page 73). Even the famous Greek Pistachio Baklava (page 76) can be made this way. Don't think that a strudel roll must always be a dessert. I have created dinner entrées that take this form, like Scrod and Spinach Strudel with Avgolemono (page 71).

One of the shapes I like best is the freestyle purse. When I have time and want to make an especially elegant presentation, I use this form to turn an ordinary dish into something unusual. Baked Egg and Ratatouille in Phyllo (page 50) and Chocolate Plum Purses (page 80) are good examples.

I am always experimenting with phyllo. I have found that stacks of six to eight buttered phyllo sheets fitted into a pie pan can make an interesting tart shell for most any sweet or savory filling. It is also great for covered pies, like the stunning Moroccan Chicken Pie known as B'stella (page 60), or an Italian-inspired Tortellini Pie (page 63).

Making phyllo from scratch can be tricky and time-consuming. Although I have included a Homemade Phyllo recipe (page 46) for the adventurous cook, I recommend using store-bought phyllo for practical purposes. If you do not happen to be lucky enough to live near a Greek pastry shop that sells freshly made phyllo, you will find frozen phyllo readily available in gourmet and specialty food shops, Middle Eastern markets, and in most large supermarkets. A one-pound box contains approximately twenty-four to thirty rolled sheets (leaves) of pastry that measure about 12 by 17 inches. Apollo is the most widely available brand.

Don't be afraid of working with phyllo. I have designed very simple wrapping techniques and if you follow the directions closely, the results will make you feel like an artist every time.

PHYLLO WRAPPING TIPS

- If the phyllo you purchase is frozen, let the unopened box of phyllo defrost in your refrigerator for at least two days before using. This way, you'll have perfectly supple phyllo to work with. Do not defrost phyllo at room temperature, because the leaves will stick to each other and working with them will be impossible. Once defrosted, phyllo will keep in the refrigerator for up to a month. Do not attempt refreezing, which will make the phyllo crumbly or pasty.
- Before unwrapping the phyllo, make sure that you have a large, dry, flat surface to work on and that all your utensils and ingredients are at hand: a baking sheet, a pastry brush (2 to 2½ inches wide), scissors or a pizza cutter, ground nuts or bread crumbs, if you are using them, and, most important, melted butter that will be brushed on each sheet of phyllo. Use a baking sheet with sides, not a cookie sheet, because the pastries will exude butter as they bake. The filling for the dish should also be ready for assembly. If you intend to bake the phyllo dish immediately after its assembly, preheat the oven.
- Once unwrapped and exposed to air, phyllo dries out very quickly. Therefore, always try to work as quickly as possible. Remove the thawed phyllo sheets from their protective plastic bag and unroll the phyllo on a flat surface. Remove only the number of sheets called for in the recipe, put them aside, and keep them well covered with a slightly damp kitchen towel to prevent them from drying out. Quickly reroll the remaining phyllo sheets, tightly wrap them in a double layer of plastic wrap, put the roll back into its box, and refrigerate.
- During assembly, work with one sheet or a piece of a sheet of phyllo at a time. Keep the remainder covered with a slightly damp kitchen towel to prevent drying out.
- If the phyllo tears while you are working with it, just match the torn edges, press them together, and proceed with the recipe.
- When buttering a sheet of phyllo, work quickly to prevent it from drying out. Begin brushing at the edges and work inward, using broad strokes to lightly coat the sheet with butter. Don't worry about covering every inch of surface; you don't want to saturate the phyllo sheet with butter. You can also dip your brush in the melted butter and sprinkle the butter generously and evenly over the phyllo.
- After assembly, it is important to brush all the unbuttered surfaces of the phyllo with melted butter. This forms a protective coating that prevents the phyllo from drying out.
- If you don't intend to bake them immediately, assembled phyllo pies or pastries can be refrigerated overnight or frozen. To refrigerate, loosely cover with foil. To freeze, refrigerate until the butter coating is firm, then wrap them either individually or together in plastic wrap or store in freezer bags.
- To bake frozen phyllo pastries, place them unthawed (they get soggy if defrosted) on a lightly buttered baking sheet and bake in a preheated 350°F oven until piping hot. Baked and refrigerated phyllo dishes can be reheated in a 350°F oven.
- Baked phyllo pastries are done when they reach a golden color. They should not brown; if the phyllo browns too fast during baking, loosely cover it with foil. Be careful not to overbake.

Homemade Phyllo

When it comes to making phyllo, Greek cooks are unsurpassed. It is traditionally prepared by combining flour, salt, water, and eggs, plus a little olive oil and/or vinegar to enrich the dough. After the dough is mixed, it is kneaded well and left to rest for an hour. It is then divided into portions, shaped into balls, and left to stand an hour longer at room temperature. Then the balls are rolled out into rough sheets, which are sprinkled with cornstarch, stacked, wrapped in plastic wrap, and left to stand overnight at room temperature.

The following day each sheet is again generously sprinkled with cornstarch and the sheets are stacked one on top of the other in a single pile. The whole stack is rolled out with a rolling pin, turned over, and rolled again. As the stack is being worked, it is frequently lifted and draped around the rolling pin and then rolled again to stretch the dough further. This process is repeated again and again until the layers are tissue-thin. The real trick is to prevent the layers from sticking to one another during the rolling and stretching process.

Now you know why I will not attempt to encourage you to make phyllo the traditional way! The hand-stretched technique described below is actually the same method used to make European strudel leaves, which are a direct descendant of phyllo. It is much more manageable and yields results almost identical to phyllo made the traditional way. Until you have practiced this technique many times and have a deft hand at stretching the dough to its limits, your sheets will be slightly thicker and heavier than traditional phyllo.

YIELD: ½ pound, enough to make eight 12- by 15-inch phyllo sheets

SPECIAL EQUIPMENT: A small kitchen table at least 40 inches square; an old clean and smooth tablecloth or sheet to cover the table; Scotch tape; small cups; a pizza cutter; and a ruler

1½ cups plus 2 tablespoons (10 ounces) unbleached all-purpose flour, plus additional as necessary
¼ cup plus 2 tablespoons hot water (110° to 115°F)
¼ teaspoon salt
1 teaspoon distilled white vinegar
1 tablespoon light olive oil, plus additional as necessary
2 large egg whites (¼ cup), lightly beaten

Cornstarch, for dusting

PREPARE THE DOUGH: Sift the flour into a mixing bowl and make a well in the middle. Blend the hot water, salt, vinegar, oil, and beaten egg whites in another bowl, and pour into the well. Use a fork to incorporate the flour into the

another bowl, and pour into the well. Use a fork to incorporate the flour into the liquid, then gather the dough into a ball with your hands. The dough should feel wet and very soft but not sticky. If it feels sticky, add a tablespoon or more of flour, until the dough no longer sticks to your hands or the bowl. Be careful not to add too much flour, or the dough will become stiff and lose its elasticity.

Lightly rub a cool work surface, preferably marble or metal, with olive oil. Lightly rub the dough with olive oil. Slap the dough down onto the oiled surface, gather it up, then slap it down again. Work the dough in this manner for about 100 strokes. This technique serves to develop the gluten in the dough. Whenever the dough begins to stick to the surface as you slap it, lightly rub the surface and your hands with a little more olive oil and lightly sprinkle the dough with flour. Do not use too much oil or flour, or the dough will become either too sticky or too stiff. The dough should be on the wet side, but not sticky.

Briefly knead the dough and shape it into a ball. Coat the dough with olive oil and place it on an oiled plate. Cover with plastic wrap and set in a warm area to allow the gluten to relax for at least 1 hour, or overnight.

STRETCH THE DOUGH: Cover the table with the tablecloth and secure the edges of the cloth by taping them underneath the edges of the table. Sprinkle the entire surface evenly with cornstarch. Sprinkle the dough lightly with cornstarch and set it in the center of the cloth. Lightly coat a rolling pin with cornstarch. Roll the dough out evenly into a thin circle, about 24 inches in diameter. Do not lift the dough from the table as you roll it or it will shrink back. If the dough starts shrinking back while you roll it, cover it with a clean towel and let it rest for about 10 minutes before continuing. If the dough sticks to the rolling pin, lightly sprinkle the dough with more cornstarch.

Lightly brush the dough circle with olive oil, being careful not to puncture the dough. Lightly oil the backs of your hands and wrists, then slide them, palms down, between the cloth and the dough. Working from the center outward, stretch the dough into a large square, using a gentle hand-over-hand motion all around the circle. When the dough becomes too thin and fragile to continue to work in this manner without tearing, lay it back on the tablecloth. Don't worry if you have a few holes in the dough; patching will do more harm than good.

Gently pull and stretch out the thicker outer edges of the dough as thin as possible with your fingers, moving around the table as you work. Do not stretch the dough in the same place for too long. If the dough begins to spring back as you stretch it, anchor the edges of the dough with floured cups. Continue stretching until you have a square of dough that is at least 40 inches across and thin enough to read through. Trim off the thicker edges of the dough with scissors or a pizza cutter. (Now you should have a square at least 36 inches across.) Cover the scraps and reserve.

cook's notes

Before you start, make sure that your fingernails are trimmed and remove all jewelry from your hands to prevent tearing the dough while you stretch it.

For best results, use a flour with a high gluten (15 to 20% protein) content, which can be found at some food specialty shops or purchased directly from a good bakery. The high gluten content in the flour will increase the stretching qualities of the dough.

Since these pastry sheets are slightly thicker than phyllo leaves, use only one sheet to every 2 or 3 leaves of store-bought phyllo called for in a recipe.

minutes. Using a ruler and a pizza cutter, cut the phyllo into six 12- by 15-inch rectangles. Reserve the scraps. Lightly sprinkle the phyllo sheets on both sides with cornstarch to prevent them from sticking together and stack. Loosely roll the stack up and wrap in plastic wrap.

Gather all the dough scraps and knead briefly into a ball. Roll and stretch the dough as above, to form a rectangle 18 by 26 inches. If the dough seems a little stiff as you stretch it, continue to oil the dough and your hands for easier handling. Trim the dough rectangle and cut out 2 more 12- by 15-inch phyllo sheets. Discard the dough scraps. Lightly sprinkle the sheets on both sides with cornstarch to prevent them from sticking together. Unroll the first batch of phyllo sheets and add the 2 sheets to the stack. Roll the stack up again and wrap in plastic wrap.

If you are not using the pastry sheets immediately, cover tightly with plastic wrap and refrigerate up to 3 days or freeze for up to 1 week. Defrost thoroughly before using.

Basil-Gorgonzola Purses

These pop-in-your-mouth hors d'oeuvres of Parmesan, Gorgonzola cheese, walnuts, and fresh basil are like tiny presents wrapped up in crackly paper-thin phyllo. Be warned! They are so addictive you will want to make lots. They are a bit time-consuming to assemble, but a snap once you get the hang of it and well worth the labor because they freeze beautifully too.

YIELD: 36 purses for hors d'oeuvres

GORGONZOLA FILLING

4 ounces Gorgonzola cheese, crumbled
4 ounces farmer's cheese or pot cheese
1 large egg, lightly beaten
2 tablespoons shredded fresh basil leaves
Cayenne pepper to taste

FOR ASSEMBLY

3 tablespoons toasted walnuts or pecans, finely ground
3 tablespoons freshly grated Parmesan cheese
9 sheets frozen phyllo pastry, fully thawed
8 tablespoons (1 stick) unsalted butter, melted

— planning ahead —

The assembled purses can be prepared a day ahead, covered, and refrigerated or frozen for up to 1 month. If they have been frozen, place them in the preheated oven without thawing and bake for 2 to 3 minutes longer than the time specified in the recipe.

MAKE THE FILLING: Combine the cheeses with a fork in a small bowl. Add the beaten egg and blend well. Stir in the basil and season with cayenne pepper. Cover and set aside.

Combine the ground nuts and Parmesan cheese in a small bowl. Set aside.

Preheat the oven to 375°F. Adjust an oven rack to the lowest position. Lightly butter a large baking sheet.

Work with one sheet of phyllo at a time, keeping the remaining sheets covered with a slightly damp kitchen towel to prevent them from drying out.

ASSEMBLE THE PURSES: Working quickly, place a sheet of phyllo on a work surface with a short side toward you. Lightly brush the sheet with melted butter and sprinkle with about 1 teaspoon of the nut-Parmesan mixture. Fold the right third of the sheet over the middle third, then fold the left third over both of these as if you were folding a business letter. You will have a 3-layer strip about 4 by 16 inches long. Lightly brush the top with melted butter. With scissors, cut the strip crosswise into four 4-inch squares. Place 1 teaspoon of the filling in the center of each square. Gather up the edges of the phyllo around and over the filling, pressing them together to seal, forming a purse-shaped pastry. Flatten the base of each purse by slightly pressing it down on the counter. Place the phyllo purses 1 inch apart on the prepared baking sheet. Brush the unbuttered surfaces of the puffs with melted butter and sprinkle a little nut-Parmesan mixture over the tops. Cover the pastries with a towel while you assemble the remaining purses.

Bake the purses until crisp and golden brown, about 10 minutes. Cool slightly before serving.

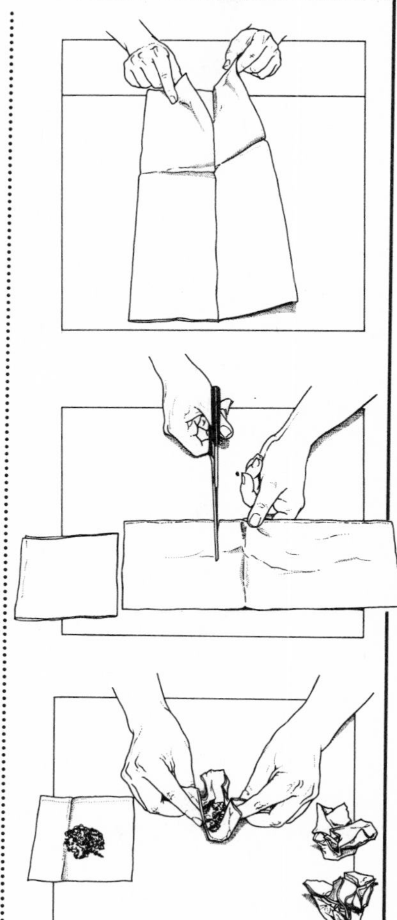

— planning ahead —

The ratatouille can be prepared a day ahead, covered, and refrigerated. The pastries can be assembled up to 2 hours ahead, loosely covered with foil, and refrigerated until ready to bake.

— cook's notes —

The ratatouille filling can be wrapped in 6 French Crêpes (page 281) and the filled crêpes served either cold with a salad or baked and served hot. To bake, place the filled crêpes on a lightly buttered baking sheet, brush with melted butter, and sprinkle generously with Parmesan cheese. Loosely cover with foil and bake in a preheated 350°F oven until heated through, about 15 minutes. Accompany with poached or fried eggs.

Baked Egg and Ratatouille in Phyllo

This Provençal-inspired recipe combines baked eggs and tender aromatic vegetables nestled in golden, flaky purse-shaped phyllo pastries. This is an ideal lighter alternative to Eggs Benedict for your favorite weekend guests as part of an elegant brunch or a light luncheon. The filling can be prepared ahead of time, but to keep the phyllo crisp, don't assemble and bake the pastries until shortly before serving. (Make sure you don't overcook the eggs!)

YIELD: 6 pastries, enough for 6 light main-course servings

RATATOUILLE

½ small eggplant (about ½ pound), peeled and cut into ½-inch cubes
2 small zucchini (about ½ pound), cut into ½-inch cubes
1¾ teaspoons salt, or more to taste
¼ cup olive oil
1 large onion, cut into ½-inch dice (about 2 cups)
1½ tablespoons minced garlic
1 pound tomatoes, peeled, seeded, and coarsely chopped
1 large green bell pepper (about 6 ounces), cut into ½-inch cubes (about 1 cup)
2 tablespoons tomato paste
¼ teaspoon crushed dried red pepper
2 tablespoons chopped fresh thyme leaves
2 bay leaves
Freshly ground black pepper to taste

FOR ASSEMBLY

12 sheets frozen phyllo pastry, fully thawed
12 tablespoons (1½ sticks) unsalted butter, melted
⅓ cup freshly grated Parmesan cheese
6 medium eggs, well chilled

MAKE THE RATATOUILLE: Toss the eggplant and zucchini in a colander with 1 teaspoon of the salt. Let drain in the sink for 30 minutes, then pat the vegetables dry with paper towels.

Heat the oil in a large skillet set over high heat. Add the onion and garlic and sauté until fragrant, about 1 minute. Add all the remaining ratatouille ingredients including the remaining ¾ teaspoon salt. Bring to a boil, lower the heat, and simmer for about

35 minutes, stirring occasionally, until thickened. Remove the pan from the heat. Taste the ratatouille and adjust the seasonings with salt and black pepper if necessary. Discard the bay leaves. Allow the ratatouille to cool, then cover and refrigerate until well chilled, or overnight.

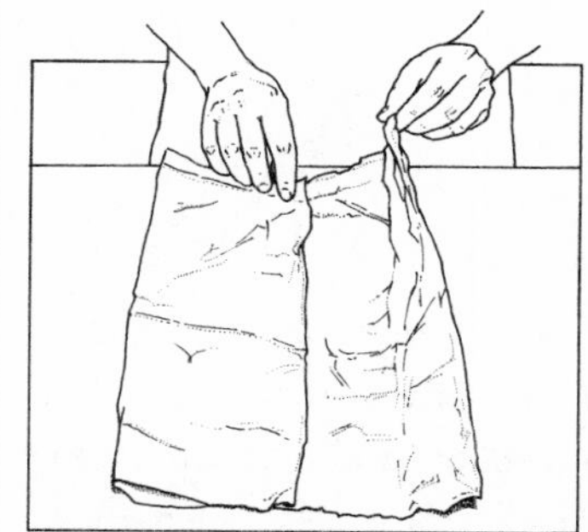

Preheat the oven to 400°F. Adjust an oven rack to the lowest position. Lightly butter a baking sheet.

Work with one sheet of phyllo at a time, keeping the remaining leaves covered with a slightly damp kitchen towel to prevent them from drying out.

ASSEMBLE THE PASTRIES: Working quickly, place a sheet of phyllo on a work surface with a long side toward you. Brush the sheet sparingly with melted butter and sprinkle with 1 teaspoon of the Parmesan cheese. Fold the right third of the sheet over the middle third, then fold the left third over both of these as if you were folding a business letter. You will have a 3-layer strip about 6 by 12 inches long. Brush the strip with melted butter and sprinkle with ½ teaspoon of the Parmesan. Prepare a second sheet of phyllo in the same fashion. Lay the second strip of phyllo across the middle of the first strip. Place ½ cup of the ratatouille in the center of the cross. With the back of a spoon, make a well large enough in the middle of the filling to accommodate an egg. Break an egg into the well. Gather up the ends of the phyllo strips around and over the filling, pressing them together to seal, forming a purse-shaped pastry. Brush the pastry with melted butter and, using a wide spatula, transfer it to the prepared baking sheet. Sprinkle 1 teaspoon of the Parmesan cheese over the pastry.

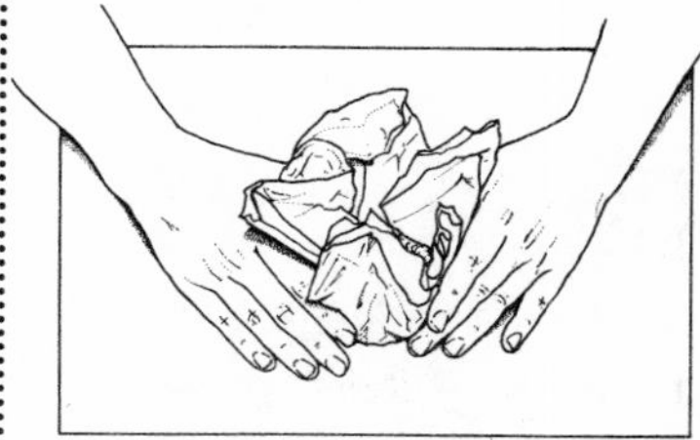

Repeat the assembly process to make 5 more pastries, placing them 2 inches apart on the baking sheet.

Bake the pastries for 15 minutes. If properly baked, the whites should be set and the yolks slightly runny. Let cool for 5 minutes before serving.

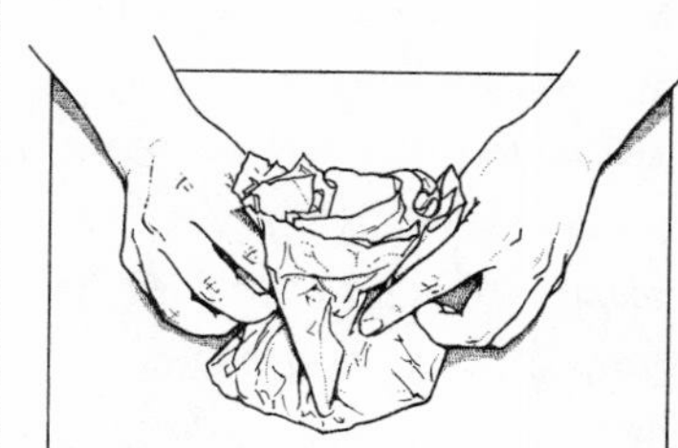

planning ahead

Spanakopetes can be assembled in advance, covered, and refrigerated for up to 2 days or frozen for up to 1 month. If they have been frozen, place them in the preheated oven without thawing and bake for about 5 to 10 minutes longer than the time specified in the recipe.

cook's notes

Feta is a Greek cheese made with sheep's milk, goat's milk, or a combination of both. White, crumbly, and salty, it is commonly used in baked savory dishes. To keep it moist, store feta tightly wrapped in plastic in the refrigerator. Use within a week. It's available in the dairy section of most supermarkets.

Spanakopetes

Spanakopetes, triangular-shaped puffs of spinach and feta cheese wrapped in flaky phyllo, are a popular Greek specialty. In my version, I add golden raisins and a hint of cinnamon to the classic filling to counterbalance the saltiness of the feta cheese. The results are utterly delicious. I have included directions for Spanakopita Pie at the end of this recipe for those who want an elegant entrée.

YIELD: 28 small puffs for hors d'oeuvres

SPINACH AND CHEESE FILLING

- ⅓ cup golden raisins
- 1¼ pounds fresh spinach, stemmed, washed, and dried, or one 10-ounce package frozen chopped spinach, thawed
- 2 tablespoons unsalted butter
- 1 cup chopped onions
- 1 tablespoon minced garlic
- 4 ounces cream cheese, softened
- 4 ounces feta cheese, crumbled
- 2 tablespoons chopped fresh dill
- 1 large egg, lightly beaten
- ½ teaspoon ground cinnamon
- Salt and freshly ground black pepper to taste

FOR ASSEMBLY

- 14 sheets frozen phyllo pastry, fully thawed
- 12 tablespoons (1½ sticks) unsalted butter, melted
- ½ cup dried bread crumbs

PREPARE THE FILLING: In a small bowl, soak the raisins in boiling water until they become plump, about 15 minutes. Drain and set aside.

If using fresh spinach, bring 3 quarts of salted water to a rolling boil in a large pot. Drop in the spinach and cook until it is just wilted, about 1 minute. Drain the spinach in a colander set in the sink, refresh under cold running water, and drain again. Squeeze the spinach dry and coarsely chop. If using frozen spinach, just squeeze the thawed spinach dry. Set aside.

In a medium skillet, melt the butter over moderate heat. Add the onions and garlic and sauté until the onions are soft, about 2 minutes. Add the spinach and sauté until it is just heated through and coated with butter, about 1 minute. Remove the pan from the heat and allow the mixture to cool slightly.

Place both cheeses in a large mixing bowl and, using a fork, mash together until they are smooth. Add the spinach mixture along with the dill, egg, cinnamon, and drained raisins. Stir to combine the filling thoroughly. Season with salt and pepper.

Preheat the oven to 375°F. Adjust an oven rack to the lowest position. Lightly butter a large baking sheet.

ASSEMBLE THE SPINACH PUFFS: Stack the phyllo sheets and cut the stack in half lengthwise with scissors.

Work with 2 rectangles of phyllo at a time, keeping the remaining sheets covered with a slightly damp kitchen towel to prevent them from drying out.

Working quickly, place 2 rectangles of phyllo on a work surface with a short side of each one toward you. Brush the rectangles generously with melted butter and sprinkle each one with ½ teaspoon of the bread crumbs. Fold each rectangle in half lengthwise to make a long thin strip about 2½ by 17 inches. Brush the strips with melted butter and sprinkle each one with ½ teaspoon bread crumbs. Place 1 tablespoon of the spinach filling about 1 inch above the lower left-hand corner of each strip. Fold up the bottom right corner of one strip diagonally over the filling so that the short edge meets the long edge of the strip, forming a triangular point. Continue folding up the triangle over itself to form a triangular package. Brush the triangle with butter and place it seam side down on the prepared baking sheet. Repeat with the second strip. Assemble the remaining puffs in the same manner.

Bake the pastries for 20 minutes, or until they are crisp and golden brown. Remove the baking sheet from the oven and allow the puffs to cool slightly before serving.

VARIATION

SPANAKOPITA PIE: Prepare a double recipe of the spinach filling. Using 8 sheets of phyllo pastry, 8 tablespoons melted butter, and ⅓ cup dried bread crumbs, assemble and bake the pie according to the directions for Tortellini Pie (page 63). Makes 6 main-course servings.

Try the chicken and smoked cheese filling for Crispy Chicken Flautas (page 202) or the curried beef filling for Jamaican Meat Patties (page 134). Follow the above instructions for preparing the phyllo and assembling the triangles.

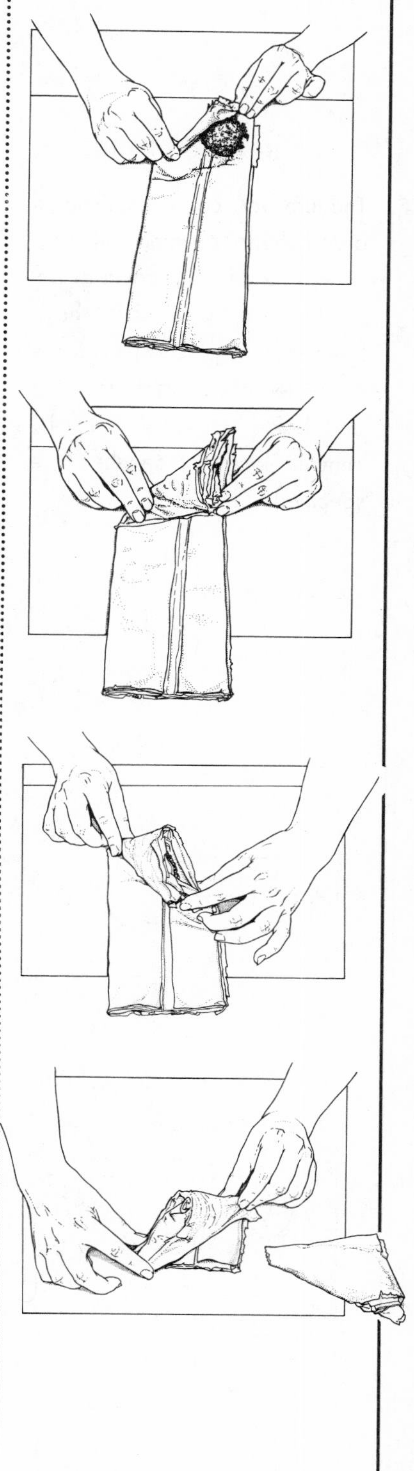

— planning ahead —

The turnovers can be assembled a day ahead, covered with plastic wrap, and refrigerated or frozen for up to a week. If they have been frozen, place them in the preheated oven without thawing and bake for about 5 to 10 minutes longer than the time specified.

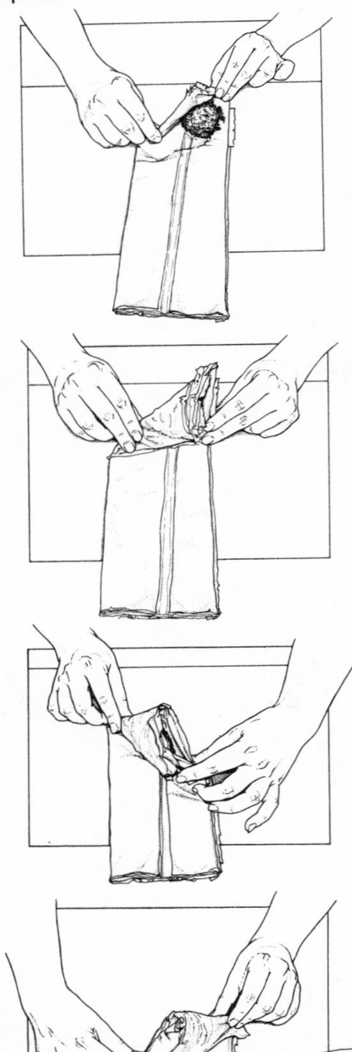

Shrimp and Eggplant Turnovers with Thai Seasoning

Growing up in Asia, I was exposed to Thai cuisine at a very young age and I have always retained a special fondness for it. Roasted curry paste, one of my favorite Thai condiments, is the secret in this dish. The inspiration for this recipe came to me one day when I saw some beautiful Japanese eggplants at a vegetable stand in New York's Chinatown. With smoky eggplants, fresh basil, and a coconut milk sauce, the sweet and hot flavor of the curry paste produces an incredible taste sensation. The flaky phyllo crust adds an extra dimension to this entrée.

YIELD: 8 turnovers, enough for 8 first-course or 4 main-course servings

ROASTED CURRY PASTE

¼ cup chopped shallots
¼ cup minced garlic
1 tablespoon minced peeled fresh ginger
4 jalapeño peppers, seeded and finely chopped
1 tablespoon curry powder, preferably Madras brand
½ teaspoon ground cumin
1 anchovy fillet packed in oil, drained and chopped
2 tablespoons peanut oil
1 tablespoon sugar
1 tablespoon fish sauce (see Cook's Notes)

CURRIED EGGPLANT FILLING

½ pounds Japanese eggplants (3 or 4 eggplants)
1½ tablespoons olive oil
¾ pound raw medium shrimp, peeled, deveined, and cut in half lengthwise
⅓ cup shredded fresh basil leaves
Salt to taste

FOR ASSEMBLY

8 sheets frozen phyllo pastry, fully thawed
8 tablespoons (1 stick) unsalted butter, melted
½ cup unsweetened shredded coconut

ROASTED CURRY SAUCE

2 cups chicken broth, homemade (page 368) or store-bought
½ cup heavy cream
½ cup canned unsweetened coconut milk (see Cook's Notes)
Shredded fresh basil leaves, for garnish

PREPARE THE CURRY PASTE: Wrap the shallots, garlic, ginger, and jalapeños in a sheet of aluminum foil, sealing well to make a flat package. Place the package directly on a gas or electric burner set at moderate heat and cook until fragrant, about 1 minute on each side, turning with tongs. Allow to cool, then unwrap and transfer the contents to a spice grinder or blender. Add the curry powder, cumin, and anchovy and process to a fine paste.

Heat the oil in a small skillet or frying pan over moderate heat and stir-fry the paste until well browned, about 3 minutes. Stir in the sugar and fish sauce, blending well. Set aside to cool.

PREPARE THE EGGPLANTS: Prick the skins of the eggplants in several places with a fork. Place the eggplants directly on a gas or electric burner set at moderate heat and grill, turning with tongs, until the flesh is soft and the skin charred, about 4 minutes. Remove to a rack and allow to cool. Peel off and discard the charred skin. The eggplant flesh should be just cooked but still firm. Cut the eggplant into ½-inch cubes. Put the cubes in a bowl and set aside.

MAKE THE FILLING: Heat the oil in a small skillet over moderate heat. Add the shrimp and stir-fry for 30 seconds. Add the eggplant and 2½ tablespoons of the curry paste and stir with a wooden spoon to mix, about 30 seconds. Add the basil and salt to taste and remove from the heat. Allow to cool.

Lightly butter a large baking sheet.

Work with one sheet of phyllo at a time, keeping the remaining leaves covered with a slightly damp kitchen towel to prevent them from drying out.

ASSEMBLE THE TURNOVERS: Working quickly, place a sheet of phyllo on a work surface with a long side toward you. Lightly brush the sheet with melted butter and sprinkle with 1 teaspoon of the shredded coconut. Fold the sheet crosswise in half. Brush with butter and sprinkle with ½ teaspoon of the coconut. Fold the sheet lengthwise in half. You will have a 4-layer strip about 4 by 12 inches. Lightly brush the strip with melted butter.

Place ¼ cup of the filling on the bottom left-hand corner of the strip. Fold the bottom right corner of the phyllo strip diagonally over the filling so that the short edge meets the long edge of the strip, forming a triangular point. Continue folding up the triangle over itself to form a triangular package. Brush the triangle with butter and place it seam side down on the prepared baking sheet. Sprinkle 1 teaspoon of the shredded coconut over the triangle. Repeat the assembly with the remaining phyllo sheets and filling. Cover and set aside until ready to bake.

MAKE THE SAUCE: Bring the chicken broth to a boil in a medium saucepan. Lower the heat to moderately high and gently boil until reduced to 1 cup, about

— cook's notes —

When buying fish sauce, look for the Squid or Tiparos brand. Once opened, fish sauce lasts indefinitely at room temperature. Fish sauce is available in Asian markets and in some well-stocked supermarkets.

Do not confuse coconut milk with coconut cream. Excellent canned unsweetened coconut milk is available in Asian markets and some supermarkets. After opening, it can be refrigerated for up to 1 week. For longer storage, freeze it in ice cube trays, then store the cubes in plastic bags. Before using, heat the frozen coconut milk until completely melted. Four cubes equal about ½ cup. You may substitute heavy cream for the coconut milk, but the taste will be slightly altered.

If you can't find Japanese eggplants, choose a large purple eggplant and allow 12 minutes to cook it.

The curry paste can be made in larger quantities. (This recipe makes about ⅓ cup.) Use it, as I do, to enhance other curried dishes. To store, put the curry paste in a glass jar. Add just enough peanut oil or vegetable oil to cover. Cover and refrigerate for up to 2 months. Do not freeze; the paste will lose its aroma.

15 minutes. Add the cream, coconut milk, and 1½ tablespoons of the curry paste and blend well with a whisk. (Save the remaining curry paste for other uses.) Continue cooking until the sauce is reduced to about 1 cup and has thickened enough to coat the back of a spoon, about 15 minutes. The sauce may appear curdled; this is natural, don't worry. Strain the sauce through a fine-mesh sieve into a small saucepan. Cover and set aside.

Preheat the oven to 375°F. Adjust an oven rack to the lowest position.

Bake the turnovers until crisp and golden brown, about 20 minutes. Let cool slightly.

TO SERVE: Gently reheat the sauce and divide it among four preheated plates. Arrange 2 turnovers on each plate and garnish with shredded basil.

Flaky Tunisian Triangles

(BRIK)

—planning ahead—

The triangles can be assembled up to 6 hours in advance, covered, and refrigerated until ready to bake.

— cook's notes —

The triangles are best baked and eaten immediately.

Brik, fried triangular turnovers stuffed with either a minted lamb mixture and whole eggs or just with eggs, are a Tunisian specialty. They are a popular first course and are always served steaming hot. In this quick and easy meatless adaptation, I have surrounded the egg with Parmesan cheese, creamy goat cheese, and nuts. Also, I find baking the pastry in a very hot oven instead of frying produces equally fine results and saves a lot of calories along the way. To be authentic, squeeze lemon juice over the pastry and eat it with your fingers. Be prepared for the soft egg to ooze out of its pastry casing and down your chin. Less adventurous diners should feel free to use a knife and fork. Served with a soup and a salad, these turnovers make a light, satisfying supper.

YIELD: 8 triangles, enough for 8 first-course or 4 light supper servings

8 sheets phyllo pastry, fully thawed
8 tablespoons (1 stick) unsalted butter, melted
⅓ cup freshly grated Parmesan cheese
1 8-ounce log goat cheese, cut into 8 slices and well chilled
8 small eggs, well chilled
Salt and freshly ground black pepper to taste
⅓ cup pine nuts (pignoli), toasted and coarsely ground
⅓ cup chopped scallions
Lemon slices (optional)

Preheat the oven to 500°F. Adjust an oven rack to the lowest position. Lightly butter a large baking sheet.

Work with one sheet of phyllo at a time, keeping the remaining sheets covered with a slightly damp kitchen towel to prevent them from drying out.

ASSEMBLE THE TRIANGLES: Working quickly, place a sheet of phyllo on a work surface with a long side toward you. Lightly brush the sheet with melted butter and sprinkle with 1 teaspoon of the Parmesan cheese. Fold the right third of the sheet over the middle third. Brush the unbuttered surface with butter. Place a slice of goat cheese on the double layer, slightly above the center, right up against the center seam. Make a deep indentation in the cheese with the back of a spoon. Carefully break an egg into the well. (Don't worry if the egg white spills over and covers the cheese.) Sprinkle the egg with salt and pepper, then top it with 2 teaspoons each of the nuts and scallions.

Fold the left third of the phyllo over, covering the filling. Lightly brush the surface with butter and sprinkle with ½ teaspoon of the Parmesan cheese. Fold the bottom right corner of the phyllo strip diagonally over the egg so that the short edge meets the long edge of the strip, forming a triangular point. Fold the top half of the phyllo strip over the triangle, then lift up the pastry and tuck the overhanging phyllo under the packet to form a triangle-shaped turnover. Brush the triangle all over with butter and place it seam side down on the prepared baking sheet. Sprinkle 1 teaspoon of the Parmesan over the triangle. Repeat the assembly with the remaining phyllo sheets, fillings, and eggs.

Bake the triangles until puffed and golden, about 10 minutes. Be careful not to overbake or the egg yolk will harden. When properly baked, the egg white should be softly set and the yolk still runny. Remove from the oven, and let cool slightly. Garnish each triangle with lemon slices if desired, and serve warm.

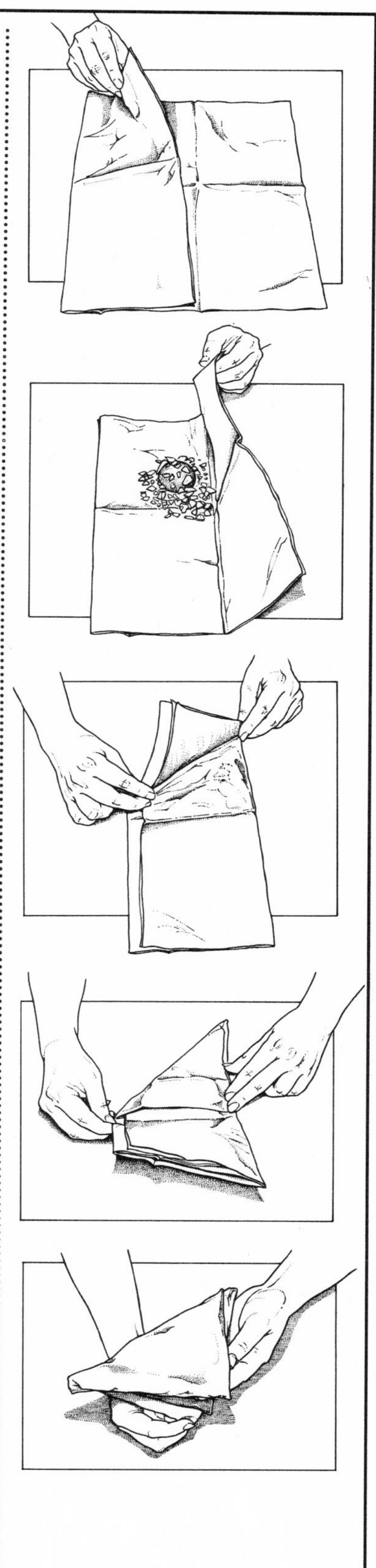

— *planning ahead* —

The filling can be prepared a day ahead, covered, and refrigerated. The pie can be assembled ahead of time, covered, and refrigerated overnight or frozen for up to 1 month. If the pie has been refrigerated, bring it to room temperature before baking. If it has been frozen, place the unthawed pie in a preheated 350°F oven and bake for 45 to 50 minutes.

— *cook's notes* —

Do try to find fresh chives or tarragon for this dish. Their fresh taste is so important. If unavailable, substitute finely sliced scallions.

Truffat

This recipe is a contemporary version of a time-honored French potato pie. Called *truffat* (because potatoes were called the truffles of the poor), the traditional pies were very heavy and solid, made with a filling of potatoes cooked in cream and encased in a puff pastry or short pie crust. In my recipe, I cook the potatoes to tenderness in chicken broth and then wrap the flavorful filling in feathery phyllo to create a lighter pie with an interesting contrast of textures.

I like to serve this as a side dish to a meat entrée. It is also marvelous at room temperature as well as piping hot. Take it on your next picnic instead of potato salad for a special treat.

YIELD: 1 large pie, enough for 6 to 8 side-dish servings

SPECIAL EQUIPMENT: A 9-inch by 1½-inch deep pie pan or round cake pan

POTATO AND BACON FILLING

3 large baking potatoes (about 1½ pounds)
6 thick slices bacon (about 6 ounces), cut crosswise into ½-inch-wide strips
2 cups chopped onions
1½ tablespoons minced garlic
⅓ cup chicken broth
1 tablespoon chopped fresh parsley
1 tablespoon chopped fresh chives or minced tarragon leaves
Salt and freshly ground black pepper to taste

FOR ASSEMBLY

8 sheets phyllo pastry, fully thawed
8 tablespoons (1 stick) unsalted butter, melted
⅓ cup freshly grated Parmesan cheese

MAKE THE FILLING: Peel the potatoes and cut them into thin slices. Rinse the slices under cold running water and pat dry with a kitchen towel. Place the potatoes in a medium bowl and cover with a towel to prevent discoloration.

Heat a large skillet or sauté pan over moderately high heat. Add the bacon and cook, stirring with a wooden spoon, until the bacon is crisp and the fat is rendered, about 5 minutes. Pour the bacon into a strainer placed over a heatproof bowl. Spread the drained bacon on paper towels, and return 3 tablespoons of the bacon fat to the skillet. Add the onions and garlic and sauté over moderately high heat for 3 minutes.

Add the potatoes and bacon, tossing to coat with the fat. Pour in the broth, lower the heat, cover, and let simmer for 5 minutes. Uncover, gently stir the mixture, cover again and continue cooking until the potatoes are tender, about 3 more minutes. Remove the pan from the heat, stir in the herbs, and season with salt and pepper. Allow to cool.

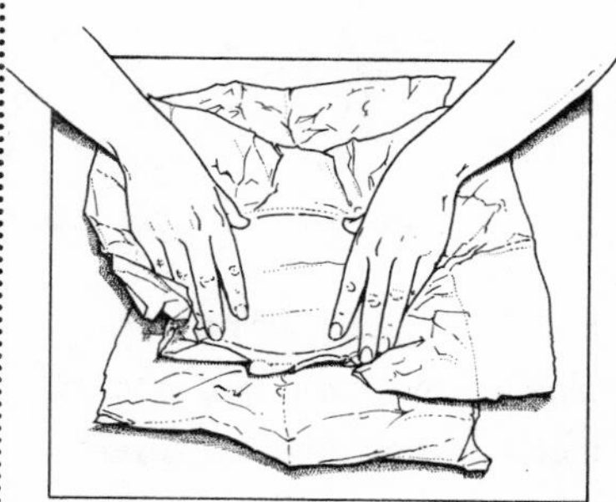

Preheat the oven to 375°F. Adjust an oven rack to the lowest position. Lightly butter the pie pan.

Work with one sheet of phyllo at a time, keeping the remaining leaves covered with a slightly damp kitchen towel to prevent them from drying out.

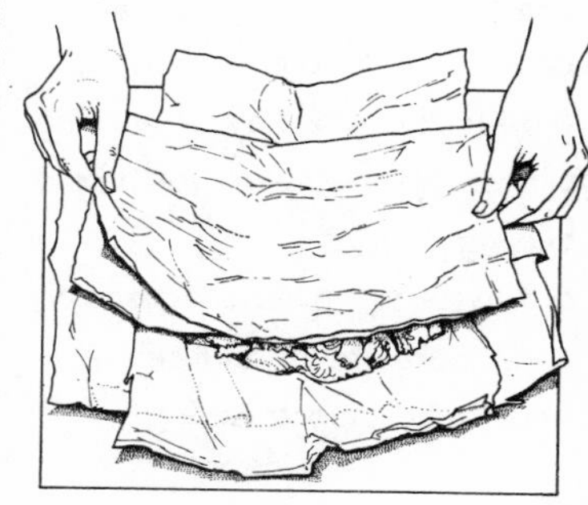

ASSEMBLE THE PIE: Working quickly, place a sheet of phyllo on a work surface. Lightly brush the sheet with melted butter and sprinkle with 1 teaspoon of the Parmesan cheese. Top with 2 more sheets, brushing each one with butter and sprinkling with Parmesan. Place the layered sheets in the bottom of the buttered pie pan with the ends extending over the sides of the pan. Layer 3 more phyllo leaves as above, brushing with melted butter and sprinkling with Parmesan. Place them in the pan across the first 3 leaves, completely covering the bottom and sides of the pan. Spoon in the filling and smooth the top. Layer the remaining 2 phyllo sheets as above, brushing each with butter and sprinkling 1 teaspoon of the Parmesan cheese over each one. Fold the leaves crosswise in half, place the folded leaves over the filling, and brush with butter. Fold the overhanging phyllo leaves over the top to completely seal the filling. Generously brush the top of the pie with melted butter and sprinkle with the remaining Parmesan cheese.

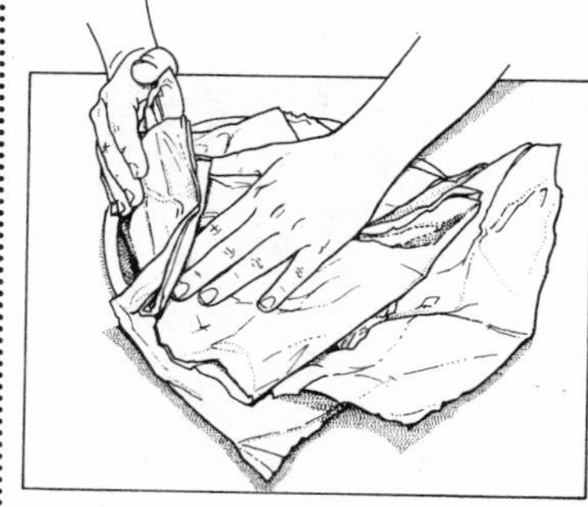

Bake the pie until crisp and golden brown, about 25 to 30 minutes. If the top of the pie begins to brown too fast during baking, loosely cover it with foil.

Remove the pie from the oven and allow it to rest on a rack for about 5 minutes. Cut into wedges and serve.

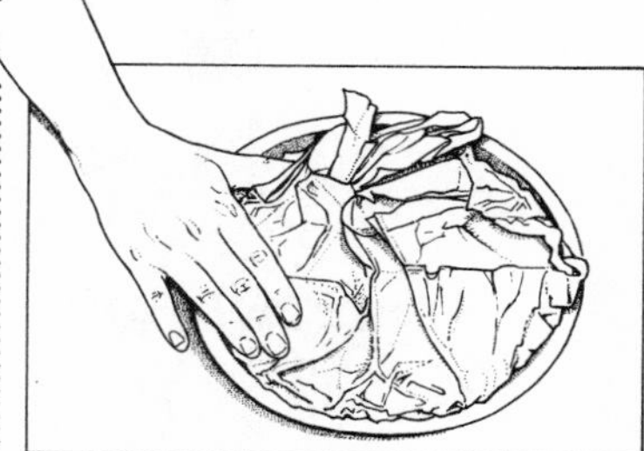

— *planning ahead* —

Both the chicken filling and the almond-cinnamon mix can be made a day ahead, covered, and refrigerated. The pie may be assembled in advance, loosely covered with foil, and refrigerated for up to 2 days. Bring the pie to room temperature before baking.

The sauce may be prepared up to 2 hours ahead and gently reheated just before serving.

Moroccan Chicken Pie

(B'STELLA)

B'stella, which derives from the Spanish word *pastilla* ("small pastry"), is one of Morocco's greatest contributions to gastronomy. I love this pie for its complex layers of taste and textures. A sumptuous and delicate deep-dish flaky pie, it is traditionally made with a filling of shredded squab meat, eggs, and almonds seasoned with an array of spices including cinnamon, saffron, coriander, and ginger. After baking, the crackly pastry crust is dusted with sugar and cinnamon. In my version, lean breasts of chicken are slowly poached in broth so the meat remains moist and very tender. Usually, b'stella is served on its own, but I prefer to accompany it with a light orange butter sauce that complements all the spices and makes it even more delicious and spectacular. Serve as an appetizer or main course or as part of a buffet.

YIELD: 1 large pie, enough for 10 appetizer or 6 main-course servings

SPECIAL EQUIPMENT: A 10-inch by 2½-inch deep pie pan or round cake pan

POACHED CHICKEN

3 cups chicken broth, homemade (page 368) or store-bought
2 2-inch cinnamon sticks
12 black peppercorns
2 boneless skinless chicken breasts (about 1 pound)

SPICE MIX

1 teaspoon ground cumin
1 teaspoon ground coriander
¾ teaspoon cayenne pepper
¼ teaspoon ground turmeric
¾ teaspoon salt

FILLING

2 tablespoons unsalted butter
1½ cups chopped onions
1 tablespoon minced garlic
1 teaspoon minced fresh ginger
½ teaspoon saffron threads, finely crushed and soaked in
2 teaspoons dry white wine (see Cook's Notes)
Salt to taste
¼ cup heavy cream
2 tablespoons finely shredded fresh mint leaves
2 tablespoons finely shredded fresh cilantro leaves

SCRAMBLED EGGS

6 large eggs
Salt to taste
2 tablespoons unsalted butter

ALMOND AND CINNAMON MIX

½ cup slivered almonds, toasted (see Cook's Notes)
1 tablespoon sugar
1 tablespoon ground cinnamon

FOR ASSEMBLY

8 sheets phyllo pastry, fully thawed
8 tablespoons (1 stick) unsalted butter, melted
⅓ cup dried bread crumbs

ORANGE SAUCE

2 large shallots, thinly sliced
1 cup fresh orange juice
½ cup dry white wine, preferably Chardonnay
8 tablespoons (1 stick) unsalted butter, at room temperature
Salt and freshly ground black pepper to taste

GARNISH

1 tablespoon confectioner's sugar
½ teaspoon ground cinnamon
1 tablespoon finely shredded fresh mint leaves

POACH THE CHICKEN: Combine the chicken broth, cinnamon sticks, and peppercorns in a large skillet. Bring to a boil over high heat. Reduce the heat to low, partially cover the pan, and simmer for 10 minutes. Add the chicken breasts, making sure that they are well immersed in the broth; if not, add water to cover. Simmer uncovered until the chicken is almost cooked through, about 10 minutes. To check the chicken for doneness, pierce the meat with a fork. The juices should run clear with no trace of blood. Remove the pan from the heat and let the chicken stand in the poaching liquid until it is cool enough to handle.

Remove the chicken to a plate. Strain and reserve the poaching liquid. Shred the chicken, cover, and set aside.

PREPARE THE SPICE MIX: Combine all the spices in a small bowl. Set aside.

PREPARE THE FILLING: Heat the butter in a large skillet over moderate heat. Add the onions, garlic, and ginger, and sauté until fragrant and soft, about 2 minutes. Add the spice mix and cook for 1 minute. Add ⅓ cup of the reserved poaching liquid and the saffron with the wine. Remove the pan from the heat, and scrape the bottom of the pan with a wooden spoon to release any browned bits. Add the shredded chicken and toss well to coat with the spices. Season to taste with salt. Transfer the filling to a shallow dish and allow to cool completely. Then add the cream, mint, and cilantro and mix well. Cover and set aside.

PREPARE THE SCRAMBLED EGGS: Break the eggs into a medium bowl. Add ¼ cup of the reserved poaching liquid and a pinch of salt. (Discard the remaining poaching liquid.) Beat the eggs with a whisk until thoroughly blended. Heat the butter in a large skillet over moderate heat and add the eggs. Stir with a rubber spatula, loosening the set eggs from the bottom and sides of the skillet. Cook the eggs first until they are softly set, about 1½ minutes. Don't worry if some liquid separates from the eggs. Remove the skillet from the heat and let the eggs cool.

continued

— cook's notes —

Saffron, a fragrant spice, is the dried stigma of the saffron crocus bulb. Because the stigmas must be handpicked, saffron is one of the world's most prized and expensive spices. The best saffron threads should look bloodred in color. They also have a pungent aroma and a slightly bitter taste, so use them sparingly. If you are lucky enough to find Kashmiri saffron, use half the amount called for in any recipe, because it has a more powerful taste and aroma than the more widely available Spanish saffron. To extract the full taste and aroma of saffron threads, pulverize them in a mortar and then soak in a little bit of warm liquid before use so the food will be evenly colored and flavored. White wine is great for drawing out all the color pigments of saffron. Avoid powdered saffron, which is not pure saffron. Dried whole saffron threads can be found in select specialty food shops. They can also be ordered from the Spice House Ltd., P.O. Box 1633, Milwaukee, WI 53201(414-768-8799).

To toast slivered almonds: Spread out on a jelly-roll pan and toast in a preheated 350°F oven until golden brown, about 6 to 8 minutes. If using whole blanched almonds, toast for 5 to 6 minutes longer.

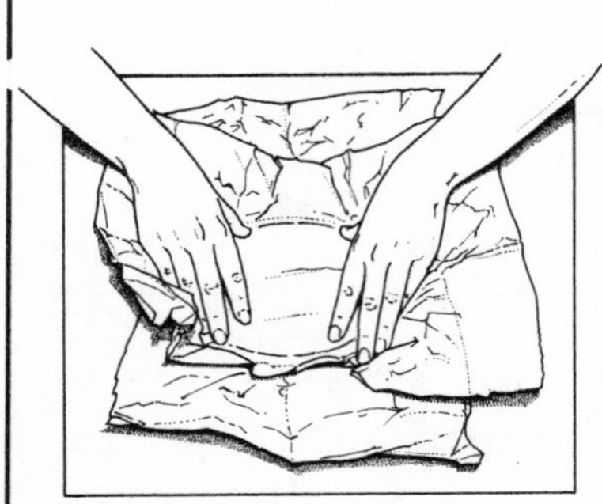

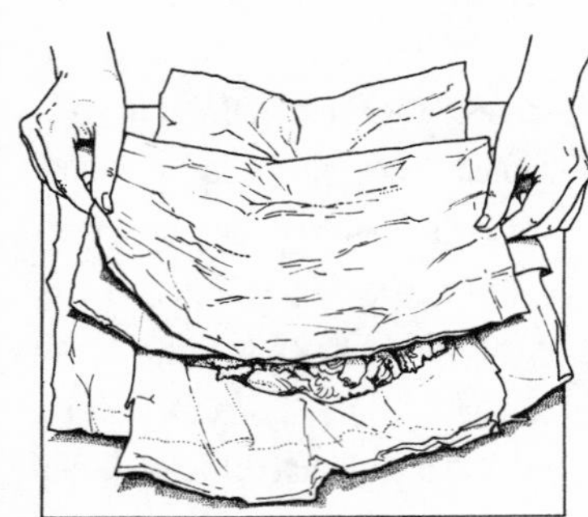

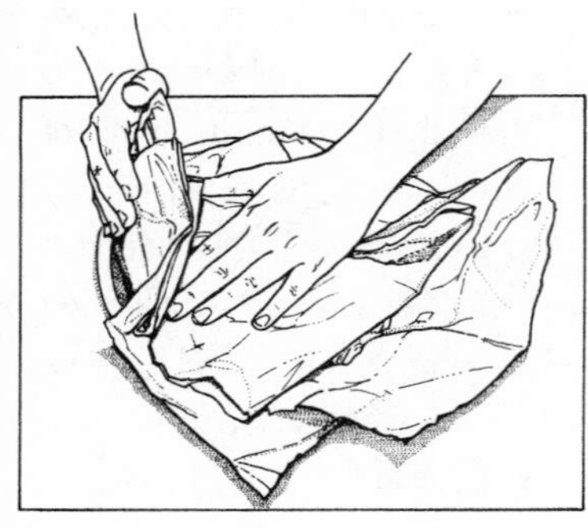

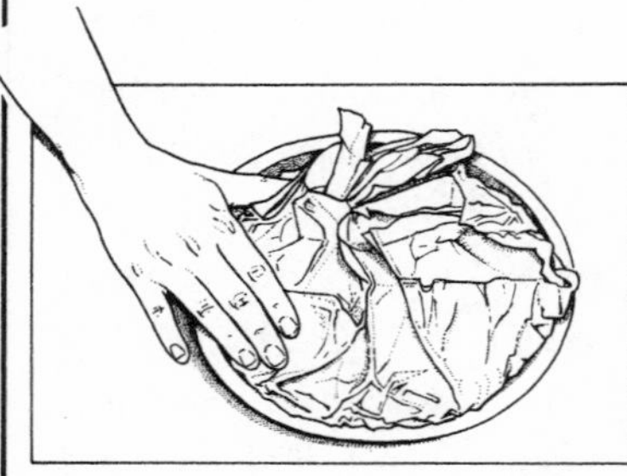

PREPARE THE ALMOND-CINNAMON MIX: Put the almonds, sugar, and cinnamon in the bowl of a food processor fitted with the metal blade and pulse until coarsely ground. Cover and set aside.

Preheat the oven to 350°F. Adjust an oven rack to the lowest position. Lightly butter the pie pan.

Work with one sheet of phyllo at a time, keeping the remaining leaves covered with a slightly damp kitchen towel to prevent them from drying out.

ASSEMBLE THE PIE: Working quickly, place a sheet of phyllo on a work surface. Lightly brush the sheet with melted butter and sprinkle with 1 teaspoon of the bread crumbs. Top with 2 more sheets, brushing each with butter and sprinkling with bread crumbs. Place the layered sheets in the bottom of the buttered pie pan with the ends extending over the sides of the pan. Layer 3 more phyllo leaves as above, brushing with melted butter and sprinkling with bread crumbs. Place them in the pan across the first 3 leaves, completely covering the bottom and sides of the pan.

Sprinkle ¼ cup of the almond-cinnamon mix over the bottom of the pie pan. Spoon half of the chicken filling evenly over the almonds. Spread half of the scrambled eggs over the chicken. Top the eggs with ¼ cup of the nut mix. Layer the remaining chicken and then the eggs in the pan and top with the remaining nut mixture. Layer the remaining 2 phyllo sheets as above, brushing with butter and sprinkling 1 teaspoon of the bread crumbs over each sheet. Fold the leaves crosswise in half, place the folded leaves over the filling, and brush with butter. Fold the overhanging phyllo leaves over the top to completely seal the filling. Generously brush the top of the pie with melted butter and sprinkle with the remaining bread crumbs.

Bake the pie until crisp and golden, about 35 to 40 minutes. If the top of the pie begins to brown too fast during baking, loosely cover it with foil. Remove the pie from the oven and allow it to rest on a rack for about 5 minutes.

Meanwhile, MAKE THE SAUCE: Combine the shallots, orange juice, and white wine in a medium-size heavy saucepan and bring to a boil over high heat. Lower the heat to moderate and simmer until the liquid is reduced by a third, about 8 minutes. Gradually whisk in the butter, about 2 tablespoons at a time. Keep the heat low enough that the butter does not melt entirely; do not allow the sauce to simmer or it will become thin and separate. Remove the pan from the heat and season with salt and pepper.

TO SERVE: Cut the pie into wedges. Place a wedge in the center of each plate and spoon the sauce around it. Combine the confectioner's sugar and cinnamon and sprinkle the mixture over the wedges. Scatter some shredded mint over the sauce.

Tortellini Pie

The Italian tradition of enclosing pasta in a short pastry crust to make a *torta* or *pasticcio* dates from medieval times. Originally a dish for the aristocracy, today pasta pies have become a staple in many parts of Italy and show up frequently at festivities. A pasta pie can include homemade tortellini, ravioli, or rectangular pasta twists called *caramelle.* The pasta is invariably combined with either a meat sauce, a white sauce, or both. Traditionally, such ingredients as mushrooms, sausages or tiny meatballs, and spices also are added, and the filling is encased in a sturdy savory pie crust. Sweet crusts or custards may be used to produce extra-special pies.

Inspired by this heritage, I offer a simplified version of such a pie. Feathery-light phyllo pastry replaces the robust pie crust, and store-bought fresh tortellini are enrobed in a simple but delicious tomato cream sauce. The result is a sensational dish that saves you some serious labor. Served with a salad and some red wine, this makes a stunning centerpiece for a grand dinner.

— planning ahead —

The tomato sauce, without the cream, can be prepared ahead, covered, and refrigerated for up to 2 days or frozen for weeks. Reheat before adding the reduced cream, basil, butter, and Parmesan cheese. The pie can be assembled up to 4 hours in advance, covered loosely with foil, and refrigerated. Bring to room temperature before baking.

YIELD: 1 large pie, enough for 8 first-course or 4 main-course servings

SPECIAL EQUIPMENT: A 9-inch by 1½-inch pie pan or round cake pan

TOMATO CREAM SAUCE

1½ tablespoons olive oil
¾ cup chopped onions
1 tablespoon minced garlic
3 medium ripe tomatoes (about 1 pound), peeled and coarsely chopped, or one 1-pound can Italian plum tomatoes in juice
¼ cup whole fresh basil leaves, plus ¼ cup minced fresh basil leaves
2 tablespoons chopped fresh parsley
1 teaspoon sugar
¾ teaspoon salt, or more to taste
About ¼ cup chicken broth (optional)
Freshly ground black pepper to taste
3 cups heavy cream
2 tablespoons unsalted butter, at room temperature
1 cup freshly grated Parmesan cheese

FILLING

1¼ pounds fresh meat- or cheese-filled tortellini

FOR ASSEMBLY

8 sheets frozen phyllo pastry, fully thawed
8 tablespoons (1 stick) unsalted butter, melted
⅓ cup freshly grated Parmesan cheese

continued

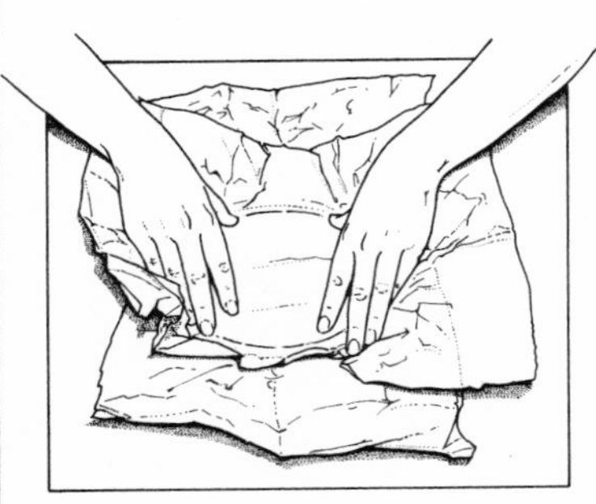

PREPARE THE TOMATO SAUCE: Heat the oil in a large saucepan set over low heat. Add the onions and garlic and cook, stirring frequently, until very soft but not browned, about 5 minutes. Add the tomatoes, whole basil leaves, parsley, sugar, and salt. Cook over low heat until slightly thickened, about 20 minutes, stirring occasionally; do not let the sauce bubble.

Transfer the sauce to the bowl of a food processor fitted with the metal blade and purée. Pass the sauce through a fine-meshed sieve, pressing on the solids to extract as much liquid as possible. Discard the pulp. If the sauce seems a little too thick, thin it with about ¼ cup chicken broth or water. You should have about 1½ cups of sauce. Taste the sauce and adjust the seasonings with salt and pepper if necessary. Cover and set aside.

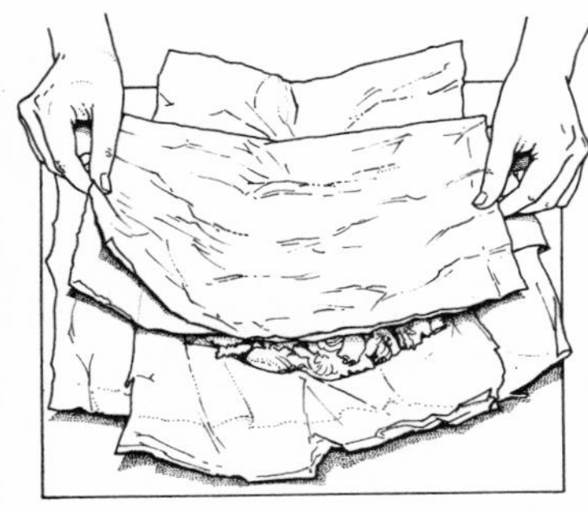

REDUCE THE CREAM: Bring the cream to a boil in a large saucepan over moderately high heat. Reduce the heat to moderate and boil the cream until reduced to 2 cups, about 10 minutes. Be careful that the cream doesn't boil over. Add the tomato sauce, stir to combine, and bring to a boil. Remove the pan from the heat and stir in the minced basil, butter, and Parmesan. Season with salt and pepper if necessary.

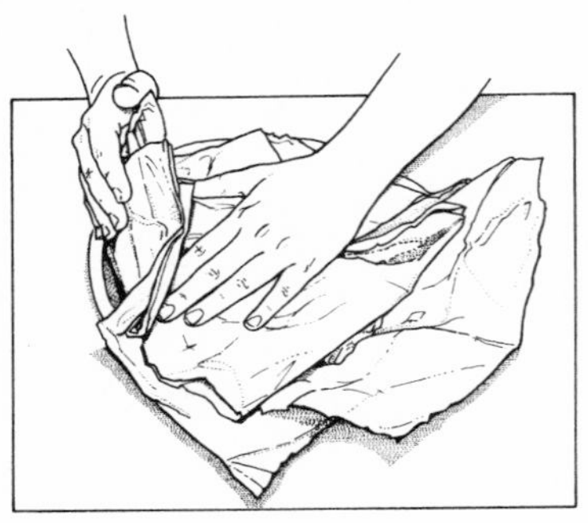

COOK THE TORTELLINI: Bring 3 quarts salted water to a boil in a large pot. Add the tortellini and cook, stirring occasionally with a wooden spoon, until they rise to the top and are cooked al dente, about 5 minutes. Drain the tortellini in a colander set in the sink, rinse under cold running water, and drain thoroughly. Transfer the tortellini to a large bowl and stir in one third of the tomato cream sauce. Set aside.

Preheat the oven to 375°F. Adjust an oven rack to the lowest position. Lightly butter the pie pan.

Work with one sheet of phyllo at a time, keeping the remaining leaves covered with a slightly damp kitchen towel to prevent them from drying out.

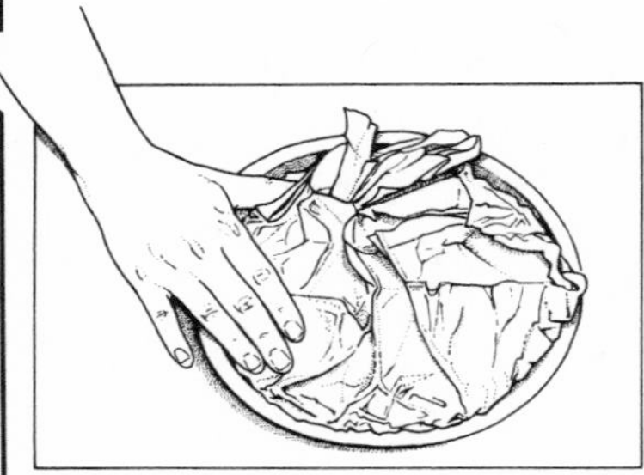

ASSEMBLE THE PIE: Working quickly, place a sheet of phyllo on a work surface. Lightly brush the sheet with melted butter and sprinkle with 1 teaspoon of the Parmesan cheese. Top with 2 more sheets, brushing each with butter and sprinkling each with Parmesan. Place the layered sheets in the bottom of the buttered pie pan with the ends extending over the sides of the pan. Layer 3 more phyllo leaves as above, brushing each with melted butter and sprinkling each with Parmesan. Place them in the pie pan across the first 3 leaves, completely covering the bottom and sides of the pan. Spoon in the tortellini filling, and smooth the top. Spoon ½ cup of the tomato cream sauce over the top, and set the remaining sauce aside.

Layer the remaining 2 phyllo sheets as above, brushing with butter and sprinkling

1 teaspoon of the Parmesan over each sheet. Fold the leaves crosswise in half, place the folded leaves over the filling, and brush with butter. Fold the overhanging phyllo leaves over the top to completely seal the filling. Generously brush the top of the pie with melted butter and sprinkle with the remaining Parmesan.

Bake the pie until crisp and golden, about 25 to 30 minutes. If the top of the pie begins to brown too fast during baking, loosely cover it with foil. Remove the pie from the oven and allow it to rest on a rack for about 5 minutes before cutting.

TO SERVE: Reheat the reserved tomato cream sauce. Cut the pie into wedges. Place a wedge in the center of each plate and spoon the sauce around it.

— *planning ahead* —

The tomato sauce can be prepared in advance, covered, and refrigerated for up to 2 days, or frozen for weeks. The pie can be assembled a day in advance, covered, and refrigerated. Bring to room temperature before baking. It can also be frozen for up to a week. If the pie has been frozen, place it unthawed in a preheated 350°F oven and bake until crisp and golden brown, about 45 to 50 minutes.

Deep-Dish Vegetarian Strudel Pie

I have combined a Turkish dried apricot and rice pie with an Italian spinach and mozzarella pie to make a very tasty deep-dish vegetarian pie. Tart, sweet, and piquant best describe its taste, which is further enhanced by a light fresh tomato-basil sauce and a hint of cinnamon. This superb phyllo-wrapped entrée has become a standard part of my repertoire and I hope it will become part of yours too. I like using a square pan to give the pie an interesting look but a round cake pan is also fine. The time it takes to make both pies is exactly the same.

YIELD: 1 pie, enough for 4 to 6 main-course servings

SPECIAL EQUIPMENT: A 9-inch by 2-inch deep square or round cake pan

TOMATO SAUCE

1½ tablespoons olive oil
¾ cup chopped onions
1 tablespoon minced garlic
3 medium ripe tomatoes (about 1 pound), coarsely chopped, or one 1-pound can Italian plum tomatoes in juice
¼ cup fresh basil leaves
2 tablespoons chopped fresh parsley
1 teaspoon sugar
¾ teaspoon salt, or more to taste
About ¼ cup chicken broth (optional)
Freshly ground black pepper to taste

SPINACH-RICE FILLING

1 cup chicken broth, homemade (page 368) or store-bought
½ cup long-grain rice
1 pound fresh spinach, stemmed, washed, and dried, or 1 10-ounce package frozen leaf spinach, thawed
2 tablespoons olive oil
½ cup chopped onion
1 tablespoon minced garlic
¾ cup golden raisins
4 ounces (about ¾ cup) dried apricots, coarsely chopped
1 tablespoon ground cinnamon
¾ teaspoon crushed dried red pepper
Salt and freshly ground black pepper to taste

FOR ASSEMBLY

8 sheets phyllo pastry, fully thawed
8 tablespoons (1 stick) unsalted butter, melted
⅓ cup freshly grated Parmesan cheese
8 ounces mozzarella cheese (preferably fresh), shredded

PREPARE THE TOMATO SAUCE: Heat the oil in a large saucepan set over low heat. Add the onions and garlic and cook, stirring frequently, until very soft but not browned, about 10 minutes. Add the tomatoes with their juices, the basil leaves, parsley, sugar, and salt. Cook over low heat until slightly thickened, about 30 minutes, stirring occasionally; do not let the sauce bubble. Transfer the sauce to the bowl of a food processor fitted with the metal blade and purée. Pass the sauce through a fine-meshed sieve, pressing on the solids to extract as much liquid as possible. Discard the pulp. If the sauce seems a little too thick, thin it with about ¼ cup chicken broth or water. You should have about 1½ cups of sauce. Taste the sauce and adjust the seasonings with salt and pepper if necessary. Cover and set aside.

PREPARE THE FILLING: Bring the broth to a boil in a medium saucepan over high heat. Add the rice, reduce the heat to low, cover, and cook until all the liquid is absorbed and the rice tender, about 18 minutes.

If using fresh spinach, bring 3 quarts salted water to a rolling boil in a large pot. Drop in the spinach and cook until just wilted, about 1 minute. Drain the spinach in a colander set in the sink, refresh under cold running water, and drain again. Squeeze the spinach dry, then coarsely chop. Set aside. If using frozen spinach, just squeeze the thawed spinach dry, then coarsely chop. Set aside.

Heat the oil in a large skillet set over moderate heat. Add the onion and garlic and cook until soft, stirring frequently, about 5 minutes. Stir in the raisins and apricots and sauté for 1 minute. Add the spinach, cinnamon, and crushed red pepper, and cook for 3 minutes, stirring occasionally. Remove from the heat. Season with salt and pepper. Set aside.

Preheat the oven to 375°F. Adjust an oven rack to the lowest position. Lightly butter the cake pan.

Work with one sheet of phyllo at a time, keeping the remaining leaves covered with a slightly damp kitchen towel to prevent them from drying out.

ASSEMBLE THE PIE: Working quickly, place a sheet of phyllo on a work surface. Lightly brush the sheet with melted butter and sprinkle with 1 teaspoon of the Parmesan cheese. Top with 2 more sheets, brushing each with butter and sprinkling with Parmesan. Place the layered sheets in the bottom of the buttered pie pan with the ends extending over the sides of the pan. Layer 3 more phyllo leaves as above, brushing with melted butter and sprinkling with Parmesan. Place them in the pan across the first 3 leaves, completely covering the bottom and sides of the pan.

Evenly spread half of the spinach mixture in the pan. Sprinkle with 1 tablespoon of the Parmesan cheese and half of the mozzarella cheese. Spread the rice evenly over the cheese, then top the rice with the remaining mozzarella. Spread the remaining vegetable mixture over the mozzarella and sprinkle with 1 tablespoon of the Parmesan

— cook's notes —

If you want, make the tomato sauce in larger quantities and store it in small containers to have on hand for impromptu meals. This delicious sauce can be served over pasta, meats, and other vegetable dishes.

cheese. Layer the remaining 2 phyllo sheets as above, brushing with butter and sprinkling 1 teaspoon Parmesan cheese over each one. Fold the leaves crosswise in half, place the folded sheets over the filling, and brush with butter. Fold the overhanging phyllo leaves over the top to completely seal the filling. Generously brush the top of the pie with melted butter and sprinkle with the remaining Parmesan cheese.

Bake the pie until crisp and golden, about 30 to 35 minutes. If the pie begins to brown too fast during baking, loosely cover it with foil. Remove the pie from the oven and allow it to rest on a rack for about 5 minutes before cutting.

TO SERVE: Reheat the tomato sauce. Cut the pie into wedges. Place a wedge in the center of each plate and spoon some sauce around it.

Roast Sesame Pork in Phyllo

This dish originated when I had a craving for roast pork one night but was tired of making it in the same old way. Fortunately, I had some unused phyllo left over from preparing another recipe in this chapter. I cooked a garlic-rubbed pork roast, wrapped it in layers of phyllo sprinkled with toasted sesame seeds, and baked it to obtain a feathery and crackly crust. This is a simple but sophisticated dish that can be prepared ahead of time so you can sit down and enjoy your meal without having to fuss at the last minute.

YIELD: 4 main-course servings

FIVE-SPICE SAUCE

1 teaspoon five-spice powder (page 70)
1 tablespoon honey
1 tablespoon tomato paste
1 tablespoon light soy sauce
1 tablespoon Oriental sesame oil
½ cup chicken broth

2 pounds rolled boneless top loin pork roast, trimmed and tied, at room temperature
Salt and freshly ground black pepper to taste
1 tablespoon peanut oil
20 garlic cloves, peeled and halved lengthwise

FOR ASSEMBLY

⅓ cup white sesame seeds
8 sheets phyllo pastry, fully thawed
6 tablespoons unsalted butter, melted

MAKE THE SAUCE: Combine all the ingredients for the sauce in a small bowl. Cover and set aside.

PREPARE THE PORK ROAST: Season the meat with salt and pepper. Heat the oil in a skillet over high heat and brown the meat on all sides, about 6 minutes. Pour off the fat from the skillet. Add the sauce and garlic to the skillet and bring to a boil. Reduce the heat to low, cover, and simmer for 20 minutes. Remove from the heat. Remove the meat to a plate to cool. Using a slotted spoon, remove the garlic pieces to a small bowl, and mash them with a fork to purée. Set aside. Taste the sauce and adjust the seasonings with salt and pepper if necessary. Cover and set aside.

TOAST THE SESAME SEEDS: Place the sesame seeds in a dry skillet over moderate heat and cook, stirring constantly, until golden brown, about 3 minutes. Transfer to a plate and allow to cool. Coarsely grind the seeds in a spice grinder or blender. Set aside.

continued

— *planning ahead* —

The pork roast can be assembled up to 6 hours in advance, loosely covered with foil, and refrigerated. Bring the roast to room temperature before wrapping it.

— *cook's notes* —

Chinese five-spice powder is a fragrant and powerful mixture of spices for poultry, fish, and meat. If you cannot locate it in a specialty market or Asian food shop, you can make it from scratch.

Preheat the oven to 400°F. Adjust an oven rack to the lowest position. Lightly butter a baking sheet.

Work with one sheet of phyllo at a time, keeping the remaining leaves covered with a slightly damp kitchen towel to prevent them from drying out.

WRAP THE ROAST: Remove and discard the butcher's string from the roast. Spread the garlic purée over the roast. Working quickly, place a sheet of phyllo on a work surface with a short side toward you. Lightly brush the sheet with melted butter and sprinkle with 2 teaspoons of the ground toasted sesame seeds. Top with 7 more sheets, brushing with butter and sprinkling each with 2 teaspoons sesame seeds. Center the roast on the short end of the pastry and fold the sides of the phyllo over the roast. Roll the roast up in the pastry, brushing the unbuttered surfaces of the phyllo with butter at each turn. Place the roll seam side down on the prepared baking sheet. Brush the entire surface of the roll with butter.

Bake the wrapped roast until crisp and nicely browned, about 25 minutes. If the phyllo begins to brown too fast during baking, loosely cover the roast with foil. Remove the roast to a cutting board and allow to cool slightly.

TO SERVE: Cut the roast into portions. Reheat the sauce, spoon it over the meat, and serve.

CHINESE FIVE-SPICE POWDER

2 teaspoons Szechuan peppercorns
2 tablespoons fennel seeds
2 tablespoons aniseed
2 star anise
1 1-inch cinnamon stick
½ teaspoon whole cloves

Grind the spices to a very fine powder in a spice grinder or blender. Sift through a fine-meshed sieve. Use it only sparingly; a little goes a long way. (There should be about 2 tablespoons.) Store the mix in an airtight jar. It will keep for weeks at room temperature.

Scrod and Spinach Strudel with Avgolemono

One day at the market, while shopping for the ingredients to make spanakopetes, I saw some beautiful scrod. I thought to myself, why not combine the two and create a main-course dish? I found that the combination of the delicate fish with spinach and feta cheese in a phyllo crust is delicious. Avgolemono, a Greek lemon and egg sauce flavored with white wine, provides just the right amount of acidity to balance the scrod.

YIELD: 1 phyllo roll, enough for 4 main-course servings

SPINACH AND CHEESE FILLING

10 ounces fresh spinach, stemmed, washed, and dried, or ½ 10-ounce package frozen leaf spinach, thawed
1 tablespoon olive oil
¼ cup chopped onion
1½ teaspoons minced garlic
2 ounces feta cheese, crumbled
2 tablespoons cottage cheese
2 tablespoons chopped fresh dill or chives
1½ teaspoons fresh lemon juice
Salt and freshly ground black pepper to taste

1 8-ounce scrod fillet
Salt and freshly ground black pepper to taste
1½ teaspoons fresh lemon juice

FOR ASSEMBLY

6 sheets phyllo pastry, fully thawed
5 tablespoons unsalted butter, melted
¼ cup dried bread crumbs

AVGOLEMONO SAUCE

1 large egg
1 tablespoon fresh lemon juice
1 cup dry white wine
1 cup bottled clam juice or chicken broth, homemade (page 368) or store-bought
2 shallots sliced
4 tablespoons unsalted butter, at room temperature
Salt and freshly ground black pepper to taste
1 tablespoon chopped fresh dill or chives

PREPARE THE FILLING: If using fresh spinach, bring 3 quarts salted water to a rolling boil in a large pot. Drop in the spinach and cook until it is just wilted, about 1 minute. Drain the spinach in a colander in the sink, refresh under cold running water, and drain again. Squeeze the spinach dry and coarsely chop. If using frozen spinach, first squeeze the thawed spinach dry, then coarsely chop. In a skillet, heat the oil over moderate heat. Add the onion and garlic and sauté until soft, about 2 minutes. Add the drained spinach and sauté until just heated through, 1 minute

— planning ahead —

The phyllo roll can be assembled up to 4 hours in advance, covered loosely with foil, and refrigerated until ready to cook. Bring to room temperature before baking.

cook's notes

Feta is a Greek cheese made with sheep's milk, goat's milk, or a combination of both. White, crumbly, and salty, it is commonly used in baked savory dishes. It is also delicious in salads. To keep it moist, store it tightly wrapped in plastic in the refrigerator. Use it within a week. It's available in the dairy section of most supermarkets.

Whitefish, salmon, cod, or tilefish fillets can be substituted for the scrod.

longer. Remove from the heat and allow to cool. When cool, stir in the cheeses, dill, and the lemon juice. Season with salt and pepper and set aside. Season the fish with salt and pepper and sprinkle with the lemon juice. Cut the fillet in half lengthwise.

Preheat the oven to 375°F. Adjust an oven rack to the lowest position. Lightly butter a baking sheet.

Work with one sheet of phyllo at a time, keeping the remaining sheets covered with a slightly damp kitchen towel to prevent them from drying out.

ASSEMBLE THE ROLL: Working quickly, place a sheet of phyllo on a work surface with a short side toward you. Lightly brush the sheet with melted butter and sprinkle with 1 teaspoon of the bread crumbs. Top this with 5 more sheets, brushing each with butter and sprinkling with bread crumbs. Lay 1 piece of scrod along the short end of the pastry, about 1½ inches in from the three edges. Spread the spinach mixture over the fish. Top the filling with the second piece of fish. Fold the sides over the fish and roll the pastry up into a log, brushing the unbuttered surfaces of the phyllo with butter at each turn. Place the roll seam side down on the baking sheet. Brush the entire surface of the roll with butter.

Bake the roll until crisp and golden, about 18 to 20 minutes.

Meanwhile, MAKE THE SAUCE: Combine the egg and lemon juice in a small bowl and whisk to blend. Set aside. Combine the white wine, clam juice, and shallots in a medium-size heavy saucepan. Bring to a boil over high heat, reduce the heat to moderately low, and simmer until the liquid is reduced to 1 cup, about 15 minutes. Remove the saucepan from the heat and gradually add the hot liquid to the egg mixture, whisking vigorously until well mixed. Pour the mixture back into the saucepan and place over low heat, swirling the sauce around the pan until just heated through. Do not let the sauce simmer or it will curdle. Add the butter to the sauce 2 tablespoons at a time and swirl until melted. Remove the sauce from the heat and season with salt and pepper. Strain the sauce through a fine-mesh strainer. Stir in the chopped dill.

Remove the baked roll from the oven and let cool slightly before cutting.

TO SERVE: Spoon the sauce into the center of four preheated dinner plates. Cut the roll into 4 pieces, place one portion on each plate, and serve immediately.

Apple-Cherry Strudel

(APFELSTRUDEL)

— *planning ahead* —

The strudel dough may be prepared a day ahead, covered, and refrigerated.

Apfelstrudel is a famous Austrian pastry consisting of a buttery, flaky dough as light and fragile as the wings of an angel, and a sumptuous apple filling. It can be made with store-bought phyllo pastry (see Cook's Notes), but I have included this made-from-scratch strudel dough recipe for those who would like to venture beyond the packaged variety. Although this old-fashioned technique for pulling strudel dough paper-thin requires time, it is do-able, lots of fun, and truly worthwhile. Take your time and you'll be amazed at the extraordinary result. There really is nothing like the real thing!

YIELD: 1 large horseshoe-shaped strudel, enough for 8 to 10 dessert servings

SPECIAL EQUIPMENT: A large baking sheet with sides; a small kitchen table at least 40 inches square; an old clean and smooth tablecloth or sheet to cover the table; Scotch tape; a pastry brush; small cups; a pair of scissors or a pizza cutter

STRUDEL DOUGH

- 1½ cups plus 2 tablespoons (10 ounces) unbleached all-purpose flour, plus additional as necessary
- ¼ cup plus 2 tablespoons hot water (110° to 115°F)
- 2 teaspoons sugar
- 1 teaspoon distilled white vinegar
- 1 tablespoon vegetable oil, plus additional as necessary
- 2 large egg whites (¼ cup), lightly beaten

APPLE FILLING

- 4 ounces dried red tart Michigan cherries (see Cook's Notes)
- 3 tablespoons brandy
- 5 Granny Smith apples (about 2½ pounds)
- 2 tablespoons fresh lemon juice
- Grated zest of 2 lemons
- ¾ cup sugar
- 1 tablespoon ground cinnamon
- 3 tablespoons unsalted butter
- 1½ cups coarsely chopped walnuts

- Cornstarch, for dusting
- 12 tablespoons (1½ sticks) unsalted butter, melted
- 3 tablespoons dried bread crumbs
- Confectioner's sugar, for dusting
- Whipped cream (optional)

MAKE THE STRUDEL DOUGH: Sift the flour into a mixing bowl and make a well in the middle. Blend the hot water, sugar, vinegar, oil, and beaten egg whites in another bowl and then pour into the well. Use a fork to incorporate the

— *cook's notes* —

Before you begin this recipe, make sure that your fingernails are trimmed and remove all jewelry from your hands to prevent tearing the dough while you stretch it.

For best results, use a flour with a high gluten (15% to 20% protein) content, which can be found at some food specialty shops or purchased directly from a good bakery. The high gluten content in the flour will increase the stretching qualities of the dough.

If you prefer to use store-bought phyllo dough for a quicker assembly, follow the wrapping instructions for strudel rolls on the phyllo pastry box. This recipe makes enough filling to fill 3 rolls; use 6 phyllo sheets per roll. Butter each sheet and sprinkle some of the dried bread crumbs between each sheet. Bake the phyllo dough strudels in a preheated 375°F oven for 35 to 40 minutes, until the tops are golden brown and the strudels are crisp.

Many specialty food stores and fine supermarkets now carry dried Michigan cherries. If they are not available locally, they can be ordered from American Spoon Foods, 411 East Lake Street, Petosky, MI 49770 (800-222-5886).

flour into the liquid. Gather the dough into a ball with your hands. The dough should feel moist and very soft but not sticky. If it feels sticky, add a tablespoon or more of flour, until the dough no longer sticks to your hands or the bowl. Be careful not to add too much flour, or the dough will become stiff and lose its elasticity.

Lightly rub a cool work surface, preferably marble or metal, with vegetable oil. Lightly rub the dough with vegetable oil. Slap the dough down onto the oiled surface, gather it up, then slap it down again. Work the dough in this manner for about 100 strokes. This technique serves to develop the gluten in the dough. Whenever the dough begins to stick to the surface as you slap it, lightly rub the surface and your hands with a little more vegetable oil and lightly sprinkle the dough with flour. Do not use too much oil or flour, or the dough will absorb them and become either too sticky or stiff. The dough should be on the wet side, but not so much that it sticks to the surface or to your hands.

Briefly knead the dough and shape it into a ball. Coat the dough with vegetable oil and place it on an oiled plate. Cover with plastic wrap and set the dough in a warm area to allow the gluten to relax for at least 1 hour, or overnight.

Combine the dried cherries and brandy in a small bowl and set aside to marinate for 30 minutes. Drain.

PREPARE THE FILLING: Peel, core, and quarter the apples. Cut into ¾-inch dice. In a mixing bowl, combine the apples with the lemon juice, zest, drained cherries, sugar, and cinnamon.

Melt the butter in a skillet over moderate heat. Add the nuts and cook until golden, about 3 minutes, stirring frequently with a wooden spoon. Drain the nuts on paper towels, then stir the nuts into the fruit mixture.

Preheat the oven to 425°F. Adjust an oven rack to the lowest position. Butter the baking sheet.

STRETCH THE DOUGH: Cover the table with the tablecloth and secure the edges of the cloth by taping them underneath the edges of the table. Sprinkle the entire surface evenly with cornstarch. Sprinkle the dough lightly with cornstarch and set it in the center of the cloth. Lightly coat a rolling pin with cornstarch. Roll the dough out evenly into a thin circle about 24 inches in diameter. Do not lift the dough from the table as you roll it or it will shrink back. If the dough starts shrinking back while you roll it, cover it with a clean towel and let it rest for about 10 minutes before continuing. If the dough sticks to the rolling pin, lightly sprinkle the dough with more cornstarch.

Lightly brush the dough circle with melted butter, being careful not to puncture the dough. Lightly oil the backs of your hands and wrists, then slide them, palms down, between the cloth and the dough. Working from the center outward, stretch the dough into a large square, using a gentle hand-over-hand motion around the circle. When the dough becomes too thin and fragile to continue to work in this manner without tearing, lay it back on the tablecloth. Don't worry if you have a few holes in the dough; patching will do more harm than good. Now, gently pull and stretch out the thicker outer edges of the dough as thin as possible with your fingers, moving around the table as you work. Do not stretch the dough in the same place for too long. If the dough begins to spring back as you stretch it, anchor the edges of the dough with floured cups. Continue stretching until you have a square of dough that is at least 40 inches across and thin enough to read through. Trim off the thicker edges of the dough with scissors or a pizza cutter and discard. (Now you should have a square at least 36 inches across.)

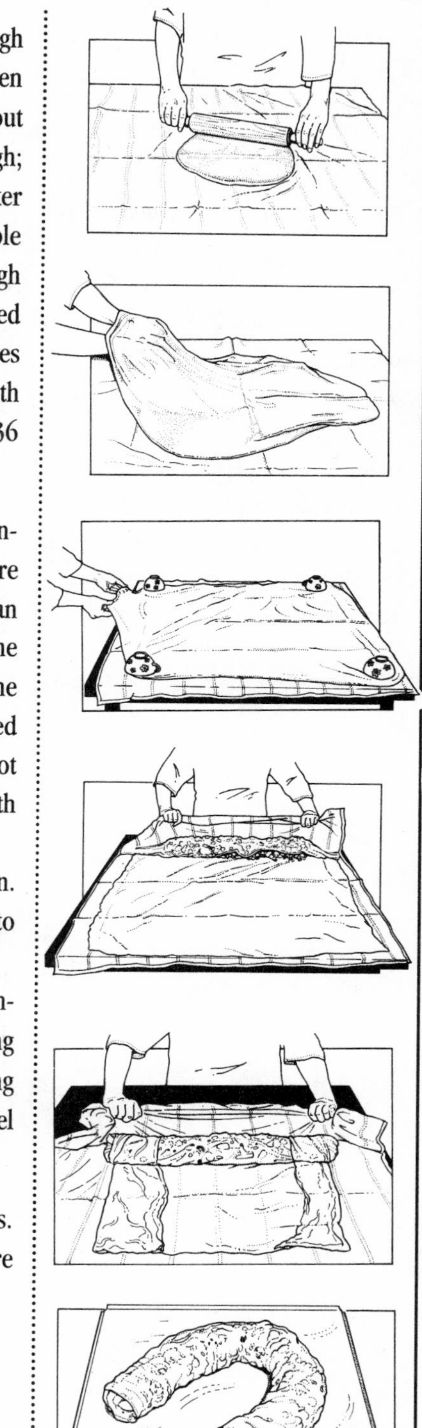

ASSEMBLE THE STRUDEL: With a pastry brush, gently brush the entire surface of the dough generously with melted butter, being careful not to puncture the dough. Evenly sprinkle the bread crumbs over the dough. Shape the filling into an even, compact roll along the bottom of the dough, leaving a 4-inch border along the bottom and side edges. Use the the tablecloth to lift and fold the dough edge over the filling. Then fold the sides over the filling. Brush the unbuttered dough with melted butter. Continue lifting the tablecloth to roll the dough over itself into a log; do not roll the strudel too tightly. As you roll, brush the unbuttered dough at each turn with melted butter.

The strudel may be rolled directly onto the prepared baking sheet, seam side down. If it is too large for the pan, bend it into a horseshoe shape before transferring it to the sheet, or cut in half if necessary. Brush the top lightly with melted butter.

Bake the strudel for 15 minutes. Brush with melted butter, reduce the oven temperature to 350°F, and bake until golden brown, about 30 minutes longer, brushing the strudel with butter every 10 minutes. If the strudel starts to brown too much during baking, loosely cover it with foil. Remove the pan from the oven and let the strudel cool slightly in the pan.

TO SERVE: Slide the strudel onto a cutting board and cut into 2½-inch pieces. Dust lightly with confectioner's sugar. The strudel may be served at room temperature or cold, but it tastes best warm. Serve with whipped cream if desired.

— *planning ahead* —

Both the syrup and the unbaked rolls can be prepared a day ahead, covered, and refrigerated. Bring the rolls to room temperature before baking. The unbaked rolls can also be frozen for up to a month. If they have been frozen, place them in the preheated 350°F oven without thawing and bake for about 15 minutes longer than the time specified.

Pistachio Baklava

The most famous Greek dessert is baklava, a pastry made with nuts and spices layered between flaky, buttery phyllo leaves and dripping with a honey syrup flavored with cinnamon and lemon. My husband has been known to haunt Greek coffee shops in New York searching for the perfect slice of baklava. I have found that the following recipe keeps him closer to home. In my version, the phyllo sheets are layered with pistachio nuts, cinnamon, and cloves and then rolled up like strudel. When the baklava is sliced, a green nut spiral filling is revealed, glistening in the honey syrup.

YIELD: 2 large rolls, enough for 24 dessert servings

HONEY SYRUP

¼ cup sugar
1 tablespoon fresh lemon juice
1 2-inch cinnamon stick
Zest of 1 lemon, removed in long strips
½ cup honey

PISTACHIO FILLING

1¼ cups (about 8 ounces) shelled, whole pistachios, unsalted (see Cook's Notes)
2 tablespoons sugar
1½ tablespoons ground cinnamon
¼ teaspoon ground cloves

FOR ASSEMBLY

12 sheets phyllo pastry, fully thawed
10 tablespoons (1¼ sticks) unsalted butter, melted

PREPARE THE SYRUP: Combine 1 cup water, the sugar, lemon juice, cinnamon stick, and lemon zest in a small saucepan and bring to a boil over high heat, stirring occasionally to dissolve the sugar. Reduce the heat to low and simmer for 8 minutes. Add the honey and simmer for 5 minutes longer. Be careful that the syrup doesn't boil over. Remove from the heat and set aside to cool.

BLANCH THE PISTACHIOS: Place the nuts in a medium saucepan, cover with cold water, and bring to a boil over high heat. Immediately drain the nuts in a colander set in the sink. Rub the nuts with a clean towel to loosen the skins, then pop off the skins with your thumb and index finger.

GRIND THE NUTS: Combine the pistachios with the sugar, cinnamon, and cloves in the bowl of a food processor fitted with the metal blade and pulse until the nuts are coarsely chopped.

Preheat the oven to 350°F. Adjust an oven rack to the lowest position. Lightly butter a large baking sheet with sides.

Work with one sheet of phyllo at a time, keeping the remaining leaves covered with a slightly damp kitchen towel to prevent them from drying out.

ASSEMBLE THE BAKLAVA ROLLS: Working quickly, place a sheet of phyllo on a work surface with a long side toward you. Lightly brush the sheet with melted butter. Top with a second sheet of phyllo and brush with melted butter. Sprinkle with ¼ cup of the pistachio filling. Top with 2 more sheets of phyllo, brushing each with butter, and sprinkle with ¼ cup nuts. Repeat the procedure with 2 more sheets, ending with a layer of nuts. Fold over about 2 inches of the dough on either side. Starting at the bottom, roll up the layered sheets jelly-roll-style. Place the roll seam side down on the baking sheet. Brush the entire roll generously with melted butter. Repeat the assembly procedure to make a second roll. Using a serrated knife, slice each roll on the diagonal into 1-inch pieces, without cutting all the way through the rolls.

Bake the baklava rolls until crisp and golden, about 25 minutes.

Remove the pan from the oven, and pour the cooled syrup evenly over the hot pastry rolls, allowing the syrup to seep down between the slices. As the syrup accumulates on the baking sheet, brush it onto the rolls. Let stand until all the syrup is absorbed. Allow the pastry rolls to cool before cutting the slices all the way through.

— cook's notes —

The pistachios available in Middle Eastern groceries are always green, fresh, and much less expensive than those found in supermarkets or health food stores. Avoid those that are dyed red. If good pistachios are unavailable, substitute chopped walnuts, pecans, or blanched almonds.

After baking, the baklava can be cooled, wrapped in foil, and stored at room temperature for 2 days or frozen for up to 1 month. If it has been frozen, thaw it overnight in the refrigerator, then bring to room temperature before serving.

— *planning ahead* —

The pastries can be assembled up to 4 hours ahead, covered loosely with foil, and refrigerated. Bring to room temperature before baking.

— *cook's notes* —

If you want a quicker assembly, follow the wrapping instructions for strudel rolls on the phyllo pastry box. There's enough filling to fill 2 rolls; use 6 phyllo sheets per roll and sprinkle the ground toasted pecans between each sheet.

If fresh kumquats are not available, substitute 1 small navel orange. Cut the unpeeled orange into ¾-inch cubes.

Harvest Fruit Pastries

This is an ideal fall or winter dessert, using the fruits of the harvest. This striking but easy to prepare pastry consists of large flaky phyllo purses filled with a mix of delectable dried fruits that have been revived by being soaked in tea, then stewed in port wine spiced with bay leaves, cinnamon, star anise, and cloves. Served slightly warm with Grand Marnier–scented Chantilly cream, they are divine!

YIELD: 8 pastries, enough for 8 dessert servings

FRUIT FILLING

2 cups freshly brewed tea
1 cup pitted prunes
1 cup dried apples
1 cup dried apricots
½ cup dried figs
2 bay leaves
1 3-inch cinnamon stick
4 cloves
3 star anise
1 cup ruby port wine
1 cup sugar
¼ pound fresh kumquats, stem ends removed, halved lengthwise, and seeded
⅓ cup heavy cream

FOR ASSEMBLY

1½ cups pecans
16 sheets phyllo pastry, fully thawed
12 tablespoons (1½ sticks) unsalted butter, melted

CHANTILLY CREAM

2 cups heavy cream, chilled
2 tablespoons sugar
3 tablespoons Grand Marnier or other orange-flavored liqueur

Confectioner's sugar, for dusting

SOAK THE FRUITS: Combine the hot tea, prunes, apples, apricots, and figs in a large pot. Let soak at room temperature for 30 minutes.

STEW THE FRUITS: Wrap the bay leaves, cinnamon stick, cloves, and star anise in a piece of clean cheesecloth or muslin and tie with kitchen string. Add the spice bag, port wine, sugar, and kumquats to the pot of soaking fruits, and bring to a boil over high heat. Reduce the heat to low and simmer, stirring occasionally, until the fruits are very soft but not mushy, about 45 minutes. There should be very little liquid left in the pot. Remove from the heat, discard the spice bag, and allow the mixture to cool completely. Stir in the heavy cream.

Preheat the oven to 350°F. Adjust an oven rack to the lowest position.

TOAST AND GRIND THE PECANS: Spread the nuts out on a baking sheet. Place them in the oven and toast until golden brown, about 12 to 15 minutes, stirring occasionally. Allow to cool, then place the toasted nuts in the bowl of a food processor fitted with the metal blade and pulse until coarsely ground. Set aside.

Increase the oven temperature to 375°F. Lightly butter a large baking sheet.

Work with one sheet of phyllo at a time, keeping the remaining leaves covered with a slightly damp kitchen towel to prevent them from drying out.

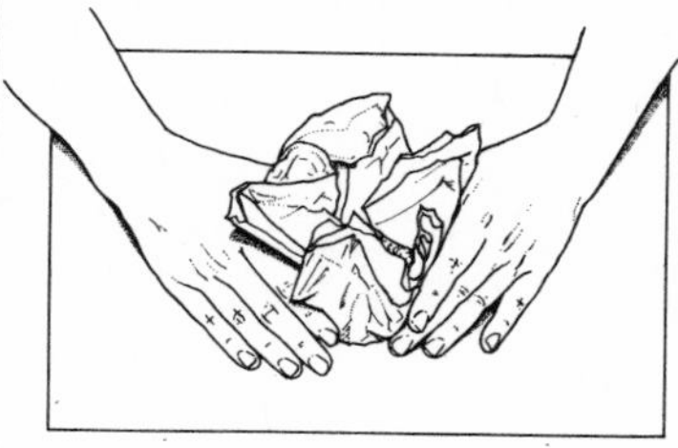

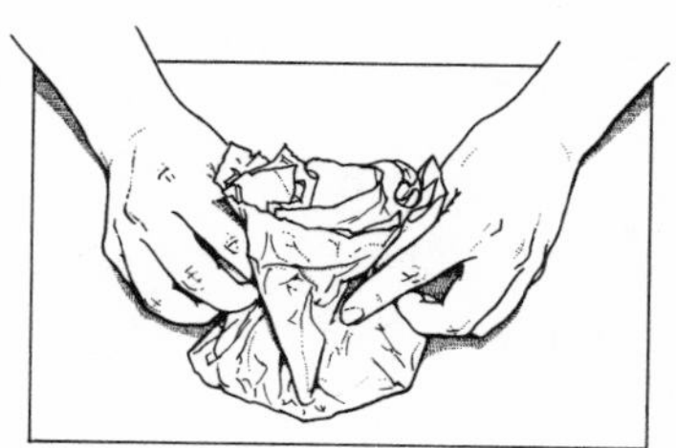

ASSEMBLE THE PASTRIES: Working quickly, place a sheet of phyllo on a work surface with a long side toward you. Lightly brush the sheet with melted butter and sprinkle with 2 teaspoons of the ground pecans. Fold the right third of the sheet over the middle third, then fold the left third over as if you were folding a business letter. You will have a 3-layer strip of about 6 by 12 inches. Lightly butter the surface and sprinkle with 1 teaspoon of the nuts. Prepare a second sheet of phyllo in the same fashion.

Lay one phyllo strip across the other, forming a cross. Place about ½ cup of the fruit compote in the center of the cross. Gather the ends of the phyllo up around the filling, pressing them together to seal, forming a purse-shaped pastry. Using a wide spatula, transfer the pastry to the prepared baking sheet, and brush the pastry all over with melted butter. Sprinkle 1 teaspoon of the ground nuts over the pastry. Repeat the assembly process to make 7 more pastries, placing them 2 inches apart on the baking sheet.

Bake the purses until they are crisp and golden brown, about 20 to 25 minutes. Remove the baking sheet from the oven and allow the pastries to cool.

PREPARE THE CHANTILLY CREAM: Put a large mixing bowl and a whisk (or the beaters of an electric hand mixer) in the freezer for 10 to 15 minutes.

Pour the cream into the chilled bowl. Using the hand whisk or electric mixer, whisk the cream, slowly at first, then gradually speed up. As soon as the cream starts to thicken, gradually add the sugar and Grand Marnier. Beat just until soft peaks form.

TO SERVE: Place a pastry on each dessert plate. Dust with confectioner's sugar and accompany with dollops of Chantilly cream.

— *planning ahead* —

The pastries can be assembled a day ahead, covered, and refrigerated. They can also be frozen for up to a month. If the pastries have been frozen, bake them unthawed in a preheated 350°F oven until the phyllo is crisp and golden brown and the plums are soft, about 20 to 25 minutes.

Chocolate Plum Purses

Years ago in Barcelona, Spain, I tasted a dessert that consisted of a dried fig stuffed with finely ground almonds and chocolate, then baked. Inspired by that unique combination, I developed this recipe, using fresh plums with chocolate wrapped in phyllo purses. This dessert is a spectacular presentation. Add a dollop of Chantilly cream or a scoop of vanilla ice cream for an extra dimension.

YIELD: 12 small pastries, enough for 6 dessert servings

STUFFED PLUMS

12 small fresh Italian prune plums or Friar plums
3 tablespoons plum brandy
¼ cup blanched sliced almonds
2 tablespoons sugar
1 ounce semisweet chocolate, finely grated
12 whole blanched almonds, toasted

FOR ASSEMBLY

6 sheets phyllo pastry, fully thawed
5 tablespoons unsalted butter, melted
¼ cup confectioner's sugar

CHANTILLY CREAM

2 cups heavy cream, chilled
2 tablespoons sugar
3 tablespoons plum brandy

Confectioner's sugar, for dusting

PREPARE THE PLUMS: With a small paring knife, make a slit along one side of each plum and remove the pit. Place the plums in a bowl, add 2 tablespoons of the brandy, and let stand for 30 minutes.

Preheat the oven to 350°F. Adjust an oven rack to the lowest position.

TOAST AND GRIND THE SLICED ALMONDS: Spread the nuts out in a pie pan. Toast them in the oven until golden brown, about 12 to 15 minutes. Let cool, then place the toasted nuts in the bowl of a food processor fitted with the metal blade and pulse until finely ground.

Increase the oven temperature to 375°F. Lightly butter a large baking sheet.

In a medium bowl, combine the ground almonds, sugar, grated chocolate, and the remaining 1 tablespoon brandy. Blend with a fork to make a soft paste. Stuff about 1 teaspoon of the nut mixture into each plum, then press in a whole almond. Press the openings of the plums together firmly to secure the filling.

Work with one sheet of phyllo at a time, keeping the remaining leaves covered with a slightly damp kitchen towel to prevent them from drying out.

ASSEMBLE THE PASTRIES: Working quickly, place a sheet of phyllo on a work surface with a long side toward you. Lightly brush the sheet with melted butter. Fold the right third of the sheet over the middle third, then fold the left third over as if you were folding a business letter. You will have a 3-layer strip about 6 by 12 inches. Lightly butter the surface. Sprinkle about 2 teaspoons of the confectioner's sugar over the phyllo strip. Using scissors, cut the strip crosswise in half into 2 squares.

Place a stuffed plum, slit side up, in the center of each phyllo square. Gather the edges of the phyllo up around and over the plum, pressing them together to form a purse-shaped pastry. Transfer the pastries to the baking sheet, placing them 1½ inches apart. Brush the purses with butter. Repeat the assembly process to make 10 more pastries.

Bake the purses until crisp and golden brown, about 13 minutes. Remove the baking sheet from the oven and allow the pastries to cool.

PREPARE THE CHANTILLY CREAM: Put a large mixing bowl and a whisk (or the beaters of an electric hand mixer) in the freezer for 10 to 15 minutes.

Pour the cream into the chilled bowl. Using the hand whisk or electric mixer, whisk the cream, slowly at first and then gradually speed up. As soon as the cream starts to thicken, gradually add the sugar and brandy. Beat just until soft peaks form.

TO SERVE: Place 2 pastries on each dessert plate. Dust with confectioner's sugar and accompany with dollops of Chantilly.

— *planning ahead* —

The pastries can be assembled a day ahead, covered, and refrigerated. They can also be frozen for up to a month. If the pastries have been frozen, bake them unthawed in a preheated 350°F oven for about 5 to 10 minutes longer than the time specified.

— *cook's notes* —

A word of caution: Don't attempt to eat the green leaves of fresh rhubarb. They can be very toxic. Only the red stalks are edible.

Do not use frozen rhubarb; the filling will be too runny.

To substitute berries, use 3 cups, preferably fresh.

Quick-cooking granulated tapioca, also called instant tapioca, is available in specialty food stores and in many supermarkets.

Lemony Rhubarb Turnovers

These turnovers are very simple to make. Rather than thickening the filling with flour, I prefer tapioca, which is much lighter and adds more texture. The lemon zest adds personality and gives a touch of freshness to the dessert. These turnovers taste just as good filled with blueberries, raspberries, or strawberries—and even better accompanied with a scoop of ice cream.

YIELD: 10 turnovers, enough for 10 dessert servings

RHUBARB FILLING

3 cups fresh rhubarb cut into ½-inch pieces (see Cook's Notes)
1 cup sugar
¼ cup quick-cooking granulated tapioca (see Cook's Notes)
2 teaspoons finely grated lemon zest

FOR ASSEMBLY

10 sheets phyllo pastry, fully thawed
12 tablespoons (1½ sticks) unsalted butter, melted
½ cup walnuts or pecans, toasted and finely ground

PREPARE THE FILLING: In a mixing bowl, mix together the rhubarb, sugar, tapioca, and lemon zest. Set aside.

Preheat the oven to 375°F. Adjust an oven rack to the lowest position. Lightly butter a large baking sheet.

Work with one sheet of phyllo at a time, keeping the remaining sheets covered with a slightly damp kitchen towel to prevent them from drying out.

ASSEMBLE THE TURNOVERS: Working quickly, place a sheet of phyllo on a work surface with a long side toward you. Lightly brush the sheet with melted butter and sprinkle with 1 teaspoon of the ground nuts. Fold the sheet crosswise in half. Brush with butter, sprinkle with ½ teaspoon of the nuts, and fold the sheet lengthwise in half. You will have a 4-layer strip about 4 by 12 inches. Lightly butter the surface of the strip.

Place ¼ cup of the filling on the bottom left-hand corner of the strip. Fold the bottom right corner of the phyllo strip diagonally over the filling so that the short edge meets the long edge of the strip, forming a triangular point. Continue folding the triangle up over itself to form a triangular package. Brush the triangle all over with butter and place it seam side down on the prepared baking sheet. Repeat the assembly with the remaining phyllo sheets and filling to form 9 more turnovers.

Bake the turnovers until crisp and golden brown, about 20 to 25 minutes. Remove from the oven and cool slightly before serving.

Serve the pastries warm, with ice cream if desired.

puff pastry

Exceptionally delicious and elegant, puff pastry is a wonderful French contribution to baking. No other dough is quite like it. It contains no sugar or leavening, yet it rises to eight times its original size and produces a crust with multiple layers of flaky dough.

Puff pastry is traditionally made by wrapping cold butter inside cold dough and then repeatedly folding and rolling it out. This process creates alternating layers of butter and dough. Under the action of intense heat in the oven, the butter "fries" the dough, releasing moisture between the layers. In turn, the pressure of the steam formed by the evaporation of the moisture pushes apart the layers of dough, causing the pastry to separate and puff, forming a "thousand-leaf" (*mille-feuilles*) effect. The result is a pastry that is flaky, buttery, and extremely tender.

In the French kitchen, puff pastry is used extensively for pie crusts, patty shells, and an endless variety of pastry confections. In this chapter, I've included such decidedly individual French favorites as Fillets of Beef en Croûte (page 99) and tempting dessert treats like Pithiviers (page 104) and Lemon Cream Chaussons (page 106).

But puff pastry is truly too good to be limited just to French dishes. I like to use puff pastry for a wide range of international dishes, from Cornish Pasties (page 97) to a Russian-style Coulibiac of Salmon (page 92), to Spanish Tomato Sardine Pie (page 95), and even an American favorite, Steak and Vegetable Pot Pie (page 101).

Until recently, I seldom made puff pastry at home. I've been spoiled by the convenience of having some of New York's wonderful French bakeries nearby. Whenever I needed some dough I would just hop over to my nearest bakery, beg them to let me purchase some dough, (perhaps surprisingly, many times they did), *et voilà!* When that failed, I would resort to packaged puff pastry. Two excellent commercial brands are Saucier and Pepperidge Farm. Saucier's puff pastry comes in one-pound boxes; Pepperidge Farm's in one-and-a-quarter-pound boxes of two prerolled 9½-inch square sheets each.

That was before I found Flo Braker's "blitz" method for producing the perfect puff pastry at home with half the fuss of the conventional method. Braker, the author of *Sweet Miniatures: The Art of Making Bite-Size Desserts* (William Morrow, 1991), transforms puff pastry making into child's play. Her pastry dough is delicious and exceptionally flaky.

The following recipes are just a few samples of what can be done with puff pastry. I'm sure you can dream up other wonderful dishes starring puff pastry. Use your creativity to impress your family and guests.

PUFF PASTRY WRAPPING TIPS

- In order to achieve flaky puff pastry, work the dough only after it has been chilled and then as quickly as possible. Avoid handling the dough too much or keeping it at room temperature too long, to ensure that the butter in the dough does not soften and become absorbed by the flour.
- Be sure to make room in the refrigerator to chill assembled puff pastry dishes before they go into the oven. Chilling allows the pastry to seal properly and prevents shrinkage during baking.
- Work with puff pastry only in a cool kitchen. The work surface on which the dough is rolled or cut should be as cool as possible. A metal surface or marble slab is ideal.
- Lightly dust the dough and the work surface with flour often to prevent the dough from sticking and tearing.
- If the dough softens and becomes difficult to work with at any point, transfer it onto a floured baking sheet, cover loosely, and refrigerate for about fifteen minutes before working with it further.
- To cut rolled-out puff pastry dough cleanly, use a pastry wheel or a very sharp knife. A dull blade will pull and distort the pastry.
- A ravioli cutter, a metal wheel with serrated teeth, is the most effective means to seal two sheets of pastry dough together.
- Be sure to preheat the oven for at least thirty minutes before baking puff pastry.
- If your oven doesn't accommodate a large baking sheet, arrange the individual pastries on two smaller baking sheets. Cover and refrigerate one sheet while you bake the items on the other. Alternatively, place the sheets on two racks in the oven. To ensure even baking, monitor the progress of the pastries and reverse the levels of the baking sheets midway through baking.
- Thaw frozen puff pastry dough in the refrigerator overnight before using.
- If you must thaw the pastry dough quickly, leave it at room temperature for about 20 minutes.
- If you like to use purchased frozen puff pastry sheets, it is most helpful to keep a box or two of it in your freezer at all times.

Homemade Puff Pastry

Thanks to Flo Braker's rapid, easy, and foolproof recipe for puff pastry, which I have adapted here to the food processor, I find myself making this buttery dough more often than ever before. And so should you! There's no longer an excuse for not making your own puff pastry. Although this dough may not rise as high as a traditional puff pastry, it is every bit as crisp, flaky, and buttery.

Plan to prepare the pastry at least one day before you use it to allow enough time between the turns for the dough to relax and become well chilled.

If you do not need a full batch of dough for your particular recipe, do not cut this recipe in half. It is better to make a full recipe and use what you need, then store the remainder, refrigerated or frozen, for future use. That way, you'll have perfect puff pastry ready any time you need an impromptu but spectacular dish.

YIELD: About 1¼ pounds

½ pound (2 sticks) unsalted butter, chilled
1¾ cups (½ pound) unbleached all-purpose flour, plus additional as necessary
½ cup ice water
½ teaspoon salt

Cut each stick of butter in half lengthwise, then crosswise into ½-inch oblong chunks. You should get 16 chunks of butter per stick. Place the pieces of butter on a baking sheet and refrigerate for at least 10 minutes to rechill and firm.

Place the flour in the bowl of a food processor fitted with the dough blade. Scatter the chunks of chilled butter over the flour. Using a rubber spatula, toss to coat the butter with the flour. Combine the ice water and salt in a small bowl and stir to dissolve the salt.

Pulsing the flour and butter mixture, pour the ice water through the feeding tube in a steady stream, neither too slowly nor too quickly. As soon as all the water has been added, stop pulsing. Most of the butter chunks should be about the same size as when you began the blending process. The mixture will appear messy and uncohesive and there will be loose flour particles in the bottom of the bowl.

Turn the rough mixture out onto a large piece of plastic wrap. Fold the ends of the plastic wrap over the dough. Use your hands to press the loose flour particles into the dough through the plastic, and then shape the dough into a compact 8- by 5- by 1-inch-thick rectangle. (If the dough resembles potato salad, you're doing just fine.)

Refrigerate the wrapped dough for 30 minutes, allowing the butter chunks to rechill and the dough to relax.

Lightly dust a work surface and rolling pin with flour. Unwrap the dough. Roll the dough into a 14- by 6-inch rectangle about ½ inch thick, with a short side facing you. Dust the work surface and dough with flour as necessary to prevent sticking while rolling. At this point the dough still won't be completely cohesive. Brush off any excess flour with a brush. Be sure the 4 corners are straight. Fold the dough in thirds, folding the bottom third up over the center, then folding the top third over all. Press any loose dry particles into the top of the dough.

Rotate the dough 90 degrees counterclockwise so the seam is on the right side. Lightly flour the work surface and the dough, and roll the dough again into a 14- by 6-inch rectangle about ½ inch thick, making sure that the corners are straight. Brush off any excess flour. Fold up the bottom half of the dough so that the edge comes to the center of the rectangle. Fold the top side down so that the two edges meet in the center. Fold the dough over in half again, forming four layers. (The dough should still be rough, not completely smooth.)

Evenly press the folded dough into a rough 4- by 7-inch rectangle, about 1¼ inches thick. You have just completed two turns of the dough. Wrap the dough in plastic wrap and refrigerate for about 20 minutes. Remember, the resting period is approximate. If the dough seems too soft after resting, a longer refrigeration period may be needed.

Lightly dust the work surface and dough with flour, and place the dough so that the seam is on the right. Roll the dough again into a 14- by 6-inch rectangle about ½ inch thick, making sure the corners are straight. Brush off any excess flour. Fold up the bottom half of the dough so that the edge comes to the center of the rectangle. Fold the top side down so that the two edges meet in the center. Fold the dough over in half again, forming four layers. This is the third turn. (You'll see that the pastry is beginning to take form.) Press the dough into a 4- by 7-inch rectangle about 1¼ inches thick. Rewrap the dough in plastic wrap, and refrigerate for 20 minutes.

Lightly dust the work surface and dough with flour, and place the dough so that the seam is on the right. Repeat the rolling and folding process as directed for the third turn above, for the fourth and final turn. Rewrap in plastic wrap, and refrigerate for at least 1 hour.

If the puff pastry is not to be used immediately after it has rested, roll it into a 12- by 8-inch rectangle. Place in a plastic bag and refrigerate for up to 3 days or freeze for up to 2 months.

— cook's notes —

Make sure that the work surface is crumb-free before you start rolling the dough.

At each turn, be sure to fold the dough evenly so that the corners align exactly.

Resting time between turns should be not less than 20 minutes but not more than 30 minutes so that the butter in the dough is cold yet pliable.

— *planning ahead* —

The puff pastry should be made ahead of time. It can be tightly sealed in plastic and refrigerated for up to 3 days or frozen for up to 2 months. The soup can be prepared up to 2 days ahead, allowed to cool, then covered and refrigerated.

Undercover Chunky Tomato Soup

Concealed under a buttery puff pastry cover is a scrumptious tomato soup. The crust serves three purposes: First, it keeps the soup hot. Second, it adds an element of suspense when the crust is broken through to reveal a steaming, velvety basil-scented tomato soup. And third, it is an elegant accompaniment to soak up all the deliciousness of the creamy soup. Serve this as a first course at a special dinner party.

YIELD: 6 first-course servings

SPECIAL EQUIPMENT: Six 8-ounce ovenproof soup bowls, about 4 inches in diameter; a 4½-inch round cookie cutter

½ recipe (about ½ pound) Homemade Puff Pastry (page 86)

CHUNKY TOMATO SOUP

3 tablespoons unsalted butter
¼ cup chopped onion
1 scallion, thinly sliced
1 shallot, thinly sliced
1 teaspoon minced garlic
1½ tablespoons all-purpose flour
1 28-ounce can crushed tomatoes
1 cup milk
1½ cups heavy cream
½ cup shredded fresh basil leaves
1 teaspoon sugar
2 teaspoons salt
Freshly ground black pepper to taste

EGG GLAZE

1 egg yolk beaten with 1 teaspoon cold water

Prepare the puff pastry dough and refrigerate until firm.

ROLL AND CUT THE PASTRY: Place the dough on a lightly floured work surface, preferably cold. Lightly dust the dough with flour. Roll the dough into a rectangle 9 by 13 inches long and about ⅛ inch thick. Using a 4½-inch cookie cutter dipped in flour, cut out 6 circles of dough. Lightly dust the circles with flour, stack them, cover the stack with plastic wrap, and refrigerate.

If you wish to enhance the final presentation, gather up and reroll the dough scraps into an ⅛-inch-thick sheet. With a small paring knife, cut the dough into decorative shapes such as leaves or diamonds for adorning the pastry covers. Cover and refrigerate.

PREPARE THE SOUP: Melt the butter in a 4-quart saucepan over moderate heat. Add the onion, scallion, shallot, and garlic and cook, stirring occasionally, until tender, about 2 minutes. Add the flour and stir until a fairly thick paste forms, about 1 minute longer. Add the tomatoes, milk, cream, basil, sugar, and salt. Stir well to blend all the ingredients, and immediately reduce the heat to as low as possible. Cook, stirring occasionally, until the soup is slightly thickened, about 30 minutes. Do not allow the soup to simmer, or it will curdle. Remove the soup from the heat and season with pepper. Allow the soup to cool.

Ladle the cooled soup into each soup bowl to about ¾ inches from the rim. Brush the rim and outside edge of the bowls with egg glaze. Firmly press a pastry circle over the top of each soup bowl, pressing the overlapping dough onto the sides of the bowls to seal.

Lightly brush the tops of the pastry with egg glaze. Press on the decorative pastry cut-outs if desired, and brush the decorations with egg glaze. Cut small slits through the top of the dough so steam can escape. Refrigerate the soup bowls for at least 30 minutes for the pastry lids to seal properly.

Preheat the oven to 400°F. Adjust an oven rack to the middle position.

For easier handling, arrange the soup bowls 2 inches apart in a large shallow baking pan. Place the baking pan in the oven and bake until the pastry is puffed and golden brown, about 20 to 25 minutes. Midway through the baking, rotate the baking pan to ensure even browning.

Remove the baking pan from the oven and allow the soup to cool for 5 minutes. Using a wide spatula, transfer the soup bowls to serving plates. Serve hot.

— cook's notes —

Purchased prerolled frozen puff pastry can be substituted for the homemade puff pastry. You will need 1 sheet (about ½ pound), thawed but kept chilled in the refrigerator until ready to use. Unfold the sheet, roll it into a 9- by 13-inch rectangle, and proceed as described above.

— planning ahead —

The puff pastry should be made ahead of time. It can be tightly sealed in plastic and refrigerated for up to 3 days or frozen for up to 2 months. The uncooked pies can be made ahead, loosely covered with foil, and refrigerated for up to a day or frozen for up to 1 month. If they have been frozen, place them in the preheated oven without thawing and bake for about 5 minutes longer than the time specified.

Miniature Curried Pâtés

The mention of pâté always makes me think of the appetizing, succulent snacks called ***pâtés chauds*** that I used to order whenever my mother took us to a fancy French restaurant in Laos. They were made with puff pastry and filled with ground beef seasoned with curry and soy sauce. These miniature pies recapture those tastes. They are so delicious that I always keep a batch of them in my freezer. In case of emergency, I just pop the frozen pies into a preheated 375°F oven, and I have perfect hors d'oeuvres for cocktails in twenty minutes.

YIELD: 12 small pies for hors d'oeuvres

SPECIAL EQUIPMENT: A 2-inch round cookie cutter

1 recipe Homemade Puff Pastry (page 86)

CURRIED MEAT FILLING

¼ pound ground chuck
¼ cup minced onion
1 scallion, chopped
2 teaspoons minced garlic
1 teaspoon sugar
1½ teaspoons curry powder, preferably Madras brand
1 tablespoon light soy sauce
1 tablespoon brandy, preferably cognac
Freshly ground black pepper to taste

EGG GLAZE

2 egg yolks beaten with 2 teaspoons water

Prepare the puff pastry dough and refrigerate until firm.

PREPARE THE FILLING: Combine all the ingredients for the filling in a mixing bowl and mix well with a wooden spoon. Cover and let stand at room temperature for 30 minutes.

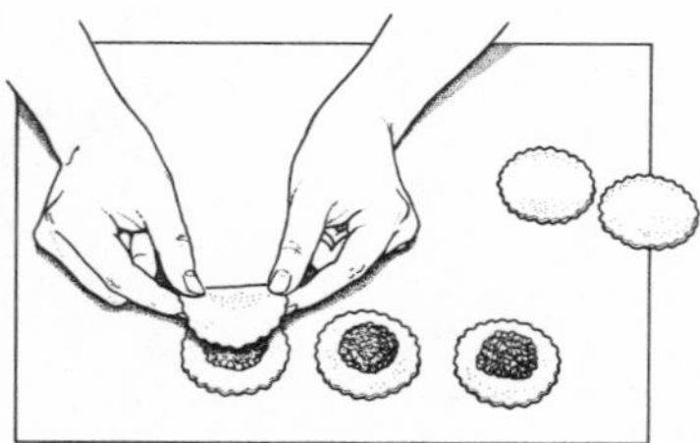

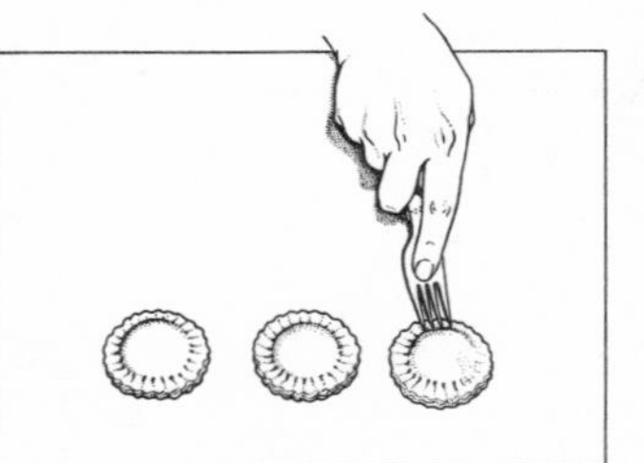

ROLL AND CUT THE PASTRY: Divide the dough evenly into 2 blocks. While working with the first half, keep the other half refrigerated.

Place a block of dough on a lightly floured work surface, preferably cold. Lightly dust the dough with flour. Roll the dough into a rectangle 7 by 9 inches long and about ⅛ inch thick. Using a 2-inch cookie cutter dipped in flour, cut out 12 circles of dough. Lightly dust the circles with flour, stack them, cover with plastic wrap, and refrigerate. Roll out the remaining dough, cut out 12 more circles, and wrap and refrigerate them. Save the pastry scraps for another use if desired.

ASSEMBLE THE MEAT PIES: Lightly grease a baking sheet or line it with parchment paper. Place 12 of the dough circles on the baking sheet and lightly brush them with egg glaze. Place 1 generous teaspoon of the filling in the center of each circle. Top the circles with the remaining 12 dough circles. Pinch the edges of the dough together and press the edges with the tines of a fork to seal. Lightly brush the pastry tops with egg glaze. Refrigerate for at least 1 hour for the borders to seal well. Refrigerate the remaining glaze.

Preheat the oven to 425°F. Adjust an oven rack to the middle position.

Brush the pastry tops again with egg glaze. Place the pastries in the oven, immediately reduce the temperature to 375°F, and bake until they are golden brown and puffy, about 20 minutes. Midway through the baking, rotate the baking sheet to ensure even browning.

Remove the baking sheet from the oven and allow the pastries to cool slightly before serving.

— cook's notes —

Purchased prerolled frozen puff pastry can be substituted for the homemade puff pastry. You will need 2 sheets (1¼ pounds.), thawed but kept chilled in the refrigerator until ready to use. Unfold the sheets and cut out the dough circles as described above.

— *planning ahead* —

The puff pastry should be made ahead of time. It can be tightly sealed in plastic and refrigerated for up to 3 days or frozen for up to 2 months. The pie can be assembled a day ahead, loosely covered with foil, and refrigerated. The sauce can be made up to 2 hours ahead of time.

Coulibiac of Salmon

Salmon pie, known in Russian as ***kulebiaka***, is one of Russia's greatest contributions to world cuisine. Traditionally, the preparation of the dish calls for an elaborate layering of fish, creamy rice with mushrooms, thin egg crêpes, vesiga (the dried spine marrow of sturgeon), and hard-boiled eggs, all of which are then encased in a rich brioche dough.

In France, the dish is called *coulibiac*, and is sometimes made with puff pastry rather than brioche. I like it better that way, because I think puff pastry enhances both the look and lightness of the dish and at the same time allows the delicate flavor of the salmon to assert itself. To make life easier, I leave out the crêpes and vesiga and replace the rice with a quicker-cooking and lighter grain such as couscous. Coulibiac is usually served with a Hollandaise or Béarnaise sauce, but I enjoy it best with a light butter sauce flavored with fresh tarragon. Since my version doesn't claim to be authentic, I even give the pie a different shape: square instead of oblong.

YIELD: 6 to 8 main-course servings

SPECIAL EQUIPMENT: A metal steamer; a ravioli or pizza cutter

1 recipe Homemade Puff Pastry (page 86)

FILLING

1½ pounds skinless salmon fillet
Salt and freshly ground black pepper to taste

COUSCOUS FILLING

⅔ cup chicken broth, homemade (page 368) or store-bought
6 tablespoons unsalted butter
¼ teaspoon salt, plus more to taste
½ cup couscous (see Cook's Notes)
½ cup chopped shallots
½ pound domestic mushrooms, sliced (about 3 cups)
Freshly ground black pepper to taste
⅓ cup chopped fresh dill
2 hard-boiled eggs, peeled and quartered lengthwise

EGG GLAZE

1 egg yolk beaten with 2 teaspoons water

TARRAGON BUTTER SAUCE

1 cup dry white wine, such as Chardonnay
2 shallots, thinly sliced
2 tablespoons chopped fresh tarragon leaves
1 cup heavy cream
8 tablespoons (1 stick) unsalted butter, cut into ½-inch-thick pieces
Salt and freshly ground white pepper to taste

Prepare the puff pastry dough and refrigerate until firm.

Lightly grease a large baking sheet or line it with parchment paper.

ROLL THE PASTRY: Divide the dough into 2 pieces, one slightly larger than the other. While working with the smaller piece, keep the larger piece refrigerated.

Place the smaller piece of dough on a lightly floured work surface, preferably cold. Lightly dust the dough with flour. Roll it into a neat 11-inch square about ⅛ inch thick. Drape the dough over the rolling pin and transfer it carefully to the center of the prepared baking sheet. Place a sheet of plastic wrap over the square and refrigerate. In the same manner, roll the larger piece of dough into a 12-inch square, slightly thicker than ⅛ inch. Lightly dust it with flour and place it on top of the plastic wrap on the first dough square. Cover loosely with plastic wrap and refrigerate.

STEAM THE SALMON: Fill the bottom of the steamer pot with 1 to 2 inches of water, and bring to a boil over moderate heat. Lightly season the salmon fillet with salt and pepper and wrap it tightly in a piece of plastic wrap. Place the fillet on the steamer rack, tightly cover the steamer, and steam the salmon until it turns opaque and the juices run clear when pierced with a fork, about 8 minutes. The fish will be baked further later, so it is preferable to slightly undercook it at this point.

Remove the fish to a shallow plate and let sit, in the plastic wrap, for about 5 minutes. Unwrap and pour off the juices. Gently separate the salmon into bite-size pieces. Cover and refrigerate.

PREPARE THE FILLING: Combine the broth, 2 tablespoons of the butter, and the salt in a medium saucepan and bring to a boil over high heat. Add the couscous, bring to a rapid boil, cover the pan, and remove from the heat. Let stand until the grains are tender, about 5 minutes. Fluff the grains with a fork and set aside to cool.

Heat the remaining 4 tablespoons butter in a large skillet over moderately high heat. Add the shallots and sauté until soft and fragrant, about 1 minute. Add the mushrooms and sauté until they are soft and render some liquid, about 3 minutes. Season with salt and pepper and remove from the heat. Transfer the shallots and mushrooms, along with any liquid, to a mixing bowl. Stir in the couscous and dill with a wooden spoon. Taste and adjust the seasoning with salt and pepper if necessary.

ASSEMBLE THE PIE: Remove the baking sheet with the dough from the refrigerator and set aside the 12-inch square. Using a spatula, pat half of the couscous mixture onto the 11-inch square on the baking sheet, leaving about a 1½-inch border all around. Be careful to keep the border crumb-free or the dough won't seal properly. Layer the salmon evenly over the couscous. Cover the salmon with the remaining couscous, patting it in place. Press the egg quarters cut side down into the couscous.

continued

cook's notes

Purchased prerolled frozen puff pastry can be substituted for the homemade puff pastry. You will need 2 sheets (1¼ pounds), thawed but kept chilled in the refrigerator until ready to use. Unfold the sheets, roll one into an 11-inch square and the other into a 12-inch square, then proceed as described above.

Couscous is a finely textured blond-colored Moroccan pasta that resembles grain. It's made from finely ground durum wheat (semolina), which has been precooked. It's available in many supermarkets and health food stores.

Leftover coulibiac can be loosely covered with foil and reheated in a 350°F oven until hot, about 15 to 20 minutes.

Lightly brush the dough border with egg glaze. Drape the 12-inch dough square over the filling. Press and mold the dough around the filling to eliminate air bubbles. Press the top and bottom sheets of dough together at the borders and seal securely by pressing the edges together with the tines of a fork. Trim the borders with a ravioli or pizza cutter to make straight edges. You should be left with a dough rim about ¾ inch. Lightly brush the top of the pie with egg glaze. Make 8 small slits in the top (between the eggs) to allow steam to escape. Loosely cover the pie with foil and refrigerate for at least 1 hour, or until the dough is firm and the edges are well sealed.

Preheat the oven to 400°F. Adjust an oven rack to the middle position.

Place the baking sheet in the oven, immediately reduce the temperature to 375°F, and bake the pie for 20 to 25 minutes, or until puffed and golden brown. Remove the pie from the oven and let cool slightly.

Meanwhile, PREPARE THE SAUCE: Combine the wine, shallots, and 1½ tablespoons of the tarragon in a medium saucepan and bring to a boil over moderately high heat. Boil until the liquid is reduced to 2 tablespoons, about 10 minutes. Reduce the heat to low, add the cream, and simmer until it is slightly thickened and reduced to ½ cup, about 10 minutes. Strain the mixture through a fine-mesh sieve set over a small bowl.

Return the liquid to the saucepan and set over moderately low heat. Whisk in the butter 1 piece at a time. Do not be tempted to add a lot of butter at once or the liquid won't be able to absorb it fast enough and the sauce will separate; be sure not to let the sauce simmer at any time or it will scorch. When all of the butter has been added, the sauce should be very smooth and creamy. If it seems too thick, thin it with up to 1 tablespoon hot water. Remove the pan from the heat and add the remaining chopped tarragon leaves. Season the sauce with salt and pepper.

TO SERVE: Cut the pie into squares. Place each portion on a warm dinner plate and spoon some sauce around it. Serve immediately, passing any remaining sauce separately.

Tomato Sardine Pie

(PASTELÓN)

Some time ago, on the Galician coast of Spain, I sampled a delicious savory pie called Pastelón à la Gallega. It was a mixture of tomato, ham, and sardines encased in a light puff pastry shell. In re-creating this dish, I have substituted the more readily available canned sardines for the traditional fresh fillets. Accompanied by sangria and a salad, this pie is ideal for a brunch gathering.

YIELD: 1 pie, enough for 4 to 6 light main-course servings

SPECIAL EQUIPMENT: A ravioli or pizza cutter

½ recipe (about ½ pound) Homemade Puff Pastry (page 86)

TOMATO FILLING

- 2 tablespoons olive oil
- 1¼ cups chopped onions
- 2 tablespoons minced garlic
- 4 ripe medium tomatoes, peeled, seeded, and coarsely chopped (about 2 cups)
- 1 teaspoon sugar
- 2 teaspoons fresh thyme leaves, finely chopped, or 1 teaspoon dried, crumbled
- 1 teaspoon crumbled fresh or dried rosemary leaves
- ½ teaspoon salt
- 1 teaspoon freshly ground black pepper
- 4 ounces sliced boiled ham, cut into ¼-inch-wide strips
- 1 4-ounce can sardines in olive oil, drained

EGG GLAZE

- 1 egg yolk beaten with 1 teaspoon water

Prepare the puff pastry dough and refrigerate until firm.

Lightly grease a baking sheet or line it with parchment paper.

ROLL THE PASTRY: Place the dough on a lightly floured work surface, preferably cold. Lightly dust the dough with flour. Roll it into a neat rectangle 11 by 12 inches and about ⅛ inch thick. Drape the dough over the rolling pin and transfer it carefully to the center of the prepared baking sheet. Cover and refrigerate.

MAKE THE FILLING: Heat the oil in a large skillet over moderately low heat. Add the onions and garlic and sauté until they are soft, about 2 minutes. Add the tomatoes and all the remaining filling ingredients except the ham. Cook, stirring fre-

— planning ahead —

The puff pastry should be made ahead of time. It can be tightly sealed in plastic and refrigerated for up to 3 days or frozen for up to 2 months. The pie can be assembled a day ahead, loosely covered with foil, and refrigerated.

— cook's notes —

Purchased prerolled frozen puff pastry can be substituted for the homemade puff pastry. You will need 1 sheet (½ pound), thawed but kept chilled in the refrigerator until ready to use. Unfold the sheet and roll it out into an 11- by 12-inch rectangle, then proceed as described above.

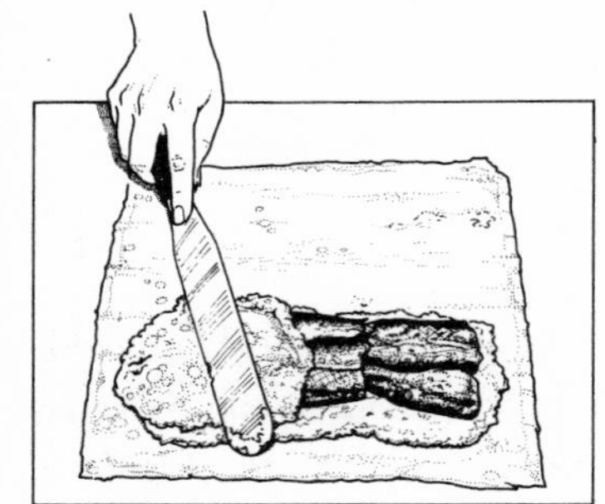

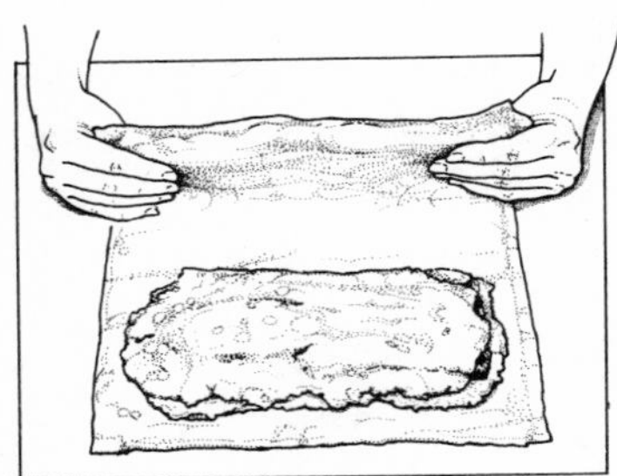

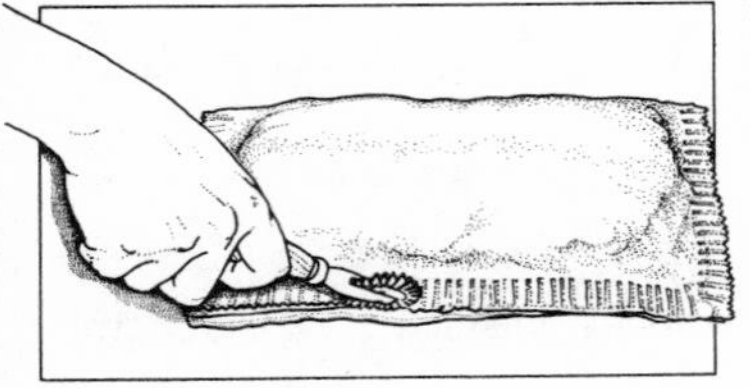

quently, until the tomatoes are soft and the mixture is thickened and any liquid has evaporated, about 5 minutes. Remove from the heat and let cool in the skillet. Stir in the ham.

ASSEMBLE THE PIE: Fold the dough in half lengthwise on the baking sheet, to make a seam, then open again. Spread half of the tomato mixture over one side of the dough, leaving about a ¾-inch margin all around. Arrange the sardines down the middle of the tomatoes. Cover the sardines with the remaining tomato mixture. Lightly brush the dough border around the filling with egg glaze. Fold the other half of the dough over the filling. (If the dough is too firm to fold over the filling, allow it to soften at room temperature for about 5 minutes.) Press the edges together and then seal securely by pressing them together with the tines of a fork. Trim the edges with a ravioli or pizza cutter.

Lightly brush the top of the pie with egg glaze. Make 3 small slits in the top to allow steam to escape. Refrigerate for at least 1 hour, or until the dough is firm and the edges are well sealed.

Preheat the oven to 400°F. Adjust an oven rack to the middle position.

Place the baking sheet in the oven, reduce the temperature to 375°F, and bake until the pie is puffed and golden brown, about 20 to 25 minutes.

Remove the pie from the oven and let cool slightly before cutting into portions. Serve hot.

Cornish Pasties

An invention of coal miners' wives, pasties are the classic meat and vegetable pies of Cornwall, England. In the old days, preparing pasties was a regular task in every proper Cornish kitchen, and they were carried off to work for the midday meal. Now they can be purchased in bake shops or ordered in pubs, and they're made with dozens of different fillings. I have even seen pasties filled with a meat mixture in one end and cinnamon-spiced apples in the other, producing a main course and a dessert in the same pie. The recipe here sticks close to the traditional basic beef and potato filling. The only change I've made is in the crust. I've substituted a lighter puff pastry for the usual sturdy pie dough. These pies are great for picnics.

YIELD: 8 large individual pies

SPECIAL EQUIPMENT: A 6-inch round plate

2 recipes (2½ pounds) Homemade Puff Pastry (page 86)

BEEF AND POTATO FILLING

2 medium potatoes (about 1 pound), peeled and cut into ½-inch cubes
2 small white turnips (about ½ pound), peeled and cut into ½-inch cubes
2 medium carrots, peeled and cut into ½-inch cubes
2 cups beef broth, homemade (page 368) or store-bought
1 pound ground lean beef (such as sirloin or round)
1½ cups finely chopped onions
1 tablespoon minced garlic
½ cup chopped fresh parsley
1 teaspoon salt
Freshly ground black pepper to taste

EGG GLAZE

2 egg yolks beaten with 2 teaspoons water

Prepare the puff pastry dough and refrigerate until firm.

ROLL AND CUT THE PASTRY: Divide the dough evenly into 2 blocks. While working with the first half, keep the other half refrigerated.

Place a block of dough on a lightly floured work surface, preferably cold. Lightly dust the dough with flour. Roll the dough into a neat 12-inch square about ⅛ inch thick. Using a knife and the 6-inch plate as a guide, cut out 4 circles from the square. Lightly dust the circles with flour, stack them, cover with plastic wrap, and refrigerate. Roll out the remaining dough, cut out 4 more dough circles, and wrap and refrigerate them. Gather up the pastry scraps, reroll, and cut out decorative leaves to affix on the pasties if desired.

continued

— *planning ahead* —

The puff pastry should be made ahead of time. It can be tightly sealed in plastic and refrigerated for up to 3 days or frozen for up to 2 months. The uncooked pasties can be made a day ahead, loosely covered with foil, and refrigerated.

— *cook's notes* —

The pasties are also delicious served at room temperature.

Purchased prerolled frozen puff pastry can be substituted for the homemade puff pastry. You will need 4 sheets (2½ pounds), thawed but kept chilled in the refrigerator until ready to use. Unfold the sheets and roll each one into a 10¼-inch square. Then cut out two 6-inch circles from each square as described above. The pasties will also taste delicious if you use the buttery pie dough on page 000; you will need a double recipe of the dough.

Although beef is still the favored meat for pasties, you may substitute ground lamb, pork, or even chicken if you prefer. Leftover roast meat is equally good.

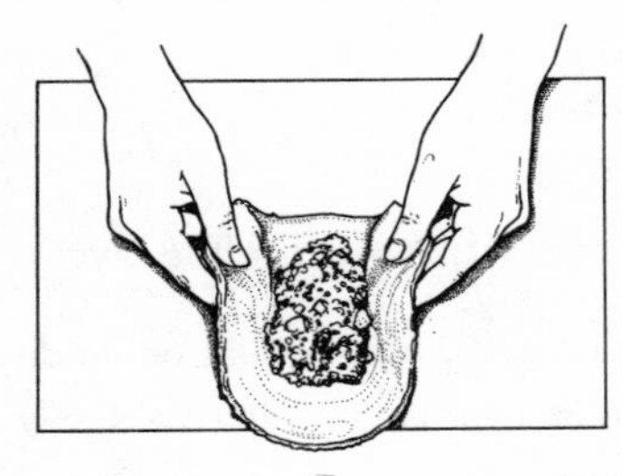

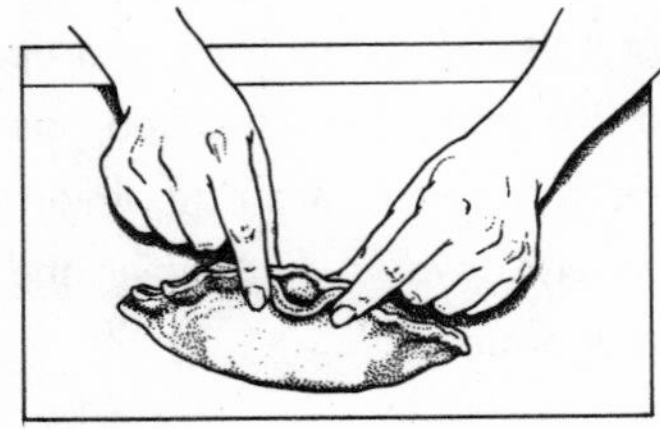

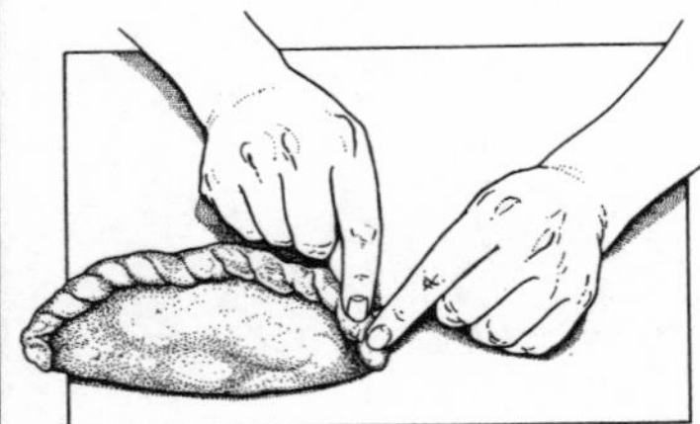

PREPARE THE FILLING: Place the potatoes, turnips, carrots, and broth in a large saucepan and bring to a boil over high heat. Reduce the heat to low and simmer until the exteriors of vegetables are just tender, about 3 minutes. Do not overcook the vegetables; they will be baked further. Use a slotted spoon to remove the vegetables to a colander set in the sink. Rinse under cold running water and drain. Reserve ¼ cup of the broth. (If you like, save the remaining broth for another use.)

In a large mixing bowl, combine the vegetables, beef, onions, garlic, parsley, salt, and the reserved ¼ cup broth. Mix well with a wooden spoon to combine. Season to taste with pepper.

Lightly grease a large baking sheet or line it with parchment paper.

ASSEMBLE THE PASTIES: Place a dough circle on a lightly floured work surface, preferably cold. Mound ½ cup of the filling in the center of the circle. Lightly brush the edges of the dough circle with egg glaze. Bring up two sides of the circle to meet over the filling, forming an upright half-moon-shaped pasty. Pinch a ½-inch border along the edges to seal. Crimp the dough along the edge. Place the pasty upright on the prepared baking sheet, loosely cover with foil, and refrigerate.

Repeat the assembly to make 7 more pasties in the same manner. Place them 1 inch apart on the baking sheet. Lightly brush the pasties with egg glaze. Decoratively affix some pastry leaves on them if desired and brush the leaves with egg glaze. Make several small slits near the top of each pasty to allow steam to escape. Loosely cover the pasties with foil and refrigerate for at least 1 hour, for the seams to seal.

Preheat the oven to 375°F. Adjust an oven rack to the middle position.

Place the baking sheet in the oven and bake the pasties until golden, about 20 minutes. Midway through the baking, rotate the baking sheet to ensure even browning.

Remove the pasties from the oven and let cool slightly. Serve hot.

Individual Fillets of Beef en Croûte with Green Peppercorn Mustard Sauce

Most people serve a fillet of beef only for large dinner parties, as a twelve-inch-long fillet will serve eight to ten guests. This fillet of beef encased in pastry crust (in French, *en croûte*) is prepared in individual portions and is ideal for a special tête-à-tête dinner. Tournedos of beef and rich, woodsy-tasting wild mushrooms and herbs are hidden under a cover of tender, flaky puff pastry. A creamy mustard sauce spiked with green peppercorns adds richness and sparkle.

YIELD: 2 main-course servings

SPECIAL EQUIPMENT: A 5½-inch and a 7½-inch round plate

½ recipe (about ½ pound) Homemade Puff Pastry (page 86)
2 teaspoons green peppercorns in brine, drained
1 teaspoon cracked black pepper
2 6-ounce tournedos of beef (see Cook's Notes)
1 teaspoon Dijon mustard
3 tablespoons unsalted butter
3 tablespoons cognac
4 ounces fresh shiitake mushrooms, stems trimmed and caps thinly sliced (see Cook's Notes)
2 teaspoons minced garlic
2 teaspoons fresh thyme leaves, finely chopped, or 1 teaspoon dried, crumbled
Salt to taste

MUSTARD CREAM SAUCE

⅓ cup beef broth
½ cup heavy cream
1 teaspoon Dijon mustard
1 teaspoon green peppercorns in brine, drained (see Cook's Notes)
Salt to taste

EGG GLAZE

1 egg yolk beaten with 1 teaspoon water

Prepare the puff pastry dough and refrigerate until firm.

ROLL THE PASTRY: Place the puff pastry on a lightly floured work surface, preferably cold. Lightly dust the dough with flour. Roll it into a neat 13-inch square about ⅛ inch thick. Using a sharp knife and the plates, cut out two 7½-inch and two 5½-inch circles. Lightly dust the circles with flour, stack them, cover with plastic wrap, and refrigerate.

If you wish to enhance the final presentation, gather up and reroll the dough scraps into an ⅛-inch-thick sheet. With a small paring knife, cut the dough into decorative shapes such as leaves and diamonds for adorning the tournedos. Cover and refrigerate.

continued

— *planning ahead* —

The puff pastry should be made ahead of time. It can be tightly sealed in plastic and refrigerated for up to 3 days or frozen for up to 2 months. Both the assembled tournedos and the sauce can be prepared up to 4 hours ahead of time.

— cook's notes —

Tournedos are thick cuts taken from the heart of a filet of beef. Usually a thin slice of fat is tied around the meat to protect it during cooking.

Green peppercorns in brine are available in specialty food shops and at some supermarkets.

Fresh shiitake mushrooms are available in many well-stocked supermarkets. Some markets call them Black Forest mushrooms.

Purchased prerolled frozen puff pastry can be substituted for the homemade puff pastry. You will need 1 sheet (½ pound), thawed but kept chilled in the refrigerator until ready to use. Unfold the sheet, roll it into a 13-inch square, and cut out the dough circles as described above.

PREPARE THE TOURNEDOS: Using a fork, lightly crush the green peppercorns on a small plate. Add the cracked black pepper and mix to combine. Brush both sides of the tournedos with the mustard. Press the tournedos into the mixed peppers, coating both sides.

Heat 1 tablespoon of the butter in a heavy-bottomed skillet set over high heat. Add the tournedos and sear on all sides, about 5 minutes. Add the cognac to the skillet and ignite it with a match. When the flames have died down, remove the tournedos to a plate to cool.

Reduce the heat under the skillet to moderate and add the remaining 2 tablespoons butter. When hot, add the mushrooms, garlic, and thyme and sauté until the mushrooms are softened and have rendered some of their liquid, about 3 minutes. Season very lightly with salt. Remove the mushrooms to a plate to cool.

MAKE THE SAUCE: Add the beef broth to the skillet, along with any juices that have collected on the plate with the meat. Bring to a boil over moderately high heat, and cook until the broth is reduced to about ¼ cup, about 1 minute. Add the cream, mustard, and peppercorns and reduce the heat to moderate. Use a fork to lightly crush the peppercorns, and let simmer until the cream is lightly thickened and reduced by almost half, about 3 minutes. The sauce should be just thick enough to coat the back of a spoon. Remove the pan from the heat. Taste the sauce and adjust the seasoning with salt if necessary. Cover and set aside.

ASSEMBLE THE TOURNEDOS: Lightly grease a baking sheet or line it with parchment paper. Spread one quarter of the mushrooms in the center of each of the 7½-inch dough circles. Remove and discard the strings and fat tied around the tournedos. Place a tournedo on each circle atop the mushrooms, then top the tournedos with the remaining mushrooms. Drape a 5-inch dough circle over each tournedo and brush the top with egg glaze. Fold the edges of the bottom dough circles up over the tops. Press the dough together to seal the edges. Lightly brush any unglazed surfaces with egg glaze. Decorate the tops with the little pastry cut-outs if desired. Transfer the tournedos to the prepared baking sheet, cover loosely with foil, and refrigerate for at least 1 hour, or until the dough is firm and edges well sealed.

Preheat the oven to 400°F. Adjust an oven rack to the middle position.

Place the tournedos in the oven and bake until golden and puffed, about 15 minutes for medium rare. Remove from the oven and let cool slightly.

Meanwhile, gently reheat the sauce.

TO SERVE: Place each tournedo in the center of a warm dinner plate. Surround the tournedos with the cream sauce and serve.

Steak and Vegetable Pot Pie

Here is my contribution to the all-American pot pie repertoire. It is made with flank steak marinated in soy and ginger, shiitake mushrooms, broccoli florets, peas, carrots, onions, and new potatoes all snuggled under a puff pastry lid. The light, flaky crust on top plays nicely against the piquant filling.

YIELD: 1 large pie, enough for 4 main-course servings

SPECIAL EQUIPMENT: A 10-inch round plate; a 9-inch by 2-inch-deep round baking dish

½ recipe (about ½ pound) Homemade Puff Pastry (page 86)

MARINADE

1 teaspoon minced garlic
1 tablespoon grated fresh ginger
2 tablespoons brandy, preferably Cognac
3 tablespoons light soy sauce
½ teaspoon sugar
2 tablespoons cornstarch
2 tablespoons peanut oil
Freshly ground black pepper to taste

STEAK AND VEGETABLE FILLING

1 pound flank steak
4 ounces fresh mushrooms (see Cook's Notes)
3 cups broccoli florets
½ cup fresh or frozen peas
2 medium carrots, cut on the diagonal into ¼-inch-thick slices
24 small pearl onions, peeled
6 small new potatoes (about 1½ inches in diameter)
3 tablespoons unsalted butter, at room temperature
3 tablespoons all-purpose flour
3 tablespoons peanut oil
1½ cups beef broth, homemade (page 370) or store-bought
¾ cup dry red wine, preferably a Bordeaux
1 teaspoon salt
Freshly ground black pepper to taste

EGG GLAZE

1 egg yolk beaten with 1 teaspoon water

Prepare the puff pastry dough and refrigerate until firm.

PREPARE THE MARINADE: Combine all the marinade ingredients in a mixing bowl.

continued

— planning ahead —

The puff pastry should be made ahead of time. It can be tightly sealed in plastic and refrigerated for up to 3 days or frozen for up to 2 months. The pot pie can be assembled a day ahead, loosely covered with foil, and refrigerated.

— *cook's notes* —

Use a combination of shiitake, wild, or domestic mushrooms as available. Or use 1 ounce dried shiitake mushrooms reconstituted in hot water: Place the dried mushrooms in a small bowl and cover with boiling water. Soak the mushrooms until softened, about 30 minutes. Drain, squeeze the mushrooms dry, and cut off and discard the stems. Shiitake mushrooms are available both fresh and dried in many well-stocked supermarkets. Some markets call them Black Forest mushrooms. The dried ones are also known as Chinese black mushrooms. Dried shiitake mushrooms can be ordered by mail from American Spoon Foods, P.O. Box 566, Petoskey, MI 49770 (616-347-9030); or from Hans Johansson, 44 West 74th Street, New York, NY 10023 (212-787-6496).

If new potatoes are not available, use 1 large potato (about 8 ounces) cut into eighths.

Purchased prerolled frozen puff pastry can be substituted for the homemade puff pastry. You will need 1 sheet (½ pound), thawed but kept chilled in the refrigerator until ready to use. Unfold the sheet, roll it into an 11-inch square, then proceed as described above.

MARINATE THE MEAT: Trim any excess fat from the flank steak. Cut the steak across the grain into ⅛-inch-thick slices, then cut the slices into pieces about 1 by 2½ inches. Add the beef to the marinade, stir well, and let marinate in the refrigerator for at least 1 hour, or overnight.

ROLL AND CUT THE PASTRY: Place the puff pastry on a lightly floured work surface, preferably cold. Lightly dust the dough with flour. Roll the dough into an 11-inch circle about ⅛ inch thick. Using a sharp knife and the 10-inch plate as a guide, cut out a circle from the pastry sheet. Lightly dust the circle with flour, cover with plastic wrap, and refrigerate.

If you wish to enhance the final presentation, gather up and reroll the dough scraps into an ⅛-inch-thick sheet. With a small paring knife, cut the dough into decorative shapes such as leaves and diamonds for adorning the pie. Cover and refrigerate.

PREPARE THE MUSHROOMS: Trim and discard the stems from the mushrooms. Cut the mushroom caps into bite-size pieces. Set aside.

PREPARE THE REMAINING VEGETABLES: Fill a large bowl with ice water and set it next to the stove. In a medium saucepan, bring 2 quarts of salted water to a rolling boil over high heat. Plunge the broccoli into the boiling water for 30 seconds. Immediately remove the florets with a slotted spoon to the bowl of cold water. If you are using fresh peas, blanch them in the same manner. Add the carrots and onions to the boiling water, and cook until just tender, about 3 minutes. Transfer the carrots and onions to the bowl of ice water. Add the potatoes and cook for about 15 minutes, or until they are tender when pierced with a paring knife. Drain the potatoes in a colander set in the sink and refresh under cold running water. Let cool, then cut the potatoes into quarters. Drain all the blanched vegetables. In a small bowl, combine the potatoes, broccoli, peas, carrots, and onions. Cover and set aside.

MAKE A BEURRE MANIÉ (see cook's notes): Using a fork, blend the butter and flour together in a small bowl to make a thick paste. Set aside.

COMPLETE THE FILLING: Heat the oil in a large skillet over high heat. Add the beef and mushrooms and cook, stirring, until the meat is seared on both sides, about 1 minute. Remove to a mixing bowl. Add the broth, wine, and salt to the skillet and bring to a boil, scraping the bottom of the pan to release any browned bits. Reduce the heat to moderate. Whisk in the beurre manié a small amount at a time until the sauce is thick and smooth. Pour the sauce over the beef and mushrooms. Season with pepper. Add the remaining vegetables, and gently stir with a wooden spoon to combine. Allow the filling to cool completely.

Transfer the filling to the baking dish. Brush the rim and outside edge of the dish with egg glaze. Place the pastry circle over the filling. Firmly press the edges of the dough onto the sides of the baking dish to seal.

Lightly brush the pastry top with egg glaze, then press on some decorative pastry cut-outs if desired. Brush the decorations with egg glaze. Cut small slits on the top of the dough so steam can escape. Refrigerate the pie for at least 30 minutes for the pastry lid to seal.

Preheat the oven to 425°F. Adjust an oven rack to the middle position.

Place the pie on a baking sheet to catch any drippings while baking. Place in the oven, reduce the heat to 375°F, and bake until the pastry is puffed and golden brown, about 30 minutes.

Remove the pie from the oven and let rest for 5 minutes before serving.

— cook's notes —

Beurre manié is a thickening and binding agent made by kneading equal amounts of soft butter and flour together to form a paste.

Any leftover beef pie can be refrigerated and then reheated, loosely covered with foil, in a 350°F oven until heated through, about 15 to 20 minutes.

Puff Pastry Cake with Almond Cream

(PITHIVIERS)

This French dessert specialty, known as a Pithiviers, is a handsome puff pastry cake filled with almond cream. It is named after the town of Pithiviers, southeast of Paris.

The cake's other name, Galette des Rois (Kings' Cake), indicates its close relationship to the Kings' Cake made with brioche (page 178), popular in the South of France and in Spain. On January 6, the French observe Epiphany. The holiday is celebrated by eating a Galette des Rois, in which a small porcelain figure or a dried bean representing the Christ child has been hidden. The person who finds the figure or bean in his or her cake slice is allowed to make a wish and is then crowned king or queen for the day. My own best memories of Epiphany date from my school years in Paris. I would bake several galettes, give some away as gifts to neighbors, and keep the rest for my sister—who could easily gobble up a whole cake by herself.

YIELD: 1 large cake, enough for 10 to 12 dessert servings

SPECIAL EQUIPMENT: An 11-inch and a 12-inch round plate

1 recipe Homemade Puff Pastry (page 86)

ALMOND CREAM FILLING

4 ounces (1¼ cups) slivered blanched almonds
½ cup sugar
8 tablespoons (1 stick) unsalted butter, cut into 8 slices, at room temperature
6 large egg yolks
⅓ cup potato starch
2 tablespoons rum
1 teaspoon almond extract
¼ teaspoon salt

1 whole almond, tightly wrapped in a small piece of foil, for the charm (optional)

EGG GLAZE

1 egg yolk, beaten with 2 teaspoons water

Confectioner's sugar, for dusting

Prepare the puff pastry dough and refrigerate until firm.

ROLL THE PASTRY: Divide the dough into 2 pieces, one slightly larger than the other. While working with the smaller piece, keep the larger piece refrigerated.

Place the smaller piece of pastry on a lightly floured work surface, preferably cold. Lightly dust the dough with flour. Roll it into an 11-inch square about ⅛ inch thick. Using a sharp knife and the 11-inch plate, cut out a circle from the dough. Lightly dust the circle with flour, cover with plastic wrap, and refrigerate. In the same manner, roll

— *planning ahead* —

The puff pastry should be made ahead of time. It can be tightly sealed in plastic and refrigerated for up to 3 days or frozen for up to 2 months. The almond cream should also be prepared a day in advance, covered, and refrigerated. The cake can be assembled ahead, covered with plastic wrap, and refrigerated overnight or frozen for up to 1 week. If the cake has been frozen, bake it unthawed for about 30 minutes, then glaze with confectioner's sugar as described in the recipe.

— *cook's notes* —

Purchased prerolled frozen puff pastry can be substituted for the homemade puff pastry. You will need 2 sheets (1¼ pounds), thawed but kept chilled in the refrigerator until ready to use. Unfold the sheets, roll one into an 11-inch square, and the other into a 12-inch square, then proceed as described above.

Hazelnuts can replace the almonds in the filling. *To skin hazelnuts,* spread them in a single layer in a small baking dish, then bake in a preheated 350°F oven, shaking the dish occasionally, for about 10 minutes. Do not allow the nuts to brown. Wrap the nuts in a clean towel and rub the cloth together to loosen the skins. Remove the nuts and discard the skins. Grind the nuts as instructed above.

the larger piece of dough into a 12-inch square slightly thicker than ⅛ inch. Cut out a 12-inch circle, cover with plastic wrap, and refrigerate.

PREPARE THE ALMOND CREAM: Place the almonds and sugar in the bowl of a food processor fitted with the metal blade. Process until finely ground. Add the butter, egg yolks, potato starch, rum, almond extract, and salt. Blend until smooth, stopping to scrape down the sides of the bowl with a rubber spatula if necessary. Transfer the almond cream to a small bowl, cover, and refrigerate until firm, about 2 hours.

Lightly grease a baking sheet or line it with parchment paper.

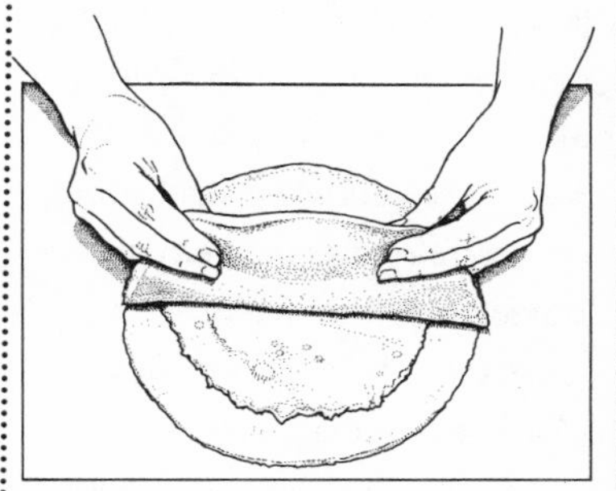

ASSEMBLE THE CAKE: Remove the dough circles from the refrigerator. Place the smaller dough circle on the prepared baking sheet. Mound the almond cream filling in the center of the dough, leaving a 2-inch margin all around. Press the foil-wrapped almond into the filling.

Lightly brush the dough margin with egg glaze. Cover the filling with the larger pastry circle. As you work, be careful that the filling doesn't spread toward the edge, or you will not be able to seal the cake properly. Press and mold the dough around the filling to eliminate any air bubbles. (If the dough is too firm to mold over the filling, allow it to soften at room temperature for about 5 minutes.) Join the top and bottom circles at the edges and seal securely by pressing them together. Using a pizza cutter, trim the edges of the cake evenly. Using a paring knife, score the dough edges at 2-inch intervals all around the cake. (This step will help the dough puff evenly.) Make a few incisions in the top of the dough to allow steam to escape.

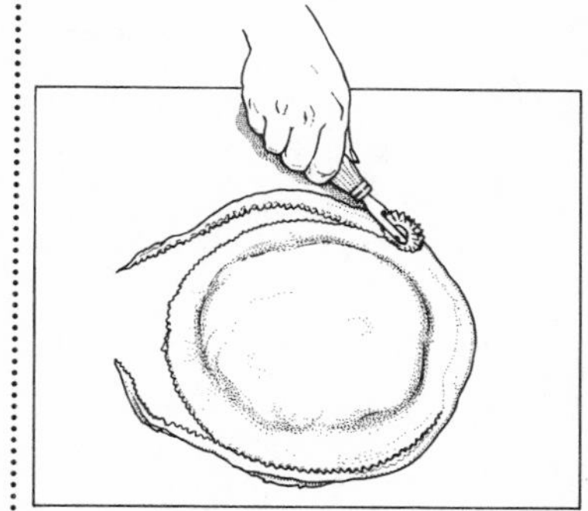

Using the unsharpened edge of a paring knife, score curved lines from the center to the edge of the top crust, without cutting through the pastry. Brush the top of the cake with egg glaze. Do not allow the egg glaze to drip down over the edges of the dough circles, or it will inhibit the pastry from puffing. Loosely cover the cake with foil and refrigerate for at least 1 hour, for the seams to seal.

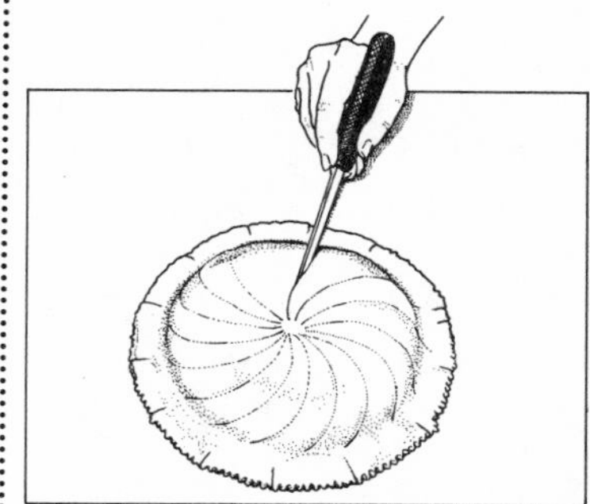

Preheat the oven to 450°F. Adjust an oven rack to the middle position.

BAKE THE CAKE: Brush the cake with any remaining egg glaze. Place it in the oven, reduce the temperature to 400°F, and bake until puffed and golden brown, about 25 minutes. Remove from the oven, and turn on the broiler.

Dust the cake with about 2 tablespoons confectioner's sugar. Place the cake under the broiler and heat, watching carefully so the sugar doesn't burn, until the sugar caramelizes slightly, about 45 seconds. Remove the cake and cool on a rack.

Serve the cake warm or at room temperature.

— *planning ahead* —

The puff pastry should be made ahead of time. It can be tightly sealed in plastic and refrigerated for up to 3 days or frozen for up to 2 months. The lemon cream can be made up to 3 days ahead, covered, and refrigerated. The unbaked chaussons can be refrigerated overnight or frozen for up to 1 month. If the chaussons have been frozen, place them in the preheated oven without thawing and bake about 5 minutes longer than the time specified.

Lemon Cream Chaussons

The traditional French dessert known as a *chausson*, "turnover" in English, is usually made with a circle of puff pastry folded over a fruit mixture, most commonly apples, baked, and served warm or cold. Chaussons are something both adults and children adore. This unusual version for sweet and tart lemon cream chaussons is my re-creation of a similar one I ate in Lyon, France, while visiting my sister.

YIELD: 8 turnovers, enough for 8 dessert servings

SPECIAL EQUIPMENT: A 5-inch round plate

1 recipe Homemade Puff Pastry (page 86)

LEMON CREAM

3 large eggs
1 large egg yolk
¾ cup confectioner's sugar
¼ cup fresh lemon juice
Grated zest of 2 lemons (about 1 tablespoon)
4 tablespoons unsalted butter, cut into 4 pieces

EGG GLAZE

1 egg yolk beaten with 2 teaspoons water

2 tablespoons confectioner's sugar

Prepare the puff pastry dough and refrigerate until firm.

ROLL AND CUT THE PASTRY: Divide the dough evenly into 2 blocks. While working with one half, keep the other half refrigerated.

Place a block of dough on a lightly floured work surface, preferably cold. Lightly dust the dough with flour. Roll the dough into a neat 11-inch square about ⅛ inch thick. Using a sharp knife and the 5-inch plate, cut out 4 circles from the dough. Lightly dust the circles with flour, stack them, cover with plastic wrap, and refrigerate. In the same manner, roll the remaining dough, cut out 4 more circles, wrap, and refrigerate them. Save the pastry scraps for another use if desired.

PREPARE THE LEMON CREAM: Put an inch or so of water in the bottom of a double boiler and bring to a boil over high heat. Reduce the heat to low to maintain a steady simmer. In the top bowl of the double boiler, off the heat, whisk the eggs, egg yolk, and confectioner's sugar gently until well combined. Stir in the lemon juice, zest, and butter. Place the top bowl into the bottom of the double boiler and cook, stirring occasionally, until the butter starts to melt. Then cook, whisking constantly, until the mixture thickens and bubbles in the center, about 10 to 12 minutes. The cream should be very smooth and shiny and thick enough to adhere to the whisk.

Remove from the heat and cool the cream quickly by placing the top of the double boiler in a bowl of cold water; stir the cream occasionally as it cools. Transfer the cream to a small bowl, cover with plastic wrap, and refrigerate until set, about 1 hour, or overnight.

Lightly grease a baking sheet or line it with parchment paper.

ASSEMBLE THE CHAUSSONS: Work with 4 dough circles at a time, keeping the remainder refrigerated.

On a cold work surface, roll out each dough circle into a slightly larger oval. Put 1 heaping tablespoon of the lemon cream on the bottom half of each oval of dough, just below center, leaving at least a ½-inch margin of dough. Moisten the exposed margin of each oval very lightly with egg glaze. Fold the top half of the oval over the cream. When you fold, be careful that the filling doesn't spread toward the edge, or you will not be able to seal the chausson properly. Join the edges and seal securely by pressing them together with the tines of a fork. Lightly brush the pastry tops with egg glaze. Make a small slit in the top of each turnover to allow steam to escape. Place the chaussons 1 inch apart on the prepared baking sheet and refrigerate.

Assemble the second batch of chaussons in the same way, and place them on the baking sheet. Refrigerate the chaussons for at least 1 hour, or until the dough is firm and the edges are well sealed.

Heat the oven to 400°F. Adjust an oven rack to the middle position.

BAKE THE CHAUSSONS: Place the baking sheet in the oven and bake until the chaussons are puffed and golden, about 20 to 25 minutes. Midway through the baking, rotate the baking sheet to ensure even browning. Remove the baking sheet from the oven, and turn on the broiler.

Dust the chaussons with the confectioner's sugar. Place the chaussons under the broiler and heat, watching carefully so the sugar doesn't burn, until the sugar caramelizes slightly, about 45 seconds. Rotate the baking sheet if necessary to ensure even browning. Remove the baking sheet from the broiler. Run a pancake turner or spatula under the chaussons to loosen them, then let cool on the baking sheet.

Serve the chaussons warm or at room temperature.

— cook's notes —

Instead of cutting out circles from the puff pastry, you can cut out 5½-inch squares, then fold them over the filling to form triangular turnovers.

Purchased prerolled frozen puff pastry can be substituted for the homemade puff pastry. You will need 2 sheets (1¼ pounds), thawed but kept chilled in the refrigerator until ready to use. Unfold the sheets, roll each into an 11-inch square, and cut out the dough circles as described above.

— planning ahead —

The puff pastry should be made ahead of time. It can be tightly sealed in plastic and refrigerated for up to 3 days or frozen for up to 2 months. The unbaked pillows can be assembled ahead, covered tightly, and refrigerated overnight or frozen for up to a week. If they have been frozen, place them in the preheated oven without thawing and bake as specified.

— cook's notes —

For a truly special dessert on Valentine's Day, trim the ravioli into heart shapes.

You may substitute blueberries for cranberries, but leave the berries whole.

Purchased prerolled frozen puff pastry can be substituted for the homemade puff pastry. You will need 1 sheet (½ pound), thawed but kept chilled in the refrigerator until ready to use. Unfold the sheet, roll it into a 14-inch square, and proceed as described above.

Sauced Cranberry Pillows

I especially love cranberries for their bursting color and tart flavor. In this dish, their acidity is nicely counterbalanced by the rich cream cheese filling. Cranberry juice imparts a piquancy to the sweet ice cream sauce. This visually stunning dessert is a knockout for small dinner parties.

YIELD: 18 pillows, enough for 4 to 6 dessert servings

SPECIAL EQUIPMENT: A ravioli or pizza cutter

½ recipe (½ pound) Homemade Puff Pastry (page 86)

ICE CREAM SAUCE

¾ cup vanilla ice cream, softened
¼ cup cranberry juice
1 tablespoon kirschwasser (cherry brandy)

CRANBERRY FILLING

½ cup fresh cranberries or frozen cranberries, partially thawed
2 ounces cream cheese, at room temperature
2 tablespoons confectioner's sugar

EGG GLAZE

1 egg yolk beaten with 1 teaspoon water

Confectioner's sugar, for dusting

Prepare the puff pastry dough and refrigerate until firm.

Lightly grease a large baking sheet or line it with parchment paper.

ROLL AND CUT THE PASTRY: Place the dough on a lightly floured work surface, preferably cold. Lightly dust the dough with flour. Roll the dough into a 14-inch square about ⅛ inch thick. Using a ravioli cutter and a ruler, cut the dough into three 4½- by 14-inch rectangles. Place the dough strips on the prepared baking sheet, cover, and refrigerate.

PREPARE THE SAUCE: Combine the softened ice cream, cranberry juice, and kirsch in the container of a blender or food processor and process until well mixed. Transfer to a glass jar, cover, and chill in the refrigerator.

PREPARE THE FILLING: Place the cranberries in the bowl of a food processor fitted with the metal blade and pulse to coarsely chop. In a small bowl, blend the cream cheese and confectioner's sugar with a fork until smooth. Using a rubber spatula, fold the chopped berries into the cream cheese.

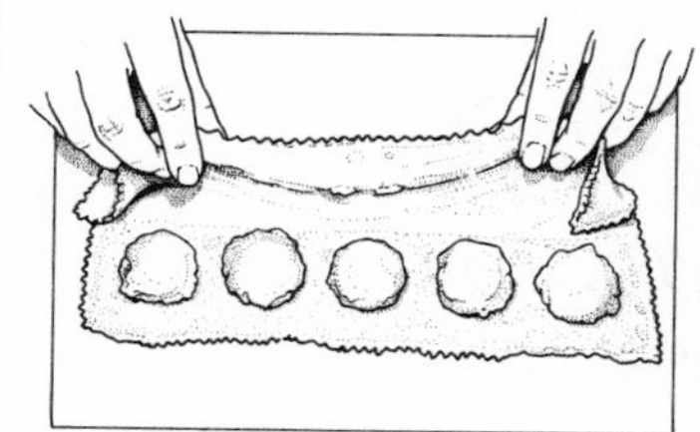

ASSEMBLE THE PILLOWS: Work with one dough strip at a time, keeping the remainder refrigerated.

Lay a strip of dough flat on a work surface with a long side toward you. Brush off the excess flour. Fold the strip in half lengthwise to make a seam, then unfold. Lightly brush the surface with egg glaze. Using a ravioli cutter, lightly score the dough at 2½-inch intervals along the bottom half of the strip to mark off 6 squares; do not cut through the dough. Place the filling in a pastry bag and pipe about 1 rounded teaspoon onto the center of each marked-off square. Fold the top half of the dough strip over the filling and join the open edges. (If the dough is too firm to mold over the filling, allow it to soften at room temperature for about 5 minutes.) Press the dough down and around each mound of filling to eliminate any air bubbles and to seal the pastry. Brush the top of the dough with egg glaze. Using the ravioli cutter, trim the edges of the pastry, then cut between the mounds of filling to separate the pillows. Place the pillows ½ inch apart on the prepared baking sheet, loosely cover with foil, and refrigerate.

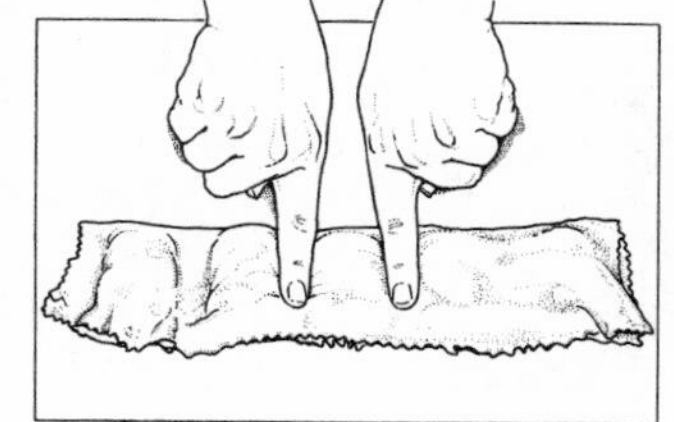

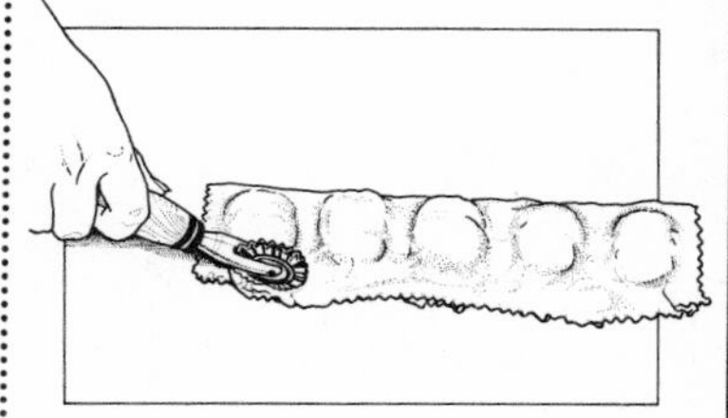

Assemble the remaining pillows in the same manner. Refrigerate for at least 1 hour, or until the pastry is firm and the edges are well sealed.

Preheat the oven to 375°F. Adjust an oven rack to the middle position.

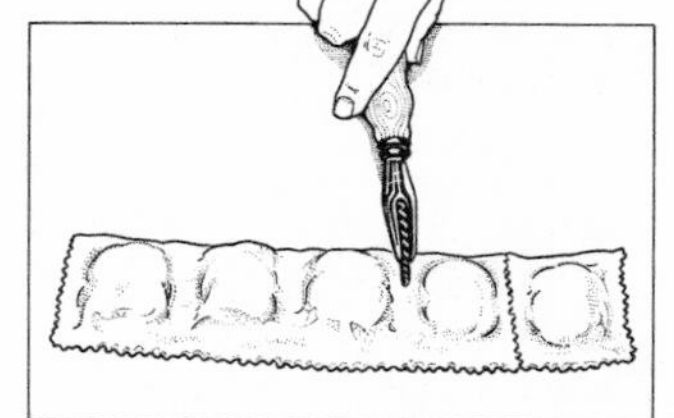

Lightly brush the tops of the pillows again with egg glaze. Bake until puffed and golden brown, about 15 minutes. Midway through the baking time, rotate the baking sheet to ensure even browning. Remove the baking sheet from the oven and allow the pillows to cool slightly.

TO SERVE: Spoon the ice cream sauce onto chilled dessert plates. Place 3 pillows on each plate and dust with confectioner's sugar.

short-dough pastries and pies

To me, pies and pastries conjure up warm, comforting images of mothers in their aprons rolling out dough and pies cooling on an open windowsill. Who among us doesn't have a favorite pastry or pie sustained in memory from childhood? Let's face it: This is universal home-style cooking that will never go out of fashion.

When hunger strikes, offer me a small pastry or piece of pie and I am appeased. Since I cannot hope to include all the wonderful savory and sweet pies and pastries that exist, I have limited the selection in this chapter to some of my favorites. My choice includes some of the most time-honored and best-loved dishes from different cultures. They range from piquant Latin American empañadas to hearty French pâté en croûte to heart-warming Russian pirozhki and good old American pot pie, to mention just a few. Of course, I have not left out some wonderful sweet pies and pastries for dessert.

The common factor in all of these dishes is that they are wrapped or covered with short-dough crusts. A short dough is an uncomplicated, quickly prepared dough that is sturdy enough to stand up to any filling, yet produces a light, flaky, and tender crust. The basic dough is made with shortening (thus, "short dough") and flour with a little liquid added to bind them together. Unlike bread doughs, which require kneading to develop the gluten, the less handling of a short dough, the better. Just as with puff pastry, too much manipulation will result in a heavy and unflaky crust.

For shortening, I use either butter or a combination of butter and vegetable shortening. Contrary to popular belief, an all-butter crust will yield a perfectly flaky crust, with a rich, buttery flavor. A mixture of half butter and half shortening creates a more tender crust, still with a good buttery flavor. In some cases, I add a little baking powder to create an even lighter crust. Whatever kind of crust you are making, be very careful when you mix the shortening into the flour. Keeping these two components somewhat separate is what creates the layers that make the crust flaky. If the fat is mixed in too well, the crust will be heavy.

Staple ingredients like salt and sugar are added to flavor the dough. Flavor and texture can be enhanced even further by adding other ingredients such as eggs, cheese, spices, herbs, citrus zests, and liquor. Sweet crusts, with sugar and egg in the dough, go particularly well with fresh fruits. They are also more delicate than the basic short crust. Add a little more sugar and egg to the dough and you will have a delicious cookie dough, which can be used for making Italian Wonder Cookies (page 153).

To make life simple, I have organized the recipes in this chapter into two separate groups. The first consists of individual pastries or turnovers that can be held and eaten out of hand, such as Spicy Chilean Empanadas (page 116), Jamaican Meat Patties (page 134), and Potato and Smoked Cheese Knishes (page 131). The second group includes single large pies, such as a wonderful Chicken Pot Pie with Herbed Crust (page 140), an unusual South African Bobotie (page 143), and a sumptuous High-Rise Peach Pie (page 149). And there are a couple of recipes that do not quite fit any category but nevertheless use a short dough, like the Chicken and Vegetable Pâté en Croûte (page 146).

Perhaps the most appealing aspect of the recipes in this chapter is that, for the most part, both the filling and dough can be made ahead, before the final assembly of the dish itself. Pies and pastries can also be prepared in advance and refrigerated or even frozen until ready to bake. They are a treasure to have in the freezer for a lunch or snack on a rainy weekend, or for a light dinner after working late. All you need to do is preheat the oven and pop in the frozen pastries, and you will have an absolutely delicious meal in about thirty minutes.

Whether you are making a whole large pie or small individual ones, let your imagination guide you from time to time. So far, I have never made exactly the same version of any of these dishes twice in a row, which makes eating them a perpetual adventure.

TIPS ON PASTRIES AND PIES

- To achieve a tender, flaky, and buttery crust, keep everything cold while you work and avoid overworking the pastry dough. The dough should be clumpy and mealy, rather than smooth and silky.
- Because of their high fat content, pie and pastry doughs need to rest in the refrigerator after being handled during preparation and in the assembly of dishes. They should be chilled before rolling out and then rolled out as quickly as possible so that they will not soften and become difficult to handle or develop gluten.
- Pastry doughs can be prepared ahead of time, placed in plastic storage bags, and refrigerated for up to a week or frozen for up to one month. Bring the dough to room temperature before rolling.
- If the chilled pastry is very hard, let it stand at room temperature for five to ten minutes before rolling.
- If you have a little pastry dough left over, reroll it and cut out small designs to affix decoratively on your pie or pastries before baking.
- All partially cooked fillings for pies and pastries should be allowed to cool completely before being encased or covered with pastry dough. Therefore, it's best to prepare them in advance, sometimes even a day ahead.
- When making turnovers, avoid putting in so much filling that the pastry cannot be sealed properly. Be sure to seal turnovers and similar pastries carefully so they don't open up while baking.
- If you have a little cooked savory filling left over from a recipe, just spread it on toast or spoon it onto lettuce leaves for an impromptu snack.
- Most pies and turnovers can be placed in plastic storage bags and refrigerated overnight or frozen for up to a month before baking. When they are ready to be used, either let them thaw in the refrigerator overnight, glaze them, and then bake, or just bake them unthawed.
- If your oven doesn't accommodate a large baking sheet, arrange individual pastries such as turnovers or cookies on two smaller baking sheets, and cover and refrigerate one sheet while you bake the items on the other. Alternatively, place the sheets on two racks in the oven, but, to ensure even baking, make sure to monitor their progress and reverse the positions of the baking sheets midway through baking.
- Most of the pies and pastries in this section will taste delicious reheated the next day, if there are any leftovers. In fact, in many cases, their flavors actually improve with sitting. To store most leftover pies and pastries, loosely cover them with foil or plastic wrap and leave at room temperature overnight, or refrigerate for up to five days. They can be served either at room temperature or reheated. To reheat, wrap the pie or pastries in foil, place in a preheated 375°F oven, and cook until they are just heated through.

— *planning ahead* —

The dough can be prepared ahead of time, wrapped well, and refrigerated for up to 1 week. The filling can be covered and refrigerated overnight. The unbaked empanadas can be tightly wrapped and refrigerated overnight or frozen for up to 1 month. If the empanadas have been frozen, bake them unthawed for 5 to 10 minutes longer than the time specified in the recipe.

Savory Pork Empanadas

In Mexican cooking, savory empanadas are frequently filled with a piquant minced meat filling called picadillo and deep-fried. This recipe is not traditional, but it's a very tasty one with a melt-in-your-mouth filling of ground pork, tomato, green chiles, oregano, and allspice. A handful of raisins is added for a pleasing sweetness. I have developed a dough for the crust that can withstand either deep-frying in hot oil or the dry heat of an oven. Whichever cooking method you choose, the empanadas will come out perfectly tender and flaky.

Serve these empanadas for late suppers or snacks, with Guacamole (page 188) or Tomato Relish (page 188) on the side if desired. You can also make them smaller for cocktails and call them *empanaditas* (tiny turnovers).

YIELD: 12 medium empanadas, enough for 4 to 6 light lunch or supper servings

DOUGH

2 cups unbleached all-purpose flour
1 teaspoon sugar
½ teaspoon salt
¼ cup cold solid vegetable shortening, cut into bits
4 tablespoons cold unsalted butter, cut into 1-inch pieces
1 large egg
¼ cup ice water

SPICY PORK FILLING

2 tablespoons unsalted butter
½ cup chopped onion
2 teaspoons minced garlic
¾ pound lean ground pork (from the shoulder or butt)
1 large tomato, seeded and finely chopped (about 1¼ cups)
1 4-ounce can chopped green chiles, undrained
¼ cup raisins, coarsely chopped
¾ teaspoon ground allspice
¾ teaspoon dried oregano leaves, crumbled
½ teaspoon salt
Cayenne pepper to taste

Vegetable oil, for deep-frying

MAKE THE DOUGH

Hand method: Combine the flour, sugar, and salt in a large mixing bowl. Scatter the shortening and butter over the flour. Using a metal pastry blender or two table knives, cut in the shortening and butter until the mixture resembles coarse meal. In a small bowl, beat the egg and ice water together. Sprinkle over the flour mixture a little at a time, working it in with a fork or your fingertips until the dough just holds together. If the dough feels too dry or crumbly, add just enough water to make it come together. Briefly knead the dough in the bowl to form a cohesive mass.

Food processor method: Put the flour, sugar, salt, shortening, and butter in the bowl of a food processor fitted with the metal blade, and pulse just until the mixture resembles coarse meal. In a small bowl, beat the egg and ice water together. With the motor on, add the liquid mixture through the feed tube. Process just until the dough barely holds together, about 10 seconds; do not overprocess. The dough should be soft, not crumbly. If it feels too dry or crumbly, add a little water and pulse until the dough just holds together. Turn the dough out onto a lightly floured surface and press it together to form a cohesive mass.

LET THE DOUGH REST: Shape the dough into a ball, then gently press it into a disk. Cover with plastic wrap and refrigerate for at least 30 minutes.

MAKE THE FILLING: Heat the butter in a large skillet over moderate heat. When hot, add the onion and garlic and cook, stirring frequently with a wooden spoon, until the onion is soft and translucent, about 2 minutes. Add the ground pork and cook, breaking up the meat lumps with the back of the spoon, until it is browned, about 5 minutes. Drain off any excess fat from the pan. Add the tomato, chiles, raisins, allspice, oregano, and salt to the pan and stir briefly to combine. Reduce the heat to low and simmer until the pork is tender and almost all the liquid has evaporated, about 15 to 20 minutes. Remove the pan from the heat. Taste and adjust the seasoning with salt and cayenne pepper. Set aside to cool completely.

ASSEMBLE THE EMPANADAS: Divide the dough into 12 pieces. Roll each piece into a ball. Work with one piece of dough at a time, keeping the remainder covered in the refrigerator.

Lightly press one portion of dough into a disk. On a lightly floured work surface, roll the dough into a 5-inch circle. Each time you roll over the dough, pick it up and rotate it a sixth of a turn to the right. This will help achieve the round shape of the dough. Put about ¼ cup of filling on the dough circle, just below the center, leaving about a ½-inch border around the bottom edge. Lightly moisten the edge of the dough with water. Fold the dough over the filling, forming a half-moon-shaped turnover. When you fold, be careful that the filling doesn't spread toward the edge, or you will not be able to seal the turnover properly. Join the edges and seal securely by pressing them together with the tines of a fork.

Place the turnover on a large platter or baking sheet. Cover with a clean towel to prevent it from drying out while you assemble the remaining empañadas in the same manner.

Preheat the oven to 250°F.

COOK THE EMPANADAS: In a deep heavy saucepan over moderate heat or in an electric fryer, slowly heat 2 to 3 inches of oil to 350°F. Gently lower the empañadas, a few at a time, into the hot oil and cook, turning occasionally, until golden brown on both sides, about 3 to 4 minutes. Use a slotted spoon to transfer the empañadas to paper towels to drain, then keep them warm in the preheated oven while you cook the remaining turnovers.

Serve hot.

— *cook's notes* —

To bake the empanadas, preheat the oven to 375°F. Arrange the empanadas on a baking sheet lined with parchment paper. Brush the top of the empanadas with egg glaze (1 egg yolk beaten with 2 teaspoons water) and bake for 20 minutes, or until golden. Midway through the baking, rotate the baking sheet to ensure even browning. (If the empanadas have been frozen, bake them for 5 to 10 minutes longer.) Serve warm.

For variation, you may substitute ground beef, veal, chicken, or turkey for the pork. If you have a little leftover filling, use it to top pieces of toast, or spoon it onto lettuce leaves and eat out of hand. It's most delicious.

— *planning ahead* —

The dough can be prepared ahead of time, wrapped well, and refrigerated for up to 1 week. The filling can be covered and refrigerated overnight. The unbaked empanadas can be tightly wrapped and refrigerated overnight or frozen for up to 1 month. If the empanadas have been frozen, fry them unthawed for 1 to 2 minutes longer than the time specified in the recipe.

Spicy Chilean Empanadas

Empanadas are delicious filled turnovers that are very popular in Latin America. The Spanish word *empanada* means "breaded," and it has come to signify a savory or sweet turnover made with either a pastry or a bread dough. These delectable Chilean beef empanadas with hard-boiled eggs and olives are called *caldudas.* You probably have never had anything like them before. The combination of hot spices with the touch of sweetness from the raisins in the rich beef filling is just heavenly. A splash of vinegar in the crust provides an extra kick. In Chile, eating these empanadas is a ritual during Fiestas Patrias, the equivalent of our July 4.

YIELD: 12 medium empanadas, enough for 4 to 6 light lunch or supper servings

SPECIAL EQUIPMENT: A 5-inch round plate

DOUGH

2½ cups unbleached all-purpose flour
1 teaspoon salt
1 teaspoon sugar
8 tablespoons (1 stick) cold unsalted butter, cut into ½-inch cubes
2 large egg yolks
2 tablespoons distilled white vinegar
⅓ cup ice water

SPICY BEEF FILLING

2 tablespoons unsalted butter
1 cup finely chopped onions
¾ pound lean ground beef chuck
1 tablespoon paprika
1 tablespoon ground cumin
2 teaspoons crushed dried red pepper
⅔ cup beef broth, homemade (page 370) or store-bought
¼ cup raisins, soaked in boiling water for 10 minutes and drained
1 teaspoon salt
Freshly ground black pepper to taste

FOR ASSEMBLY

2 7-minute hard-boiled eggs, peeled and cut lengthwise into 6 wedges each
12 small pitted green Spanish olives, halved lengthwise

EGG GLAZE

1 egg yolk beaten with 2 teaspoons water

Paprika, for sprinkling

MAKE THE DOUGH

Hand method: Combine the flour, salt, and sugar in a large mixing bowl. Scatter the butter over the flour. Using a metal pastry blender or two table knives, cut in the butter until the mixture resembles coarse meal. In a small bowl, beat together the egg yolks, vinegar, and ice water. Sprinkle over the flour mixture a little at a time, working it in with a fork or your fingertips until the dough just holds together. If the dough feels too dry or crumbly, add just enough water to make it come together. Briefly knead the dough in the bowl to form a cohesive mass.

Food processor method: Put the flour, salt, sugar, and butter in the bowl of a food processor fitted with the metal blade, and pulse just until the mixture resembles coarse meal. In a small bowl, beat together the egg yolks, vinegar, and ice water. With the motor on, add the liquid mixture through the feed tube. Process just until the dough barely holds together, about 10 seconds; do not overprocess. The dough should be soft, not crumbly. If it feels too dry or crumbly, add a little water and pulse until the dough just holds together. Turn the dough out onto a lightly floured surface and press it together to form a cohesive mass.

LET THE DOUGH REST: Divide the dough in half. Shape each half into a ball, then gently press it into a disk. Cover with plastic wrap and refrigerate for at least 30 minutes.

MAKE THE FILLING: In a large skillet, melt the butter over moderate heat. When hot, add the onions and cook, stirring frequently with a wooden spoon, until they are very tender and lightly browned, about 15 minutes. Add the ground beef, paprika, cumin, and crushed red pepper and cook, breaking up the meat lumps with the back of the spoon, until the meat is browned, about 3 minutes. Stir in the broth, raisins, and salt and cook until almost all the liquid has evaporated, about 5 minutes. Remove the pan from the heat and season the mixture with pepper. Set aside to cool.

ROLL AND CUT THE DOUGH: Work with one portion of dough at a time, keeping the remaining piece refrigerated.

On a lightly floured surface, roll one disk of dough into a circle slightly larger than 12 inches in diameter and about ⅛ inch thick. As you roll, lift up the dough from time to time and sprinkle a light dusting of flour under it to prevent the dough from sticking. Using a sharp paring knife and the 5-inch plate, cut out 4 circles. Gather the dough scraps into a ball, reroll into a ⅛-inch-thick circle, and cut out another circle. Reroll and cut the dough scraps to make one more circle. Lightly dust the 6 dough circles with flour, stack them on a plate, cover with plastic wrap, and refrigerate.

Roll and cut the remaining piece of dough to make 6 more circles in the same manner, and refrigerate. Make sure the dough circles are well chilled before filling them.

Preheat the oven to 375°F. Adjust an oven rack to the middle shelf. Lightly grease a baking sheet or line it with parchment paper.

ASSEMBLE THE EMPANADAS: Work with half the dough circles at a time, keeping the remainder refrigerated.

continued

cook's notes

To change the character of the dough, substitute 2 tablespoons dry sherry for the white vinegar.

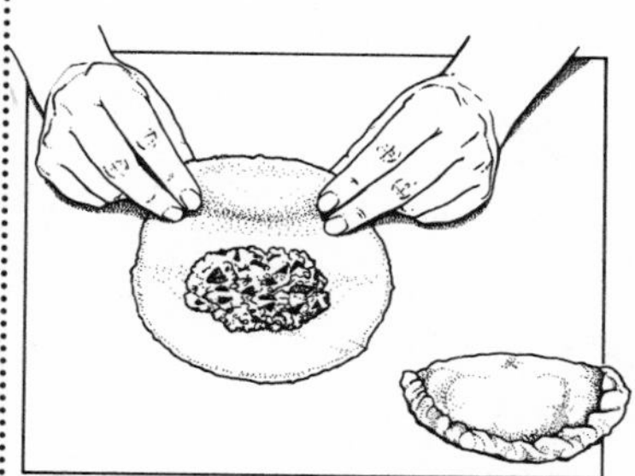

Place 6 dough circles on a lightly floured work surface. Put about 1 tablespoon of filling on each circle, just below the center, leaving about a 1-inch border around the bottom edge. Press an egg wedge and 2 olive halves into each mound of filling. Lightly brush the edge of the dough with egg glaze. Fold the dough over the filling, forming a half-moon-shaped turnover. When you fold, be careful that the filling doesn't spread toward the edge, or you will not be able to seal the turnover properly. Join the edges and seal securely by pressing them together with the tines of a fork. Decoratively crimp the edges if desired. Arrange the empanadas on the prepared baking sheet and cover with a clean towel to prevent them from drying out.

Assemble the remaining empanadas in the same manner and place them on the baking sheet. Lightly brush the pastries with egg glaze and sprinkle with paprika.

Place the baking sheet in the oven and bake until the empanadas are lightly browned, about 20 minutes. Remove the baking sheet from the oven and let the empanadas cool slightly. Serve warm.

Curried Duck Empanadas with Parsley-Mint Sauce

I love empanadas so much that I often try different fillings and flavors, seeking to take this wonderful pastry form to new heights. This recipe is the result of one such experiment. The filling includes duck, potato, and raisins. To make the filling even more lively, I flavor it with ginger and curry. Served with a zesty parsley and mint sauce, these baked turnovers are utterly delicious. The slightly sweet, spicy, and sour taste combinations make them most memorable.

YIELD: 12 medium turnovers, enough for 12 first-course or 6 luncheon servings

DOUGH

1¾ cups unbleached all-purpose flour
1 teaspoon baking powder
½ teaspoon salt
½ teaspoon sugar
4 tablespoons cold unsalted butter, cut into ½-inch cubes
¼ cup cold solid vegetable shortening, cut into bits
¼ cup ice water

PARSLEY-MINT SAUCE

½ cup extra-virgin olive oil
¼ cup red wine vinegar or fresh lemon juice
2 teaspoons minced garlic
½ cup chopped fresh parsley
½ cup minced shallots
¼ cup shredded fresh mint leaves
Salt and cayenne pepper to taste

CURRIED DUCK FILLING

2 tablespoons olive oil
¾ cup chopped onions
1 tablespoon minced garlic
2 teaspoons grated fresh ginger
½ pound boneless skinless duck breast meat (from 1 large breast), finely ground
2 tablespoons curry powder, preferably Madras brand
2 teaspoons ground cumin
1 teaspoon ground coriander
¼ cup raisins, coarsely chopped
½ baking potato (4 ounces), peeled and shredded
⅓ cup beef or chicken broth
½ teaspoon salt, or more to taste
Freshly ground black pepper to taste
2 tablespoons shredded fresh coriander leaves

EGG GLAZE

1 egg yolk beaten with 2 teaspoons water

continued

— planning ahead —

The dough can be prepared ahead of time, wrapped well, and refrigerated for up to 1 week. The filling can be covered and refrigerated overnight. The unbaked empanadas can be tightly wrapped and refrigerated overnight or frozen for up to 1 month. If the empanadas have been frozen, bake them unthawed for 5 to 10 minutes longer than the time specified in the recipe.

— cook's notes —

The same amount of ground lamb, beef, pork, or chicken may be substituted for the duck.

MAKE THE DOUGH

Hand method: Combine the flour, baking powder, salt, and sugar in a large mixing bowl. Scatter the butter and shortening over the flour. Using a metal pastry blender or two table knives, cut the butter and shortening into the flour until the mixture resembles coarse meal. Sprinkle the ice water over the flour mixture a little at a time, working it in with a fork or your fingertips until the dough just holds together. If the dough feels too dry or crumbly, add just enough water to make it come together. Briefly knead the dough in the bowl to form a cohesive mass.

Food processor method: Put the flour, baking powder, salt, sugar, butter, and shortening in the bowl of a food processor fitted with the metal blade. Pulse just until the mixture resembles coarse meal. With the motor on, add the ice water through the feed tube. Process just until the dough barely holds together, about 10 seconds; do not overprocess. The dough should be soft, not crumbly. If it feels too dry or crumbly, add a little water and pulse until the dough just holds together. Turn the dough out onto a lightly floured work surface and press into a mass.

LET THE DOUGH REST: Shape the dough into a rectangle, then slightly flatten it. Cover it with plastic wrap and refrigerate for at least 30 minutes.

Meanwhile, MAKE THE SAUCE: In a medium bowl, mix together the olive oil, vinegar, garlic, parsley, shallots, and mint. Season with salt and cayenne pepper. Cover and let stand at room temperature for at least 1 hour for the flavors to develop.

MAKE THE FILLING: Heat the oil in a large skillet over moderate heat. When hot, add the onions, garlic, and ginger. Cook, stirring frequently with a wooden spoon, until soft and lightly browned, about 5 minutes. Add the duck meat, curry, cumin, and coriander and cook, breaking up the meat lumps with the back of the spoon, until the meat is browned, about 5 minutes. Add the raisins, potato, broth, and salt. Reduce the heat to low and cook, stirring occasionally, until almost all the liquid has evaporated, about 10 minutes. Remove the pan from the heat. Taste and adjust the seasonings with salt and pepper if necessary. Stir in the coriander and let the filling cool thoroughly.

ROLL AND CUT THE DOUGH: On a well-floured work surface, roll the dough into a rectangle approximately 14 by 18 inches long and about ⅛ inch thick. Using a ruler and a pastry wheel, cut out twelve 4½-inch squares. (Save any dough scraps for another use, if desired.) Lightly dust the dough squares with flour, stack them on a plate, cover with plastic wrap, and refrigerate. Make sure the dough is well chilled before assembling the empanadas.

Preheat the oven to 375°F. Adjust an oven rack to the middle shelf. Lightly grease a baking sheet or line it with parchment paper.

ASSEMBLE THE EMPANADAS: Work with half the dough squares at a time, keeping the remainder refrigerated.

Place 6 of the dough squares on a work surface, each with a point toward you. Put about 2 tablespoons of the filling on each square, just below the center, leaving about a ½-inch border around the bottom edge. Lightly brush the edge of the dough with egg glaze. Fold the dough over the filling, forming a triangular turnover. When you fold, be careful that the filling doesn't spread toward the edge, or you will not be able to seal the turnover properly. Join the edges and seal securely by pressing them together with the tines of a fork. Arrange the empanadas on the prepared baking sheet and cover with a clean towel to prevent them from drying out.

Assemble the remaining empanadas in the same manner and place them on the baking sheet. Lightly brush the empanadas with egg glaze.

BAKE THE EMPANADAS: Place the baking sheet in the oven and bake until the empanadas are lightly browned, about 20 minutes. Midway through the baking, rotate the baking sheet ensure even browning. Remove the baking sheet from the oven and let the turnovers cool slightly.

Serve the empanadas warm, passing the sauce separately.

— *planning ahead* —

The dough can be prepared ahead of time, wrapped well, and refrigerated for up to 1 week. The filling can be covered and refrigerated overnight. The unbaked turnovers can be tightly wrapped and refrigerated overnight or frozen for up to 1 month. If the rissoles have been frozen, bake them unthawed for 5 to 10 minutes longer than the time specified in the recipe.

Chicken and Mushroom Rissoles

Rissoles could be considered the French version of empanadas. In France, home cooks may decide to make rissoles after checking their refrigerator or pantry for leftovers. Guided by their palate and imagination, they can transform just about any ingredients on hand into fabulous fillings for these rissoles. My approach to making rissoles is no different. This filling, made with ground chicken, is rich with mushrooms and cream and flavored with thyme. The name ***rissole,*** by the way, comes from the verb ***rissoler,*** "to cook to completion." It signifies that although a cooked filling is used, the filled pastry itself must be cooked to completion in the oven.

YIELD: 14 medium turnovers, enough for 14 first-course or 6 to 7 lunch servings

SPECIAL EQUIPMENT: A 5-inch round plate or saucer

DOUGH

2½ cups unbleached all-purpose flour
1 teaspoon salt
1 teaspoon sugar
½ pound (2 sticks) cold unsalted butter, cut into ½-inch cubes
½ cup ice water

CHICKEN FILLING

4 tablespoons unsalted butter
1 tablespoon minced garlic
⅔ cup chopped onions
1 pound ground chicken
⅔ cup sliced domestic mushrooms
1½ tablespoons chopped fresh thyme or 2 teaspoons dried, crumbled
¼ cup chicken broth
¾ cup heavy cream
½ cup chopped fresh parsley
Salt and freshly ground black pepper to taste

EGG GLAZE

1 egg beaten with 2 teaspoons water

MAKE THE DOUGH

Hand method: Combine the flour, salt, and sugar in a large mixing bowl. Scatter the butter over the flour. Using a metal pastry blender or two table knives, cut the butter into the flour until the mixture resembles coarse meal. Sprinkle the ice water over the flour mixture a little at a time, working it in with a fork or your fingertips until the dough just holds together. If the dough feels too dry or crumbly, add just enough cold water to make it come together. Briefly knead the dough in the bowl to form a cohesive mass.

Food processor method: Put the flour, salt, sugar, and butter in the bowl of a food processor fitted with the metal blade. Pulse just until the mixture resembles coarse meal. With the motor on, add the ice water through the feed tube. Process just until the dough holds together, about 10 seconds; do not overprocess. The dough should be soft, not crumbly. If it feels too dry or crumbly, add a little water and pulse until the dough just holds together. Turn the dough out onto a lightly floured work surface and press it together to form a cohesive mass.

LET THE DOUGH REST: Divide the dough in half. Shape each half into a ball, then gently press it into a disk. Cover with plastic wrap and refrigerate for at least 30 minutes.

MAKE THE FILLING: Heat the butter in a large skillet over moderate heat. Add the garlic and onions and cook, stirring with a wooden spoon, until the onions are soft and translucent, about 2 minutes. Add the chicken meat and cook, breaking up the meat lumps with the back of the spoon, until the chicken is no longer pink, about 3 minutes. Add the mushrooms and thyme and sauté until the mushrooms are soft, about 2 minutes. Stir in the broth and cream, and bring to a boil over high heat. Reduce the heat to low and simmer until the mixture thickens and most of the liquid has evaporated, about 15 minutes. Remove the pan from the heat. Stir in the parsley, season the filling with salt and pepper, and set aside to cool.

ROLL AND CUT THE DOUGH: Work with one piece of dough at a time, keeping the remaining dough refrigerated.

On a lightly floured surface, roll one piece of dough into a circle slightly larger than 13 inches in diameter and about ⅛ inch thick. As you roll, lift up the dough from time to time and sprinkle a light dusting of flour under it to prevent the dough from sticking. Using a knife and the 5-inch plate, cut out 4 circles of dough. Gather the pastry scraps into a ball and reroll into a ⅛-inch-thick circle. Cut out 2 more circles. Then reroll and cut the dough scraps to make one more circle. Lightly dust the 7 dough circles with flour, stack them on a plate, cover with plastic wrap, and refrigerate.

Roll and cut the remaining piece of dough to make 7 more circles in the same manner and refrigerate. Make sure the dough circles are well chilled before filling them.

Preheat the oven to 400°F. Adjust an oven rack to the middle shelf. Lightly grease a baking sheet or line it with parchment paper.

ASSEMBLE THE RISSOLES: Work with half the dough circles at a time, keeping the remainder refrigerated.

Place 7 dough circles on a work surface. Mound about ¼ cup of the filling on each circle, just below the center, leaving about a 1-inch border around the bottom edge. Lightly brush the edge of the dough with egg glaze. Fold the dough over the filling, forming a half-moon-shaped turnover. When you fold, be careful that the filling doesn't

— cook's notes —

If you have leftover roast beef, lamb, pork, or chicken on hand, grind it yourself and measure out about 2½ cups. Skip browning the ground meat in the butter; add it after you sauté the mushrooms and proceed with the recipe as directed.

spread toward the edge, or you will not be able to seal the turnover properly. Join the edges and seal securely by pressing them together with the tines of a fork. Arrange the rissoles on the prepared baking sheet and cover with a clean towel to prevent them from drying out.

Assemble the remaining turnovers in the same manner and place them on the baking sheet. Lightly brush the pastries with egg glaze. Make a small slit in the top of each turnover to allow steam to escape.

BAKE THE RISSOLES: Place the baking sheet in the oven and bake until the turnovers are golden brown, about 25 minutes. Midway through the baking, rotate the baking sheet to ensure even browning. Remove the baking sheet from the oven, and let the turnovers cool slightly.

Serve warm.

Spiced Tuna and Chickpea Samosas

What the empanada is to South America and the rissole is to France, the samosa is to India. Samosas are little conical pastries prepared with a variety of savory fillings, usually meat or potato, wrapped in a flaky pastry crust made with melted butter (ghee) or shortening. The dough is kneaded a little to make it smoother than most short doughs.

For a change of pace, I enjoy filling this Indian specialty with tuna, chickpeas, and carrots. To balance the rich, spicy samosas, I serve raita, an Indian side dish of yogurt, chopped cucumber, tomato, and fresh cilantro. I also find samosas as addictive when they are served with Tomato Relish (page 188) or Parsley-Mint Sauce (page 119). Who says there is just one way of doing things?

YIELD: 12 small samosas for hors d'oeuvres, or enough for 6 first-course servings

DOUGH

2 cups unbleached all-purpose flour, plus additional if necessary
½ teaspoon salt
½ teaspoon sugar
4 tablespoons melted butter
½ cup cold water

RAITA

1 small cucumber
1 teaspoon salt
½ cup yogurt
¼ teaspoon sugar
2 tablespoons ground coriander
⅓ teaspoon ground cumin
¼ teaspoon cayenne pepper
½ medium tomato, seeded and finely diced
1 tablespoon finely shredded fresh cilantro leaves
Salt to taste

SPICED TUNA FILLING

1 teaspoon cumin seeds
1 tablespoon vegetable oil
½ cup chopped onion
1 teaspoon minced garlic
1 teaspoon grated fresh ginger
1 cup canned chickpeas, drained
½ teaspoon ground coriander
¼ teaspoon cayenne pepper
1 6½-ounce can tuna packed in oil, drained
1 scallion, thinly sliced
⅓ cup grated carrot
Salt and freshly ground black pepper to taste

Vegetable oil, for deep-frying

continued

— *planning ahead* —

The dough can be prepared ahead of time, wrapped well, and refrigerated for up to 2 days. The filling can be covered and refrigerated overnight. The uncooked pastries can be tightly wrapped and refrigerated overnight or frozen for up to 1 month. If the samosas have been frozen, fry them unthawed for 1 to 2 minutes longer than the time specified in the recipe.

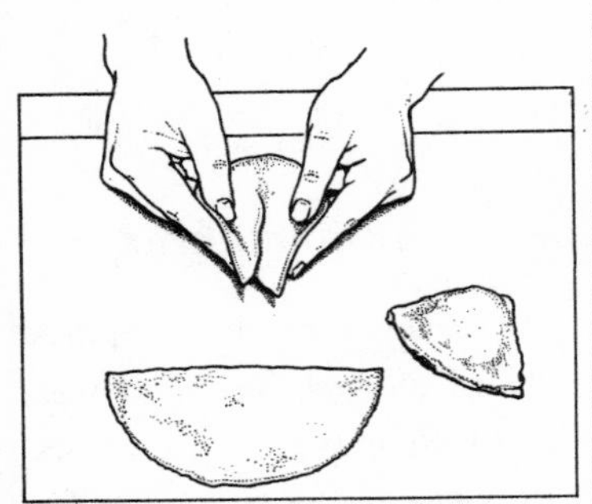

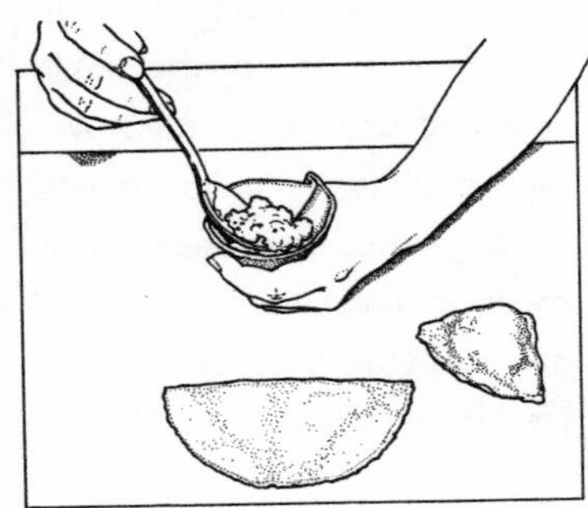

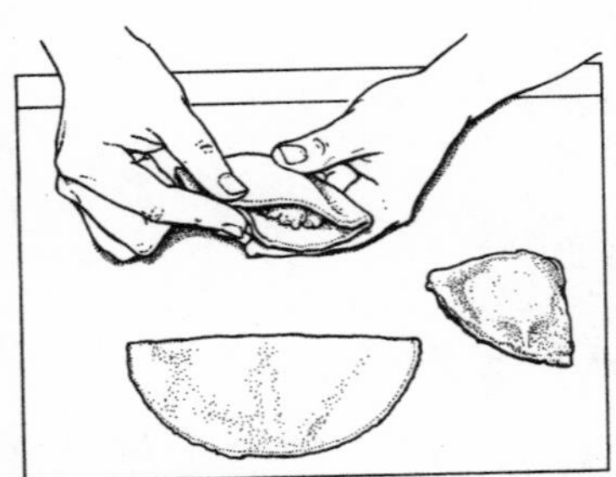

MAKE THE DOUGH

Hand method: Combine the flour, salt, and sugar in a large mixing bowl. Sprinkle the melted butter over the flour. Using a metal pastry blender or fork, blend the butter into the flour until the mixture resembles coarse meal. Sprinkle the water over the flour and, using your fingertips, work it into the mixture until you have a soft dough. If the dough feels too dry or crumbly, add just enough water to make the dough hold together. If it feels sticky, add just enough flour to make a soft dough. Turn the dough out onto a lightly floured work surface. Knead until smooth, about 2 minutes.

Food processor method: Put the flour, salt, and sugar in the bowl of a food processor fitted with the metal blade. Drizzle the melted butter over the flour. Pulse just until the mixture resembles coarse meal. With the motor on, add the water through the feed tube, and process until the dough is soft and smooth, about 20 seconds. If it feels too dry or crumbly, add a little water and pulse until the dough just holds together. If it feels sticky, add just enough flour to make a soft dough. Turn the dough out onto a lightly floured work surface and briefly knead to form a cohesive mass.

LET THE DOUGH REST: Divide the dough into 6 pieces. Roll each piece into a ball, then flatten it slightly and lightly dust with flour. Lay the pieces of dough on a plate, cover with plastic wrap, and refrigerate for 30 minutes.

Meanwhile, PREPARE THE RAITA: Peel and seed the cucumber, and cut it into ¼-inch dices. Place the cucumber in a colander, sprinkle the salt over, toss well, and let stand for 15 minutes in the sink. Rinse off the salt with cold water, and pat the cucumber dry with paper towels.

In a medium bowl, combine the cucumber with all the remaining raita ingredients. Stir well to blend, cover, and refrigerate.

MAKE THE FILLING: Place the cumin seeds in a large dry skillet set over moderate heat and toast until fragrant, about 3 minutes, shaking the pan frequently. Add the oil, onions, garlic, and ginger and cook, stirring frequently, until the onions are soft and translucent, about 2 minutes. Stir in the chickpeas, coriander, and cayenne pepper. Using the back of a spoon, coarsely mash the chickpeas. Add the tuna along with 1 tablespoon water and stir to combine. Remove the pan from the heat and stir in the scallion and grated carrot. Season with salt and pepper, cover, and set aside to cool completely.

ASSEMBLE THE SAMOSAS: Work with one portion of dough at a time, keeping the remainder refrigerated.

On a lightly floured work surface, roll one piece of dough into an 8-inch circle, lifting and turning the dough frequently and dusting the work surface with flour as needed to prevent sticking. Cut the circle in half. Moisten the straight edge of one semicircle with water and roll it up into a loose cone, overlapping the cut edges. Firmly press the seam to seal. Hold the cone in one hand with the open end up and fill it with 2 tablespoons of the filling. Moisten the inside edges of the open end with water and pinch together to seal. Repeat with the second semicircle.

Place the samosas on a large platter and cover with a clean towel to prevent them from drying out while you assemble the remaining samosas in the same manner.

Preheat the oven to 250°F.

COOK THE SAMOSAS: In a deep heavy saucepan over moderate heat or in an electric fryer, slowly heat 2 to 3 inches of oil to 350°F. Add a few samosas at a time and cook, turning occasionally, until they are golden, about 3 to 4 minutes. Using a slotted spoon, transfer the samosas to a baking sheet lined with paper towels to drain. Keep them warm in the oven while you cook the remainder.

Serve the samosas hot, passing the raita on the side.

— *planning ahead* —

The dough can be prepared ahead of time, wrapped well, and refrigerated for up to 2 days. The filling can be covered and refrigerated overnight. The unbaked pastries can be tightly wrapped and refrigerated overnight or frozen for up to 1 month. If the pirozhki have been frozen, bake them unthawed for 5 to 10 minutes longer than the time specified in the recipe.

Beef and Egg Pirozhki

A traditional Russian favorite, pirozhki are crisp finger-length filled oval pastries, usually served along with a clear soup. The filling varies to complement the soup, but typical fillings include minced fish, meat, liver, mushrooms, hard-boiled eggs, rice, and cheese. My recipe for pirozhki offers a filling of ground beef and egg, scented with fresh dill. I also use an unusual flaky crust made with sour cream. I serve these for supper with just a tossed salad, but they also make excellent finger food.

YIELD: About 24 small pastries for hors d'oeuvres, or enough for 10 to 12 side-dish servings

SPECIAL EQUIPMENT: A 3½-inch round cookie cutter

DOUGH

1½ cups unbleached all-purpose flour
½ teaspoon salt
¼ teaspoon baking powder
7 tablespoons cold unsalted butter, cut into 1-inch cubes
1 egg yolk
⅓ cup sour cream

BEEF AND EGG FILLING

4 cloves
2 bay leaves
½ small onion
¾ pound beef chuck, cut into ¾-inch cubes
1 tablespoon unsalted butter
1¼ cups finely chopped onions
2 tablespoons sour cream
2 tablespoons beef broth
2 hard-boiled eggs, peeled and finely chopped
3 tablespoons chopped fresh dill
Salt and freshly ground black pepper to taste

EGG GLAZE

1 egg yolk beaten with 2 teaspoons water

Sour cream or applesauce, for serving (optional)

MAKE THE DOUGH

Hand method: Combine the flour, salt, and baking powder in a large mixing bowl. Scatter the butter over the flour. Using a metal pastry blender or two table knives, cut the butter into the flour until the mixture resembles coarse meal. In a small bowl, whisk the egg yolk and sour cream together. Pour the mixture over the flour. Using a fork or your fingertips, work the mixture until it just holds together. Gather it together and briefly knead in the bowl until the mixture forms a soft dough. If the dough feels too dry or crumbly, add just enough cold water to make the dough hold together. If it feels sticky, add just enough flour to make a soft dough. Press the dough together to form a cohesive mass.

Food processor method: Place the flour, salt, baking powder, and butter in the bowl of a food processor fitted with the metal blade. Pulse just until the mixture resembles coarse meal. In a small bowl, whisk the egg yolk and sour cream together. Pour the mixture over the flour, and pulse until the dough just holds together. If it feels too dry or crumbly, add a little water and pulse until it holds together. If it feels sticky, add just enough flour to make a soft dough. Turn the dough out onto a lightly floured work surface and press it together to form a cohesive mass.

LET THE DOUGH REST: Divide the dough in half. Shape each half into a ball, then gently press it into a disk. Cover with plastic wrap and refrigerate for at least 1 hour.

PREPARE THE FILLING: Use the cloves to pin the bay leaves to the flat surface part of the onion. Place the meat and studded onion in a medium saucepan and add enough water to cover. Bring the mixture to a boil over moderately high heat, skimming the foam from the surface as it forms. Reduce the heat to low, cover, and let simmer until the meat is very tender, about 40 to 45 minutes. Remove the pot from the heat and drain the meat, discarding the onion and cooking liquid. Allow the meat to cool slightly.

Place the meat in the bowl of a food processor fitted with the metal blade, and process until the meat is finely ground. Measure out 1¼ cups for the filling, and reserve any remaining ground beef for another use.

Heat the butter in a large skillet over moderately low heat. Add the onions and cook, stirring frequently with a wooden spoon, until very soft and golden brown, about 15 minutes. Transfer to a medium mixing bowl, and add the ground beef, sour cream, broth, chopped eggs, and dill. Season with salt and black pepper and mix well with a wooden spoon. Cover and refrigerate.

ROLL AND CUT THE DOUGH: Work with one piece of dough at a time, keeping the remainder refrigerated.

On a lightly floured surface, roll one piece of dough into a 12-inch circle about ⅛ inch thick. As you roll, lift up the dough from time to time and sprinkle a light dusting of flour under it to prevent the dough from sticking.

Using the 3½-inch cookie cutter (or the top of a drinking glass), cut out 6 circles. Gather the dough scraps into a ball and reroll into a ⅛-inch-thick circle. Cut out as many circles as you can. Repeat rolling the dough out to a ⅛-inch thickness and cutting out more circles until all the dough is used; you should have about 12 dough circles. Lightly dust the dough circles with flour, stack them on a plate, cover with plastic wrap, and refrigerate.

continued

cook's notes

If you have any leftover filling, use it to top pieces of toast. It's delicious.

Roll and cut the remaining piece of dough to make 12 or so more circles in the same manner, and refrigerate. Make sure the dough circles are well chilled before filling them.

Preheat the oven to 350°F. Adjust an oven rack to the middle shelf. Lightly grease a baking sheet or line it with parchment paper.

ASSEMBLE THE PIROZHKI: Work with 8 of the dough circles at a time, keeping the remainder refrigerated.

Place 8 dough circles on a lightly floured work surface. Spread about 1 tablespoon of the filling over the center of each circle, leaving about a 1-inch margin at the edges. Lightly brush the edges of the dough with egg glaze. Bring up the two sides of each circle to meet over the filling, forming an upright half-moon-shaped purse. Pinch a ¼-inch seam along the edges to seal, then lightly press down on the pastry, forming an oval shape. Arrange the pastries seam side down on the prepared baking sheet and cover with a clean towel to prevent them from drying out.

Assemble the remaining pirozhki in the same manner and place them on the baking sheet. Lightly brush the pastries with egg glaze.

BAKE THE PIROZHKI: Place the baking sheet in the oven and bake until the pirozhki are golden brown, about 25 minutes. Midway through the baking, rotate the baking sheet to ensure even browning. Remove the baking sheet from the oven, and let the pastries cool slightly.

Serve the pirozhki warm, with sour cream or applesauce on the side if desired.

Potato and Smoked Cheese Knishes

Like their cousins, Russian pirozkhi, knishes, the classic Jewish-American dish, are traditionally made from a pastry dough or a potato dough rolled very thin and wrapped around a filling of either mashed potatoes, kasha, mixed vegetables, ground meat, or cheese. I consider knishes the epitome of Jewish cooking. They are rich but simple and have an irresistible homey appeal. I prefer my knishes filled with mashed potatoes made with lots of caramelized onions and smoked cheese. The mild, smoky flavor of the cheese enhances the potato considerably. As with Indian samosas, the dough for knishes is kneaded a little to make it smoother than most short doughs. Made into finger-size servings, knishes are ideal for cocktails.

YIELD: 8 medium knishes; enough for 8 light lunch or snack servings

DOUGH

1 cup unbleached all-purpose flour, plus additional if necessary
½ teaspoon baking powder
¼ teaspoon salt
1 large egg
2 tablespoons vegetable oil
1½ tablespoons hot water

POTATO AND CHEESE FILLING

2 large potatoes (about 1½ pounds)
3 tablespoons vegetable oil
3 cups finely chopped onions
6 ounces smoked cheese (such as Gouda or Bruder Basil), grated
¼ cup cottage cheese
2 tablespoons snipped fresh chives
Salt and freshly ground black pepper to taste

EGG GLAZE

1 egg yolk beaten with 1 teaspoon water

MAKE THE DOUGH

Hand method: Combine the flour, baking powder, and salt in a large mixing bowl. In a small bowl, whisk the egg, oil, and hot water together. Pour over the flour and, using a fork or your fingertips, work the mixture until it just holds together. Gather it together and briefly knead in the bowl until it forms a soft dough. If the dough feels too dry or crumbly, add just enough water to make the dough hold together. If it feels sticky, add just enough flour to make a soft dough. Turn the dough out onto a lightly floured work surface. Knead until smooth, about 2 minutes.

continued

— planning ahead —

The dough can be prepared ahead of time, wrapped well, and refrigerated for up to 2 days. The filling can be covered and refrigerated overnight. The unbaked knishes can be tightly wrapped and refrigerated overnight or frozen for up to 1 month. Thaw frozen knishes overnight in the refrigerator, then bake as specified in the recipe.

Food processor method: Place the flour, baking powder, and salt in the bowl of a food processor fitted with the metal blade. Pulse to blend the ingredients. In a small bowl, whisk the egg, oil, and hot water together. With the motor on, gradually add the liquid through the feed tube, and process until the dough is soft and smooth, about 20 seconds. If it feels too dry or crumbly, add a little water and pulse until it just holds together. If it feels sticky, add just enough flour to make a soft dough. Turn the dough out onto a lightly floured work surface and briefly knead to form a cohesive mass.

LET THE DOUGH REST: Divide the dough into 8 pieces. Roll each piece into a ball, then flatten it slightly and lightly dust with flour. Place the pieces of dough on a plate, cover with plastic wrap, and refrigerate for at least 1 hour.

PREPARE THE FILLING: Peel and quarter the potatoes. Place them in a medium saucepan and add salted water to cover. Bring to a boil over high heat, then reduce the heat to moderate and cook until the potatoes are fork-tender but not mushy, about 20 to 25 minutes. Drain the water from the saucepan, reduce the heat to low, and shake the pan over the heat to dry the potatoes.

Using a potato masher, food mill, or electric mixer, mash the potatoes thoroughly, until no lumps remain. Measure out 2 cups of mashed potatoes for the filling and place in a large mixing bowl. (Save the remainder for another use.)

Heat the oil in a large skillet over moderately low heat. Add the onions and cook, stirring frequently with a wooden spoon, until very soft and well browned, about 20 minutes. Transfer the onions to the bowl of mashed potatoes. Add the smoked cheese, cottage cheese, and chives to the potatoes, and blend thoroughly with a wooden spoon. Season with salt and pepper. Cover and chill well before filling the knishes.

Preheat the oven to 400°F. Lightly grease a baking sheet or line it with parchment paper.

ASSEMBLE THE KNISHES: Work with one portion of dough at a time, keeping the remainder refrigerated.

On a lightly floured work surface, roll a portion of dough into a 6-inch circle, lifting and turning the dough frequently and dusting the work surface with flour as needed to prevent sticking. Mound ⅓ cup of the filling in the center of the circle. Lightly flatten the filling into a 3-inch patty, leaving a 1½-inch margin around the edges of the dough. Moisten the edges of the dough circle with water. Working your way around the circle, fold and pleat the dough over the filling, covering it completely and forming a round pastry. Invert the knish on the prepared baking sheet and cover with a towel to prevent it from drying out.

Assemble the remaining knishes in the same manner. Lightly brush the knishes with egg glaze.

BAKE THE KNISHES: Place the baking sheet in the oven and bake until the knishes are golden brown, about 20 minutes. Midway through the baking, rotate the baking sheet to ensure even browning. Remove the baking sheet from the oven and allow the knishes to cool slightly.

Serve warm.

VARIATION

KNISHES WITH BROCCOLI AND CHEDDAR: Substitute 1 cup chopped cooked broccoli for 1 cup of the mashed potatoes and use Cheddar cheese instead of the smoked cheese.

— *planning ahead* —

The dough can be prepared ahead of time, wrapped well, and refrigerated for up to 2 days. The filling can be covered and refrigerated overnight. The uncooked patties can be wrapped individually in plastic wrap and frozen for up to 1 month. Fry frozen patties unthawed for a minute longer than the time specified in the recipe.

Jamaican Meat Patties

These savory meat patties are popular street food throughout Jamaica and there are as many variations as there are cooks. They have their origins in Spain, in the form of meat pies, or *pasteles,* but have been transformed into something uniquely Jamaican with the use of native ingredients and the seasonings favored by the island's African and Indian populations. This recipe is my re-creation of a similar pastry I enjoyed at the Sugar Reef restaurant in New York. The dough is easy to handle, neither fragile nor firm, and it produces one of the most tender meat pies ever. Curry and hot chile peppers add a welcome bite to the fragrant beef filling.

YIELD: 12 patties, enough for 12 first-course or 6 light supper servings

DOUGH

2 cups unbleached all-purpose flour, plus additional if necessary
2 teaspoons sugar
1 teaspoon salt
1 teaspoon baking powder
½ teaspoon turmeric
1 large egg
3 tablespoons unsalted butter, at room temperature

SPICY BEEF FILLING

4 tablespoons unsalted butter
2 medium white onions, finely chopped (about 2 cups)
1 tablespoon minced garlic
½ Scotch bonnet pepper (see Cook's Notes), seeded and minced
1 pound ground beef, preferably round or sirloin
1 tablespoon curry powder, preferably Madras brand
1 tablespoon chopped fresh thyme leaves or 1 teaspoon dried, crumbled
½ teaspoon salt, or more to taste
1 teaspoon freshly ground black pepper, or more to taste
1 teaspoon sugar
⅔ cups beef broth, homemade (page 370) or store-bought
½ cup dried bread crumbs

EGG GLAZE

1 egg yolk beaten with 2 teaspoons water

Vegetable oil, for deep-frying
Tabasco sauce or West Indian hot sauce, such as jerk sauce, for serving (optional)

MAKE THE DOUGH

Hand method: Combine the flour, sugar, salt, baking powder, and turmeric in a large mixing bowl, and make a well in the middle. In a small bowl, whisk together the egg and ⅔ cup water. Pour the mixture into the well. Using a wooden spoon, draw the flour into the liquid to blend until it clumps together into a rough, shaggy mass. Gather it together and briefly knead in the bowl until it forms a soft dough. The dough should be soft and damp but not sticky. If it feels sticky, knead in about a tablespoon more flour. Turn the dough out onto a well-floured work surface. Knead the softened butter into the dough. Continue kneading the dough until it is very soft and smooth, about 2 to 3 minutes. If the dough feels sticky as you knead, dust it with a little flour. Shape the dough into a smooth ball.

Food processor method: Place the flour, sugar, salt, baking powder, and turmeric in the bowl of a food processor fitted with the metal blade. Pulse to blend the ingredients. In a small bowl, whisk together the egg and ⅔ cup water. With the motor on, gradually add the mixture through the feed tube. Process until the dough forms a soft ball, about 10 seconds. Scatter the softened butter over the dough. Process until the dough is very soft and moist but not sticky, about 5 seconds. If the dough feels sticky, add about 1 tablespoon flour and pulse until it is no longer sticky. Turn the dough out onto a lightly floured work surface and shape it into a ball.

LET THE DOUGH REST: Cover the dough with plastic wrap and set it aside to rest for at least 1 hour.

MAKE THE FILLING: Heat the butter in a large skillet over moderate heat. Add the onions, garlic, and Scotch bonnet pepper, and cook, stirring with a wooden spoon, until the onions are soft and translucent, about 2 minutes. Add the meat, curry, thyme, salt, pepper, and sugar, and cook, breaking up the meat lumps with the back of the spoon, until the meat is browned, about 5 minutes. Add the broth and reduce the heat to low. Cover and simmer until the beef is tender, about 8 minutes. Add the bread crumbs, stir well to combine, and continue to simmer until all the liquid is absorbed, about 2 minutes longer. Remove the pan from the heat. Taste and adjust the seasonings with salt and pepper if necessary. Let cool thoroughly.

ASSEMBLE THE PATTIES: Divide the dough into 12 pieces. Work with one piece of dough at a time, keeping the remainder covered in the refrigerator.

Shape one piece of dough into a rough square. On a lightly floured work surface, roll the dough into a rectangle 5 by 7 inches, with a short side toward you. Put about ¼ cup of the filling on the bottom half of the dough, just below the center, leaving about a ½-inch margin of dough exposed around the filling. Moisten the exposed dough with water. Fold the top half of the dough over the filling, forming a rectangular turnover. When you fold, be careful that the filling doesn't spread toward the edges, or you will not be able to seal the turnover properly. Join the edges and seal securely by pressing them together with the tines of a fork.

Place the patty on a lightly floured platter or baking sheet. Cover with a clean towel to prevent it from drying out while you assemble the remaining patties in the same manner. Then lightly brush the surface of the patties with egg glaze.

continued

— *cook's notes* —

Scotch bonnet is the world's hottest chile pepper, so called because its shape resembles a Scotsman's bonnet. It is commonly used in tropical cooking. Fresh Scotch bonnet peppers and West Indian jerk sauce are available in Caribbean markets and some Latin American markets. You may substitute 2 jalapeño peppers for the Scotch bonnet.

The patties may be generously brushed with melted butter and baked in a preheated 400°F oven until light golden, about 20 minutes.

The beef filling in this recipe is so good that I often use it to fill phyllo triangles and then bake them for hors d'oeuvres. To make them, follow the instructions for assembling Spanakopetes (page 52).

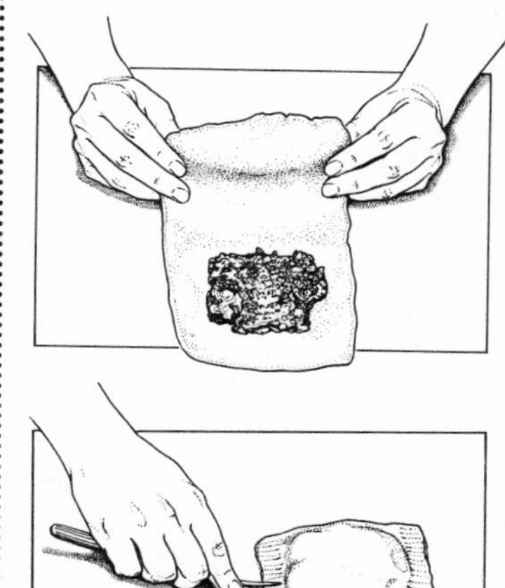

Preheat the oven to 250°F.

COOK THE PATTIES: In a deep heavy saucepan over moderate heat or in an electric fryer, slowly heat 2 to 3 inches of oil to 350°F. Gently lower the patties, a few at a time, into the hot oil. Cook, turning occasionally with tongs, until the patties are golden brown on both sides, about 3 to 4 minutes. Using the tongs, remove them to paper towels to drain. Keep the fried patties warm in the oven while you cook the remaining patties in the same manner.

Serve the patties hot, passing Tabasco sauce or hot sauce on the side if desired.

French-Canadian Meat Pie

(TOURTIÈRE)

This savory Quebécois meat pie is traditionally served at Christmas. It takes its name from the pan (*tourtière*) in which it is baked. Here, I have substituted a less starchy sweet potato for the traditional white potato in the filling. Thyme, allspice, and ground cinnamon add a snappy bite that offsets the richness of the filling.

YIELD: One pie, enough for 4 to 6 main-course servings

SPECIAL EQUIPMENT: A 9-inch round pie pan

DOUGH

- 1½ cups unbleached all-purpose flour
- ⅓ cup grated sharp Cheddar cheese
- ½ teaspoon salt
- ½ teaspoon sugar
- 4 tablespoons cold unsalted butter, cut into 1-inch pieces
- ¼ cup cold solid vegetable shortening, cut into bits
- ¼ cup ice water

SAVORY MEAT FILLING

- 2 tablespoons vegetable oil
- 2 cups chopped onions
- 1 tablespoon minced garlic
- ½ pound ground pork
- ½ pound ground beef, preferably round or sirloin
- 1 cup chopped fresh tomatoes
- ¾ cup chicken broth, homemade (page 368) or store-bought, or water
- 1 teaspoon dried thyme leaves, crumbled
- 1 teaspoon ground allspice
- 1 teaspoon ground cinnamon
- 2 bay leaves
- ½ teaspoon salt
- Freshly ground black pepper to taste

- 1 large sweet potato (about ½ pound), peeled and cut into 2-inch chunks

EGG GLAZE

- 1 egg yolk beaten with 1 teaspoon water

MAKE THE DOUGH

Hand method: Combine the flour, cheese, salt, and sugar in a large mixing bowl. Scatter the butter and shortening over the flour. Using a metal pastry blender or two table knives, cut the butter and shortening into the flour until the mixture resembles coarse meal. Sprinkle the ice water over the mixture a little at a time, working it into the mixture with a fork or your fingertips until the dough just holds together. If the dough feels too dry or crumbly, add just enough water to make it stick together. Briefly knead the dough in the bowl to form a cohesive mass.

continued

— *planning ahead* —

The dough can be prepared ahead of time, wrapped well, and refrigerated for up to 1 week. The filling can be covered and refrigerated overnight. The unbaked pie can be tightly wrapped and refrigerated overnight or frozen for up to 1 month. If the pie has been frozen, bake it unthawed for 5 to 10 minutes longer than the time specified in the recipe.

— cook's notes —

If you have any leftover pie, it will taste delicious reheated the next day.

Food processor method: Put the flour, cheese, salt, sugar, butter, and shortening in the bowl of a food processor fitted with the metal blade. Pulse until the mixture resembles coarse meal. With the motor on, gradually add the ice water through the feed tube. Process just until the dough barely holds together, about 10 seconds; do not overprocess. The dough should be soft, not crumbly. If it feels too dry or crumbly, add a little water and pulse until it just holds together. Turn the dough out onto a lightly floured surface and press it together to form a cohesive mass.

LET THE DOUGH REST: Cut the dough into 2 pieces, one twice as large as the other. Shape each portion into a ball, then lightly press each piece into a disk. Cover with plastic wrap and refrigerate for at least 30 minutes.

PREPARE THE FILLING: Heat the oil in a large skillet over moderate heat. Add the onions and garlic and cook, stirring frequently with a wooden spoon, until the onions are soft and translucent, about 2 minutes. Add the pork and cook, breaking up the meat lumps with the back of the spoon, until the meat loses its pink color, about 2 minutes. Add the beef and tomatoes, and cook, stirring frequently, just until the tomatoes are soft and the beef loses its pink color, about 1 minute. Add the broth, thyme, allspice, cinnamon, bay leaves, and salt. Stir well and bring the mixture to a boil over high heat. Reduce the heat to low and simmer, uncovered, until the meat is very tender and most of the liquid has evaporated, about 30 minutes. Remove the pan from the heat. Taste and adjust the seasoning with salt and pepper if desired. Set aside to cool.

Meanwhile, put the sweet potato pieces in a medium saucepan and add enough water to cover. Bring to a boil over high heat. Reduce the heat to moderate and cook until the potato is fork-tender, about 10 minutes. Drain the sweet potato and place in a large mixing bowl. Using a potato masher or a fork, mash the potato thoroughly.

Add the cooled meat mixture to the mashed sweet potato and stir to combine. Cover and chill well before filling the pie.

Preheat the oven to 400°F. Adjust an oven rack to the middle shelf.

ASSEMBLE THE PIE: On a lightly floured work surface, roll the larger dough piece into a circle slightly larger than 13 inches in diameter and about ⅛ inch thick. As you roll, lift and turn the dough frequently, dusting the work surface with flour as necessary to prevent the dough from sticking. Gently fold the dough circle in half, and then in half again. Lift the folded circle and place it in the pie pan with the point in the center. Unfold the dough to line the pie plate, leaving the excess dough overhanging the rim. Pack the filling into the dough shell and smooth the top.

Roll the remaining piece of dough into a 10-inch circle. Gently fold the circle in half, and then in half again. Transfer the folded circle to the pie plate and unfold it so that it covers the filling. Using scissors, trim the excess pastry from the bottom round of dough, leaving a ½-inch overhang. Reserve the dough trimmings to decorate the pie. Brush the pastry top with egg glaze. Fold the pastry overhang up over the top of the pie, and crimp to seal. Brush the crimped edges with egg glaze.

Gather the dough scraps into a ball, reroll into a sheet ⅛ inch thick, and cut out several decorative leaf shapes. Arrange the leaves atop the pie and brush them with egg glaze. Make several small incisions in the crust to allow steam to escape.

BAKE THE PIE: Place the pie in the oven and bake for 10 minutes. Then reduce the oven temperature to 350°F and continue baking until the crust is golden brown, about 35 minutes. Remove the pie from the oven, and let cool slightly on a rack before serving.

— *planning ahead* —

The dough can be prepared ahead of time, wrapped well, and refrigerated for up to 1 week. The filling can be covered and refrigerated overnight. The unbaked pie can be tightly wrapped and refrigerated overnight; I do not recommend freezing this pie.

Chicken Pot Pie with Herbed Crust

After two years of study at the Culinary Institute of America and countless chicken pot pies, both good and bad, served at student meals, I thought I could never face another pot pie as long as I lived. Lucky me: That was the very first dish I was asked to put on a restaurant menu when I started out as a professional chef. Still, something tells me that many people will be disappointed if I don't offer a recipe for chicken pot pie in this book. Therefore, here is my version of the American classic.

When making chicken pot pie, I use dark chicken meat, which I think is much more tasty and juicier than white meat. I also avoid cooking the meat to death, as is often the case. In this recipe, the parsnips and sweet potato provide the right balance of sharp and sweet flavors against the rich white sauce in the filling. Once you serve this creamy chicken pot pie, with a crust redolent of fresh thyme, your family will never be satisfied with a store-bought frozen pie again.

YIELD: One large pie, enough for 5 to 6 main-course servings

SPECIAL EQUIPMENT: A 9-inch deep-dish pie pan

DOUGH

1½ cups unbleached all-purpose flour
2 tablespoons chopped fresh thyme leaves or 1½ teaspoons dried, crumbled
1 teaspoon sugar
½ teaspoon salt
4 tablespoons cold unsalted butter, cut into 1-inch pieces
¼ cup cold solid vegetable shortening, cut into bits
¼ cup ice water

CHICKEN FILLING

4 large chicken legs (about 2½ pounds), well rinsed
5 cups chicken broth, homemade (page 368) or store-bought
2 teaspoons black peppercorns
2 bay leaves
4 sprigs fresh thyme or 1 teaspoon dried thyme leaves
3 large garlic cloves, crushed
2 small carrots, peeled and cut into ¾-inch cubes (about ¾ cup)
1 small leek, halved lengthwise and cut crosswise into ½-inch-thick pieces (about 2 cups), well rinsed
2 large parsnips, peeled and cut into ¾-inch cubes (about 1½ cups)
1 small sweet potato (about 8 ounces), peeled and cut into ¾-inch cubes
½ cup fresh or frozen peas

SAUCE

4 tablespoons unsalted butter
5 tablespoons all-purpose flour
1 cup heavy cream
2 tablespoons chopped fresh thyme leaves or 1 teaspoon dried
Salt and freshly ground black pepper to taste
Tabasco sauce to taste

MAKE THE DOUGH

Hand method: Combine the flour, thyme, sugar, and salt in a large mixing bowl. Scatter the butter and shortening over the flour. Using a metal pastry blender or two table knives, cut the butter and shortening into the flour until the mixture resembles coarse meal. Sprinkle the ice water over the mixture a little at a time, working it into the mixture with a fork or your fingertips until the dough just holds together. If the dough feels too dry or crumbly, add just enough water to make it stick together. Briefly knead the dough in the bowl to form a cohesive mass.

Food processor method: Put the flour, thyme, sugar, salt, butter, and shortening in the bowl of a food processor fitted with the metal blade. Pulse until the mixture resembles coarse meal. With the motor on, gradually add the ice water through the feed tube. Process just until the dough barely holds together, about 10 seconds; do not overprocess. The dough should be soft, not crumbly. If it feels too dry or crumbly, add a little water and pulse until the dough just holds together. Turn the dough out onto a lightly floured surface and press it together to form a cohesive mass.

LET THE DOUGH REST: Shape the dough into a ball and lightly press it into a disk. Cover with plastic wrap and refrigerate for at least 30 minutes.

PREPARE THE FILLING: Put the chicken legs in a 5-quart soup pot. Add the broth, peppercorns, bay leaves, thyme sprigs, and garlic. Bring to a boil over high heat, skimming the foam from the surface as it forms. Reduce the heat to low and simmer very gently until the chicken legs are fork-tender, about 35 to 40 minutes.

Remove the pot from the heat. Using tongs, remove the chicken legs to a plate and set them aside to cool. Strain the broth through a fine-mesh strainer into a medium bowl. You should have about 3½ cups. Return the broth to the soup pot and set aside.

When the chicken legs are cool enough to handle, remove and discard the skin. Tear the meat into bite-size pieces and discard the bones. Put the chicken meat into a large mixing bowl, cover, and set aside.

Bring the reserved broth in the pot to a boil over high heat. Add the carrots and leek. As soon as the broth returns to a boil, reduce the heat to moderate, and cook until the leek is soft and the carrots just tender, about 4 minutes. Add the parnips and sweet potato; if using fresh peas, add them as well. Once the broth returns to a full boil, cook until the sweet potatoes are just cooked through, about 2 minutes longer. Using a slotted spoon, transfer all the vegetables to the bowl with the chicken, and set aside uncovered. Reduce the heat to moderately low and let the broth simmer as you begin to prepare the sauce.

MAKE THE SAUCE: Melt the butter in a heavy medium saucepan over low heat. Make a roux by adding the flour and then cooking, stirring frequently with

— *cook's notes* —

Do try to find fresh thyme, which is essential for the delicate balance of flavors in this dish.

If you have any leftover pie, it will taste delicious reheated the next day.

a whisk, until the mixture develops a nutty smell, about 2 minutes. Slowly add half of the hot broth to the roux, whisking constantly until the sauce thickens. Add the rest of the broth along with the cream and chopped thyme. Increase the heat to moderate and allow the sauce to simmer, stirring occasionally, until it is well steeped with the flavor of thyme, about 5 minutes. Remove the pan from the heat. Add the vegetables and chicken to the sauce. If using frozen peas, add them now. Season the mixture with salt, pepper, and Tabasco. Set aside to cool slightly.

Preheat the oven to 375°F. Adjust an oven rack to the middle shelf.

ROLL THE DOUGH: On a lightly floured work surface, roll the dough into a 12-inch circle about ⅛ inch thick. As you roll, lift and turn the dough frequently, dusting the work surface with flour as necessary to prevent the dough from sticking.

ASSEMBLE THE PIE: Spoon the filling into the pie pan. Drape the dough over the rolling pin and transfer it carefully to the pie pan to cover the filling. Trim the overhanging pastry to about 1 inch. Tuck the edges of the dough inside the rim of the pie pan to seal the pie. Reroll the dough trimmings and cut out several leaf shapes to decorate the pie if you wish. Make several small incisions in the crust to allow steam to escape.

BAKE THE PIE: Place the pie in the oven and bake until the crust is light golden brown, about 50 minutes. Remove the pie from the oven, and let cool slightly on a rack before serving.

Bobotie

Out of South Africa comes a most distinguished culinary delight by the Afrikaan name ***bobotie***. Bobotie is a succulent minced meat casserole of Malaysian origin. Traditionally, it was made with hard-boiled eggs, onions, tomatoes, lemons, lemon leaves, curry, milk, and minced game meat. Today, lamb is the more favored ingredient. Midway through the baking, the mincemeat mixture is removed from the oven and topped with beaten eggs, then returned to the oven. The casserole is served over rice.

I think bobotie is just too exquisite to serve as a casserole. I found that covering it with a light, flaky crust transforms it into a dish suitable for a most elegant meal. My version of bobotie uses ground venison, plus raisins in the filling and almonds sprinkled over the crust. The combination of sweet, nutty, and tart flavors is an exciting sensation on the palate.

YIELD: 1 large pie, enough for 8 main-course servings

SPECIAL EQUIPMENT: A 9-inch deep-dish pie pan

DOUGH

2 cups unbleached all-purpose flour
1 teaspoon baking powder
1 teaspoon salt
1 teaspoon sugar
5 tablespoons cold unsalted butter, cut into ½-inch cubes
5 tablespoons cold solid vegetable shortening, cut into bits
¼ cup ice water

SPICE MIXTURE

2 teaspoons turmeric
2 teaspoons ground cumin
2 teaspoons ground coriander
1 teaspoon ground cinnamon
1 teaspoon ground ginger
1 teaspoon salt

VENISON FILLING

2 tablespoons unsalted butter
2 cups chopped onions
1 tablespoon minced garlic
1½ pounds ground venison (see Cook's Notes)
5 tablespoons fresh lemon juice
3 tablespoons light brown sugar
¾ cup beef broth, homemade (page 370) or store-bought
½ cup golden raisins
Grated zest of 2 lemons (about 2 tablespoons)
½ cup dried bread crumbs
Salt and freshly ground black pepper to taste
5 hard-boiled eggs, peeled

EGG GLAZE

1 egg yolk beaten with 2 teaspoons water

2 tablespoons sliced almonds

continued

— *planning ahead* —

The dough can be prepared ahead of time, wrapped well, and refrigerated for up to 1 week. The filling can be covered and refrigerated overnight. The unbaked pie can be tightly wrapped and refrigerated overnight or frozen for up to 1 month. If the pie has been frozen, bake it unthawed for 5 to 10 minutes longer than the time specified in the recipe.

— cook's notes —

If possible, have the butcher grind the venison meat for you. Otherwise, use 1½ pounds of meat from the forequarter, shanks, or any other inexpensive cuts of the venison. Trim off any visible fat and cut the meat into 1-inch pieces. Put the meat twice through a grinder fitted with the medium blade. The ground meat should have the texture of raw hamburger. Alternatively, chop the meat in a food processor.

You may substitute ground lamb for the venison.

If you have access to fresh lemon, orange, or lime leaves, be sure to add a few of them to the filling for an unusual and exciting citrusy flavor.

MAKE THE DOUGH

Hand method: Combine the flour, baking powder, salt, and sugar in a large mixing bowl. Scatter the butter and shortening over the flour. Using a metal pastry blender or two table knives, cut the butter and shortening into the flour until the mixture resembles coarse meal. Sprinkle the ice water over the mixture a little at a time, working it into the mixture with a fork or your fingertips until the dough just holds together. If the dough feels too dry or crumbly, add just enough water to make it stick together. Briefly knead the dough in the bowl to form a cohesive mass.

Food processor method: Put the flour, baking powder, salt, sugar, butter, and shortening in the bowl of a food processor fitted with the metal blade. Pulse just until the mixture resembles coarse meal. With the motor on, gradually add the ice water through the feed tube. Process just until the dough barely holds together, about 10 seconds; do not overprocess. The dough should be soft, not crumbly. If it feels too dry or crumbly, add a little water and pulse until it just holds together. Turn the dough out onto a lightly floured surface and press it together to form a cohesive mass.

LET THE DOUGH REST: Cut the dough into 2 pieces, one twice as large as the other. Shape each portion into a ball, then lightly press each piece into a disk. Cover with plastic wrap and refrigerate for at least 30 minutes.

MIX THE SPICES: In a small bowl, blend all the spice mixture ingredients together. Cover and set aside.

MAKE THE FILLING: Heat the butter in a large skillet over moderate heat. When hot, add the onions and garlic, and cook, stirring frequently with a wooden spoon, until the onions are soft and translucent, about 2 minutes. Add the spice mixture and stir well to combine. Add the ground venison and cook, breaking up the meat lumps with the back of the spoon, until no traces of pink remain, about 3 minutes.

In a small bowl, stir the lemon juice and sugar together until the sugar is dissolved. Add the sweetened lemon juice, the broth, raisins, and lemon zest to the skillet, stir, and reduce the heat to low. Cover the pan and simmer until the meat is tender, about 8 minutes. Stir in the bread crumbs. (Most of the liquid in the pan will be absorbed by the crumbs.) Cover the pan and continue simmering for 2 minutes longer. Remove the pan from the heat, uncover, and allow the mixture to cool completely. Taste and adjust the seasoning with salt and pepper if necessary.

Preheat the oven to 375°F. Adjust an oven rack to the middle shelf.

ASSEMBLE THE PIE: On a lightly floured work surface, roll the larger piece of dough into a 13-inch circle about ⅛ inch thick. As you roll, lift and turn the dough frequently, dusting the work surface with flour as necessary to prevent the dough from sticking. Gently fold the dough circle in half, and then in half again. Lift the folded circle and place it in the pie pan, with the point in the center. Unfold the dough to line the pan, leaving the excess dough overhanging the rim.

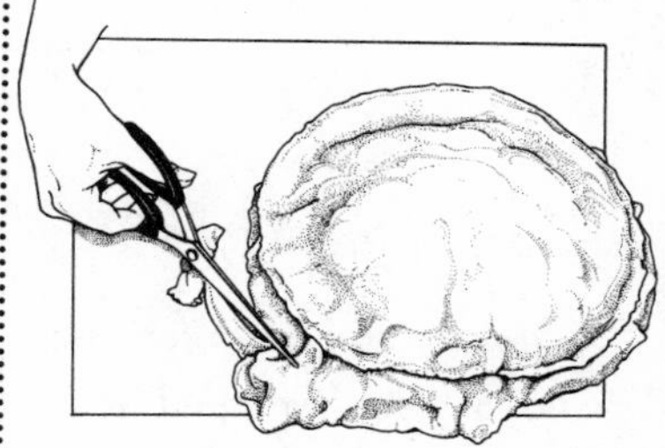

Spread half of the filling over the pastry. Cut each egg in half lengthwise and arrange them, cut side down, over the filling. Cover the eggs with the remaining filling and smooth the top.

Roll the remaining piece of dough into a 10-inch circle. Gently fold the circle in half, and then in half again. Transfer the folded circle to the pie plate and unfold it so that it covers the filling. Brush the pastry top with egg glaze. Bring the overhanging pastry from the bottom up over the top of the pie and crimp the edges to seal. Brush the crimped edges with egg glaze. Sprinkle the sliced almonds over the pie. Make several small incisions in the crust to allow steam to escape.

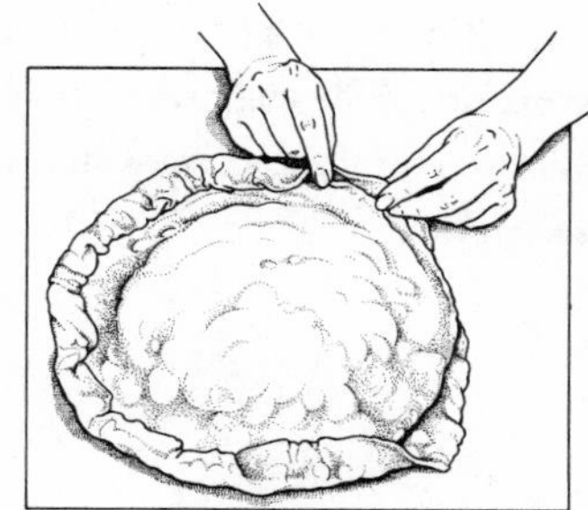

BAKE THE PIE: Place the pie in the oven and bake for 10 minutes. Then reduce the oven temperature to 350°F and continue baking until the pie is golden brown, about 35 minutes. Remove the pie from the oven and allow it to cool slightly on a rack before serving.

VARIATION

HUNTER'S PIE: Omit the pastry dough. Layer the filling and eggs in a pie pan as indicated above, then top with mashed potatoes (made with 2 pounds potatoes, 1 cup milk, 4 tablespoons melted butter, and salt and freshly ground black pepper to taste). Sprinkle 3 tablespoons freshly grated Parmesan cheese over the top. Bake the pie in a preheated 400°F oven for 20 minutes. Turn on the broiler, and place the pie under the broiler until the potato crust turns golden brown, about 5 minutes. Serve hot.

— *planning ahead* —

The dough can be prepared ahead of time, wrapped well, and refrigerated for up to 1 week. Tightly wrapped in plastic wrap and foil, the baked pâté will keep for up to a week in the refrigerator.

Chicken and Vegetable Pâté en Croûte

The term *pâté* is most frequently used to refer to mixtures of ground meat, game, or fish, prepared in a round or rectangular mold or in an earthenware dish called a terrine. By definition, however, a pâté is any variation on a filling baked in a casing of pastry dough. When pâté is served cold, it is usually known as pâté en croûte.

Here is a wonderfully light and very tasty pâté en croûte made with colorful vegetables held in suspension in a ground chicken forcemeat. The delicate flavors of both the chicken and the vegetables are further heightened by the mix of fresh herbs, including dill, tarragon, thyme, and basil. Serve this elegant pâté warm as a main course or cold as a first course or at a buffet.

YIELD: One 12-inch-long pâté, enough for 12 appetizer or 6 main-course servings

SPECIAL EQUIPMENT: A 2-quart hinged pâté mold or loaf pan

DOUGH

2¾ cups unbleached all-purpose flour
2 teaspoons salt
2 teaspoons sugar
9 tablespoons unsalted butter, cut into ½-inch pieces
2 large eggs
⅓ cup ice water

CHICKEN FORCEMEAT

2 boneless skinless chicken breasts (about ¾ pound)
1 large egg white
½ cup heavy cream, well chilled
¾ teaspoon salt
¼ teaspoon ground white pepper
1 tablespoon chopped fresh dill
1 tablespoon chopped fresh basil leaves
1 tablespoon chopped fresh thyme leaves
1 tablespoon chopped fresh tarragon leaves

VEGETABLES

2 medium red bell peppers
2 tablespoons unsalted butter
1 tablespoon minced garlic
3 medium carrots, peeled and cut into ¼-inch cubes (1¼ cups)
1 small yellow squash, cut into ½-inch cubes (about ¾ cup)
1 10-ounce package frozen artichoke hearts, thawed and cut into ½-inch pieces
½ 10-ounce package frozen chopped spinach, thawed and squeezed dry
Salt and freshly ground black pepper to taste

EGG GLAZE

1 egg yolk beaten with 2 teaspoons water

MAKE THE DOUGH

Hand method: Combine the flour, salt, and sugar in a large mixing bowl. Scatter the butter over the flour. Using a metal pastry blender or two table knives, cut the butter into the flour until the mixture resembles coarse meal. In a small bowl, whisk together the eggs and ice water. Pour the liquid over the flour mixture and work it in with a fork or your fingertips until the dough just holds together. If the dough feels too dry or crumbly, add just enough water to make it stick together. Briefly knead the dough in the bowl to form a cohesive mass.

Food processor method: Put the flour, salt, sugar, and butter in the bowl of a food processor fitted with the metal blade. Pulse until the mixture resembles coarse meal. In a small bowl, whisk together the eggs and ice water. With the motor on, add the liquid through the feed tube. Process just until the dough holds together, about 10 seconds; do not overprocess. The dough should be soft, not crumbly. If it feels too dry or crumbly, add a little water and pulse until the dough just holds together. Turn the dough out onto a lightly floured surface and press it together to form a cohesive mass.

LET THE DOUGH REST: Shape the dough into a rough rectangle. Cover with plastic wrap and refrigerate until the dough is firm, at least 1 hour.

PREPARE THE CHICKEN FORCEMEAT: Trim any visible fat from the chicken. Cut the chicken into 1-inch pieces and place them in a small bowl. Cover the bowl and put it in the freezer until the chicken is well chilled, about 20 minutes.

Put the chilled chicken meat in the bowl of a food processor fitted with the metal blade. Pulse just until the chicken is ground and the texture resembles that of raw hamburger meat. Add the egg white to the ground chicken and process to a purée, about 10 seconds. With the motor on, gradually add the heavy cream through the feed tube and process until the cream is just incorporated and the mixture is light and fluffy, about 10 seconds. Do not overprocess. Add the salt, pepper, and all the herbs and pulse until just blended. Transfer the chicken forcemeat to a medium mixing bowl, cover, and refrigerate.

PREPARE THE VEGETABLES: Place the bell peppers directly over a gas or electric burner set at moderate heat and grill, turning the peppers with tongs, until the peppers are soft and their skin charred, about 5 minutes. Let the peppers cool, then hold the peppers under cold running water and rub the skin off. Pat dry, core, and seed. Cut the peppers into ¼-inch-wide strips. Put the sliced peppers in a small bowl, cover, and set aside.

continued

— *cook's notes* —

Avoid freezing pâté en croûte as its texture will be altered and the thawed pâté will be soggy.

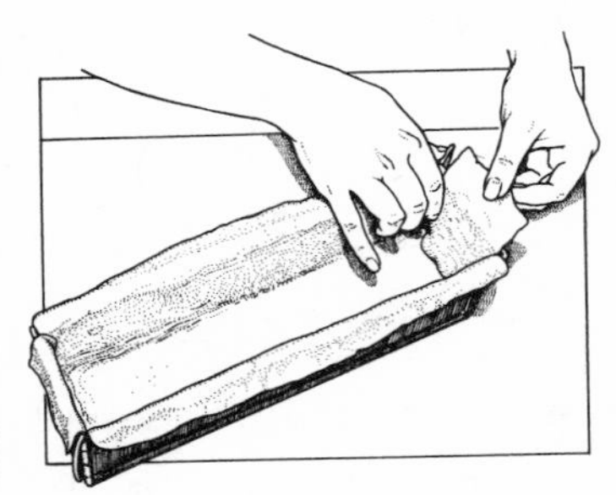

Melt the butter in a large skillet over moderately low heat. When the butter is hot, add the garlic and carrots. Sauté until the carrots are barely cooked, about 2 minutes. Add the squash and sauté until it is just tender, about 2 minutes. Add the artichoke hearts and sauté until they are heated through, 2 minutes longer. Add the spinach and sauté until it is just heated through, 1 minute longer. Remove the pan from the heat. Season the mixture with salt and pepper. Set aside to cool thoroughly.

Fold the cooled sautéed vegetables into the chicken forcemeat with a rubber spatula. Cover and refrigerate.

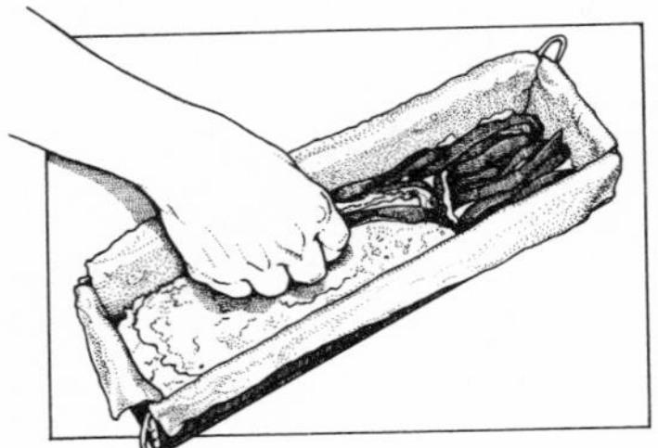

Preheat the oven to 400°F. Adjust an oven rack to the middle shelf. Lightly butter the pâté mold.

ROLL AND CUT THE DOUGH: On a lightly floured work surface, roll the dough into a large rectangle about 12 by 22 inches and ⅛ inch thick. Using a ruler and a sharp paring knife, cut out 4 pieces as follows: a 12-inch square, a 2¾- by 11½-inch rectangle, and two 3- by 4-inch rectangles. Save the dough trimmings.

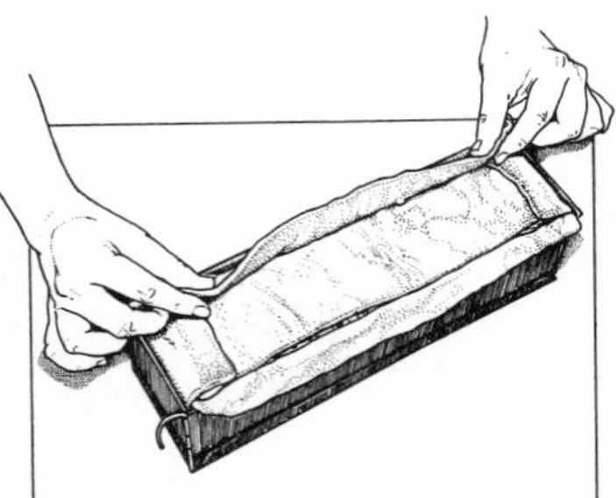

ASSEMBLE THE PÂTÉ: Press the large rectangle of dough into the bottom and up the long sides of the prepared mold. The dough should overhang the edges of the mold by about ¾ inch. Press a small dough rectangle into each end of the mold, leaving about a ¾-inch overhang. Using a fork, spread half of the filling into the bottom of the mold. Arrange the red pepper strips lengthwise on top of the filling, covering it completely. Cover the peppers with the remaining filling, and smooth the surface. Lay the remaining rectangle of dough over the filling, and lightly brush with egg glaze. Fold back the dough overhanging the sides of the mold to seal the pâté. Lightly brush any unglazed surfaces of dough with egg glaze.

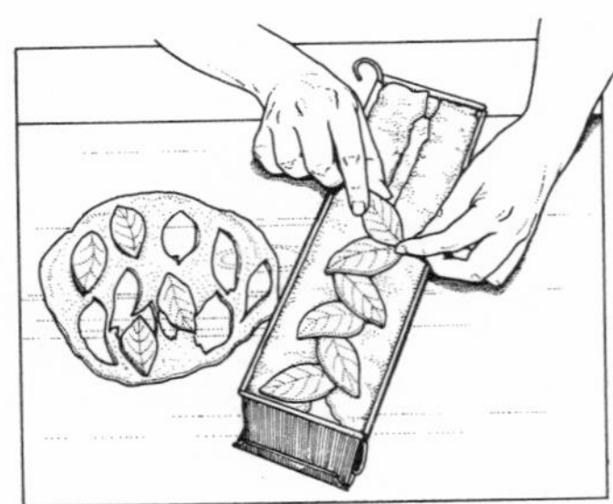

Reroll the dough trimmings to a thickness of ⅛ inch. Using a small paring knife, cut out several decorative leaf shapes. Arrange the cut-out leaves in a decorative manner over the top of the pâté. Lightly brush the leaves with egg glaze. Using a wooden skewer, puncture a few holes in the top of the pastry to allow steam to escape while the pâté is baking.

BAKE THE PÂTÉ: Place the pâté in the oven and bake for about 15 minutes, or until the dough is light golden brown. Reduce the oven temperature to 350°F and continue baking until the pâté is cooked through, about 30 minutes longer, or until an instant-read thermometer inserted into the pâté reaches 140°F.

Remove the pâté from the oven and allow it to cool slightly in the mold, then carefully unmold the pâté and let it cool on a rack.

TO SERVE: For a warm entrée, serve the pâté cut into ½-inch-thick slices. For appetizers, allow the pâté to cool completely, or refrigerate it, and then cut into ¼-inch slices.

High-Rise Peach Pie

What makes this pie so irresistible is the light, flaky, and buttery crust hiding a heaping mound of luscious peaches, made special by a hint of ginger. Make this pie in the summer when peaches are at their best and full of flavor. The trick here is to choose peaches that are just ripe and not too juicy and to leave their skins on. The pie crust is so delicious you will want to use it for other types of fruit pies as well.

YIELD: One pie, enough for 6 to 8 dessert servings

SPECIAL EQUIPMENT: A 9-inch pie pan

DOUGH

2½ cups unbleached all-purpose flour
2 tablespoons sugar
½ teaspoon salt
½ pound (2 sticks) cold unsalted butter, cut into ½-inch cubes
1 large egg yolk
½ cup ice water

PEACH FILLING

4 pounds ripe but firm peaches, rinsed and patted dry (*do NOT peel*)
1 cup sugar
⅓ cup all-purpose flour, plus additional if necessary
2 teaspoons ground ginger
4 tablespoons unsalted butter, cut into small pieces

2 tablespoons heavy cream
Sugar, for dusting (optional)

PREPARE THE DOUGH

Hand method: Combine the flour, sugar, and salt in a large mixing bowl. Scatter the butter over the flour. Using a metal pastry blender or two table knives, cut the butter into the flour until the mixture resembles coarse meal. In a small bowl, whisk together the egg yolk and water. Pour the liquid over the flour mixture and work it in with a fork or your fingertips until the dough just holds together. If the dough feels too dry or crumbly, add just enough water to make it stick together. Briefly knead the dough in the bowl to form a cohesive mass.

Food processor method: Put the flour, sugar, salt, and butter in the bowl of a food processor fitted with the metal blade. Pulse until the mixture resembles coarse meal. In a small bowl, whisk together the egg yolk and water. With the motor on, add the liquid through the feed tube. Process just until the dough holds together, about 10 seconds; do not overprocess. The dough should be soft, not crumbly. If it feels too dry or crumbly, add a little water and pulse until it just holds together. Turn the dough out onto a lightly floured surface and press it together to form a cohesive mass.

continued

— *planning ahead* —

The dough can be prepared ahead of time, wrapped well, and refrigerated for up to 1 week. The filling can be covered and refrigerated overnight, leaving just a quick assembly and the baking for the day you serve it.

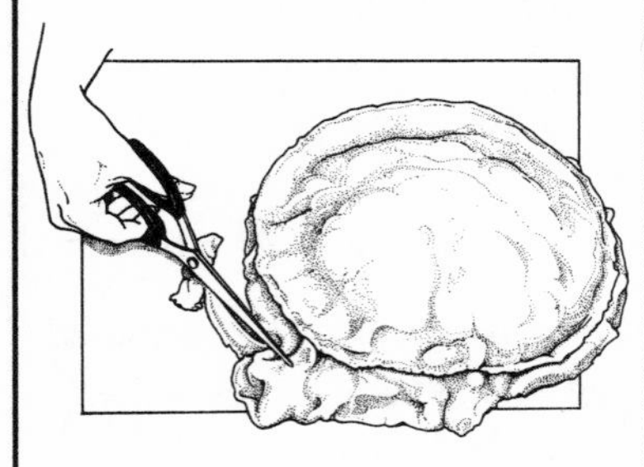

LET THE DOUGH REST: Cut the dough into 2 pieces, one twice as large as the other. Shape each portion into a ball, then lightly press each piece into a disk. Cover with plastic wrap and refrigerate for at least 30 minutes.

Preheat the oven to 400°F. Adjust an oven rack to the middle shelf.

Cut the peaches into ½-inch-thick wedges and place them in a large mixing bowl. In a medium bowl, mix the sugar, flour, and ground ginger together. Make sure that no lumps remain. Sprinkle the mixture over the peaches and toss well to coat the fruit. If the peaches are very juicy, add about 2 more tablespoons flour, and toss well.

ASSEMBLE THE PIE: On a lightly floured work surface, roll the larger piece of dough into a 13-inch circle about ⅛ inch thick. As you roll, lift and turn the dough frequently, dusting the work surface with flour as necessary to prevent the dough from sticking.

Gently fold the dough circle in half, and then in half again. Lift the folded circle and place it in the pie pan, with the point in the center. Unfold the dough to line the pie plate, leaving the excess dough overhanging the rim. Mound the peaches into the dough shell. Dot with the butter.

Roll the remaining piece of dough into a 11-inch circle. Drape the dough over the rolling pin and transfer it carefully to the pie pan to cover the filling. Using scissors, trim the bottom pastry, leaving a 1-inch overhang. Reserve the dough trimmings to decorate the pie. Brush the pastry top with the heavy cream. Bring the pastry overhang up over the edge of the pie, and crimp the edges to seal. Brush the crimped edges with heavy cream.

Gather the dough scraps into a ball, reroll into a sheet ⅛ inch thick, and cut out several decorative leaf shapes. Arrange the leaves atop the pastry and brush them with heavy cream. Make several small incisions in the crust to allow steam to escape. The top of the pie can be lightly dusted with sugar if desired.

BAKE THE PIE: Place the pie in the oven and bake until the crust is nicely browned and the juices are bubbling, about 45 to 50 minutes. If the crust begins to brown too quickly, loosely cover the top of the pie with aluminum foil. Remove the pie from the oven, and let cool slightly on a rack before serving.

Baked Pear Dumplings with Bourbon-Cinnamon Sauce

This extremely good, simple, and handsome dessert may be just the exclamation point you need to end a meal. It consists of wedges of pears encased in a flaky, buttery pie crust and baked in a bourbon-cinnamon sauce until caramelized. Delicious aromas will fill your home as the dumplings bake. If you like, serve with a scoop of vanilla ice cream.

YIELD: 6 dumplings, enough for 6 dessert servings

DOUGH

3¾ cups unbleached all-purpose flour
2 tablespoons sugar
¼ teaspoon salt
¾ pound (3 sticks) cold unsalted butter, cut into ½-inch cubes
¾ cup ice water

BOURBON-CINNAMON SAUCE

⅔ cup apricot preserves
⅔ cup bourbon
⅓ cup port
1 tablespoon plus 1 teaspoon fresh lemon juice
½ teaspoon ground cinnamon
¼ teaspoon ground cloves
¼ teaspoon ground ginger
8 tablespoons (1 stick) unsalted butter, cut into 8 pieces, at room temperature

3 large ripe pears (about 1½ pounds), such as Bartlett or Anjou
1 egg yolk beaten with 2 teaspoons milk, for egg glaze
Ice cream or sweetened whipped cream (optional)

PREPARE THE DOUGH

Hand method: Combine the flour, sugar, and salt in a large mixing bowl. Scatter the butter over the flour. Using a metal pastry blender or two table knives, cut the butter into the flour until the mixture resembles coarse meal. Sprinkle the ice water over the mixture a little at a time, working it into the mixture with a fork or your fingertips until the dough just holds together. If the dough feels too dry or crumbly, add just enough water to make it stick together. Briefly knead the dough in the bowl to form a cohesive mass.

Food processor method: Put the flour, sugar, salt, and butter in the bowl of a food processor fitted with the metal blade. Pulse until the mixture resembles coarse meal. With the motor on, gradually add the ice water through the feed tube. Process just until the dough barely holds together, about 10 seconds; do not overprocess. The dough should be soft, not crumbly. If it feels too dry or crumbly, add a little water and pulse until it just holds together. Turn the dough out onto a lightly floured surface and press it together to form a cohesive mass.

continued

— planning ahead —

The dough can be prepared ahead of time, wrapped well, and refrigerated for up to 1 week. The sauce can be covered and refrigerated overnight. The unbaked dumplings can be tightly wrapped and refrigerated overnight or frozen for up to 1 month. If the dumplings have been frozen, bake them unthawed for 5 to 10 minutes longer than the time specified in the recipe.

— cook's notes —

For simpler dumplings, just wrap each dough square around a whole pear or apple that has been peeled and cored. Bake the dumplings for about 10 minutes longer than the time specified above.

Puff pastry may replace the buttery pie crust.

LET THE DOUGH REST: Divide the dough in half. Shape each half into a ball, then lightly press each into a disk. Cover with plastic wrap and refrigerate for at least 30 minutes.

MAKE THE SAUCE: Combine the apricot preserves, bourbon, port, lemon juice, cinnamon, cloves, and ginger in a medium saucepan. Bring the mixture to a boil over moderately high heat, reduce the heat to moderate, and gently boil until the sauce is slightly thickened and syrupy, about 5 to 6 minutes. Whisk in the butter, one piece at a time, until it is well incorporated. Remove the pan from the heat and set aside to cool.

Peel, core, and cut the pears into ½-inch-thick wedges. Cover and set aside.

ROLL AND CUT THE DOUGH: On a lightly floured surface, roll one portion of the dough into a rectangle about 7 by 21 inches long and 3⁄16 inch thick. Using a sharp paring knife and a ruler, cut out three 7-inch squares. Lightly dust the dough squares with flour, stack them on a plate, cover with plastic wrap, and refrigerate. Roll and cut the remaining piece of dough in the same manner to make 3 more squares, and refrigerate. Make sure the dough is well chilled before assembling the dumplings.

Lightly grease a baking sheet or line it with parchment paper.

ASSEMBLE THE DUMPLINGS: Arrange one sixth of the pears (about ½ cup) in the center of one of the dough squares. Lightly brush the dough edges with egg glaze. Drizzle 1 tablespoon of the bourbon sauce over the pears; make sure that the sauce doesn't spread toward the edge or you will not be able to seal the dumpling properly. Bring the four corners of the dough together over the filling to meet in the center. Pinch the edges together at the seams to seal completely, forming a square dumpling. Transfer the dumpling to the prepared baking sheet.

Assemble the remaining dumplings in the same manner, placing them 1 inch apart on the baking sheet. Reserve the remaining bourbon sauce for serving. Lightly brush the dumplings with egg glaze. Loosely cover the dumplings with foil and refrigerate until the dough seams are well sealed, at least 30 minutes.

Preheat the oven to 375°F. Adjust an oven rack to the middle shelf.

BAKE THE DUMPLINGS: Place the baking sheet in the oven and bake until the dumplings are nicely browned, about 30 minutes. Midway through the baking, rotate the baking sheet to ensure even browning. Remove the baking sheet from the oven and set it on a rack. Allow the dumplings to cool on the baking sheet.

TO SERVE: Reheat the reserved bourbon sauce over low heat. Spoon it over the dumplings. Serve with vanilla ice cream or whipped cream if desired.

Italian Wonder Cookies

This recipe comes from my friend Anna-Lisa Bassotti, who got it from her mother, a native of Genoa, Italy. These little wonders have been a tradition at Christmas in her family for as long as she can remember. Nutty and chocolatey with a hint of lemon and brandy, these crumbly little cookies are shaped into little squares to resemble ravioli. Keep a sharp eye on them, as they may disappear before you know it. The sweet short dough for these cookies contains potato flour, egg, and a good amount of sugar, making it slightly sticky. Work quickly but carefully when you roll and mold the squares, as the dough tends to break easily.

YIELD: About 40 cookies

SPECIAL EQUIPMENT: A pastry bag fitted with a ½-inch plain nozzle

DOUGH

1¼ cups unbleached all-purpose flour
1 cup potato flour (see Cook's Notes)
8 tablespoons (1 stick) unsalted butter, at room temperature
½ cup sugar
1 large egg
2 tablespoons brandy, preferably cognac
1 teaspoon grated lemon zest
1 teaspoon vanilla extract
⅛ teaspoon salt

CHOCOLATE ALMOND FILLING

2 tablespoons finely diced mixed dried fruit, such as apples, apricots, and raisins
1 tablespoon brandy, preferably cognac
½ cup ricotta cheese
¼ cup confectioner's sugar
¼ cup blanched slivered almonds, toasted and finely chopped
1 ounce good-quality semisweet chocolate, finely chopped

FOR DUSTING

2 tablespoons confectioner's sugar
2 tablespoons Dutch-process cocoa powder

MAKE THE DOUGH: Combine both flours in a medium bowl. In a large mixing bowl, cream together the butter and sugar with an electric mixer until light and fluffy, about 2 minutes. At low speed, blend in the egg, brandy, lemon zest, vanilla extract, and salt. Gradually add the flour mixture, ½ cup at a time, and blend at medium speed until you have a soft dough. Gather the dough together and briefly knead it in the bowl to make a compact mass. Cover with plastic wrap and refrigerate overnight.

continued

— planning ahead —

Both the dough and the filling should be prepared a day in advance, covered, and refrigerated. The baked cookies can be frozen for up to 2 months if they are securely wrapped. Thaw them at room temperature.

— cook's notes —

Potato flour, also known as potato starch, is available in the kosher products section of most supermarkets.

As a filling alternative, you may use homemade fruit preserves or jam.

The cookies can be stored between sheets of waxed paper in an airtight jar or tin for up to 2 weeks at room temperature.

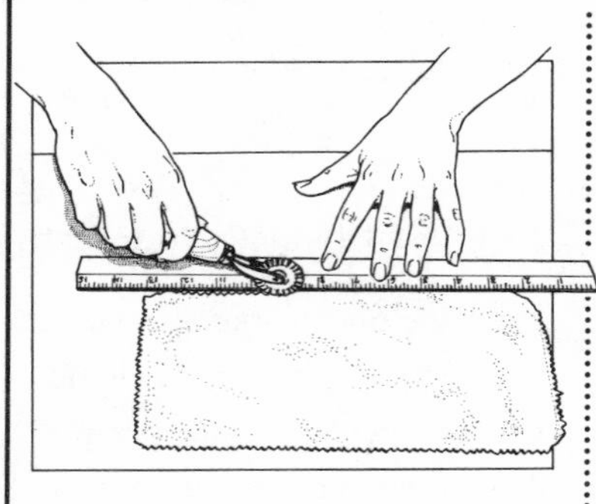

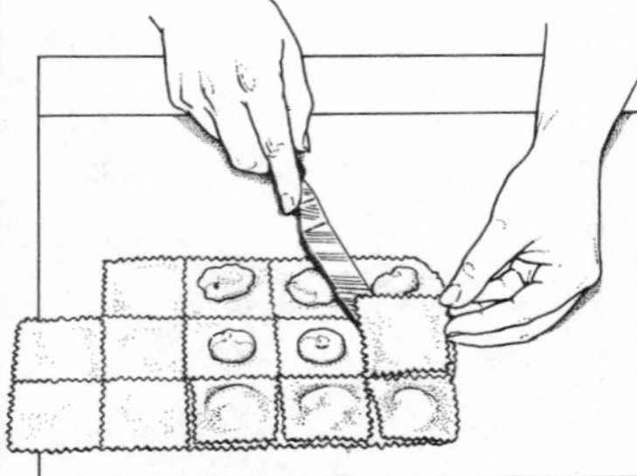

MAKE THE FILLING: In a small cup, mix the dried fruit with the brandy. Cover and let sit for 30 minutes. Drain the fruit, discarding the liquid. Finely chop the fruit and place it in a medium mixing bowl along with all the remaining filling ingredients. Mix well with a rubber spatula to combine. Cover and refrigerate overnight.

Preheat the oven to 350°F. Adjust an oven rack to the middle shelf. Lightly grease two baking sheets or line them with parchment paper.

ASSEMBLE THE COOKIES: Divide the dough into 4 pieces. Work with one piece of dough at a time, keeping the remaining dough covered and refrigerated.

Shape one portion of dough into a rough rectangle. On a well-floured surface, gently roll the dough into a rectangle slightly larger than 6 by 12 inches and about ⅛ inch thick. As this is a fragile dough, don't apply too much pressure while rolling it. If it cracks, gather the dough into a ball and reroll.

Using a fluted pastry wheel and a ruler, trim the edges of the dough to make a neat 6- by 12-inch rectangle. Cut the dough into eighteen 2-inch squares. (Do not separate the squares.) Wrap and refrigerate the dough trimmings.

Place the filling in the pastry bag. Pipe out about ½ teaspoon of filling onto the center of 9 of the squares. Slightly flatten each mound of filling with the back of a spoon. Lightly brush the dough margins around the filling with water. Using a metal spatula, carefully lift the unfilled dough squares, one at a time, and place them over the squares with the filling, making sure to align the edges. Gently press the edges of each cookie together to seal in the filling. Using the spatula, transfer the cookies to a prepared baking sheet, placing them 1 inch apart. Loosely cover with plastic wrap and refrigerate.

Assemble 27 more cookies with the remaining portions of dough in the same manner and place them on the baking sheets. Combine all the reserved dough trimmings, and reroll into a rectangle slightly larger than 4 by 8 inches and about ⅛ inch thick. Cut 8 more squares to make 4 additional cookies.

BAKE THE COOKIES: Place the baking sheets in the oven and bake until the cookies are pale golden and crisp, about 20 minutes. (If your oven is not large enough to accommodate both sheets on one shelf, keep the second baking sheet covered in the refrigerator while the first batch of cookies bakes.) Midway through the baking, rotate the baking sheets to ensure even cooking. Remove the baking sheets from the oven and cool on a rack.

TO SERVE: Combine the confectioner's sugar and cocoa powder. Sift the mixture lightly over the cooled cookies before serving.

breads, buns, and brioches

I find making bread to be a most stimulating experience. It involves all of the senses: sight, hearing, touch, smell, and taste. To me, the sight and sound of yeast bubbling and dough rising is magical, and there's no better therapy than kneading or punching into a plump mass of dough and feeling its soft, spongelike texture. And what a fragrance as it bakes! Finally, who can resist the taste of bread that is just out of the oven? Certainly there is nothing in the world like it.

All the recipes in this chapter are made with yeasted doughs. These doughs can be grouped into two categories: basic doughs, made with just yeast, water, and flour, and enriched doughs, with eggs and/or butter added.

A basic dough produces dense and slightly chewy bread with a crisp and firm crust. An excellent example is Pizza Dough (page 160), which I use to make calzoni, like the Shrimp and Cheese Calzoni (page 166), or rolled bread loaves, like Scoubidou (page 168).

A little egg added to a basic dough yields a light, moist, and fine-textured white bread. This enriched dough forms the basis for wonderful Chinese dim sum, such as Baked Pork Buns (page 170).

A standout among enriched doughs is Brioche (page 164). Brioche, a uniquely French culinary invention, is a yeasted bread dough with lots of eggs and butter added. In France, there are as many formulas and methods for making brioche as there are bakers, but they all involve three basic steps: making a sponge with yeast and flour, incorporating butter and eggs into the dough, and allowing the dough to rise twice. This process results in a buttery, tender, and fluffy dough that is ideal for encasing relatively dry ingredients such as sausages, cheese, or puréed dried fruits. I have included a few of my favorite recipes in this chapter, including savory Sausage in Saffron Brioche (page 174), Chocolate Buns (page 176), and festive Kings' Cake (page 178).

A yeast dough can be manipulated in different ways to change its flavor, alter its color, or modify its texture. For example, herbs, seeds, nuts, or ground spices can be added to the dough. Another technique I often use is to infuse a small amount of hot oil with the seasonings to intensify their flavors. Once the flavored oil has cooled to room temperature, I add it to the dough. Interesting tastes and textures can also be created by combining different types of flour. This approach is used to produce a corn bread that can be wrapped around Barbecued Chicken (page 172).

While making most of the specialties in this section requires patience, the recipes are not really all that difficult and your efforts will be amply rewarded. With a little practice, you will soon begin to invent your own flavorful bread-wrapped specialties for unique meals. And there's nothing like the aroma of freshly baked bread wafting through your home. It evokes memories of something old, caring, and secure.

BASIC TECHNIQUES FOR MAKING YEASTED DOUGHS

The following basic guidelines for making yeasted doughs will help you to understand and successfully prepare the recipes in this chapter.

Yeast is a living organism. In the presence of flour, sugar, and water, it swells and produces a gas that makes the dough rise and expand. I generally use granulated active dry yeast, which is packaged in foil packets and sold in supermarkets. You can also buy it in health food stores. I find it easy to handle, and it produces a wonderful and distinctive smell in yeasted breads. Each packet contains two teaspoons (one quarter ounce) yeast. The expiration date should be clearly marked on the packets. Store them in the refrigerator and use before the date expires to ensure that the yeast is still fresh and potent.

The first step in preparing a dough is proofing the yeast. The yeast is dissolved in lukewarm water or milk, along with a little sugar. If the yeast bubbles within five or ten minutes, it is alive (you can almost hear it activate) and usable.

I use a sponge starter in all my yeasted doughs to increase the lightness of the end product. Basically, a sponge is yeast proofed with the addition of a little flour to create a loose batter. A spoonful of sugar is also added to induce a quick fermentation. When used in small quantities, sugar helps the yeast grow and leaven the dough. It also adds flavor and makes the crust brown. Too much sugar, however, will slow down the proofing action.

I use all-purpose flour (wheat flour) in all of the dough recipes. I prefer the unbleached variety, which yields a more tender baked product. I measure flour by the dip and sweep method, which means that I dip the measuring cup into a bin of flour and sweep off the excess with a long flat spatula or knife.

With the exception of brioche, which uses milk, the yeast doughs in this chapter are made with water. Milk gives a soft crust to brioche, while water produces a crusty bread.

Enriching a dough with eggs increases its tenderness, flavor, and color. Eggs also have a slight leavening effect that contributes to making a lighter and softer bread.

Butter and olive oil improve the flavor of a yeast dough and help it stretch more easily. Fat also lubricates the gluten in the dough so that it is free to rise. Furthermore, it makes the bread tender and helps it stay soft longer.

Most yeasted doughs must be kneaded to develop gluten, the elastic network of cells that traps the carbon dioxide produced by the yeast. To knead the dough, place it on a lightly floured work surface and flatten it slightly into a disk. Hold the bottom edge of the dough with one hand. Press down into the dough with the heel of your other hand and push away from you to stretch out the dough. Fold the dough in half toward you. Rotate the dough a quarter turn and repeat stretching, folding, and turning, dusting the work surface and your hands occasionally as needed to keep the dough from sticking.

When kneading is completed, the dough should be very smooth and elastic with little blisters under the surface. It shouldn't stick to the work surface or to your hands. When dough is made by hand, it generally requires kneading for about ten minutes. When the dough is made using a food processor, most of the kneading is done by the machine and little extra kneading is required.

Shape the dough into a ball by pulling the sides of the dough under itself until the mass is evenly rounded and tight and smooth on top. Place it in a lightly oiled mixing bowl, smooth side up. Lightly brush the top with some oil so that it doesn't dry out, and cover the bowl tightly with plastic wrap. The dough is ready for the rising.

Place the bowl in a warm, draft-free place to rise, at a temperature of about 80° to 85°F. If your kitchen is cool, place the bowl in an unheated oven with a large pan of hot water on the shelf below, replacing the water as it cools. Or place the bowl on a wire rack set over a large roasting pan filled two-thirds full with hot tap water. During the rising period, the yeast cells are continuing to give off carbon dioxide to expand and puff the dough, making it lighter.

In general, yeast dough should double in volume in about 1 to 1½ hours if ideal conditions are met. To check, make an indentation by pressing a finger lightly in the top of the dough. If the dough springs back, it has not risen enough. If the indentation remains, the rising is complete.

Brioche dough should be left to rise at cool room temperature rather than in a warm area to prevent the butter in the dough from separating. Brioche dough may take as long as three to four hours to rise in summer, or five to six hours in winter.

After the dough has risen once, it is necessary to punch it down, which stops the rising process instantly. Simply punch the dough down in the bowl with your fist until all the air has been released. Pull the dough from the edges to the center to re-form a ball shape, and turn the dough over in the bowl. For brioche, instead of punching, just stir the batter down with a wooden spoon.

After punching down, most doughs are ready to be used. In the case of brioche, the dough must rest in the refrigerator to firm up the butter and make it more workable.

Once the dough has been rolled and filled, it is often allowed to rise a second time until it has almost doubled in volume before it is baked. This process produces light, spongy breads with an even crumb.

A glaze is generally a mixture of egg yolk and a little bit of liquid, such as water, milk, or cream, which is brushed over the dough before it is baked. Beside protecting the dough crust from cracking during its final rising, it also gives the bread a glossy sheen and an appetizing golden color once baked.

BREAD-MAKING TIPS

- Time and temperature are key factors in successful bread making. The first step is to check that you have on hand all the ingredients needed for your recipe. Take them out of the refrigerator and let them reach room temperature if they are cold. Try to keep the kitchen at approximately 75°F, or even warmer, and close any windows if it's cool outside. A yeasted dough doesn't like a cold, drafty kitchen.
- For best results, always cover a yeast sponge with plastic wrap to trap the warm heat of the mixture inside.
- If your sponge doesn't expand or your dough won't rise, your best bet is to start all over again. Some of the reasons for failure to rise are:

  The liquid used was too cold or too warm. When proofing yeast, dissolve the yeast called for in the recipe in liquid that is 105° to 115°F. For accuracy, use an instant-read thermometer. Remember that temperatures over 120°F kill yeast.

  The yeast was too old. Always check the expiration date on the yeast package before using it. If the yeast bubbles within five or ten minutes, it is alive and usable. Otherwise, discard the yeast and use a fresher package.

  The flour was too cold. If you keep your flour in the refrigerator or a cold pantry, make sure to take it out in time to reach room temperature before you start to bake.

  The room was too cold. The dough was left to rise in an area that was too cold or too drafty for it to rise.
- Salt and fat inhibit the growth of yeast and therefore should not be added to the dough until the yeast has come to full potency.
- Keep in mind that a filling for any type of bread dough, especially in those recipes calling for a second rise, should not be too wet, or it will exude juices that will inhibit the rising process and produce a soggy mess.
- If the breads seems to brown too quickly in the oven, cover with a piece of foil or lower the oven temperature by 25°F.

- When done, baked breads should sound hollow when you tap them with your finger and they should shrink from the sides of the baking pan.
- Remove individual buns from the baking sheet right after they come out of the oven and cool them on a wire rack. Otherwise, steam will collect on the bottom of the breads and make the crust soggy.
- In general, filled breads are at their best when eaten while still warm. That's when the natural flavors of all the ingredients inside are released, producing an intense taste sensation. Some bread dishes improve with reheating the following day. If you wish to store filled and baked breads, allow them to cool first. Then, wrap them in foil and seal in a plastic bag. Refrigerate for up to three days or freeze and use within one month.
- To defrost frozen breads, thaw them overnight in the refrigerator.
- To reheat baked breads that have been refrigerated, wrap them individually in foil and place in a preheated 375°F oven for about twenty minutes, or until they are heated through.

— cook's notes —

You can use this basic dough with your favorite toppings to make four 10- to 11-inch round pizzas. You can also make delicious bread by shaping the dough into two round or elongated loaves, letting them rise a second time, then baking in a preheated 400°F oven for about 25 minutes.

Pizza Dough

If the dough is not to be used immediately, punch it down after its first rise, put it in a plastic storage bag, and refrigerate it overnight or freeze for up to one month. If the dough has been frozen, thaw it overnight in the refrigerator before use. Always bring the dough to room temperature before use, but do not let it rise again before assembling or filling it.

YIELD: About 1¾ pounds

SPONGE

1 envelope active dry yeast
1 teaspoon sugar
2 tablespoons unbleached all-purpose flour
¼ cup very warm water (105° to 115°F)

DOUGH

3 cups unbleached all-purpose flour, plus additional for dusting and kneading
1 cup lukewarm water
1½ teaspoons salt
1 teaspoon sugar
2 tablespoons olive oil

MAKE THE SPONGE: Combine the yeast, sugar, flour, and warm water in a small bowl. Stir to dissolve the sugar. Tightly cover with plastic wrap and let the mixture proof until it has doubled in volume, about 10 minutes.

MAKE THE DOUGH

Hand method: Place the flour in a large mixing bowl and make a well in the center. Add the water, salt, sugar, oil, and the sponge to the well. Using a wooden spoon, stir the flour into the liquids until the mixture clumps together into a rough, shaggy dough. Gather the dough into a ball. If the dough feels sticky, sprinkle on a little flour. If it seems dry or flaky, add about a teaspoon or so more water. Briefly knead the dough in the bowl until it forms a soft ball. Turn the dough out onto a lightly floured work surface and knead with a strong push-fold-and-turn motion, bearing down heavily on the dough, until it is firm and elastic, about 10 minutes, adding a little more flour whenever the dough feels sticky.

Food processor method: Place the flour in the bowl of a food processor fitted with the metal blade. Using a rubber spatula, scrape the sponge onto the flour. Combine the water, salt, sugar, and oil in a small bowl, and stir to dissolve the salt and sugar. With the motor on, gradually add the liquid mixture through the feed tube, and process until the dough cleans the sides of the bowl and rides on the blade, about 10 seconds. The dough should be soft but not sticky. Continue to process for about 45 to 50 seconds. If the dough sticks to the bowl, add about a teaspoon or so more flour and process until the dough cleans the sides of the bowl. Turn the dough out onto a lightly floured surface and knead briefly until firm and elastic.

LET THE DOUGH RISE: Form the dough into a ball, rub it all over with oil, and place it in a large greased bowl. Cover tightly with plastic wrap and let the dough rise in a warm place until it has doubled in bulk, about 1½ hours.

VARIATION

HERB-FLAVORED PIZZA DOUGH: You can change the character of the dough by flavoring the oil added to the dough with fresh or dried herbs such as thyme, rosemary, oregano, or sage. Combine 1 tablespoon chopped fresh herbs or 2 teaspoons crumbled dried herbs and the 2 tablespoons olive oil in a small saucepan over moderately low heat. Heat until the herb begins to turn golden, about 1½ to 2 minutes. Remove the pan from the heat and let the mixture steep at room temperature until completely cool. Add the flavored oil mixture to the flour along with the water, salt, and sugar as instructed above.

White Bread Dough

This dough is lighter and more tender than a standard bread dough. You can use this dough to make your own Chinese dim sum buns or to make bread loaves filled with all kinds of moist and wonderful fillings. Be sure that the filling is not too wet or the dough will become soggy.

If the dough is not to be used immediately, punch it down after its first rise, put it in a plastic storage bag, and refrigerate it overnight or freeze for up to one month. If the dough has been frozen, thaw it overnight in the refrigerator before use. Always bring the dough to room temperature before use, but do not let it rise again before assembling or filling it.

YIELD: About 1¼ pounds, enough for 8 buns or one 9-inch round loaf

SPONGE

1 envelope active dry yeast
1 teaspoon sugar
2 tablespoons unbleached all-purpose flour
¼ cup very warm water (105° to 115°F)

DOUGH

2¼ cups unbleached all-purpose flour, plus additional for dusting and kneading
1 egg, lightly beaten, at room temperature
¼ cup lukewarm water
2 teaspoons sugar
¾ teaspoon salt
2 tablespoons vegetable oil

MAKE THE SPONGE: Combine the yeast, sugar, flour, and warm water in a small bowl. Stir to dissolve the sugar. Tightly cover with plastic wrap and let the mixture proof until it has doubled in volume, about 10 minutes.

MAKE THE DOUGH

Hand method: Place the flour in a large mixing bowl and make a well in the center. Add the beaten egg, water, sugar, salt, oil, and the sponge to the well. Using a wooden spoon, stir the flour into the liquids until the mixture clumps together into a rough, shaggy dough. Gather the dough into a ball. If the dough feels sticky, sprinkle on a little flour. If it seems dry or flaky, add about a teaspoon or so more water. Briefly knead the dough in the bowl until it forms a soft ball. Turn the dough out onto a lightly floured work surface and knead with a strong push-fold-and-turn motion, bearing down heavily on the dough, until it is smooth and elastic, about 10 minutes. Add a little more flour whenever the dough feels sticky.

Food processor method: Place the flour in the bowl of a food processor fitted with the metal blade. Using a rubber spatula, scrape the sponge onto the flour. In a small bowl, combine the beaten egg, water, sugar, salt, and oil, and stir to dissolve the sugar and salt. With the motor on, gradually add the liquid mixture through the feed tube, and process until the dough cleans the sides of the bowl and rides on the blade, about 10 seconds. Continue to process for about 45 to 50 seconds. If the dough sticks to the bowl, add about a teaspoon or so more flour and process until the dough cleans the sides of the bowl. The dough should be soft but not sticky. Turn the dough out onto a lightly floured work surface and knead briefly until smooth and soft.

LET THE DOUGH RISE: Form the dough into a ball, rub it all over with oil, and place it in a large greased bowl. Cover tightly with plastic wrap and let the dough rise in a warm place until it has doubled in bulk, about 1 hour.

VARIATIONS

HERB-FLAVORED DOUGH: You can change the character of the dough by flavoring the oil added to the dough with fresh herbs such as scallion, thyme, oregano, or sage, or dried spices such as caraway seeds, cumin seeds, or chili powder. Use 1 tablespoon fresh herbs or 2 teaspoons dried spices per 2 tablespoons oil.

SCALLION-FLAVORED DOUGH: Heat the 2 tablespoons oil in a small saucepan until hot but not smoking, about 300°F. Remove the pan from the heat and add 1 sliced scallion. Let steep at room temperature until completely cooled.

CUMIN AND CHEDDAR-FLAVORED CORNMEAL DOUGH: Heat the 2 tablespoons oil for the dough in a small saucepan until hot but not smoking, about 300°F. Remove the pan from the heat and add 2 teaspoons cumin seeds. Let the mixture steep at room temperature until completely cooled. Instead of 2¼ cups flour for the dough, use 2 cups flour and ½ cup yellow cornmeal. Increase the sugar added to the dough to 2 tablespoons, and add 1 cup grated sharp Cheddar cheese to the flour.

— *cook's notes* —

You can make delicious soft bread or rolls by shaping this dough into one round loaf or 8 small buns. Cover and let rise until doubled in bulk, then bake in a preheated 350°F oven for 25 to 30 minutes.

Brioche Dough

With the food processor, excellent brioche dough can be made in a matter of just minutes. It is no longer a task that only professional bakers can master. I also find making brioche dough in the food processor less messy than the old-fashioned way, which requires repeated slapping of the sticky dough by hand onto the counter.

Brioche should be made over a two-day period. The dough is made the first day and allowed to rise, then stirred down and refrigerated overnight. The next day it is shaped, allowed to rise again, and baked. Avoid making brioche in very hot weather. The butter will get too soft and make the dough greasy.

This dough will keep for two days in the refrigerator or one week frozen. As it sits in the refrigerator, the dough develops more flavor. If the brioche dough has been frozen, thaw it overnight in the refrigerator before use. Do not let it rise again before shaping or filling it.

YIELD: About 1¼ pounds

SPONGE

¼ cup milk
1½ teaspoons active dry yeast
1 teaspoon sugar
2 tablespoons unbleached all-purpose flour

DOUGH

1½ cups unbleached all-purpose flour
2 tablespoons sugar
1 teaspoon salt
8 tablespoons (1 stick) unsalted butter, cut into 8 pieces, at room temperature
2 large eggs, at room temperature

MAKE THE SPONGE: Heat the milk in a small saucepan over low heat until it is very warm, about 105 to 115°F. Transfer the milk to a small bowl and add the yeast, sugar, and flour. Stir to dissolve the sugar. Tightly cover with plastic wrap and let the mixture proof until it has doubled in volume, about 10 minutes.

MAKE THE DOUGH: Place the flour, sugar, and salt in the bowl of a food processor fitted with the metal blade. Pulse to blend. Scatter the butter over the dry ingredients. Break the eggs over the butter. Using a rubber spatula, scrape the sponge into the food processor. Process for 20 seconds, or until the dough is smooth and looks like a thick, sticky cake batter; do not stop the motor until the batter forms. (The dough should not make a ball on the blade.)

LET THE DOUGH RISE: Using a rubber spatula, scrape the batter into a medium mixing bowl. Tightly cover the bowl with plastic wrap and let the dough rise at room temperature until it has doubled in volume, about 2 to 3 hours, depending on the humidity of the room.

After the dough has risen, stir it down with a rubber spatula. Cover the bowl with plastic wrap, then seal in a plastic bag. Refrigerate until firm, at least 2 to 3 hours, or overnight.

You can make a brioche loaf or individual brioches as follows:

BRIOCHE LOAF: On a well-floured work surface, shape the dough into a roll about 8 inches long. Place it into a buttered 8½- by 4½-inch 2½-quart loaf pan. Cover with a towel and let rise for 2 to 3 hours, or until doubled in bulk. Make an egg glaze by beating together 1 egg yolk and 2 teaspoons milk, and brush the loaf with the glaze. Bake the brioche in a preheated 375°F oven until the top is well browned and a wooden skewer inserted into the center comes out clean, about 30 minutes. Cool slightly before unmolding. Serve warm.

INDIVIDUAL BRIOCHES: Divide the dough into 6 equal portions. Cut each portion into 2 pieces, one twice as large as the other. Shape the larger pieces into round balls, place them in buttered brioche molds or muffin tins, and make an indentation in the center of each one. Form the smaller pieces of dough into balls and lightly press them onto the tops of the large balls. Cover the brioches with a towel and let rise for about 1 hour, or until doubled in bulk. Make an egg glaze by beating together 1 egg yolk and 2 teaspoons milk. Brush the brioches with the glaze and bake in a preheated 400°F oven until the tops are browned and a wooden skewer inserted into the center of a brioche comes out clean, 15 to 20 minutes. Cool slightly before unmolding. Serve warm.

VARIATIONS

LEMON BRIOCHE DOUGH: Add 1½ teaspoons grated lemon zest to the flour in the food processor.

SAFFRON BRIOCHE DOUGH: Add ½ teaspoon crumbled saffron threads to the warm milk before combining it with the remaining ingredients for the sponge.

cook's notes

The temperature of the ingredients is very important in making brioche dough. The butter must be at room temperature or it will not incorporate properly into the flour. If you forget to put the eggs out to reach room temperature, submerge them in warm water for 10 minutes.

Do not use quick-rising yeast. If the dough rises too fast, it gets a sour taste.

Let the brioche rise at cool room temperature (about 78°F) rather than in a warm area to prevent the butter from separating.

If you wish to make a larger amount of brioche, make it in successive batches rather than doubling the recipe.

— *planning ahead* —

The dough can be prepared in advance, covered, and refrigerated for 1 day or frozen for up to 1 month.

— *cook's notes* —

To produce calzoni with crisp, golden crusts, bake them on a preheated ceramic pizza brick or baking stone, available in kitchenware stores, or heat a baking sheet before placing the calzoni on it to simulate the dry, intense, radiant heat of old-fashioned brick ovens.

If the dough becomes too elastic to roll, cover it with a towel and let it relax for 10 minutes before continuing.

If you are short on time, you can substitute freshly made pizza dough from your favorite pizza parlor or frozen white bread dough from the supermarket. You will need about 1¾ pounds of dough.

I do not recommend storing or freezing calzoni. They are best eaten hot from the oven.

Shrimp and Cheese Calzoni

To me, a calzone is the perfect finger food. I think it must have been invented to make eating pizza even easier by baking it with the crust folded over the topping. Calzoni are fun to make but even more fun to eat. Almost any pizza topping makes a suitable filling, but it should not be too wet or runny, or the dough will become soggy and the filling will ooze out of the calzoni during baking.

It may not occur to most people to pair shrimp and cheese, but I love this unusual combination. Sautéed shrimp, onions, strips of red bell pepper, and mushrooms mixed with mild Fontina and mozzarella cheese make these calzoni colorful and filling. To further enhance the flavor, I brush the calzoni crust with flavored garlic oil.

YIELD: 4 large calzoni, enough for 4 light main-course servings

SPECIAL EQUIPMENT: A baking stone (see Cook's Notes)

1 recipe Pizza Dough (page 160)

SHRIMP AND CHEESE FILLING

2 tablespoons olive oil
½ pound raw medium shrimp, peeled and deveined
½ cup sliced onion
1 tablespoon minced garlic
1 medium red bell pepper, cut into julienne strips
1 cup sliced domestic mushrooms
1 tablespoon chopped fresh oregano leaves or 2 teaspoons dried, crumbled
3 scallions, thinly sliced
½ teaspoon crushed dried red pepper
Salt and freshly ground black pepper to taste
6 ounces Fontina cheese, cut into ½-inch cubes
6 ounces mozzarella cheese, cut into ½-inch cubes

OREGANO-FLAVORED OLIVE OIL

1 teaspoon minced garlic
2 teaspoons chopped fresh oregano leaves or 1 teaspoon dried, crumbled
⅓ cup olive oil

Flour, for dusting
Freshly grated Parmesan cheese (optional)

Prepare the dough and let it rise.

PREPARE THE FILLING: Heat 1 tablespoon of the olive oil in a skillet over high heat. Add the shrimp and sauté until they turn pink, about 1 minute. Remove to a bowl. Add the remaining 1 tablespoon oil to the skillet and reduce the heat to moderately high. When the oil is hot, stir in the onion, garlic, red pepper, and mushrooms and sauté until the vegetables are soft, about 2 minutes. Transfer the mixture to the bowl with the shrimp. Add the oregano, scallions, and crushed red pepper and toss to mix. Season with salt and pepper. Allow the mixture to cool to room temperature, then stir in the Fontina and mozzarella.

PREPARE THE FLAVORED OIL: Combine the garlic, oregano, and olive oil in a small heavy saucepan. Place the pan over low heat and simmer for 4 to 5 minutes. Remove the pan from the heat and set aside for at least 30 minutes so the flavors continue to infuse the oil. Strain the oil through a fine-mesh sieve into a small bowl. Discard the solids. Cover the oil and set aside.

Remove all the racks from the oven. At least 30 minutes before baking, place a pizza stone or a large baking sheet on the oven floor and preheat the oven to 500°F.

ROLL THE DOUGH: After the pizza dough has risen, punch it down. Divide it evenly into 4 pieces. Briefly knead each piece, then form it into a smooth, tight ball. Place the dough balls on a lightly floured work surface, cover with a clean towel, and let them relax for 10 minutes.

On a lightly floured work surface, roll out each ball of dough into a 6-inch circle. Cover the dough circles with towels and allow to relax for 10 minutes more before assembly.

ASSEMBLE THE CALZONI: Work with one dough circle at a time, keeping the remaining dough covered. Roll the dough out into a 10-inch circle. Brush a little water all around the edge of the dough. Mound one quarter of the filling on the bottom half of the dough, leaving a 1-inch border. Fold the top half of the dough over the filling without stretching it. Firmly press the edges together to seal the dough. Crimp the edges. Assemble the remaining calzoni in the same manner.

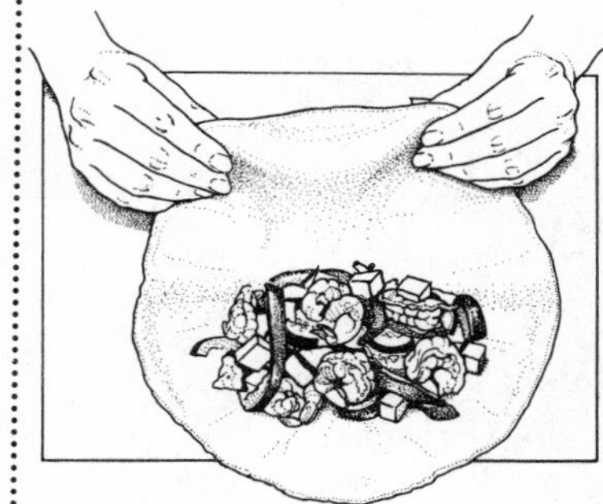

Brush the calzoni with some of the flavored oil. Reserve the remaining oil. With the tines of a fork, poke a few holes in the top of each calzone to allow steam to escape.

BAKE THE CALZONI: Sprinkle the baking stone or baking sheet with flour. Using a wide spatula, transfer the calzoni onto the stone or baking sheet, and bake for 10 minutes. Brush the calzoni again with the flavored oil, and continue to bake until the crust is crisp and golden brown, about 10 minutes longer.

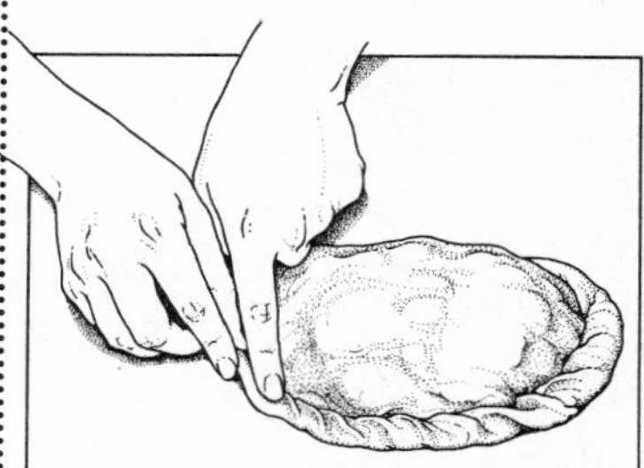

As soon as the calzoni come out of the oven, brush them with the remaining flavored oil. Sprinkle with Parmesan cheese if desired. Serve hot.

VARIATION

CALZONCINI: To make cocktail-size calzoncini, use a 4-inch cookie cutter and cut out as many circles as possible from the rolled-out pizza dough. Fill each with 1 tablespoon of your favorite filling. Fold each circle into a half-moon and seal well before baking or deep-frying in vegetable oil.

— *planning ahead* —

The dough can be prepared in advance and refrigerated for a day or frozen for up to 1 month. The filling can be prepared a day in advance, covered, and refrigerated.

Scoubidou

When I lived in Nice, one of my daily chores was to pick up our bread at the local *boulangerie* on the way home from school. That suited me just fine, because at the same time I could get a delicious rolled bread filled with tender onions, black olives, and anchovies to munch on. At the *boulangerie*, it was nicknamed "scoubidou," a Provençal term for an elongated bread roll.

In making my own scoubidou, I first flavor a basic pizza dough with a rosemary oil before rolling it into a large sheet. Then I spread it with an herbed onion and anchovy filling and roll the whole thing up into a large jelly roll. The wonderful, sweet smell of onions, olive oil, and yeasty bread baking in the oven is enough to make anyone hungry. It is delicious as an accompaniment to any meal or by itself as a snack or light meal.

YIELD: 1 large roll, enough for 8 to 10 side-dish servings

1 recipe Herb-Flavored Pizza Dough (page 161), made with rosemary

ONION FILLING

⅓ cup olive oil
2 pounds onions, chopped
3 tablespoons minced garlic
1 2-ounce can anchovy fillets, drained and finely chopped
2 tablespoons tomato paste
2 large bay leaves, finely crumbled
2 tablespoons chopped fresh thyme leaves or 2 teaspoons dried, crumbled
2 teaspoons sugar
½ teaspoon salt, or more to taste
½ teaspoon freshly ground black pepper, or more to taste
½ cup chopped pitted black brine-cured olives, such as Niçoise or Kalamata

Flour, for dusting
⅓ cup olive oil, for brushing

Prepare the dough and let it rise.

PREPARE THE FILLING: Heat the olive oil in a large skillet over moderate heat. Add the onions and garlic and cook, stirring frequently with a wooden spoon, until the onions are very soft and browned, about 20 minutes. Add the anchovies, tomato paste, bay leaves, thyme, sugar, salt, and pepper and cook for 5 minutes longer, stirring frequently and scraping up any browned bits adhering to the bottom of the pan. Stir in the olives and remove the pan from the heat. Taste the filling and adjust the seasoning with salt and pepper if necessary. Set aside to cool.

Preheat the oven to 400°F. Adjust an oven rack to the lowest position. Lightly grease a large baking sheet or line it with parchment paper.

After the pizza dough has risen, punch it down. Briefly knead, then form it into a smooth, tight ball. Cover and let the dough relax for 15 minutes.

ASSEMBLE THE BREAD ROLL: On a well-floured work surface, roll the dough into a large 13- by 20-inch rectangle about ¼-inch thick. Position the dough with a long side toward you. Lightly brush the dough with olive oil. Evenly spread the filling over the dough, leaving a 2-inch border all around. Starting at a long edge, gently roll the dough up, like a giant jelly roll, being careful not to roll it too tightly. (You do not want to end up with a roll that will burst in the oven.) Pinch the ends together to prevent the filling from leaking out, and crimp the ends. Press along the seam to seal. Carefully transfer the scoubidou, seam side down, to the prepared baking sheet, slightly curving the roll to fit it onto the baking sheet, forming a wide crescent. Do not curve the bread roll too much or the dough will stretch during cooking and burst open.

BAKE THE SCOUBIDOU: Brush the roll all over with about 1 tablespoon of the olive oil. Place the roll in the preheated oven, reduce the oven temperature to 350°F, and bake for 1 hour and 15 minutes, brushing the roll every 15 minutes with olive oil. Midway through the baking, rotate the baking sheet in the oven to ensure even browning. If the roll begins to brown too fast, reduce the oven temperature to 325°F. The bread is done when it is golden brown and sounds hollow when tapped on the crust.

Remove the bread from the oven. If any oil has accumulated in the pan, brush the roll with it. Allow the bread to cool on the pan for about 20 minutes before cutting.

TO SERVE: Remove the bread to a cutting board and cut into 2-inch-thick slices.

cook's notes

If the dough becomes too elastic to roll, cover it with a towel and let it relax for 10 minutes before continuing.

If you are short on time, you can substitute freshly made pizza dough from your favorite pizza parlor or frozen white bread dough from the supermarket. You will need about 1¾ pounds of dough.

— *planning ahead* —

The dough can be prepared in advance and refrigerated for a day or frozen for up to 1 month. The filling can be prepared a day in advance, covered, and refrigerated.

Baked Pork Buns

(BAO)

This recipe is my adaptation of the classic char sui baos, the popular steamed dim sum buns served in Cantonese teahouses. A convenient way to use up leftovers, these buns may be filled with stir-fried minced pork and mushrooms, diced chicken in oyster sauce, or any suitable items a cook might have on hand. I usually prepare the filling with cubes of lean pork cooked in a soy, honey, and ketchup sauce laced with sherry, vinegar, and sesame oil. To make the buns even tastier, I flavor the dough with scallion oil. I find that baking the buns rather than steaming them results in a more flavorful product.

These buns are so delicious they will disappear in a trice. They are wonderful when served as a brunch or light meal, accompanied by a salad and/or a soup. I personally like them for breakfast with tea, while my husband finds them perfect as a snack with beer.

YIELD: 8 buns, enough for 8 first-course or 4 main-course servings

1 recipe Scallion-Flavored Dough (page 163)

PORK FILLING

1 pound boneless pork butt, cut into ¼-inch cubes
1½ tablespoons dry sherry
5 tablespoons light soy sauce
⅓ cup ketchup
3 tablespoons honey
¼ cup sugar
1½ tablespoons red wine vinegar
2 tablespoons vegetable oil
1½ cups chopped onions
2 tablespoons minced garlic
½ cup frozen peas
½ teaspoon Oriental sesame oil
Freshly ground black pepper to taste

EGG GLAZE

1 egg yolk beaten with 2 teaspoons water

Prepare the dough and let it rise.

PREPARE THE FILLING: In a mixing bowl, combine the pork, sherry, and 2 tablespoons of the soy sauce, and toss to coat the pork. Set aside to marinate for 30 minutes.

In another bowl, combine the remaining 3 tablespoons soy sauce, the ketchup, honey, sugar, and vinegar. Set aside.

Heat the oil in a large skillet set over high heat. Add the pork and stir-fry until it is lightly browned, about 2 minutes. Add the onions and garlic and stir-fry until they are tender and fragrant, about 2 minutes. Stir in the soy sauce mixture. Reduce the heat to low and simmer uncovered, stirring occasionally, for 20 minutes or until thickened.

Remove the pan from the heat. Stir in the frozen peas and sesame oil. Season with black pepper, then set aside to cool completely.

Lightly dust a baking sheet with flour or line it with parchment paper.

Punch the dough down, and divide it into 8 pieces. Work with one piece of dough at a time, keeping the remainder covered with a towel to prevent it from drying out.

FILL AND SHAPE THE BUNS: On a lightly floured work surface, roll one piece of dough into a 5-inch circle, rolling the edges of the dough slightly thinner than the center. Mound about 2 tablespoons of the filling in the center of the dough. Gather the edges of the dough over the filling, pleating and pinching them together. To seal, twist the gathered dough firmly in a clockwise direction, forming a topknot. Place the filled bun upside down on the prepared baking sheet and cover with a dry towel.

Assemble the remaining buns in the same manner, spacing the buns 2 inches apart on the baking sheet and covering them with the towel. Let the buns rise, under the towel, until almost doubled in volume, about 35 to 45 minutes, depending on the temperature of the room.

Preheat the oven to 350°F.

Brush the buns with the egg glaze. Bake in the center of the oven until lightly golden, about 25 minutes. Midway through the baking, rotate the baking sheet to ensure even browning.

Remove the buns from the oven, and transfer to a wire rack to cool. The buns are delicious either warm or at room temperature.

cook's notes

After baking, the buns can be tightly wrapped and stored at room temperature for 2 days or frozen for up to 1 month. If the buns have been frozen, thaw them overnight in the refrigerator, then reheat them, wrapped in foil, in a preheated 350°F oven for about 20 minutes.

Instead of shaping individual buns, you can make a single loaf by rolling the dough into a 16-inch circle. Mound all of the filling in the center. Gather the edges of the dough over the filling, and tie the gathered dough with kitchen string to form a topknot. Using two wide spatulas, transfer the loaf topknot side up onto the floured baking sheet for the final rising. Bake for 35 to 40 minutes, or until a bamboo skewer inserted into the thickest part of the loaf comes out clean. If the loaf begins to brown too fast, reduce the oven temperature to 325°F. Let cool on a wire rack, remove the string, and serve. Tied with a red ribbon, this stuffed loaf makes a beautiful gift for the Chinese New Year!

— *planning ahead* —

Both the dough and the filling can be prepared a day in advance, covered, and refrigerated.

Barbecued Chicken in Corn Bread

Imagine the tastes of succulent caramelized onions and slow-cooked chicken barbecued in a fragrant and spicy chili sauce and you will have the filling for this Southwestern-inspired bread loaf. A cornmeal crust with Cheddar cheese and cumin seeds gives the loaf a very distinctive texture and flavor. Moist, slightly sweet, and wonderful, the loaf increases in flavor as it sits overnight. This is the kind of dish you can make the day before and take with you to a picnic.

YIELD: 1 loaf, enough for 8 first-course or 4 main-course servings

1 recipe Cumin and Cheddar-Flavored Cornmeal Dough (page 163)

BARBECUED CHICKEN FILLING

½ cup chicken broth
¾ cup ketchup
⅓ cup chili sauce
2 teaspoons cider vinegar
2 teaspoons sugar
2 teaspoons ground cumin
1½ teaspoons chili powder
2 pickled jalapeño peppers, minced (1 tablespoon)
4 thin slices bacon, cut crosswise into ½-inch-wide strips
2 boneless skinless chicken breasts (about 1¼ pounds), cut into ½-inch cubes
1½ cups chopped onions
2 tablespoons minced garlic
Salt to taste
Tabasco sauce to taste (optional)

EGG GLAZE

1 egg yolk beaten with 2 teaspoons water

Prepare the dough and let it rise.

PREPARE THE FILLING: In a small bowl, mix together the chicken broth, ketchup, chili sauce, vinegar, sugar, cumin, chili powder, and jalapeño. Set aside.

Heat a large skillet or sauté pan over moderately high heat. Add the bacon and cook, stirring with a wooden spoon, until the bacon is crisp and the fat is rendered, about 5 minutes. Pour the bacon into a strainer placed over a heatproof bowl. You should have about 3 tablespoons of rendered fat. Set the bacon aside.

Return 2 tablespoons of the bacon fat to the skillet. Add the chicken and sauté over moderately high heat until it is no longer pink, about 2 minutes. Remove the chicken to a bowl. Add the remaining rendered bacon fat to the skillet and reduce the heat to moderate. Add the onions and garlic. Cook, stirring frequently, until tender and lightly browned, about 5 minutes. Add the ketchup-chili mixture and the chicken, along with any juices that have collected in the bowl, to the skillet. Reduce the heat to low and simmer uncovered, stirring occasionally, until the mixture is thickened, about 5 minutes. Remove the pan from the heat, and stir in the bacon. Season with salt and with Tabasco sauce if desired. Allow the mixture to cool completely.

Preheat the oven to 350°F. Lightly dust a baking sheet with flour or line it with parchment paper.

FILL AND SHAPE THE LOAF: Punch the dough down. On a lightly floured work surface, roll the dough into a 16-inch circle about ¼ inch thick. Lightly brush the dough with egg glaze. Mound all of the filling in the center. Gather the edges of the dough over the filling, then tie the gathered dough with kitchen string to form a topknot. Using two wide spatulas, transfer the loaf onto the baking sheet and cover it with a towel. Let the loaf rise until almost doubled in volume, about 35 to 45 minutes, depending on the temperature of the room.

BAKE THE LOAF: Lightly brush the loaf with egg glaze. Bake the loaf in the center of the oven until lightly golden and a bamboo skewer inserted into the thickest part of the loaf comes out clean, about 35 to 40 minutes. If the loaf begins to brown too fast, reduce the oven temperature to 325°F. Midway through the baking, rotate the baking sheet to ensure even browning.

Remove the loaf from the oven, transfer to a wire rack, and let cool for about 1 hour. Remove and discard the kitchen string before cutting the loaf into wedges.

— cook's notes —

After baking, the loaf can be wrapped and stored at room temperature for 2 days or frozen for up to 1 month. If the loaf has been frozen, thaw it overnight in the refrigerator, then reheat, wrapped in foil, in a preheated 350°F oven for about 30 minutes.

— *planning ahead* —

The uncooked sausage should be prepared at least 3 days in advance and refrigerated to develop flavor. The brioche dough can also be prepared in advance, tightly wrapped in plastic, and refrigerated for up to 3 days or frozen for 1 week. The sausage can be cooked a day in advance, covered, and refrigerated.

Sausage in Saffron Brioche

Saucisson en brioche, sausage encased in a brioche loaf, is an epicurean French specialty. Sausage is a humble food by itself, but encased in sophisticated brioche dough, it emerges as a proud dish that is rich, delicious, and great for entertaining. Slicing the brioche becomes a dramatic act: a revelation of riches within.

In this recipe, I have enhanced the brioche dough with saffron, which provides an intriguing flavor and a festive golden hue. Like a treasure, hidden inside is a homemade brandy-flavored pork sausage. A mild mustard sauce makes this brioche-based creation one of the best you'll ever taste.

This recipe may seem elaborate, but, in fact, although time-consuming, it's relatively easy and provides enough food for a crowd. With careful planning, it can be done leisurely over a period of several days.

YIELD: 1 large loaf, enough for 10 to 12 first-course servings

SPECIAL EQUIPMENT: A meat grinder with medium and fine blades; a triple layer of cheesecloth about 12 by 15 inches; a large shallow baking pan at least 13 inches long and 2 inches deep; a 12-inch-long 6-cup sandwich bread pan

PORK SAUSAGE

1¼ pounds pork butt, cut into 1-inch cubes
4 ounces pork fatback, finely diced (about ⅔ cup)
¼ cup brandy, preferably cognac
1 tablespoon minced garlic
1½ tablespoons salt, or more to taste
1 teaspoon black peppercorns, coarsely crushed
1 tablespoon potato starch or cornstarch

1 recipe Saffron Brioche Dough (page 165)

POACHING LIQUID

9 cups chicken broth, homemade (page 368) or store-bought, plus additional if necessary
3 cups dry white wine, preferably Chardonnay, plus additional if necessary
1 large onion, cut into eighths
2 teaspoons black peppercorns
2 large bay leaves

Flour, for rolling
1 egg white, lightly beaten
1 egg yolk beaten with 2 teaspoons water, for egg glaze

MUSTARD SAUCE

3 tablespoons Dijon mustard
2 teaspoons cornstarch
1 cup reserved sausage poaching liquid
⅓ cup heavy cream
Salt and freshly ground black pepper to taste

PREPARE THE SAUSAGE: Fit a meat grinder with a medium blade. Grind the pork and fatback together. Remove the medium blade, attach the fine blade, and grind half of the ground meat a second time.

Combine all the ground meat, the brandy, garlic, salt, crushed peppercorns, and potato starch in a mixing bowl. Mix well by hand. To check for seasoning, pinch off a small piece of the mixture and fry in a dry skillet on both sides until cooked through. Taste, then add salt if necessary.

Lay the layered cheesecloth on a work surface. Place the sausage mixture in the center of the cheesecloth and shape into a 12-inch-long cylinder. Tightly wrap the cheesecloth around the sausage. Twist the ends of the cheesecloth in opposite directions and tie the ends with kitchen string. Roll the sausage back and forth on the work surface to form a compact, even cylinder and to eliminate any air trapped in the sausage. Place the wrapped sausage, uncovered, in the refrigerator for 3 days to develop flavor and dry slightly.

Prepare the brioche dough and refrigerate until firm.

Preheat the oven to 400°F.

POACH THE SAUSAGE: In the baking pan, combine all the ingredients for the poaching liquid. Bring to a boil over moderately high heat. As soon as the liquid comes to a boil, carefully add the sausage. Add more chicken broth and/or wine to cover the sausage, if necessary.

Cover the pan with a lid or foil, transfer it to the center of the oven, and bake for 20 minutes. Using tongs, carefully turn the sausage over in the liquid. Cover and continue poaching the sausage for 20 to 25 minutes longer, or until the juices from the sausage run clear when pierced with a wooden skewer. Remove the pan from the oven. Uncover and let the sausage cool completely in the poaching liquid.

Remove the sausage to a platter. Strain the poaching liquid through a fine sieve into a large bowl. Reserve 1 cup of the liquid for the mustard sauce. Freeze the remaining liquid in batches for making sauces.

Butter the loaf pan. Remove and discard the cheesecloth from the sausage.

ASSEMBLE THE BRIOCHE: Sprinkle a work surface with about 3 tablespoons flour. Lightly dust the brioche dough with flour and roll the chilled dough into a 14-inch square. Cut off a 2-inch-wide strip from the top of the square and reserve it for decoration.

Brush the entire surface of the sausage with the beaten egg white. Place the sausage lengthwise across the bottom edge of the dough square. Roll the dough up into a cylinder. Fold the ends under the loaf. Place the loaf seam side down in the loaf pan. Brush the top with egg glaze.

continued

cook's notes

As an alternative to the homemade sausage, you can buy a good boiling garlic sausage in French specialty food stores or by mail from Trois Petits Cochons, 17 East 13th Street, New York, NY 10003 (212-255-3844). A fresh unsmoked Polish kielbasa sausage will do nicely too.

If the brioche dough softens too much as you roll it, place it on a baking sheet and freeze for 10 to 15 minutes to firm the butter. Use a minimal amount of flour when dusting or rolling the brioche dough. Too much flour will make the dough heavy.

After baking, the sausage loaf can be wrapped and stored in the refrigerator for 2 days or frozen for up to 1 month. If it has been frozen, thaw it overnight in the refrigerator, then reheat, wrapped in foil, in a preheated 375°F oven for about 30 to 35 minutes.

Using a ruler as a guide, cut the reserved dough strip lengthwise into 3 equal strips. Braid the strips together. Affix the braid on top of the loaf. Brush the braid with egg glaze. Refrigerate the remaining egg glaze. Place the loaf pan in a large plastic bag, being careful to leave space for the dough to rise without touching the plastic. Set aside in a warm area to let the brioche rise until it has expanded to almost fill the pan up to 3 or 4 hours, depending on the temperature of the room.

Preheat the oven to 350°F.

BAKE THE LOAF: Brush the surface of the loaf with egg glaze. Place the loaf in the center of the oven and bake for 30 to 35 minutes, or until a wooden skewer inserted into the center comes out clean. Remove the pan from the oven and allow the loaf to cool on a rack for at least 45 minutes.

MAKE THE MUSTARD SAUCE: Mix the mustard and cornstarch together in a small bowl. Place the reserved cup poaching liquid in a small saucepan and bring to a boil over moderate heat. Whisk about ⅓ of the hot liquid into the mustard mixture, then stir the mustard mixture and the cream into the saucepan. Cook over low heat, stirring frequently, until slightly thickened, about 5 minutes. Taste the sauce and adjust the seasonings with salt and pepper if necessary. Remove from the heat.

TO SERVE: Unmold the loaf. Place it right side up on a cutting board and cut into ¾-inch slices. Serve warm with the mustard sauce.

— *planning ahead* —

The brioche dough can be made in advance, tightly wrapped in plastic, and refrigerated for up to 3 days or frozen for 1 week.

Chocolate Buns

(PETITS PAINS AU CHOCOLAT)

When I was a schoolgirl in Cannes, I carried little chocolate buns, *pains au chocolat,* in the pockets of my school apron to sustain me during afternoon recess at four o'clock. These sweet treats, sometimes made with brioche dough, sometimes with croissant dough, and yet other times with white bread dough and baked with a slim bar of chocolate inside, were my favorite *goûter* (snack).

Make these buns with brioche for your children's lunch boxes and you will win their hearts. But you don't have to be a child to treat yourself to some of these buns. I like them best when they've just come out of the oven, still oozing with melting bittersweet chocolate. My husband thinks he is being very French when he dunks them in his coffee at breakfast.

YIELD: 8 small buns

1 recipe Brioche Dough (page 164)

1 7-ounce bittersweet chocolate bar, such as Lindt or Tobler

EGG GLAZE

1 egg yolk beaten with 2 teaspoons milk

Prepare the brioche dough and refrigerate until firm.

Lightly grease a large baking sheet or line it with parchment paper.

Cut the chocolate bar into 8 equal fingers, 1 by 4 inches each. Divide the dough evenly into 8 portions.

ASSEMBLE THE CHOCOLATE BUNS: Work with one portion of dough at a time, keeping the remaining dough covered.

On a lightly floured work surface, roll one portion of dough into a 4- by 5-inch rectangle about ¼ inch thick. Position the dough with a short side of the rectangle toward you and place a chocolate finger across the center. Lightly brush the top and bottom margins of the dough with egg glaze. Fold the bottom third of the dough over the chocolate, then fold the top over so that the dough overlaps in the center by about ½ inch. Press the dough together at the seam to seal.

Assemble the remaining buns in the same manner. Refrigerate the remaining egg glaze. Space the buns, seam side down, 2 inches apart on the prepared baking sheet. Cover with a towel and let rise in a warm area until they have almost doubled in volume, about 45 minutes to 1 hour, depending on the temperature of the room.

Preheat the oven to 375°F.

BAKE THE BUNS: Brush the buns again with egg glaze. Place the baking sheet in the center of the oven and bake until the rolls are golden brown and firm to the touch and the chocolate is melted, about 20 to 25 minutes. Midway through the baking, rotate the baking sheet to ensure even browning. If the buns begin to brown too fast, reduce the oven temperature to 350°F.

Remove the buns from the oven and let them cool on the baking sheet. The chocolate buns are delicious either warm or at room temperature.

— cook's notes —

After baking, the chocolate buns can be wrapped and stored at room temperature for 2 days or frozen for up to 1 month. If they have been frozen, thaw them overnight in the refrigerator, then reheat them wrapped in foil in a preheated 350°F oven for about 20 minutes.

— planning ahead —

The brioche dough can be made in advance, tightly wrapped in plastic, and refrigerated for up to 3 days or frozen for up to 1 week. The filling can be prepared up to 2 days in advance, covered, and refrigerated.

— cook's notes —

Good-quality glacéed fruits are available at specialty food stores or through Maid of Scandinavia, 32-44 Raleigh Avenue, Minneapolis, MN 55416 (800-328-6722).

After baking, the cake can be wrapped and stored at room temperature for 2 days or frozen for up to 1 month. If it has been frozen, thaw it overnight in the refrigerator. To reheat the cake, wrap it in foil and place in a preheated 350°F oven for about 30 minutes.

Tying a red satin bow at one end of the crown makes this cake an ideal gift for Christmas.

KINGS' CAKE

Recently, I happened to be in Spain on January 6, Kings' Day as it is known there. This holiday commemorates the visit of the three Wise Men to the infant Jesus. In Spanish tradition presents are given not at Christmas but on Kings' Day. On the afternoon of January 5, men dressed as the Three Kings parade through the streets, bearing gifts that will be distributed to children's homes that evening.

On this festive occasion, a traditional cake called Roscon de Reyes, much like the French Pithiviers (page 104), is served. It is a ring-shaped cake made of brioche, filled with nuts and raisins and scented with lemon zest. Hidden inside is a charm boding good luck for the one who finds it. The finished loaf is glazed with a lemon icing and crowned with candied fruits, such as green angelica, red cherries, and glacéed lemon, to simulate gems. The result is a cake every bit as precious looking as it is delicious, really fit for a king.

YIELD: 1 large ring, enough for 10 to 12 dessert servings

1 recipe Lemon Brioche Dough (page 165)

ALMOND AND FRUIT FILLING

2 tablespoons golden raisins
2 tablespoons chopped mixed candied fruits
2 tablespoons brandy, preferably cognac
4 ounces (1¼ cups) slivered blanched almonds
½ cup sugar
4 tablespoons unsalted butter, cut into 4 pieces, at room temperature
1 large egg
1 egg yolk
3 tablespoons potato starch
½ teaspoon almond extract
¼ teaspoon salt
¼ cup coarsely chopped blanched almonds

Flour, for rolling

1 egg yolk beaten with 2 teaspoons water, for egg glaze
1 whole almond, tightly wrapped in a small piece of foil, for the charm (optional)

LEMON GLAZE

¼ cup sugar
2 tablespoons fresh lemon juice
1 tablespoon unsalted butter

FOR DECORATION

3 glacéed red cherries, cut in half
6 glacéed green angelica, each cut into 3 diamond shapes
6 slices glacéed citron

Prepare the lemon brioche dough and refrigerate until firm.

PREPARE THE FILLING: Mix the raisins, candied fruits, and 1 tablespoon of the brandy in a small bowl. Cover and set aside to marinate for 30 minutes; drain.

Place the slivered almonds and sugar in the bowl of a food processor fitted with the metal blade. Process until finely ground. Add the butter, egg, egg yolk, potato starch, the remaining 1 tablespoon brandy, the almond extract, and salt. Blend until smooth, stopping to scrape down the sides of the bowl with a rubber spatula if necessary. Transfer this almond paste to a small bowl and add the drained fruits and the chopped almonds. Mix well with a rubber spatula. Cover and refrigerate until the paste is firm, about 2 hours.

Lightly grease a baking sheet or line it with parchment paper.

ASSEMBLE THE BRIOCHE: Sprinkle about 3 tablespoons flour on a work surface. With floured hands, roll the brioche into a long roll, about 22 inches long. Then, with a rolling pin, roll the dough into a 6- by 22-inch rectangle about ¼ inch thick. Brush the dough with egg glaze.

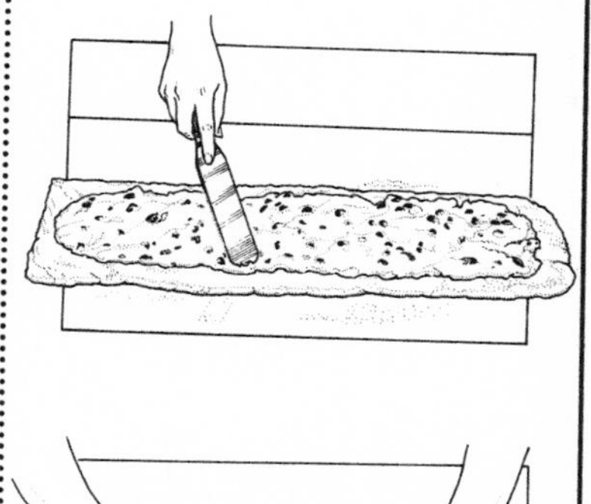

Evenly spread the almond and fruit filling over the dough, leaving a 1-inch border all around. Press the foil-wrapped almond into the filling. Gently but tightly roll the dough up lengthwise, like a jelly roll, into a compact roll. Be careful not to stretch the dough, as it could easily rip—but you do not want to end up with a roll that is loose with lots of air spaces. Pinch the dough together at the ends to prevent the filling from leaking out. Press the seam together to seal.

Brush the ends of the roll with egg glaze, and join the ends to form a ring about 9 inches in diameter. Press the ends together well to adhere. Carefully transfer the ring, seam side down, to the prepared baking sheet. Shape the ring if necessary into a uniform round. Brush the surface with egg glaze. Cover the ring with a large bowl and let it rise in a warm area until almost doubled in volume, about 45 minutes to 1 hour, depending on the temperature of the room.

Preheat the oven to 350°F.

BAKE THE CAKE: Place the baking sheet in the center of the oven and bake the cake for about 30 minutes, or until the cake is golden brown and a wooden skewer inserted into the ring comes out clean. Midway through the baking, rotate the baking sheet to ensure even browning. If the crust begins to brown too fast during baking, cover the cake loosely with foil.

Meanwhile, MAKE THE LEMON GLAZE: Combine the sugar, lemon juice and butter in a small saucepan over medium heat and cook, stirring occasionally, until the butter melts and the sugar is completely dissolved, about 3 minutes. Remove the pan from the heat and let cool slightly.

continued

When the cake is done, remove it from the oven, and let cool slightly on the baking sheet. Brush all of the lemon glaze over the cake. As the glaze accumulates on the baking sheet, brush it onto the cake again. Decorate the cake with candied cherries, angelica, and citron. Serve at room temperature.

Be prepared to celebrate and wish good luck to whomever finds the charm!

flatbreads

When I think of the cuisines of Mexico, India, and the Middle East, flatbreads come immediately to mind. So many of the specialties from these regions feature flat rounds of unleavened bread as an integral part of the meal. These and other cultures have been using flatbreads for centuries, not only as sources of nourishment but also as edible utensils, substituting for both fork and plate. I imagine that early cooks found it convenient to hold and eat their food wrapped in a soft bread that could be quickly made from just flour and water and cooked on a heated stone. Once you try some of the recipes in this chapter, you will find that this still holds true today. You will also experience the fun that comes from eating with your hands.

Today, for better taste and texture, flatbreads are generally made with the addition of shortening, salt, and/or either baking powder or soda. With no added yeast or eggs, the dough does not have to be allowed to rise, making flatbreads quick and simple to prepare. Because they are flat, they also cook much faster than loaf-shaped breads. Start to finish, perfect rounds of flatbreads from the recipes in this section can be produced in less than forty minutes.

The simplest and most common cooking method for flatbreads is griddle-baking, whereby rounds of dough are quickly cooked on both sides on a hot, dry surface. No special equipment is required, since a dry skillet makes a perfect griddle. This technique is used for Mexican tortillas, Chinese po ping, Indian naan, and Middle Eastern pocketless pita bread. Sometimes a small amount of butter is brushed on the surface of the bread or the griddle during baking, as in the preparation of West Indian puries.

Here in the United States, Mexican cuisine has been a major contributor to popularizing flatbread-wrapped foods. Since Mexican specialties based on flour and corn tortillas alone could fill an entire cookbook, I include here only a few of my favorites, like Crispy Chicken Flautas (page 202), but I confess the choice has not been easy. However, I use familiar Mexican techniques to explore a wide range of fillings, even experimenting with the tastes of other countries, like Roast Duck Burritos, Chinese Style (page 190), or Grilled Beef Fajitas, Vietnamese Style (page 192).

Flatbreads make excellent wrappers for all kinds of fillings. They are sturdy enough to be wrapped around stews, as in Indian Spiced Lamb Curry in Yogurt Bread (page 206) or Chimichangas with Pork and Black Bean Chili (page 196). Moreover, their neutral taste allows the assertive flavors in a filling to take center stage, as in the Curried Chicken Rotis (page 209) of the West Indies.

Wonderful turnovers can also be made from flatbread doughs. Sample the delights of these half-moon-shaped pastries by making Corn Quesadillas with Wild Mushrooms and Cheese (page 200) as hors d'oeuvres, Chinese Griddle Cakes Gone American (page 222) for a light meal, or delicious Strawberry Empanadas (page 226) for dessert. Just don't try them all at once, as even I think there can be too much of a good thing.

Most if not all of the dishes in this chapter share a common trait: They make great entertaining fare. The various components for these recipes, the fillings, accompaniments, and the flatbreads themselves, can be conveniently prepared well ahead of time. Some of the dishes will actively involve your guests in putting the ingredients together. Lay the components out at the table or at an outdoor barbecue buffet. Your guests will help themselves, transforming the soft flatbreads into edible envelopes by wrapping them around the various ingredients on display and eating them out of hand. This wrap-it-yourself concept may sound messy, but it translates into fun and informality—and may even save you some serious dishwashing, part of the appeal.

MEXICAN TERMS

Since many of the recipes in this chapter are based on Mexican specialties, I am including this brief overview of the basic language of this cuisine. I hope it will serve as an introduction for those who may be unfamiliar with the sometimes subtle distinctions among the dishes.

BURRITO Common throughout northern Mexico, a burrito, or taco de harina, is a flour tortilla wrapped around a filling of meat, beans, or cheese, or any combination of these.

CHIMICHANGA The name used in the southwestern United States for a fat, crisp-fried burrito. In Mexico, a slimmer version goes by the name *chivichanga.*

EMPANADA The Spanish word for "breaded," *empanada* refers to a pastry turnover surrounding a savory or sweet filling. The pastry is either baked or fried.

ENCHILADA A corn tortilla coated with a highly seasoned sauce, usually containing chiles, rolled around a filling made from meat, chicken, vegetables, and/or other ingredients.

FAJITA A fajita dish traditionally consists of marinated skirt or flank steak that has been charcoal-grilled, thinly sliced, and wrapped in warm flour tortillas. Nowadays, fillings of chicken or lamb are popular too. The dish is usually served with condiments such as salsa, onions, and guacamole. Or it may simply be accompanied by lime wedges to squeeze over it.

FLAUTA In northern Mexico, a flauta ("flute") indicates a cigar-shaped dish such as corn tortillas that have been stuffed and fried.

QUESADILLA The Spanish word for "little cheese bites." In Mexico, a quesadilla is a small fried turnover made with fresh corn dough (masa) that has been stuffed with a variety of ingredients and almost always contains cheese. In the southwestern United States, it refers to a filled pancake in which a cheese-based filling is sandwiched between two flour tortillas.

TACO Traditionally, a taco is a corn tortilla wrapped around a meat filling, seasoned with fresh herbs, and served with a spicy sauce. In practice, almost anything wrapped, rolled, or folded in a corn tortilla may be referred to as a taco.

TORTILLA A round, thin, unleavened griddle-baked cake. There are two types of tortilla: Tortillas made with wheat flour (tortillas de harina) are a specialty of northern Mexico; those made with corn dough (tortillas de masa) are found throughout Mexico.

FLATBREAD WRAPPING TIPS

- To keep flatbreads soft and warm after they are cooked, wrap them in a clean cloth and keep them in a warm place in a covered container or bread basket. This way, they will keep warm for as long as 1 hour. But they are best if served immediately after they have been cooked.
- If you are using thawed frozen corn tortillas and they start to crack as you fold them, put them briefly into a steamer or colander over boiling water, or immerse them in hot fat for just a few seconds. This will make them softer and more flexible.
- I use all-purpose flour in all my flatbread recipes. I prefer the unbleached variety, which yields a more tender baked product.
- I measure flour by the dip-and-sweep method, which means that I dip the measuring cup into a bin of flour and sweep off the excess with a long flat spatula or knife.

Homemade Flour Tortillas

Tortillas de harina, a basic staple of northern Mexico, are made from a flour dough rolled into thin 8-inch or larger rounds and cooked briefly on both sides on a griddle. Exceptionally versatile, these flexible flatbreads may be stuffed, rolled, layered, or simply served plain as bread.

To store tortillas, allow them to cool, stack them, and then seal in a plastic storage bag. They can be refrigerated for up to a week, or frozen for up to one month. Defrost frozen tortillas overnight in the refrigerator before reheating. To reheat, wrap stacks of three or four tortillas in foil. Place the foil-wrapped tortillas in a preheated 400°F oven just until they soften and are heated through, about ten to fifteen minutes.

YIELD: Twelve 8-inch tortillas or six 10-inch tortillas

DOUGH

3 cups unbleached all-purpose flour, plus additional if necessary

1 teaspoon baking powder

3 tablespoons cold solid vegetable shortening

1 teaspoon salt dissolved in ¾ cup plus 2 tablespoons warm water

MAKE THE DOUGH

Hand method: Sift the flour and baking powder together into a large mixing bowl. Using a fork or metal pastry blender, blend in the shortening until the mixture resembles fine meal. Sprinkle the salted water a little at a time over the mixture, using your fingertips to work the dough into a rough dough. After the mixture has clumped together into a rough, shaggy dough, gather it together and briefly knead in the bowl until the dough forms a soft ball. The dough should be moist but not sticky. If it feels sticky, knead in about a tablespoon more flour. If it feels dry or flaky, knead in up to 1 tablespoon more water a teaspoon at a time. Turn the dough out onto a lightly floured work surface and knead until it is shiny and smooth, about 2 to 3 minutes. Shape the dough into a ball.

Food processor method: Place the flour, baking powder, and shortening in the bowl of a food processor fitted with the metal blade. Pulse to blend the ingredients until the mixture resembles coarse meal. With the motor on, gradually add the salted water through the feed tube, and process until the dough cleans the sides of the bowl and rides on the blade, about 10 seconds. The dough should be moist but not sticky. If it feels sticky, add about a tablespoon more flour. If it feels dry or flaky, add up to 1 tablespoon more water a teaspoon at a time. Turn the dough out onto a lightly floured work surface and shape it into a smooth ball.

LET THE DOUGH REST: Divide the dough evenly into 12 pieces (or 6 pieces for 10-inch tortillas). Roll each piece into a ball. Place the dough balls on a lightly floured baking sheet and cover with a clean kitchen towel. Allow the dough to relax at room temperature for at least 30 minutes, or up to 1 hour.

ROLL THE DOUGH: Work with one piece of dough at a time, keeping the remainder covered with a towel to prevent them from drying out.

Lightly press one ball of dough into a disk. On a lightly floured work surface, roll the dough into an 8-inch (or 10-inch) round about 1⁄16 inch thick. Each time you roll over the dough, pick it up and rotate it a sixth of a turn to the right. This will help achieve the round shape of the tortilla. (Don't worry if the tortillas are not perfectly round; they will taste just as good.) Roll the remaining dough balls in the same manner, lightly dusting each tortilla with flour and stacking them on a large plate.

COOK THE TORTILLAS: Heat a griddle or large dry skillet over moderately low heat until hot. Be sure the griddle is not too hot or the tortillas will brown too quickly without cooking through. Place a tortilla on the hot griddle and cook until lightly browned on the bottom, about 20 seconds. The surface will blister slightly as it cooks; use the back of a spatula or spoon to press down on it to keep the tortilla flat. Turn the tortilla over with your fingers or a wide spatula and cook for 20 seconds longer. Remove the tortilla to a large plate or bread basket and cover with a cloth napkin to keep warm. Cook the remaining tortillas in the same manner.

The tortillas will stay warm for hours if you wrap them, napkin and all, in foil and put them into a barely warm (150°F) oven.

cook's notes

For those who don't want to make them at home, flour tortillas are readily available in packages of a dozen at most supermarkets.

Homemade Pita Breads

Unlike the pocketed variety of pita bread, which is made with yeast and oven-baked, this pocketless bread is made with baking powder and is griddle-baked. It is more tender and flexible than pocket pita. Rolled into large 8-inch rounds, it can easily be wrapped around morsels of food.

To store the pitas, allow them to cool, stack them, and then seal in a plastic storage bag. They can be refrigerated for up to a week or frozen for up to one month. Defrost frozen pitas overnight in the refrigerator. To reheat, wrap stacks of two or three pitas in foil and place in a preheated 400°F oven just until heated through, about ten to fifteen minutes.

YIELD: Eight 8-inch round breads

DOUGH

4 cups unbleached all-purpose flour, plus additional if necessary
2 teaspoons baking powder
1 teaspoon baking soda
2 teaspoons sugar
1 teaspoon salt
⅓ cup light olive oil
1⅓ cups warm water

MAKE THE DOUGH

Hand method: Sift the flour, baking powder, and baking soda together into a large mixing bowl. Make a well in the middle. Put the sugar, salt, olive oil, and water into the well. Using a wooden spoon, stir to dissolve the sugar and salt. Then stir to draw the flour into the liquid to blend until the mixture clumps together into a rough, shaggy dough. Gather it together and briefly knead by hand in the bowl until the dough forms a soft ball. The dough should be moist but not sticky. If it feels sticky, knead in about a tablespoon more flour. If it feels dry or flaky, knead in up to 1 tablespoon more flour a teaspoon at a time. Turn the dough out onto a lightly floured work surface and knead until it is shiny and smooth, about 2 to 3 minutes. Shape the dough into a ball.

Food processor method: Place the flour, baking powder, and baking soda in the bowl of a food processor fitted with the metal blade. Pulse to blend. In a small bowl, combine the sugar, salt, olive oil, and warm water. Stir to dissolve the salt and sugar. With the motor on, pour the liquid through the feed tube of the food processor, and process until the dough forms a ball and rides on the blade, about 10 seconds. The dough should be moist but not sticky. If it feels sticky, add about a tablespoon more flour. If it feels dry or flaky, add up to 1 tablespoon water a teaspoon at a time. Turn the dough out onto a lightly floured work surface and shape it into a smooth ball.

LET THE DOUGH REST: Divide the dough into 8 pieces. Roll each piece into a ball. Place the dough balls on a lightly floured baking sheet and cover with a clean kitchen towel. Allow the dough to relax for at least 30 minutes, or up to 1 hour.

ROLL THE DOUGH: Work with one piece of dough at a time, keeping the remainder covered with a towel to prevent them from drying out.

Lightly press one ball of dough into a disk. On a lightly floured work surface roll the dough into an 8-inch round about 3⁄16 inch thick. Each time you roll over the dough, pick it up and rotate it a sixth of a turn to the right. This will help achieve the round shape of the pita. (Don't worry if they are not perfectly round; they will taste just as good.)

Roll the remaining dough balls in the same manner, lightly dusting each pita with flour and stacking them on a large plate.

COOK THE PITAS: Heat a griddle or a large dry skillet over moderately low heat until it is hot. Be sure the griddle is not too hot or the pitas will brown too quickly without cooking through. Place a pita on the hot griddle and cook until lightly browned on the bottom, about 2 minutes. Turn the pita over with your fingers or a wide spatula and cook for 2 minutes longer. The pita may puff slightly as it cooks, but it will deflate after cooking. Remove the pita to a large plate or bread basket and cover with a cloth napkin to keep warm. Cook the remaining pitas in the same manner.

The pitas will stay warm for hours if you wrap them, napkin and all, in foil and put them into a barely warm (150°F) oven.

— cook's notes —

It is possible to buy ready-made pocketless pita breads in some supermarkets.

— *planning ahead* —

The homemade tortillas can be prepared ahead of time, covered, and refrigerated for up to a week or frozen for up to 1 month. Both the guacamole and tomato relish can be prepared up to 6 hours before serving, covered, and refrigerated.

Smoked Chicken Burritos

No compilation of food under wraps would be complete without the popular burrito. While to most people a burrito conjures up an image of a banal filling of refried beans wrapped in a flour tortilla and topped with melted cheese and shredded lettuce, this is definitely a limited perception.

In this version, I use guacamole, smoked chicken meat, and tomato relish as a filling, a winning flavor combination. This refreshing and simple-to-make dish has become a favorite of mine for entertaining in the summer. For a large group, double or triple the recipe and present each component separately at the table for a wrap-it-yourself dinner party. Serve these burritos with pickled vegetables and chilled Mexican beer, tequila, or margaritas.

YIELD: 6 burritos, enough for 6 light main-course servings

GUACAMOLE

4 small ripe avocados
¼ cup fresh lime juice
3 fresh or pickled jalapeño peppers, seeded and minced
¼ cup chopped fresh cilantro leaves
2 teaspoons minced garlic
1 teaspoon ground cumin
1 teaspoon salt
Freshly ground black pepper to taste

TOMATO RELISH

4 ripe plum tomatoes, seeded and finely diced
1 large red onion, finely diced
2 fresh or pickled jalapeño peppers, seeded and minced
2 teaspoons minced garlic
3 tablespoons fresh lime juice
⅓ cup light olive oil
2 tablespoons chopped fresh cilantro leaves
2 tablespoons chopped fresh mint leaves
Salt and freshly ground black pepper to taste

1½ pounds smoked boneless chicken breast (see Cook's Notes)
12 8-inch Homemade Flour Tortillas (page 184)

ACCOMPANIMENTS

1 small head romaine lettuce, thinly shredded
1 cup sour cream

PREPARE THE GUACAMOLE: Cut the avocados in half and remove the pits, reserving them. Using a spoon, scoop the avocado flesh into a large nonreactive mixing bowl. Mash the avocados with a fork or potato masher; they should remain chunky. Add the lime juice, jalapeño peppers, cilantro, garlic, cumin, and salt. Season with black pepper. Place the avocado pits in the guacamole. (The pits help prevent the avocados from oxidizing and turning brown.) Cover the bowl with plastic wrap and let stand at room temperature for about 1 hour to develop flavor.

PREPARE THE TOMATO RELISH: Place all the relish ingredients in a small nonreactive bowl and stir to combine. Cover and refrigerate until ready to serve.

Remove and discard the skin and any excess fat from the smoked chicken. Cut the chicken meat lengthwise into thin slices, then cut each slice into 1-inch-wide strips. Place the chicken on a plate, cover, and refrigerate until ready to serve.

Prepare the flour tortillas. Stack them, place in a serving basket, and cover with a clean kitchen towel to keep them soft and warm.

TO SERVE: Set out the tortilla basket, smoked chicken, guacamole, relish, lettuce, and sour cream at the table for guests to help themselves. To eat, spread some sour cream and guacamole evenly over a tortilla. Distribute a few strips of chicken over the tortilla and top with some lettuce and relish. Roll up the tortilla and eat the burrito out of hand.

— cook's notes —

Smoked chicken breast is available at smokehouses and gourmet shops. It can also be ordered from D'Artagnan, Inc., 399-419 St. Paul Avenue, Jersey City, NJ 07306 (Tel. 800-DAR-TAGN or 201-792-0748; Fax 201-792-0113).

If you use store-bought rather than homemade flour tortillas, reheat them before serving. To reheat, wrap the tortillas in foil in stacks of 4 and heat in a preheated 400°F oven until they soften, about 10 to 15 minutes. If the tortillas are very dry to begin with, place a dampened paper towel between each one before stacking them.

Fresh jumbo crabmeat or grilled or poached shrimp may be substituted for the chicken.

— *planning ahead* —

The homemade tortillas can be prepared ahead of time, covered, and refrigerated for up to a week or frozen for up to 1 month. The salad can be prepared up to 6 hours before serving, covered, and refrigerated.

Roast Duck Burritos, Chinese Style

There's really no reason to limit the burrito to Mexican-style fillings. In this recipe, I use leftover roast duck to make a Chinese-style salad flavored with hoisin sauce and ground peanuts. The combination of crunchy vegetables, tender meat, and a sweetish sauce, all wrapped up in a flour tortilla, makes for an experience you'll find very satisfying.

These rolls are ideal for a picnic or eating on the run. They can be rolled up early in the day and wrapped in plastic wrap, ready for transportation. Another great way to serve them is at a buffet. Simply set out the filling ingredients on the sideboard, keep the tortillas warm in a basket, and let your guests assemble their own rolls.

YIELD: 8 burritos, enough for 8 light first-course or 4 main-course servings

DUCK SALAD

- 1 cup fresh bean sprouts or 1 stalk celery, cut into thin 2-inch-long strips
- 2 cups thinly shredded cold roast duck meat, skin removed
- 1 medium carrot, peeled and cut into thin 2-inch-long strips
- 1 medium cucumber, peeled, seeded, and cut into thin 2-inch-long strips
- 4 scallions, trimmed, cut into 2-inch-long lengths, and finely shredded
- 1 cup fresh cilantro leaves

- 8 8-inch Homemade Flour Tortillas (page 184)
- ½ cup or more hoisin sauce, for serving
- ¼ cup unsalted dry-roasted peanuts, coarsely ground

PREPARE THE DUCK SALAD: Drop the bean sprouts or celery into a small pot of boiling water. Immediately drain the bean sprouts in a colander set in the sink. Refresh them under cold running water. Drain well.

In a large mixing bowl, combine the blanched bean sprouts or celery, the shredded duck, carrot, cucumber, scallions, and cilantro leaves. Toss well to mix, cover, and refrigerate until ready to serve.

Prepare the flour tortillas. Stack them, place in a serving basket, and cover with a clean kitchen towel to keep them soft and warm.

TO SERVE: Set out the tortilla basket, salad, the hoisin sauce, and the ground peanuts on the table. To eat, spread 1 tablespoon of the hoisin sauce over a tortilla and sprinkle on ½ tablespoon of the ground peanuts. Place some of the salad on the tortilla. Roll the tortilla and eat out of hand; dip the rolls in additional hoisin sauce if desired.

— cook's notes —

If you use store-bought rather than homemade flour tortillas, reheat them before serving. To reheat, wrap the tortillas in foil in stacks of 4 and heat in a preheated 400°F oven until they soften, about 10 to 15 minutes. If the tortillas are very dry to begin with, place a dampened paper towel between each one before stacking them.

Roast chicken, turkey, veal, or pork can replace the duck in the salad.

For a delicious variation, you can create the equivalent of mock Peking Duck: Spread about a tablespoon of hoisin sauce on a warm flour tortilla, then place a few slices of either roasted, grilled, or barbecued duck or chicken meat in the middle, along with a few strips of cucumbers and finely shredded scallions (white part only). Roll the tortilla up tightly to enclose the filling and eat out of hand.

— planning ahead —

The homemade tortillas can be prepared ahead of time, covered, and refrigerated for up to a week or frozen for up to 1 month. Both the dressing and salad mix can be prepared up to 6 hours ahead, tightly covered, and refrigerated until serving time.

Grilled Beef Fajitas, Vietnamese Style

Mexican and Vietnamese cuisines are similar in many ways. Not only do they share many of the same ingredients, such as cilantro, chiles, and limes, they also share the practice of enveloping cooked food in an edible wrapper and eating it out of hand. In my cooking, I often like to cross these two styles, as this dish demonstrates.

In Mexican cooking, a dish made with thin strips of grilled or stir-fried beef with onions and bell peppers wrapped in a flour tortilla is called a *fajita.* Here, a delicate flour tortilla is wrapped around an uncommon filling of grilled flank steak, charred peppers, and lettuce tossed in a lively Vietnamese-style dressing accented with chiles, lemongrass, and mint. Don't worry about the long ingredient list. These are really easy to prepare.

YIELD: 12 fajitas, enough for 6 light main-course servings

CHILE DRESSING

1 stalk lemongrass, minced (see Cook's Notes), or grated zest of 1 lime
3 tablespoons fresh lime juice
3 tablespoons fish sauce (see Cook's Notes) or light soy sauce
1 tablespoon sugar
1 jalapeño pepper, minced
1 teaspoon freshly ground black pepper
¼ cup olive oil
2 teaspoons minced garlic
1 small red onion, sliced paper-thin

SALAD MIX

1 medium green or red bell pepper
2 cups shredded romaine lettuce
3 plum tomatoes, cored, seeded, and finely diced
¼ cup chopped fresh cilantro leaves
⅓ cup finely shredded fresh mint leaves

12 8-inch Homemade Flour Tortillas (page 184)
4 6-ounce skirt steaks or 1½ pounds flank steak
Salt and freshly ground black pepper to taste
2 tablespoons olive oil
2 teaspoons minced garlic
1 large avocado

PREPARE THE DRESSING: In a small bowl, whisk together all the dressing ingredients. Cover and set aside.

PREPARE THE SALAD MIX: Place the bell pepper directly on a gas or electric burner at moderate heat and grill, turning the pepper with tongs, until the flesh is soft and the skin charred, about 4 minutes. Alternatively, cut the pepper in half lengthwise, place it skin side up under a preheated broiler, and broil until the skin is blackened. Place the pepper on a plate and let it stand for 5 minutes to cool. Then hold the pepper under cold running water and rub the skin off. Pat dry, then core, seed, and cut into ¼-inch-wide strips. Place in a mixing bowl. Add the lettuce, tomatoes, cilantro, and mint and toss to mix. Cover and refrigerate until ready to serve.

Prepare the flour tortillas. Stack them, place in a serving basket, and cover with a clean kitchen towel to keep them soft and warm.

GRILL THE STEAKS: Prepare a fire in an outdoor grill, or heat a griddle or heavy nonstick skillet over moderately high heat. Season the steaks with salt and pepper. In a small bowl, combine the oil and garlic. Brush both sides of the meat with the mixture. Place the steaks on the grill or in the pan and cook to the desired degree of doneness, about 4 to 5 minutes per side for medium rare. Remove the steaks to a cutting board and let stand for 5 to 10 minutes.

Holding a carving knife at a slight angle, slice the steak across the grain into thin slices. Add the meat to the salad mix. Pour the dressing over the salad and toss gently to coat all the ingredients. Turn the salad onto a serving platter.

Cut the avocado in half lengthwise and remove the pit. Peel, then cut the avocado into ¼-inch-thick slices. Place the avocado on a small plate.

TO SERVE: Set out the tortilla basket, beef salad, and sliced avocado on the table. To eat, place a portion of the salad on a tortilla, along with a few slices of avocado. Roll up the tortilla and eat out of hand.

— cook's notes —

Lemongrass is available in Asian markets. Since it freezes well, buy several bunches at a time. Cut to separate the bottom stalk where the leaves begin to branch, and discard the loose leaves. Freeze the stalks in plastic bags. To use, peel the tough outer layer from the stalk to disclose the white under layer. Crush lightly before chopping to release maximum flavor. If fresh lemongrass is unavailable, substitute grated lime zest, using the zest of 1 lime for each stalk of lemongrass required.

When buying fish sauce, look for the Squid or Tiparos brand. Once opened, fish sauce lasts up to 1 year at room temperature. Fish sauce is available in Asian markets and in some well-stocked supermarkets.

If you use store-bought rather than homemade flour tortillas, reheat them before serving. To reheat, wrap the tortillas in foil in stacks of 4 and heat in a preheated 400°F oven until they soften, about 10 to 15 minutes. If the tortillas are very dry to begin with, place a dampened paper towel between each one before stacking them.

— planning ahead —

The homemade tortillas can be prepared ahead of time, covered, and refrigerated for up to a week or frozen for up to 1 month. Both the marinated chicken and pickled vegetables can be prepared up to 6 hours ahead, tightly covered, and refrigerated until serving time.

— cook's notes —

Lemongrass is available in Asian markets. Since it freezes well, buy several bunches at a time. Cut to separate the bottom stalk where the leaves begin to branch, and discard the grassy tops. Freeze the stalks in plastic bags. To use, peel the tough outer layer from the stalk to disclose the white under layer. Crush lightly before chopping to release maximum flavor. If fresh lemongrass is unavailable, substitute grated lime zest, using the zest of 1 lime for each stalk of lemongrass required.

When buying fish sauce, look for the Squid or Tiparos brand. Once opened, fish sauce lasts up to a year at room temperature. Fish sauce is available in Asian markets and in some well-stocked supermarkets.

Grilled Chicken Fajitas, Thai Style

Here is another one of my cross-cultural ideas. When I have company for dinner and I'm in the mood for a very light but flavorful meal, this is the kind of dish I like to prepare. Skinless chicken breasts are marinated in a blend of Thai spices and grilled or broiled. The moist chicken is then snuggled into a soft flour tortilla along with crunchy marinated cucumber and eaten out of hand. Served with a simple soup, these bundles are so light and irresistible you could easily gobble up several.

YIELD: 12 fajitas, enough for 6 light main-course servings

4 boneless skinless chicken breast halves (about 1½ pounds)

MARINADE

1 teaspoon minced garlic
1 tablespoon grated fresh ginger
¼ cup chopped shallots
½ cup chopped fresh cilantro leaves
1 stalk lemongrass, minced (see Cook's Notes), or grated zest of 1 lime
2 teaspoons brown sugar
½ cup unsweetened coconut milk (see Cook's Notes)
1 tablespoon fresh lime juice
1 tablespoon fish sauce (see Cook's Notes)
1 tablespoon light soy sauce
¼ cup peanut oil
½ teaspoon Oriental sesame oil

PICKLED VEGETABLES

1 cup rice vinegar or distilled white vinegar
¼ cup sugar
1 teaspoon salt
¼ cup fish sauce
1 teaspoon crushed dried red pepper
4 medium cucumbers, peeled, seeded, and thinly sliced
4 medium carrots, peeled and thinly sliced
2 small red onions, peeled and thinly sliced
⅓ cup chopped fresh cilantro leaves

12 8-inch Homemade Flour Tortillas (page 184)

MARINATE THE CHICKEN: Remove any excess fat from the chicken breasts. Rinse and pat them dry. Place the chicken pieces in a shallow dish. In a blender or food processor, purée all the marinade ingredients. Pour the marinade over the chicken, and use your hands to coat the chicken with the marinade. Cover and let sit at room temperature for 2 hours or refrigerate overnight, turning the chicken at least once in the marinade.

PREPARE THE PICKLED VEGETABLES: Combine the vinegar, sugar, and salt with ½ cup hot water in a small saucepan, and stir until the sugar is dissolved. Bring the mixture to a boil over moderately high heat. Immediately remove from the heat and pour into a large mixing bowl. Stir in the fish sauce and crushed red pepper, and allow to cool. Add the vegetables and cilantro and stir with a fork to combine. Cover and let the vegetables marinate at room temperature for at least 1 hour.

Prepare the flour tortillas. Stack them, place in a serving basket, and cover with a clean kitchen towel to keep them soft and warm.

GRILL THE CHICKEN: Prepare a fire in an outdoor grill, or heat a griddle or heavy nonstick pan over moderately high heat.

Drain the chicken, discarding the marinade. Place the chicken on the grill or in the pan and cook until the meat is no longer pink at the center of the thickest part, about 4 minutes per side. Remove the chicken pieces to a cutting board and let rest for 5 minutes. Thinly slice the chicken and arrange the slices on a platter.

TO SERVE: Drain the pickled vegetables, discarding the marinade. Set out the tortilla basket, sliced chicken, and vegetables on the table. To eat, place a few slices of the chicken and some pickled vegetables on a tortilla. Roll up the tortilla and eat out of hand.

Do not confuse coconut milk with coconut cream. Excellent canned unsweetened coconut milk is available in Asian markets and some supermarkets. After opening, it can be refrigerated for up to 1 week. For longer storage, freeze it in ice cube trays, then store the cubes in plastic bags. Before using, heat the frozen coconut milk until completely melted. Four cubes equal about ½ cup. You may substitute heavy cream for the coconut milk, but the taste will be slightly altered.

If you use store-bought rather than homemade flour tortillas, reheat them before serving. To reheat, wrap the tortillas in foil in stacks of 4 and heat in a preheated 400°F oven until they soften, about 10 to 15 minutes. If the tortillas are very dry to begin with, place a dampened paper towel between each one before stacking them.

The chicken can also be broiled.

Turkey or pork cutlets, or lamb or beef steaks may replace the chicken.

— planning ahead —

The homemade tortillas can be prepared ahead of time, covered, and refrigerated for up to a week or frozen for up to 1 month. The cooked chili can be covered and refrigerated for up to 2 days. The uncooked chimichangas can be wrapped in plastic wrap and refrigerated for a day or frozen for up to 1 month. If they have been frozen, thaw them overnight in the refrigerator before deep-frying.

Chimichangas with Pork and Black Bean Chili

Every now and then I find myself craving a good, hearty fried tortilla roll. These chimichangas are the answer to such cravings.

A chimichanga is nothing more than a burrito filled with a dense meat stew laced with beans, cheese, and chiles and deep-fried. In this variation, I use a well-seasoned chili made with pork and black beans, two elements that are traditional in Mexican cuisine. Serve the chimichangas with dollops of sour cream and tomato relish on the side, if you wish.

YIELD: 10 chimichangas, enough for 4 to 5 main-course servings

PORK AND BLACK BEAN CHILI

2 tablespoons olive oil
1 pound lean boneless pork stew meat, trimmed of fat and cut into ¾-inch cubes
1 large onion, sliced (about 2 cups)
1 tablespoon minced garlic
2 teaspoons ground cumin
1 teaspoon ground coriander
1 jalapeño pepper, seeded and minced
2 cups chicken broth, homemade (page 368) or store-bought
¼ cup dry sherry
½ teaspoon salt
1½ cups cooked black beans (see Cook's Notes)
2 tablespoons fresh lemon juice
1 cup shredded Monterey Jack cheese
1 scallion, finely chopped
2 tablespoons chopped fresh cilantro leaves

10 10-inch Homemade Flour Tortillas (page 184)
Corn oil, for deep-frying

ACCOMPANIMENTS

Sour cream, for serving (optional)
Tomato Relish (page 188), for serving (optional)

PREPARE THE CHILI: Heat the oil in a 5- to 6-quart pot or Dutch oven over high heat. Add the pork and cook, stirring with a wooden spoon, until browned on all sides, about 5 minutes. Using a slotted spoon, remove the meat to a bowl, leaving as much of the oil as possible in the pot. Add the onion and garlic to the pot, lower the heat to moderately high, and cook, stirring occasionally, until the onion is limp, about 3 minutes. Add the cumin and coriander and stir until the mixture is fragrant, about 2 minutes. Return the pork and any juices that have collected in the bowl to the pot, along with the jalapeño, chicken broth, sherry, and salt. Bring the mixture to a boil, reduce the heat to low, cover the pot, and simmer for 1 hour, or until the meat is almost tender.

Uncover the pot and stir in the beans and lemon juice. Simmer, uncovered, for 30 minutes more or until the pork is very tender and all the liquid has evaporated. Remove from the heat and allow to cool.

Use two forks to shred the pieces of pork. Stir in the cheese, scallion, and cilantro. Cover and refrigerate.

Prepare the flour tortillas. Stack them on a large plate and cover with a clean kitchen towel to keep them soft and warm.

ASSEMBLE THE ROLLS: Work with one tortilla at a time, keeping the remaining tortillas covered with the towel.

Place a tortilla flat on a work surface. Fold over the bottom third, as if you were beginning to fold a letter, to make a solid base. Spread ¼ cup of the chili on the folded base, then roll the base over once. Fold the sides of the tortilla over and roll the tortilla up to make a neat, compact package. Fasten the seam with toothpicks. Place the roll on a large plate. Assemble the remaining rolls in the same manner.

Preheat the oven to 250°F.

FRY THE ROLLS: Heat about 3 inches of oil in a deep-fryer or a large heavy saucepan over moderate heat to 350°F. Deep-fry the rolls, in batches, until crisp and golden, about 5 minutes, turning them occasionally with tongs. Drain each batch well on paper towels, then keep warm in the oven while you fry the remainder.

TO SERVE: Arrange the chimichangas on a warm serving dish. Garnish with sour cream and tomato relish if desired.

— cook's notes —

To cook black beans, soak 1 cup dried beans in 3 cups hot water for at least 2 hours, or, preferably, overnight. Drain the beans. Place them in a saucepan, cover with 3 cups cold water, and bring to a boil over moderate heat. Reduce the heat to low and cook until tender, about 40 minutes, adding more water if necessary to keep the beans covered. Drain in a colander set in the sink, rinse with cold water, and drain well.

If you prefer to use canned black beans, drain a 15-ounce can of black beans, rinse, and drain well before adding to the chili.

If you use store-bought rather than homemade flour tortillas, reheat them before serving. To reheat, wrap the tortillas in foil in stacks of 4 and heat in a preheated 400°F oven until they soften, about 10 to 15 minutes. If the tortillas are very dry to begin with, place a dampened paper towel between each one before stacking them.

Veal, lamb, or beef stewing meat may replace the pork.

— planning ahead —

The homemade tortillas can be prepared ahead of time, covered, and refrigerated for up to a week or frozen for up to 1 month. The assembled quesadillas can be covered and left at room temperature for up to 4 hours before cooking.

Griddle-Baked Apple and Cheese Quesadillas

In the hands of a Mexican cook, a quesadilla takes the form of a fried half-moon turnover made from fresh masa dough. As the dish moves across the border into the southwestern United States, it turns into something totally different—a flat pancake of two flour tortillas filled with cheese and chiles and fried or griddle-baked.

This version of quesadillas belongs in the second category. In it, I use mozzarella cheese and thin slices of apple as a simple but deliciously refreshing filling. These are ideal for cocktails.

If you wish, serve the quesadillas with sour cream, guacamole, and tomato relish.

YIELD: 34 quesadillas, or 32 wedges for hors d'oeuvres

8 8-inch Homemade Flour Tortillas (page 184)
1 medium red Delicious apple
4 tablespoons unsalted butter, melted
8 ounces fresh mozzarella cheese, preferably buffalo, thinly sliced
2 tablespoons shredded fresh cilantro leaves
2 tablespoons chopped scallions
Salt and freshly ground black pepper to taste
Sour cream, for serving (optional)
Guacamole (page 188), for serving (optional)
Tomato Relish (page 188), for serving (optional)

Prepare the flour tortillas. Stack them on a plate and cover with a clean kitchen towel to keep them soft and warm.

Peel, quarter, and core the apple. Cut each quarter lengthwise into thin slices, but keep the slices next to each other, to prevent them from turning brown.

ASSEMBLE THE QUESADILLAS: Work with one tortilla at a time, keeping the remaining tortillas covered with the towel.

Place a tortilla on a work surface and brush with melted butter. Arrange a few slices of the cheese over the buttered tortilla, leaving a 1 inch border all around. Distribute one quarter of the sliced apple over the cheese. Sprinkle ½ tablespoon each of cilantro and scallions over all, then season with salt and pepper. Top with a few more slices of cheese. Brush one side of a second tortilla with melted butter and place it over the filling, buttered side down. Press the edges of the tortillas together to seal; if necessary, secure the quesadilla by weaving a few toothpicks around the edges of the tortillas. Place the assembled quesadilla on a large baking sheet and cover with a towel. Assemble the remaining quesadillas in the same manner.

Preheat the oven to 250°F.

COOK THE QUESADILLAS: Heat a large griddle or 2 large nonstick skillets over low heat. Brush 2 of the quesadillas on both sides with melted butter and place them on the griddle. Cook them until the bottoms are lightly browned, about 2 minutes. Using a wide spatula, turn the quesadillas over and cook for another 2 minutes. Remove the quesadillas to the baking sheet and keep warm in the oven while you cook the remainder.

TO SERVE: Cut each quesadilla into 8 wedges and arrange them on a large platter. Serve hot. Pass guacamole, tomato relish, and sour cream, if desired.

— cook's notes —

If you use store-bought rather than homemade flour tortillas, reheat them before serving. To reheat, wrap the tortillas in foil in stacks of 4 and heat in a preheated 400°F oven until they soften, about 10 to 15 minutes. If the tortillas are very dry to begin with, place a dampened paper towel between each one before stacking them.

Fresh goat cheese may be used as a substitute for the mozzarella, and thin slices of peeled jicama for the apple.

For variation, try the chicken and cheese filling for Crispy Chicken Flautas (page 202) or the filling for Corn Quesadillas with Wild Mushrooms and Cheese (page 200) instead of apples and mozzarella cheese.

planning ahead

The filling for the quesadillas can be prepared a day in advance, covered with plastic wrap, and refrigerated. The uncooked quesadillas can be wrapped individually in plastic wrap and refrigerated overnight or frozen for up to 3 months. If the frozen quesadillas are to be fried, thaw them overnight in the refrigerator. Otherwise, brush both sides with melted butter and cook, unthawed, over a hot griddle for about 5 minutes per side.

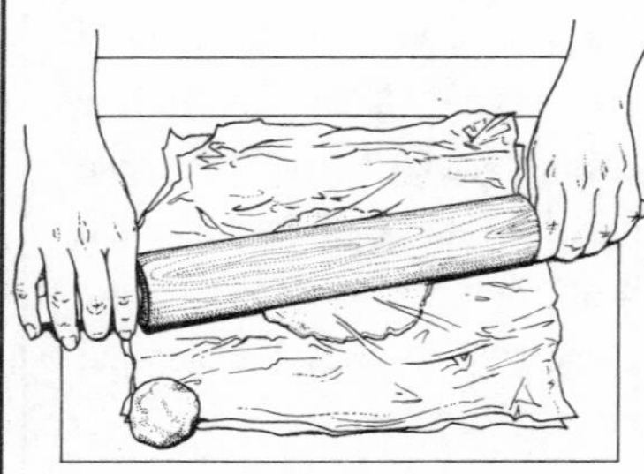

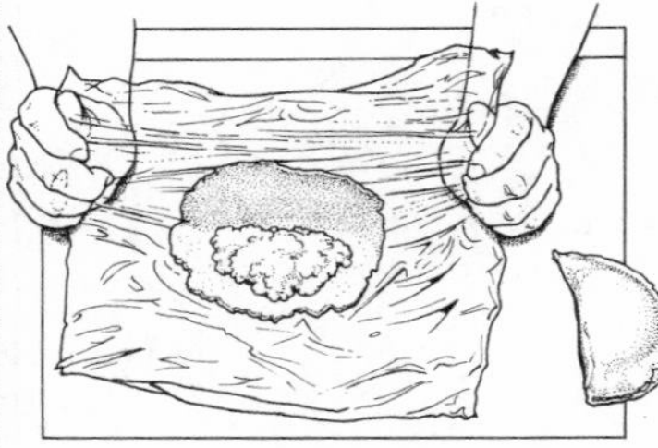

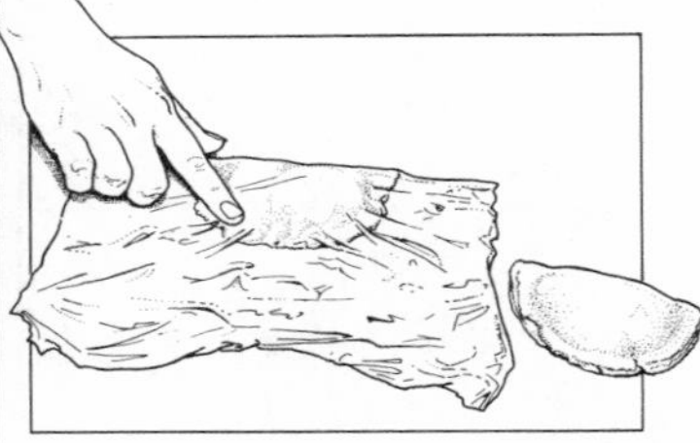

Corn Quesadillas with Wild Mushrooms and Cheese

A favorite snack in central Mexico is a fried turnover called a *quesadilla frita.* A corn dough called *masa* forms the crust, which is typically filled with cheese and any of a number of other ingredients, such as chiles, well-spiced vegetables, sausages, or other meats. Instead of rolling the dough, Mexican cooks form the masa dough by hand. With quick, deft movements they pass a small ball of dough from one hand to the other, flattening it between their palms into a disk and then transforming it in no time at all into a thin pancake, which is then filled and fried.

In this meatless quesadilla, I use shiitake mushrooms and a mild white Monterey Jack cheese for the filling. If, like me, you have not mastered the art of flattening the dough by hand, use a tortilla press or a rolling pin to roll it between two sheets of plastic wrap. Either baked or fried, these creamy and nutty-tasting quesadillas are so terrific you can never make enough. Set the pastries in a bread or straw basket on the table to serve with drinks as an informal appetizer or as a light lunch or supper with a soup.

If you wish, serve the quesadillas with Tomato Relish (page 188) or your favorite store-bought salsa and sour cream.

YIELD: 16 quesadillas for hors d'oeuvres, or enough for 8 first-course servings

MUSHROOM AND CHEESE FILLING

3 tablespoons unsalted butter
1 cup minced onions
1 tablespoon minced garlic
1 jalapeño pepper, seeded and minced
1 pound fresh shiitake mushrooms, stems removed and caps sliced (see Cook's Notes)
1 large tomato, peeled, seeded, and finely chopped
½ teaspoon salt, or more to taste
½ pound Monterey Jack cheese, grated
2 tablespoons chopped fresh cilantro leaves
Freshly ground black pepper to taste

DOUGH

2 cups masa harina (see Cook's Notes)
¼ cup unbleached all-purpose flour, plus additional if necessary
1 teaspoon baking powder
1 teaspoon salt
1 teaspoon sugar
2 teaspoons solid vegetable shortening
1¼ cups hot water

¼ cup melted butter, for griddle-baking, or vegetable oil, for deep-frying

PREPARE THE FILLING: Melt the butter in a large skillet over moderate heat. Add the onions, garlic, and jalapeño. Sauté until the onions are softened, about 2 minutes. Add the mushrooms and cook until they are soft, about 5 minutes. Add the tomato and salt and cook until the tomato is soft, about 3 minutes. Remove the pan from the heat and set aside to cool, then mix in the cheese and cilantro. Taste the filling and adjust the seasoning with salt and pepper if necessary. Cover and set aside.

PREPARE THE DOUGH: Place the masa harina, flour, baking powder, salt, sugar, and shortening in a large mixing bowl. Using a fork, blend the shortening into the masa and flour. Sprinkle the hot water a little at a time over the mixture, using your fingertips to work the dough into a ball. After the mixture has clumped together into a rough, shaggy dough, gather it together and briefly knead in the bowl until the dough forms a soft ball. The dough should be moist but not sticky or crumbly. If the dough feels sticky, knead in additional flour a teaspoon at a time until the dough is no longer sticky. If it feels dry or flaky, knead in more water a teaspoon at a time until the dough is soft and holds together without crumbling.

Remove the dough from the bowl and lightly press it into a flat disk. Cover with plastic wrap and allow it to rest at room temperature for 30 minutes.

ASSEMBLE THE QUESADILLAS: Divide the dough into 16 pieces. Roll each portion of dough into a ball. Work with one piece of dough at a time, keeping the remainder covered with a clean kitchen towel to prevent them from drying out.

Using a tortilla press or a flat saucer, flatten a dough ball between two sheets of plastic wrap to a 5-inch circle. Or use a rolling pin to gently roll the dough between the plastic wrap. Don't be concerned if the dough border looks jagged.

Peel off the top piece of plastic. Put 1 tablespoon of the filling on the dough circle, just below the center, leaving about a ¾-inch margin around the bottom edge. Lightly moisten the exposed margin of dough with water. Lift the plastic wrap and use it to fold the dough over the filling, forming a half-moon-shaped turnover. Firmly press the edges of the dough together around the filling, through the plastic wrap, to seal the quesadilla. Peel off the plastic. Trim the edges of the quesadilla with a sharp knife or large cookie cutter to make a neat border. Place the quesadilla on a baking sheet lined with plastic wrap, and cover with a towel to prevent drying. Assemble the remaining quesadillas in the same manner.

Preheat the oven to 250°F.

TO GRIDDLE-BAKE THE QUESADILLAS: Heat a large griddle or two 10- to 12-inch skillets over moderate heat until hot. Be sure the surface is not too hot or the quesadillas will brown too quickly before they cook through. Lightly brush the griddle and both sides of the quesadillas with melted butter. Place as many

— *cook's notes* —

Fresh shiitake mushrooms are available in many well-stocked supermarkets. Some markets call them Black Forest mushrooms.

Masa harina is made from fresh corn that has been soaked in water, dried, and ground to a powder. I use Quaker Oats Masa Harina, which is available in many supermarkets. If you have access to Mexican groceries, look for the Maseca brand. After opening, wrap the container tightly and store it in a dry area. Masa will last for at least a year.

If you are lucky enough to find epazote (called *pazote* in some parts of the United States), use it instead of the cilantro. Epazote is a tall, greenish plant with flat, pointed leaves that give a distinctive pungent flavor to many Mexican dishes.

As a variation, try the chicken and cheese filling for Crispy Chicken Flautas (page 202).

quesadillas as will fit on the griddle, and cook until lightly browned on the bottom, about 3 to 4 minutes. Using a metal spatula, turn the quesadillas over and cook until the second side is lightly browned, about 3 to 4 minutes. Remove the quesadillas to a baking sheet and keep warm in the oven while you cook the remaining quesadillas.

TO FRY THE QUESADILLAS: In a deep heavy saucepan or an electric fryer, heat 2 to 3 inches of oil to 350°F. Slide in a few quesadillas at a time and fry until crisp and golden brown, about 3 minutes. Use a slotted spoon to transfer the quesadillas to paper towels to drain. Keep the turnovers warm in the oven while you fry the rest.

TO SERVE: Place the quesadillas in a bread basket and cover with a cloth napkin to keep warm. Serve immediately.

Crispy Chicken Flautas

— planning ahead —

Although it is best to fry the flautas immediately after assembling them, they may be rolled up to an hour ahead, tightly covered with plastic wrap, and kept at room temperature. Do not refrigerate, or the tortillas will crack.

Flautas (literally, "flutes") are cylindrical meat-filled crispy fried tacos. Although almost any kind of firm ingredient can be used to stuff flautas, I find that roast chicken, smoked cheese, chiles, and a hint of cumin make one of the simplest and most addictive fillings. Serve these crunchy, irresistible little rolls as soon as they are cooked.

YIELD: 12 flautas, enough for 12 first-course or 6 light luncheon servings

CHICKEN AND SMOKED CHEESE FILLING

¾ pound cooked chicken meat, shredded (about 3 cups)
6 ounces smoked cheese, such as Gouda or Bruder Basil, grated (1½ cups)
1 4-ounce can chopped green chiles, drained
1 teaspoon ground cumin
Salt and freshly ground black pepper to taste

2 corn tortillas (1 12-ounce package)
Vegetable oil, for frying
Sour cream, for garnish (optional)

MAKE THE FILLING: In a mixing bowl, mix together the chicken, cheese, chiles, and cumin. Season with salt and pepper.

ASSEMBLE THE FLAUTAS: Work with one tortilla at a time, keeping the remaining tortillas covered with a clean kitchen towel.

Soften a tortilla by heating it briefly in a lightly greased skillet over moderate heat. Lay the tortilla flat on a plate. Spread about ¼ cup of the filling in a log shape across the bottom half of the tortilla, leaving about a ½-inch border. Roll the tortilla up tightly to form a cylinder. Fasten the seam shut with a toothpick. Assemble the remaining flautas in the same manner.

Preheat the oven to 250°F.

FRY THE FLAUTAS: Put slightly less than ¼ inch of oil in a 10- to 12-inch skillet set over moderately low heat, and heat to 365°F. (If the oil level is too high, the oil will seep right through the flautas and result in greasy rolls.)

Fry the flautas, a few at a time, until golden and crisp on the bottom, 1 to 2 minutes. Using tongs, turn the flautas over and cook for another minute or so. Transfer each batch to a baking sheet lined with paper towels to drain, and keep warm in the oven while you cook the remainder.

TO SERVE: Remove and discard the toothpicks. Place the flautas on a warm serving dish and top each with a dollop of sour cream if desired. Serve hot.

VARIATION

TEX-MEX CHICKEN TURNOVERS: Use the above filling and phyllo pastry to form Tex-Mex Chicken Turnovers. Follow the wrapping and baking instructions for Spanakopetes (page 52).

— cook's notes —

This is a dish to be eaten immediately after it is cooked. Do not reheat the flautas, or they will become leathery.

Cooked shredded turkey, pork, or veal can be used instead of chicken.

planning ahead

The mole sauce can be made a day ahead, covered, and refrigerated. The assembled enchiladas can be wrapped airtight in the pan with foil and refrigerated overnight or frozen for up to 1 month. Thaw in the refrigerator before baking.

Veal Enchiladas in Mole Sauce

I love making enchiladas because they are a lot of fun and naturally messy but oh, so good! In this recipe, I succeeded in matching some of my favorite ingredients, mole sauce, veal, and avocado, to come up with a sensational dish. The mole sauce may seem elaborate because of the number of ingredients, but it's easy and adds considerably to the flavor of the enchiladas. Try it!

YIELD: 12 enchiladas, enough for 12 first-course or 4 to 6 main-course servings

MOLE SAUCE

2 tablespoons olive oil
2 cups chopped onions
1 tablespoon minced garlic
2 teaspoons all-purpose flour
2 teaspoons dried oregano leaves
2 tablespoons chili powder
2 teaspoons ground cumin
2 teaspoons ground coriander
1 teaspoon cayenne pepper, or more to taste
2 cups canned tomatoes, undrained
2 cups chicken broth, homemade (page 368) or store-bought
1 teaspoon salt, or more to taste
1 tablespoon sugar, or more to taste
2 squares (2 ounces) semisweet chocolate, grated

VEAL FILLING

1 small veal roast (about 1 pound), preferably from the loin
1 teaspoon minced garlic
½ teaspoon ground cumin
½ teaspoon salt, plus more to taste
Freshly ground black pepper to taste
3 tablespoons olive oil
2 medium onions, sliced
1 large avocado, peeled, quartered, and cut into ½-inch pieces
8 ounces Monterey Jack cheese, shredded

FOR ASSEMBLY

12 corn tortillas (1 12-ounce package)
¼ cup grated mild Cheddar cheese

GARNISH

Sour cream
Diced tomatoes
Fresh cilantro sprigs

MAKE THE MOLE SAUCE: Heat the oil in a 10- to 12-inch nonreactive skillet over moderately low heat. When hot, add the onions and garlic and cook until the onions are soft, about 5 minutes. Whisk in the flour, oregano, the spices, tomatoes, and chicken broth and bring to a boil. Reduce the heat to low, cover, and simmer for 15 minutes, stirring occasionally. Whisk in the salt, sugar, and grated chocolate, cover, and continue to simmer until the sauce is slightly thickened, about

10 minutes longer. Transfer the sauce to a blender or a food processor fitted with the metal blade and purée. Taste the sauce and adjust the seasoning with salt, cayenne pepper, and a pinch of sugar if necessary. Return the sauce to the skillet, cover, and set aside.

MAKE THE FILLING: Trim off any excess fat from the veal. In a small bowl, mix together the garlic, cumin, salt, and black pepper. Rub the spice mixture over the veal.

Heat 1 tablespoon of the olive oil in a skillet set over moderately high heat. When the oil is hot, add the veal and brown it quickly on all sides, about 2 minutes. Cover the skillet, reduce the heat to moderately low, and cook the meat until it is well browned and cooked through, about 30 to 35 minutes; turn the meat every 5 minutes to prevent scorching. Remove the meat to a plate and cover with foil to keep warm.

Pour off the oil from the pan. Increase the heat to moderate and add the remaining 2 tablespoons oil. When the oil is hot, add the onions and sauté, scraping the bottom of the pan with a wooden spoon to release any browned bits, until the onions are lightly browned, about 3 minutes. Add the avocado, season with salt and pepper to taste, and cook until the avocado is just heated through, about 1 minute. Transfer to a large bowl and let cool.

Preheat the oven to 400°F.

Cut the veal into very thin slices, then cut the slices in half. Pour any juice from the meat into the mole sauce. Add the veal and Jack cheese to the onion mixture. To facilitate assembly, divide the filling into 12 equal portions on a baking sheet.

ASSEMBLE THE ENCHILADAS: Work with one tortilla at a time, keeping the remaining tortillas covered with a clean kitchen towel.

Lightly cover the bottom of a 9- by 13-inch baking pan with some mole sauce. Place the skillet with the remaining mole sauce over moderately low heat and heat until the sauce is just hot. Press a tortilla into the hot mole sauce. Let it sit until just softened, about 10 seconds. Using tongs, lift the tortilla and lay it flat on a plate. Scatter one portion of the filling across the bottom half of the tortilla. Roll the tortilla up around the filling, forming a tight cylinder. Place the roll seam side down in the prepared pan.

Assemble the remaining enchiladas in the same manner, placing them side by side in the pan. Pour the remaining mole sauce evenly over the enchiladas. Sprinkle with the Cheddar cheese.

Bake the enchiladas, uncovered, until the filling is heated through and the cheese melted, about 15 minutes.

TO SERVE: Place a dollop of sour cream on each enchilada and garnish with diced tomatoes and a sprig of cilantro.

— planning ahead —

The curry can be prepared ahead of time, covered, and refrigerated for up to 3 days or frozen for up to 1 month. If it has been frozen, thaw it overnight in the refrigerator before reheating.

Spiced Lamb Curry in Yogurt Bread

Naan, a flatbread made from wheat flour, is a staple food of northern India. It is traditionally baked in a special clay oven called a *tandoor.* The oven is shaped rather like a large barrel and is usually buried in sand or soil. The clay conducts the heat of the charcoal fire on the flat bottom of the tandoor up to its top. This oven is also used for baking other breads, such as tandoori roti, and for roasting meat and fish.

Fortunately, naan can be successfully made by cooking it on an ungreased griddle. This recipe uses a soft, slightly chewy naan made with yogurt for wrapping around the deliciously aromatic northern Indian lamb curry called Roghan Josh. A simple salad is all you need to complement this dish.

YIELD: 4 to 6 main-course servings

MARINADE

5 pods green cardamom (see Cook's Notes)
2 tablespoons coriander seeds
2 tablespoons cumin seeds
4 cloves
2 bay leaves, crumbled
1 cup low-fat yogurt, at room temperature
1 teaspoon salt

2½ pounds lean boneless lamb, preferably from the leg, cut into 1½-inch cubes

CURRY

4 tablespoons unsalted butter
2 medium onions, finely chopped
2 tablespoons minced garlic
1 2-inch piece fresh ginger (about 1 ounce), crushed and finely chopped
4 green chiles, coarsely chopped
1 large ripe tomato, peeled, seeded, and coarsely chopped (about 1¼ cups)
¼ cup tomato paste
1 teaspoon ground turmeric
1 teaspoon paprika
2 2-inch cinnamon sticks
Salt and freshly ground black pepper to taste

8 8-inch rounds of Naan (Indian Yogurt Bread) (page 207)

PREPARE THE MARINADE: Split the cardamom pods open and remove the seeds. Discard the pods. Put the cardamom, coriander, and cumin seeds into a dry skillet over moderate heat. Heat for about 5 minutes, shaking the pan constantly, until the seeds give off a fragrant aroma. Transfer the seeds to a mortar, add the cloves and bay leaves, and, using a pestle, crush the spices until they are finely ground. Or finely grind the spice mixture in a spice grinder. Combine the ground spices, the yogurt, and salt in a large mixing bowl.

MARINATE THE LAMB: Add the lamb cubes to the marinade. Using your hands, toss well to coat the lamb. Cover the bowl and let marinate at room temperature for at least 2 hours, or refrigerate overnight.

PREPARE THE CURRY: Melt the butter in a Dutch oven over moderate heat. Add the onions, garlic, ginger, and chiles. Cook, stirring frequently with a wooden spoon, until the vegetables are tender and fragrant, about 2 minutes. Add the tomato, tomato paste, turmeric, paprika, and cinnamon sticks and cook, stirring, until a thick paste is formed, about 3 minutes. Add the lamb along with the marinade to the pan, and stir to blend all the ingredients. When the mixture begins to bubble, reduce the heat to low, cover the pot, and simmer, stirring occasionally, until the lamb is very tender, about 1 hour and 15 minutes.

Meanwhile, prepare the naans. Stack them, place in a serving basket, and cover with a clean kitchen towel to keep them soft and warm.

When the curry is done, remove from the heat. Taste and adjust the seasonings with salt and pepper if necessary. Ladle the curry into a serving bowl.

TO SERVE: Each diner should spoon a small amount of lamb curry into a round of bread, fold the bread up to enclose the filling, and eat out of hand.

cook's notes

Cardamom, a highly aromatic spice, is widely used in India as a flavoring, particularly in rice dishes and curries. Dried green cardamom is available in Indian markets. Each pod contains two clusters of approximately six dark seeds each. In order to preserve their aromatic flavor, do not take the seeds out of the pods until they are ready for use. If the pods are not available, use ground cardamom, which is less aromatic.

Beef, veal, or pork may be used instead of lamb. As an alternative to the homemade naan bread, use warmed flour tortillas or pocketless pita bread.

NAAN (INDIAN YOGURT BREAD)

To store naans, cool to room temperature, wrap in a plastic bag, refrigerate for up to a week or freeze for up to 1 month. To reheat, wrap stacks of 2 or 3 naans in foil, and place the foil-wrapped breads in a preheated 400°F oven just until heated through, about 10 to 15 minutes.

YIELD: Eight 8-inch rounds

DOUGH

3½ cups unbleached all-purpose flour, plus additional if necessary
2 teaspoons sugar
1½ teaspoons salt
1 teaspoon baking powder
½ teaspoon baking soda
1½ cups yogurt

continued

MAKE THE DOUGH

Hand method: Sift the flour, sugar, salt, baking powder, and baking soda together into a large mixing bowl. Make a well in the middle and add the yogurt to the well. Using a wooden spoon, draw the flour into the yogurt to blend until the mixture clumps together into a rough dough. Gather it together and briefly knead in the bowl until the dough forms a soft ball. If the dough feels sticky, sprinkle on a little flour. If it feels dry or flaky, add up to 1 tablespoon water a teaspoon at a time. Turn the dough out onto a lightly floured work surface and knead for 8 to 10 minutes, or until smooth and elastic.

Food processor method: Place the flour, sugar, salt, baking powder, and baking soda in the bowl of a food processor fitted with the metal blade. Pulse to blend. Add the yogurt and process until the dough forms a soft ball and rides on the blade, about 10 seconds. The dough should be soft but not sticky; if it seems too sticky, add about 1 tablespoon flour and process until the dough leaves the sides of the bowl. Continue to process the dough for 45 seconds, or until very smooth and elastic. Turn the dough out onto a lightly floured work surface and shape it into a ball.

LET THE DOUGH REST: Divide the dough into 8 pieces. Roll each piece into a ball. Place the dough balls on a lightly floured baking sheet and cover with a towel. Allow the dough to relax at room temperature for 30 minutes.

ROLL THE DOUGH: Work with one piece of dough at a time, keeping the remainder covered with a towel to prevent them from drying out.

Lightly press one ball of dough into a disk. On a lightly floured work surface, roll the dough into an 8-inch round about ⅛ inch thick. Each time you roll the dough, pick it up and rotate it a sixth of a turn to the right. This will help achieve the round shape of the naan (don't worry if they are not perfectly round; they will taste just as good).

Roll the remaining dough portions in the same manner, lightly dusting each naan with flour and stacking it on a large plate.

COOK THE NAANS: Heat a griddle or a large dry skillet over moderately low heat until it is hot. Be sure the griddle is not too hot or the bread will brown too quickly before it cooks through. Place a naan on the hot griddle and cook until the bread puffs up lightly and browns on the bottom, about 2 minutes. Turn the naan with your fingers or a wide spatula and cook for 2 minutes longer. Remove the naan to a large plate or bread basket and cover with a cloth napkin to keep warm. Cook the remaining naans in the same manner.

The naans will stay warm for hours if you wrap them, napkin and all, in foil and put them into a barely warm (150°F) oven.

PHOTOGRAPH BY BETH GALTON

Moroccan Chicken Pie
(page 60)

PHOTOGRAPH BY BETH GALTON

Whole Red Snapper en Papillote, Mediterranean Style

(page 320)

PHOTOGRAPH BY BETH GALTON

Panfried Lamb Manti with Yogurt Sauce
(page 258)

PHOTOGRAPH BY BETH GALTON

Chocolate Purses with Rhubarb-Raspberry Mousse
(page 362)

Lobster Belle Nicole
(page 243)

Smoked Turkey Rolls with Basil Sauce
(page 292)

Asian Appetizers (*clockwise from top*):
Vietnamese Spring Rolls (page 294);
Grilled Beef and Scallion Rolls (page 342);
Shao Mai with Chicken, Shrimp, and Mushrooms (page 260);
and Spiced Tuna and Chickpea Samosas (page 125)

Green Pasta Crab Rolls with Spinach Broth
(page 240)

Sausage in Saffron Brioche
(page 174)

Trio of Phyllo Desserts (*clockwise from left*):
Pistachio Baklava (page 76), Lemony Rhubarb Turnovers (page 82),
and Chocolate Plum Purses (page 80)

Individual Fillets of Beef en Croûte with
Green Peppercorn Mustard Sauce
(page 99)

Lemon Cheese Blintzes with Blueberry Sauce
(page 308)

Herbed Venison Roast in Salt Crust
(page 328)

Deep-Dish Vegetarian Strudel Pie
(page 66)

Roast Sesame Pork in Phyllo
(page 69)

Undercover Chunky Tomato Soup (page 88)
and Knishes with Broccoli and Cheddar (page 131)

Molded Rice Salad Provençale
(page 18)

Veal and Mashed Potato Loaf
(page 340)

Latin-American Party (*clockwise from top*):
Spicy Chilean Empanadas (page 116);
Grilled Beef Fajitas, Vietnamese Style (page 192);
Corn Quesadillas with Wild Mushrooms and Cheese (page 200);
and Crispy Chicken Flautas (page 202)

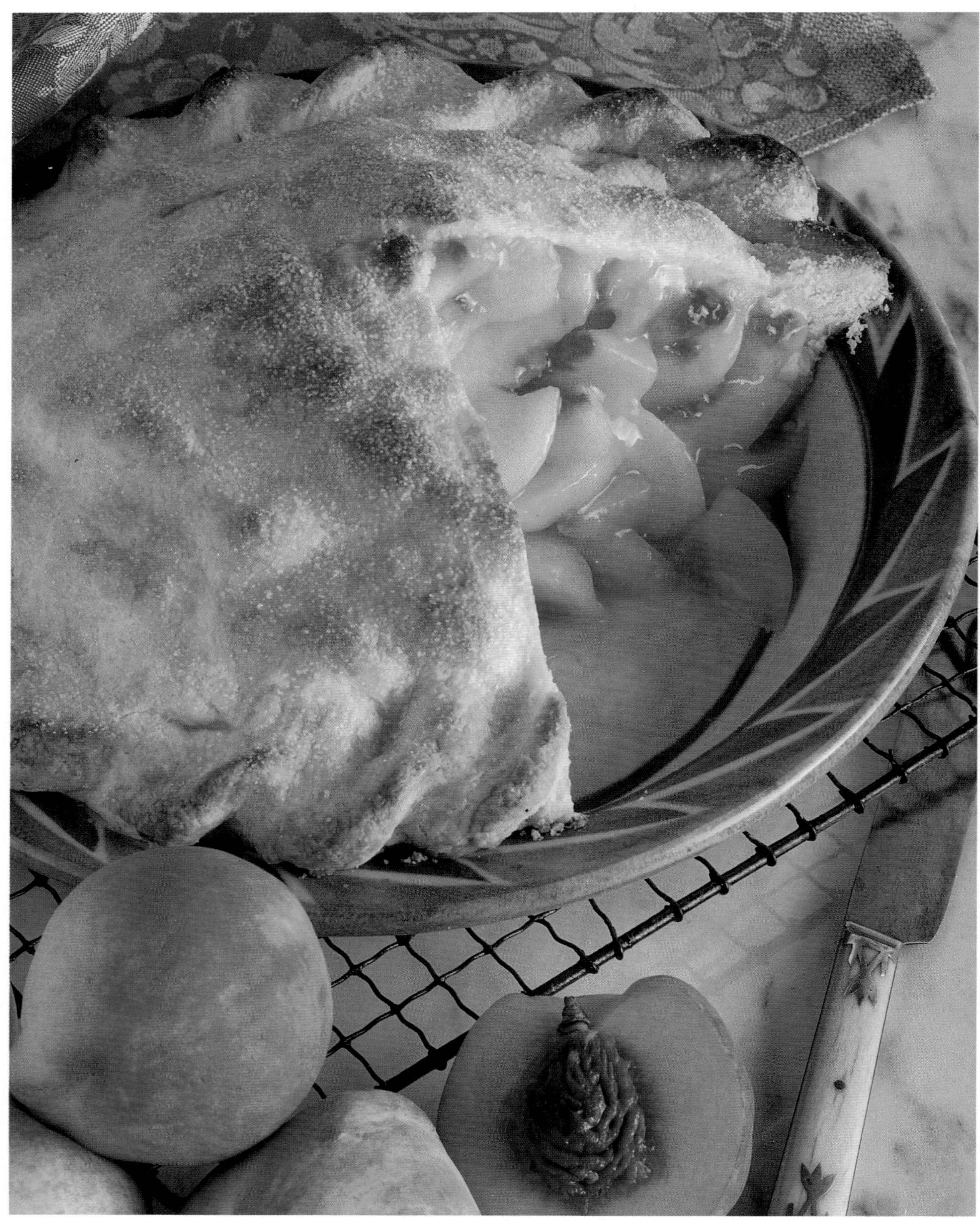

High-Rise Peach Pie
(page 149)

Barbecued Chicken in Corn Bread
(page 172)

Lobster and Scallops Grilled in Corn Husks
(page 32)

Smoked Chicken Burritos
(page 188)

Potato Pirogi with Smothered Onions and Cabbage
(page 266)

Curried Chicken Rotis

Roti is a delectable flatbread-wrapped curry sandwich made popular in the West Indies by the islands' Indian population. Although it takes its name from a type of Indian griddle bread, roti is a local invention, with no equivalent in India. The flatbread itself is called a purie, but it resembles the Indian poorie in name only. A poorie is a small, deep-fried flatbread, and a purie is a large round of griddle-baked flatbread.

In Trinidad's roti shops, a round of purie dough is first slapped on a griddle and allowed to cook until the bread is bubbly. The soft purie is then wrapped like a blanket around a curried filling, usually goat, fish, or vegetable, and the hot sandwich is eaten out of hand.

These rotis are made with a truly special version of chicken and potato curry, for which I prepare my own curry paste. Since rotis can be very filling, I serve them as a main course, either for lunch or dinner. You will find making and serving rotis to be an experience in itself, every bit worth your time. Make sure you have lots of napkins and beer on hand!

YIELD: 6 rotis, enough for 6 main-course servings

ROASTED CURRY PASTE

¼ cup chopped shallots
¼ cup minced garlic
1 tablespoon minced peeled fresh ginger
4 jalapeño peppers, seeded and finely chopped
1 tablespoon curry powder, preferably Madras brand
½ teaspoon ground cumin
1 anchovy fillet packed in oil, drained and chopped
2 tablespoons peanut oil
1 tablespoon sugar
½ teaspoon salt

CURRIED CHICKEN FILLING

1 pound chicken thighs, boned, skinned, and cut into 1-inch pieces
3 tablespoons vegetable oil
1 large russet potato (about 10 ounces), peeled and cut into ¾-inch cubes
1 cup chopped onions
2 teaspoons minced garlic
2 scallions, thinly sliced
1 tablespoon curry powder, preferably Madras brand
¼ teaspoon turmeric
1 cup chicken broth, homemade (page 368) or store-bought
¼ cup unsweetened coconut milk (see Cook's Notes) or heavy cream
⅓ cup fresh or frozen green peas
Salt to taste

1 recipe Puries (page 211)

— *planning ahead* —

The curry paste can be prepared up to a week in advance, covered, and refrigerated. Both the dough for the puries and the chicken curry can be prepared a day in advance, covered, and refrigerated. The puries can be cooked several hours before serving, wrapped in foil, and kept warm in a low oven.

— cook's notes —

Do not confuse coconut milk with coconut cream. Excellent canned unsweetened coconut milk is available in Asian markets and some supermarkets. After opening, it can be refrigerated for up to 1 week. For longer storage, freeze it in ice cube trays, then store the cubes in plastic bags. Before using, heat the frozen coconut milk until completely melted. Four cubes equal about ½ cup. You may substitute heavy cream for the coconut milk, but the taste will be slightly altered.

The curry paste can be made in larger quantities if desired, because it keeps very well in the refrigerator. (The recipe makes about ⅓ cup.) Use it, as I do, to enhance other curried dishes. To store, put the curry paste in a glass jar and add just enough peanut oil or vegetable oil to cover the paste. Cover and refrigerate for up to 2 months. Do not freeze, or the curry paste will lose its aroma.

If you like your food extra spicy, add some chopped Scotch Bonnet peppers (known as the world's hottest peppers!) or hot pepper sauce to the chicken curry.

As an alternative to homemade puries, you can use store-bought Indian chappati or paratha breads, available in Indian grocery stores. Heat them before serving.

PREPARE THE CURRY PASTE: Wrap the shallots, garlic, ginger, and jalapeños in a sheet of aluminum foil, making a flat package, and seal well. Place the package directly on a gas or electric burner set at moderate heat and cook until fragrant, about 1 minute on each side, turning with tongs. Allow the package to cool. Unwrap and transfer the contents to a spice grinder or blender. Add the curry powder, cumin, and anchovy, and process to a fine paste.

Heat the oil in a small skillet or frying pan over moderate heat. Add the paste and stir-fry until brown and fragrant, about 3 minutes. Stir in the sugar and salt. Transfer the curry paste to a small container.

PREPARE THE FILLING: In a medium bowl, combine the chicken, 2 tablespoons of the curry paste, and 1 tablespoon of the oil and toss to mix well. Cover and let marinate at room temperature for 30 minutes. Cover the remaining curry paste and set aside.

Heat 1 tablespoon of the oil in a large frying pan set over high heat. When the oil is hot, add the marinated chicken and sauté until lightly browned, about 1 minute. Add the potato cubes and sauté, stirring, until they are well coated with oil and spices, about 1 minute longer. (The chicken and potatoes will not be completely cooked at this point.) Transfer the mixture to a bowl.

Add the remaining 1 tablespoon oil to the skillet and reduce the heat to moderate. When the oil is hot, add the onions, garlic, and scallions. Cook until the vegetables are soft, about 2 minutes. Add the reserved curry paste, the curry powder, and turmeric. Cook, stirring with a wooden spoon, until the spices turn golden brown, about 5 minutes. Add the chicken broth and coconut milk and bring to a boil over moderately high heat, scraping the bottom of the pan to release any browned bits. Return the chicken and potato mixture to the skillet. Cook uncovered, stirring occasionally, until the chicken is cooked through and the potatoes are tender, about 15 minutes. Add the peas and cook until the sauce is thickened, about 5 minutes longer. Remove from the heat. Taste and adjust the seasoning with salt if necessary. Cover and set aside until ready to serve.

Prepare the puries. Fold them into quarters, then place in a serving basket and cover with a clean kitchen towel to keep warm.

TO SERVE: Reheat the filling over moderate heat. Place one sixth of the filling in the center of each purie. Fold over the bottom and sides of the purie to enclose the filling, forming a package like an unsealed envelope. Wrap a napkin around each roti and eat out of hand.

PURIES

Puries do not store well. They are best eaten the day they are made.

YIELD: 6 large puries

2 cups unbleached all-purpose flour, plus additional if necessary
1 teaspoon baking powder
1 teaspoon salt
½ teaspoon turmeric
2 tablespoons unsalted butter, at room temperature
6 tablespoons unsalted butter, melted, for cooking

MAKE THE DOUGH

Hand method: Sift the flour and baking powder together into a large mixing bowl. Make a well in the middle. Add the salt, turmeric, and ¾ cup plus 1 tablespoon water to the well. Using a wooden spoon, stir the liquid in the well to dissolve the salt and turmeric. With the spoon, draw the flour into the liquid to blend until the mixture clumps together into a rough dough. Gather it together and briefly knead in the bowl until the dough forms a soft ball. The dough should be moist and very soft but not sticky. If it feels sticky, knead in about a tablespoon more flour. Turn the dough out onto a well-floured work surface. Place the 2 tablespoons butter on the dough and knead until it is incorporated. If the dough feels sticky, sprinkle on a little flour. Knead the dough until it is smooth and shiny, about 5 minutes. Shape the dough into a ball.

Food processor method: Place the flour and baking powder in the bowl of a food processor fitted with the metal blade. In a small bowl, combine the salt, turmeric, and ¾ cup plus 1 tablespoon water. Stir to dissolve the salt and turmeric. With the motor on, gradually add the liquid through the feed tube of the food processor, and process until the dough cleans the sides of the bowl and rides on the blade, about 10 seconds. Add the softened butter and continue to process until it is incorporated into the dough, about 10 seconds longer. The dough should be very moist but not sticky. If it feels sticky, add about a tablespoon more flour. Turn the dough out onto a lightly floured work surface and shape it into a smooth ball.

LET THE DOUGH REST: Divide the dough into 6 pieces. Roll each piece into a ball and lightly dust with flour. Place the balls in an oiled bowl, cover with a damp towel, and set aside for 1 to 3 hours to allow the dough to relax.

ROLL THE DOUGH: Work with one piece of dough at a time, keeping the remainder covered with a towel to prevent them from drying out.

Lightly flatten one ball of dough into a disk. On a lightly floured work surface, roll the dough into a thin 9-inch round about 1⁄16 inch thick. Each time you roll over the dough, pick it up and rotate it a sixth of a turn to the right. This will help achieve the round shape of the purie. (Don't worry if it is not perfectly round; it will taste just as good.) Dust the work surface with flour as necessary to prevent the dough from sticking. Roll the remaining dough in the same manner, lightly dusting each purie with flour and stacking them on a large plate.

COOK THE PURIES: Generously brush a large skillet or griddle with melted butter and set it over moderately high heat. When hot, place a purie on the skillet and cook until it is light golden brown on the bottom and small bubbles appear on the surface, about 1 minute. Use the back of a spatula or spoon to press down on the purie to flatten it. Generously brush the top side with melted butter and, using a spatula or your fingers, turn the purie over. Cook until the second side is light golden brown, about 1 minute. (When cooked, the bread should feel like a damp cloth.) Fold the purie into quarters, then place on a large plate or in a bread basket and cover with a cloth napkin to keep warm. Cook the remaining puries in the same manner, brushing the pan with more butter before adding each one.

The puries will stay warm for an hour or so if you wrap them, napkin and all, in foil and put them into a barely warm (150°F) oven.

Falafel with Yogurt-Tahini Sauce

Falafel is a favorite Middle Eastern vegetarian treat made of a mixture of highly spiced ground chickpeas and wheat, formed into balls, and deep-fried. Although the fritters can be served on their own as appetizers, they become really interesting when they are stuffed into pita bread and topped with a tahini sauce. Serving falafel this way is especially popular in Israel, where it is sold on every street corner as the "Israeli hot dog."

In my adaptation of this dish, the falafel is wrapped in pocketless pita bread instead of being stuffed in a pita pocket. The interesting contrast between the crunch of the fritters, the chewiness of the bread, and the nutty, cooling yogurt and tahini sauce make this tasty sandwich all the more delightful.

YIELD: 24 fritters, enough for 6 to 8 light main-course servings or 24 hors d'oeuvres

FALAFEL FRITTERS

½ cup chickpeas
1½ tablespoons bulghur or cracked wheat
1 tablespoon all-purpose flour
2 tablespoons wheat germ
2 tablespoons minced onion
2 tablespoons chopped fresh parsley
½ teaspoon baking soda
1 tablespoon minced garlic
1 teaspoon light soy sauce
¼ teaspoon salt
¼ teaspoon crushed dried red pepper
1 tablespoon ground cumin
¼ teaspoon ground coriander
½ teaspoon turmeric

YOGURT-TAHINI SAUCE

1½ cups yogurt
½ cup tahini paste (see Cook's Notes)
2 teaspoons minced garlic
2 tablespoons minced fresh parsley
½ teaspoon fresh lemon juice
Salt and cayenne pepper, to taste
8 8-inch Homemade Pita Breads (page 186)
Corn oil, for deep-frying

ACCOMPANIMENTS

1 red onion, finely diced
1 small green bell pepper, finely diced
3 small tomatoes, finely diced
1 small cucumber, peeled, seeded, and finely diced

Place the chickpeas in a small bowl and cover with water. Let soak for at least 6 hours at room temperature, or overnight in the refrigerator.

In a medium bowl, soak the bulghur or cracked wheat in water to cover for 1 hour at room temperature.

continued

— planning ahead —

The chickpeas should be soaked for at least 6 hours, or overnight. Both the homemade pita breads and yogurt sauce can be prepared a day in advance, covered, and refrigerated. The uncooked falafel balls and the accompaniments can be prepared up to 4 hours ahead of time, covered, and refrigerated.

— *cook's notes* —

Do not use canned chickpeas for this recipe. They lack the crunch that gives the sandwich its special texture.

As a quick alternative to the fritters, instant falafel mix can be used. Both falafel and tahini paste are available in health food stores and in many supermarkets.

If you use store-bought instead of homemade pocketless pita breads, reheat them before serving. To reheat, wrap them in foil in stacks of 2. Place the foil-wrapped pita breads in a preheated 400°F oven until they are soft, about 15 minutes.

The fritters, accompanied by the sauce, make perfect hors d'oeuvres.

PREPARE THE FRITTERS: Drain the chickpeas and bulghur. Place them in the bowl of a food processor fitted with the metal blade. Process until finely ground but not puréed, stopping to scrape down the sides of the bowl with a rubber spatula as necessary. Transfer to a mixing bowl and stir in the remaining fritter ingredients until well mixed.

Moisten your hands with water. Shape about 1 tablespoon of the fritter mixture into a compact ball and place it on a large plate. Make the remaining balls in the same manner. You should have 24 balls. Cover with plastic wrap and refrigerate.

PREPARE THE YOGURT-TAHINI SAUCE: Combine the yogurt, tahini paste, garlic, parsley, and lemon juice in the container of an electric blender. Blend until smooth. Pour the sauce into a small bowl. Season with salt and cayenne pepper, cover, and refrigerate.

Prepare the pita breads. Wrap them in foil and keep warm in a preheated 250°F oven while you cook the fritters.

COOK THE FRITTERS: In a deep heavy saucepan or an electric fryer, heat about 3 inches of oil to 350°F. Add the fritters in batches and fry until golden brown and crisp, about 1 minute. Remove the fritters with a slotted spoon and drain on paper towels. Keep the deep-fried fritters warm in the oven while you cook the remainder.

TO SERVE: Set out the fritters, pita breads, yogurt-tahini sauce, and the diced onion, pepper, tomatoes, and cucumber on the table. To eat, slightly crush a few fritters and put them on one half of a pita bread. Add some of the diced vegetables and top with some yogurt sauce. Fold the pita up to enclose the filling and eat out of hand.

Souvlaki Gyros

Popular street food in Greece, gyros are rapidly becoming familiar fare in large cities throughout the United States. A gyro is a superb sandwich loaded with thin slices of grilled sausage or souvlaki, chunks of lamb grilled on skewers like shish kebab. It is usually topped with plenty of fresh vegetables, such as onions, lettuce, tomatoes, and peppers, and seasoned with either hot sauce or a garlicky yogurt and cucumber sauce called tzatziki. I like to use a red pepper mayonnaise to give this pushcart staple more depth of taste. Here I offer recipes for both the mayonnaise and tzatziki so you can experiment.

Gyros make a perfect dish for backyard entertaining. Round off the meal with French fries (try making them with sweet potatoes) sprinkled with Cajun spices and a bottle of fruity red wine.

YIELD: 8 main-course servings

SPECIAL EQUIPMENT: 8 metal skewers or presoaked 10-inch-long bamboo skewers

2 pounds lean boneless lamb, preferably from the leg, cut into 1½-inch cubes

MARINADE

⅔ cup chopped onions
⅔ cup chopped fresh parsley
⅔ cup olive oil
⅓ cup fresh lemon juice
2 tablespoons minced garlic
2 tablespoons dried oregano leaves
1 tablespoon freshly ground black pepper
1 teaspoon salt

Red Pepper Mayonnaise or Tzatziki (pages 216 and 217)
1 medium onion, thinly sliced
1 tablespoon red wine vinegar
8 8-inch Homemade Pita Breads (page 186)
2 cups shredded romaine lettuce
2 medium tomatoes, halved and thinly sliced
Tabasco or hot sauce (optional)

MARINATE THE LAMB: Place the lamb cubes in a large nonreactive mixing bowl. Combine all the marinade ingredients in the bowl of a food processor fitted with the metal blade, and process to a purée. Pour the marinade over the lamb. Using your hands, toss the meat to coat well with the marinade. Cover and let marinate for at least 4 hours at room temperature, or refrigerate overnight.

continued

— planning ahead —

The marinated lamb, homemade pita breads, and mayonnaise or yogurt sauce can be prepared a day in advance, covered, and refrigerated. The accompaniments can be prepared up to 4 hours ahead of time, covered, and refrigerated.

If you are using bamboo skewers, they must be presoaked in water for 30 minutes.

— cook's notes —

Cubes of marinated pork loin or boneless chicken thighs can be substituted for the lamb.

If you don't have a grill, the brochettes can be broiled in the oven.

If you use store-bought instead of homemade pocketless pita breads, reheat them before serving. To reheat, wrap them in foil in stacks of 2. Place the foil-wrapped pita breads in a preheated 400°F oven until they are soft, about 15 minutes.

Prepare the mayonnaise and/or tzatziki, cover, and refrigerate.

Toss the onion with the vinegar, cover, and refrigerate.

Prepare the pita breads. Wrap in foil and keep warm in a preheated 250°F oven while you cook the lamb.

Bring the lamb to room temperature. Thread the lamb cubes onto the skewers.

COOK THE LAMB: Prepare a medium-hot fire in a grill. Place the lamb brochettes on the grill and cook, turning them frequently, until the lamb is medium rare, about 7 minutes. Transfer the brochettes to a warm platter, and remove the lamb from the skewers.

TO SERVE: Set out the pita breads, lamb, the mayonnaise and/or tzatziki, onion, lettuce, and tomatoes at the table for guests to help themselves. To eat, spread some mayonnaise or tzatziki over a pita. Distribute a few cubes of lamb on the bread and top with onion, lettuce, and tomatoes. Sprinkle with a few drops of Tabasco sauce, if desired, roll up the pita, and eat the sandwich out of hand.

RED PEPPER MAYONNAISE

YIELD: About 2 cups

1 medium red bell pepper
1 fresh or pickled jalapeño pepper, seeded and chopped
2 large egg yolks
2 teaspoons minced garlic
1 tablespoon Dijon mustard
1 tablespoon red wine vinegar
1 teaspoon Tabasco sauce
½ teaspoon dried oregano leaves
¼ teaspoon dried basil leaves
½ teaspoon sugar
¼ teaspoon salt, or more to taste
Pinch of cayenne pepper, or more to taste
1¼ cups vegetable oil

Place the bell pepper directly on a gas or electric burner set at moderate heat and grill, turning the pepper with tongs, until the flesh is soft and the skin charred, about 4 minutes. Alternatively, cut the pepper in half lengthwise, place it in skin side up under a preheated broiler, and broil until the skin is blackened. Place the pepper on a plate and let stand for 5 minutes. Hold the pepper under cold running water and rub the skin off. Pat dry, core, seed, and coarsely chop.

Place the chopped bell pepper in a food processor or a blender. Add all the remaining ingredients except the oil, and process to a purée. With the motor on, slowly drizzle in the oil and blend until thickened. Taste and adjust the seasoning with salt and cayenne pepper if necessary. Transfer to a small container, cover, and refrigerate. The mayonnaise will keep for up to 2 weeks in the refrigerator.

TZATZIKI (CUCUMBER AND YOGURT SAUCE)

YIELD: About 2½ cups

1 small cucumber
2 cups yogurt
2 teaspoons minced garlic
2 teaspoons distilled white vinegar
3 tablespoons extra-virgin olive oil
Salt and freshly ground white pepper to taste

Peel, seed, and coarsely grate the cucumber. Squeeze the cucumber between your hands to extract as much liquid as possible. You should have about ½ cup cucumber.

Place the cucumber and the remaining ingredients in the container of an electric blender. Pulse to blend. Transfer the sauce to a bowl, cover, and refrigerate for at least 2 hours, or overnight, for the flavors to meld. This sauce will keep for up to 1 week in the refrigerator.

— *planning ahead* —

The shrimp and chicken can be marinated a day ahead, covered, and refrigerated. The sauce for the stir-fry and the pancakes can be made a day in advance, covered, and refrigerated.

Dragon and Phoenix in Lotus Leaves

To most people, mu shu is a fairly ordinary Chinese dish made with a stir-fry of shredded pork, beef, or chicken wrapped in flexible pancakes. By making it at home, you can bring it to new heights with a more inventive filling, such as the succulent tangerine-flavored shrimp and chicken mixture in this recipe. Following the Chinese style of giving metaphoric and poetic terms to their food, the "lotus leaves" refer to the po ping pancakes, "dragon" to the shrimp, and "phoenix" to the chicken. As far as I'm concerned, one of the most delicious things about this dish is the informal and messy way of eating it out of hand.

YIELD: 4 main-course or 6 first-course servings

8 ounces raw medium shrimp, peeled, deveined, and halved lengthwise
8 ounces skinless boneless chicken thighs (about 4), cut into ¼-inch-thick strips about 2½ inches long

MARINADE

1 tablespoon dry sherry
1 tablespoon light soy sauce
1 egg white, lightly beaten
1 tablespoon cornstarch

TANGERINE SAUCE

¼ cup chicken broth
2 tablespoons fresh tangerine juice or orange juice
2 tablespoons dry sherry
2 tablespoons oyster sauce
2 tablespoons hoisin sauce
1 teaspoon sugar
2 teaspoons Oriental sesame oil
1 tablespoon cornstarch
¼ teaspoon Szechuan hot chili bean paste

½ cup unsalted roasted peanuts

Po Ping Pancakes (page 219)

STIR-FRY

¼ cup peanut oil
1 tablespoon shredded peeled fresh ginger
1 tablespoon minced garlic
1 tablespoon minced fresh tangerine or orange peel
2 ounces fresh snow peas, cut into julienne strips
10 fresh or canned water chestnuts, peeled and sliced
4 scallions, cut into 1-inch lengths
1 red bell pepper, cut into julienne strips
Hoisin sauce, for serving

MARINATE THE SHRIMP AND CHICKEN: Place the shrimp, chicken, and all the marinade ingredients in a mixing bowl. Using your hands, toss well to coat the chicken and shrimp with the marinade. Cover and refrigerate.

PREPARE THE SAUCE: Combine all ingredients for the sauce in a small bowl. Cover and set aside.

TOAST THE PEANUTS: Place the nuts in a dry skillet over moderate heat and cook, stirring constantly, until light golden and fragrant, about 3 minutes. Remove the pan from the heat and set aside to cool.

Prepare the pancakes. Wrap them in foil and keep warm in a preheated 250°F oven.

COOK THE STIR-FRY: Place 2 tablespoons of the oil in a wok or large skillet over high heat. When the oil is very hot, add the marinated chicken and shrimp. Stir-fry until the chicken turns white and the shrimp pink, about 2 minutes. Remove to a bowl. Add the remaining 2 tablespoons oil to the wok. When hot, add the ginger, garlic, and tangerine peel. Stir-fry for about 5 seconds, then add the snow peas, water chestnuts, scallions, and bell pepper. Stir-fry until the vegetables are just soft, about 1 minute. Return the shrimp and chicken to the wok. Add the tangerine sauce and peanuts, and stir-fry until the sauce thickens slightly, about 1 minute. Transfer to a warm platter.

TO SERVE: Set out the stir-fry, hot pancakes, and a dish of hoisin sauce at the table for guests to help themselves. To eat, spread some hoisin sauce on a pancake. Spoon some of the stir-fry onto the middle of the pancake. Fold up the pancake to enclose the filling and eat out of hand.

VARIATION

STIR-FRIED SHRIMP AND CHICKEN IN LETTUCE CUPS: Brush the inside of crisp lettuce leaves (such as Bibb, iceberg, or Italian radicchio) with hoisin sauce, then spoon some of the stir-fry onto them. Sprinkle with ground toasted peanuts. Fold over the lettuce to eat out of hand. Serve as a first course.

PO PING PANCAKES

These sophisticated Chinese pancakes are also known as Mandarin pancakes or mu shu pancakes. They are also sometimes called Peking pancakes because they are served with the famous Peking duck, to be wrapped around pieces of crackling roast duck skin, strips of fresh cucumbers, and scallions.

The boiling water added to the dough for these pancakes yields wrappers that are slightly resilient to the bite.

continued

To store the pancakes, allow them to cool, stack them, and then seal in a plastic storage bag. They can be refrigerated for up to 2 days or frozen for up to 1 month. Defrost frozen pancakes overnight in the refrigerator before reheating. To reheat, line a flat-bottomed steamer with a clean wet cloth. Stack the pancakes on the cloth and fold the cloth over them. Cover and steam until the pancakes are warm and soft, about 5 minutes. Transfer the pancakes to a serving basket and cover with a clean kitchen towel.

Since the pancakes dry out quickly, serve just a few at a time, keeping the remainder covered.

It is possible to buy mu shu pancakes in packages of a dozen at most Chinese markets. Just be aware that they are virtually lifeless on the tastebuds!

YIELD: Twelve 6½-inch pancakes

1 cup unbleached all-purpose flour, plus additional if necessary
½ cup less 1 tablespoon boiling water
Oriental sesame oil, for rolling

MAKE THE DOUGH

Hand method: Place the flour in a mixing bowl. Drizzle the boiling water over the flour. Using a fork, blend until all the liquid has been absorbed and the dough clumps together. Allow the dough to cool slightly, then gather the dough into a soft ball in the bowl. If the dough feels sticky, add a little flour. If it feels dry or flaky, add up to 1 tablespoon more hot water a teaspoon at a time. Turn the dough out onto a lightly floured work surface and knead until smooth and satiny, about 5 minutes. Shape the dough into a smooth ball.

Food processor method: Place the flour in the bowl of a food processor fitted with the metal blade. With the motor on, gradually add the boiling water through the feed tube, and process until the dough cleans the sides of the bowl and rides on the blade, about 10 seconds. The dough should be smooth and supple. If the dough sticks to the bowl, add about a tablespoon of flour and process until the dough cleans the sides of the bowl. Turn the dough out onto a lightly floured surface and shape it into a smooth ball.

LET THE DOUGH REST: Cover the dough with a damp kitchen towel and let it rest at room temperature for at least 30 minutes, or up to 1 hour.

ROLL THE DOUGH: Roll the dough into a 12-inch-long log. Divide it evenly into 12 portions, and roll each portion into a ball. Flatten each ball into a 2½-inch disk. Work with 2 dough rounds at a time, keeping the remaining dough covered with a towel.

Generously grease a work surface with sesame oil. Place one round of dough on the surface and generously brush sesame oil over it. Place another round of dough on top of it and press down to seal the two and prevent slipping. With a rolling pin, roll the dough from the center out to a very thin 6½-inch circle. Place the rolled-out dough on a plate and cover with a piece of waxed paper. Roll the remaining dough in the same manner, stacking and separating the circles with wax paper. (Each dough circle will make two pancakes.)

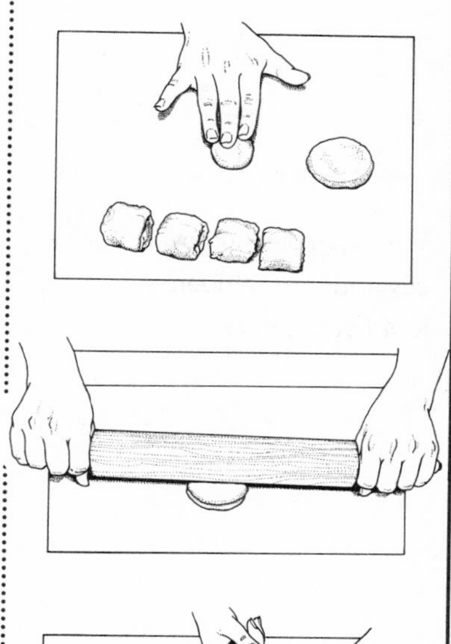

COOK THE PANCAKES: Heat a large ungreased skillet or griddle over moderately low heat until hot. Add a dough circle and cook for about 30 seconds, then turn and cook for about 10 seconds longer, taking care not to let the dough brown. Slide the circle onto a plate or into a bread basket. Let cool for about 15 seconds. Separate the 2 pancakes at the edges and gently peel apart. Cover with a cloth napkin to keep warm. Cook the remaining pancakes in the same manner.

The pancakes will stay warm for hours if you wrap them, napkin and all, in foil and put them into a barely warm (150°F) oven.

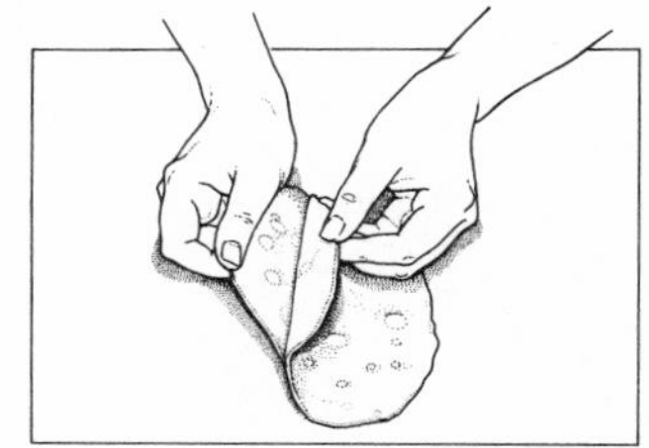

— *planning ahead* —

The assembled turnovers can be covered and refrigerated for up to 4 hours before cooking.

Chinese Griddle Cakes Gone American

This title says it all. The dough is Chinese inspired, the filling, American. A luscious mixture of eggs, smoked salmon, apples, cream cheese, and scallions is encased in a crisp chewy crust, similar to a calzone. They are absolutely delicious for brunch, accompanied with sausage or bacon, a salad, and chilled Champagne.

YIELD: 4 large turnovers, enough for 4 brunch or light lunch servings

DOUGH

2 cups unbleached all-purpose flour, plus additional if necessary
1½ teaspoons baking powder
½ teaspoon salt
½ cup plus 3 tablespoons boiling water

SMOKED SALMON FILLING

8 large eggs
2 tablespoons heavy cream
2 tablespoons chopped scallions
2 tablespoons unsalted butter
1 Granny Smith apple, peeled, cored, and cut into medium dice
6 ounces cream cheese, cut into ½-inch cubes, at room temperature
4 ounces smoked salmon, cut into thin strips
Salt and freshly ground black pepper to taste

Flour, for dusting
Vegetable oil, for cooking
Sour cream, for garnish
2 tablespoons chopped scallions, for garnish

MAKE THE DOUGH

Hand method: Sift the flour, baking powder, and salt together into a large mixing bowl. Drizzle the boiling water over the flour. Using a fork, blend until all the liquid has been absorbed and the dough clumps together. Allow the dough to cool slightly, then gather the dough into a soft ball in the bowl. If the dough feels sticky, add about a tablespoon of flour. Turn the dough out onto a lightly floured work surface and knead until it is smooth and satiny, about 5 minutes. Shape the dough into a smooth ball.

Food processor method: Place the flour, baking powder, and salt in the bowl of a food processor fitted with the metal blade. Pulse to blend. With the motor on, gradually add the boiling water through the feed tube, and process until the dough cleans the sides of the bowl and rides on the blade, about 10 seconds. The dough should be smooth and supple. If the dough sticks to the bowl, add about a tablespoon of flour and process until the dough cleans the sides of the bowl. Turn the dough out onto a lightly floured surface and shape it into a smooth ball.

LET THE DOUGH REST: Place the dough on a lightly floured plate and cover with a damp kitchen towel. Allow the dough to relax for at least 30 minutes, or up to 1 hour.

MAKE THE FILLING: Combine the eggs, cream, and chopped scallions in a mixing bowl. Using a fork or wire whisk, beat the mixture until well blended.

Melt the butter in a 12-inch nonstick skillet set over moderately high heat. Add the diced apple and sauté until slightly soft, about 1 minute. Reduce the heat to moderately low and pour in the egg mixture. Cook, stirring gently with a rubber spatula, until the eggs are softly set but not runny, about 3 to 4 minutes. Do not overcook. Scatter the cream cheese cubes evenly over the eggs, then immediately remove the pan from the heat and fold in the salmon, being careful not to break up the cheese too much. Season with salt and pepper. Set aside to cool.

Divide the dough into 4 pieces. Roll each piece into a ball. Work with one piece of dough at a time, keeping the remainder covered with a towel to prevent drying.

FILL AND SHAPE THE TURNOVERS: Lightly press one ball of dough into a disk. On a lightly floured work surface, roll it into an 8-inch circle about ⅛-inch thick. Each time you roll over the dough, pick it up and rotate it a sixth of a turn to the right. This will help achieve a perfectly round shape. If necessary, trim the edges to make the circle even.

Place about ½ cup of filling just below the center of the dough circle, leaving about a 1 inch margin around the bottom edge. Lightly moisten the bottom edge of dough with water. Fold the top half of the dough over the filling to form a half-moon-shaped pastry. Using the tines of a fork dipped in flour, press the edges firmly together to seal. Fold and crimp the edges as for a calzone, if desired. Gently press down on the turnover so that it will sit flat on the griddle. Place the turnover on a lightly floured baking sheet, and assemble the remaining turnovers in the same manner.

COOK THE TURNOVERS: Brush a griddle or large nonstick skillet with vegetable oil and set over moderately low heat. Dredge each turnover in flour and shake off the excess. Place the turnovers on the griddle, in batches if necessary. Cook until the bottoms are lightly browned, about 4 minutes, pressing gently on the turnovers with a spatula to flatten and adjusting the heat as necessary to maintain a gentle sizzle. Using a wide spatula, carefully turn the turnovers over, and continue to cook until golden brown on the other side, about 4 minutes longer. Transfer the turnovers to warm dinner plates.

TO SERVE: Garnish each turnover with a dollop of sour cream and ½ tablespoon of the scallions. Serve immediately.

— cook's notes —

For variation, wrap the egg filling in Buckwheat Crêpes (page 281). Place the stuffed crêpes in a lightly buttered baking pan, brush with melted butter, and sprinkle with Parmesan cheese. Cover and bake in a preheated 350°F oven until heated through, about 15 to 20 minutes.

For a quick breakfast, wrap warmed flour tortillas around the filling.

— *planning ahead* —

The uncooked tortillas may be covered and refrigerated for up to a day.

Mozzarella Tortilla Puffs

I devised these utterly delicious little puffs for one of my cocktail parties by wrapping bits of mozzarella cheese and anchovies in fresh tortilla dough. Surprise your guests by not divulging the ingredients until they ask what gives them their wonderful flavor.

YIELD: 32 tortillas for hors d'oeuvres

TORTILLA DOUGH

1 cup unbleached all-purpose flour, plus additional if necessary
½ teaspoon baking powder
1 tablespoon cold solid vegetable shortening
1½ teaspoons sugar dissolved in ¼ cup plus 2 teaspoons warm water

FILLING

6 ounces mozzarella cheese, shredded
16 anchovy fillets, cut crosswise in half

Vegetable oil, for deep-frying

MAKE THE DOUGH

Hand method: Sift the flour and baking powder together into a small mixing bowl. Using a fork or metal pastry blender, blend in the shortening until the mixture resembles fine meal. Sprinkle the sweetened water a little at a time over the mixture, using your fingertips to work the mixture into a rough dough. After the mixture clumps together into a rough, shaggy mass, gather it together and briefly knead in the bowl until the dough forms a soft ball. The dough should be moist but not sticky. If it feels sticky, knead in a little flour. If it feels dry or flaky, knead in about a teaspoon of water. Turn the dough out onto a lightly floured work surface and knead until shiny and smooth, about 2 to 3 minutes. Shape the dough into a ball.

Food processor method: Place the flour, baking powder, and shortening in the bowl of a food processor fitted with the metal blade. Pulse until the mixture resembles coarse meal. With the motor on, gradually add the sweetened water through the feed tube, and process until the dough cleans the sides of the bowl and rides on the blade, about 10 seconds. The dough should be moist but not sticky. If it feels sticky, blend in a little flour. If it feels dry or flaky, add about a teaspoon of water. Turn the dough out onto a lightly floured work surface and shape it into a smooth ball.

LET THE DOUGH REST: Divide the dough into 32 pieces. Roll each piece into a ball. Place the dough balls on a lightly floured baking sheet and cover with plastic wrap. Allow the dough to relax at room temperature for at least 30 minutes, or up to 1 hour.

SHAPE THE TORTILLAS: Work with one piece of dough at a time, keeping the remainder covered with a towel to prevent drying.

Lightly press one ball of dough into a disk. On a lightly floured work surface, roll the dough into an almost paper-thin 4- to 4½-inch circle. Scatter 1 teaspoon of the mozzarella over the dough and place 1 piece of anchovy in the center. Lightly moisten the edges with water if necessary, and roll the dough up into a cigar shape. Press the seam and the ends together to seal in the filling. Curve the roll, seam side toward the inside, into a ring and pinch the ends together. Assemble the remaining tortillas in the same manner.

COOK THE TORTILLAS: In a deep heavy saucepan or an electric fryer, heat 2 to 3 inches of oil over moderate heat to 350°F. Cook the tortillas in batches without crowding, as they will expand while cooking: Gently lower the tortillas into the hot oil, and fry until puffed and golden brown, about 1½ minutes. Using a slotted spoon, transfer the tortillas to paper towels to drain. Serve hot.

— cook's notes —

Instead of deep-frying, you may brush the tortillas with olive oil or melted butter and bake them on a baking sheet in a preheated 400°F oven until slightly puffed and browned, about 15 minutes. Baked tortillas will be slightly drier than the deep-fried ones.

— planning ahead —

The uncooked empanadas can be individually wrapped in plastic wrap and refrigerated overnight or frozen for up to 3 months. Griddle-bake or fry them without thawing.

— cook's notes —

You may substitute slightly tart fruits such as pineapple, rhubarb, blueberries, raspberries, or Italian plums for the strawberries.

To make traditional fried empanadas, heat 2 to 3 inches of oil to 350°F in a deep heavy saucepan or an electric fryer over moderate heat. Gently lower the empanadas, a few at a time, into the hot oil. Cook until the turnovers are golden brown on both sides, about 2 minutes, spooning the oil over the top to encourage puffing. Use a slotted spoon to transfer the empanadas to paper towels to drain.

Strawberry Empanadas

In Mexico and other Latin American countries, empanadas can be made with either a bread dough, such as the tortilla dough in this recipe, or a flaky pastry crust containing shortening. The filling variations can be endless. Here I have created a dessert with a simple but delicious blending of cream cheese, brown sugar, and fresh strawberries. Since most people, including myself, shy away from fried foods, I griddle-bake these empanadas instead of deep-frying them.

YIELD: 8 empanadas, enough for 8 dessert servings

DOUGH

1½ cups unbleached all-purpose flour, plus additional if necessary
½ teaspoon baking powder
1½ tablespoons cold solid vegetable shortening
1½ teaspoons sugar dissolved in ½ cup warm water

STRAWBERRY FILLING

1 8-ounce package cream cheese, cut into small pieces, at room temperature
⅓ cup light brown sugar
1 cup coarsely chopped fresh strawberries

4 tablespoons unsalted butter, melted
Confectioner's sugar, for dusting
Ice cream (optional)

MAKE THE DOUGH

Hand method: Sift the flour and baking powder together into a small mixing bowl. Using a fork or metal pastry blender, blend in the shortening until the mixture resembles fine meal. Sprinkle the sweetened water a little at a time over the mixture while using your fingertips to work the mixture into a rough dough. After the mixture has clumped together into a rough, shaggy mass, gather it together and briefly knead in the bowl until the dough forms a soft ball. The dough should be moist but not sticky. If it feels sticky, knead in a little flour. If it feels dry or flaky, knead in about a teaspoon of water. Turn the dough out onto a lightly floured work surface and knead until it is shiny and smooth, about 2 to 3 minutes. Shape the dough into a ball.

Food processor method: Place the flour, baking powder, and shortening in the bowl of a food processor fitted with the metal blade. Pulse to blend until the mixture resembles coarse meal. With the motor on, gradually add the sweetened water through the feed tube, and process until the dough cleans the sides of the bowl and rides on the blade, about 10 seconds. The dough should be moist but not sticky. If it feels sticky, blend in a little flour. If it feels dry or flaky, add about a teaspoon of water. Turn the dough out onto a lightly floured work surface and knead it into a smooth ball.

LET THE DOUGH REST: Divide the dough into 8 pieces. Roll each piece into a ball. Place the dough balls on a lightly floured baking sheet and cover with plastic wrap. Allow the dough to relax at room temperature for at least 30 minutes, or up to 1 hour.

PREPARE THE FILLING: In a mixing bowl, blend the cream cheese and brown sugar together with a fork or electric hand mixer until smooth. Using a rubber spatula, fold in the chopped strawberries.

ASSEMBLE THE EMPANADAS: Work with one piece of dough at a time, keeping the remainder covered with a towel to prevent drying.

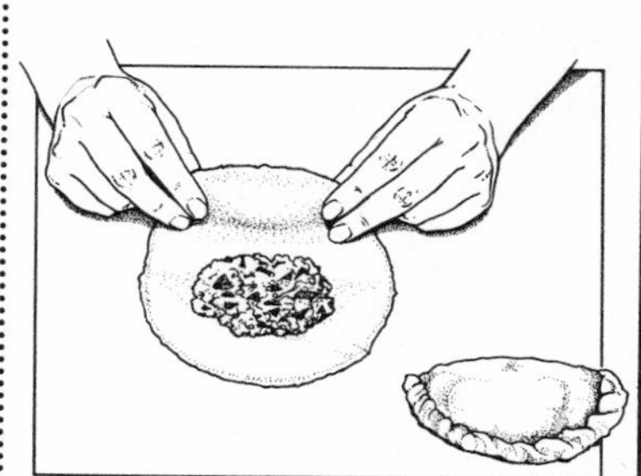

Lightly press one ball of dough into a disk. On a lightly floured surface, roll the dough into a 5½ inch circle about ¹⁄₁₆ inch thick. Each time you roll over the dough, pick it up and rotate it a sixth of a turn to the right. This will help achieve the round shape.

Put about 2 heaping tablespoons of the fruit filling on the dough circle, just below the center, leaving a 1-inch border around the bottom edge. Form a half-moon-shaped pastry by folding the other half of the dough over the filling, leaving a ¼-inch border of dough exposed around the bottom edge. When you fold over the dough, be careful that the filling doesn't spread toward the edge, or you will not be able to seal the turnover properly. Press the dough together around the filling, and secure the seam by folding the exposed rim of dough over. Decoratively seal the pastry by crimping the edges of the dough. Place the empanada on a lightly floured platter or baking sheet. Assemble the remaining empanadas in the same manner.

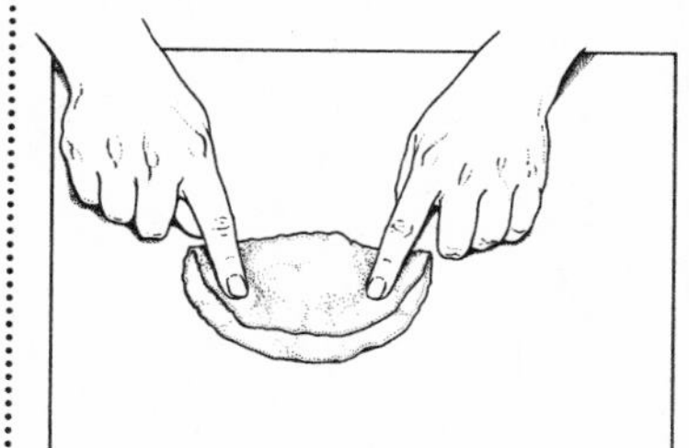

COOK THE EMPANADAS: Heat a large griddle or two 10- to 12-inch skillets over moderate heat until hot. Be sure the surface is not too hot or the empañadas will brown too quickly without cooking through. Generously brush the griddle and both sides of the empañadas with the melted butter. Place as many empañadas as will fit on the griddle, and cook until the turnovers are lightly browned and crisp on the bottom, about 3 to 4 minutes. Using a metal spatula, turn the empañadas over and cook until the second side is lightly browned and crisp, about 3 to 4 minutes longer. Transfer the cooked empañadas to a platter, and cook the remaining empañadas in the same manner.

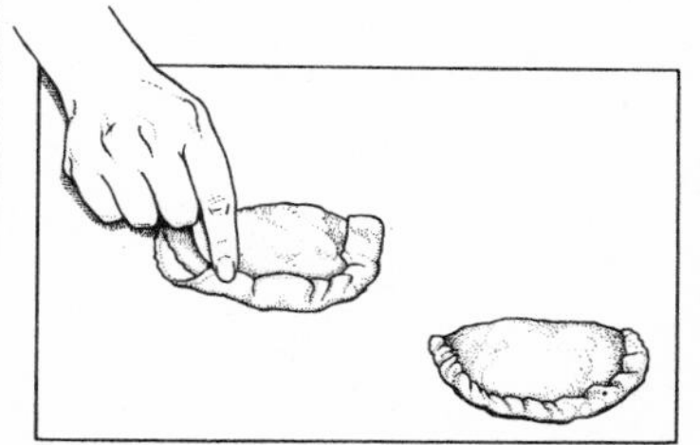

TO SERVE: Lightly dust the turnovers with confectioner's sugar and serve hot, with a scoop of ice cream if desired.

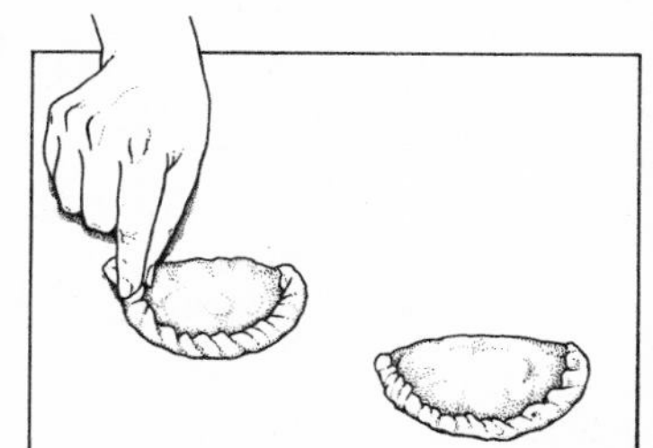

— *planning ahead* —

The uncooked tortillas may be prepared a day in advance, stacked between sheets of plastic wrap, covered, and refrigerated.

Chocolate Mango Tortillas

I so much enjoyed a fruit-filled chocolate tortilla served for dessert at Dallas's popular Routh Street Cafe that I decided to re-create it at home. Although my tortillas sometimes come out slightly cracked, they taste every bit as wonderful as the originals.

In this unusual, easy-to-prepare, and visually striking dessert, delicate cocoa-flavored tortillas are folded over a filling of juicy mangoes and whipped cream. The rum flavor in both the fruit filling and the whipped cream contributes to making the tortillas a sensation.

YIELD: 4 tortillas, enough for 4 dessert servings

DOUGH

½ cup unbleached all-purpose flour
2 tablespoons Dutch-process cocoa powder
2 tablespoons sugar
¾ teaspoon baking powder
¼ teaspoon salt
2 tablespoons unsalted butter, at room temperature
2 tablespoons warm water

MANGO FILLING

2 ripe mangoes, peeled and cut into ½-inch pieces
2 teaspoons rum or tequila
1 tablespoon plus 1 teaspoon sugar
1 tablespoon plus 1 teaspoon fresh lemon juice

WHIPPED CREAM

½ cup heavy cream, well chilled
2 teaspoons rum or tequila
2 teaspoons confectioner's sugar

PREPARE THE DOUGH: Sift the flour, cocoa powder, sugar, baking powder, and salt together into a medium bowl. Using a fork or metal pastry blender, cut in the butter until the mixture resembles coarse meal. Sprinkle the water over the mixture and mix until the dough is evenly moistened and clumps together. If the mixture seems a little dry, add just a few drops of water—no more than ¼ teaspoon. Turn the dough out onto a lightly floured board and knead until smooth, about 1 minute. The dough should be firm and moist but not sticky. Shape it into a flat disk, wrap in plastic, and refrigerate for at least 1 hour, or overnight.

MARINATE THE MANGOES: In a bowl, toss together the mangoes, rum, sugar, and lemon juice. Cover with plastic wrap and let marinate for at least 30 minutes in the refrigerator.

MAKE THE WHIPPED CREAM: Just before serving, whip the cream with the rum in a mixing bowl until soft peaks form. Add the sugar and continue whipping until stiff peaks form. Cover and refrigerate.

MAKE THE TORTILLAS: Divide the dough into 4 portions. Roll each portion into a ball, then flatten it into a round disk. Work with one portion at a time, covering the remainder with a towel to prevent them from drying out.

Lightly dust a board and rolling pin with flour. Roll one portion of dough into a 6-inch circle about ⅛ inch thick. Each time you roll over the dough, pick it up and rotate it a sixth of a turn to the right. This will help achieve the round shape of the tortilla. Transfer the tortilla onto a plate and cover with a piece of wax paper. Roll out the remaining tortillas in the same fashion, stacking them between pieces of wax paper.

COOK THE TORTILLAS: Heat a dry nonstick 6½-inch omelet pan or skillet over moderately low heat until very hot. Add a tortilla to the pan and cook for 30 seconds. Do not overcook, or the tortilla will dry out and crack. Slide a wide spatula under the tortilla, carefully turn it over, and cook for 10 seconds longer. The tortilla should still be slightly soft and moist. Slide it onto a plate and cover with a piece of aluminum foil to prevent drying. Cook the remaining tortillas in the same fashion, stacking them between pieces of foil.

TO SERVE: Place the tortillas on four dessert plates. Spoon one quarter of the mango filling over one half of each tortilla, then fold the other half over the mangoes. (The tortillas may crack as you fold them, which is natural. This slight imperfection adds a homemade feel to the dessert that will be appreciated by your guests.) Serve with dollops of the whipped cream.

— cook's notes —

As these tortillas are quite fragile and it may take you a few tries to get a feel for making them, it's a good idea to start out with a double batch of dough.

Fresh, juicy peaches, papaya, or nectarines may be used instead of mangoes.

Use unsweetened alkalized (Dutch-process) cocoa powder, such as Hershey's European-style or Dröste, an imported Dutch brand. Dutch-process cocoa has had alkali added to make it darker and less acidic.

pasta and noodles

If we choose to believe the legend that Marco Polo brought noodles back to Italy from China, then the recipes in this chapter allow us to follow him on a culinary journey from Asia to Europe. What we will find along the way is that using pastas and noodles to wrap different fillings in a variety of shapes is common to many cuisines.

Very few of us take the time to make our own filled pasta and noodles. This is a shame. Even the very best packaged ravioli or wontons can never equal the scrumptious flavor and moist texture of homemade Three-Cheese Ravioles with Walnut Sauce (page 241) or Crisp-Fried Shrimp Wontons (page 254).

Pasta and *noodle* are different names for the same thing, a dough paste (hence the word *pasta*) made with flour and either egg and/or water. The final taste and texture of a particular pasta or noodle is determined by whether the dough is rolled thick or thin, how it is shaped, and the way it is cooked.

To me the ultimate stuffed pasta and noodle foods are dumplings: plump, velvety-tasting morsels with savory or sweet fillings. I generally try to have different kinds, like Shao Mai with Chicken, Shrimp, and Mushrooms (page 260) or Kreplach (page 264), on hand in my freezer for impromptu festivities.

Since nothing can match the satisfaction of making something from scratch, fresh homemade doughs are generally my first choice for preparing the dishes in this chapter. However, this may not always be practical for today's busy cooks. Therefore, in many recipes I have suggested store-bought wrappers as substitutions for the fresh doughs. The final results may be slightly different but the significant savings in time may make certain recipes more approachable.

The choice of the type of wrapper to use is usually determined by the texture, shape, and cooking method of the final product. Pasta and noodle wrappers are generally unsuitable for baking because of their low-fat composition. They would become hard and unpalatable in the dry oven heat. Instead, these wrappers lend themselves to moist cooking methods like steaming, boiling, deep-frying, and panfrying. In some cases, two methods may be combined, as with Beef Potstickers with Warm Spicy Dipping Sauce (page 256), which are panfried and then steamed. The descriptions of the various types of dough wrappers that follow will help you better understand their nature and how they are particularly appropriate for certain preparations.

HOMEMADE NOODLE DOUGH WRAPPERS As much as pasta is associated with Italian-style dishes, noodle-based dishes are associated with Asian, Russian, German, and Eastern European cuisines. Fresh noodle dough, made of flour, eggs, and water or milk, is prepared and used much the same way as fresh pasta dough. In the recipes in this chapter, noodle dough is usually rolled to ¹⁄₁₆ inch thick, then wrapped around different types of fillings to form little dumplings. The appeal of noodle dough comes from its unique smoothness and chewiness. Because of its strong, smooth, and elastic qualities, noodle dough is ideal for many cooking techniques, such as boiling, steaming, and panfrying. However, I cannot recommend deep-frying fresh noodle dough because it contains too much moisture and will not be as crispy as deep-fried pasta dough, for example. There are really no commercial wrappers that approximate the texture of fresh noodle dough.

HOMEMADE PASTA DOUGH WRAPPERS Starting with a basic dough made with flour and eggs, wrappers of various shapes and sizes can be made for Italian-style stuffed pasta dishes. In general, the thickness for rolled-out dough used in the preparation of stuffed pastas is about ¹⁄₁₆ inch (the thickness of a quarter). For fried wonton and tortellini-style dishes, a slightly thinner dough is more appropriate. Stuffed pasta is usually boiled first before being combined with a sauce or baked in the oven. As long as you don't overboil it, cooked fresh pasta dough has a firm texture. Store-bought fresh lasagna sheets, Chinese egg roll wrappers, and the smaller wonton wrappers can be used as a substitute for fresh pasta dough when making filled pasta dishes.

FRESH LASAGNA SHEETS Fresh lasagna sheets are rolled-out fresh pasta sheets that can be purchased in Italian specialty stores. They usually are available as 9- by 4½-inch rectangles (about 1⁄16 inch thick) and can be either plain (made with egg only) or flavored with such ingredients as spinach or tomato. When I need larger pasta sheets and am too lazy to make my own, I call the pasta store a day or so in advance to place my order. Do not use the dried lasagna available in packages at supermarkets; it is much too thick.

WONTON WRAPPERS (OR SKINS) These paper-thin sheets (1⁄32 inch thick) of pasta dough, made from flour, eggs, and salt, are useful and convenient stand-ins for 3-inch dumpling wrappers made from homemade pasta dough. The texture and taste will not differ much; the only difference is that purchased wonton skins will save you some precious time. Wonton wrappers stand up beautifully to boiling, steaming, and deep-frying.

EGG ROLL WRAPPERS These are made from a soft dough of flour and eggs, rolled into sheets about 1⁄16 inch thick, and then cut into 8-inch squares. They can be purchased in most supermarkets and Asian markets. They should not be confused with spring roll wrappers or Shanghai egg roll wrappers, which are much thinner (1⁄32 inch) and drier and contain no egg. Egg roll wrappers are a convenient store-bought substitute for homemade pasta dough wrappers when a thicker dough is needed. In traditional Chinese cuisine, foods encased in egg roll wrappers are invariably deep-fried. But I have found that after boiling, egg roll dough can be as good as homemade pasta, if not better, because it retains its slightly resilient texture and holds its shape beautifully.

HOMEMADE POTSTICKER DOUGH WRAPPERS Nothing tastes as good as potstickers, the popular Chinese dumplings, when the dough is made from scratch. Made of flour, salt, and boiling water, the smooth, silken dough forms a strong "skin" that will stand up to panfrying. Although most cooks roll the dough to a thickness of 1⁄16 inch, I prefer to make it a little thicker, about ⅛ inch, so it will yield a moister and more meaty texture. Although gyoza wrappers can be used as a convenient substitute, the texture is not the same.

GYOZA WRAPPERS Also labeled as gyoza skins, these are round, eggless Japanese dumpling wrappers. They are thinner (a little less than 1⁄32 inch thick) and silkier than Chinese wonton wrappers and more resilient in texture. They can be used as a substitute for homemade potsticker wrappers or in dishes where an eggless dough wrapper is preferred.

Although I have happily eaten and cooked pasta- and noodle-wrapped foods for many years, I am incapable of telling you why I prefer a certain kind of dough wrapper over another in any given dish. I know it has a lot to do with personal taste and experience. Therefore, I have come to the conclusion that the only rule when preparing a dish is that you do what pleases you most.

Experiment and decide for yourself which dough wrapper goes best with which filling. Don't feel bound to do things the classic way. Give free rein to your individual taste, creativity, and pleasure.

NOTES ON STORE-BOUGHT DUMPLING WRAPPERS

Before you buy any of the following wrappers, test for freshness. Try to feel through the package to see whether they are soft and supple. They should bend easily, without cracking.

EGG ROLL WRAPPERS These are commonly available fresh or frozen in one-pound packages (ten 8-inch-square sheets) in Asian markets and in the produce section of many supermarkets. If they are frozen, remove the package from the freezer and allow it to thaw fully in the refrigerator before using. Open the bag and cover the wrappers with a clean damp cloth to prevent them from drying out. Carefully separate the wrappers sheet by sheet as you use them. Unused wrappers should be sealed in a plastic bag and stored in the refrigerator, where they will keep for up to three days, or frozen for up to two months.

GYOZA WRAPPERS These are sold in Asian markets in one-pound packages (about fifty to seventy-five 3½-inch rounds) either fresh or frozen. Store them (wrapped airtight) in the refrigerator for up to a week, or freeze them for up to two months.

WONTON WRAPPERS OR SKINS These are found in Chinese markets and in the refrigerator sections of many supermarkets. They come in two shapes, square and round, but the round shape, which is a little thicker, is rarely available. The wonton wrappers sold in Chinese groceries are superior to the kind sold in supermarkets, which tend to be thicker and doughy tasting, but if the supermarket kind is all that is available to you, don't hesitate to use them. Those available in Chinese groceries range from fifty to seventy-five sheets per pound. Store wonton wrappers (wrapped airtight) in the refrigerator for up to a week, or freeze for up to two months.

PASTA AND NOODLE WRAPPING TIPS

- Since commercially made wrappers (lasagna sheets, egg roll, wonton, and gyoza skins) can be used as stand-ins for many of the homemade doughs in this chapter, I urge you to keep a package of each type in your freezer. You will find them a handy means of producing an exciting meal for family or friends.
- Before freezing wrappers, divide each package in halves, thirds, or quarters to speed thawing time. This also reduces waste, since most wrappers don't refreeze successfully. They often dry out, crack, or become pasty and stick together.
- All frozen dough wrappers must be thoroughly defrosted before being used. Otherwise, they will not pull apart easily and will tear or break when filled. Defrost them (still in their protective wrapping) in the refrigerator or at room temperature. Exposure to the air will dry the dough and make it brittle.
- Fresh homemade dough may be rolled and cut into the appropriate shape for a given recipe up to a day in advance. To store, lightly dust the cut-out dough pieces with cornstarch or flour to prevent them from sticking together. Stack them, seal in a plastic storage bag, and refrigerate until ready to use.

- To prevent pasta and noodle wrappers from drying out while you prepare a recipe, keep them covered with plastic wrap or a damp kitchen towel or in a plastic bag.
- To properly seal a stuffed dough or noodle wrapper, apply a little water or egg glaze to the edges. Make sure that the edges are crumb-free or they will not stick together.
- Uncooked filled pasta and noodle items may be prepared one day in advance, tightly wrapped, and refrigerated. This will not affect their taste or texture; in fact, the filling inside may develop more flavor from sitting. To store, place them half an inch apart on a lightly floured baking sheet, cover, and refrigerate. Many of these items can also be frozen for up to one month. Place the baking sheet in the freezer until the pieces are solidly frozen, then transfer them to storage containers or freezer bags. They need not be thawed before cooking (unless they are to be deep-fried), but they will need to cook a few minutes longer than the time specified in the recipe.

— cook's notes —

It is important to knead the dough well, then allow it to relax for at least 1 hour or, better yet, overnight. You'll find it much easier to roll after it rests. If the dough starts shrinking back when you roll it, cover it with plastic wrap or a clean towel and let it rest for about 10 minutes before continuing.

Homemade Pasta Dough

This recipe makes rich, deep golden pasta with a texture slightly resilient to the bite. A hand-cranked pasta machine is helpful but not necessary for rolling out the dough.

YIELD: ½ pound

1 cup unbleached all-purpose flour, plus additional for dusting and kneading
2 large eggs, lightly beaten
¼ teaspoon salt
½ teaspoon distilled white vinegar

MAKE THE DOUGH

Hand method: Place the flour in a large mixing bowl and make a well in the center. Put the beaten eggs, salt, and vinegar into the well. Using a fork, gradually draw the flour into the eggs to blend until the mixture clumps together into a rough, shaggy dough. Gather it in the bowl into a ball. If the dough feels sticky, sprinkle on a little flour. If it feels dry or crumbly, add just enough water to make the dough stick together. Briefly knead the dough in the bowl until it forms a soft mass. Transfer the dough to a well-floured surface and knead by pressing down on the dough with the heels of your hands, then folding the dough in half over itself. Give the dough a half turn and repeat the kneading procedure until the dough feels very smooth and soft but not sticky, about 10 minutes. Dust with a little more flour whenever the dough starts to feel sticky.

Food processor method: Place the flour in the bowl of a food processor fitted with the metal blade. In a small bowl, combine the eggs, salt, and vinegar. With the motor on, gradually add the egg mixture through the feed tube. Process until the dough cleans the sides of the bowl and rides on the blade, about 10 seconds. Continue to process for about 30 seconds. If the dough starts to stick to the bowl, add a little more flour and process until the dough cleans the sides of the bowl. Turn the dough out onto a lightly floured work surface and knead briefly until smooth and firm.

LET THE DOUGH REST: Shape the dough into a ball and dust it lightly with flour. Cover the dough with an inverted bowl or wrap in plastic wrap and let it relax at room temperature for at least 1 hour, or wrap in plastic and refrigerate overnight.

VARIATION

GREEN PASTA DOUGH: Squeeze dry ¼ cup (about 2 ounces) blanched fresh or defrosted frozen spinach (or blanched Swiss chard leaves). Chop very fine and add to the beaten eggs. Proceed as instructed above.

Homemade Noodle Dough

This recipe makes rich, pale golden noodles with a slightly resilient texture. A hand-cranked pasta machine is helpful but not necessary for rolling out the dough.

YIELD: 1 pound

2 cups unbleached all-purpose flour, plus additional for dusting and kneading

2 large egg yolks, lightly beaten

½ cup milk

1 teaspoon salt

MAKE THE DOUGH

Hand method: Place the flour in a large mixing bowl and make a well in the center. Put the beaten egg yolks, milk, and salt into the well. Using a fork, gradually draw the flour into the eggs to blend until the mixture clumps together into a rough, shaggy dough. Gather it in the bowl into a ball. If the dough feels sticky, sprinkle on a little flour. If it feels dry or crumbly, add just enough water to make the dough stick together. Briefly knead the dough in the bowl until it forms a soft mass. Transfer the dough to a well-floured surface and knead by pressing down on the dough with the heels of your hands, then folding the dough in half over itself. Give the dough a half turn and repeat the kneading procedure until the dough feels very smooth and soft but not sticky, about 10 minutes. Dust with a little more flour whenever the dough starts to feel sticky.

Food processor method: Place the flour in the bowl of a food processor fitted with the metal blade. In a small bowl, combine the egg yolks, milk, and salt. With the motor on, gradually add the egg mixture through the feed tube. Process until the dough cleans the sides of the bowl and rides on the blade, about 10 seconds. Continue to process for about 30 seconds. If the dough starts to stick to the bowl, add a little more flour and process until the dough cleans the sides of the bowl. Turn the dough out onto a lightly floured work surface and knead briefly until smooth and firm.

LET THE DOUGH REST: Shape the dough into a ball and dust it lightly with flour. Cover the dough with an inverted bowl or wrap in plastic wrap and let it relax at room temperature for at least 1 hour, or wrap in plastic and refrigerate overnight.

— cook's notes —

It is important to knead the dough well, then allow it to relax for at least 1 hour or, better yet, overnight. You'll find it much easier to roll after it rests. If the dough starts shrinking back when you roll it, cover it with plastic wrap or a clean towel and let it rest for about 10 minutes before continuing.

— *planning ahead* —

The noodle-wrapped meat patties can be assembled a day ahead, covered, and refrigerated until ready to fry. The sauce can also be prepared 1 day in advance, covered, and refrigerated. Bring the sauce to room temperature before serving.

— *cook's notes* —

Dried shiitake mushrooms, also known as Chinese black mushrooms, are available in many supermarkets and in Asian markets. They can also be ordered by mail from American Spoon Foods, P.O. Box 566, Petoskey, MI 49770 (616-347-9030), or from Hans Johansson, 44 West 74th Street, New York, NY 10023 (212-787-6496).

Spanish fideos, similar to very thin vermicelli, are readily available in supermarkets; Goya is a popular brand.

When buying fish sauce, look for the Squid or Tiparos brand. Once opened, fish sauce lasts up to a year at room temperature. Fish sauce is available in Asian markets and in some well-stocked supermarkets.

Ladies in a Sarong

(MOO SARONG)

Moo Sarong, peppery little meatballs wrapped in Asian flat egg noodles, are popular snacks in Thailand. They are crisp-fried and served with a spicy, sweet, and tangy sauce. Combining different flavors and textures in one dish is typical of Thai cuisine. For easy handling, I flatten the meatballs slightly into little patties before wrapping them in a very thin pasta such as Italian vermicelli or Spanish fideos. Traditionally, the "ladies" are dressed again by being wrapped in lettuce leaves along with a few sprigs of mint and cilantro before being dipped in the sauce and popped into one's mouth. Serve as an hors d'oeuvre or an appetizer.

YIELD: 20 meat patties, enough for 40 hors d'oeuvres or 6 appetizer servings

THAI DIPPING SAUCE

1 cup distilled white vinegar
½ cup plus 4 teaspoons light brown sugar
1½ tablespoons minced garlic
1 tablespoon crushed dried red pepper
⅓ cup fish sauce (see Cook's Notes)

FILLING

6 dried shiitake mushrooms (see Cook's Notes)
1 6-ounce package vermicelli or fideos (see Cook's Notes)
1 teaspoon vegetable oil
2 tablespoons chopped fresh coriander leaves and stems
1 tablespoon minced garlic
½ teaspoon black peppercorns
1 small onion, chopped
10 ounces ground pork
1 tablespoon light soy sauce
1 large egg yolk
½ teaspoon sugar
¼ teaspoon salt
1 tablespoon cornstarch

Vegetable oil, for deep-frying
Fresh coriander sprigs, for garnish (optional)

PREPARE THE DIPPING SAUCE: Stir the vinegar and sugar together in a small saucepan. Bring to a boil over moderate heat, and boil just until the sugar has dissolved. Transfer to a bowl. Add the garlic, crushed pepper, and fish sauce. Set aside.

PREPARE THE FILLING: Place the dried mushrooms in a small bowl and cover with boiling water. Let soak until softened, about 30 minutes; drain. Squeeze the mushrooms dry. Cut off and discard the stems, finely chop the caps, and set aside.

Bring 3 quarts water to a rolling boil in a large pot. Add the pasta and return to a boil, then reduce the heat to moderate and cook for 5 minutes, stirring occasionally to separate the pasta. Drain in a colander, rinse the pasta under cold running water, and drain well. Toss the noodles with the 1 teaspoon vegetable oil to prevent them from sticking together. Set aside.

Combine the coriander, garlic, and black peppercorns in a nut grinder or food processor and grind to a paste. Transfer to a bowl and add the mushrooms and all the remaining filling ingredients. Mix well to blend thoroughly.

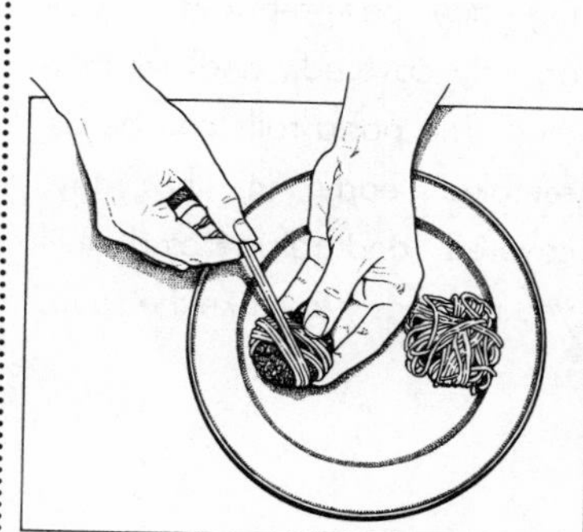

ASSEMBLE THE PATTIES: Roll about 1 tablespoon of the meat mixture between your palms to form a little meatball, then lightly press it to form a patty. Repeat until all of the meat mixture is used up.

Pick up a few strands of noodles, and wrap them around one patty. Continue wrapping with noodles until the patty is covered completely. Place the wrapped patty on a baking sheet. Wrap the remaining patties in the same manner.

FRY THE PATTIES: In a wok or heavy-bottomed saucepan over moderately high heat, heat 2 to 3 inches of vegetable oil to 350°F. Fry the patties, a few at a time, for about 1½ minutes on each side, or until golden brown. Transfer with a slotted spoon to paper towels to drain.

TO SERVE: For hors d'oeuvres, cut each patty in half and arrange on a platter with a small bowl of the dipping sauce. For appetizers, serve the patties whole with individual small bowls of dipping sauce for each person. Garnish with coriander leaves if desired.

— *planning ahead* —

Both the pasta dough and the filling may be prepared a day ahead, covered, and refrigerated. The pasta rolls can be assembled early in the day, covered, and refrigerated until you are ready to make the soup.

Green Pasta Crab Rolls in Spinach Broth

Sometimes my Asian heritage sneaks into my pasta creations. I start out with a classic Italian tortellini shape but end up with something that looks like a Chinese egg roll. That's what happened in this recipe. Here, green pasta rolls hold a crabmeat filling delicately flavored with fresh basil and then floated in green spinach broth. The effect of green on green is stunning. Light and elegant, this soup is an exciting start to a fancy dinner.

YIELD: 12 small pasta rolls, enough for 6 first-course servings

1 recipe Green Pasta Dough (page 236)

CRABMEAT FILLING

1 tablespoon olive oil
⅔ cup chopped shallots
½ pound fresh lump crabmeat, well picked over
2 teaspoons minced garlic
Salt and cayenne pepper to taste
2 tablespoons shredded fresh basil leaves or chopped fresh chives

BROTH

6 cups chicken broth, homemade (page 368) or store-bought
½ pound fresh spinach, cleaned, or 1 10-ounce package frozen leaf spinach, thawed
Salt and freshly ground black pepper to taste

Freshly grated Parmesan cheese

Prepare the pasta dough. Cover and set aside.

PREPARE THE FILLING: Heat the oil in a skillet over moderately high heat. Add the shallots and sauté until soft, about 1 minute. Add the crabmeat and garlic and sauté until the garlic is soft and fragrant, about 1 minute. Transfer to a bowl. Season with salt and cayenne pepper, and stir in the basil. Allow the filling to cool. Cover and refrigerate.

ROLL AND CUT THE PASTA: Divide the pasta dough into 2 portions. Keep one covered while you work with the other.

On a lightly floured surface, roll one portion of dough into a very thin sheet about 10 by 14 inches and a little less than 1⁄16 inch thick. Trim the edges and, using a knife and ruler, cut six 4½-inch squares. Keep the squares covered while you roll and cut the remaining dough.

PARBOIL THE PASTA: In a large pot, bring about 4 quarts salted water to a rolling boil. Place a large bowl of cold water next to the stove. Add 2 or 3 of the dough squares to the pot and cook for 30 seconds. Using a slotted spoon, transfer the cooked pasta to the bowl of cold water. Cook the remaining squares in the same manner. Drain the dough squares and dry them between two clean towels.

PREPARE THE PASTA ROLLS: Position a square of pasta on a work surface with one point toward you. Spread 1 tablespoon of the filling just below the center of the sheet. Roll up the pasta and filling one turn to the center and widest part of the square. Fold the sides over the center and roll up to make a neat, compact cylinder. Place the filled roll seam side down on a lightly floured baking sheet or platter and keep covered with a clean towel while you fill and roll the remaining squares. Cover and refrigerate until ready to use.

MAKE THE SOUP: In a large soup pot, bring the broth to a boil. Add the spinach, reduce the heat, and simmer until the leaves are tender, about 2 minutes. Add the pasta rolls and simmer until they are heated through, about 2 minutes. Season with salt and pepper.

TO SERVE: Place 2 rolls each in six warm soup bowls. Ladle some of the broth and spinach into each bowl. Sprinkle with Parmesan cheese and serve at once.

— cook's notes —

Store-bought egg roll wrappers or fresh green lasagna sheets are excellent substitutes for the homemade pasta in this recipe. If using them, you will need 3 egg roll sheets or six 9 by 4½-inch lasagna sheets. Cut the dough sheets into approximately 4½-inch squares and parboil them as described in the recipe before assembling the rolls; if using egg roll sheets, parboil for 1 minute.

Fresh chives can be used instead of basil for a different but just as interesting flavor.

Three-Cheese Ravioles with Walnut Sauce

Although there are innumerable variations in the way the celebrated ravioli is prepared, there are really only two differences: the filling and the sauce. Having shared its border with Italy over the centuries, the Savoy region of France has adopted many of northern Italy's best dishes. Ravioles are the French version of ravioli. In my adaptation of a classic Savoie preparation, the sublime creamy filling consists of goat cheese, Gruyère, and Parmesan, flavored with fresh chives. The ravioles are served in a brown butter sauce with sautéed walnuts and additional Parmesan. The final result is a scrumptious pairing of the tender and the crunchy.

This is a simple dish, and therefore demands the finest ingredients: the best cheeses and the best butter. I like to accompany it with a salad of Belgian endive dressed with lemon and walnut oil.

YIELD: 22 ravioles, enough for 6 to 7 appetizer or 4 main-course servings

— planning ahead —

The dough can be prepared up to 2 days ahead, covered, and refrigerated. The ravioles may be assembled early in the day, covered, and refrigerated until ready to cook.

continued

—— *cook's notes* ——

You may substitute Jarlsberg cheese for the Gruyère.

If fresh chives are unavailable, substitute 1 tablespoon chopped scallions.

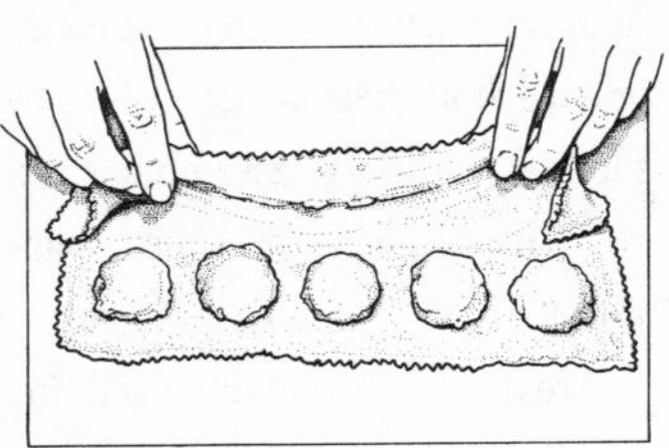

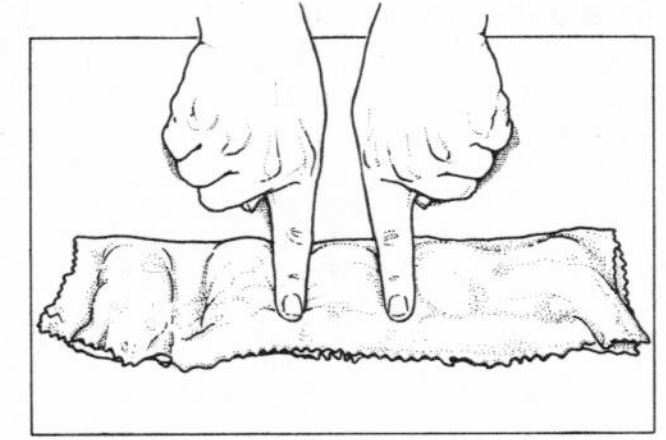

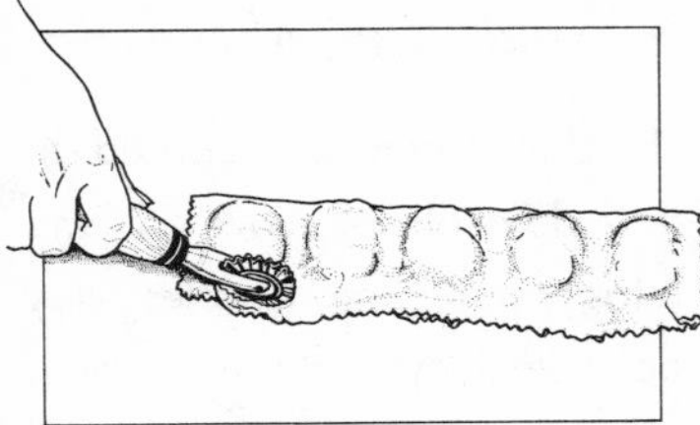

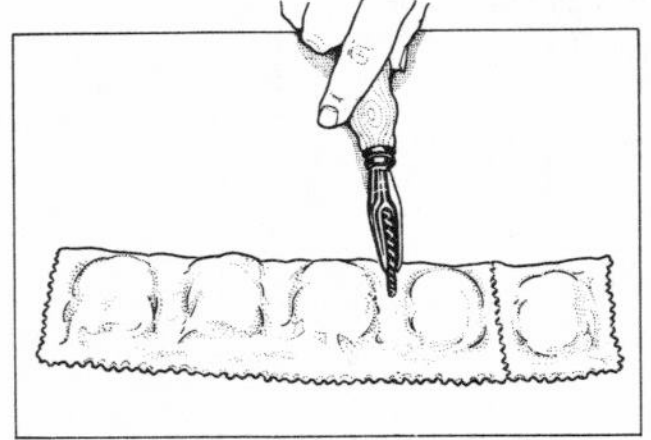

1 recipe Homemade Pasta Dough (page 236)

CHEESE FILLING

4 ounces soft white goat cheese, such as Montrachet
4 ounces Gruyère cheese, shredded
2 tablespoons freshly grated Parmesan cheese
1 medium egg, lightly beaten
1 tablespoon chopped fresh chives

WALNUT SAUCE

4 tablespoons unsalted butter
½ cup coarsely chopped walnuts

⅓ cup freshly grated Parmesan cheese
Salt and freshly ground black pepper to taste

Prepare the dough. Cover and set aside.

MAKE THE FILLING: Place the goat cheese in a medium mixing bowl and mash with a fork. Add the Gruyère, Parmesan, beaten egg, and chives and mix well. Cover and refrigerate until ready to use.

ASSEMBLE THE RAVIOLES: Divide the dough into 2 portions. Keep one portion covered with a damp cloth while you work with the other.

On a well-floured surface, roll one portion of dough into a 5½- by 20-inch rectangle about ⅛ inch thick. Lightly brush the dough with water. Put 2 teaspoons of the cheese filling at one end of the strip of pasta, placing it 1 inch from the end of the strip and 1 inch in from one of the long sides. Leaving a 1-inch space between them, place another mound of filling next to the first one. Repeat to make a row of 10 mounds of filling along one half of the strip of dough. Fold the dough in half over the mounds of filling. Press the dough around the mounds to seal on all sides.

Using a ravioli cutter or fluted pastry wheel, trim off the excess dough along the edges. Then cut between the mounds to obtain 2-inch-square ravioles. Make sure the edges of the ravioles are well sealed, or they will open when boiling. Place them ½ inch apart on a lightly floured baking sheet and cover with a kitchen towel. Roll, fill, and cut the remaining dough to make 10 more ravioles. Gather all the dough scraps, reroll, and fill and cut to make 2 more ravioles.

COOK THE PASTA: In a large pot, bring 4 quarts salted water to a rolling boil. Add all the ravioles. As soon as the water returns to a boil, reduce the heat and gently boil until the pasta is just tender but still firm to the bite, about 5 minutes.

Meanwhile, MAKE THE SAUCE: Melt the butter in a large saucepan set over moderate heat. Add the walnuts and sauté until the butter is browned and the nuts are golden, about 2 minutes.

TO SERVE: Drain the pasta and toss it in the sauce. Add the Parmesan cheese and toss again. Season with salt and pepper and serve

Lobster Belle Nicole

I developed this recipe when I was executive chef at Sarabeth's Restaurant in New York City. It became an instant hit and remained on the menu many years. This elegant dish consists of large lobster-filled ravioli bathed in a plush lobster sauce accented with lemongrass and a hint of curry. Lobster meat, asparagus, shiitake mushrooms, and tree ear mushrooms add not only intriguing textures and flavors but also contrasting colors to the pinkish background of the sauce. This is truly an outstanding eating experience!

— *planning ahead* —

Both the sauce and the filled ravioli can be made a day ahead, covered, and refrigerated. Bring the sauce to room temperature before completing the dish.

YIELD: 16 ravioli, enough for 8 appetizer or 4 to 5 main-course servings

1 recipe Homemade Pasta Dough (page 236)
16 dried shiitake mushrooms (see Cook's Notes)
3 tablespoons small dried tree ear mushrooms (see Cook's Notes)
18 asparagus spears

LOBSTER FILLING

4 live Maine lobsters (about 1½ to 2 pounds each)
4 shallots, coarsely chopped
4 garlic cloves, coarsely chopped
2 teaspoons fish sauce (see Cook's Notes)
Freshly ground black pepper to taste

Cornstarch, for dusting
1 egg beaten with 1 teaspoon water, for egg glaze

LOBSTER SAUCE

Reserved shells and heads from lobsters
2 tablespoons vegetable oil
4 small carrots, peeled and coarsely chopped
2 medium onions, coarsely chopped
2 cups canned crushed tomatoes
2 tablespoons tomato paste
3 stalks lemongrass, finely chopped (about 1 cup) (see Cook's Notes)
2 cups heavy cream
2 tablespoons fish sauce
2 teaspoons curry
¼ teaspoon turmeric
Cayenne pepper to taste

Fresh coriander leaves, for garnish

Prepare the dough. Cover and set aside.

PREPARE THE VEGETABLES: Place the shiitake mushrooms and tree ear mushrooms in two separate bowls. Pour 3 cups boiling water into each bowl and let the mushrooms soak for 30 minutes.

Drain the tree ear mushrooms, discarding the liquid, and squeeze them dry. Drain the shiitake mushrooms, reserving the liquid. Squeeze dry, and remove and discard the tough stems. Coarsely chop 4 of the shiitake mushroom caps with ½ cup of the

— cook's notes —

Store-bought wonton wrappers (preferably round) may be substituted for the homemade dough wrappers. If using square wonton wrappers, trim the corners with a sharp paring knife, or use a cookie cutter to obtain rounds. You will need 32 wrappers.

Live lobsters should be cooked as soon as they come from the market. I find the meat of Maine lobsters to be the most succulent. If you cannot cook them immediately, rinse them under cold water and drain. Transfer to a large pan, cover with a moistened towel, and refrigerate until cooking time. Rinse again, and remove the rubber bands from the claws with scissors just before cooking.

Dried shiitake and tree ear mushrooms are available in many supermarkets and in Asian markets; dried shiitakes are also known as Chinese black mushrooms. Dried mushrooms can be ordered by mail from American Spoon Foods, P.O. Box 566, Petoskey, MI 49770 (616-347-9030); or from Hans Johansson, 44 West 74th Street, New York, NY 10023 (212-787-6496).

When buying fish sauce, look for the Squid or Tiparos brand.

tree ear mushrooms. Cover and set aside for the filling. Cover the remaining whole mushrooms and reserve for the sauce.

Cut off the asparagus stalks 3 inches from the tips and discard the tough stems. Blanch the tips in boiling salted water until crisp-tender, 2 to 3 minutes depending on their thickness. Refresh under cold running water, cover, and refrigerate.

PREPARE THE LOBSTER MEAT: In a large pot, bring 8 quarts salted water to a rolling boil. With tongs, lower the live lobsters headfirst into the pot. Bring back to a boil and cook the lobsters for 2 minutes more. Drain the lobsters in a colander set in the sink and let cool. (Note that the lobster meat is not fully cooked at this point.)

Using kitchen gloves to protect your hands, twist the claws off the lobsters. Gently crack the claw shells with a hammer or the back of a heavy cleaver, being careful not to damage the meat. Use a small fork to remove the meat, which should come out in a single piece. Place the claw meat in a small bowl, cover, and refrigerate. Reserve the shells.

Gently detach the lobster tails from the heads. To remove the meat from the tails, use scissors to cut lengthwise through the underside of the tail, being careful not to damage the meat. Remove the tail meat in a single piece. With a small knife or toothpick, remove and discard the long, thin intestinal tract running the length of the meat. Reserve the shells. Slice the meat from two tails into 12 medallion-shaped pieces. Add the medallions to the bowl with the claw meat, cover, and refrigerate. Set the remaining tail meat aside.

Using a sharp heavy knife, split each lobster head lengthwise. Remove and discard the lumpy sac located near the eyes. Do not remove the soft green strip of tomalley (liver) or the dark green coral that runs parallel to the liver. Set the heads and all the shells aside for the sauce.

PREPARE THE FILLING: Cut the reserved tail meat into small chunks and place them in the bowl of a food processor fitted with the metal blade. Pulse to a coarse paste. Don't overprocess; you want to retain some of the texture of the lobster meat. Transfer the lobster to a medium mixing bowl. Add the reserved chopped mushrooms, the shallots, and garlic to the food processor. Pulse to finely chop. Add the mixture to the chopped lobster. Stir in the fish sauce and season with black pepper. Cover and refrigerate.

ROLL AND CUT THE DOUGH: Divide the pasta dough into 2 portions. Cover one portion with a damp cloth while you work on the other.

Sprinkle a work surface with 1 tablespoon cornstarch and roll one portion of dough into a very thin sheet about 6 by 24 inches and 1⁄16 inch thick. Sprinkle the dough with cornstarch. Using a 3-inch round cookie cutter, cut out 16 circles. Sprinkle the dough circles with cornstarch to prevent them from sticking together, stack them, and cover with the damp cloth while you roll and cut the remaining dough.

ASSEMBLE THE RAVIOLI: Spread 5 of the dough circles on a work surface. Lightly brush the edges of each one with egg glaze. Place about 1 tablespoon of filling in the center of circle, and top each one with another circle. Press the edges of the wrappers together, pressing around the filling to seal. Place the filled ravioli on a tray and cover with a kitchen towel to keep them from drying out. Assemble the remaining ravioli in the same manner. Cover with plastic wrap and refrigerate until ready to use.

PREPARE THE SAUCE: Crush the reserved lobster shells with a mallet. In a large heavy saucepan, heat the oil over moderately high heat. When the oil is hot, add the crushed lobster shells and the heads. Using a wooden spoon, stir the shells until they turn red, about 5 minutes. Add the carrots and onions and cook until the vegetables are soft, about 3 minutes. Add the reserved shiitake mushroom liquid along with the crushed tomatoes, tomato paste, lemongrass, and 2 cups water. Bring to a boil, reduce the heat to low, and simmer until the sauce is quite flavorful, about 30 to 35 minutes.

Strain the sauce through a large fine-mesh sieve set over a saucepan. Discard the solids. Set the sauce over high heat and cook until the liquid is reduced to about 2½ cups, about 10 minutes.

Meanwhile, place the cream in a medium saucepan and boil over moderately high heat until reduced by half, about 5 minutes.

Reduce the heat under the lobster sauce to low and whisk in the reduced cream. Add the fish sauce, curry, and turmeric, and season with cayenne pepper. Add the reserved lobster meat, asparagus tips, and whole mushrooms. Simmer until the lobster meat is cooked through and the vegetables are just tender, about 3 to 4 minutes. Remove from the heat and cover to keep warm.

POACH THE RAVIOLI: Bring 2 large pots filled with 3 quarts salted water each to a rolling boil. Add half of the ravioli to each pot and cook until just firm to the bite, about 3 minutes. Drain into a colander set in the sink.

TO SERVE: Place 2 ravioli for an appetizer or 3 to 4 for a main-course serving on a preheated plate. Spoon some sauce, along with pieces of lobster and vegetables, onto each plate. Garnish with coriander leaves. Serve at once.

Once opened, fish sauce lasts for up to 1 year at room temperature. Fish sauce is available in Asian markets and in some well-stocked supermarkets.

Lemongrass gives a very distinctive flavor to the sauce; don't leave it out. Lemongrass is available in Asian markets. Since it freezes well, buy several bunches at a time. Cut to separate the bottom stalk where the leaves begin to branch, and discard the grassy top. Freeze the stalks in plastic bags. To use, peel the tough outer layer from the stalk to disclose the white under layer. Crush lightly before chopping to release the maximum flavor.

— *planning ahead* —

The sauce can be prepared up to 1 week in advance, stored in a jar, and refrigerated. After reheating, if the sauce is too thick, thin with a little chicken broth or water. It should be slightly runny, just enough to coat the pasta. The filling can be made 1 day ahead. The pasta twists can be assembled early in the day they are to be served, covered, and refrigerated until ready to cook.

Stuffed Pasta Twists in Spicy Peanut Sauce

This recipe combines two of my favorite foods: pasta and peanut sauce. The dish is similar to Dan Dan, Szechuan-style dumplings served in a rich and spicy sesame and peanut sauce. Here, shrimp and chicken are the surprise filling for small pasta cylinders that are twisted shut at each end. They are then placed in a spicy peanut sauce laced with coconut. A final sprinkling of ground roasted peanuts completes this exciting medley of flavors and textures.

This is one instance where a pasta dish is better made with store-bought wrappers instead of homemade pasta dough. Egg roll wrappers yield the perfectly smooth and silken texture after boiling that is essential for these pasta twists.

YIELD: 24 twists, enough for 8 appetizer or 4 main-course servings

3 tablespoons unsalted dry roasted peanuts

PEANUT SAUCE

1 tablespoon vegetable oil
2 teaspoons minced garlic
¼ teaspoon Szechuan hot chili bean paste
½ cup chicken broth
¼ cup unsweetened coconut milk (see Cook's Notes)
3½ tablespoons creamy peanut butter
1 tablespoon light soy sauce
1 teaspoon sugar

SHRIMP AND CHICKEN FILLING

6 ounces shelled raw shrimp
2 ounces ground chicken meat
½ large egg white, lightly beaten
½ teaspoon sugar
¼ teaspoon salt
1½ teaspoons grated fresh ginger
1½ teaspoons dry sherry or vermouth
1½ teaspoons cornstarch
1 teaspoon light soy sauce
1 teaspoon Oriental sesame oil
2 tablespoons chopped scallions
Freshly ground black pepper to taste

6 egg roll wrappers, thawed if frozen
Shredded or sliced scallions, for garnish

TOAST THE PEANUTS: Place the peanuts in a dry skillet over moderate heat. Cook, shaking the pan constantly, until the nuts are heated through and fragrant, about 2 to 3 minutes. Let cool, then transfer the nuts to a spice grinder and process until coarsely chopped. Cover and set aside at room temperature.

PREPARE THE SAUCE: Heat the oil in a small saucepan set over moderate heat. When the oil is hot, add the garlic and chili paste. Sauté until the garlic is fragrant and lightly browned, about 30 seconds. Stir in the remaining sauce ingredients. Whisk to blend, and bring to a boil. Lower the heat and simmer, stirring occasionally, until the sauce has thickened slightly, about 2 minutes. Remove from the heat and set aside.

PREPARE THE FILLING: Devein and rinse the shrimp. Pat dry and dice coarsely. In a bowl, mix the shrimp with the remaining filling ingredients. Cover and let stand for 30 minutes.

Cut each egg roll into 4 squares.

ASSEMBLE THE PASTA TWISTS: Spread 2 teaspoons of the filling across the bottom edge of a wrapper square, leaving a ½-inch border. Shape the filling into a log approximately 2½ inches long. Lightly moisten the edges of the dough with water and roll the dough up around the filling into a cylinder. Gently twist the ends of the cylinder in opposite directions, then pinch the seam and both ends firmly to seal. Place the filled pasta seam side down on a lightly floured baking sheet. Cover with a clean towel while you fill and wrap the remaining pasta.

COOK THE PASTA: Bring 2 large pots filled with 4 quarts salted water each to a rolling boil. Add half of the pasta to each pot, reduce the heat, and gently boil until just tender but still firm to the bite, about 5 to 6 minutes. Drain well.

TO SERVE: Reheat the peanut sauce and divide it among warmed plates. Arrange the pasta twists, 3 for an appetizer or 6 for a main-course serving, on top of the sauce. Sprinkle with the ground toasted peanuts and garnish with shredded scallions. Serve at once.

— *cook's notes* —

Do not confuse coconut milk with coconut cream. Excellent canned unsweetened coconut milk is available in Asian markets and some supermarkets. After opening, it can be refrigerated for up to 1 week. For longer storage, freeze it in ice cube trays, then store the cubes in plastic bags. Before using, heat the frozen coconut milk until completely melted. Four cubes equal about ½ cup. You may substitute heavy cream for the coconut milk, but the taste will be slightly altered.

If egg roll wrappers are unavailable, Homemade Pasta Dough (page 236) is acceptable.

Prepare a double recipe of pasta, divide the dough into 4 portions, and roll each portion into a rectangle about 4 by 24 inches and slightly less than ⅛ inch thick. Cut each sheet of pasta into six 4-inch squares, for a total of 24 squares, and assemble the pasta twists as directed above.

— planning ahead —

The tomato sauce, without the cream, can be made weeks ahead and frozen. Reheat it before adding it to the reduced cream. The filling and homemade pasta dough can be prepared 1 day ahead, covered, and refrigerated. The pasta roll can also be assembled early in the day it is to be served, covered, and refrigerated until ready to cook.

Salmon Pasta Roll

This is one of the most delicious pasta dishes I have ever made. Instead of the classic ricotta cheese and spinach filling often used in ravioli and other Italian-style stuffed pastas, I have chosen a salmon mousse, subtly flavored with ginger and nutmeg, and I've added bits of spinach, shrimp, and scallops for texture. To complement the pink and green colors swirling through the roll, I accompany it with a luscious tomato cream sauce flavored with fresh basil. This is a light, melt-in-your-mouth delicacy that you will want to add to your entertaining repertoire.

YIELD: 1 large roll, enough for 8 appetizer or 4 to 5 main-course servings

SPECIAL EQUIPMENT: A large flameproof rectangular baking dish, about 9 by 16 inches and at least 3 inches deep

1 recipe Homemade Pasta Dough (page 236)

TOMATO CREAM SAUCE

3 tablespoons olive oil
1¼ cups chopped onions
2 tablespoons minced garlic
5 medium ripe tomatoes (about 2 pounds), coarsely chopped, or 1 2-pound can Italian plum tomatoes with their juices
½ cup tightly packed fresh basil leaves
¼ cup chopped fresh parsley
2 teaspoons sugar
1½ teaspoons salt, or more to taste
Freshly ground black pepper to taste
3 cups heavy cream

SEAFOOD FILLING

½ pound salmon fillet, cut into ½-inch pieces and well chilled
1 large egg
½ teaspoon ground ginger
⅛ teaspoon freshly grated nutmeg
½ teaspoon salt
⅛ teaspoon cayenne pepper
¼ teaspoon freshly ground black pepper
½ cup heavy cream, well chilled
½ pound sea scallops, cut into ½-inch pieces
4 ounces shelled raw shrimp, deveined and cut into ½-inch pieces
2 scallions, thinly sliced
½ cup finely diced carrots, blanched in boiling water
1 10-ounce package frozen leaf spinach, thawed, squeezed dry, and coarsely chopped

Prepare the pasta dough. Cover and set aside.

PREPARE THE TOMATO SAUCE: Heat the oil in a large saucepan set over low heat. Add the onions and garlic and cook, stirring frequently, until very soft but not browned, about 10 minutes. Add the tomatoes, basil leaves, parsley, sugar, and salt. Cook over low heat, stirring occasionally, until slightly thickened, about 30 minutes.

Transfer the sauce to the bowl of a food processor fitted with the metal blade, and purée. Pass the sauce through a fine-meshed sieve, pressing on the solids to extract as much liquid as possible. Discard the pulp. If the sauce seems a little too thick, thin it with a little water. You should have about 3 cups of sauce. Taste the sauce and adjust the seasoning with salt and pepper if necessary. Allow to cool. Cover and set aside.

PREPARE THE FILLING: Purée the salmon in a food processor until very smooth. Add the egg, ginger, nutmeg, salt, and cayenne and black peppers and process until well mixed. With the motor running, slowly add the cream through the feed tube and blend until very smooth. Transfer to a large mixing bowl and fold in the remaining filling ingredients. Cover and refrigerate.

Preheat the oven to 375°F. Adjust an oven rack to the middle position.

ASSEMBLE THE PASTA ROLL: Flatten the dough into a disk and place it on a well-floured work surface. Using a long rolling pin, roll out the dough to an approximately 18-inch square sheet a little less than 1⁄16 inch thick, dusting the work surface with more flour whenever the dough feels sticky.

Spread the filling evenly over the pasta sheet, tapering off toward the edges. Starting with the end nearest you, roll up the pasta sheet jelly-roll fashion. Trim the ends. Wrap the pasta roll in a double layer of cheesecloth and tie both ends securely with butcher's twine.

POACH THE PASTA ROLL: In the baking dish, bring approximately 3 quarts salted water to a simmer over moderately high heat. Add the pasta roll, making sure it is completely covered with water. Cover the pan with foil and carefully transfer it to the oven. Cook for 30 minutes. Uncover, carefully turn the roll over, and continue cooking for 30 minutes longer. Remove the pasta roll from the water and set it aside to rest for 10 minutes.

COMPLETE THE SAUCE: Meanwhile, bring the heavy cream to a boil in a large saucepan over moderately high heat. Reduce the heat to moderate and let the cream boil until it is reduced to about 2 cups, about 10 minutes; be careful the cream doesn't boil over. Stir in the tomato sauce and bring to a quick boil. Remove the pan from the heat. The sauce should be just thick enough to coat the back of a spoon. Taste and adjust the seasoning with salt and pepper if necessary.

TO SERVE: Carefully ladle the sauce onto preheated dinner plates. Unwrap the pasta roll and cut it into 1-inch-thick slices. Place 2 slices for an appetizer or 3 to 4 slices for a main-course serving over the sauce and serve.

cook's notes

Large fresh pasta sheets are an excellent substitute for homemade pasta dough in this recipe. They can be obtained from Italian specialty stores, if you are lucky enough to live near one. Be prepared to place your order at least a day in advance, as the large sheets are not always readily available. For this recipe, you will need 1 lasagna sheet trimmed to an 18-inch square.

If you wish for an even more flavorful and colorful dish, use homemade Green Pasta Dough (page 236).

— *planning ahead* —

The ragoût is best if made a few days before serving, then reheated the day it is to be eaten. Both the pasta dough and ragoût may be prepared up to 2 days in advance, covered, and refrigerated, leaving just a short assembly and baking to be done right before serving. The pouches can be assembled early in the day, covered, and refrigerated until ready to bake.

Pasta Pouches with Chunky Ragoût Filling

This dish is inspired by cannelloni, the Piedmontese specialty in which rectangles of cooked pasta are stuffed with a meat filling, rolled into tube shapes, and baked. In this delicious variation, a ragoût of short ribs is exotically flavored with a blend of cinnamon, ginger, curry, and anise. Purse-shaped pasta pouches hold the chunky ragoût filling. I like to serve this dish as an entrée, accompanied by a simple tossed salad.

YIELD: 8 pouches, enough for 8 appetizer or 4 main-course servings

1 recipe Homemade Pasta Dough (page 236)

RAGOÛT

2 pounds short ribs, cut into individual ribs
2 tablespoons minced garlic
2 tablespoons grated fresh ginger
2 teaspoons ground cinnamon
2 teaspoons curry powder
2 teaspoons sugar
½ teaspoon salt, plus more to taste
Cayenne pepper to taste
¼ cup olive oil
2 cups finely chopped onions
1 cup finely chopped carrots
1 cup finely chopped celery
⅔ cups dry red wine
6 cups beef broth, homemade (page 370) or store-bought
¼ cup tomato paste
4 star anise, tied up in a piece of cheesecloth
1 cup chopped scallions

8 scallions, trimmed and blanched in boiling water

Prepare the pasta dough. Cover and set aside.

MARINATE THE MEAT: Place the ribs in a large mixing bowl. Combine 1 tablespoon of the garlic, the ginger, cinnamon, curry, sugar, salt, and cayenne pepper in a small bowl. Sprinkle the spice mixture over the ribs and toss thoroughly with your hands. Let sit for at least 30 minutes.

MAKE THE RAGOÛT: Heat 2 tablespoons of the olive oil in an ovenproof casserole or Dutch oven. In batches, brown the meat on all sides. Transfer the browned meat to a bowl, leaving as much of the oil in the pan as possible.

Add the remaining 2 tablespoons oil to the pan. Add the remaining 1 tablespoon minced garlic, the onions, carrots, and celery. Sauté until the vegetables are soft, about 5 minutes. Turn the heat to high, add the wine, and let it bubble for 1 minute. Scrape the bottom of the pan with a wooden spoon to loosen any browned bits. Stir in 4 cups of the broth, the tomato paste, star anise, and the browned meat with its juices, and bring the mixture to a boil. Cover the pan, turn the heat to very low, and simmer for 30 minutes. Season with salt to taste, cover, and simmer for 30 more minutes. Remove from the heat and allow the ragoût to cool.

Remove the meat from the cooking liquid and remove all the meat from the bones. Discard the bones and the anise. Cut the meat into ¾-inch cubes. Place the meat in a medium bowl, and add ½ cup of the cooking liquid and ¾ cup of the chopped scallions. Set aside.

MAKE THE SAUCE: Place the reserved cooking liquid and the remaining 2 cups beef broth in a blender and process until finely puréed. Cover and refrigerate.

ROLL AND CUT THE PASTA: Divide the pasta dough into 2 portions. Keep one portion covered with a damp cloth while you work with the other.

On a lightly floured surface, roll one portion of dough into a very thin 14-inch square sheet a little less than 1/16 inch thick. Cut out four 7-inch circles, and discard the dough scraps. Keep the rounds covered with a damp cloth while you roll and cut the remaining dough in the same manner.

PARBOIL THE PASTA ROUNDS: In a large pot, bring about 4 quarts salted water to a rolling boil over moderately high heat. Place a large bowl of cold water next to the stove. Add 2 rounds of pasta to the boiling water and cook for 30 seconds. Using a slotted spoon, transfer the cooked dough to the bowl of cold water. Cook the remaining wrappers in the same manner. Drain the dough sheets and dry them between two clean towels.

Preheat the oven to 400°F.

ASSEMBLE THE POUCHES: Set a pasta circle into a ramekin or rice bowl. Fill with ⅓ cup of the ragoût. Gather the edges of the dough up around the filling and tie shut with 1 of the blanched scallions. Place the pouch in a lightly oiled large shallow baking dish. Form the remaining pouches in the same manner.

COOK THE POUCHES: Drizzle the sauce over the purses. Cover the baking dish with foil and bake until the pasta is cooked through, about 20 minutes.

TO SERVE: Transfer the purses and sauce to warmed plates and serve immediately, sprinkled with the remaining ¼ cup chopped scallions.

— cook's notes —

Store-bought egg roll wrappers are excellent substitutes for the home-made pasta in this recipe. They will be slightly thicker and have a more resilient texture. You will need 8 sheets. Trim into 7-inch rounds and parboil them for 1 minute before assembling the pouches.

Rabbit, chicken, stewing beef, and lamb are good substitutes for the short ribs.

For a simpler version of this dish, just layer the parboiled pasta sheets and the filling like a lasagna in an ovenproof dish and bake.

— planning ahead —

The salsa can be made ahead of time, stored in a jar, and refrigerated for up to 1 week. Bring it to room temperature before serving. The dough can be prepared up to 2 days ahead, covered, and refrigerated. The tortellini can be assembled early in the day they are to be served, covered, and refrigerated, leaving just a quick deep-frying for the last minute.

— cook's notes —

Store-bought square wonton wrappers may be substituted for the homemade dough wrappers. You will need 32 wrappers.

Tex-Mex Tortellini with Spicy Tomato-Coriander Salsa

This recipe consists of a crisp-fried wrapper and a flavorful, mild green chile and Jack cheese filling. For a more complex flavor, I like to dip these fried tortellini in a slightly spicy tomato and coriander salsa. These irresistible Southwestern-style treats make fabulous hors d'oeuvres.

YIELD: 32 tortellini for hors d'oeuvres

1 recipe Homemade Pasta Dough (page 236)

TOMATO-CORIANDER SALSA

2 small ripe tomatoes, peeled, seeded, and coarsely chopped (about 1¼ cups)
1 jalapeño pepper, seeded and finely chopped
2 tablespoons ketchup
2 tablespoons chopped green bell pepper
2 tablespoons chopped onion
½ teaspoon minced garlic
1 teaspoon sugar
½ teaspoon salt, or more to taste
2 tablespoons chopped fresh coriander leaves

GREEN CHILE AND CHEESE FILLING

1 4-ounce can chopped green chile peppers, drained
½ cup grated Monterey Jack cheese (about 2 ounces)
½ cup grated Cheddar cheese (about 2 ounces)
1 teaspoon ground cumin

Cornstarch, for dusting
Vegetable oil, for frying

Prepare the dough. Cover and set aside.

PREPARE THE SALSA: In a medium saucepan, combine all the salsa ingredients except the coriander. Bring to a boil over moderately high heat. Reduce the heat to low and simmer, stirring occasionally, until the mixture is slightly thickened and the vegetables are soft, about 5 minutes. Remove from the heat and allow the salsa to cool. Stir in the coriander. Taste and adjust the seasoning with salt if necessary. Transfer to a small bowl, cover, and refrigerate until needed.

PREPARE THE FILLING: In a mixing bowl, combine the green chiles with the cheeses and cumin.

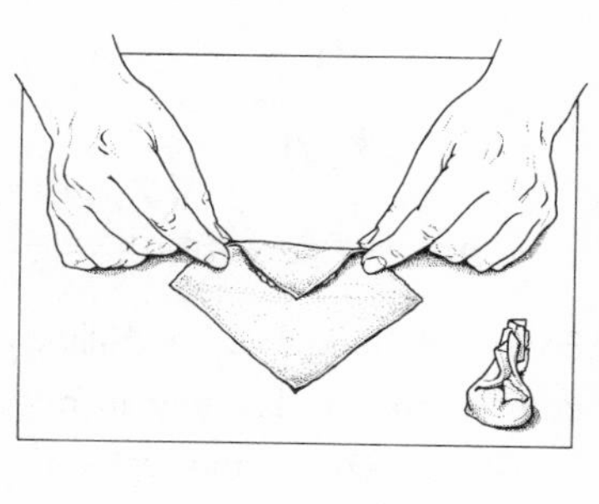

ROLL AND CUT THE DOUGH: Divide the pasta dough into 2 portions. Keep one portion covered with a damp cloth while you work with the other.

Sprinkle a work surface with 1 tablespoon cornstarch. Roll one portion of dough into a very thin sheet about 6 by 24 inches and 1⁄16 inch thick. Sprinkle the dough with cornstarch. Using a ruler and a paring knife or pastry cutter, cut the sheet into sixteen 3-inch squares. Keep the squares covered with a clean towel while you roll and cut the remaining dough.

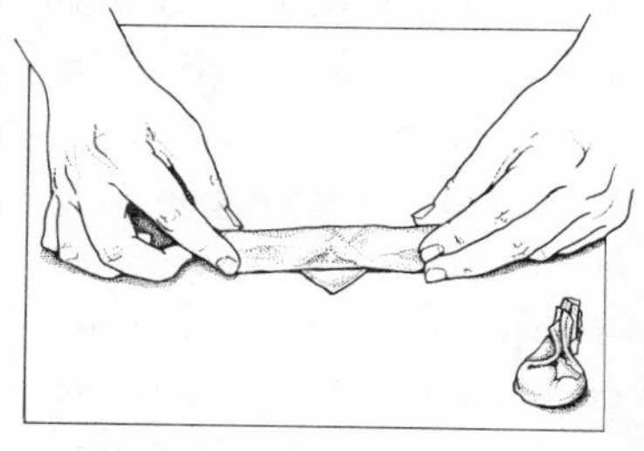

ASSEMBLE THE TORTELLINI: Position a dough square with one point toward you. Place 1 rounded teaspoon of the filling just below the center of the square. Lightly moisten the edges of the dough with water, and fold the dough in half over the filling to form a triangle. Be careful that the filling doesn't spread toward the edges, or you will not be able to seal the tortellini properly. Press the edges together and press around the filling to seal. Fold over the filled portion so that the bottom edge is within ½ inch of the tip of the triangle. Moisten the side points with water, then overlap them over the filled portion to form a ring. Pinch the overlapping edges firmly together to seal. Place the filled pasta on a lightly floured baking sheet and keep covered while you fill and fold the remaining tortellini.

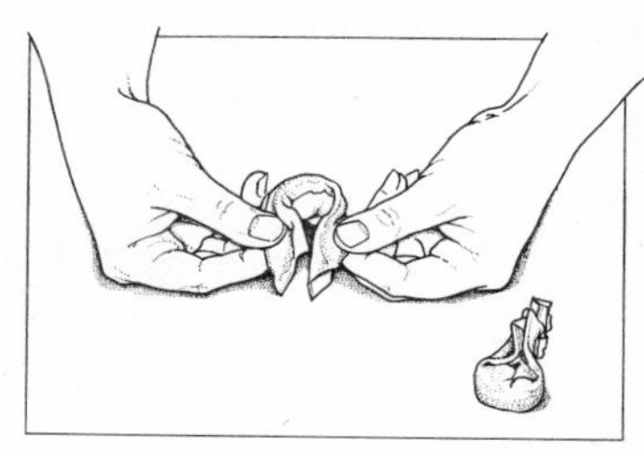

FRY THE TORTELLINI: In a wok or heavy-bottomed saucepan over moderately high heat, heat 2 to 3 inches of oil to 350°F. Add the tortellini a few at a time and fry until golden, about 1 to 1½ minutes. With a slotted spoon, remove the tortellini to paper towels to drain.

Serve hot with the salsa for dipping.

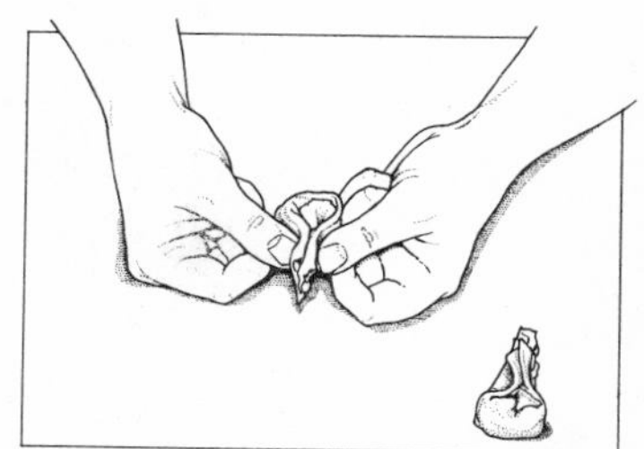

— planning ahead —

Both the dipping sauce and filling can be prepared a day in advance, covered, and refrigerated. Bring the sauce to room temperature before serving. The dough can be prepared up to 2 days ahead, covered, and refrigerated. The wontons can be assembled ahead of time, covered, and refrigerated overnight or frozen for up to 1 month. Thaw them first before deep-frying.

Crisp-Fried Shrimp Wontons

Wontons are just one of the many dumplings that make up the Chinese dim sum repertoire. They are shaped like Italian tortellini and usually stuffed with ground seasoned meats. They can be fried or steamed and served with a tangy dipping sauce, or boiled and added to noodles in broth or to stir-fried dishes. These wontons are filled with shrimp and a bit of pork and flavored with ginger, sherry, and sesame oil. They make very tasty hors d'oeuvres.

YIELD: 28 wontons for hors d'oeuvres

1 recipe Homemade Pasta Dough (page 236)

SHRIMP FILLING

6 ounces shelled raw shrimp
2 ounces ground pork
½ large egg white, lightly beaten
½ teaspoon sugar
¼ teaspoon salt
1½ teaspoons grated fresh ginger
1½ teaspoons dry sherry or vermouth
1½ teaspoons cornstarch
1 teaspoon light soy sauce
1 teaspoon Oriental sesame oil
2 tablespoons chopped scallions
Freshly ground black pepper to taste

SOY DIPPING SAUCE

¼ cup light soy sauce
¼ cup rice vinegar
2 teaspoons sugar
1 tablespoon chopped scallion
2 teaspoons finely shredded fresh ginger
½ teaspoon Oriental sesame oil
½ teaspoon chili oil

Cornstarch, for dusting
Vegetable oil, for frying

Prepare the dough. Cover and set aside.

PREPARE THE FILLING: Devein and rinse the shrimp. Pat dry and dice coarsely. In a bowl, mix the shrimp with the remaining filling ingredients. Let stand for 30 minutes.

PREPARE THE DIPPING SAUCE: Place the soy sauce, vinegar, sugar, and ¼ cup water in a small saucepan over moderate heat and bring to a boil. Remove the saucepan from the heat. Stir in the scallion, ginger, sesame oil, and chili oil. Cover and set aside.

ROLL AND CUT THE DOUGH: Divide the pasta dough into 2 portions. Keep one portion covered with a damp cloth while you work with the other.

Sprinkle a work surface with 1 tablespoon of cornstarch. Roll one portion of dough into a very thin rectangle about 6 by 24 inches. Sprinkle the dough with cornstarch. Using a ruler and a paring knife or pastry cutter, cut the sheet into sixteen 3-inch squares. Keep the squares covered with a clean towel while you roll and cut the remaining dough in the same manner.

ASSEMBLE THE WONTONS: Position a dough wrapper with one point toward you. Place 1 rounded teaspoon of the filling just below the center of the wrapper. Lightly moisten the edges of the dough with water. Fold the wrapper in half over the filling to form a triangle. Press the edges together and around the filling to seal. Moisten the 2 side points with water and overlap them over the filled portion. Pinch the overlapping edges firmly together to seal. Place the filled wonton on a lightly floured baking sheet and keep covered while you fill and fold the remaining wontons.

FRY THE WONTONS: In a wok or heavy-bottomed saucepan over moderately high heat, heat 2 to 3 inches of oil to 350°F. Add the wontons a few at a time and fry until golden, about 1 to 1½ minutes. With a slotted spoon, remove the wontons to paper towels to drain.

Serve hot with the dipping sauce.

— cook's notes —

Store-bought square wonton wrappers may be substituted for the homemade dough wrappers. You will need 28 wrappers.

In place of the shrimp, you may use 6 ounces fresh lump crabmeat or 6 ounces coarsely chopped sea scallops.

— *planning ahead* —

The dipping sauce and filling can be prepared a day ahead and refrigerated. Although it is preferable to use the potsticker dough immediately, it can be wrapped and stored in the refrigerator overnight. Once the dough is rolled and cut, the dumplings should be assembled immediately. They can be assembled ahead of time, covered, and refrigerated overnight or frozen for up to 1 month. There is no need to thaw them before frying, but increase the cooking time by 2 to 3 minutes.

Beef Potstickers with Warm Spicy Dipping Sauce

Known to the Japanese as *gyoza* and translated from the Chinese as "potstickers," these tasty dumplings have really caught on in America. They are traditionally panfried over high heat in a little oil to brown them, and their bottoms tend to stick to the pan, hence the name. Once they become crisp, water or broth is added to steam the dumplings to tenderness.

My version, which is very easy to make, yields pyramid-shaped parcels instead of the usual time-consuming pleated purses. Since the dough is bland, I make a highly seasoned filling of beef, water chestnuts, and shiitake mushrooms flavored with ginger, sherry, and sesame oil. I also find a richer flavor can be given to the dumplings by heating them briefly in their soy dipping sauce before serving.

YIELD: 24 dumplings, enough for 4 to 5 appetizer servings

POTSTICKER DOUGH

2 cups unbleached all-purpose flour, plus additional if necessary
¼ teaspoon salt
¾ cup boiling water

SOY DIPPING SAUCE

¼ cup light soy sauce
¼ cup rice vinegar
2 teaspoons sugar
1 tablespoon chopped scallion
2 teaspoons finely shredded fresh ginger
½ teaspoon Oriental sesame oil
½ teaspoon chili oil

BEEF FILLING

4 dried shiitake mushrooms (see Cook's Notes)
½ pound ground beef chuck
4 fresh or canned water chestnuts, peeled and chopped
½ large egg white, lightly beaten
½ teaspoon sugar
¼ teaspoon salt
1½ teaspoons grated fresh ginger
1½ teaspoons dry sherry or vermouth
1½ teaspoons cornstarch
1 teaspoon light soy sauce
1 teaspoon Oriental sesame oil
2 tablespoons chopped scallions
Freshly ground black pepper to taste

1 cup chicken broth, homemade (page 368) or store-bought
¼ cup peanut oil

PREPARE THE DOUGH: Place the flour and salt in the bowl of a food processor fitted with the metal blade. With the motor on, pour the boiling water through the feed tube. Process until the dough cleans the sides of the bowl and rides on the blade, about 10 seconds. If the dough sticks to the bowl, add a little more flour and process until the dough cleans the sides of the bowl. Transfer the dough to a well-floured surface and knead until very soft and silky but not sticky, about 5 minutes. Form the dough into a ball, cover with an inverted bowl, and let rest for 30 minutes.

Knead the dough a second time until quite elastic, about 3 minutes. Cover and let rest for 1 hour.

PREPARE THE DIPPING SAUCE: Place the soy sauce, vinegar, sugar, and ¼ cup water in a small saucepan over moderate heat and bring to a boil. Remove the saucepan from the heat. Stir in the scallion, ginger, sesame oil, and chili oil. Cover and set aside.

PREPARE THE FILLING: Put the mushrooms in a small bowl, cover with boiling water, and soak until soft, about 30 minutes. Drain, discarding the liquid, and squeeze the mushrooms dry. Cut off and discard the stems. Mince the mushroom caps and place them in a large mixing bowl. Add all the remaining filling ingredients and mix well. Cover and let stand for 30 minutes for the flavors to blend.

ROLL AND CUT THE DOUGH: Divide the dough into 2 portions. Keep one portion covered with a damp cloth while you work with the other.

On a well-floured surface, roll one portion of dough into a 6- by 18-inch rectangle about ⅛ inch thick. Using a knife and a ruler, cut out twelve 3-inch squares.

ASSEMBLE THE DUMPLINGS: Place 2 level teaspoons of the filling in the center of each square. Moisten the edges of one square lightly with water. Bring up and join 2 opposite corners of the square over the filling. Bring up the other 2 corners and pinch all 4 together in a point to make a pyramid-shaped parcel. Pinch the seams firmly together to seal. Place the dumpling on a lightly floured baking sheet. Assemble the remaining dumplings in the same manner. Cover with a kitchen towel while you roll and cut the remaining dough in the same manner and assemble the remaining dumplings.

FRY THE DUMPLINGS: In a small saucepan over moderate heat, bring the chicken broth to a boil. Cover and reduce the heat to just high enough to keep the broth simmering. Put 2 tablespoons of the oil into each of two 12-inch skillets set over moderately high heat. When the oil is very hot and hazy, add the dumplings to the skillets, flat bottom down. Fry until the bottoms are brown and very crisp, about 2 minutes. Add half the simmering broth to each skillet, pouring it around the dumplings. Cover and cook until the broth is absorbed, about 3 minutes. Uncover and let the dumplings fry for 1 or 2 minutes to recrisp the bottoms.

Reserve half of the dipping sauce and pour the remaining sauce over the dumplings in both skillets. Bring to a rapid boil, toss the dumplings in the sauce, and remove from the heat. Serve the dumplings immediately with the reserved sauce on the side.

— cook's notes —

Although freshly made potsticker dough is better because of its moist texture and thickness, store-bought gyoza wrappers may be substituted. You will need 24 wrappers. Place the filling in the center of each wrapper, moisten the edges with water, and fold up the sides of the dough over the filling to form a flat-bottomed, half-moon purse. Press the edges firmly to seal.

Dried shiitake mushrooms, also known as Chinese black mushrooms, are available in many well-stocked supermarkets and in Asian markets. They can also be ordered by mail from American Spoon Foods, P.O. Box 566, Petoskey, MI 49770 (616-347-9030); or from Hans Johansson, 44 West 74th Street, New York, NY 10023 (212-787-6496).

If a more assertive flavor is desired, replace the beef in the filling with ground lamb.

planning ahead

The dough, yogurt sauce, and filling can be prepared a day in advance, covered, and refrigerated. Bring the sauce to room temperature before serving. The manti can be assembled ahead of time, covered, and refrigerated overnight or frozen for up to 1 month. There is no need to thaw them before frying, but increase the cooking time by 2 to 3 minutes.

cook's notes

Store-bought square wonton wrappers may be substituted for the homemade dough wrappers. You will need 32 wrappers.

Panfried Lamb Manti with Yogurt Sauce

Manti are small pasta dumplings found throughout Central Asia, most notably in Uzbekistan, Armenia, and Turkey. They usually hold a subtly spiced filling of minced lamb, but they may also be filled with beef, pork, seafood, curd cheese, potatoes, or mushrooms. Manti can be simmered and served in a broth, deep-fried, or boiled and then baked with a sour cream sauce. In this version, I panfry them like Chinese potstickers and serve them with a garlicky yogurt sauce. They are divine!

YIELD: 32 dumplings, enough for 8 appetizer or 4 main-course servings

1 recipe Homemade Pasta Dough (page 236)

YOGURT SAUCE

2 cups yogurt
1 teaspoon minced garlic
Salt and cayenne pepper to taste

LAMB FILLING

¾ pound ground lamb
½ cup chopped fresh parsley
2 teaspoons minced garlic
2 teaspoons ground cumin
2 teaspoons ground coriander
Salt to taste
Tabasco to taste

Cornstarch, for dusting
2 cups beef broth, homemade (page 370) or store-bought
6 tablespoons unsalted butter
¼ cup chopped fresh mint leaves

Prepare the dough. Cover and set aside.

MAKE THE YOGURT SAUCE: Combine the yogurt, garlic, salt, and cayenne pepper in a bowl and blend well. Cover and refrigerate until ready to use.

MAKE THE FILLING: Combine all the filling ingredients in a mixing bowl and mix with your hands until blended. Cover and refrigerate until ready to use.

ROLL AND CUT THE DOUGH: Divide the pasta dough into 2 portions. Keep one portion covered with a damp cloth while you work with the other.

Sprinkle a work surface with 1 tablespoon cornstarch. Roll one portion of dough into a very thin sheet about 6 by 24 inches and 1⁄16 inch thick. Sprinkle the dough with cornstarch. Using a ruler and a paring knife or pastry cutter, cut the dough into sixteen 3-inch squares. Keep the squares covered with a clean towel while you roll and cut the remaining dough.

ASSEMBLE THE DUMPLINGS: Put 2 teaspoons of the filling in the center of a dough wrapper. Lightly moisten the edges of the dough with water. Bring the 4 corners over the filling to meet in the center. Pinch the edges together at the seams to seal the filling completely, forming a square dumpling. Place the dumpling on a lightly floured baking sheet and cover with a kitchen towel while you fill the remaining dumplings in the same manner.

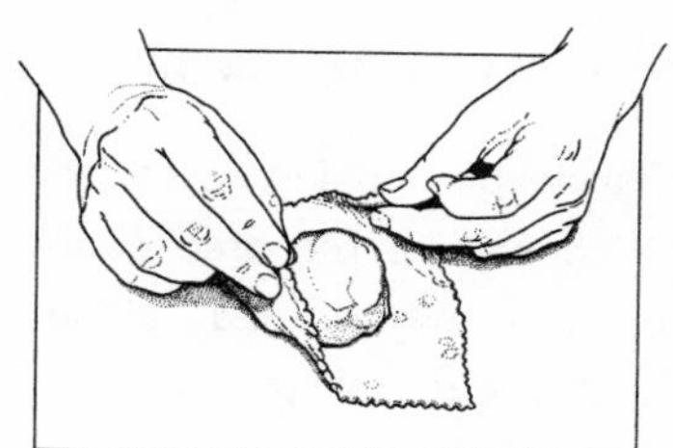

Place the broth in a medium saucepan and bring to a boil over high heat. Reduce the heat and keep the broth at a bare simmer.

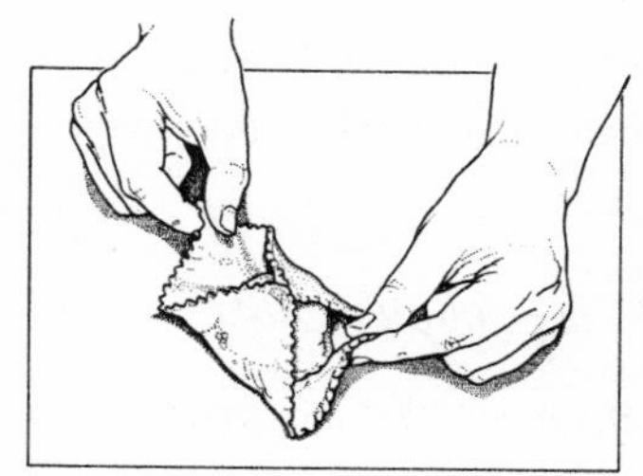

COOK THE DUMPLINGS: Melt 1 tablespoon of the butter in each of two large deep skillets over moderately low heat. When the butter foam subsides, add the manti, flat bottom down, and fry for 2 minutes without turning. Pour the hot broth over the dumplings, adding half to each pan. Cover the skillets and steam the dumplings for 5 minutes, or until all the broth has been absorbed.

TO SERVE: Meanwhile, melt the remaining 4 tablespoons butter in a skillet, and add the mint. Divide the manti among individual serving bowls and spoon the yogurt sauce over. Pour the flavored butter over the manti. Serve hot.

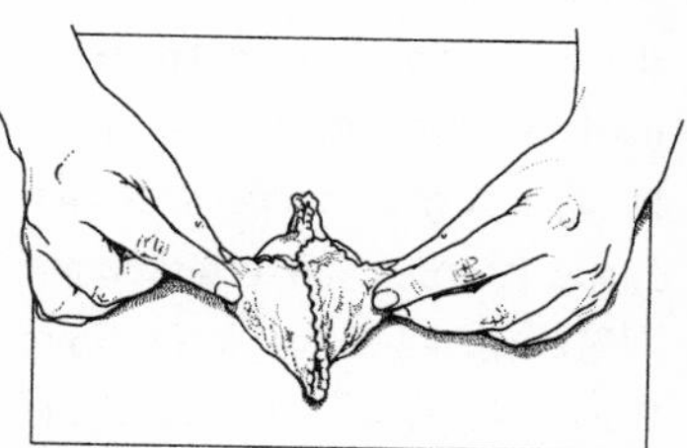

— planning ahead —

The dough, dipping sauce, and filling can be prepared a day ahead, covered, and refrigerated. The dumplings can be assembled ahead of time, covered, and refrigerated overnight or frozen for up to 1 month. Thaw them in the refrigerator before steaming.

— cook's notes —

Dried shiitake mushrooms, also known as Chinese black mushrooms, are available in many well-stocked supermarkets and in Asian markets. They can also be ordered by mail from American Spoon Foods, P.O. Box 566, Petoskey, MI 49770 (616-347-9030); or from Hans Johansson, 44 West 74th Street, New York, NY 10023 (212-787-6496).

For a different taste, replace the shrimp in the filling with cooked lobster meat or well-picked-over crabmeat.

In this recipe, gyoza wrappers should be used because of their resilient and silky texture and their ultrathin quality. If gyoza wrappers are unavailable, wonton wrappers or homemade pasta dough cut into 3-inch rounds will do as convenient stand-ins but the texture will be slightly different. If using square wonton wrappers, trim the corners with a sharp paring knife, or use a 3-inch cookie cutter, to make rounds.

Shao Mai with Chicken, Shrimp, and Mushrooms

Shao mai are steamed Chinese dumplings made up of a tasty filling, usually ground pork, inside very thin round dough wrappers. The wrapper is shaped around the filling and pinched near the top so as to have a "waist," creating a basket-shaped morsel that can stand upright on the steamer rack. I'm addicted to these dumplings and you will be too once you've tried them. Instead of a pork filling, I prefer this pleasingly textured and fragrant mixture of chicken, shrimp, shiitake mushrooms, and water chestnuts. Served with a garlicky soy dipping sauce, these shao mai are just great. You may wish to double this recipe and freeze some for impromptu hors d'oeuvres.

YIELD: 16 dumplings for hors d'oeuvres

SPECIAL EQUIPMENT: A metal steamer

CHICKEN AND SHRIMP FILLING

4 dried shiitake mushrooms (see Cook's Notes)
6 ounces ground chicken meat (preferably from the thigh)
2 ounces raw shrimp, shelled, deveined, and coarsely chopped
4 fresh or canned water chestnuts, peeled and chopped
½ large egg white, lightly beaten
½ teaspoon sugar
¼ teaspoon salt
1½ teaspoons grated fresh ginger
1½ teaspoons dry sherry or vermouth
1½ teaspoons cornstarch
1 teaspoon light soy sauce
1 teaspoon Oriental sesame oil
2 tablespoons chopped scallions
Freshly ground black pepper to taste

SOY DIPPING SAUCE

¼ cup light soy sauce
¼ cup rice vinegar
2 teaspoons sugar
1 tablespoon chopped scallion
2 teaspoons finely shredded fresh ginger
½ teaspoon Oriental sesame oil
½ teaspoon chili oil

16 gyoza wrappers
16 fresh or frozen green peas

PREPARE THE FILLING: Put the mushrooms in a small bowl, add boiling water to cover, and soak until soft, about 30 minutes. Drain, discarding the liquid. Squeeze the mushrooms dry. Cut off and discard the stems. Mince the mushroom caps and place them in a mixing bowl. Add the chicken and all the remaining filling ingredients, and mix well. Let stand for at least 30 minutes to allow the flavors to marry.

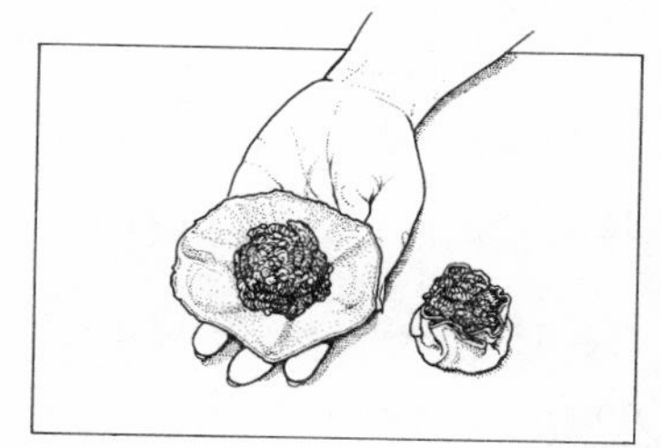

PREPARE THE DIPPING SAUCE: Place the soy sauce, vinegar, sugar, and ¼ cup water in a small saucepan over moderate heat and bring to a boil. Remove the saucepan from the heat. Stir in the scallion, ginger, sesame oil, and chili oil. Cover and set aside.

ASSEMBLE THE SHAO MAI: Place 1 tablespoon of the filling in the center of a wrapper. Gather the edges of the wrapper up around the filling. Then, holding the little packet in the palm of your hand, lightly squeeze the dumpling between your index finger and thumb to form a "waistline." Use a teaspoon dipped in hot water to press the filling down so that it is smooth on top and compact. Lightly press 1 pea into the center of the filling. Place the filled dumpling on a lightly floured baking sheet. Cover with a clean towel while you fill and wrap the remaining dumplings.

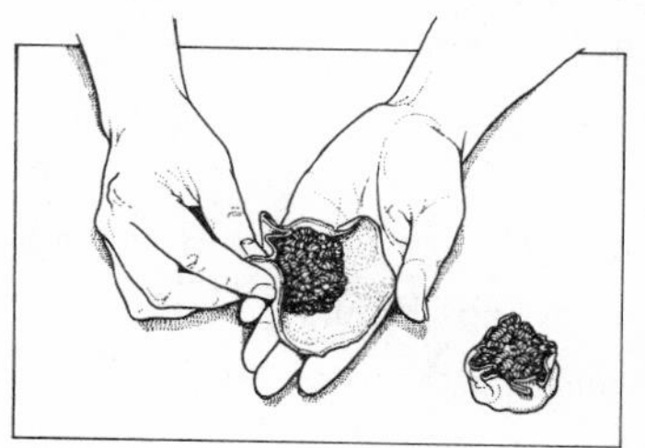

STEAM THE DUMPLINGS: Fill the bottom of the steamer pot with 1 to 2 inches of water. Bring to a boil over moderate heat. Stand the dumplings upright on an oiled steamer tray, ½ inch apart, cover, and steam for 5 minutes over high heat.

Serve hot with the dipping sauce.

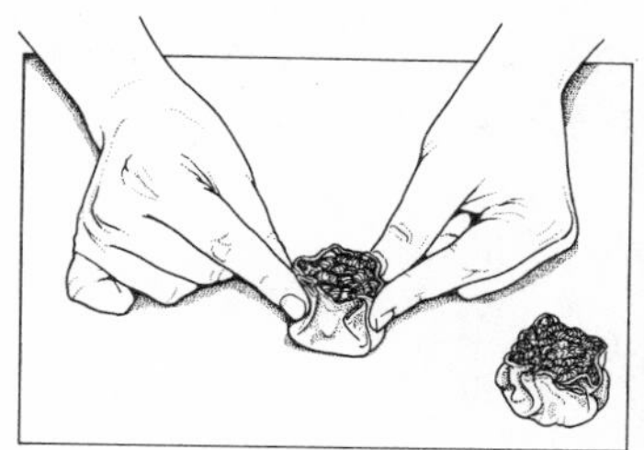

— planning ahead —

The filling can be prepared a day ahead, covered, and refrigerated. Although it is preferable to use the dough as soon as you make it, it can be wrapped and stored in the refrigerator overnight. Once rolled and cut, the dumplings should be assembled immediately. The dumplings can be assembled ahead of time, covered, and refrigerated overnight or frozen for up to 1 month. Thaw them before frying.

Sesame Beef Mandu in Broth

Mandu are the Korean version of Chinese wontons. Though influenced by Chinese and Japanese cuisines, Korean cooking is typified by a fondness for beef and bold seasonings of soy, sesame, and hot red pepper, as this dish demonstrates. I recommend serving these dumplings in a highly seasoned beef broth as a hearty whole-meal soup. However, they are just as tasty panfried and eaten on their own as hors d'oeuvres with a soy dipping sauce.

YIELD: 24 mandu, enough for 4 to 6 main-course servings

DOUGH

1 cup unbleached all-purpose flour, plus additional if necessary
¼ teaspoon salt
6 tablespoons boiling water

BEEF FILLING

2 cups finely shredded Nappa cabbage
1 teaspoon salt
¼ pound ground beef chuck
¼ cup chopped shallots or scallions
1 teaspoon minced garlic
1 tablespoon light soy sauce
2 teaspoons toasted sesame seeds, crushed (see Cook's Notes)
2 teaspoons Oriental sesame oil
Cayenne pepper to taste

BROTH

6 cups homemade beef broth (page 370) or 2 13 ¾-ounce cans beef broth diluted with 3 cups water
2 quarter-size slices fresh ginger, crushed
¼ cup light soy sauce
1 tablespoon sugar
1½ teaspoons minced garlic
¼ teaspoon cayenne pepper
2 teaspoons Oriental sesame oil

GARNISH

2 scallions, thinly sliced, for garnish
2 teaspoons toasted sesame seeds, crushed (see Cook's Notes)

PREPARE THE DOUGH: Place the flour and salt in the bowl of a food processor fitted with the metal blade. With the motor on, pour the boiling water through the feed tube. Process until the dough cleans the sides of the bowl and rides on the blade, about 10 seconds. If the dough sticks to the bowl, add a little more flour and process until the dough cleans the sides of the bowl. Transfer the dough to a well-floured surface and knead until very soft and silky but not sticky, about 5 minutes. Form the dough into a ball, cover with an inverted bowl, and let rest for 30 minutes.

Knead the dough a second time for about 3 minutes, or until the dough is quite elastic. Cover and let rest for at least 1 hour.

Meanwhile, MAKE THE FILLING: Toss the cabbage with the salt in a colander, and let stand for 15 to 20 minutes, until it has wilted. Rinse the cabbage and squeeze dry.

In a mixing bowl, combine the cabbage with the remaining filling ingredients. Cover and refrigerate.

PREPARE THE BROTH: In a 4- to 5-quart pot, combine the beef broth, ginger, soy sauce, sugar, and garlic and bring to a boil over moderately high heat. Reduce the heat to low and simmer until the broth is well flavored with the ginger and garlic, about 10 minutes. Stir in the cayenne pepper and sesame oil. Remove from the heat, cover, and set aside until ready to use.

ASSEMBLE THE DUMPLINGS: Divide the dough into 2 portions. Keep one portion covered with a damp cloth while you work with the other.

On a well-floured surface, roll one portion of dough into a 6- by 18-inch rectangle about 1⁄16 inch thick. Using a 3-inch round cookie cutter, cut out 12 circles. Place 2 level teaspoons of filling in the center of each circle. Moisten the edges of one circle of dough lightly with water. Fold the wrapper over the filling to form a half-moon. When you fold, be careful that the filling doesn't spread toward the edges or you will not be able to seal the dumpling properly. Pinch the edges firmly together to seal. Place the dumpling on a lightly floured baking sheet. Assemble the remaining dumplings in the same manner. Cover with a kitchen towel.

Roll and cut the remaining dough and assemble the remaining dumplings in the same manner.

COOK THE DUMPLINGS: Bring two large pots of 4 quarts salted water each to a rolling boil. Add half of the dumplings to each pot and boil until tender, about 3 minutes. Drain the dumplings in a colander.

TO SERVE: Bring the soup to a boil over moderately high heat. Add the dumplings and cook just until they are heated through, about 2 minutes. Ladle the soup and 4 to 5 dumplings into each soup bowl. Sprinkle the scallions and toasted sesame seeds over the soup. Serve hot.

— *cook's notes* —

Although freshly made potsticker dough is better because of its moist texture and thickness, store-bought gyoza wrappers may be substituted. If using gyoza wrappers, you will need 24.

To toast sesame seeds, place them in a dry skillet over moderate heat and cook, stirring constantly, until golden brown, about 3 minutes. Cool before using.

To serve the mandu as hors d'oeuvres: Cook the mandu in boiling water as above; drain. Heat 2 tablespoons peanut oil in each of two large skillets set over moderate heat. Add half of the boiled dumplings to each skillet and fry until golden, about 1 minute on each side. With a slotted spoon, remove the dumplings to paper towels to drain. Serve the mandu hot with a bowl of Soy Dipping Sauce (page 260) that has been sprinkled with 1 teaspoon crushed toasted sesame seeds.

— planning ahead —

The dough and filling can be prepared a day in advance, covered, and refrigerated. The dumplings can be assembled ahead of time, covered, and refrigerated overnight or frozen for up to 1 month. There is no need to thaw them before boiling, but increase the boiling time by 2 to 3 minutes.

Kreplach

Kreplach, a staple of Jewish cuisine, are small pillow-shaped noodle dumplings stuffed with cooked ground beef, chicken, or liver. They are boiled and then either added to chicken soup or sautéed and eaten on their own as hors d'oeuvres.

Although their origin is obscured in Jewish history, they are a traditional part of the meal on certain holidays and festivals. My husband's grandmother would tell me that the dough wrapper symbolizes the protection the Jewish people need from a harsh world and the filling inside represents the hidden nature of the festival being celebrated. She also said that kreplach are too good to wait for a special occasion to serve them, and I agree.

What is the best stuffing for kreplach? Since I can't decide, I've provided both a robust beef filling and a milder chicken or turkey one (page 265), both flavored with dill.

YIELD: 36 kreplach for hors d'oeuvres, or enough for 6 to 8 side-dish servings

1 recipe Homemade Noodle Dough (page 237)

BEEF FILLING

4 whole cloves
2 bay leaves
½ medium onion, peeled
10 ounces not-too-lean beef chuck, cut into ¾-inch cubes
3 tablespoons vegetable oil
¾ cup chopped onions
2 tablespoons chopped fresh dill
Salt and freshly ground black pepper to taste

4 tablespoons unsalted butter

Prepare the dough. Cover and set aside.

Using the cloves, pin the bay leaves to the cut surface of the onion.

MAKE THE FILLING: Place the meat and studded onion in a medium saucepan and cover with cold water. Bring to a boil over moderately high heat, skimming off the foam as it forms on the surface. Reduce the heat to low, cover, and simmer for 40 to 45 minutes, or until the meat is very tender. Drain the meat, discarding the onion, and set aside to cool.

In a medium skillet, heat the oil over moderately low heat. Add the chopped onions and cook, stirring occasionally, until golden brown, about 10 minutes. Transfer the fried onions and the oil to the bowl of a food processor fitted with the metal blade. Add the cooked beef and process just until the mixture forms a mass; the texture should be fairly soft but not a purée. Remove the filling to a bowl and mix in the dill. Season with salt and pepper, cover, and refrigerate until ready to use.

ROLL AND CUT THE DOUGH: On a lightly floured surface, roll the dough into a very thin sheet about 18 inches square and 1⁄16 inch thick. Using a ruler and a paring knife or pastry cutter, cut out thirty-six 3-inch squares. Keep the squares covered with a clean towel while you assemble the kreplach.

ASSEMBLE THE KREPLACH: Position a dough square with one point toward you. Place 1 rounded teaspoon of the filling just below the center of the square. Lightly moisten the edges of the dough with water. Fold the dough in half over the filling to form a triangle. When you fold, be careful that the filling doesn't spread toward the edge, or you will not be able to seal the dumpling properly. Using the tines of a fork, press the edges of the dumpling to seal. Place the kreplach on a lightly floured baking sheet and cover with a kitchen towel while you continue filling the remaining dumplings in the same manner.

COOK THE KREPLACH: Bring two large pots of 4 quarts salted water each to a rolling boil over moderately high heat. Add half of the kreplach to each pot. As soon as the water returns to a boil, reduce the heat to moderately low and gently boil until the kreplach are cooked but firm to the bite, about 3 to 4 minutes. Drain the dumplings in a colander set in the sink.

TO SERVE: Melt 2 tablespoons of the butter in each of two large skillets over moderate heat. When the butter foam subsides, add the boiled kreplach to the two pans in a single layer and sauté for 1 minute on each side or until golden brown. Season with salt and pepper. Serve at once.

VARIATION

CHICKEN AND ONION FILLING

1½ cups minced cooked chicken or turkey, preferably white meat (¾ pound)

½ cup minced onion

1 small egg, lightly beaten

2 tablespoons chopped fresh dill

Salt and freshly ground black pepper to taste

Combine all the ingredients in a small mixing bowl. Mix well, cover, and refrigerate until ready to use.

cook's notes

For those who prefer serving kreplach in chicken soup, add the boiled kreplach to about 6 cups piping-hot homemade chicken broth (page 368). Ladle some of the soup and 4 to 5 dumplings into each soup bowl, sprinkle with chopped fresh dill, and serve hot.

— *planning ahead* —

Both the filling and the dough can be prepared a day in advance, covered, and refrigerated. The dumplings can be assembled ahead of time, covered, and refrigerated overnight or frozen for up to 1 month. There's no need to thaw them before boiling. Just cook them 2 or 3 minutes longer. The smothered onions and cabbage can be prepared early in the day, covered, and reheated before serving.

Potato Pirogi with Smothered Onions and Cabbage

In Poland, stuffed noodle dumplings called *pirogi* are a familiar dish. There they are almost always homemade. Traditional fillings include ground meat, mashed potatoes, mushrooms, sauerkraut, or farmer's cheese. They are served in soup or tossed with buttered bread crumbs or bacon fat and served as a side dish with dollops of sour cream. In my version, a creamy and rich-tasting filling of mashed potatoes, enhanced by a smoky cheese flavor, contrasts nicely with the slightly chewy outer wrapper. To me, eating these pirogi with caramelized onions and tender but robust cabbage is soul-satisfying.

YIELD: 16 pirogi, enough for 8 side-dish or 4 main-course servings

½ recipe Homemade Noodle Dough (page 237)

POTATO AND CHEESE FILLING

1 large potato (about ¾ pound), peeled and quartered
1½ tablespoons vegetable oil
1½ cups finely chopped onions
3 ounces smoked cheese, such as Gouda or Bruder Basil, grated
2 tablespoons cottage cheese or sour cream
1 tablespoon snipped fresh chives

Salt and freshly ground black pepper to taste

SMOTHERED ONIONS AND CABBAGE

1 tablespoon olive oil
1 tablespoon unsalted butter
2 large onions (about 1 pound), thinly sliced
1 tablespoon minced garlic
4 cups coarsely chopped cabbage (about ½ pound)
¼ cup dry red wine
¼ cup chicken broth or water

Salt and freshly ground black pepper to taste

Prepare the dough. Cover and set aside.

PREPARE THE FILLING: Place the potato in a medium saucepan and cover with salted water. Bring to a boil over high heat, then reduce the heat to medium and cook until the potato is fork-tender but not mushy, about 20 minutes.

Drain the water from the saucepan, reduce the heat to low, and heat, shaking the pan to dry the potato. Transfer the potato to a medium mixing bowl. Using a potato masher, food mill, or electric mixer, mash the potato thoroughly until no lumps remain. Cover and set aside to cool.

In a large skillet, heat the oil over moderate heat. Add the onions and fry, stirring frequently, until very soft and brown, about 15 minutes. Remove from the heat and allow to cool. Add the fried onions to the mashed potato, along with the remaining filling ingredients. Blend well with a wooden spoon. Cover and chill.

ROLL AND CUT THE DOUGH: On a lightly floured surface, roll the dough into a circle about 16 inches in diameter and about 1⁄16 inch thick. Using a 3½-inch round cookie cutter, cut out as many circles as you can; you should get about 14. Gather the scraps into a ball, reroll, and cut out 2 or 3 more circles, for a total of 16. Keep the circles covered with a clean towel while you assemble the pirogi.

ASSEMBLE THE PIROGI: Place 1 level tablespoon of the filling just below the center of one dough circle. Lightly moisten the dough edges with a little water, then fold over to form a half-moon. When you fold, be careful that the filling doesn't spread toward the edge, or you will not be able to seal the dumpling properly. Pinch the edges firmly together to seal. Place the pirogi on a lightly floured baking sheet and cover with a kitchen towel while you continue to fill and shape the remaining dumplings in the same manner. Set aside.

COOK THE ONIONS AND CABBAGE: Heat the oil and butter in a large skillet over moderate heat. Add the onions and sauté until very brown, about 15 minutes, stirring frequently to prevent burning. Add the garlic and cook for 5 minutes. Add the cabbage and cook until wilted, about 2 minutes. Stir in the wine and broth, scraping the bottom of the pan to loosen the browned bits. Cover the skillet, reduce the heat to low, and cook until the cabbage is tender but not too soft, about 10 to 15 minutes.

Meanwhile, COOK THE DUMPLINGS: Bring two large pots of 4 quarts salted water each to a rolling boil over moderately high heat. Add half of the dumplings to each pot. As soon as the water returns to a boil, reduce the heat to moderately low and gently boil until the pirogi are cooked but still firm to the bite, about 5 to 6 minutes. Drain the dumplings in a colander set in the sink.

When the cabbage is tender, add the drained pirogi to the skillet. Season with salt and pepper and cook over low heat, stirring occasionally, for about 5 minutes. Transfer the pirogi and cabbage to a heated serving platter and serve at once.

— cook's notes —

If you own a pasta machine with a ravioli attachment and you are really pressed for time, you may use the machine to assemble these dumplings. Follow the manufacturer's directions for making ravioli. With the machine, of course, you will get ravioli shapes instead of half-moon shapes. Made this way, there will be almost enough filling to stuff a double batch of noodle dough.

— *planning ahead* —

Both the filling and the dough can be prepared a day ahead of time, covered, and refrigerated. The dumplings can be assembled ahead of time, covered, and refrigerated overnight or frozen for up to 1 month. There's no need to thaw them before boiling. Just cook them a minute or 2 longer.

— *cook's notes* —

If you own a pasta machine with a ravioli attachment and you are really pressed for time, you may use the machine to assemble these dumplings. Follow the manufacturer's directions for making ravioli. With the machine, of course, you will get ravioli shapes instead of half-moon shapes. Made this way, there will be almost enough filling to stuff a double batch of noodle dough.

Pel'meni with Vinegar and Mustard Sauce

Pel'meni are tiny button-size noodle dumplings shaped like tortellini. Originally from Mongolia, these dumplings are now a Siberian staple. They are prepared in large quantities and kept in sacks outdoors to last through the whole winter, ready to be cooked as needed. In Russian cities, pel'meni are sold in special cafés called *pel'mennay* and are served in several ways. They can be coated with butter and eaten as a delicious main course with sour cream. Siberian-style, they are sprinkled with vinegar and freshly ground black pepper and accompanied by a glass of beer or vodka. Or they may be simply added to piping-hot beef consommé and eaten as a soup.

Making pel'meni into small little button shapes is laborious, but I have found that making them larger saves time and takes nothing away from their taste and texture. Pel'meni are traditionally filled with shaved frozen horsemeat, bits of beef suet, and onions. As horsemeat and beef suet are hard to find here (I didn't look very hard), I have substituted ground chuck. The taste of the final dish will depend mostly on the accompaniments. Here, I have prepared a vinegar and mustard sauce. Feel free to experiment with some of the other ways of serving I mention above.

YIELD: 28 dumplings, enough for 4 appetizer or 2 main-course servings

½ recipe Homemade Noodle Dough (page 237)

BEEF FILLING

4 ounces ground chuck, well chilled
¼ cup very finely chopped onion
⅓ teaspoon salt
Freshly ground black pepper to taste
3 tablespoons ice water

VINEGAR AND MUSTARD SAUCE

¼ cup of good malt vinegar
2 tablespoons Dijon mustard

4 tablespoons unsalted butter
Sour cream (optional)

Prepare the dough. Cover and set aside.

MAKE THE FILLING: Place the ground beef, onion, salt, and pepper in a medium mixing bowl. Using an electric mixer, blend the ingredients at low speed. Gradually add the ice water and beat just until the mixture is fluffy. Cover and refrigerate.

ROLL AND CUT THE DOUGH: On a lightly floured surface, roll the dough into a circle about 16 inches in diameter and about 1/16 inch thick. Using a 3-inch round cookie cutter, cut out as many circles as you can; you should get about 23. Gather the scraps into a ball, reroll, and cut out 5 or 6 more circles, for a total of 28. Keep the circles covered with a clean towel while you assemble the pel'meni.

ASSEMBLE THE DUMPLINGS: Place 1 teaspoon of the filling just below the center of one dough circle. Lightly moisten the dough edges with a little water, and fold over to form a half-moon. Pinch the edges firmly together to seal. Moisten the 2 corners with a little water and bring them together, overlapping them just below the filled portion of the dumpling. Pinch the overlapped corners firmly together to seal. Place the pel'meni on a lightly floured baking sheet and cover with a kitchen towel while you continue to fill and shape the remaining dumplings in the same manner.

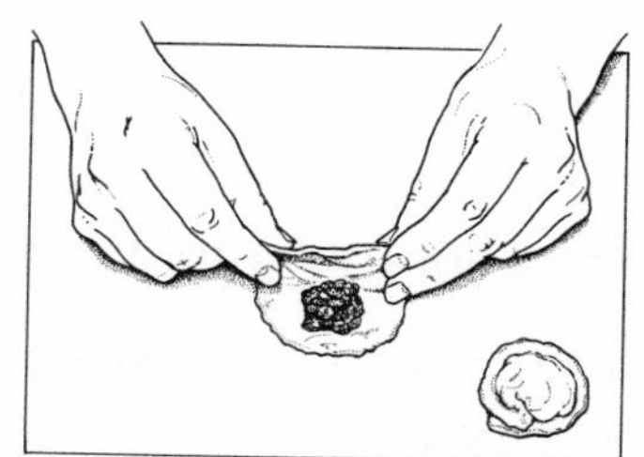

MAKE THE SAUCE: Combine the vinegar and mustard in a small saucepan and bring to a boil over moderately low heat. Remove from the heat, cover, and set aside.

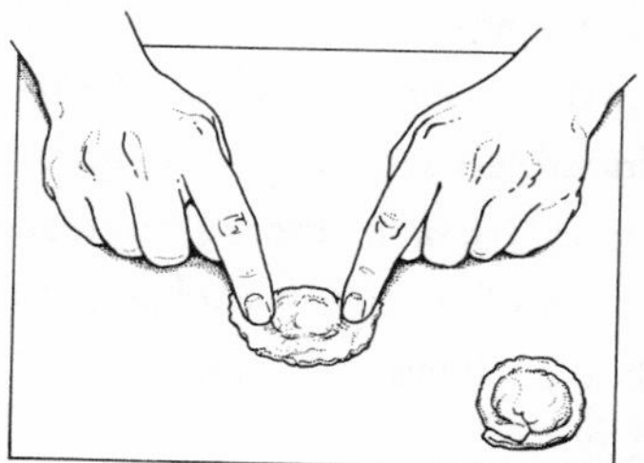

COOK THE PEL'MENI: Bring two large pots of 4 quarts salted water each to a rolling boil over moderately high heat. Add half of the dumplings to each pot. As soon as the water returns to a boil, reduce the heat to moderately low and gently boil until the dumplings are cooked but still firm to the bite, about 3 to 4 minutes. Drain the dumplings in a colander set in the sink.

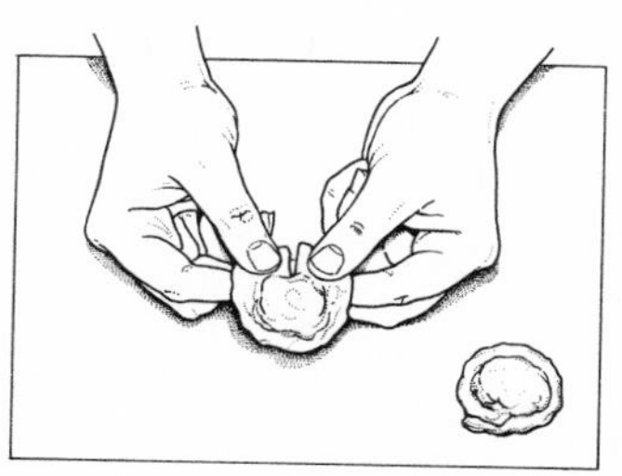

TO SERVE: In a large pot, melt the butter over moderate heat. Add the pel'meni and toss well to coat with butter. Transfer the buttered pel'meni to heated pasta bowls. Sprinkle with the vinegar and mustard sauce. If desired, top with dollops of sour cream.

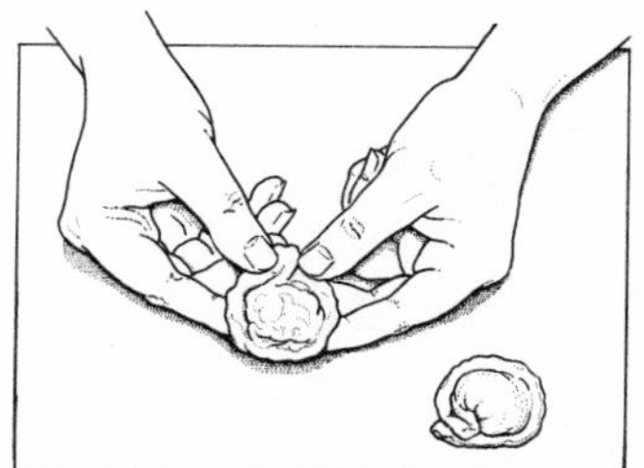

— planning ahead —

Both the filling and the dough can be prepared a day ahead, covered, and refrigerated. The dumplings can be assembled ahead of time, covered, and refrigerated overnight or frozen for up to 1 month. There's no need to thaw them before cooking. Just boil a minute or 2 longer.

Bavarian Dumplings

(MAULTASCHEN)

The first time I ate these little triangular noodle dumplings was on a bicycle trip with German friends through the Black Forest in southwestern Bavaria. During a stop at a village inn, we feasted on a sumptuous dinner of roast venison. These plump, delicious meat-filled triangles were featured as a side dish. Like pirogi, maultaschen may accompany meat dishes. Or, like kreplach and tortellini, they can be served in a clear broth. The delicate chicken and spinach filling in this recipe combines wonderfully with the slightly smoky, crunchy bread crumb topping. Serve these tasty morsels as the first course of a light supper.

YIELD: 36 dumplings, enough for 6 first-course servings

1 recipe Homemade Noodle Dough (page 237)

CHICKEN AND SPINACH FILLING

2 slices white bread
¼ cup milk
1 10-ounce package frozen chopped spinach, thawed
½ cup minced cooked chicken or turkey (about ¼ pound)
½ cup minced onions
¼ teaspoon freshly grated nutmeg
1 small egg, lightly beaten
Salt and freshly ground black pepper to taste

8 tablespoons (1 stick) unsalted butter
½ cup fine bread crumbs
½ cup chopped fresh parsley
Salt and freshly ground black pepper to taste

Prepare the dough. Cover and set aside.

MAKE THE FILLING: Soak the bread in the milk for 3 minutes. Squeeze dry. Reserve ¼ cup of the spinach for another use. Squeeze dry the remaining spinach and place in a bowl. Add the bread and the remaining filling ingredients and mix well.

ROLL AND CUT THE DOUGH: On a lightly floured surface, roll the dough into a very thin sheet about 18 inches square and 1/16 inch thick. Using a ruler and a paring knife or pastry cutter, cut out thirty-six 3-inch squares. Keep the squares covered with a clean towel while you assemble the dumplings.

ASSEMBLE THE DUMPLINGS: Position a dough square with one point toward you. Place 1 rounded teaspoon of the filling just below the center of the square. Lightly moisten the edges of the dough with water. Fold the dough in half over the filling to form a triangle. When you fold, be careful that the filling doesn't spread toward the edge, or you will not be able to seal the dumpling properly. Using the tines of a fork, press the edges of the dumpling to seal. Place the dumpling on a lightly floured baking sheet and cover with a kitchen towel. Fill the remaining dumplings in the same manner.

MAKE THE BUTTERED BREAD CRUMBS: Melt the butter in a skillet set over low heat. Add the bread crumbs and sauté for 5 minutes, or until lightly toasted, stirring constantly to prevent burning. Stir in the parsley and season with salt and pepper. Remove from the heat and cover to keep warm.

COOK THE DUMPLINGS: Bring two large pots of 4 quarts salted water each to a rolling boil over moderately high heat. Add half of the dumplings to each pot. As soon as the water returns to a boil, reduce the heat to moderately low and gently boil until the dumplings are cooked but still firm to the bite, about 3 to 4 minutes. Drain the dumplings in a colander set in the sink.

TO SERVE: Place the dumplings in heated pasta bowls and top with the buttered crumbs. Serve at once.

cook's notes

This recipe is a perfect way to use up leftover cooked chicken. It can be made as well with cooked beef, ham, or veal.

— *planning ahead* —

Both the filling and the dough can be prepared a day in advance, covered, and refrigerated. The dumplings can be assembled ahead of time, covered, and refrigerated overnight or frozen for up to 1 month. Thaw them in the refrigerator before boiling.

Glazed Potato Dumplings

(KARTOFFELNUDELN)

What pirogi are to Poland, kartoffelnudeln are to Germany. My first memory of eating these delicious potato-filled dumplings was actually in Belgium, when a German neighbor brought them over for my family to taste. To me, these robust dumplings capture the rustic heartiness of traditional German food. With their soul-satisfying starchy warmth and a crusty, creamy topping, they are the perfect comfort food. I have added Gruyère and Parmesan cheeses to the cream, neither of which is a traditional ingredient in German cooking, but they provide an absolutely sublime flavor to the cooked dumplings.

YIELD: 12 large dumplings, enough for 6 appetizer or 4 main-course servings

1 recipe Homemade Noodle Dough (page 237)

POTATO FILLING

2 large baking potatoes (about 1½ pounds), peeled and quartered
1½ tablespoons olive oil
1½ tablespoons unsalted butter
3 cups finely chopped onions
2 tablespoons snipped fresh chives or chopped scallions
Salt and freshly ground black pepper to taste

GLAZE

1 cup heavy cream
¼ cup chopped fresh parsley
¼ cup grated Gruyère or Swiss cheese
¼ cup freshly grated Parmesan cheese
Cayenne pepper to taste

Prepare the dough. Cover and set aside.

PREPARE THE FILLING: Place the potato in a medium saucepan and cover with salted water. Bring to a boil over high heat. Reduce the heat to medium and cook until the potato is fork-tender but not mushy, about 20 minutes.

Drain the water from the saucepan, reduce the heat to low, and heat, shaking the pan to dry the potato. Transfer the potato to a medium mixing bowl. Using a potato masher, food mill, or electric mixer, mash the potato thoroughly until no lumps remain. Cover and set aside to cool.

In a large skillet, heat the oil and butter over moderate heat. Add the onions and fry, stirring frequently, until very soft and brown, about 15 minutes. Remove from the heat and allow to cool. Stir in 2 cups of the mashed potatoes (any extra potato can be saved for other use). Stir in the chives and season with salt and pepper. Transfer to a bowl, cover, and refrigerate until ready to use.

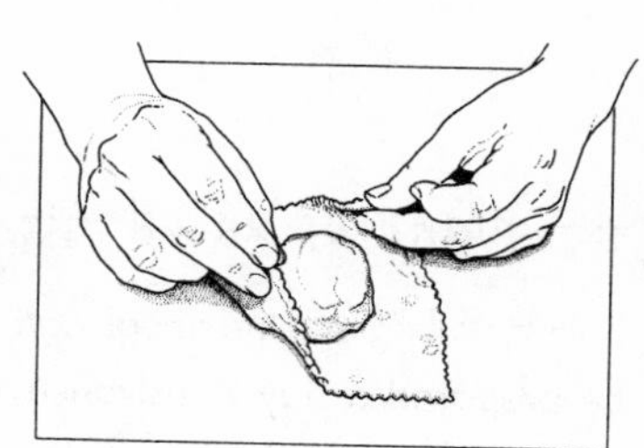

ROLL AND CUT THE DOUGH: On a lightly floured surface, roll the dough into a 15- by 20-inch rectangle about ⅛ inch thick. Using a ruler and a paring knife or pastry cutter, cut out twelve 5-inch squares. Keep the squares covered with a clean towel while you assemble the dumplings.

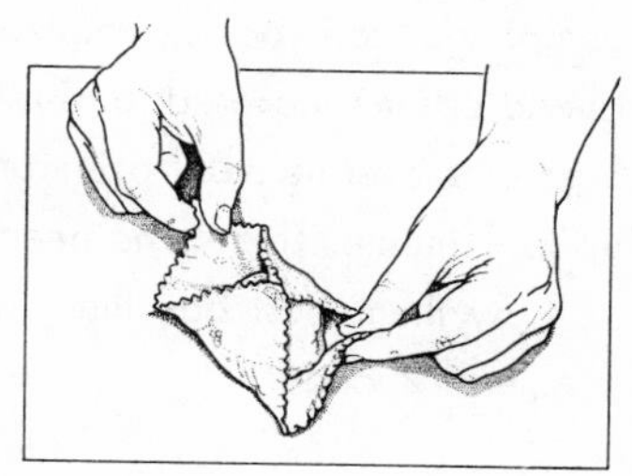

ASSEMBLE THE DUMPLINGS: Divide the potato filling into 12 equal portions. Mound one portion of filling in the center of a dough square. Lightly moisten the edges of the dough with water. Bring the 4 corners over the filling to meet in the center. Pinch the edges together at the seams to seal the filling completely, forming a pyramid-shaped dumpling. Place the dumpling on a lightly floured baking sheet and cover with a kitchen towel while you continue filling the remaining dumplings in the same manner.

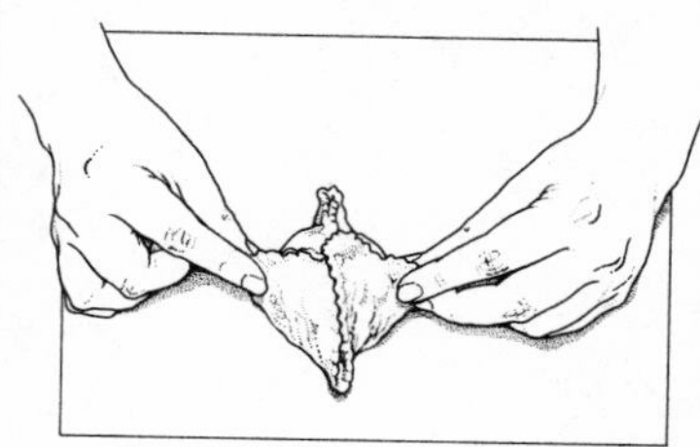

COOK THE DUMPLINGS: Bring two large pots of 4 quarts salted water each to a rolling boil over moderately high heat. Add half of the dumplings to each pot. As soon as the water returns to a boil, reduce the heat to moderately low and gently boil until the dumplings are cooked but still firm to the bite, about 6 to 8 minutes. Using a slotted spoon, carefully transfer the dumplings to a colander set in the sink to drain.

Meanwhile, preheat the broiler.

GLAZE THE DUMPLINGS: Arrange the dumplings in a single layer in a large baking dish. Pour the cream over the dumplings. Sprinkle with the parsley, the cheeses, and cayenne pepper. Broil until the topping is bubbly and lightly browned, about 2 minutes. Serve at once.

— *planning ahead* —

Both the filling and the dough can be prepared a day in advance, covered, and refrigerated. The dumplings can be assembled ahead of time, covered, and refrigerated overnight or frozen for up to 1 month. There's no need to thaw them. Just boil them a minute or 2 longer.

Cherry Variniki with Whipped Sour Cream

A Ukrainian specialty, variniki are close cousins to the Polish pirogi. When stuffed with a sweet filling, they make a delicious and easy dessert. This dish may be the ultimate pleasure for pasta lovers. It resembles ravioli that have been filled with cherries. Cut into, they reveal a precious jewellike interior awash in a rich ruby syrup. Whipped sour cream with cherry brandy and brown sugar caps the variniki with just the right touch. Be sure to warn your guests to save room for dessert when you are planning to serve this remarkable finale to a meal.

YIELD: 16 dumplings, enough for 4 to 6 dessert servings

½ recipe Homemade Noodle Dough (page 237)

CHERRY FILLING

½ pound fresh cherries, pitted and halved, or frozen cherries, thawed and drained
1 tablespoon kirschwasser (cherry brandy)
⅓ cup cherry, strawberry, or raspberry preserves

WHIPPED SOUR CREAM

1 cup sour cream
1 teaspoon kirschwasser
¼ cup light brown sugar

Prepare the dough. Cover and set aside.

MAKE THE FILLING: Combine the cherries and kirschwasser in a bowl, and set aside to marinate for 15 minutes. Stir in the preserves. Cover and refrigerate.

ROLL AND CUT THE DOUGH: On a lightly floured surface, roll the dough into a circle about 16 inches in diameter and about 1/16 inch thick. Using a 3½-inch round cookie cutter, cut out as many circles as you can; you should get about 14. Gather the scraps into a ball, reroll, and cut out 2 or 3 more circles, for a total of 16. Keep the circles covered with a clean towel while you assemble the variniki.

ASSEMBLE THE VARINIKI: Place 1 teaspoon of the filling just below the center of a dough circle. Lightly moisten the dough edges with a little water, then fold over to form a half-moon. When you fold, be careful that the filling doesn't spread toward the edge, or you will not be able to seal the dumpling properly. Pinch the edges firmly together to seal. Place the dumpling on a lightly floured baking sheet and cover with a kitchen towel while you continue to fill and shape the remaining dumplings in the same manner.

PREPARE THE SOUR CREAM TOPPING: In a mixing bowl, combine the sour cream, kirschwasser, and sugar. Whip until the cream is smooth and stiff. Cover and refrigerate until ready to serve.

COOK THE DUMPLINGS: Bring 4 quarts salted water to a rolling boil in a large pot over moderately high heat. Add the dumplings. As soon as the water returns to a boil, reduce the heat to moderately low and gently boil until the dumplings are cooked but still firm to the bite, about 5 minutes. Carefully transfer the dumplings, using a slotted spoon, to a colander set in the sink.

TO SERVE: Place the variniki in dessert bowls and top with the whipped sour cream. Serve immediately.

crêpes

Which came first: French crêpes, Filipino lumpias, Eastern European blintzes, or Vietnamese steamed rice pancakes? My guess is none of them. Thin pliant circular wrappers like these were probably developed independently and simultaneously in the cuisines of many countries and cultures.

I tend to equate all of these wrappers with the crêpe, however, as they are so similar in nature. They are all made from a batter of flour and either eggs or water that is poured sparingly into a crêpe pan or frying pan and cooked on one or both sides. The end results are paper-thin, flexible pancakes that can be used to wrap up all sorts of food and can be eaten hot or cold, with a knife and fork or out of hand. They are versatile, to say the least. Savory or sweet in taste and light in texture, they lend themselves to a variety of intriguing, often elegant, presentations. Best of all, they are extremely easy to prepare and require no tricky techniques or special kitchen equipment.

I have included recipes using store-bought Asian spring roll wrappers and rice paper rounds in this chapter because they have many elements in common with homemade crêpes and are used in a similar fashion. The following background information will help you understand the nature of all of the crêpelike wrappers.

FRENCH CRÊPES In France, especially in Brittany, crêpe making is a time-honored tradition. A French crêpe is made from a batter of wheat or buckwheat flour, eggs, milk, and melted butter. The crêpe is lightly fried on both sides until it just begins to brown. The French will fill a crêpe with just about anything, and so should you. Among my favorite crêpe dishes are Smoked Salmon Crêpes with Tender Greens (page 283) and Buckwheat Crêpes with Scampi (page 298).

BLINTZES What crêpes are to France, blintzes are to Russia. Blintz pancakes are similar to crêpes but with some important differences. A blintz is slightly thicker than a crêpe, is cooked only on one side, and is not allowed to brown like its French relative. Most people know blintzes as thin pancakes wrapped around sweetened pot cheese, panfried in butter, and served with either a fruit sauce or a dollop of sour cream. The blintz pancake is too versatile to be limited to this single filling. Personally, I like to make Ice Cream Blintzes (page 310) and serve them flambéed in a fruit sauce.

LUMPIA Like the words *crêpes* and *blintzes, lumpia* refers both to Filipino lumpia wrappers and the dishes made with them. Fresh lumpia wrappers are delicate, thin pancakes made from a batter of cornstarch, eggs, and water and cooked on one side only. For assembly, a lettuce leaf is placed on each wrapper and a filling of choice is placed in the center of the leaf. The filling can be a simple salad or a mixture of cooked meat and vegetables. The wrapper is folded around the filling to form a compact bundle, which is dipped into a sauce and eaten out of hand. My recipe for Grilled Shrimp and Pineapple Lumpia on (page 302) illustrates this style of eating.

You may also find frozen lumpia wrappers in Asian markets. Drier and more chewy than homemade lumpia, they are very similar to the semidried spring roll wrappers described below. They are used solely for deep-frying.

VIETNAMESE STEAMED RICE CRÊPES Vietnamese rice pancakes (banh uot) are made from a rice flour batter that contains no egg or milk. Traditionally, they are prepared by spreading the batter onto a muslin cloth stretched over a pot of simmering water and covering with a lid to steam-cook the pancakes. For the home kitchen, it's more practical to make them like crêpes by pouring the batter into a pan set over low heat. I cover the pan so that the crêpe is steamed and fried simultaneously. This produces translucent, soft, and very moist crêpes with a noodlelike texture. To experiment with them, try the recipes for Grilled Lime Chicken in Rice Crêpes (page 288) or Rice Paper Raviolis (page 290).

VIETNAMESE DRIED RICE PAPER Dried rice paper (banh trang), a uniquely Vietnamese wrapper, is used much like the other crêpes in this chapter for wrapping and eating foods. It is made by spreading a paste of rice flour, salt, and water into paper-thin translucent rounds on bamboo mats and drying them under the sun. The drying process imprints the papers with their characteristic and intriguing crosshatched bamboo pattern.

Banh trang are available in Asian markets in one-pound packages. Although dried rice papers come in different sizes, 8- and 12-inch diameters are most common. They must be stored at room temperature in airtight plastic bags or they will curl from contact with the air. They will keep for up to one year.

Dried rice paper must be rehydrated before use by briefly dipping it in hot water. Once this is done, you will have a wrapper that is very flexible and, when wrapped around a filling, adheres to itself to seal the food inside. It may be eaten without further cooking, as in my Smoked Turkey Rolls with Basil Sauce (page 292). When fried or baked, rice paper develops a crisp and brittle texture, as in the famous Vietnamese Spring Rolls (page 294). I have found rice paper to be extremely versatile, excellent for most cooking techniques, and wonderful for experimenting. This has led to such tempting dishes as Apple and Tarragon Rice Paper Crêpes (page 304).

SPRING ROLL WRAPPERS Available in Asian groceries in 8-inch square sheets, these paper-thin semi-dried crêpes are made by flattening a ball of wet flour-and-water dough into a hot skillet to produce a very thin pancake. Do not confuse these with egg roll wrappers, which are a lot thicker and moister and contain egg. Because of their lack of egg, spring roll wrappers produce a crisper, more delicate crust after frying. They come frozen in packages of four ounces (ten sheets) or twelve ounces (twenty-five sheets).

Spring roll wrappers are most commonly used in Chinese, Filipino, and Thai cooking, where they are invariably wrapped around a precooked meat, fish, or vegetable filling and deep-fried. The end result is usually just called a spring roll. When fried, these wrappers produce crisp, brittle crusts. To the best of my knowledge, they are uniquely suited for this cooking method. Any other method yields unsatisfactory results. Although spring roll wrappers are usually associated only with spring rolls, they can definitely be used for more exciting creations, ranging from Tempura Shrimp Toasts (page 284) to Tropical Strudels (page 306).

As you can see, crêpes can belong to many nationalities. Because some of the wrappers in this chapter may be unfamiliar to many cooks, I have chosen to demonstrate their versatility by using them in both traditional and untraditional ways. As always, my aim is to encourage experimentation with other food cultures.

CRÊPE WRAPPING TIPS

- When using frozen spring roll wrappers, allow them to thaw fully in their protective bag before using. To use, remove from the bag and cover the contents with a clean damp cloth to prevent them from drying out. Carefully remove the wrappers sheet by sheet as required. Tightly seal any unused wrappers in a plastic bag and freeze (for no more than one month) for future use or store in the refrigerator and use within three days.
- To store uncooked spring rolls, arrange them half an inch apart on a plastic-lined baking sheet, cover, and refrigerate for up to twenty-four hours. Or, place the baking sheet in the freezer until the items are solidly frozen, then transfer them to storage containers or freezer bags for up to one month. Thaw them before deep-frying.

- When you are ready to assemble a dish using rice paper, open the package and remove as many sheets as required. Rewrap the remaining sheets. Cover the sheets you need at all times with a clean damp cloth or plastic wrap to prevent them from drying out while you work.
- Dried rice paper wrappers must be rehydrated before use by dipping them briefly in a large bowl of hot water. If the wrappers are to be deep-fried, a little sugar added to the water will give a golden color and extra crunch to the fried wrapper.
- If you are a beginning crêpe maker, you may want to use only one pan. But once you have gotten into the special rhythm and ease of crêpe making, you will feel comfortable and efficient keeping two pans going at once. This is especially useful if you are producing crêpes in quantity.
- Reserve two nonstick or Teflon-coated frying pans or special crêpe pans about 8½ inches (or 6½ inches) in diameter solely for crêpe making if you want the crêpes to come out of the pan perfectly every time.
- If calories are your concern, use a good quality oil or butter spray to coat the pans in which the crêpes are to be cooked.

French Crêpes

YIELD: About eighteen 8-inch crêpes

1 cup unbleached all-purpose flour
½ cup milk
4 large eggs
½ teaspoon salt
6 tablespoons unsalted butter, melted

MAKE THE BATTER: Combine the flour, milk, eggs, and salt with 1 cup water in the container of a blender or food processor. Blend at high speed, scraping down the sides as necessary, until the batter is well mixed; do not overblend. Pour the batter through a fine-mesh sieve into a mixing bowl. Whisk in 3 tablespoons of the melted butter. Allow the batter to rest, covered, at room temperature for at least 1 hour so that the gluten will relax, or the crêpes will be rubbery.

COOK THE CRÊPES: Heat an 8-inch crêpe pan or nonstick omelet pan over moderately high heat. Brush the pan lightly with some of the remaining melted butter and heat until a drop of water sizzles on contact. Stir the batter. Fill a ⅓-cup liquid measure about two-thirds full with batter. Lift the pan from the heat and add the batter. Quickly tilt and rotate the pan to cover the bottom evenly with the batter. Return the pan to the heat and cook until the edges and underside of the crêpe are lightly browned, about 1 minute. Loosen the edges of the crêpe with the tip of a metal spatula, then lift up the crêpe and quickly turn it with your fingers. Brown the crêpe lightly on the other side and slide it onto a plate.

Continue making crêpes with the remaining batter in the same manner, brushing the pan lightly with butter each time. Allow the crêpes to cool before using.

VARIATIONS

DILLED CRÊPES: Just before you cook the crêpes, stir 2 tablespoons chopped fresh dill into the batter. Chopped fresh chives, thyme, or oregano can replace the dill.

BUCKWHEAT CRÊPES: Replace ¼ cup of the all-purpose flour with buckwheat flour (available in health food stores).

DESSERT CRÊPES: Add 2 tablespoons sugar to the batter and decrease the salt to ¼ teaspoon.

cook's notes

Letting the batter stand produces better-textured, lighter crêpes.

To make the most delicate crêpes, make sure the pan is hot enough to make a thin, even layer stick when the batter is swirled around the pan.

Although crêpes are best when fresh, they can be kept in the refrigerator for a few days or frozen for up to 2 weeks. To store the crêpes, layer them between waxed paper, seal them in a plastic bag, and refrigerate for up to 3 days or freeze for future use. Defrost thoroughly before using. To reheat, wrap the crêpes in foil and place in a preheated 350°F oven until thoroughly heated, about 10 to 15 minutes.

The basic crêpe can be used both for entrées and desserts. When making dessert crêpes, add 2 tablespoons sugar to the batter and decrease the salt to ¼ teaspoon. You may flavor the batter to taste with vanilla extract, finely grated lemon or orange zest, or liquor, such as Curaçao, cognac, or rum.

— cook's notes —

Rice flour is available in 1-pound bags at Asian markets and some health food stores. Potato flour, also known as potato starch, is available in the kosher products section of many supermarkets and in health food stores.

This batter may be used immediately or kept in a jar in the refrigerator for up to 2 days. Bring to room temperature before using.

To successfully prepare these wrappers, use fairly low heat and make sure that the pan is well brushed with oil and heated for 15 seconds before adding each batch of well-stirred batter. To speed up the preparation time, use two pans at a time. While one crêpe is being steamed, start the next one in the other pan, and so on until all the batter is used.

The steamed crêpes may be prepared early in the day, covered with plastic wrap, and kept at room temperature until ready to be used. Do not refrigerate or freeze the crêpes or they will tear. The rice flour and cornstarch in the batter don't like cold temperatures.

Steamed Rice Crêpes

YIELD: About twenty-eight 6-inch crêpes

BATTER

1 cup rice flour (see Cook's Notes)
½ cup potato flour (see Cook's Notes)
½ cup cornstarch
½ teaspoon salt
¼ cup vegetable oil

Vegetable oil, for coating

MAKE THE BATTER: In a large mixing bowl, combine the flours, cornstarch, salt, the ¼ cup oil, and 3 cups cold water. Blend well with a wire whisk. Set aside.

Generously oil a baking sheet and set it next to the stove, along with a small bowl of vegetable oil and a pastry brush.

COOK THE CRÊPES: Brush a 6½-inch nonstick omelet pan with oil and set it over low heat for 2 minutes. Stir the batter. Half-fill a ¼-cup liquid measure with batter and pour the batter into the pan. Tilt the pan and swirl to distribute the batter evenly. Cover the pan tightly and steam for about 2 minutes, or until the crêpe looks bubbly and translucent. Remove the lid, being careful not to allow the condensed moisture to drip onto the crêpe. Loosen the edges of the crêpe with the tip of a spatula, lift the crêpe from the pan, and place it upside down on the oiled baking sheet. Allow the crêpe to cool slightly, then turn it a few times to coat both sides with oil. Transfer the cooled crêpe to an oiled plate. Generously oil the baking sheet again.

Continue making the crêpes, taking care to stir the batter thoroughly each time before adding it to the pan. Allow the crêpes to cool thoroughly before stacking them, or they will stick together.

Smoked Salmon Crêpes with Tender Greens

Sometimes the simplest recipes turn out to be the best. I'm sure you will find this light and refreshing dish as pleasing to look at as it is to eat. It is just the right item for an elegant Sunday brunch or a light lunch. The smoky taste and creamy texture of the salmon is nicely counterbalanced by the light, lemony salad. It would be de rigueur to serve cold vodka, chilled champagne, or both with this dish.

YIELD: 8 crêpes, enough for 4 light main-course servings

½ recipe Dilled Crêpes (page 281)

SMOKED SALMON FILLING

1 cup crème fraîche, store-bought or homemade (see Cook's Notes)
1 tablespoon chopped fresh dill
16 thin slices smoked salmon (about ¾ pound)

SALAD

1 tablespoon fresh lemon juice
1 tablespoon finely chopped shallots
2 teaspoons Dijon mustard
⅓ cup light olive oil
Salt and freshly ground black pepper to taste
½ pound mixed leafy greens, such as red oak leaf lettuce, mâche, baby butter lettuce, and radicchio
Salmon caviar, for garnish (optional)
Fresh dill sprigs, for garnish (optional)

Prepare the crêpes. You will need 8 crêpes for this recipe. Cover and refrigerate.

PREPARE THE FILLING: In a bowl, whip ¾ cup of the crème fraîche until slightly thick. Stir in the dill.

ASSEMBLE THE CRÊPES: Spread about 2 tablespoons of the whipped crème fraîche over each crêpe. Top with 2 slices of the salmon. Fold the crêpes into quarters. Place the crêpes on a large platter, cover, and refrigerate until ready to serve.

PREPARE THE SALAD: Whisk the lemon juice, shallots, mustard, and olive oil in a salad bowl. Season with salt and pepper. Add the mixed greens and gently toss to coat with the dressing.

Divide the mixed greens among four dinner plates and top each salad with 2 folded crêpes. Garnish each crêpe with a dollop of the remaining crème fraîche, and with some salmon caviar and a sprig of dill if desired.

— planning ahead —

The crêpes can be prepared a day ahead, covered, and refrigerated. Both the assembled crêpes and dressing may be prepared a few hours in advance, covered, and refrigerated, leaving just a quick tossing of the salad before serving.

If you wish to make your own crème fraîche (page 372), it must be prepared at least 2 days in advance.

— cook's notes —

The filled crêpes gain in flavor if removed from the refrigerator 5 to 10 minutes before serving.

— *planning ahead* —

Both the sauce and the filling can be prepared a day ahead, covered, and refrigerated. The tempura batter and assembled shrimp toasts can be made up to 2 hours ahead, covered, and refrigerated, leaving just a quick deep-frying before serving.

Tempura Shrimp Toasts

As a tempura lover, I couldn't resist using it to give shrimp toast a new twist. I also like to wrap the fragrant shrimp filling in delicate spring roll sheets instead of spreading it on pieces of white bread, which tend to absorb too much oil. These shrimp toasts are then coated with a tempura batter and fried until crisp and golden brown. The crunchy toasts dipped in a light and tangy sauce are really addictive, so be sure to prepare plenty, as they will disappear in no time. Serve them as hors d'oeuvres.

YIELD: 12 large toasts for hors d'oeuvres

SOY DIPPING SAUCE

¼ cup light soy sauce
¼ cup rice vinegar
2 teaspoons sugar
1 tablespoon chopped scallion
2 teaspoons finely shredded fresh ginger
½ teaspoon Oriental sesame oil
½ teaspoon chili oil

SHRIMP FILLING

2 tablespoons coarsely chopped coriander leaves and stems
2 teaspoons chopped garlic
½ small onion, coarsely chopped
¼ teaspoon cracked black pepper
4 ounces raw medium shrimp, shelled, deveined, and cut into ½-inch pieces
2 ounces ground pork
1½ teaspoons light soy sauce
¼ teaspoon sugar
⅛ teaspoon salt

TEMPURA BATTER

1 small egg
¾ cup ice water
1 cup cake flour, sifted

3 8-inch square spring roll wrappers
Fresh coriander sprigs
Vegetable oil, for deep-frying

PREPARE THE SAUCE: Place the soy sauce, vinegar, sugar, and ¼ cup of water in a small saucepan and bring to a boil over moderate heat. Remove the saucepan from the heat. Stir in the remaining ingredients, cover, and set aside.

MAKE THE FILLING: Place the coriander, garlic, onion, and pepper in the bowl of a food processor fitted with the metal blade and process until finely minced. Transfer the mixture to a small mixing bowl. Process the shrimp in the food processor until finely minced. Add the shrimp, pork, soy sauce, sugar, and salt to the onion mixture and mix well to combine. Set aside.

MAKE THE BATTER: In a mixing bowl, beat the egg thoroughly with a wire whisk. Whisk in the ice water until blended. Sprinkle the flour evenly over the liquid. Using the whisk, stir the mixture only until the flour is moistened and the larger lumps disappear. The batter should remain very lumpy. Set aside; do not stir the batter again.

ASSEMBLE THE SHRIMP TOASTS: Work with one spring roll wrapper at a time, keeping the remaining wrappers covered with a kitchen towel to prevent drying. Cut the sheet into 4 squares. Brush each square lightly with some of the batter. Spread 1 tablespoon of the filling over each square, leaving a ½-inch border all around. Scatter a few coriander sprigs on top of the filling. Fold each square in half to form a triangle, pressing on the edges and around the filling to seal. Repeat the process with the remaining spring roll wrappers.

COOK THE TOASTS: In a deep heavy saucepan or an electric fryer, slowly heat about 2 inches of oil to 350°F. Hold a shrimp triangle by one corner and dip it into the batter. Gently shake off the excess batter and slide the triangle into the hot oil. Repeat with 2 or 3 more triangles. Fry the toasts for about 1 minute, turn over, and fry 1 minute longer, or until they are lightly golden brown. Using a slotted spoon, remove the toasts to paper towels to drain. If necessary, skim off any pieces of cooked batter from the oil with a wire mesh strainer before adding the next batch of toasts.

Serve hot with the dipping sauce.

— planning ahead —

The dipping sauce can be made a day ahead, stored in a jar, and refrigerated. Bring to room temperature before serving. The assembled rolls may also be prepared ahead, covered, and refrigerated overnight or frozen for up to 2 weeks. Bring the rolls to room temperature, or thoroughly defrost them, before frying.

— cook's notes —

When buying fish sauce, look for the Squid or Tiparos brand. Once opened, fish sauce lasts up to a year at room temperature. Fish sauce is available in Asian markets and in some well-stocked supermarkets.

Cooked salmon, lobster meat, or chicken may be substituted for the crabmeat.

For additional flavor and texture, wrap the fried rolls in tender lettuce leaves, along with some sprigs of mint and coriander, before dipping into the sauce.

Thai Crab Rolls

These savory packets are my updated version of the popular Thai spring rolls. I give the crabmeat filling a French twist by using butter, carrots, and celery. Depending on my mood, I enjoy these crisply fried morsels with either a sweet and piquant Thai dipping sauce, a less traditional Red Pepper Mayonnaise (page 216), or simply with hot mustard and ketchup. Whichever way you choose to serve these spring rolls, they are delicious!

YIELD: 20 rolls for hors d'oeuvres, or enough for 4 to 6 appetizer servings

THAI DIPPING SAUCE

1 cup distilled white vinegar
½ cup plus 4 teaspoons light brown sugar
1½ tablespoons minced garlic
1 tablespoon crushed dried red pepper
⅓ cup fish sauce (see Cook's Notes)

CRABMEAT FILLING

2 tablespoons unsalted butter or olive oil
2 teaspoons minced garlic
⅓ cup chopped onion
⅓ cup chopped celery
⅓ cup shredded carrot
3 large fresh shiitake mushroom caps, coarsely chopped
1 cup fresh or drained canned lump crabmeat, well picked over
1 tablespoon fish sauce (see Cook's Notes), or salt to taste
Freshly ground black pepper to taste

10 8-inch square spring roll wrappers
1 tablespoon all-purpose flour mixed with 1 tablespoon cold water to form a paste

Vegetable oil, for deep-frying

PREPARE THE SAUCE: Combine the vinegar and sugar in a small saucepan and bring the mixture to a boil over moderate heat. Boil just until the sugar is dissolved. Transfer the liquid to a small bowl. Add the garlic, pepper, and fish sauce. Set aside.

MAKE THE FILLING: Melt the butter in a skillet over moderate heat. Add the garlic and onion and cook until the onion is translucent, about 2 minutes. Add the celery, carrot, and mushrooms, and sauté until the vegetables are soft but not browned, about 2 minutes. Add the crabmeat, fish sauce, and black pepper and toss well. Transfer the filling to a bowl and cool completely.

ASSEMBLE THE ROLLS: Stack the spring roll wrappers. Using a sharp knife or scissors, cut the stacked wrappers in half along the diagonal. Work with one triangle at a time, keeping the remaining wrappers covered with a damp kitchen towel to prevent drying.

Place a triangle smooth side down on a work surface, with the long edge nearest you. Lightly brush the sheet with the flour paste. Place 2 heaping teaspoons of the filling along the lower edge of the wrapper, and shape the filling into a 2-inch-long log. Fold over the sides of the wrapper, and then roll up from the bottom to enclose the filling. Place the roll seam side down on a large plate and keep covered with a damp towel while you fill and roll the remaining triangles.

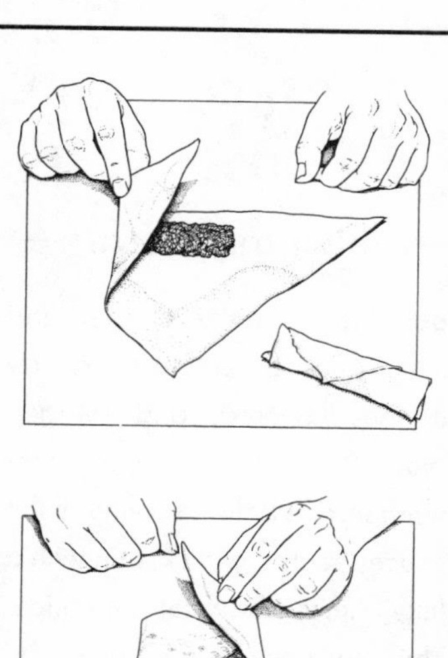

Preheat the oven to 250°F. Line a baking sheet with paper towels.

COOK THE ROLLS: Heat 2 inches of oil in a wok or deep heavy skillet to 350°F. Gently add the rolls in batches and cook, turning occasionally, until golden brown, about 2 minutes. Remove with a slotted spoon to a sieve set over a large bowl to drain. Transfer the rolls to the baking sheet and keep warm in the oven while you cook the remaining rolls.

Serve the rolls with the dipping sauce.

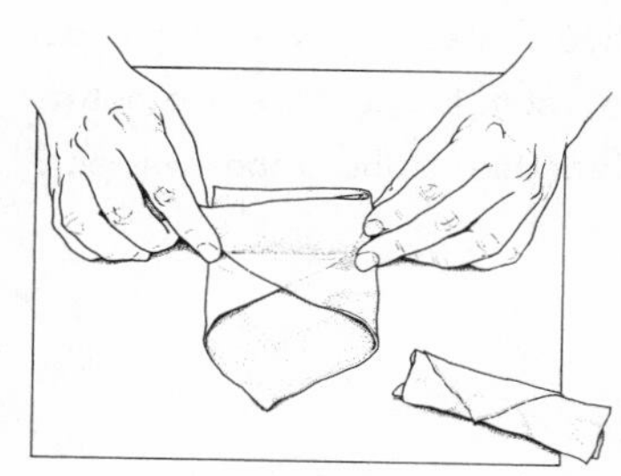

VARIATION

CRABMEAT TRIANGLES: Cut each spring roll wrapper into 3 strips. Place 2 teaspoons of the filling on a bottom corner of each strip and fold up and over flag-style to form triangles. Brush the end with flour paste before the last fold to seal. Fry and serve with the sauce as above.

If you prefer to bake rather than fry these treats, wrap up the filling flag-style in strips of phyllo pastry to form triangles, spray or brush with butter, and bake in a preheated 375°F oven until golden brown, about 15 to 20 minutes. Serve the triangles on their own, without sauce.

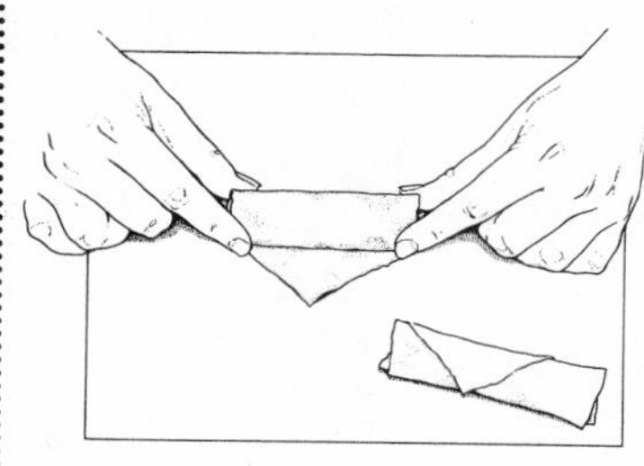

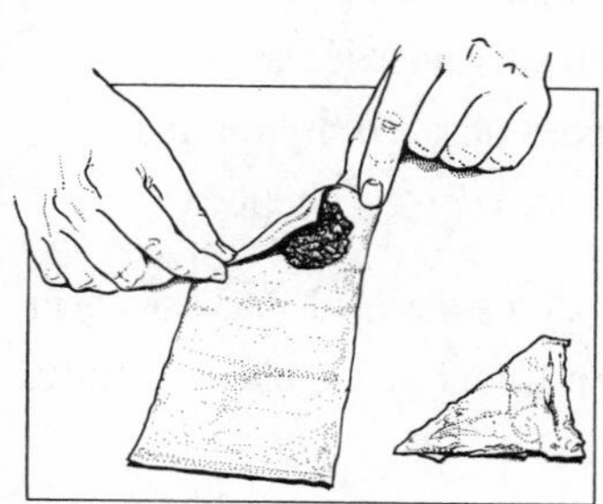

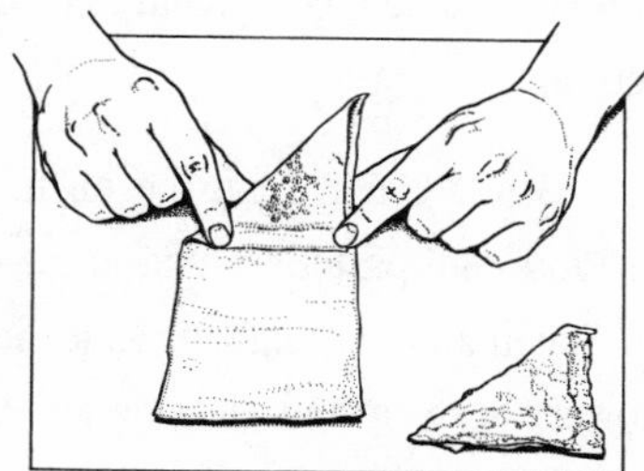

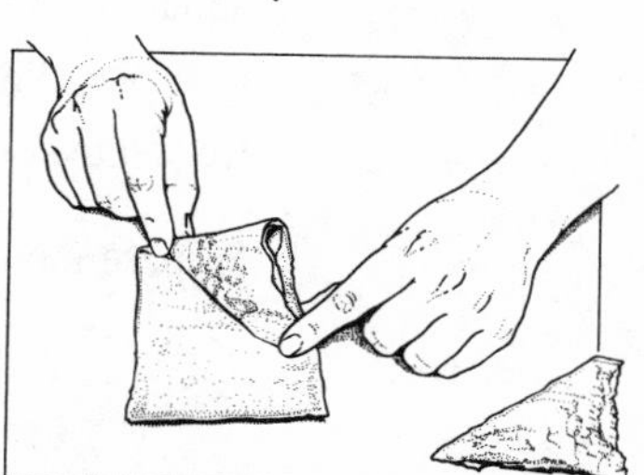

Crabmeat Triangles Variation

— planning ahead —

Both the marinated chicken and sauce may be prepared a day ahead, covered, and refrigerated. Bring the sauce to room temperature before serving. If the sauce seems too thick, thin with a little chicken broth or lime juice. The sesame seeds may be toasted early in the day and kept covered at room temperature until ready to use. The assembled crêpes may be prepared up to 6 hours ahead, covered, and kept at room temperature. Do not refrigerate, or the crêpes will tear.

Grilled Lime Chicken in Rice Crêpes

You will find these clean-tasting Vietnamese crêpes irresistible. Boneless breasts of chicken are marinated in lime juice, grilled, and encased in delicate fresh rice crêpes. Toasted sesame seeds, fresh mint, coriander, and a spicy peanut sauce add terrific character to these crêpes, creating an explosion of flavors and textures. The rolls can be eaten like burritos out of hand, or they may be cut into smaller "bites" and served as hors d'oeuvres.

YIELD: 12 crêpes, enough for 3 to 4 appetizer servings

MARINADE

2 tablespoons light soy sauce
1 teaspoon minced garlic
1 tablespoon plus 1 teaspoon sugar
2 tablespoons peanut oil
2 tablespoons fresh lime juice
Grated zest of 1 lime
Freshly ground black pepper to taste

3 boneless skinless chicken breast halves (about 1 pound)

PEANUT SAUCE

1 tablespoon vegetable oil
2 teaspoons minced garlic
¼ teaspoon Szechuan hot chili bean paste
½ cup chicken broth
¼ cup unsweetened coconut milk (see Cook's Notes)
3 tablespoons creamy peanut butter
1 tablespoon light soy sauce
1 teaspoon sugar

½ recipe Steamed Rice Crêpes (page 282)
¼ cup white sesame seeds
1 cup fresh mint leaves
1 cup fresh coriander leaves
3 tablespoons unsalted dry-roasted peanuts, coarsely chopped

MARINATE THE CHICKEN: Combine all the marinade ingredients in a mixing bowl. Add the chicken, cover, and marinate for 1 hour at room temperature, or refrigerate overnight.

MAKE THE SAUCE: Heat the oil in a small saucepan. When the oil is hot, add the garlic and chili paste. Fry until the garlic is fragrant and lightly browned, about 30 seconds. Stir in all the remaining sauce ingredients and whisk to blend. Bring to a boil, then lower the heat and simmer for about 2 minutes to thicken, stirring frequently. Cover and set aside at room temperature.

Prepare the crêpes; you will need 12 for this recipe. Cover and set aside.

TOAST THE SESAME SEEDS: Place the seeds in a dry skillet over moderate heat and cook, stirring constantly, until golden brown, about 3 minutes. Allow to cool. Set aside.

COOK THE CHICKEN: Prepare a moderately hot fire in a grill or preheat a broiler.

Drain the marinade from the chicken and grill or broil the chicken 4 inches from the heat source for about 4 minutes per side, or until the juices run clear when pierced with a fork. Transfer the chicken to a platter and let rest for 5 minutes.

ASSEMBLE THE CRÊPES: Cut each chicken breast lengthwise into 4 strips about ¾ inch thick. Sprinkle ½ teaspoon of the toasted sesame seeds over each crêpe. Place a strip of grilled chicken on each crêpe, sprinkle with a few mint and coriander leaves, and roll up to form a cigar shape.

Sprinkle the chopped peanuts over the sauce. Serve the crêpes with the sauce.

— cook's notes —

Peeled and deveined whole shrimp or strips of beef tenderloin can replace the chicken; add 1 teaspoon Oriental sesame oil to the marinade.

This dish is usually served at room temperature but you can reheat the assembled crêpes very briefly in a microwave oven or steamer before serving.

Do not confuse coconut milk with coconut cream. Excellent canned unsweetened coconut milk is available in Asian markets and some supermarkets. After opening, it can be refrigerated for up to 1 week. For longer storage, freeze it in ice cube trays, then store the cubes in plastic bags. Before using, heat the frozen coconut milk until completely melted. Four cubes equal about ½ cup. You may substitute heavy cream for the coconut milk, but the taste will be slightly altered.

— planning ahead —

The sauce, garnish, and filling may be prepared a day ahead, covered, and refrigerated. Bring the sauce to room temperature before serving. The assembled ravioli may be prepared up to 6 hours ahead, covered, and kept at room temperature. Do not refrigerate, or the crêpes will tear.

Rice Paper Raviolis

One of my strongest memories of my mother's cooking is her famous rolled rice paper crêpes. This recipe is based on that dish but with my own twist. I use the soft and silky steamed rice crêpes to wrap an Italian-style filling of porcini mushrooms, onions, and prosciutto instead of the traditional ground pork. A flavorful and unusual garnish of crisp-fried shallots, Nappa cabbage, and sweet basil adds a pleasing crunch and texture to the ravioli. To further enhance the clean, sparkling taste of the ravioli, a light and lemony sauce is ladled over them just before serving.

YIELD: 24 ravioli, enough for 8 appetizer or 4 main-course servings

GARLIC-VINEGAR SAUCE

6 tablespoons balsamic vinegar
2 tablespoons sugar
2 garlic cloves, minced
6 tablespoons light soy sauce
2 tablespoons fresh lemon juice

6 cups finely shredded Napa cabbage or 1 pound fresh bean sprouts
½ cup shredded fresh basil leaves
½ cup vegetable oil
½ cup thinly sliced shallots

MUSHROOM FILLING

1 ounce dried porcini mushrooms or cèpes (see Cook's Notes)
1 small onion, finely chopped
2 shallots, minced
2 garlic cloves, minced
8 ounces prosciutto (in one piece)
2 tablespoons unsalted butter
1 teaspoon light soy sauce
Freshly ground black pepper to taste

1 recipe Steamed Rice Crêpes (page 282)

PREPARE THE SAUCE: Combine the vinegar, 6 tablespoons water, and the sugar in a small saucepan and bring to a boil over high heat, swirling the liquid in the pan until the sugar is dissolved. Remove the pan from the heat and allow to cool. Transfer the liquid to a small bowl. Stir in the remaining sauce ingredients. Set aside.

PREPARE THE GARNISH: Drop the cabbage (or bean sprouts) into a large pot of boiling salted water, then immediately drain in a colander set in the sink. Refresh under cold running water, then drain thoroughly. Transfer to a bowl and stir in the basil. Cover and refrigerate.

Heat the oil in a small saucepan until hot but not smoking, about 320°F. Add the sliced shallots and fry over moderate heat just until crispy and golden brown, about 5 minutes. Do not overcook, or they will taste bitter. Remove the shallots with a slotted spoon and drain on paper towels. Cover and set aside at room temperature.

MAKE THE FILLING: Place the mushrooms in a small bowl, add 1½ cups boiling water, and let soak for 30 minutes, or until they are softened. Drain the mushrooms, squeeze them dry, and chop fine. (If desired, strain the mushroom liquid and save it for soups or sauces.) Combine the mushrooms, onion, minced shallots, and garlic in a small bowl, cover, and set aside.

Cut the prosciutto into small cubes and coarsely grind them in a food processor. Set aside.

Heat the butter in a skillet over moderate heat. Add the mushroom mixture and sauté until fragrant, about 2 minutes. Add the soy sauce and stir to combine. Add the prosciutto and cook very briefly, about 30 seconds, breaking up the lumps of meat with a wooden spoon. Make sure that you don't cook the prosciutto through or it will taste salty; the meat should remain pink. Transfer the mixture to a bowl and allow to cool. Season with black pepper. Cover and set aside.

Prepare the rice crêpes.

FILL THE RAVIOLI: Place a crêpe on an oiled work surface. Spread 1 teaspoon of the filling over the crêpe, leaving a 1½-inch border all around. Fold over the sides to enclose the filling, then roll the crêpe up to make a neat roll. Fill the remaining crêpes in this manner. Set the ravioli on a platter, cover, and set aside at room temperature until ready to serve.

TO SERVE: Place 3 ravioli for an appetizer, or 6 for a main course, on each plate. Top with ¼ cup of the cabbage mixture and a sprinkling of crisp-fried shallots. Ladle some sauce over and serve.

— cook's notes —

Porcini mushrooms, also known as cèpes, have an intense flavor. They are available at some supermarkets and many specialty grocers. They can also be ordered by mail from: American Spoon Foods, P.O. Box 566, Petoskey, MI 49770 (616-347-9030); or from Hans Johansson, 44 West 74th Street, New York, NY 10023 (212-787-6496). Dried shiitake mushroom caps may replace the porcini. You will need about 6 caps.

These ravioli are usually served at room temperature but you can reheat them very briefly in a microwave oven or steamer before serving.

— planning ahead —

The dressing can be made up to a week ahead, covered, and refrigerated. The filling can be prepared early on the day you are going to serve this dish. The assembled rolls are at their best if served immediately, but they can be placed in plastic bags and kept at room temperature for up to 2 hours before serving. Do not refrigerate, as the rice paper will harden and tear.

Smoked Turkey Rolls with Basil Sauce

This recipe is one of my signature dishes. It has received rave reviews, both from my cooking students and my dinner guests. These rolls are really a cold salad of angel hair pasta with mixed raw vegetables, fresh basil, and smoked turkey, all wrapped in soft, slightly resilient rice paper. To accentuate the colorful rolls, I serve them on a pool of pastel green garlic and basil dressing, giving the dish a stunning visual effect. This cold dish makes a great addition to any fancy meal but I like it best as an appetizer or light main course in the summer.

YIELD: 8 rolls, enough for 8 appetizer or 4 main-course servings

BASIL DRESSING

⅔ cup tightly packed fresh basil leaves
2 large eggs
2 tablespoons Dijon mustard
1 tablespoon minced garlic
1 tablespoon sugar
¼ cup rice vinegar
1 cup vegetable oil
Salt and freshly ground white pepper

SMOKED TURKEY FILLING

4 ounces fresh angel hair pasta
1 large carrot (or 2 medium), peeled and cut into fine julienne strips
1 medium cucumber, peeled, seeded, and cut into fine julienne strips
1 large tomato, seeded and cut into fine julienne strips
2 cups tightly packed fresh basil leaves, shredded
4 large Boston lettuce leaves, thick stems removed and thinly shredded
1 cup fresh bean sprouts
16 very thin slices smoked turkey breast (about 8 ounces)

16 8-inch round sheets dried rice paper (banh trang)

PREPARE THE DRESSING: Place the basil, eggs, mustard, garlic, sugar, and vinegar in a blender. Process until the basil is finely puréed. With the motor on, add the oil in a steady stream and blend until well mixed. Transfer to a small bowl or jar, season with salt and pepper, cover, and refrigerate.

PREPARE THE FILLING: Bring 2 quarts salted water to a rolling boil in a large pot. Drop in the pasta and cook until al dente, about 1 to 1½ minutes. Drain in a colander set in the sink. Refresh under cold running water, then drain thoroughly. Using scissors, cut the pasta strands into 5- to 6-inch lengths.

Place the pasta in a large mixing bowl and add the carrot, cucumber, tomato, basil, lettuce, and bean sprouts. Toss to mix, cover, and refrigerate.

Stack 2 slices of the smoked turkey and roll into a cigar shape. Repeat with the remaining slices to make 7 more rolls. Cover and refrigerate until you are ready to assemble the rice paper rolls.

ASSEMBLE THE RICE PAPER ROLLS: Divide the pasta salad into 8 portions. Fill a large bowl with 8 cups hot water. Work with 2 sheets of the rice paper at a time, keeping the remaining sheets covered with a barely damp cloth to prevent them from curling.

Immerse a sheet of rice paper in the hot water for 2 seconds. Remove from the water and lay it flat on a clean kitchen towel. The rice paper should become pliable within seconds. Moisten another sheet of rice paper and place it alongside the first sheet on the towel.

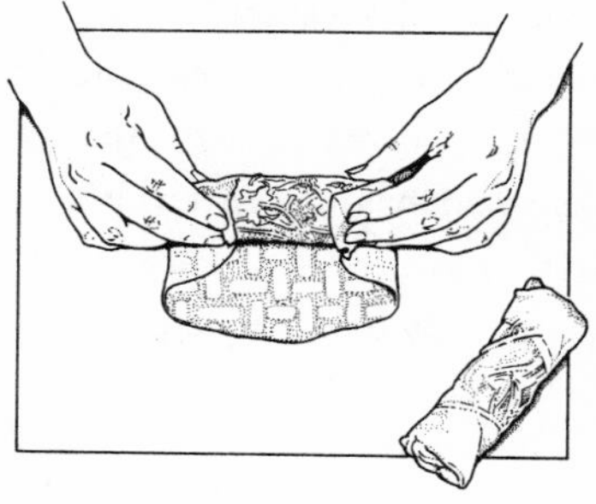

Shape one portion of the pasta salad into a log along the bottom of one sheet, about 1½ inches from the edge. Top the salad with a turkey roll. Tightly roll the rice paper into a cylinder, stopping at the center of the paper. Fold the sides of the wrapper over the filling and continue rolling into a neat cylinder. Wrap the cyclinder in the second sheet to secure the roll. Place the roll seam side down on a large platter and cover with a damp towel to keep it moist while you fill the remaining wrappers in the same manner.

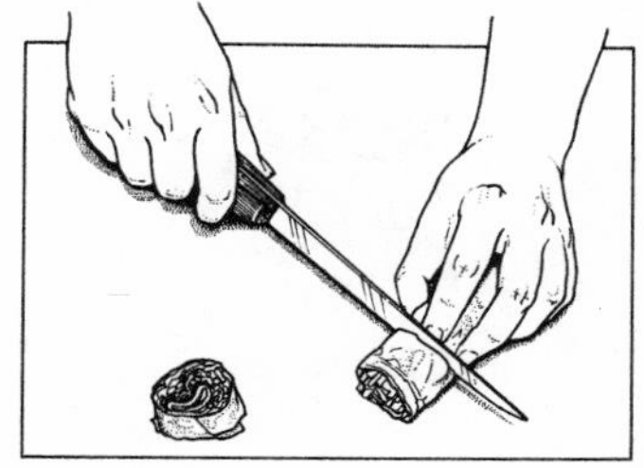

TO SERVE: Cut the rolls crosswise in half or into bite-size pieces, sushi fashion. To serve as a main course, ladle the dressing onto chilled plates and arrange the rolls over the dressing. To serve as hors d'oeuvres, pour the dressing into small individual bowls. Let your guests dip the rolls into the dressing and eat out of hand.

— planning ahead —

The dipping sauce can be prepared a day ahead, covered, and refrigerated. Bring to room temperature before serving. The rolls can be assembled 1 day ahead, covered with plastic wrap, and refrigerated. The assembled rolls may also be frozen for up to 2 weeks. Defrost them thoroughly before frying.

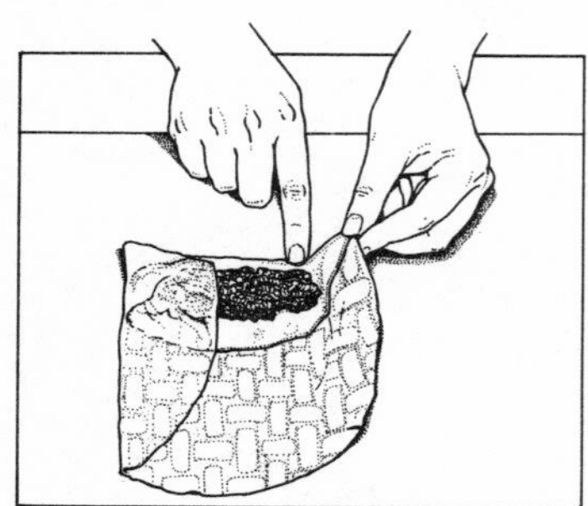

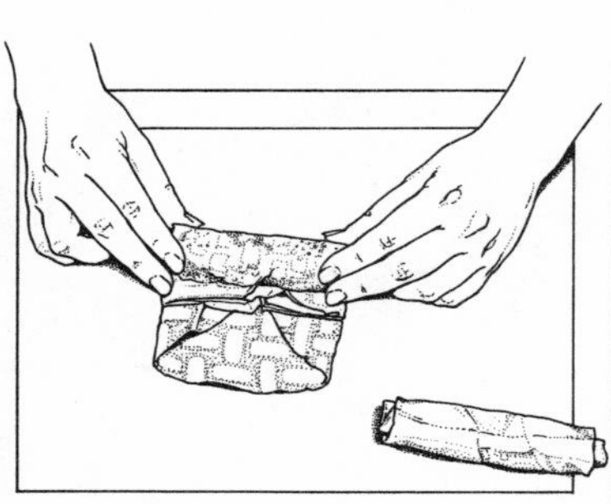

Vietnamese Spring Rolls

(CHA GIO)

Spring rolls are considered the national dish of Vietnam. Cha gio are totally different from Chinese spring rolls, from the filling inside to the outside wrapping, and even in the manner in which they are eaten.

I developed this recipe for an article in *Bon Appétit* magazine. The dish consists of a filling of chicken, shrimp, pork, and dried shiitake mushrooms wrapped in delicate rice paper and then deep-fried until very crispy. For additional flavor and texture, the rolls are wrapped in soft lettuce with sprigs of fresh mint and coriander before dipping into a sweet and tangy sauce.

YIELD: 26 rolls, enough for 52 hors d'oeuvres or 6 to 8 light main-course servings

CHILE DIPPING SAUCE

½ cup rice vinegar
½ cup fish sauce (see Cook's Notes)
½ cup hot water
¼ cup sugar
¼ cup fresh lime juice
2 teaspoons minced garlic
3 small fresh hot red chiles (such as jalapeño or serrano), seeded and chopped
½ cup finely shredded carrot
½ cup finely shredded daikon (Japanese white radish) or white turnip

SPRING ROLL FILLING

6 dried shiitake mushrooms (see Cook's Notes)
1 ounce cellophane noodles (see Cook's Notes)
1 large skinless boneless chicken breast half (about 6 ounces), coarsely chopped
10 ounces raw medium shrimp, shelled, deveined, and coarsely chopped
4 ounces ground pork
1½ cups packed coarsely chopped fresh bean sprouts
1½ cups packed shredded carrots
1 cup minced onions
2 tablespoons minced garlic
¼ cup fish sauce (see Cook's Notes)
2 teaspoons sugar
½ teaspoon salt
½ teaspoon freshly ground black pepper
3 large eggs, lightly beaten

1 cup sugar
26 8-inch round sheets dried rice paper (banh trang)
Peanut oil, for frying

GARNISH

Boston lettuce leaves
Fresh mint sprigs
Fresh coriander sprigs

PREPARE THE DIPPING SAUCE: Combine all the ingredients except the carrot and daikon in a blender or food processor, and process until well blended and the sugar is dissolved. Pour into a bowl and stir in the carrot and daikon. Cover and set aside.

MAKE THE FILLING: Soak the mushrooms and cellophane noodles in separate bowls of hot water until they soften, about 30 minutes. Drain the mushrooms and discard the soaking liquid. Squeeze the mushrooms dry, cut off and discard the stems, and mince the caps. Drain the noodles and discard the soaking liquid. Cut into 1-inch-long pieces (there should be about ½ cup). Place the mushrooms and noodles in a large bowl, add all the remaining filling ingredients, and mix well.

ASSEMBLE THE ROLLS: Fill a large bowl with 8 cups hot water, add the sugar, and stir to dissolve. Work with 1 sheet of the rice paper at a time, keeping the remaining sheets covered with a barely damp cloth to prevent them from curling.

Completely immerse a sheet of rice paper in the hot water for 2 seconds. Remove from the water and place it on a damp kitchen towel. The rice paper should become pliable within seconds. Fold over the bottom third of the rice paper round. Place about 3 tablespoons of the filling atop the center of the folded portion. Shape the filling into a 4-inch-long log. Fold the sides of the rice paper over the filling and roll up the rice paper into a cylinder, enclosing the filling completely. Place the roll seam side down on a baking sheet lined with plastic wrap. Repeat with the remaining rice paper and filling.

Preheat the oven to 250°F. Line a baking sheet with paper towels.

FRY THE ROLLS: Pour about 2 inches of oil into each of two large heavy skillets and heat to 325°F. Add as many of the rolls as will fit comfortably to each skillet (do not crowd or the rolls will stick together) and fry over moderate heat, turning often, until golden and crisp, about 20 minutes. Remove the rolls with tongs to the baking sheet. Keep warm in the oven while you fry the remaining rolls.

TO SERVE: Cut the rolls in half and arrange on a large platter. Surround with the lettuce leaves and mint and coriander sprigs. Serve the dipping sauce on the side. Encourage your guests to wrap a lettuce leaf along with some herbs around a roll before dipping the packet into the sauce.

— cook's notes —

When buying fish sauce, look for the Squid or Tiparos brand. Once opened, fish sauce lasts up to a year at room temperature. Fish sauce is available in Asian markets and in some well-stocked supermarkets.

Dried shiitake mushrooms, also known as Chinese black mushrooms, are available in many well-stocked supermarkets and in Asian markets. They also can be ordered by mail from American Spoon Foods, P.O. Box 566, Petoskey, MI 49770 (616-347-9030); or from Hans Johansson, 44 West 74th Street, New York, NY 10023 (212-787-6496).

Cellophane noodles, also called bean threads, are used in stuffings primarily for their texture. They are sold in 1-pound or 2-ounce packages in Asian stores and some supermarkets.

As rice paper is very delicate, it needs to be fried at a low to medium heat and therefore takes comparatively longer to brown and crisp. Make sure that the oil is not too hot when you add the rolls to it. Don't be tempted to take shortcuts by cooking the rolls at a high temperature: You will end up with blistered, burnt, or torn wrappers as the filling inside expands too rapidly under the intense heat.

— planning ahead —

The vinaigrette may be prepared up to 2 days in advance and refrigerated. The citrus fruits may be cut up to 2 hours before serving, covered, and refrigerated. Bring the vinaigrette to room temperature before stirring into the fruits. The assembled salmon fillets may be prepared early on the day you are going to serve them, covered, and refrigerated until ready to cook.

Roast Salmon in Rice Paper with Citrus Vinaigrette

I am always intrigued to discover the uses other cooks find for Asian ingredients. This dish is prepared by one of the most skillful artists in the kitchen that I know, Jean-Georges Vongerichten, chef and owner of Jo Jo, his extraordinary restaurant in New York City. He graciously allowed me to share his recipe with you.

This smashing entrée starts with fillets of salmon that are wrapped in translucent rice paper rounds and then pan-roasted. I have made one small change; instead of roasting the salmon in the oven as the chef does, I cook it in a skillet over the stove. The result is an exceptionally moist fish on the inside with a surprising crunch on the outside. The salmon is then served with a delicate citrus vinaigrette. This simple, great-tasting, and elegant dish will be a surefire hit at your next dinner party!

YIELD: 4 main-course servings

CITRUS VINAIGRETTE

½ cup extra-virgin olive oil
3 tablespoons light soy sauce
1 tablespoon plus 1 teaspoon sherry vinegar or balsamic vinegar
1 tablespoon plus 1 teaspoon finely shredded peeled ginger
¼ teaspoon salt
½ teaspoon Tabasco sauce
2 tablespoons boiling water
1 medium lime, peeled, sectioned, and cut into medium dice
1 medium lemon, peeled, sectioned, and cut into medium dice
1 medium orange, peeled, sectioned, and cut into medium dice
1 medium pink grapefruit, peeled, sectioned, and cut into medium dice
20 black peppercorns, cracked
2 tablespoons shredded fresh coriander leaves

RICE-PAPER-WRAPPED SALMON

4 6-ounce skinless salmon fillets
Salt and freshly ground black pepper to taste
3 tablespoons olive oil
4 8-inch round sheets dried rice paper (banh trang)

PREPARE THE VINAIGRETTE: Combine the olive oil, soy sauce, vinegar, ginger, salt, Tabasco sauce, and boiling water in a medium jar. Cover the jar and shake well. Set aside until you are ready to serve.

Place the diced citrus fruits, cracked pepper, and coriander in a small nonreactive mixing bowl. Cover and set aside.

Season the salmon fillets with salt and pepper. Rub the fillets on both sides with 2 tablespoons of the oil.

WRAP THE SALMON FILLETS: Fill a large bowl with 8 cups hot water. Work with 1 sheet of the rice paper at a time, keeping the remaining sheets covered with a barely damp cloth to prevent them from curling.

Completely immerse a sheet of rice paper in the hot water for 2 seconds. Remove and place on a damp kitchen towel. The rice paper should become pliable within seconds. Place a salmon fillet in the center of the softened rice paper. Fold the four sides of the rice paper tightly over the fish to completely enclose it. Form 3 more packets in this manner. Place the wrapped fillets seam side down on a plate, cover, and refrigerate until ready to cook.

COOK THE SALMON: In a large nonstick skillet, heat the remaining 1 tablespoon oil over moderately high heat. Add the salmon packets and cook for 1 minute. Turn the fillets over and cook 1 minute longer. Cover the pan, reduce the heat to low, and cook for 1 minute. Turn the fillets and continue cooking, covered, for 1 more minute. Remove the pan from the heat and let sit, covered, for 2 minutes.

Meanwhile, stir the vinaigrette into the citrus fruits.

TO SERVE: Place each packet on a warmed dinner plate, spoon a portion of citrus vinaigrette over the fish, and serve immediately.

— *cook's notes* —

Catfish, red snapper, or mahimahi may be prepared the same way. Adjust the cooking time according to the thickness of the fillets.

— *planning ahead* —

The crêpes may be prepared a day ahead, covered, and refrigerated. The filling may be prepared up to 2 hours in advance, covered, and refrigerated. Bring both the crêpes and filling to room temperature before assembling the dish.

Buckwheat Crêpes with Scampi

The French region of Brittany is the land of crêpes. Wherever you go, crêperies (crêpe shops) beckon you. The last time I was in St. Malo, I tasted delicious buckwheat crêpes amply filled with a creamy mixture of lobster and mushrooms. My re-creation of that dish combines mushrooms, brandy-laced cream, and flambéed shrimp instead of lobster. The light and inimitable nutlike taste of the buckwheat crêpes is nicely balanced by the sweet flavor of the shrimp and cream.

This dish is ideal for company because all the components can be prepared in advance, leaving just a quick rolling and a reheating of the crêpes in the oven before serving. Served with a soup, salad, and white wine, this rich yet light dish makes a terrific supper.

YIELD: 8 crêpes, enough for 4 main-course servings

½ recipe Buckwheat Crêpes (page 281)

FILLING

4 tablespoons unsalted butter
6 ounces domestic mushrooms, sliced
¾ cup sliced shallots
1 cup heavy cream
¼ cup brandy, preferably cognac
Salt and freshly ground black pepper to taste
1½ pounds raw medium shrimp, shelled and deveined
⅓ cup dry white wine
2 tablespoons freshly grated Parmesan cheese

Prepare the buckwheat crêpes. You will need only 8 crêpes for this recipe. Cover and set aside.

PREPARE THE FILLING: Heat 2 tablespoons of the butter in a large skillet set over moderately high heat. Add the mushrooms and half of the shallots and sauté until the mushrooms render their liquid, about 2 minutes. Add ⅓ cup of the cream. Cook until the cream is slightly thickened and reduced to about ¼ cup, about 2 minutes. Remove the pan from the heat. Stir in 1 tablespoon of the brandy and season with salt and pepper. Transfer the mixture to a large bowl, cover, and set aside. Wipe the skillet clean.

Heat the remaining 2 tablespoons of butter in the skillet over high heat. Add the shrimp and remaining shallots and sauté until the shrimp turn pink, about 2 minutes. Remove from the heat and add the remaining 3 tablespoons brandy. Ignite the brandy to flambé the mixture. When the flames die out, return the pan to the heat. Add the wine and cook the shrimp for another minute. Use a slotted spoon to remove the shrimp to the mushroom mixture. Cook the liquid remaining in the pan until syrupy and almost evaporated, about 2 minutes. Add the remaining ⅔ cup heavy cream and cook until thickened and reduced by almost half, about 2 minutes; be careful the cream doesn't boil over. The sauce should be thick enough to coat the back of a spoon. Stir half of the sauce into the shrimp and mushroom mixture. Set the remaining sauce aside.

Preheat a broiler.

ASSEMBLE THE CRÊPES: Spread one eighth of the shrimp filling over each crêpe, and roll up into a cylinder. Place the rolled crêpes seam side down in a lightly buttered baking dish just large enough to accommodate all the crêpes side by side. Spoon the reserved sauce over the crêpes. Sprinkle with the Parmesan cheese.

Broil until the sauce is nicely glazed and the filling is heated through, about 2 minutes. Serve hot.

— cook's notes —

To prevent sogginess, do not assemble the crêpes and broil them until ready to serve.

You may substitute fresh sea scallops for the shrimp.

— planning ahead —

The batter can be prepared up to 3 days in advance and kept covered in the refrigerator. Bring it to room temperature before making the crêpes. The chicken, onion, and mushroom mixture can be prepared a day ahead, covered, and refrigerated. Bring to room temperature before assembling the crêpes.

Rice Crêpes with Pulled Chicken and Cheese

With my Vietnamese and French background, it's not surprising that I often mix the two cuisines. If you like chicken, cheese, fried onions, and crispy crêpes, you will love this unusual Eurasian dish. Crunchy on the outside and tender on the inside, these crêpes, folded like an omelet, have a mild and succulent filling of poached chicken, caramelized onions, and sautéed mushrooms that oozes with melting cheese. The crêpe batter is very simple, just rice flour and water with a hint of curry. Serve this dish for brunch or supper.

YIELD: 4 large crêpes, enough for 4 main-course servings

CRÊPE BATTER

1 cup rice flour
½ teaspoon curry powder, preferably Madras brand
¼ teaspoon turmeric
½ teaspoon salt
½ teaspoon sugar
1 scallion, thinly sliced

POACHED CHICKEN

2 cups chicken broth, homemade (page 368) or store-bought
½ cup dry white wine
½ teaspoon black peppercorns
2 small bay leaves
½ pound chicken breast tenderloins (see Cook's Notes)

CARAMELIZED ONIONS AND MUSHROOMS

3 tablespoons extra-virgin olive oil
1½ cups thinly sliced onions
1½ cups thinly sliced domestic mushrooms
3 tablespoons dry sherry
1 tablespoon red wine vinegar
½ teaspoon sugar
Salt and freshly ground black pepper to taste

3 tablespoons extra-virgin olive oil
4 ounces Gruyère or Swiss cheese, shredded (about 1 cup)

PREPARE THE CRÊPE BATTER: In a medium bowl, combine the rice flour, curry powder, turmeric, salt, and sugar. Add 1 cup water and whisk until well blended. Stir in the scallion. Cover and set aside.

POACH THE CHICKEN: In a large skillet, combine the broth, wine, peppercorns, and bay leaves. Bring the mixture to a boil, lower the heat, and simmer for 5 minutes. Bring the liquid back to a boil, then remove from the heat. Add the chicken in one layer, cover the pan, and set aside to let the chicken poach in the hot liquid; let cool completely.

Meanwhile, COOK THE ONIONS AND MUSHROOMS: In a large nonstick skillet, heat 2 tablespoons of the olive oil over high heat. Add the onions and cook, stirring frequently, until browned, about 5 minutes. Add the remaining 1 tablespoon oil and the mushrooms and sauté for 2 minutes, or until the mushrooms are soft and lightly browned. Add the sherry. Cook, stirring, until the liquid is evaporated, about 1 minute. Add the vinegar and sugar. Cook for 1 minute longer. Remove the pan from the heat.

Remove the chicken from the poaching liquid and shred the meat by pulling it apart with your fingers. Stir the shredded chicken into the caramelized onions and mushrooms. Season with salt and pepper. Allow to cool, then cover and set aside until ready to assemble the crêpes.

MAKE THE CRÊPES: In an 8-inch nonstick omelet pan, heat 2 teaspoons of the olive oil over moderately high heat. When the oil is very hot, stir the crêpe batter and ladle ⅓ cup of batter into the pan. Quickly tilt the pan to distribute the batter evenly. Cover the pan and cook for 2 minutes. Scatter ½ cup of the chicken mixture over the bottom half of the crêpe and sprinkle one quarter of the shredded cheese over the filling. Cover the pan and continue cooking for 2 more minutes, or until the bottom of the crêpe is deep brown and crispy. Fold the unfilled half over the filling and slide the crêpe onto a warm platter. Keep warm in a low oven while you make the remaining crêpes in the same manner.

Serve immediately.

— cook's notes —

A chicken breast tenderloin, or tender, is the tender strip of meat attached to the underside of the chicken breast. You can substitute 2 small boneless breasts of chicken by cutting them into ½-inch-thick strips for the tenderloins.

The poaching liquid used for the chicken, known as a court bouillon, can be strained and refrigerated for use in sauces or soups where chicken broth is called for.

Danish Fontina cheese or Monterey Jack cheese may be substituted for the Gruyère or Swiss cheese.

The secret to making crunchy crêpes is to keep the heat moderately high throughout the cooking process. Covering the crêpe as it cooks also helps create the distinctive hard crust on the bottom.

To speed up the preparation time of the crêpes, use two pans at a time; while one crêpe is cooking, use the other pan to start the next crêpe and so on until all the batter is used.

— planning ahead —

The sauce can be prepared a day in advance, covered, and refrigerated. Bring the sauce to room temperature before serving. If the sauce seems a little thick, thin it with about a tablespoon of chicken broth or hot water. The lumpia batter may be made ahead and kept covered in the refrigerator for up to 2 days. Bring to room temperature before using. The lumpia crêpes can be made early in the day, covered, and kept at room temperature. Do not attempt to refrigerate or freeze them, or they will tear.

If using bamboo skewers, soak them in water for 30 minutes before use.

Grilled Shrimp and Pineapple Lumpia

In the Philippines, a moist, soft crêpe known as a lumpia is used much like the Chinese mu shu pancake to wrap morsels of stir-fried seafood or pork for eating out of hand. *Lumpia* also refers to a dish using such a wrapper and to this style of eating. There are as many variations for lumpia as there are cooks in the Philippines.

My version of lumpia is a mixture of Filipino, Southeast Asian, and Western ingredients. Moist lumpia crêpes and crisp lettuce leaves are wrapped around succulent pieces of grilled shrimp and pineapple. Soft pasta and crunchy peanuts are added for more body and texture. A flavorful peanut dipping sauce completes the dish.

This fun dish is ideal for a party: Just lay out all the various components for the dish at the table. Also make sure you have plenty of napkins on hand.

YIELD: 10 lumpia, enough for 4 to 5 light main-course servings

SPECIAL EQUIPMENT: 10 metal or presoaked 10-inch bamboo skewers

LUMPIA BATTER

2 large eggs, lightly beaten
1 cup cornstarch
¾ teaspoon salt
1 tablespoon vegetable oil, plus additional for greasing the pan

PEANUT SAUCE

1 tablespoon vegetable oil
2 teaspoons minced garlic
¼ teaspoon Szechuan hot chili bean paste
½ cup chicken broth
¼ cup unsweetened coconut milk (see Cook's Notes)
3½ tablespoons creamy peanut butter
1 tablespoon light soy sauce
1 teaspoon sugar

¼ cup unsalted dry-roasted peanuts
9 ounces fresh angel hair pasta
1 teaspoon plus 2 tablespoons light olive oil
1 large head Boston lettuce, separated into leaves and tough stems removed
1 small bunch fresh coriander, trimmed into sprigs
1 pound raw large shrimp, peeled and deveined
2 tablespoons light olive oil
Salt and freshly ground black pepper to taste
8 plum tomatoes, quartered
1 medium ripe pineapple, peeled and cut lengthwise into eighths and crosswise into ½-inch-thick pieces

PREPARE THE LUMPIA CRÊPES: In a medium mixing bowl, combine the eggs, 1 cup cold water, the cornstarch, salt, and oil and blend well with a wire whisk.

Lightly brush an 8-inch nonstick omelet pan or crêpe pan with oil and set over moderately low heat for about 2 minutes, or until a drop of water sizzles on contact. Stir the batter and fill a ⅓ liquid measure cup about two-thirds full with batter. Lift the pan from the heat and add the batter. Quickly tilt and rotate the pan to cover the bottom evenly with the batter. Return the pan to the heat and cook until the batter is set and the crêpe looks dry on top, about 1½ minutes; do not let the crêpe brown. Loosen the edges of the crêpe with a spatula and slide it out onto a platter to cool. Continue making the crêpes, taking care to stir the batter thoroughly each time before adding more to the pan. Let the crêpes cool, then stack them on a serving platter, cover, and set aside at room temperature until ready to serve.

PREPARE THE PEANUT SAUCE: Heat the vegetable oil in a small saucepan over moderate heat. When the oil is hot, add the garlic and chili paste. Fry until the garlic is fragrant and lightly browned, about 30 seconds. Stir in the remaining sauce ingredients. Whisk to blend, and bring to a boil. Lower the heat and simmer for about 2 minutes to thicken, stirring occasionally. Allow the sauce to cool, pour it into small bowls, cover, and set aside.

TOAST THE PEANUTS: Place the peanuts in a dry skillet set over moderate heat and cook, stirring constantly, until the nuts are heated through, about 2 to 3 minutes. Let cool. Transfer to a spice grinder and process until coarsely chopped. Set aside.

COOK THE PASTA: Bring 3 quarts salted water to a rolling boil in a large pot. Add the pasta and cook for 1 to 1½ minutes, stirring occasionally. Drain the pasta in a colander set in the sink and refresh under cold running water. Using scissors, cut the pasta strands into 4- or 5-inch lengths. Toss the pasta with 1 teaspoon olive oil to prevent sticking. Put the pasta in a shallow bowl, cover, and refrigerate.

PREPARE THE GREENS: Arrange the lettuce leaves and coriander sprigs on a platter, cover, and refrigerate.

GRILL THE SHRIMP: Toss the shrimp with the 2 tablespoons olive oil and season with salt and pepper. Thread 3 pieces each of tomato and pineapple and 3 shrimp alternately onto each skewer.

Prepare a medium-hot fire in a grill or preheat a broiler. Grill or broil the brochettes 4 inches from the heat source until the shrimp turn pink and the tomato and pineapple are heated through, about 2 minutes on each side. Unskewer the brochettes onto a large serving platter.

TO SERVE: Present the hot grilled food, lumpia crêpes, peanut sauce, ground peanuts, pasta, and the lettuce platter at the table for guests to help themselves. To eat,

— cook's notes —

The soft, moist nature of this dish demands freshly made lumpia crêpes. Do not attempt to use store-bought lumpia or mu shu wrappers. They are unsuitable for this recipe.

Do not confuse coconut milk with coconut cream. Excellent canned unsweetened coconut milk is available in Asian markets and some supermarkets. After opening, it can be refrigerated for up to 1 week. For longer storage, freeze it in ice cube trays, then store the cubes in plastic bags. Before using, heat the frozen coconut milk until completely melted. Four cubes equal about ½ cup. You may substitute heavy cream for the coconut milk, but the taste will be slightly altered.

spread a crêpe with some of the peanut sauce. Sprinkle some ground peanuts over the sauce. Set a lettuce leaf on the crêpe, then top with pieces of shrimp, pineapple, and tomato along with some pasta and coriander sprigs. Fold the right side of the crêpe over the filling, then roll the crêpe up from the bottom edge to form a cylinder. Dip the lumpia into the peanut sauce and eat out of hand.

— planning ahead —

The filled rice paper crêpes can be prepared early in the day or a day ahead, covered, and refrigerated, leaving just the baking for the last minute.

If you wish to make your own crème fraîche (page 372), it must be prepared at least 2 days in advance.

Apple and Tarragon Rice Paper Crêpes

After you have used dried rice paper for the first time, you will be eager to experiment again. Once moistened, the rice paper becomes so smooth and flexible that it entices you to touch and play with it more than you should. To demonstrate its versatility, I created this dessert in which I use the rice paper much like a French crêpe.

Borrowing from the Asian tradition of combining the flavors of fruits and herbs, I season an apple filling with fresh tarragon. Rice paper crêpes are folded around the fruit filling and then baked, a cooking method not usually associated with rice paper. Served with a dollop of sweetened crème fraîche and accompanied by mugs of hot apple cider, this soft and crispy dessert is irresistible!

YIELD: 12 rolled crêpes, enough for 6 dessert servings

APPLE FILLING

2 medium Granny Smith apples, peeled, cored, and coarsely chopped
2 teaspoons minced fresh tarragon leaves
1 tablespoon sugar
1 tablespoon unsalted butter, melted
2 tablespoons crème fraîche, store-bought or homemade (see Cook's Notes)

¼ cup sugar
12 8-inch round sheets dried rice paper (banh trang)
4 tablespoons unsalted butter, melted

½ cup crème fraîche, store-bought or homemade (see Cook's Notes)
1 tablespoon light brown sugar

MAKE THE FILLING: Mix the apples, tarragon, and sugar in a small bowl. Let stand for 20 minutes. Stir in the melted butter and crème fraîche.

ASSEMBLE THE CRÊPES: Fill a large bowl with 8 cups hot water. Add the sugar and stir to dissolve. Work with 1 sheet of the rice paper at a time, keeping the remaining sheets covered with a barely damp cloth to prevent curling.

Completely immerse a sheet of rice paper in the hot water for 2 seconds. Remove from the water and place it on a damp kitchen towel. The rice paper should become pliable within seconds. Brush the sheet with melted butter. Place ¼ cup of the filling on the bottom half of the rice paper round about 1½ inches from the edge. Fold the bottom edge of the rice paper over, then fold the sides over the filling. Brush the unbuttered surfaces of the rice paper with melted butter and roll up into a compact cylinder. Brush the roll all over with melted butter. Place the roll seam side down on a nonstick baking sheet. Continue assembling the remaining rolls in the same manner.

Preheat the oven to 400°F.

Bake the crêpes until they are crisp and golden brown, about 20 minutes.

Meanwhile, mix the crème fraîche and brown sugar in a small bowl.

Serve the crêpes with the crème fraîche mixture on the side.

— cook's notes —

I prefer fresh tarragon for this recipe; if you cannot find it, just omit it.

— *planning ahead* —

The sauce may be prepared up to a week ahead, stored in a jar, and refrigerated. The assembled strudels may be prepared early in the day, covered, and refrigerated.

Tropical Strudels

In the Philippines, these unusual and delicious strudels, known as *turon,* are a favorite for *merienda*, an important meal between lunch and dinner, which can best be compared to an English high tea. Traditionally, small fragrant cooking bananas called *sabas* are used to stuff these tropical-style strudels. But almost any fresh, firm fruit, such as apples, pears, or peaches, will do. Adding a simple raspberry sauce turns this traditional Asian sweet into an elegant dessert.

YIELD: 12 small strudels, enough for 4 dessert servings

RASPBERRY SAUCE

2 cups fresh or thawed frozen raspberries
½ cup plus 1 tablespoon confectioner's sugar

PINEAPPLE STRUDELS

⅓ cup light brown sugar
½ ripe pineapple, peeled, cored, and cut into 12 sticks about 4 inches long and ¾ inch thick
6 8-inch square spring roll wrappers
1 tablespoon all-purpose flour mixed with 1 tablespoon cold water to form a paste

Vegetable oil, for deep-frying
Confectioner's sugar, for dusting

MAKE THE SAUCE: Combine the raspberries and confectioner's sugar in a small saucepan and cook over low heat until the berries are soft, about 3 to 4 minutes. Transfer to a food processor or blender and purée. Strain into a small bowl and discard the seeds. Stir 2 tablespoons cold water into the sauce to thin slightly. Transfer to a jar and refrigerate.

ASSEMBLE THE STRUDELS: Spread the brown sugar in a shallow dish. Gently roll the pineapple sticks in the sugar to coat.

Stack the spring roll sheets. Using a sharp knife or scissors, cut the stack in half along the diagonal into triangles. Work with one triangle at a time, keeping the remaining sheets covered with a damp kitchen towel to prevent drying.

Place a spring roll triangle smooth side down on the work surface with the longest edge nearest you. Place 1 pineapple stick along the lower edge of the wrapper. Brush the edges of the wrapper with flour paste, fold the sides over the pineapple, and roll up into a tight cylinder. Put the roll seam side down on a large platter. Assemble the remaining strudels in the same manner.

COOK THE STRUDELS: Heat about 2 inches of oil in a wok or heavy deep skillet to 365°F, or until a dry bread cube browns instantly when dropped into the oil. Gently add the strudels in batches (do not crowd) and fry until golden brown, turning occasionally, about 2 to 3 minutes. Drain the strudels on paper towels and let cool slightly. Dust with confectioner's sugar.

TO SERVE: Ladle some raspberry sauce onto chilled dessert plates and arrange 3 strudels on each plate.

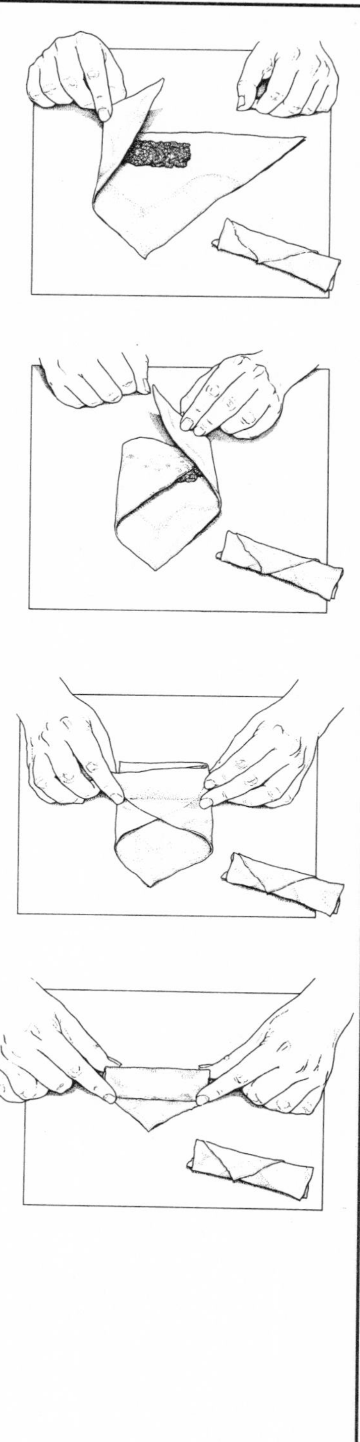

— planning ahead —

The blueberry sauce can be prepared up to 2 days ahead, covered, and refrigerated. Bring to room temperature before serving. The assembled blintzes can be stored in the refrigerator for a day or so, covered with plastic wrap. They can also be frozen for up to a month.

Lemon Cheese Blintzes with Blueberry Sauce

Blintzes are delicate egg-rich pancakes rolled around a plain cheese filling and then lightly fried. They are the direct descendants of Russian blinis, small crêpes often made of buckwheat flour and served with princely caviar.

Blintzes may be served for lunch or dinner, but I think they are in their glory when served for brunch. Lemon-flavored cheese blintzes are one of my favorite dishes to serve when entertaining at brunches. Napped with a delicious and striking blueberry sauce, these sweet blintzes never fail to draw praise. I find that what makes them taste particularly wonderful is the suggestive smell of coffee brewing while you gobble them up.

YIELD: 10 blintzes, enough for 5 light brunch or main-course servings

BLINTZ PANCAKES

- 2 large eggs
- 1 cup milk
- ⅔ cup unbleached all-purpose flour
- 4 tablespoons unsalted butter, melted and cooled

LEMON CHEESE FILLING

- 8 ounces farmer's cheese or pot cheese
- 2 ounces cream cheese, at room temperature
- 1 large egg, lightly beaten
- 1½ teaspoons finely grated lemon zest
- 1 teaspoon sugar
- ¼ teaspoon vanilla extract

BLUEBERRY SAUCE

- ½ pound (about 1¾ cups) fresh or frozen blueberries
- ¼ cup sugar
- 3 tablespoons confectioner's sugar
- 1 tablespoon fresh lemon juice

FOR PAN-FRYING

- 2 tablespoons unsalted butter

GARNISH

- ⅔ cup sour cream
- Confectioner's sugar

PREPARE THE BLINTZ BATTER: Combine the eggs, milk, 3 tablespoons water, and the flour in a blender or food processor. Blend until the batter is well mixed, scraping down the sides of the container as necessary. Transfer the batter to a medium bowl. Mix in 2 tablespoons of the melted butter. Cover and let stand for 1 hour.

PREPARE THE FILLING: Place both cheeses in a large mixing bowl and, using an electric mixer at medium speed, beat until smooth. Add the beaten egg, lemon zest, sugar, and vanilla and beat until well combined. Cover and refrigerate until ready to assemble the blintzes.

MAKE THE SAUCE: Combine the sauce ingredients in a small heavy saucepan. If using frozen berries, add 1 tablespoon water. Bring to a boil over moderately high heat, stirring frequently. Reduce the heat to low and cook, crushing some of the berries with a fork, until they are soft, about 2 minutes. Remove from the heat and cool.

MAKE THE BLINTZ PANCAKES: Heat a 6½-inch nonstick omelet or crêpe pan over moderate heat. Brush the pan lightly with some of the remaining 2 tablespoons melted butter and heat until a drop of water sizzles on contact. Stir the batter and fill a ⅓ liquid measure cup about two-thirds full with batter. Lift the pan from the heat and add the batter. Quickly tilt and rotate the pan to cover the bottom evenly with the batter. Return the pan to the heat and cook until the batter is set and the crêpe looks dry on top, about 45 seconds. Loosen the edges of the pancake with the tip of a knife, then slide the crêpe onto a kitchen towel laid out on the counter. Continue making the pancakes, taking care to stir the batter thoroughly each time before adding more to the pan. Let the pancakes cool, then stack, cover, and set aside at room temperature until ready to assemble.

ASSEMBLE THE BLINTZES: Place a pancake browned side up on a flat surface. Place 2 tablespoons of the cheese filling in the center of the pancake. Shape the filling with the back of the spoon into a 3-inch-long log. Fold the bottom of the pancake over to cover the filling, then fold the sides over and roll up from the bottom to seal. Place the blintz, seam side down, on a large plate lined with waxed paper. Continue to assemble the remaining blintzes in the same manner.

PANFRY THE BLINTZES: Place 1 tablespoon of butter each in two large skillets set over moderately low heat. When the butter is hot, add 5 blintzes to each pan and fry until the bottoms of the blintzes are golden brown, about 2 minutes. Carefully turn the blintzes over and fry for 2 minutes longer.

TO SERVE: Place 2 blintzes side by side on each serving plate. Surround the blintzes with 2 tablespoons of blueberry sauce, then top with 2 tablespoons of the sour cream. Lightly dust with confectioner's sugar and serve immediately.

cook's notes

To freeze blintzes, line them well apart in rows on waxed paper on a small baking sheet, cover, and freeze until firm, about 4 hours. Transfer the blintzes to freezer bags, and freeze for up to 1 month. Defrost them thoroughly in the refrigerator before frying. Blintzes freeze so well you may consider making them in quantity to have on hand for impromptu brunch or breakfast gatherings.

If you do not care for sweet blintzes, turn them into savory blintzes by omitting the sugar and vanilla extract in the filling. Instead of lemon zest, use one of your favorite fresh herbs to flavor the filling and then season it with salt to taste. Serve the fried savory blintzes on their own with sour cream and fresh fruit, or applesauce if desired.

— planning ahead —

The ice cream blintzes can be made up to 1 week ahead, covered, and frozen. The Grand Marnier Sauce with Peaches can be made a day ahead and kept in a jar in the refrigerator.

Ice Cream Blintzes Flambé

When I was living in Nice, France, I used to await Mardi Gras with great excitement. It meant participating in the flower parade on the Promenade des Anglais, then rushing home afterwards with friends for our crêpe-making party, a French Mardi Gras tradition. While the crêpes were being flipped in the air, each of us would touch the crêpe pan's handle to wish for luck. We often made crêpes "en surprise," filled with ice cream and flambéed.

Through experimentation, I have found that the dessert is even better made with blintz pancakes, which are firmer than French crêpes and excellent for sealing the ice cream inside. I can't decide on a favorite topping, so here I give you two equally sinful sauces to try. One is an orange-flavored Grand Marnier sauce with peaches, the other a rum-flavored banana sauce.

Speed is crucial when preparing these blintzes. You must work very quickly to keep the ice cream hidden inside frozen.

YIELD: 8 blintzes, enough for 8 dessert servings

BLINTZ PANCAKES

2 large eggs
1 cup milk
⅔ cup unbleached all-purpose flour
4 tablespoons unsalted butter, melted and cooled

1 pint vanilla (or chocolate) ice cream

PREPARE THE BLINTZ BATTER: Combine the eggs, milk, 3 tablespoons water, and the flour in a blender or food processor. Blend until the batter is well mixed, scraping down the sides of the container as necessary. Transfer the batter to a medium bowl. Stir in 2 tablespoons of the melted butter. Cover and let stand for 1 hour.

MAKE THE BLINTZ PANCAKES: Heat an 8-inch nonstick omelet or crêpe pan over moderate heat. Brush the pan lightly with some of the remaining 2 tablespoons melted butter and heat until a drop of water sizzles on contact. Stir the batter, lift the pan from the heat, and pour ¼ cup batter into the pan. Quickly tilt and rotate the pan to cover the bottom evenly with the batter. Return the pan to the heat and cook until the batter is set and the crêpe looks dry on top, about 45 seconds. Loosen the edges of the pancake with the tip of a knife, then slide the crêpe onto a kitchen towel laid out on the counter. Continue making the pancakes, taking care to stir the batter thoroughly each time before adding more to the pan. Let the pancakes cool, then stack, cover, and set aside at room temperature until ready to assemble.

ASSEMBLE THE BLINTZES: Place a pancake browned side up on a flat surface. Using a ¼ cup scoop or measure, place a scoop of ice cream on the cooled pancake, just above the bottom edge. Using your hands, quickly shape the ice cream into a 4-inch-long log. Fold the sides over to cover the ice cream, then roll up from the bottom to seal. Wrap the blintz in plastic wrap and immediately place in the freezer. Continue to assemble the remaining blintzes in the same manner.

TO SERVE: Prepare Flaming Banana Sauce or Grand Marnier Sauce (recipes follow), and finish the blintzes as directed in the recipe.

FLAMING BANANA SAUCE

YIELD: About 3 cups

4 ripe bananas, peeled and cut into ½-inch slices
¼ cup fresh lemon juice
1½ teaspoons ground cinnamon
8 tablespoons (1 stick) unsalted butter
¾ cup packed light brown sugar
⅓ cup rum

Toss the bananas with the lemon juice and cinnamon.

Divide the butter and brown sugar between two large skillets and heat over moderate heat, stirring occasionally, until both the butter and sugar are melted. Add half of the banana mixture to each pan and sauté until just heated through, about 1 minute.

Push the bananas to the side of the pans, and add 4 of the frozen blintzes to each pan. Cook for 30 seconds, turn the blintzes over, and cook for 30 seconds longer. Remove the skillets from the heat. Pour half of the rum into each pan, ignite, and flambé, shaking the pans gently to distribute the liquor. As soon as the flames begin to die out, remove the blintzes to dessert plates. Spoon the bananas and sauce over the blintzes and serve immediately.

GRAND MARNIER SAUCE WITH PEACHES

YIELD: About 4 cups

1 cup sugar
½ cup Grand Marnier
Juice of 2 oranges (about ⅔ cup)
2 tablespoons minced fresh ginger
6 medium peaches, cut into ½-inch wedges
2 tablespoons unsalted butter
¼ cup cognac

continued

cook's notes

Remove the ice cream container from the freezer 5 minutes before assembling the blintzes. This will take the "frost" out of the ice cream and make it easier to handle.

If you wish, use a thin plastic bag as a "glove" to shape the ice cream into a log.

In a medium saucepan, combine the sugar, Grand Marnier, orange juice, and ginger and bring to a boil over high heat. Lower the heat and simmer until the syrup is well flavored, about 5 minutes. Strain the sauce and discard the ginger. Return the sauce to the pan, add the peaches, set the pan over moderate heat, and cook until the peaches are just heated through, about 2 to 3 minutes. Remove from the heat and set aside.

Divide the butter between two large skillets and melt over moderately high heat. Add 4 of the frozen blintzes to each skillet. Cook for 30 seconds, turn the blintzes over, and cook for 30 seconds longer. Remove the skillets from the heat. Pour half of the cognac into each pan, ignite, and flambé, shaking the pans gently to distribute the liquor. As soon as the flames begin to die out, remove the blintzes to dessert plates. Pour the Grand Marnier sauce mixture into one of the skillets, heat briefly, and then spoon the warm sauce over the blintzes. Serve immediately.

cooking en papillote

I love food cooked in its natural juices, so to me almost everything seems to taste a little better when it's prepared *en papillote.* This French term describes a dish baked in the oven in a sealed envelope of parchment paper. The paper inflates under the action of the heat, which creates steam around the food. This style of cooking also offers the advantage of a complete low-fat meal in one dish.

This technique belongs almost exclusively to classical French cooking. The nonabsorbent parchment is cut into a heart shape and lightly greased with butter. The light coating of butter helps seal the papillote while enhancing the flavor of the food inside. The food, usually a fillet of fish or a small bird, plus vegetables and a sprinkling of lemon juice or wine, is placed on one half of the heart. The other half of the heart is folded over like a book, and the edges folded and crimped to tightly seal the food inside.

Then the sealed bag is briefly baked in a very hot oven. The intense heat releases the natural juices from the food as steam. The expanding packet creates a chamber in which the steam circulates without dilution or evaporation, retaining all of the nutrients within.

For a dramatic effect, the sealed papillote is presented on its serving plate to the guest at the table. He or she opens the package to inhale its tantalizing aromas and to discover what is hidden inside.

Parchment paper is available in rolls or sheets at cake-decorating supply houses, specialty stores, and some supermarkets. I have also found that freezer wrap, available in supermarkets, can be used with great success. Although traditionally the package is made from paper, aluminum foil can be substituted in a pinch. The foil will not expand and allow the air to circulate as the paper will, but it will steam the enclosed food.

This "wet" method of cooking is most suitable for lean fish, such as Cod en Papillote, New England Style (page 318). A fatty food may release unwanted fats or oils inside the parchment. This undesirable effect can be overcome by precooking, as demonstrated in the recipe for Herbed Lemon Chicken and Corn Ragoût en Papillote (page 316).

En papillote cooking does not have to be limited to fish and poultry. Try a dessert in which fruits are given extra flavor and sophistication, such as Pineapple and Banana en Papillote (page 322).

Once you have tried this method of cooking, I'm sure you will devise your own recipes. Not only are these dishes easy to prepare, they make such a wonderful presentation at the table that en papillote will surely become part of your repertoire for entertaining.

Paper-Wrapped Ham and Pineapple, Hong Kong Style

This recipe is a good example of how an ancient technique of cooking can be adapted to new ingredients. It originated with Chinese cooks, who wrapped little morsels of food in pieces of cellophane to prevent the food inside from absorbing the cooking oil during deep-frying. The benefits of this technique have only been reinforced by today's tastes and health concerns. Here in the West, cellophane has been replaced by the more readily available parchment paper. Hidden inside these paper parcels are succulent morsels of ham and pineapple, accented with allspice. Since unfolding and eating this paper-wrapped appetizer can be a little messy, make sure there are plenty of napkins on hand.

YIELD: 16 mini-packets, enough for 4 to 5 appetizer servings

¼ of a fresh pineapple, peeled, cored, and cut crosswise into ¼-inch-thick slices
2 teaspoons light brown sugar
1 teaspoon light soy sauce
¼ teaspoon ground allspice
2 tablespoons unsalted butter, melted

2 ¼-inch-thick slices honey-baked ham (about 6 ounces), each cut into 8 strips about 2 by 2½ inches
16 sprigs fresh coriander or flat-leaf parsley

Vegetable oil, for frying

16 6¼-inch squares cooking parchment or foil

Place the pineapple slices in a shallow dish. Combine the sugar, soy sauce, and allspice in a small bowl and pour over the pineapple. Carefully turn the slices to coat with the sauce. Let stand for 15 minutes.

ASSEMBLE THE PACKETS: Lay a parchment paper square on the counter with one corner pointing toward you and lightly brush with melted butter. Lay a strip of ham across the bottom of the paper, 1½ inches from the bottom corner. Top with a slice of pineapple and a coriander sprig. Fold the bottom corner over the filling. Crease sharply. (When creasing, run your nail along each seam twice to sharpen the folds, so the package will not unfold during deep-frying.) Fold the package up and over, and crease the fold sharply. Fold the two side points over the center, crossing one another, and crease sharply along the two sides; the package should look like an envelope with the top flap open. Tuck the top flap as far as it will go down into the envelope between the filling and the two crossed sides, then crease it to seal. Firmly crease all folds again, and set aside on a platter. Repeat with the remaining paper squares and filling ingredients.

continued

— *planning ahead* —

The parcels can be assembled a few hours in advance, placed on a platter, and refrigerated. Bring to room temperature before frying or baking.

— *cook's notes* —

Honey-baked ham is available at the deli section of most supermarkets. If unavailable, use a low-salt type of ham, such as boiled ham, and lightly brush the slices with honey before wrapping.

Thin slices of fresh salmon or sea scallops may be used instead of ham.

TO FRY THE PARCELS: Heat ½ inch of oil in a large skillet to 365°F. Gently slide 6 or 8 parcels, smooth side down, into the hot oil and fry until the parcels are lightly browned, about 2 minutes. Using a slotted spoon, drain the parcels on paper towels, pressing them lightly to blot the excess oil. Fry the remaining packets.

TO BAKE THE PARCELS: Preheat the oven to 450°F. Place the parcels on a baking sheet and bake until slightly browned and puffed, about 8 to 10 minutes.

TO SERVE: Let each person open his or her own parcels and pop the contents into his or her mouth.

Herbed Lemon Chicken and Corn Ragoût en Papillote

— planning ahead —

It's best to allow the chicken to marinate overnight in the refrigerator. Bring to room temperature before assembling the packets.

The sealed papillotes may be prepared a few hours before serving and refrigerated. Bring to room temperature before baking.

Three of my favorite ingredients are combined in this simple but delicious dish: chicken, corn, and herbes de Provence, a blend of Mediterranean herbs typically including thyme, basil, rosemary, savory, and marjoram. Before wrapping the chicken, I like to partly grill it to seal in the flavor and give it a beautiful color and markings. When the papillote is cut open, it reveals an aromatic and moist chicken that almost falls off the bone.

YIELD: 4 main-course servings

MARINADE

⅓ cup fresh lemon juice
⅓ cup olive oil
1 tablespoon Dijon mustard
1 teaspoon paprika
1 tablespoon minced garlic
2 tablespoons herbes de Provence (see Cook's Notes)
1 teaspoon salt
Freshly ground black pepper to taste

8 chicken legs (drumsticks and thighs)

CORN RAGOÛT

2 tablespoons olive oil
2 small onions, chopped
1 tablespoon minced garlic
4 small ears fresh corn, kernels cut off the cob, or 2 cups frozen corn kernels, thawed
4 ripe plum tomatoes, cut into medium dice
1 tablespoon chopped fresh thyme leaves or 1 teaspoon dried, crumbled
¼ cup chopped fresh flat-leaf parsley
Salt and freshly ground black pepper to taste

4 tablespoons unsalted butter, melted

4 15-inch squares cooking parchment or foil

MARINATE THE CHICKEN: Place all the marinade ingredients in a large shallow dish and mix well. Add the chicken legs and turn to coat them with the mixture. Cover and marinate for at least 2 hours, or overnight, in the refrigerator.

PRECOOK THE CHICKEN: Drain the chicken legs, discarding the marinade. Heat a grill or a greased skillet set over moderately high heat, and cook the legs for about 5 minutes on each side (see Cook's Notes). Remove the legs to a platter and set aside. (The legs are only partially cooked at this point: the cooking will be completed in the oven.)

MAKE THE CORN RAGOÛT: Heat the oil in a large skillet over moderately high heat. Add the onions and garlic and sauté until translucent, about 1 minute. Add the corn and tomatoes and cook until heated through, about 1 minute. Stir in the herbs, and remove the pan from the heat. Season with salt and pepper. Drain any juices from the chicken platter into the corn mixture. Set aside.

Preheat the oven to 425°F.

ASSEMBLE THE PACKETS: Brush a sheet of parchment paper with melted butter. Fold in half and reopen to reveal a center fold line. Place one quarter of the corn ragoût on the bottom half of the sheet, leaving a 1- to 1½-inch border. Top the ragoût with 2 chicken legs, skin side up. Fold the other half of the parchment paper over, and fold and crimp the edges to seal, forming a rectangular packet. Set the packet on a baking sheet. Repeat with the remaining packets.

BAKE THE PACKETS: Place the packets in the oven and bake for about 30 to 35 minutes, or until an instant-read thermometer inserted through a papillote into a chicken thigh reads 175°F to 180°F.

TO SERVE: Transfer the papillotes to serving plates. Cut an "X" in the top of each papillote to reveal the filling. Present the chicken in the packets or slide each serving onto the plate and discard the paper.

— cook's notes —

Dried herbes de Provence are available at gourmet and specialty food shops. To make your own, combine equal portions of crumbled dried thyme, rosemary, basil, fennel, savory, and marjoram. If you like the floral taste of lavender and have access to some, by all means add some to the blend. If you can obtain these herbs fresh, it will be even better.

If assembling the packets with foil, use a sturdy foil that will not rip or tear and will hold the weight of the food inside.

Use a cast-iron pan with raised grids on the bottom to skillet-grill the meat in order to obtain attractive grill marks.

Split pigeon, Rock Cornish hens, or pheasant breasts may replace the chicken legs in this recipe. If you like, remove their skins before wrapping.

— planning ahead —

The sealed papillotes may be prepared a few hours before serving and refrigerated. Bring to room temperature before baking.

— cook's notes —

If assembling the packets with foil, use a sturdy foil that will not rip or tear and will hold the weight of the food inside. Do not cut into heart shapes. Place the ingredients on one half of the foil square and fold the other half over the food. Fold and crimp the edges to form a rectangular packet.

Halibut or monkfish may be used instead of codfish.

Cod en Papillote, New England Style

Codfish, a staple in this country since before the American Revolution, is a highly versatile, economical, and healthful fish. It lends itself beautifully to various methods of preparation, and cooking in parchment is one of them. To make this dish even more special, I bake the fish on a bed of bacon-flavored potatoes and roast bell peppers. When opened, the papillote will exude a fragrant aroma and reveal a spectacular, steaming piece of fish. Given that this dish contains both fish and vegetables, you've got an entire meal in one packet!

YIELD: 2 main-course servings

- 1 large red bell pepper
- 4 thin slices bacon, cut crosswise into thin strips
- 1 medium Idaho potato, peeled and cut into ½-inch cubes
- 1 cup chopped onions
- 1 teaspoon minced garlic
- 4 scallions, sliced
- Salt and freshly ground black pepper to taste
- 2 tablespoons unsalted butter, melted
- 2 4-ounce cod fillets
- 2 teaspoons olive oil

- 2 15-inch squares cooking parchment or foil

PREPARE THE FILLING: Place the bell pepper directly over a gas flame or an electric burner and char it, turning frequently until the skin blackens all over, about 5 minutes. Using tongs, transfer the pepper to a plate and let it cool. Peel off the skin, halve the pepper lengthwise, and remove the seeds. Set aside. Alternatively, cut the pepper in half lengthwise, place it skin side up under a preheated broiler, and broil until the skin is blackened. Peel off the skin, remove the seeds, and set aside.

Heat a large skillet over moderately high heat. Add the bacon and cook, stirring with a wooden spoon, until the bacon is crisp and the fat is rendered, about 5 minutes. With a slotted spoon, remove the bacon to paper towels to drain. Pour off all but 1 tablespoon of the fat from the skillet. Add the potato to the pan and sauté over moderate heat until slightly colored, about 2 minutes. Stir in the onions and garlic and cook until the onions are soft and lightly browned, about 2 minutes. Stir in the scallions and bacon, and remove the pan from the heat. Season with salt and pepper. Set aside.

Preheat the oven to 425°F.

ASSEMBLE THE PACKETS: Lightly brush the parchment sheets with melted butter and fold them in half. Cut a half-heart shape out of each one, with the widest point measuring 7½ inches, and open each paper into a full heart shape.

Place a red pepper half on one side of each paper, near the center fold. Lightly season the fillets with salt and pepper, and top the peppers with the cod fillets. Top each fillet with half of the potato mixture. Fold the other side of each paper over, and, starting at the wide end of the heart, fold and crimp along the edges to seal. Place the packets on a baking sheet.

Bake the packets for about 15 minutes, or until the papillotes puff and the paper is slightly browned.

TO SERVE: Transfer each papillote to a preheated dinner plate. Cut an "X" in the top of each packet and sprinkle the exposed filling with 1 teaspoon of the olive oil. Present the fish in the packet or slide each serving onto the plate and discard the paper.

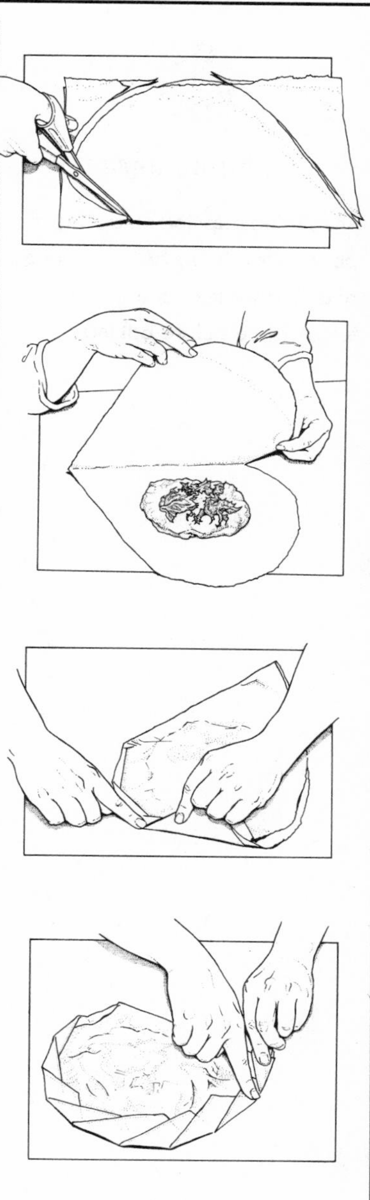

— *planning ahead* —

The sealed papillotes may be prepared a few hours before serving and refrigerated. Bring to room temperature before baking.

Whole Red Snapper en Papillote, Mediterranean Style

This is a quick, simple, and elegant recipe that demands no particular technical skills. Just make sure you have the freshest of red snapper. I have noticed that anchovies, a staple of Mediterranean-style cooking, are greatly underappreciated in this country. Since I love them, they found their way into this recipe. The snapper, flavored with vinegar, capers, olives, and a hint of fresh basil, takes on a new dimension. Offer garlic bread or steamed rice on the side to soak up the delicious juices from the fish.

YIELD: 2 main-course servings

1 small head of garlic, separated into cloves and peeled
2 tablespoons olive oil
1 tablespoon balsamic vinegar
2 medium tomatoes, diced
2 tablespoons capers, drained and coarsely chopped
¼ cup pitted Kalamata olives, coarsely chopped (see Cook's Notes)
½ teaspoon anchovy paste or 2 anchovy fillets, finely chopped
¼ teaspoon crushed dried red pepper
¼ cup shredded fresh basil leaves
2 1-pound red snapper, gutted and scaled, heads left on, tails and fins trimmed
2 tablespoons unsalted butter, melted
Salt and freshly ground black pepper to taste

2 15-inch squares cooking parchment or foil

Preheat the oven to 425°F.

PARBOIL THE GARLIC: Bring a small saucepan of water to a boil, add the garlic, and boil for 1 minute. Drain, discarding the liquid. Set aside.

In a small bowl, combine the olive oil, vinegar, tomatoes, capers, olives, anchovy paste, crushed pepper flakes, and basil leaves. Set aside.

Rinse the fish thoroughly inside and out until there is no trace of blood remaining. If the gills have not been removed, do so to avoid bitterness. Pat the fish dry.

ASSEMBLE THE PACKETS: Lightly brush the parchment sheets with melted butter. Fold each in half and reopen to reveal a center fold line. Lightly season the fish inside and out with salt and pepper. Place a fish on the bottom half of each sheet of paper, leaving a 1- to 1½-inch border. Spoon the tomato mixture and the garlic cloves over the fish. Fold the other half of each parchment paper over, and fold and crimp the edges to seal, forming a rectangular packet. Place the packets on a baking sheet.

Bake the packets for about 20 minutes, or until the papillotes puff and the paper is slightly browned.

TO SERVE: Transfer each papillote to a preheated dinner plate. Cut an "X" in the top of each packet to reveal the filling. Present the fish in the packet or slide each serving onto the plate and discard the paper.

— cook's notes —

Kalamata olives are small purple-black Greek olives.

If assembling the packets with foil, use a sturdy foil that will not rip or tear and will hold the weight of the food inside.

— planning ahead —

The packages can be assembled a few hours ahead and refrigerated. Bring them to room temperature before baking.

— cook's notes —

You may also try different combinations of seasonal fruits, such as apples and pears, peaches and strawberries or pitted cherries, mangoes and oranges, or figs and raspberries.

Pineapple and Banana en Papillote

This "wet" method of cooking fruit results in an especially moist and fragrant dessert. The robust ginger syrup adds a slight pungent accent to the subtle flavors of the fruits. This is one of my favorite ways to conclude a meal, especially on cold winter nights.

YIELD: 4 dessert servings

GINGER SYRUP

½ cup pure maple syrup
2 teaspoons finely grated fresh ginger

2 tablespoons unsalted butter, melted
4 small bananas
1 ripe pineapple, peeled, cored, and quartered lengthwise

¼ cup rum or tequila
4 tablespoons unsalted butter
¼ cup shredded coconut, toasted

4 15-inch squares cooking parchment or foil

MAKE THE SYRUP: In a small saucepan, combine the syrup, grated ginger, and 2 tablespoons water. Bring to a boil, then reduce the heat and simmer until the syrup is well flavored with ginger, about 5 minutes. Strain the syrup through a fine-mesh sieve, pressing on the ginger to extract all the liquid. Discard the ginger and set the syrup aside.

Preheat the oven to 425°F.

ASSEMBLE THE PACKETS: Lightly brush a parchment sheet with melted butter. Fold in half and reopen to reveal a center fold line. Peel one banana and cut into diagonal slices. Fan out the banana slices on the bottom half of the parchment, near the center fold line. Slice a pineapple quarter and fan the slices on top of the bananas. Drizzle 2 tablespoons of the syrup and 1 tablespoon of the rum over the fruits. Dot with 1 tablespoon of the butter. Fold the outer half of the parchment paper over, and fold and crimp the edges to seal, forming a rectangular packet. Set the packet on a baking sheet. Repeat with the remaining packets.

Bake the packets for about 6 minutes, or until the papillotes puff and the paper is lightly browned.

TO SERVE: Place a papillote on each serving plate. Cut a small "X" in the top of each and sprinkle the exposed fruits with toasted coconut. Let the guests serve themselves from the papillotes.

cooking in salt crusts

Baking food hermetically sealed in a salt crust is a cooking style that is probably unfamiliar to most people in America, whereas in Europe it has long been a culinary tradition. Even today, in many elegant restaurants in France and Spain, small birds are cooked in a salt crust, which becomes the serving vessel at the table. Once cracked open, the crust releases the aroma of the food inside and sets the diners' appetites astir.

As with a parchment paper papillote, the purpose of baking with a salt crust is to cook the encased food slowly and evenly in an environment where it retains its moisture and gains a dramatic depth of flavor. Unlike papillotes, which are generally prepared with individual portions, a salt vessel is well suited for a whole fish, game bird, or a filet of beef or venison. Because of their lean and delicate nature, these foods actually fare best when cooked in this fashion. They don't run the risk of drying out or getting tough even if they are slightly overcooked.

A salt crust is made by simply kneading flour with water, egg white, and coarse salt. Sometimes chopped fresh herbs are added to the dough so that the food inside is infused with their wonderful flavor while it cooks. The egg white in the dough helps to seal the crust during baking.

During baking, the salt dough hardens under the intense heat. It then acts as a moist oven, conducting the heat with maximum efficiency around the food. This method yields exceptionally tender, juicy, and flavorful meats without requiring additional fats or oils during cooking. After baking, the hardened crust feels much like a coat of plaster. When cut open, it separates easily from the food and comes off without crumbling. Despite what you might think, the food sealed inside the salt crust does not end up tasting particularly salty. (The salt crust itself is not edible.)

For salt crusts, I prefer using coarse kosher salt because it is far less expensive and tastes milder than refined sea salt. To judge for yourself, I suggest that you taste-test the different salts, first on their own and then by cooking the same dish using each of them. This is the best way to understand the character of these salts and how they taste under various conditions.

The following recipes are just a few examples of how to cook game meat and fish in a salt crust. Once you realize how delicious and easy this cooking method can be, I'm sure you'll prepare your food this way often, as I do.

COARSE KOSHER SALT VERSUS SEA SALT

COARSE KOSHER SALT is a pure, distinctly mild-tasting salt with a flavor that balances well with any type of food. It is available in three-pound boxes in large supermarkets, often located on a shelf with other Jewish food products. It is half as salty as table salt or sea salt.

COARSE SEA SALT has an assertive character of its own. As it is twice as salty as coarse kosher salt, if you decide to use it instead of kosher salt, begin with only half as much as the recipe calls for. It comes in two forms: refined and unrefined. Unrefined sea salt is more suitable for making salt crusts because it will be used solely as a cooking vessel and won't be consumed. Refined sea salt is generally reserved for cooking.

SALT CRUST TIPS

- It is important that you allow a salt dough to relax for at least thirty minutes or, better yet, overnight. You'll find it much easier to roll. It can be left either at room temperature or refrigerated. If the dough starts shrinking back while you roll it, cover it with plastic or wrap a clean towel and let it rest for about ten minutes more before continuing.
- Use an accurate, instant-read thermometer to check for doneness. Remove the food from the oven, and insert the thermometer through the crust into the thickest part of the fish, poultry, or meat. The internal temperature of cooked fish should be 125°F, of poultry should be 175° to 180°F, and of pork should be 150° to 155°F. Red meats (fillet of beef, venison, or lamb) should be 125°F for rare, 135°F for medium rare, 145°F for medium, and 150°F for well done. Note that as all these foods rest, their internal temperature will increase by 5 to 10 degrees.
- Once the dish is cooked, allow it to rest for at least thirty minutes before opening the crust. Opening the crust as soon as it comes out of the oven may result in steam burns if you are not careful. The resting time also allows the juices that accumulate in the center of meat to spread throughout, which will make for more tender meat that is easier to carve.

— *planning ahead* —

The bird can marinate overnight in the refrigerator. The salt dough can be prepared a day ahead, covered, and refrigerated. Bring the dough and the fowl to room temperature before proceeding with the recipe. The roast bird can sit in the crust on the baking sheet at room temperature for up to 1 hour before serving.

Honey-Roasted Guinea Hen in Salt Crust

I think guinea hen is one of the most delicious, tender, and delicate of the domestically raised game birds available. Sometimes referred to as guinea fowl or as *pintade,* its French name, it is rich, plump, faintly gamey, and firm in texture. It stands somewhere between a pheasant and a chicken.

Here, a guinea hen is marinated in a tantalizing Asian-flavored sauce of honey, soy sauce, sherry, hoisin, ginger, and sesame oil. When cooked, the salt crust is opened to reveal succulent and moist meat that almost falls off the bone. This dish is ideal for entertaining since the cooked fowl can sit in the salt crust for up to an hour and still emerge hot and delicious. Serve rice and a simple vegetable dish with the hen.

YIELD: 4 main-course servings

1 young guinea hen (about 3 pounds) (see Cook's Notes)

MARINADE

3 scallions, chopped
2 tablespoons honey
2 tablespoons light soy sauce
2 tablespoons dry sherry
2 tablespoons hoisin sauce
2 tablespoons grated fresh ginger
1 tablespoon minced garlic
½ teaspoon Oriental sesame oil
Freshly ground black pepper to taste

SALT DOUGH

2½ cups all-purpose flour, plus additional if necessary
1 cup coarse kosher salt
2 large egg whites

Oriental sesame oil, for brushing

MARINATE THE FOWL: Rinse the hen well, remove and discard any excess fat, and pat dry with paper towels. Carefully loosen the skin on the breast and legs of the bird by pushing your fingers between the skin and meat to form a pocket. In a shallow dish large enough to hold the hen, whisk all the ingredients for the marinade together. Place the hen in the dish. Rub the marinade generously inside the hen cavity, over the skin, and under the loosened skin. Tuck the wings under the bird. Secure the legs by tying them with kitchen string. Cover and set aside to marinate at room temperature for at least 2 hours, or refrigerate overnight, turning the bird occasionally in the marinade.

PREPARE THE SALT DOUGH: Place the flour and salt in the bowl of a food processor fitted with the metal blade and pulse to blend. Beat the egg whites and ⅔ cup water together in a bowl. With the motor running, add the egg and water mixture through the feed tube and blend just until the dough holds together and rides on the blade. The dough should be firm and moist, not sticky. If the dough is a little flaky, add about 1 tablespoon more water. If it is sticky, add about 1 tablespoon flour. Turn the dough out onto a lightly floured work surface. Gather the dough together, briefly knead it, and shape it into a smooth, flat disk. Cover with plastic wrap and let rest at room temperature for at least 30 minutes.

Preheat the oven to 400°F.

WRAP THE BIRD: Remove the hen from the marinade and place it breast side up in the center of a foil-lined baking sheet. Reserve the marinade for the sauce.

Lightly dust a work surface with flour. Roll the dough from the center out toward the edges to form a circle large enough to envelop the bird, about 16 inches in diameter. Lift the dough from the board by wrapping it loosely around the rolling pin. Carefully unroll it over the hen, completely covering it. Tuck the excess dough under the hen.

ROAST THE HEN: Place the baking sheet with the hen in the oven and bake for about 1 hour and 30 minutes, or until an instant-read thermometer inserted through the crust into an inner thigh reads 175°F to 180°F. Remove the hen and allow it to rest in the crust on the baking pan for at least 30 minutes but no longer than an hour. The hen will remain warm for up to an hour.

Meanwhile, MAKE THE SAUCE: Pour the juices collected in the baking pan into a skillet. Skim off any excess fat. Add the reserved marinade to the pan and bring to a boil. Cook over moderately high heat until the sauce is slightly reduced, about 2 minutes. Remove from the heat, taste the sauce, and adjust the seasoning if necessary.

TO SERVE: Cut open the salt crust with a pair of scissors and remove the hen to a cutting board. If you are opening the crust soon after it comes out of the oven, be careful of the escaping steam. Discard the crust. Brush sesame oil over the hen and quarter it. Transfer the pieces to a warmed platter, spoon the sauce over, and serve.

— cook's notes —

Top-quality fresh guinea hens can be found in many select butcher shops, supermarkets, and specialty stores. It can also be ordered from D'Artagnan, Inc., 399–419 St. Paul Avenue, Jersey City, NJ 07306 (Tel. 800-DAR-TAGN or 201-792-0748; Fax 201-792-0113).

A 3-pound pheasant or roasting chicken can be prepared the same way as the guinea hen.

— planning ahead —

The salt dough can be prepared a day ahead, covered with plastic wrap, and refrigerated. Bring to room temperature before rolling. The cooked venison can rest in the crust on the baking sheet at room temperature for up to 1 hour before serving.

Herbed Venison Roast in Salt Crust

This absolutely terrific and easy-to-prepare dish deserves to be served at your most important dinner party or holiday celebration. A moist and tender venison loin infused with the wonderful flavors of fresh thyme and garlic is roasted to perfection under a salt crust.

Very lean and low in cholesterol, venison, no longer hard to find, is the perfect alternative for red-meat lovers. For roasting in a salt crust, I use a shortloin cut, which is as tender as the tenderloin but slightly less expensive. Do make a special effort to get fresh thyme for this dish. Although the dried version can be used, the end result will not approach the taste obtained with fresh herbs.

YIELD: 4 main-course servings

SALT DOUGH

2½ cups all-purpose flour, plus additional if necessary
1 cup coarse kosher salt
2 large egg whites

1 boneless venison shortloin (about 2 pounds), at room temperature (see Cook's Notes)
1 tablespoon unsalted butter
1 tablespoon extra-virgin olive oil
⅓ cup dry white wine, such as Chardonnay
⅓ cup beef broth
2 teaspoons finely chopped fresh thyme leaves
2 teaspoons minced garlic
Salt and freshly ground black pepper to taste

PREPARE THE SALT DOUGH: Place the flour and salt in the bowl of a food processor fitted with the metal blade and pulse to blend. Gently beat the egg whites and ⅔ cup water together in a bowl. With the motor on, add the egg and water mixture through the feed tube and blend just until the dough holds together and rides on the blade. The dough should be firm and moist, not sticky. If the dough is too dry or crumbly, add about 1 tablespoon more water. If it's too sticky, add about 1 tablespoon of flour.

Turn the dough out onto a lightly floured work surface. Gather the dough together, briefly knead it, and shape it into a smooth flat disk. Cover with plastic wrap and let rest at room temperature for at least 30 minutes.

PREPARE THE VENISON: Rinse the shortloin thoroughly and pat dry with paper towels. Trim the silverskin and any visible fat from the meat. Tuck the long ends of the meat under the loin to make a neat roll. Tie the roll in several places with kitchen string.

Put the butter and oil in a roasting pan large enough to hold the venison and heat over moderately high heat. When hot, add the venison and sear well on both sides, about 2 minutes per side. Transfer the loin to a platter to cool. (Reserve the pan drippings to make the sauce.)

PREPARE THE SAUCE: Add the white wine to the roasting pan with the drippings and bring to a boil over moderately high heat. Scrape the bottom of the pan with a wooden spoon to release any browned bits, and cook until the wine is reduced by half, about 1 minute. Add the beef broth. Cook until the liquid is reduced by half, about 1 minute. Pour the reduced liquid into a small saucepan, cover, and set aside.

Preheat the oven to 400°F.

WRAP THE VENISON: Lightly dust a work surface with flour. Roll the dough out to a rectangle about 11 by 15 inches long and 3⁄16 inch thick, large enough to envelop the piece of venison without stretching the dough.

Drain the meat juices that have collected on the venison platter into the saucepan of reduced liquid. Place the loin in the center of the dough. Mix the thyme and garlic together and pat the mixture over the meat. Fold one long side of the dough over the meat and lightly moisten the top surface with water. Fold the other side over to enclose the meat, and press the dough together to seal. Lightly moisten the ends of the dough, fold the ends up, and press to completely seal the package. Transfer the wrapped loin, seam side up, to an ungreased baking sheet.

ROAST THE VENISON: Place the baking sheet with the venison in the oven. For rare meat, roast for 15 minutes (about 8 minutes per pound), or until an instant-read thermometer inserted in the meat reads 115°F. For medium rare, roast an additional 5 minutes, or until the meat's internal temperature reaches 120°F. Remove the roast from the oven and let it rest in the crust on the baking sheet for at least 30 minutes but no more than one hour. The meat will remain warm for up to an hour.

TO SERVE: Cut open the salt crust at one end with a pair of scissors. If you are opening the crust soon after it comes out of the oven, be careful of the escaping steam. Remove the venison to a cutting board, being careful to save all the meat juices collected in the crust. Drain the juices into the sauce and discard the crust. Briefly reheat the sauce. Taste and adjust the seasonings with salt and pepper if necessary. Cut the venison into 8 thick slices and arrange them on warmed dinner plates. Spoon the sauce over the meat and serve at once.

cook's notes

Venison can be ordered from D'Artagnan, Inc., 399-419 St. Paul Avenue, Jersey City, NJ 07306 (Tel. 800-DAR-TAGN or 201-792-0748; Fax 201-792-0113). Ask for shortloin of venison imported from New Zealand. The venison arrives vacuum-packed in heavy plastic, and, unopened, has about a 10-day shelf life.

The same size veal loin or beef tenderloin can be substituted for the venison loin.

— *planning ahead* —

Both the aïoli and the salt dough can be prepared a day in advance, covered, and refrigerated. Bring them to room temperature before use. The baked fish can sit in the crust on the baking sheet at room temperature for up to 1 hour before serving.

Whole Sea Bass in Salt Crust with Aïoli

I will never forget my first encounter with aïoli. When my family moved from Laos to Cannes, we stayed in a family inn called Soleil d'Azur. The chef there frequently served cold or baked fish with aïoli, a mayonnaise assertively flavored with garlic. I liked it so much that I decided I must learn how to make it. Little by little, I convinced the chef to let me help with small chores, like washing dishes and making mayonnaise. After a few flops and with much help from the chef, I finally got my first decent batch of aïoli. I can't begin to tell you the pride that I felt. I knew then that my true calling in life would be to be a cook.

One of the purest and easiest ways to cook sea bass, or *loup* as it is called in Provence, is to bake it whole, buried in a mound of coarse sea salt. This style of cooking fish is immensely popular in the South of France, especially along the Spanish-French border. The fish may be served with just a sprinkling of fruity olive oil and lemon juice, or accompanied by an emulsified sauce such as mayonnaise or bèarnaise. My version calls for a salt crust, which is much easier to break through after baking, and takes nothing away from the dish in terms of flavors. Garlicky aïoli best complements the mild, sweet taste of this sea bass and at the same time brings the flavors of Provence to your table.

YIELD: 4 light main-course servings

SALT DOUGH

3¾ cups all-purpose flour, plus additional if necessary
1½ cups coarse kosher salt
3 large egg whites

AÏOLI

3 large garlic cloves
½ teaspoon salt
2 large egg yolks
1 teaspoon fresh lemon juice
1 cup extra-virgin olive oil
Freshly ground white pepper to taste

1 3-pound sea bass, gutted and scaled, gills removed, head left on, and tail and fins trimmed

PREPARE THE SALT DOUGH: Place the flour and salt in the bowl of a food processor fitted with the metal blade and pulse to blend. Beat the egg whites and 1 cup water in a bowl. With the motor running, add the egg and water mixture through the feed tube and blend just until the dough holds together and rides on the blade. The dough should be firm and moist, not sticky. If the dough is a little flaky, add about 1 tablespoon more water. If it is too moist, add about 1 tablespoon flour.

Turn the dough out onto a lightly floured work surface. Gather the dough together, briefly knead it, and shape it into a smooth, flat disk. Cover with plastic wrap and let it rest at room temperature for at least 30 minutes.

PREPARE THE AÏOLI: Using the flat side of a cleaver or mallet, smash the garlic cloves. Peel the garlic, combine with the salt, and mince to make a very fine paste. You should have about 2½ teaspoons of garlic paste.

Put the garlic paste, egg yolks, and lemon juice in the container of a blender. With the motor running, slowly drizzle in the oil and blend until thick. If the mixture seems to be too thick as you blend it, add about ½ teaspoon or so of water. The finished aïoli should be dense, mayonnaise-like, and highly fragrant. Transfer it to a small bowl. You should have about 1 cup of aïoli. Cover with plastic wrap and refrigerate.

Rinse the fish thoroughly inside and out until there is no trace of blood remaining. Pat dry with paper towels.

Preheat the oven to 400°F.

WRAP THE FISH: Lightly dust a work surface with flour. Roll the dough to form a rectangle about 12 by 18 inches long, large enough to envelop the whole fish without stretching the dough. Place the fish in the center of the dough. Fold one long side over the fish and lightly moisten the top surface with water. Fold the other side over to enclose the fish. Press the dough together to seal. Lightly moisten the ends of the dough, fold up, and press to completely seal the package. Transfer the wrapped fish, seam side up, to an ungreased baking sheet.

Bake the fish for 35 to 40 minutes, or until an instant-read thermometer inserted through the dough into the thickest part of the fish (near the head) reads 125°F. Remove the fish from the oven and let it rest in the crust on the baking sheet for at least 30 minutes but no more than an hour. The fish will remain warm for up to 1 hour.

TO SERVE: With a pair of scissors, cut open the salt crust to reveal the fish. If you are opening the crust soon after it comes out of the oven, be careful of the escaping steam. Some of the fish skin will come off with the crust. Using a fork, carefully remove any skin left on the top of the fish and discard. Using a large spoon and a fork, split the top fillet in half lengthwise along the center bone. Gently remove each half, in a single piece if possible, and transfer to a warmed dinner plate. Carefully remove the center bones and discard. Split the bottom fillet to obtain two more portions.

Serve immediately with the aïoli on the side.

— cook's notes —

If by any chance the aïoli should curdle as you are blending it, add about 1 teaspoon hot water and process until the mixture is smooth again.

For a much lighter and simpler meal, instead of preparing the aïoli, just drizzle a little bit of fruity olive oil over the cooked fillets and serve them with wedges of lemon.

If there's any leftover aïoli, transfer it to a glass jar. It will keep in the refrigerator for up to 2 weeks. Serve it as a condiment for any roast or as a tasty spread for sandwiches.

A whole red snapper, small salmon, or tilefish can replace the sea bass. If you are preparing a slightly smaller or larger fish, adjust the baking time by 5 minutes either way for each ½ pound of fish.

fish, poultry, and meat wrappers

In classical French cooking, thin slices of meat or fish rolled around a stuffing are called *paupiettes* or *oiseaux sans tête* ("headless birds"). In the English-speaking world, these dishes are simply known as "birds." One can safely assume that the term *bird* refers to the shape of the bundle, which resembles a stuffed quail or woodcock without its head. This style of cooking has its main roots in European cuisines, where meat is generally the focus of a meal.

For meat to be used as a wrapper, it must be tender and thin enough to be flexible. Poultry breasts, lean pieces of veal, pork, or lamb, or beef slices from the shell or flank steak are most appropriate. Often, the meat is transformed into a large, paper-thin sheet by pounding it with a mallet. That is how the delicate texture of Chicken Kiev (page 346) is achieved. Sometimes, instead of pounding, the meat is cut very thin and overlapping slices are laid out to form a single sheet, as in Grilled Beef and Scallion Rolls (page 342). Another method is to roll ground meat into a sheet before molding it around a filling. This method can be used to transform an ordinary egg into a wonderful brunch dish, Scotch Eggs (page 338).

Fillets of fish are ideal for making paupiettes. Naturally thin and flexible, they do not need to be pounded, which would ruin their delicate texture in any case. By combining the clean fresh taste of the fish with a sophisticated filling like the scallop mousse in Paupiettes of Sole in Crabmeat Sauce (page 336), you can create a dish that will stand out on special occasions.

The cooking method for dishes wrapped with meat or fish depends on what's outside and what's inside. Many of the meat-wrapped dishes with fillings that just need to be heated through are great for grilling, like the Grilled Braccioletini of Pork (page 344). On the other hand, the raw sausage stuffing in the Paupiettes of Turkey, Cajun Style (page 350) demands thorough cooking. The most suitable method for this and similar dishes is braising, which allows the stuffed rolls to cook slowly and evenly. The presence of a braising liquid prevents the thin meat wrapper from drying out during the long cooking process.

Although most of the recipes in this chapter are for light entrées or main courses, excellent hors d'oeuvres can also be prepared using thin slices of smoked fish or meats. Smoked Salmon Rolls with Eggplant Caviar (page 335) are one of my favorites. These are great for cocktails, as they can be prepared well in advance, ready to serve as soon as company arrives.

The recipes in this chapter illustrate the diversity of taste and techniques that the wrapped form style of cooking can lead to. All the dishes can be easily prepared and they all are so good to eat, too.

Smoked Salmon Rolls with Eggplant Caviar

I like to say good-bye to the old year and ring in the new by serving these tasty, elegant little rolls with Champagne on New Year's Eve. Inspired by the classic combination of smoked salmon and caviar, I roll the salmon around a light purée of eggplant that in France is known as "poor man's caviar." The eggplant is grilled to bring out its sweetness and amplify its flavor, and then assertively seasoned with garlic, lemon juice, capers, and chives to stand up to the smoky flavor of the salmon. Simple to prepare, these rolls are also excellent served on a bed of mixed greens as an entrée for a light luncheon (see Cook's Notes), accompanied by Champagne.

YIELD: 36 small rolls for hors d'oeuvres, or enough for 6 light lunch servings

SPECIAL EQUIPMENT: A pastry bag fitted with a 1-inch plain nozzle

EGGPLANT PURÉE

- 1 medium eggplant (about 12 ounces)
- 1 teaspoon minced garlic
- 1 tablespoon capers, drained and coarsely chopped
- 1 tablespoon fresh lemon juice
- 1 tablespoon chopped fresh chives
- 1½ tablespoons olive oil
- Salt and freshly ground black pepper to taste
- 18 slices cocktail rye bread or pumpernickel bread
- 2 tablespoons unsalted butter, at room temperature
- 18 large paper-thin slices (about 3 by 4 inches each) smoked salmon (about ½ pound)
- Very thin lemon slices, for garnish
- Fresh chives, for garnish

PREPARE THE PURÉE: Prick the skin of the eggplant in several places with a fork. Place the eggplant directly on a gas burner and grill over a moderately hot flame, turning occasionally with tongs, until the flesh is soft and the skin is charred all over, about 10 minutes. Alternatively, place the eggplant directly on an electric burner and grill as above. Remove the eggplant to a rack and allow to cool.

Peel off and discard the charred skin from the eggplant. Coarsely chop the meat and place it in a bowl. Stir in the garlic, capers, lemon juice, and chives. Whisk in the olive oil and season with salt and pepper. Cover with plastic wrap and chill well before using.

Stack the slices of bread and trim the crusts. Spread the slices with the butter and then cut them in half to obtain thirty-six 1- by 2-inch rectangles. Cover with plastic wrap and set aside.

ASSEMBLE THE SALMON ROLLS: Cut each slice of salmon crosswise in half to obtain 36 rectangles about 2 by 3 inches each. Arrange the salmon

— planning ahead —

The eggplant purée may be prepared a day ahead, covered, and refrigerated. The stuffed salmon rolls may be prepared early on the day you are going to serve them, covered with plastic wrap, and refrigerated until ready to serve. The buttered pieces of bread may be prepared up to 2 hours before serving. Place them in a single layer on a baking sheet, cover with plastic wrap, and set aside at room temperature until ready to use.

— cook's notes —

To facilitate the assembly of the rolls, I recommend using a pastry bag fitted with a 1-inch nozzle. If a pastry bag is not available, place about a teaspoon of the purée on each salmon rectangle before rolling.

If you serve these rolls as a light lunch with mixed greens, leave the salmon slices whole. Fill each with about a tablespoon of the filling, then roll up.

rectangles with a short edge facing you. Place the eggplant purée in the pastry bag and pipe a length of eggplant mixture just above the bottom edge of each salmon rectangle. Roll the salmon up around the purée to form a small cylinder.

Place the salmon rolls seam side down on the buttered bread. Garnish with lemon slices and chives. Chill before serving.

Paupiettes of Sole in Crabmeat Sauce

— *planning ahead* —

The paupiettes can be assembled up to 4 hours in advance, covered, and refrigerated until you are ready to bake them.

To me, one of the tastiest ways of serving fish is to spread a fillet with seafood mousse, roll it up, bake it in a court bouillon made with white wine, and then present it in a rich, velvety sauce. Fillets of fish prepared in this fashion are called *paupiettes,* and it's the kind of dish that you would expect to find only in a fine French restaurant. The surprise is that it can be made at home quite simply with results that will please the eye as well as the palate. Rich yet light, this delicious dish of sole with a scallop mousse is served with a creamy crabmeat sauce, intensified by the flavorful cooking liquor from the fish.

YIELD: 4 large paupiettes, enough for 4 main-course servings

SPECIAL EQUIPMENT: A 10-inch square or round baking dish with a lid

SCALLOP MOUSSE

¾ pound sea scallops, well chilled
1 large egg white
½ teaspoon salt
½ teaspoon freshly ground white pepper
¼ teaspoon freshly grated nutmeg
1 teaspoon sugar
¼ cup heavy cream, well chilled

COURT BOUILLON

2 tablespoons unsalted butter
1 cup dry white wine, preferably Chardonnay
¼ cup finely chopped shallots

4 6-ounce skinless fillets of sole (about 1½ pounds)
Salt and freshly ground white pepper to taste

CRABMEAT SAUCE

1½ tablespoons unsalted butter
1½ tablespoons all-purpose flour
¼ cup clam juice
¼ cup heavy cream
1 teaspoon tomato paste
4 ounces fresh lump crabmeat, well picked over
Salt to taste
Tabasco sauce to taste

Small bunch of fresh chervil or sprigs of flat-leaf parsley, for garnish

PREPARE THE MOUSSE: Rinse the scallops and pat dry. Remove and discard the little muscles on the side of the scallop. Purée the scallops in a food processor until very smooth. Add the egg white, salt, pepper, nutmeg, and sugar and process until well blended. With the motor running, slowly add the cream through the feed tube and process until very smooth. Transfer the mousse to a small bowl, cover, and refrigerate for at least 1 hour for the mousse to firm.

PREPARE THE COURT BOUILLON: Melt the butter in the baking dish over low heat, then remove the dish from the heat. Pour in the white wine and sprinkle on the shallots. Set aside.

Preheat the oven to 375°F.

ASSEMBLE THE PAUPIETTES: Lightly season the fillets with salt and white pepper. Lay the fillets skin side up on a work surface, with the thick ends nearest you. (This way, the paupiettes will contract during cooking and keep their shape. If placed skin side down, they would open during cooking.) Spread about ¼ cup of the mousse over each fillet. Starting from the thick end of a fillet, roll up the fillet, without squeezing out any of the mousse. There is no need to tie the paupiettes as the fish will adhere to itself. Place the paupiettes in the court bouillon.

COOK THE PAUPIETTES: Place the baking dish over high heat and bring the liquid to a boil. Cover the dish and transfer it to the oven. Bake until the fish flakes easily when tested with a fork, about 20 minutes.

Meanwhile, PREPARE THE SAUCE: Melt the butter in a small stainless steel or enamel saucepan set over medium heat. Add the flour and whisk the mixture into a paste, being careful that it does not brown. Add the clam juice and cream and whisk constantly until the mixture thickens lightly. Add the tomato paste, whisking until well blended. The sauce should be just thick enough to lightly coat the back of a spoon. Remove the pan from the heat and set aside.

When the paupiettes are done, remove the baking dish from the oven. Using a wide spatula, transfer the paupiettes to a large platter and cover loosely with foil to keep warm while you finish the sauce.

Using a fine-mesh sieve, strain the court bouillon into the sauce. Discard the shallots. Place the saucepan over moderate heat and whisk until the sauce is smooth and creamy. Make sure that the sauce doesn't boil. Add the crabmeat and stir until it is just heated through. Remove from the heat and season with salt and Tabasco.

TO SERVE: Place a paupiette on each of four warmed dinner plates. Spoon the sauce over the fish and garnish with the herbs.

— *planning ahead* —

The breaded eggs may be assembled up to a day ahead, covered, and refrigerated. Bring to room temperature before cooking.

Scotch Eggs

Scotch eggs are nothing but hard-boiled eggs wrapped in sausage meat and deep-fried to give more "body" to the outside crust. A traditional staple in most British pubs, this indulgent but delicious dish is uncomplicated to make. Scotch eggs may be served simply with hot English mustard and pickles, or as a sophisticated brunch item with a light tomato-cream sauce.

YIELD: 4 light main-course servings

2 raw eggs
½ cup milk
1½ cups all-purpose flour
1½ cups dried bread crumbs
Salt and freshly ground black pepper to taste
4 medium hard-boiled eggs (boiled for 7 minutes), peeled
1 pound bulk pork sausage or sweet Italian sausages, casings removed
Vegetable oil, for deep-frying

Break the raw eggs into a bowl, add the milk, and lightly beat to blend. Place the flour and the bread crumbs in separate bowls. Season the flour with salt and pepper.

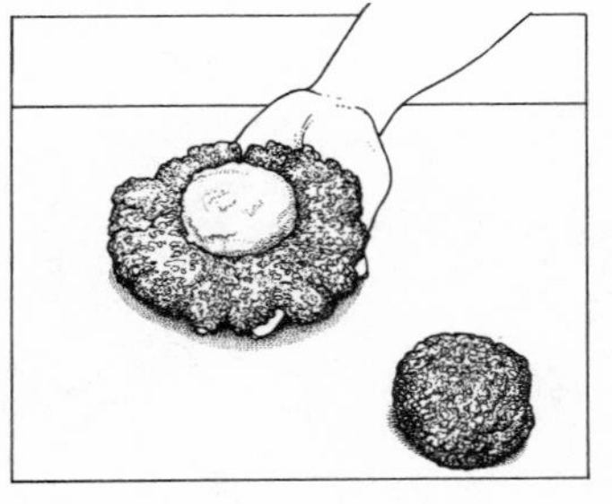

COAT THE EGGS: Dip each boiled egg into the egg mixture, roll in the seasoned flour, and then repeat. The eggs must be dipped twice in the beaten eggs and flour or the flour won't stick to the eggs. Place the eggs on a platter and set aside. Reserve the beaten eggs and seasoned flour.

ASSEMBLE THE SCOTCH EGGS: Divide the sausage meat into 4 equal portions. Shape each portion into a tight ball. On a well-floured surface, lightly press one sausage ball into a patty. Dust a rolling pin with flour and roll the patty into a 6-inch circle about ¼ inch thick. Place a flour-coated egg in the middle of the sausage circle. Bring the sides up to completely seal the egg. Squeeze gently to eliminate any air pockets. Make sure that it is well sealed by pressing the meat together, or the meat will shrink during cooking and expose the egg. Repeat with the remaining sausage and eggs.

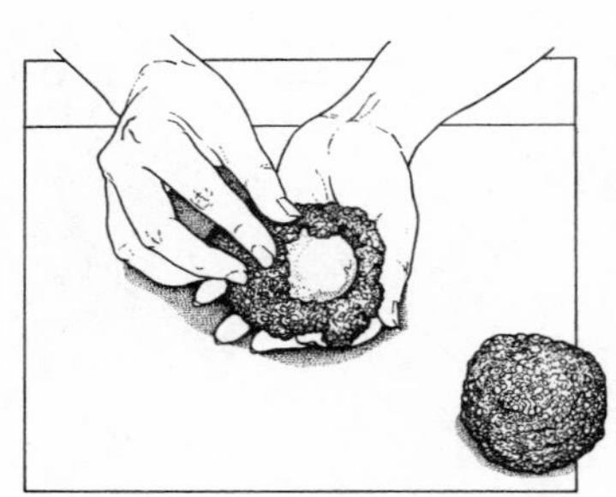

BREAD THE EGGS: Roll each sausage-wrapped egg first in the flour, then in the beaten egg, and finally in the bread crumbs, coating the surface completely. Place the breaded eggs on a plate, cover, and set aside until ready to cook.

FRY THE EGGS: In a large deep heavy skillet or an electric fryer, slowly heat about 2 inches of oil to 350°F. Carefully add the eggs and fry, turning them occasionally, until golden brown, about 6 to 7 minutes. If the eggs begin to brown too quickly, reduce the heat accordingly. Properly fried eggs should be a deep golden brown but not too dark. Use a slotted spoon to transfer the eggs to paper towels to drain.

TO SERVE: Halve each egg and serve hot or at room temperature with the desired accompaniments.

cook's notes

If you are concerned about calories, bake the Scotch eggs instead of deep-frying them. Place the breaded eggs in a lightly oiled baking dish, put in a preheated 400°F oven, and bake until the sausage meat is cooked through, about 20 minutes.

Ground lamb can be substituted for the pork sausage.

— planning ahead —

The mashed potatoes can be prepared a day in advance, covered, and refrigerated. Both the assembled loaf and the sauce can be prepared up to 4 hours in advance, covered, and refrigerated until ready to bake. Reheat the sauce before serving.

Veal and Mashed Potato Loaf

If you know someone whose culinary tastes are limited to meat and potatoes, this dish is for them. It will also silence your family's woeful cries of "What, meat loaf again?" In this quick and easy-to-prepare dish, an ordinary meat loaf is transformed into a sophisticated meal by wrapping lean ground veal around creamy mashed potatoes that have been subtly flavored with fresh thyme leaves. Served with a light sauce of red wine and shallots, this loaf sets itself apart from its unsophisticated cousin.

YIELD: 4 main-course servings

SPECIAL EQUIPMENT: A 1½-quart loaf pan

MASHED POTATOES

2 medium potatoes (about ¾ pound)
1 tablespoon unsalted butter
⅓ cup hot milk
2 teaspoons chopped fresh thyme leaves or ½ teaspoon dried, crumbled
Salt and freshly ground black pepper to taste

VEAL MIXTURE

1 tablespoon unsalted butter
1 cup chopped onions
2 teaspoons minced garlic
1 pound ground veal
1 egg, lightly beaten
2 slices white bread, crusts removed
1 teaspoon chopped fresh thyme leaves or ½ teaspoon dried, crumbled
1 teaspoon salt
Freshly ground black pepper to taste
2 tablespoons dried bread crumbs
3 slices bacon

RED WINE SAUCE

1 tablespoon unsalted butter, plus 2 tablespoons softened unsalted butter
2 tablespoons finely chopped shallots
1 cup dry red wine, preferably Bordeaux
1 cup homemade beef broth (page 370) or ½ cup canned beef broth mixed with ½ cup water
1 tablespoon all-purpose flour

Fresh thyme sprigs, for garnish (optional)

PREPARE THE MASHED POTATOES: Peel and quarter the potatoes. Place them in a medium saucepan and add salted water to cover. Bring to a boil over high heat, reduce the heat to medium, and cook until the potatoes are fork-tender but not mushy, about 20 to 25 minutes.

Drain the water from the saucepan, reduce the heat to low, and shake the pan over the heat to dry the potatoes. Using a potato masher, food mill, or electric mixer, mash the potatoes thoroughly, until no lumps remain. Beat in the butter, milk, and thyme. Season with salt and pepper. Cover and set aside.

Preheat the oven to 350°F.

PREPARE THE VEAL MIXTURE: Heat the butter in a small skillet over moderate heat. Add the onions and garlic and sauté until the onions are tender and lightly browned, about 5 minutes. Transfer to a large mixing bowl and add the ground veal and beaten egg.

Briefly dip the bread slices in a bowl of water to soften them, then squeeze to remove excess water. Add the bread to the meat. Add the thyme, salt, and pepper, and, using your hands, combine the mixture thoroughly.

ASSEMBLE THE LOAF: Spread the bread crumbs over a sheet of wax paper. Press the meat out on the crumbs to make an 8- by 11- by ½-inch-thick rectangle. Spread the mashed potatoes over the meat, leaving a ½-inch border all around. Using the waxed paper as an aid, roll up the meat and potatoes from a short side, jelly-roll fashion. Pat and press the ends to make a compact loaf. Place the loaf seam side down into a loaf pan. Cover the loaf with the bacon.

Bake the loaf until the juices run clear when pierced with a skewer, about 45 minutes. Remove from the oven and allow the loaf to rest for about 10 to 15 minutes.

Meanwhile, PREPARE THE SAUCE: Melt the 1 tablespoon butter in a medium saucepan over moderate heat. Add the shallots and sauté for 1 minute. Add the wine and simmer, uncovered, until the liquid is reduced to ¼ cup, about 10 minutes. Add the beef broth and simmer for about 2 minutes. Knead the 2 tablespoons softened butter into the flour to make a paste. Whisk the paste into the sauce, bit by bit, until the sauce is smooth and glossy and no lumps remain. Remove the pan from the heat.

TO SERVE: Cut the veal loaf into 8 slices. Ladle some sauce onto four warmed dinner plates. Place 2 slices of the loaf on each plate, garnish with a thyme sprig if desired, and serve at once. Pass the remaining sauce on the side.

— cook's notes —

This dish is ideal for using leftover mashed potatoes. You will need about 1½ cups. Make sure to adjust the seasonings with salt and pepper and mix in the thyme before spreading over the meat.

— *planning ahead* —

The beef may be marinated a day ahead, covered, and refrigerated overnight. Bring it to room temperature before proceeding with the recipe. The beef rolls may also be prepared a day in advance, covered, and refrigerated. Bring to room temperature before grilling.

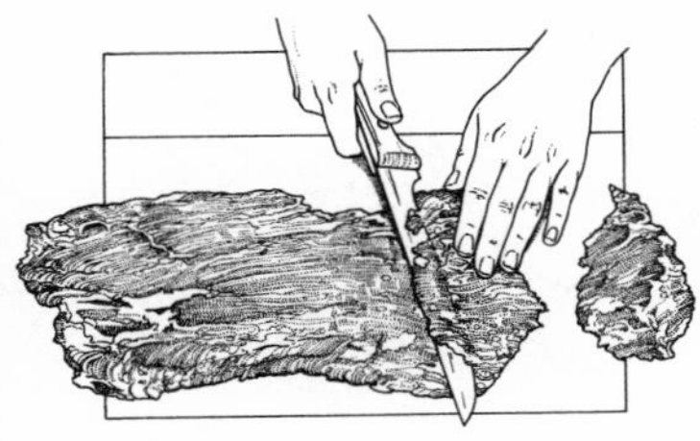

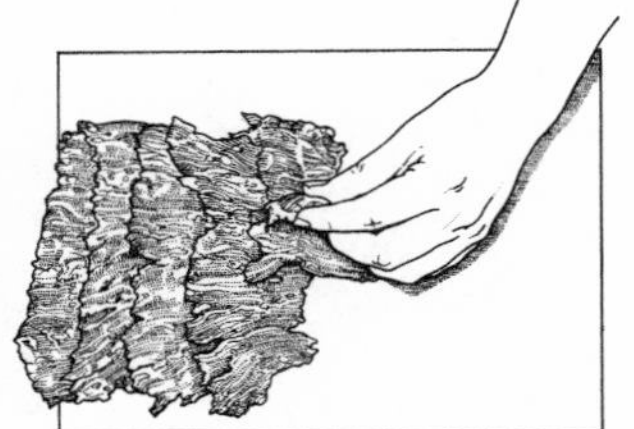

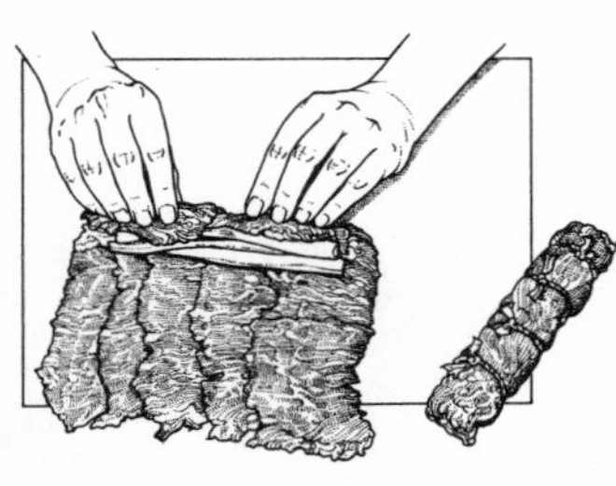

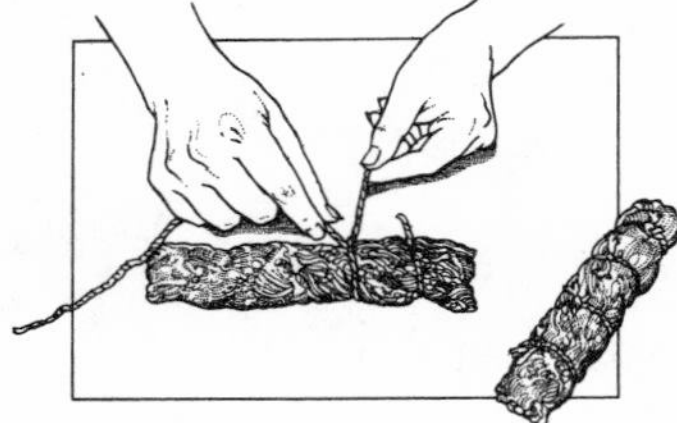

Grilled Beef and Scallion Rolls

(NEGE-MAKE)

One of my husband's favorite Japanese dishes is nege-maki, in which paper-thin slices of marinated beef are wrapped around scallions, pan-fried, and then simmered in a sweet soy sauce. The contrast of flavors between the tangy beef and the sharp-tasting scallions makes this a tantalizing dish. In this adaptation, the rolls are grilled to seal in the juices and served with a light, warm soy sauce. For a complete meal, serve these delicious rolls as an entrée with steamed rice and fresh cucumber slices. They also make excellent hors d'oeuvres.

YIELD: 4 large rolls, enough for 4 main-course servings or 48 hors d'oeuvres

1 pound flank steak

MARINADE

¼ cup soy sauce
¼ cup sake or dry white wine
2 tablespoons sugar
1 tablespoon grated fresh ginger
1 tablespoon minced garlic

8 scallions, trimmed to 12-inch lengths
2 tablespoons olive oil
Wasabi (optional; see Cook's Notes)

Freeze the beef until just firm, not hard, about 2 hours, to facilitate slicing.

Meanwhile, MAKE THE MARINADE: Combine the soy sauce, sake, ¼ cup water, the sugar, ginger, and garlic in a small saucepan. Stir to dissolve the sugar, and bring to a boil. Remove from the heat and allow to cool.

Using a very sharp knife, cut the beef on an angle, against the grain, into wide thin slices, about ⅛ inch thick. Place the beef slices in a mixing bowl and pour half of the marinade over. Reserve the remaining marinade for the sauce. Using your hands, gently turn the beef in the marinade to coat. Cover and let stand for at least 30 minutes.

Drop the scallions into a pot of boiling salted water. Immediately remove from the heat and drain the scallions in a colander set in the sink. Refresh the scallions under cold running water. Squeeze the scallions dry and cut them crosswise in half.

ASSEMBLE THE NEGE-MAKI: Lay out 4 or 5 slices of beef, overlapping their long edges to make a sheet about 6 inches wide. Place 2 scallions across the bottom edges of the meat and roll up tightly. Tie the roll in several places with kitchen string. Repeat with the remaining beef and scallions, making 3 more rolls.

Prepare a medium-hot fire in the grill.

COOK THE NEGE-MAKI: Brush the beef rolls with the oil, place them on the grill 4 inches above the heat, and grill for 6 to 7 minutes, turning once. (Alternately, cook the rolls under a broiler for about 4 to 5 minutes.) Remove the rolls to a cutting board and allow to cool slightly.

Meanwhile, place the reserved marinade in a small saucepan. Set over moderate heat and gently warm the sauce. Remove from the heat and cover to keep warm.

TO SERVE: Carefully remove the string from the rolls. Using a sharp knife, cut the rolls into ½-inch pieces and arrange them on warm plates. Drizzle the sauce over the beef and serve hot or at room temperature. Accompany with wasabi if desired.

— *cook's notes* —

Wasabi tastes like horseradish but is more pungent, with a very strong, sharp flavor. It is available in Japanese groceries and many supermarkets in paste and powdered form. The ready-to-use paste, packaged in a tube, keeps in the refrigerator for months. The green powder, which comes in small cans or jars, must be mixed with water to form a paste; use about 1½ teaspoons water per tablespoon of wasabi powder.

For a change of pace, thin, pounded slices of shell steak, chicken, pork, or lamb may be used instead of flank steak. Blanched carrots, leeks, asparagus, or green beans are good alternatives for the scallions.

— *planning ahead* —

The marinade may be prepared a day ahead and refrigerated. The pounded pork medallions may be kept between the sheets of plastic wrap and stacked, covered, and refrigerated for up to 1 day. The braccioletini may be assembled a day in advance, covered, and refrigerated. Bring them to room temperature before you skewer and grill them.

If you use bamboo skewers, they must be presoaked in water for 30 minutes.

Grilled Braccioletini of Pork

These wonderful skewered little bundles (*braccioletini*) of pork are ideal for outdoor grilling. This is a typical Italian dish that doesn't require a great deal of work and produces stupendous results. Along with mozzarella cheese, most Italian cooks include prosciutto or pancetta inside these flavorful packets, but I find them less salty without, and that's how I prefer them. Accompanied by a green salad and plenty of iced tea, braccioletini are perfect for an evening meal outdoors.

YIELD: 8 braccioletini, enough for 4 main-course servings

SPECIAL EQUIPMENT: 4 metal skewers or presoaked 10-inch bamboo skewers

MARINADE

⅓ cup olive oil
⅓ cup corn oil
4 large garlic cloves, peeled
½ cup coarsely chopped flat-leaf parsley
Salt and freshly ground black pepper to taste

BRACCIOLETINI

¾ pound center-cut pork loin (in 1 piece)
Salt and freshly ground black pepper to taste
2 tablespoons freshly grated Parmesan cheese
2 tablespoons dried bread crumbs
4 ounces fresh mozzarella cheese, cut into 8 sticks about 2½ inches long by ½ inch thick
1 loaf day-old bread, preferably sourdough, cut into 24 1½-inch cubes
32 fresh sage leaves (optional)

PREPARE THE MARINADE: Place both oils, the garlic, and parsley in a blender or food processor and process to a fine purée. Season with salt and pepper. Cover and set aside.

ASSEMBLE THE BRACCIOLETINI: Trim the pork loin of excess fat. Cut crosswise into 8 thin medallions, about ¼ inch thick. Using a meat mallet or the flat side of a meat cleaver, pound each medallion between two sheets of plastic wrap into thin slices about 4 to 5 inches across, being careful not to tear the meat.

Arrange the slices on a work surface, and peel the plastic wrap off the tops. Sprinkle salt and pepper over the meat. Spread about 1 teaspoon of the marinade over each slice. Reserve the remaining marinade. Combine the Parmesan cheese and bread crumbs in a small bowl, and sprinkle each slice with 1½ teaspoons of the mixture. Place 1 stick of the mozzarella cheese across the bottom edge of each slice. Fold about

1 inch from each side over the cheese, and, starting from the bottom, roll the meat up to enclose the cheese, forming a neat little bundle.

Thread 3 bread cubes and 2 braccioletini alternately onto each skewer, skewering a sage leaf between each bread cube and meat roll if desired. Cover and set aside until ready to grill.

Prepare a medium-hot fire in the grill.

Brush the skewers with the remaining marinade, place them on the grill 4 inches above the heat, and cook, turning often, until they are golden brown and look glossy and succulent, about 10 minutes. Transfer to a warm platter and serve immediately.

— cook's notes —

Cooking braccioletini in a broiler is perfectly acceptable but they will lack the tantalizing smoky flavor from the coals. The braccioletini can also be breaded and deep-fried for 5 to 6 minutes, then served with lemon wedges.

Pounded pieces of chicken breast, veal medallions, or shell steak may be substituted for the pork. You may use Fontina or Gruyère cheese instead of mozzarella and pesto sauce instead of the marinade. If fresh sage leaves are not available, use bay leaves.

— *planning ahead* —

The unbreaded chicken rolls may be wrapped individually in plastic wrap and frozen for up to 1 week. Bring to room temperature before breading and deep-frying.

For best results, refrigerate the breaded rolls for at least 2 hours before deep-frying to ensure that the crumbs adhere to the chicken.

Chicken Kiev

This dish was created during the czarist days in Russia and is still a favorite with Russian emigrés everywhere. Tarragon-laced butter is hidden inside a rolled boneless breast of chicken. The rolls are then breaded and deep-fried. Serving such a dish may throw your diet out the window but there's nothing wrong with indulging yourself once in a while. I can guarantee you this is well worth the indulgence.

YIELD: 8 rolls, enough for 4 main-course servings

- 4 boneless skinless chicken breasts (about 1½ pounds)
- Salt and freshly ground black pepper to taste
- 1 tablespoon plus 1 teaspoon chopped fresh tarragon leaves
- 1 tablespoon plus 1 teaspoon minced garlic
- 8 tablespoons (1 stick) unsalted butter, well chilled
- ½ cup all-purpose flour
- 2 eggs
- 2 cups dried bread crumbs
- Vegetable oil, for deep-frying

PREPARE THE CHICKEN: Split the chicken breasts in half and trim off any fat. Remove the tenderloins from under the breasts and reserve them for another use. Using a meat mallet or the flat side of a meat cleaver, pound each chicken cutlet between two sheets of plastic wrap into a paper-thin slice about 6 to 7 inches across and ⅛ inch thick, being careful not to tear the meat.

ASSEMBLE THE CHICKEN ROLLS: Arrange the chicken pieces on a work surface with a short side toward you. Peel the plastic wrap off the tops. Sprinkle each cutlet with salt and pepper and ½ teaspoon each of the tarragon and garlic.

Cut the stick of butter in half crosswise and then quarter each half lengthwise to obtain eight 2½-inch-long finger-shaped pieces. Place a piece of butter across the middle of each breast. Fold about 1 inch from each side over the butter and roll the meat up from the bottom to enclose the butter, forming a neat little bundle. The soft chicken flesh will adhere to itself without skewers or string. Arrange the bundles seam side down on a plate.

COAT THE CHICKEN ROLLS: Place the flour in a shallow pan. Break the eggs into a small shallow bowl and beat lightly. Spread the bread crumbs on a baking sheet or a large piece of wax paper. Roll each chicken roll in the flour to coat on all sides, and pat to leave a thin even dusting of flour all over the roll. Using your left hand, roll a piece of chicken in the beaten eggs to coat evenly, then transfer the roll to the bread crumbs. Using your right hand, quickly and lightly roll the chicken in the bread crumbs, being sure that every bit of it is covered. Place the breaded chicken roll seam side down on a large platter. Repeat with the remaining rolls. Cover with plastic wrap and chill in the refrigerator for at least 2 hours so the crumbs will adhere.

Preheat the oven to 250°F. Line a baking sheet with paper towels.

FRY THE ROLLS: In a large deep heavy skillet or an electric fryer, slowly heat about 2 inches of oil to 350°F. Carefully add the rolls in batches, without crowding, and fry, turning occasionally, until golden brown, about 3 to 4 minutes. If the rolls begin to brown too quickly, reduce the heat accordingly. Properly fried chicken rolls should be a deep golden brown, but not too dark. Use a slotted spoon to transfer the fried rolls to the prepared baking sheet, and keep them warm in the oven while you cook the remaining rolls.

Serve immediately.

cook's notes

If you are really concerned with calories, sprinkle the breaded chicken rolls with melted butter or olive oil and bake in a preheated 375°F oven until golden brown, about 20 to 25 minutes.

A chicken tenderloin, also known as a breast tender, is the tender strip of meat attached to the underside of the chicken breast.

Other fresh herbs, such as chives or thyme, may be used instead of tarragon.

— planning ahead —

The uncoated chicken rolls may be wrapped individually in plastic wrap and frozen for up to 1 week. Bring them to room temperature before coating and deep-frying.

For best results, refrigerate the coconut-coated rolls for at least 2 hours before deep-frying to ensure that the coconut adheres to the chicken.

— cook's notes —

If you are concerned with calories, sprinkle the coconut-coated chicken rolls with melted butter or olive oil and bake in a preheated 375°F oven until golden brown, about 20 to 25 minutes.

A chicken tenderloin, also known as a breast tender, is the tender strip of meat attached to the underside of the chicken breast.

Hawaiian Chicken Rolls

While on a trip to Hawaii, I sampled a most memorable dish at a small restaurant in Honolulu. Offered on the menu as Coconut and Banana Chicken, it consisted of boneless rolled chicken cutlets seasoned with herbs and a touch of curry, stuffed with ham and ripe banana, rolled in coconut flakes, and deep-fried.

This recipe is my interpretation of that dish. The nutty and crunchy coconut coating, the salty prosciutto, and the sweetness of the banana unite to create a distinctive combination of tastes and textures. The thyme and curry powder add a subtle nuance to this easy-to-make supper offering.

YIELD: 8 large rolls, enough for 4 main-course servings

SEASONING MIX

2 tablespoons chopped fresh thyme leaves or 1 tablespoon dried, crumbled
2 teaspoons curry powder
1½ teaspoons salt
½ teaspoon freshly ground black pepper

8 boneless skinless chicken breast halves (about 1½ pounds)
8 paper-thin slices prosciutto (about 3 ounces)
2 medium bananas, peeled and cut into 4 pieces each
½ cup all-purpose flour
2 large eggs
2½ cups shredded coconut
Vegetable oil, for deep-frying

PREPARE THE SEASONING MIX: Combine the thyme, curry powder, salt, and pepper in a small bowl. Set aside.

PREPARE THE CHICKEN: Remove the tenderloins from under the chicken breasts and reserve them for another use. Using a meat mallet or the flat side of a meat cleaver, pound each chicken cutlet between two sheets of plastic wrap into a paper-thin slice about 6 to 7 inches across and ⅛ inch thick, being careful not to tear the meat.

ASSEMBLE THE CHICKEN ROLLS: Arrange the chicken pieces on a work surface. Peel the plastic wrap off the tops. Sprinkle half of the seasoning mix over the chicken. Top each chicken piece with a slice of prosciutto, folding the prosciutto over if necessary to leave a ¼-inch border all around. Place 1 piece of banana in the center of each prosciutto slice. Fold about 1 inch from each side over the filling and roll the meat up from the bottom to enclose the filling, forming a neat little bundle. The soft chicken flesh will adhere without skewers or string. Arrange the bundles seam side down on a plate and set aside.

COAT THE CHICKEN ROLLS: Place the flour in a shallow pan and blend in the remaining seasoning mix. Break the eggs into a small shallow bowl and beat lightly. Spread the coconut on a baking sheet or a large piece of wax paper. Roll each chicken bundle in the flour to coat on all sides, patting it so there is a thin even dusting of flour all over the roll. Using your left hand, roll a piece of chicken in the beaten eggs to coat evenly, then transfer the roll to the shredded coconut. Using your right hand, quickly roll the chicken in the coconut, lightly pressing the chicken into the coconut so that every bit of chicken is covered. Place the coated chicken roll seam side down on a large platter. Repeat with the remaining rolls. Cover with plastic wrap and chill in the refrigerator for at least 2 hours so the coconut will adhere.

Preheat the oven to 350°F. Line a baking sheet with paper towels.

FRY THE ROLLS: In a large deep heavy skillet or an electric fryer, slowly heat about 2 inches of oil to 350°F. Carefully add the rolls in batches, without crowding, and fry, turning occasionally, until golden brown, about 5 to 6 minutes. If the rolls begin to brown too quickly, reduce the heat accordingly. Properly fried chicken rolls should be a deep golden brown, but not too dark. Use a slotted spoon to transfer the fried rolls to the prepared baking sheet, and keep them warm in the oven while you cook the remaining rolls.

TO SERVE: Cut each roll crosswise into 3 pieces and arrange them, cut sides up, on warmed dinner plates. Serve hot.

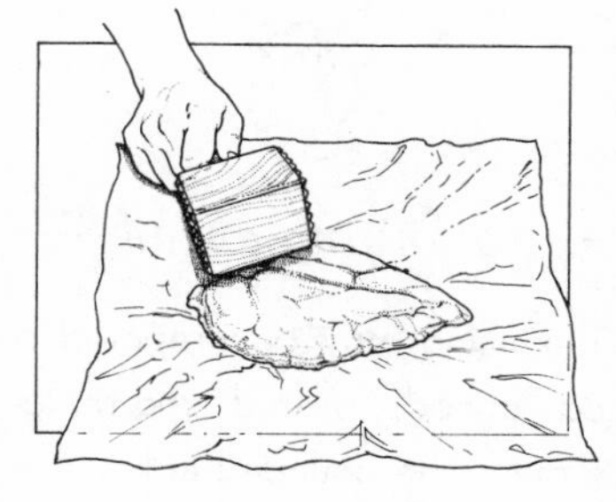

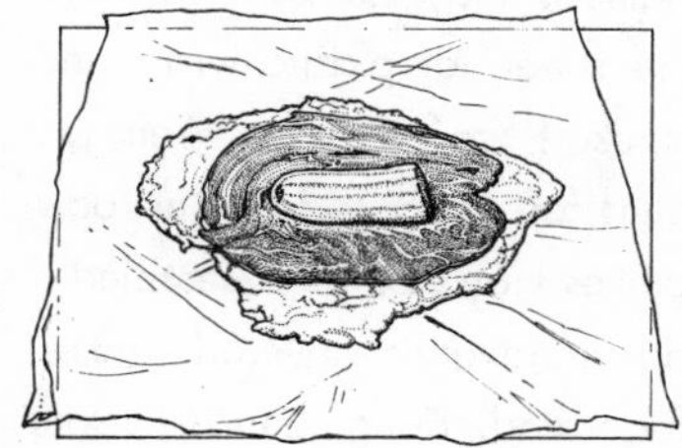

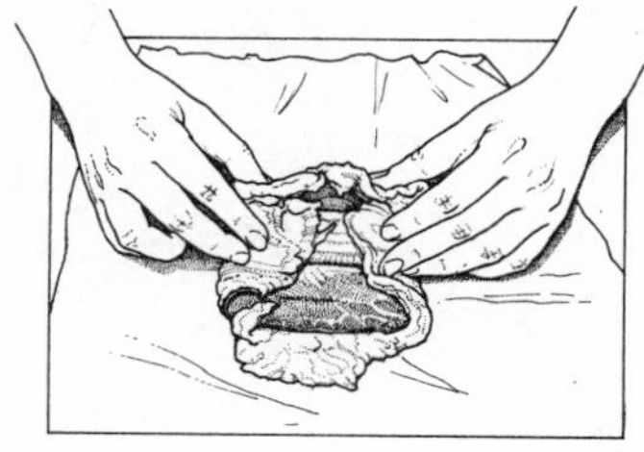

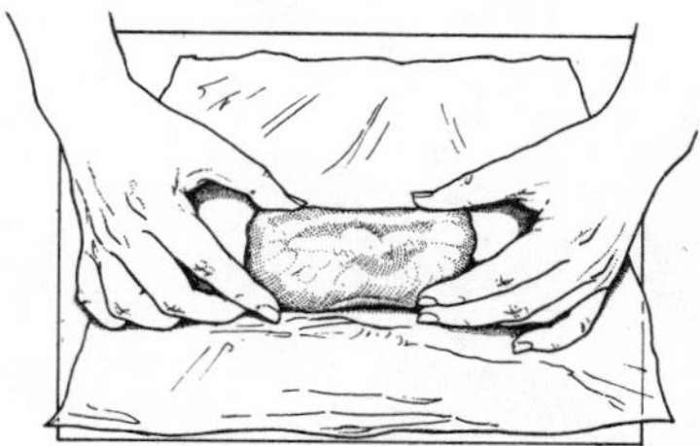

— planning ahead —

The filling may be prepared a day ahead, covered, and refrigerated. The pounded turkey medallions may be kept between the sheets of plastic wrap and stacked, covered, and refrigerated for up to 1 day. The paupiettes may also be assembled a day in advance, covered, and refrigerated. Bring them to room temperature before cooking.

Paupiettes of Turkey, Cajun Style

My love for Cajun flavors is combined here with the classic French country-style dish of meat rolled around a succulent stuffing known as a paupiette. The flavors begin with a subtle contrast between the natural sweetness of the sausage-filled turkey rolls and the tang of the tomato sauce. The liberal use of three different kinds of peppers, plus dried thyme and basil, all favorite condiments in Cajun cooking, adds a clean, sparkling taste. One bite of this piquant dish and I guarantee your taste buds will stay awake after the meal!

I use lean turkey cutlets here, but it could just as well be lamb, veal, or beef. Serve these paupiettes over noodles or with mashed potatoes and a green vegetable.

YIELD: 6 paupiettes, enough for 3 main-course servings

SPICE MIX

¾ teaspoon dried basil leaves, crumbled
¾ teaspoon dried thyme leaves, crumbled
½ teaspoon cayenne pepper
¼ teaspoon freshly ground black pepper
¼ teaspoon ground white pepper
¼ teaspoon freshly grated nutmeg

SAUSAGE FILLING

2 tablespoons unsalted butter
½ cup finely chopped onion
½ cup finely chopped green bell pepper
¼ cup finely chopped celery
1½ teaspoons minced garlic
Salt to taste
½ pound sweet Italian sausage, casings removed

6 4-ounce turkey cutlets
Salt to taste
4 tablespoons unsalted butter
1 tablespoon minced garlic
1 cup finely chopped onions
2 scallions, thinly sliced
4 large ripe tomatoes (about 1½ pounds), peeled, seeded, and finely chopped (about 3 cups)
½ cup dry white wine, preferably Chardonnay
1 cup chicken broth, homemade (page 368) or store-bought
1 teaspoon arrowroot or cornstarch mixed with 1 tablespoon cold water
1 tablespoon chopped fresh parsley

PREPARE THE SPICE MIX: Combine all the spice mix ingredients in a small bowl. Set aside.

PREPARE THE FILLING: Heat the butter in a medium skillet set over moderately high heat. Add the onion, pepper, celery, and garlic and sauté until the vegetables are soft and lightly browned, about 2 minutes. Add half of the spice mix and sauté for 1 minute more. Transfer the mixture to a small mixing bowl, season with salt, and allow to cool.

Add the sausage meat to the vegetable mixture and mix with a fork or wooden spoon until well combined. Cover and set aside until ready to use.

ASSEMBLE THE PAUPIETTES: Using a meat mallet or the flat side of a meat cleaver, pound each turkey cutlet between two sheets of plastic wrap into paper-thin slices about 6 to 8 inches across and ⅛ inch thick, being careful not to tear the meat.

Arrange the slices on a work surface. Peel the plastic wrap off the tops. Lightly season the turkey with salt. Pat about ¼ cup of the filling into a small mound in the middle of each slice. Fold about 2 inches from each side over the filling and roll the meat up to enclose the filling, forming a neat little bundle. Tie each bundle with kitchen string. Cover and set aside until ready to cook.

Preheat the oven to 350°F. Adjust an oven rack to the middle shelf.

COOK THE PAUPIETTES: Heat the butter in a large skillet over moderately high heat. Add the paupiettes and brown them on both sides, about 2 minutes. Remove the paupiettes to a platter and set aside.

Reduce the heat to medium. Add the garlic, onions, and scallions to the skillet and sauté until soft, about 3 minutes. Add the remaining spice mix and the tomatoes and sauté 2 minutes longer. Add the white wine and stir with a wooden spoon, scraping the bottom of the pan to loosen any browned bits. Cook until the wine is almost evaporated, about 2 minutes. Add the chicken broth and the paupiettes, and season the sauce with salt. Bring to a boil and immediately transfer the skillet to the oven.

Bake, uncovered, for 10 minutes. Turn the rolls over in the sauce and continue baking for 10 minutes more. Remove the skillet from the oven.

With a slotted spoon, transfer the paupiettes to a warm platter. Stir the arrowroot mixture into the sauce and bring to a gentle simmer over moderate heat. Cook until slightly thickened, about 1 minute.

TO SERVE: Remove the strings from the paupiettes. Spoon the sauce over the paupiettes and sprinkle with the parsley. Serve immediately.

— planning ahead —

The beef roll may be assembled a day ahead, covered, and refrigerated. Bring it to room temperature before grilling.

— cook's notes —

If you don't have a grill, cook the beef roll on a griddle. Set the griddle over low heat, cover (use a large metal bowl if necessary), and griddle-cook the beef roll for about 30 minutes, turning frequently, until medium rare; an instant-read thermometer inserted into the rotolo should read 120° to 125°F. The flavor will approximate that of a charcoal-grilled steak.

For an even more special meal, serve this dish with Red Pepper Mayonnaise (page 216).

Grilled Rotolo of Flank Steak with Mozzarella

I love beef cooked over live coals, especially right off the grill. Nothing tastes like it, it's so tantalizing and sensuous! This Italian-inspired rolled steak is perfectly suited to this style of cooking and is simplicity itself to make. It uses flank steak, a popular cut of meat that is flavorful and not too expensive. Either ask the butcher to butterfly it for you or follow the instructions below. To complete the meal, surround the grilled steak with a supporting cast of French fries and marinated tomatoes.

YIELD: 1 large roll, enough for 4 main-course servings

1 2-pound flank steak, trimmed of fat
Salt and freshly ground black pepper to taste
3 tablespoons minced garlic
1 cup coarsely chopped flat-leaf parsley
8 ounces fresh mozzarella cheese, cut into thin slices
Olive oil, for brushing

BUTTERFLY THE STEAK: Place the steak on a cutting board and hold it firmly so it does not slide, placing your palm on the top surface. Using a long, sharp knife, slice into the steak along one long side and cut it horizontally almost in half, but not quite all the way through (leaving about ½ inch uncut on the far side). As you cut, lift the upper meat flap to have a better view of what you are doing. Open the steak like a book (its shape will be similar to that of a butterfly) and place it between two large sheets of plastic wrap. Using a meat mallet or the flat side of a meat cleaver, pound the meat to flatten it slightly. Remove the plastic wraps.

ASSEMBLE THE ROTOLO: Sprinkle salt and pepper over the meat. Combine the garlic and parsley and spread the mixture over the meat. Arrange the mozzarella slices in a single layer over the steak. Check the way in which the grain of the meat runs, and position the meat so that the grain runs horizontally. Starting from the bottom, roll the steak up tightly into a thick cylinder. Tie the roll securely with butcher's twine at 2-inch intervals and brush with a little olive oil. Season with salt and pepper, cover, and set aside until ready to grill.

Prepare a medium-hot fire in the grill.

COOK THE ROTOLO: Place the rotolo on the grill 4 inches above the heat, cover, and grill until medium rare and the cheese is melted, about 20 minutes. (The time will vary slightly depending on the thickness of the meat.) Baste occasionally with olive oil and turn to brown the meat on all sides.

Remove the beef roll to a cutting board and allow to rest for 5 minutes. Remove the string and cut the roll into 1-inch slices. Transfer to warm dinner plates and serve immediately.

Matahambre

Matahambre (literally, "kill hunger") is a tempting meat roll popular in Argentina, Uruguay, and Brazil. It starts with a butterflied flank steak that is marinated overnight in wine and vinegar. The steak is then spread out flat and layered with fresh spinach leaves, onions, hard-boiled eggs, and blanched carrots. The meat is rolled up with the vegetables inside, tied with string, and poached in seasoned beef broth. In Argentina, the poached matahambre is generally pressed under weights until the juices drain off, refrigerated, and served cold as an appetizer.

Since I prefer to serve the matahambre hot as a main course, I slowly pan-roast it with a little beef broth. When the roast is cut, the alternating layers of spinach, carrots, and eggs are revealed in an eye-appealing spiral pattern. To make the juicy and tender matahambre even more flavorful, I serve chimichurri, a favorite piquant Argentinian sauce of onion and parsley, on the side. The result is a dish that tastes every bit as good as it looks.

— planning ahead —

Both the chimichurri sauce and the beef roll may be prepared a day ahead, covered, and refrigerated. Bring the meat to room temperature before roasting.

YIELD: 1 large roll, enough for 4 main-course servings

SPECIAL EQUIPMENT: A Dutch oven, preferably oval, with a lid

1 2-pound flank steak, trimmed of fat
¼ cup red wine vinegar
¼ cup dry red wine, such as Bordeaux
¼ cup vegetable oil
Salt and freshly ground black pepper to taste
2 teaspoons chopped fresh thyme leaves
1 tablespoon minced garlic

CHIMICHURRI SAUCE

⅓ cup extra-virgin olive oil
¼ cup red wine vinegar
½ cup minced onion
½ cup chopped fresh parsley
2 teaspoons minced garlic
2 teaspoons chopped fresh thyme leaves
¼ teaspoon crushed dried red pepper
Salt and freshly ground black pepper to taste

SPINACH STUFFING

4 medium carrots, halved lengthwise
2 ounces (about 2 cups) fresh spinach leaves, stemmed and washed
2 hard-boiled eggs, peeled and cut lengthwise into quarters
½ medium Spanish or Bermuda onion, thinly sliced
Salt and freshly ground black pepper to taste

2 tablespoons unsalted butter
Salt and freshly ground black pepper to taste
½ cup beef broth

BUTTERFLY THE STEAK: Place the steak flat on a cutting board and hold firmly so it does not slide, placing your palm on the top surface. Using a long,

— cook's notes —

Have your butcher butterfly the steak if you prefer.

A butterflied shoulder veal roast may be used instead of flank steak.

sharp knife, slice into the steak along one long side and cut it horizontally almost in half, but not all the way through (leaving about ½ inch uncut on the far side). As you cut, lift up the upper meat flap to have a better view of what you are doing. Open the steak like a book (its shape will be similar to that of a butterfly) and place it between two large sheets of plastic wrap. Using a meat mallet or the flat side of a meat cleaver, pound the meat to flatten it slightly. Remove the plastic wrap and place the opened-out steak in a shallow baking pan large enough to hold it. Pour the vinegar, wine, and oil over the meat. Turn the meat to coat both sides with the marinade. Sprinkle salt and pepper over the meat. Spread thyme and garlic over the cut side of the meat, then close the steak. Cover the pan and let the steak marinate for 6 to 8 hours at room temperature, or overnight in the refrigerator.

MAKE THE CHIMICHURRI SAUCE: In a small bowl, combine all the sauce ingredients. Stir to mix well. Cover and refrigerate for at least 2 hours for the flavors to blend.

COOK THE CARROTS: Bring 2 quarts of salted water to a rolling boil over high heat. Add the carrots, lower the heat to moderate, and cook until fork-tender, about 8 to 9 minutes. Carefully drain the carrots in a colander set in the sink, refresh under cold running water, and drain well again.

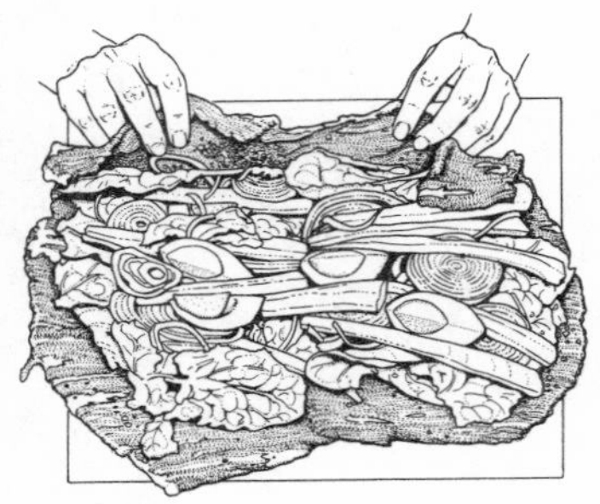

ASSEMBLE THE BEEF ROLL: Drain the steak, discarding the marinade. Open the steak and lay it cut side up on a flat surface. Check the direction the grain of the meat runs, and position the meat so that the grain runs horizontally. Spread the spinach leaves evenly over the meat. Arrange the carrots across the meat in rows about 3 inches apart. Place the eggs in rows between the rows of carrots. Scatter the onion slices over all. Sprinkle the vegetables with salt and pepper. Starting from the bottom, roll the steak up tightly into a thick cylinder. Tie the roll securely with butcher's twine at 2-inch intervals.

ROAST THE MATAHAMBRE: Melt the butter in the Dutch oven over moderately high heat. When hot, add the beef roll and brown the meat well all over, about 3 to 4 minutes. Season the roll with salt and pepper, then add the beef broth. Reduce the heat to low and partially cover the pot with the lid.

Cook, turning the roll from time to time, until the meat is tender when pricked with a fork, about 1 hour and 15 minutes. Remove from the heat and let the roast rest in the cooking liquid for 10 minutes.

Transfer the roll to a carving board, reserving the pan juices, and remove the string. With a sharp knife, cut the matambre into 1-inch-thick slices, taking care not to squeeze the stuffing out.

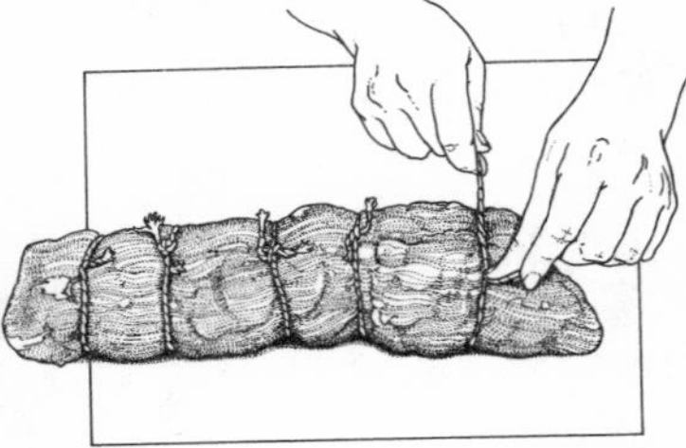

TO SERVE: Arrange the slices on a warmed serving platter and spoon the pan juices over them. Pass the chimichurri sauce at the table.

chocolate

Since no serious discussion of food would be complete without mentioning chocolate, I have dreamed up three distinctive desserts in which the focal point is chocolate molded or wrapped around various tempting fillings. These recipes range from the heavenly Christmas cake known as Bûche de Noël (page 358) to spectacular Chocolate Purses with Rhubarb-Raspberry Mousse (page 362) to sinfully rich Chocolate Sushi Truffle (page 364).

The molding chocolate is made by melting chocolate in the top of a double boiler. When the chocolate has melted, light corn syrup is stirred in to form a soft, malleable paste. The paste is then rolled and set aside until partially set. When the chocolate reaches the consistency of soft clay, it is briefly kneaded, and then rolled into thin sheets. It can then be cut into various shapes and sizes and wrapped around other sweet confections. This chocolate is so pliable that it can be molded into almost any shape that you wish.

None of the following desserts is difficult, but they do require some advance planning. If you approach them step by step and allow ample time, you'll produce masterpieces. The best reward for me would be to know that these recipes inspired you to create your own memorable desserts under wraps.

NOTES ON CHOCOLATE AND COCOA

Chocolate is produced from the beans of the cacao tree, native to tropical Central America and the Caribbean islands. Each tree produces only twenty to thirty pods a year, and each pod just twenty-five to forty beans. It takes about four hundred beans to make a pound of chocolate.

Chocolate is produced by roasting the cacao beans. They are then shelled, pressed, and heated until they break down, at which point the chocolate liquor and cocoa butter in the beans can be extracted. Generally, the more cocoa butter in a chocolate, the better the quality. The cocoa butter's presence in chocolate gives it its silky texture and a long shelf life.

Cocoa is a form of powdered chocolate from which most of the cocoa butter or fat has been removed. In baking, it is used for dusting cakes or coating truffles, or it may be added to melted chocolate when a stronger chocolate taste is desired. Look for unsweetened alkalized (Dutch-process) cocoa powder, such as Hershey's European-style or Dröste, an imported Dutch brand. Dutch-process cocoa has had alkali added to make it darker and less acidic.

Unsweetened (bitter) chocolate is pure chocolate with no other ingredients added. It is also known as baking chocolate. Do not confuse it with bittersweet chocolate, which has sugar added. Look for the widely available Baker's, Hershey, and Nestlé brands, which come packed in eight-ounce packages of eight 1-ounce squares. I've used them in baking with excellent results. If you have access to European brands like Tobler, Lindt, or Suchard, however, use them by all means.

Semisweet and bittersweet chocolate are chocolates with cocoa butter, sugar, and vanilla added. Bittersweet chocolate contains less sugar than semisweet chocolate.

White chocolate is "false" chocolate in that it contains no chocolate liquor. It is just cocoa butter, milk solids, sugar, and flavorings. The best white chocolate is made with just cocoa butter; look for Callebaut or Tobler Narcisse.

CHOCOLATE TIPS

There are a few things to keep in mind when you are working with chocolate:

- Chocolate melts most easily if it is grated or chopped first.
- When grating chocolate, hold it with a paper towel so the heat of your hand doesn't warm and melt the chocolate.
- When you need a large quantity of grated chocolate, coarsely chop the chocolate, place it in a food processor, and pulse until it is finely ground.
- Melting chocolate at a very low temperature is critical to the final texture. It should be melted gradually in a warm water bath or chocolate warmer until the temperature reaches approximately 86°F. If over- or underheated, the chocolate will turn gray and lose its gloss. Temperatures over 115°F will make the chocolate thick and coarse.
- Make sure that the water in the bottom of the double boiler barely simmers and doesn't boil. Do not let the hot water touch the bottom of the pan containing the chocolate, because too high heat will scorch the chocolate.
- While the chocolate is melting, it must be protected from any contact with water or any other liquid, which would tend to cause the chocolate to stiffen and "seize."
- For the smoothest melted chocolate, stir it constantly; do not leave it unattended.
- Chocolate can also be melted in a microwave: Put the grated chocolate in a glass bowl, cover with plastic wrap, and microwave on high power for 30 seconds. Stir, and continue to microwave and stir at 30-second intervals until the chocolate is completely melted and smooth.

— *planning ahead* —

The mocha cream can be made up to 2 days ahead, covered, and refrigerated. The assembled cake, without the molding chocolate, should be prepared a day ahead, loosely covered, and refrigerated. The molding chocolate should be prepared and used the day you plan to serve the cake.

Chocolate Christmas Log

(BÛCHE DE NOËL)

Bûche de Noël, or Yule Log, is the traditional dessert served in French homes on Christmas Eve. This festive and delicious fantasy creation consists of rolled layers of moist sponge cake and rich mocha buttercream shaped to resemble a small log. The log is then covered with more buttercream patterned to resemble tree bark and decorated with meringue mushrooms, marzipan leaves, and fresh holly leaves. When sliced, the spiral layers of cake and cream suggest the growth rings of a tree.

One Christmas, instead of the traditional log shape, I made a large, round bûche resembling a slice through a tree trunk. I replaced the heavy buttercream with whipped cream slightly thickened with gelatin for body, flavored it with coffee and cinnamon, and used a chocolate wrapping crimped to resemble bark on the outside of the cake.

You will probably find yourself looking forward to making this bûche each year. It is as much fun to make as it is to eat and the results always guarantee rave reviews.

YIELD: 14 to 16 dessert servings

SPECIAL EQUIPMENT: A 17- by 11- by 1-inch jelly-roll pan; a 13- by 19-inch sheet of parchment paper (or wax paper)

MOCHA CREAM

2 teaspoons unflavored gelatin (1 envelope)
2 cups heavy cream, well chilled
3 tablespoons instant espresso powder
1 teaspoon ground cinnamon
1 cup confectioner's sugar, sifted

SPONGE CAKE

½ cup (3 ounces) slivered blanched almonds (see Cook's Notes)
½ cup sugar
6 large eggs, separated
1 egg white
¼ teaspoon salt
½ cup plus 2 tablespoons cake flour, sifted
2 tablespoons unsalted butter, melted and cooled
Unsweetened cocoa powder, for dusting

RUM SYRUP

¼ cup sugar
2 tablespoons rum

Confectioner's sugar, for dusting

MOLDING CHOCOLATE

7 ounces semisweet chocolate, grated
2 ounces unsweetened chocolate, grated
¼ cup light corn syrup
1½ teaspoons rum or cognac
Confectioner's sugar, for kneading and rolling

2 tablespoons confectioner's sugar
2 tablespoons unsweetened cocoa powder
Meringue mushrooms, marzipan leaves, and/or fresh pine sprigs (see Cook's Notes)

Place a large mixing bowl and the beaters of your electric mixer in the refrigerator to chill for at least 30 minutes.

PREPARE THE MOCHA CREAM: Put ¼ cup cold water in a small saucepan, and sprinkle the gelatin over. Set aside and let soften for 5 minutes. Then heat the mixture over low heat, swirling until the gelatin is completely dissolved and no grains remain. Remove from the heat and let cool for 5 minutes.

In the chilled bowl, place the cream, espresso powder, cinnamon, and confectioner's sugar, and stir with a spatula to combine. Whip the cream with an electric mixer at low speed until slightly thickened, about 3 minutes. While beating, drizzle in the dissolved gelatin in a slow, steady stream. Then increase the speed to high and continue to whip the cream until it holds stiff peaks, about 2 to 3 minutes longer. Stop once or twice to scrape down the sides of the bowl with the spatula. Do not overbeat, or the cream will turn into butter. Cover and refrigerate the mocha cream until set, about 2 to 3 hours, or overnight.

Preheat the oven to 400°F. Adjust a rack one third up from the bottom of the oven. Lightly grease the jelly-roll pan. Line the bottom and sides of the pan with the piece of parchment paper; the paper should overhang the short ends by 1 inch. Grease and lightly flour the paper. Set the pan aside.

PREPARE THE SPONGE CAKE: Spread the almonds in a small baking dish. Place the dish in the oven and toast, shaking the dish and checking the nuts occasionally to make sure they don't burn, until the nuts are fragrant and golden brown, about 8 minutes. Remove from the oven and allow the nuts to cool. Place the nuts and 2 tablespoons of the sugar in a food processor. Process until finely ground. Set aside.

In the large bowl of an electric mixer, beat the egg yolks with 1 teaspoon hot water at high speed until lemon-colored, about 3 minutes. Gradually beat in the remaining 6 tablespoons sugar and continue to beat at high speed for 5 minutes longer, or until the mixture has the consistency of thick cream and is ivory-colored. Set aside.

In a large, clean, dry copper, glass, or stainless steel mixing bowl, beat the 7 egg whites and the salt with an electric mixer at high speed until the whites hold stiff peaks, about 1½ to 2 minutes. Do not overbeat, or the mixture will be dry.

Place half the whites on top of the beaten yolks. Sift half the flour over and sprinkle half the ground nuts on top. With a spatula, gently fold the mixture together just until blended. Fold in the remaining whites, flour, and nuts in the same manner. Transfer half of the batter into the egg white bowl and fold in the melted butter. Fold in the remaining batter.

Pour the batter into the prepared pan and spread it evenly with a metal spatula. Bake the cake for 6 or 7 minutes, or until it is just set, lightly puffed, and browned

— cook's notes —

Meringue mushrooms and marzipan leaves are available in gourmet shops and in some French-style bakeries around Christmastime.

Assemble all the ingredients and equipment before you begin.

It is best to use the molding chocolate right after it has been rolled out, while it's still soft and pliable.

Hazelnuts can replace the almonds in the sponge cake. *To toast hazelnuts,* spread them, with their skins on, in a single layer in a small baking dish and bake in a preheated 350°F oven, shaking the dish occasionally, until the nuts are golden under the skin (rub off some skin to test), about 15 minutes. Wrap the nuts in a clean towel and rub the cloth to loosen the skins. Remove the nuts one by one and rub off and discard the skins. Grind the nuts as instructed above.

on top. Remove the pan from the oven. Let the cake cool slightly in the pan on a rack, about 2 to 3 minutes.

Lightly dust the top of the cake with cocoa powder. Grasping the paper overhangs, lift the cake out of the pan and place it on a work surface, with a long side facing you. Starting at a long side, firmly roll up the cake and paper, jelly-roll fashion. Wet and wring out a large clean kitchen towel. Wrap it around the rolled cake. Place the roll seam side down on a rack to cool completely.

PREPARE THE RUM SYRUP: In a small saucepan, combine the sugar and ½ cup water. Bring the liquid to a boil over moderately high heat and boil until it is syrupy and reduced to about ¼ cup, about 5 minutes. Remove from the heat and stir in the rum. Cool.

ASSEMBLE THE CAKE: Unroll the cake, leaving it on the paper. Brush the cake all over with the rum syrup. Evenly spread half of the mocha cream over the cake. Using a long sharp knife, cut the cake crosswise into eleven 1½-inch-wide strips. Cut through the paper as well, but do not separate the strips at this point.

Grasping the ends of the strip of paper, slide one strip away from the others. Roll up the strip tightly into a coil, removing the paper as you roll. Place the coil faceup in the middle of a doily-lined cake stand or a large serving platter. Using a cake spatula, pick up a second cake strip and, starting at the end of the first coil, wrap the strip around the coil, cream side in. Continue wrapping the remaining cake strips around the coil in the same manner to form a large spiral.

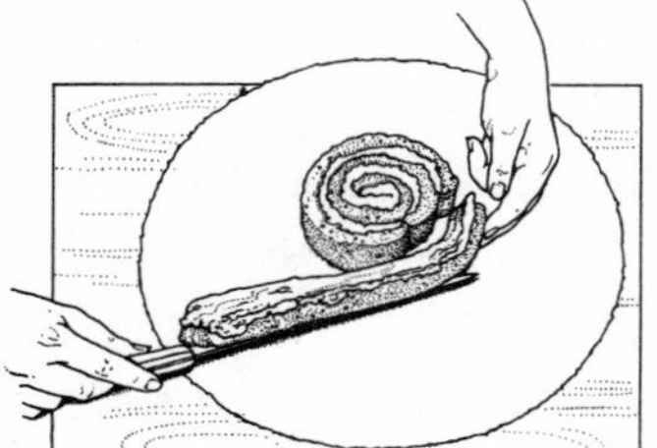

Spread the remaining mocha cream over the top and sides of the cake, smoothing it with a spatula. Dust the top of the cake generously with confectioner's sugar. To create the "tree rings," spread some cocoa powder on a large piece of wax paper. Dip the rims of various cups, bowls, and plates of increasing diameters into the cocoa powder, then press each lightly on top of the cake in order to mark a series of rings. Refrigerate the cake.

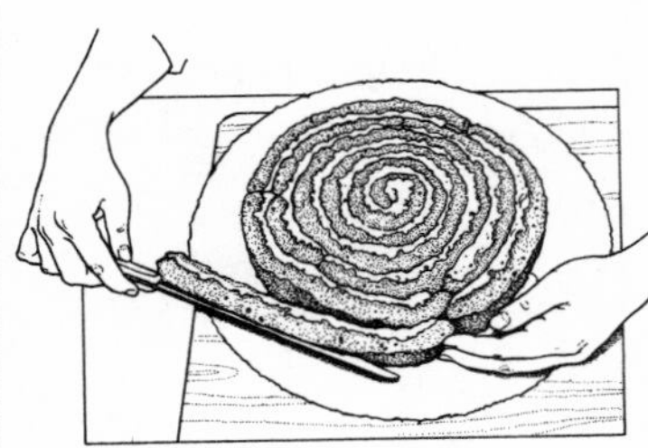

PREPARE THE MOLDING CHOCOLATE: Put both chocolates in the top of a small double boiler over simmering water. Melt over low heat, stirring constantly with a spatula or wooden spoon until the chocolate is very smooth and shiny. Remove from the heat and add the corn syrup and liquor. Using a wooden spoon, mix the chocolate vigorously (the chocolate will start to "seize"; don't worry, you are doing just fine) until the chocolate gradually thickens and leaves the sides of the bowl to form a loose, soft mass. The stirring should take no longer than a minute; do not overwork the chocolate or its oils may separate.

Place the chocolate in the center of an 11- by 16-inch-long sheet of plastic wrap on a cool flat surface. Level the chocolate with a spatula. Cover the chocolate with a second sheet of plastic wrap the same size as the first sheet. Using a rolling pin, gently roll the chocolate into a rectangle about 10 by 15 inches and ⅛ inch thick. Leaving the chocolate covered, set aside at room temperature away from any heat source for 1 to 1½ hours to partially set, until the chocolate is no longer wet but still very pliable. If at first it's still too wet to handle, let it sit for 5 to 10 minutes more but do not allow it to harden or it will become difficult to knead.

Remove the plastic wrap from the chocolate. Generously dust a work surface with confectioner's sugar. Gather the chocolate into a ball. If the chocolate has dried out and cracks or crumbles a little, don't be concerned. The chocolate will soften and come together again after kneading. Knead it briefly, pressing it into the confectioner's sugar as you knead, until soft and no longer sticky. Knead in a little more confectioner's sugar. The molding chocolate should feel very soft and smooth.

Brush off any chocolate crumbs left on the work surface; the surface should be dry, or the chocolate will stick.

Lightly dust the work surface and a rolling pin with confectioner's sugar, and roll the chocolate out into a rectangle about 10 by 20 inches long. As you roll the chocolate, lift the sheet of chocolate from time to time and dust the surface underneath with a little more confectioner's sugar to prevent sticking.

Using a sharp paring knife, cut the chocolate rectangle lengthwise into two bands measuring about 5 by 20 inches. Cover one band with a kitchen towel to prevent drying out. Loosely wrap the other chocolate band halfway around the sides of the cake, pleating and crimping the chocolate to simulate tree bark. Repeat with the second chocolate band in the same fashion to completely cover the sides of the cake. Press the ends of the chocolate bands together so they meet and adhere to the cake.

Decorate the cake with meringue mushrooms, marzipan leaves, and/or fresh pine sprigs. Dust the mushrooms with additional cocoa. Refrigerate until ready to serve.

— planning ahead —

The mousse is better if allowed to sit overnight, or even up to 2 days. It can be frozen as well. Bring it to room temperature before filling the purses. The raspberry sauce can be made 1 day ahead, covered, and refrigerated. The molding chocolate should be prepared and used the day you plan to serve this dessert. The assembled purses can be frozen very successfully. Before serving, thaw them in the refrigerator overnight.

Chocolate Purses with Rhubarb-Raspberry Mousse

I love everything about this dessert. Its look is chocolatey, sophisticated, and mysterious. Its texture is firm on the outside and soft on the inside. Its taste is not too rich or too sweet, but soul-satisfying. The winning flavor combination of sweet raspberries, tart rhubarb, and slightly bitter chocolate, with the striking presentation, will make a spectacular impression on your guests.

YIELD: 4 purses, enough for 4 dessert servings

RHUBARB-RASPBERRY MOUSSE

1½ cups (about ½ pound) fresh or frozen rhubarb, finely diced
⅓ cup sugar
1 teaspoon unflavored gelatin
¼ cup sour cream
½ cup fresh raspberries
½ cup heavy cream, well chilled

RASPBERRY SAUCE

2 cups fresh raspberries
5 tablespoons confectioner's sugar

MOLDING CHOCOLATE

7 ounces semisweet chocolate, grated
2 ounces unsweetened chocolate, grated
¼ cup light corn syrup
1½ teaspoons rum or cognac
Confectioner's sugar, for kneading and rolling

Place a medium mixing bowl and the beaters of your electric mixer in the refrigerator to chill for at least 30 minutes.

MAKE THE MOUSSE: Combine the rhubarb and sugar in a medium saucepan. Cover and bring to a simmer over low heat. Cook for 8 to 10 minutes, or until the rhubarb is very soft. Transfer to the bowl of a food processor and purée. Transfer the purée to a medium nonreactive mixing bowl and set aside.

Put 2 tablespoons cold water in a small saucepan, and sprinkle the gelatin over. Set aside and let soften for 5 minutes. Heat the mixture over low heat, swirling until the gelatin is completely dissolved and no grains remain. Stir the gelatin into the puréed rhubarb and allow to cool. Then fold the sour cream and berries into the purée.

In the chilled bowl, whip the cream with an electric mixer at high speed until it holds soft peaks. Do not overbeat. Gently fold the whipped cream into the fruit mixture with a rubber spatula. Cover the mousse and refrigerate until it sets, about 4 hours, or overnight.

MAKE THE SAUCE: Combine the raspberries and confectioner's sugar in a small saucepan. Cook over low heat until the berries are soft, about 3 to 4 minutes. Transfer to a food processor or blender and purée. Strain through a fine-mesh strainer into a small bowl and discard the seeds. Stir 2 tablespoons of cold water into the sauce to thin. Transfer to a jar and refrigerate.

PREPARE THE MOLDING CHOCOLATE: Put both chocolates in the top of a small double boiler over simmering water. Melt over low heat, stirring constantly with a spatula or wooden spoon until the chocolate is very smooth and shiny. Remove from the heat and add the corn syrup and liquor. Using a wooden spoon, mix the chocolate vigorously (the chocolate will start to "seize"; don't worry, you are doing just fine) until the chocolate gradually thickens and leaves the sides of the bowl to form a loose, soft mass. The stirring should take no longer than a minute; do not overwork the chocolate or its oils may separate.

Divide the chocolate into 2 equal portions. Place one portion in the center of an 11- by 16-inch-long sheet of plastic wrap on a cool flat surface. Level the chocolate with a spatula. Cover the chocolate with a second sheet of plastic wrap the same size as the first sheet. Using a rolling pin, gently roll the chocolate into a rectangle about 10 by 15 inches and 1⁄16 inch thick. Leaving the chocolate still covered, set aside at room temperature away from any heat source for 30 to 45 minutes to partially set. Repeat with the remaining chocolate. When the chocolate is partially set, it should be no longer wet but still very pliable. If at first it's still too wet to handle, let it sit for about 5 minutes more but do not allow it to harden or it will become difficult to knead.

Remove the plastic wrap from one sheet of chocolate. Generously dust a work surface with confectioner's sugar. Gather the chocolate into a ball. If the chocolate has dried out and cracks or crumbles a little, don't be concerned. The chocolate will soften and come together again after kneading. Knead it briefly, pressing it into the confectioner's sugar as you knead, until soft and no longer sticky. If it feels sticky, knead in a little more confectioner's sugar. The molding chocolate should feel very soft and smooth.

Divide the chocolate in half and shape each half into a ball. Cover the balls with plastic wrap and set aside. Knead and shape the remaining sheet of chocolate in the same manner, for a total of 4 chocolate balls.

ASSEMBLE THE PURSES: Brush off any chocolate crumbs left on the work surface; the surface should be dry, or the chocolate will stick. Lightly dust the work surface and a rolling pin with confectioner's sugar. Slightly flatten one chocolate ball and gently roll it out into a circle about 9 inches in diameter. As you roll the chocolate, be sure to lift it from time to time and dust the surface underneath with a little more confectioner's sugar to prevent the chocolate from sticking.

continued

— *cook's notes* —

It is best to use the molding chocolate right after it has been rolled out, while it's still soft and pliable.

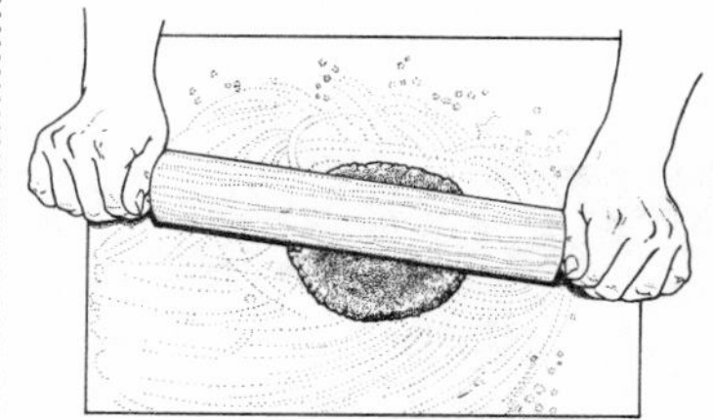

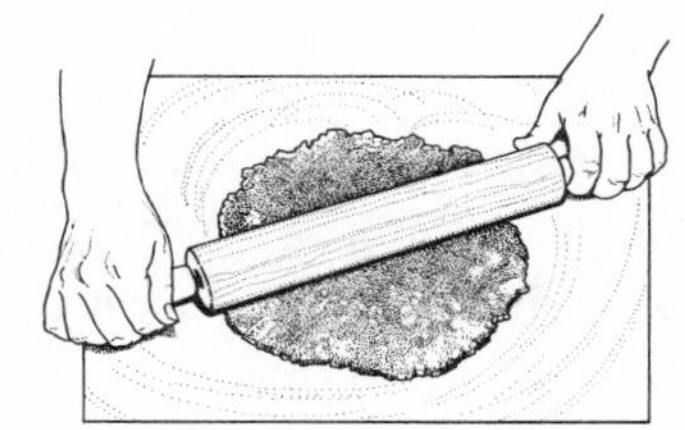

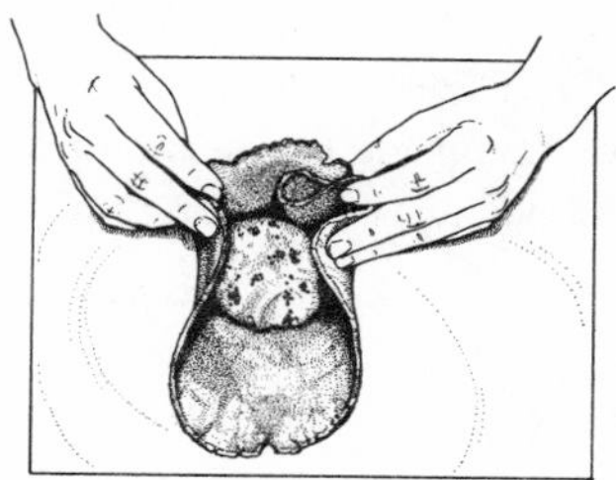

Place one quarter (about ⅓ cup) of the mousse in the center of the chocolate circle. Gather the sides up to enclose the filling. Pinch the purse at the neck to seal in the mousse, allowing the top edges of the purse to fan out. Transfer the purse to a large platter, loosely cover with plastic wrap, and refrigerate.

Repeat rolling and filling the remaining balls of chocolate to make 3 more purses. Cover and refrigerate until ready to serve.

TO SERVE: Place a chocolate purse on each chilled dessert plate and spoon some raspberry sauce around it.

Chocolate Sushi Truffle

— planning ahead —

The white and dark chocolate truffle should be made up to 2 days ahead, covered, and refrigerated. The molding chocolate should be prepared and used the day you plan to serve this dessert. The chocolate logs can be tightly sealed in a plastic bag and frozen for up to 1 month. Thaw them overnight in the refrigerator before cutting into sushi.

These are pop-in-your-mouth sweets with layers of dark and white chocolate truffle wrapped in a sheet of firm chocolate. When cut, the "sushi" displays two dramatic, yin-yang colors.

With flavors reminiscent of a rich fudge bar, this deeply chocolatey dessert definitely falls into the "death by chocolate" category. The sushi also make splendid gifts for holidays or special occasions.

YIELD: Four 10-inch-long rolls, or about 60 "sushi"

WHITE CHOCOLATE TRUFFLE

8 ounces top-quality white chocolate (such as Callebaut or Tobler Narcisse), grated
¼ cup hot water
3 tablespoons unsalted butter, at room temperature
1½ tablespoons Grand Marnier, rum, or cognac

DARK CHOCOLATE TRUFFLE

⅓ cup plus 2 tablespoons heavy cream
1½ tablespoons unsalted butter, at room temperature
4 ounces top-quality semisweet chocolate, grated
1 tablespoon unsweetened Dutch-process cocoa powder
2 teaspoons Grand Marnier, rum, or cognac

Confectioner's sugar, for kneading and rolling
Unsweetened cocoa powder, for dusting

MOLDING CHOCOLATE

7 ounces semisweet chocolate, grated
2 ounces unsweetened chocolate, grated
¼ cup light corn syrup
1½ teaspoons rum or cognac

MAKE THE WHITE CHOCOLATE TRUFFLE: Place the white chocolate and hot water in the top of a small double boiler over simmering water. Melt over low heat, stirring constantly with a spatula or wooden spoon until the chocolate is very smooth and shiny. Remove from the heat and stir in the butter and liquor. Continue to stir until the mixture is perfectly smooth. Cover and refrigerate until set, about 6 hours, or overnight.

MAKE THE DARK CHOCOLATE TRUFFLE: Place the cream and butter in a saucepan and bring to a boil over moderate heat. Remove from the heat and stir in the chocolate, cocoa, and liquor. Continue to stir until the chocolate is completely melted and the mixture thickens slightly. Cover and refrigerate until set, about 6 hours, or overnight.

SHAPE THE TRUFFLE LOGS: Dust a piece of wax paper with confectioner's sugar. Divide the white chocolate truffle mixture into 4 portions. Dust your hands with additional confectioner's sugar, then roll out each portion of chocolate on the dusted wax paper to form a 10-inch-long log. Cover with plastic wrap and refrigerate to firm.

Dust another piece of wax paper with cocoa powder. Divide the dark chocolate truffle mixture into 4 portions, and repeat the rolling process to form 4 more logs. Cover and refrigerate until ready to wrap the logs.

PREPARE THE MOLDING CHOCOLATE: Put both chocolates in the top of a small double boiler over simmering water. Melt over low heat, stirring constantly with a spatula or wooden spoon until the chocolate is very smooth and shiny. Remove from the heat and add the corn syrup and liquor. Using a wooden spoon, mix the chocolate vigorously (the chocolate will begin to "seize"; don't worry, you are doing just fine) until the chocolate gradually thickens and leaves the sides of the bowl to form a loose, soft mass. The stirring should take no longer than a minute; do not overwork the chocolate or its oils may separate.

Divide the chocolate into 2 equal portions. Place one portion in the center of an 11- by 16-inch-long sheet of plastic wrap on a cool flat surface. Level the chocolate with a spatula. Cover the chocolate with a second sheet of plastic wrap the same size as the first sheet. Using a rolling pin, gently roll the chocolate into a rectangle about 10 by 15 inches and 1/16 inch thick. Roll the remaining chocolate in the same manner. Leaving the rolled chocolate covered, set aside at room temperature away from any heat source for 30 to 45 minutes to partially set, until the chocolate is no longer wet but still very pliable. If at first it's still too wet to handle, let it sit for about 5 minutes more but do not allow to harden or it will become difficult to knead.

continued

— cook's notes —

It is best to use the molding chocolate right after it has been rolled out, while it's still soft and pliable.

Remove the plastic wrap from one sheet of chocolate. Generously dust a work surface with confectioner's sugar. Gather the chocolate into a ball. If the chocolate has dried out and cracks or crumbles a little, don't be concerned. The chocolate will soften and come together again after kneading. Knead it briefly, pressing it into the confectioner's sugar as you knead, until it is soft and no longer sticky. If it feels sticky, knead in a little more confectioner's sugar. The chocolate should feel very soft and smooth. Shape the chocolate into a ball, cover with plastic wrap, and set aside. Knead and shape the remaining sheet of chocolate in the same manner.

Brush off any chocolate crumbs left on the work surface; the work surface should be dry, or the chocolate will stick as you roll it. Lightly dust the work surface and a rolling pin with confectioner's sugar. Slightly flatten one chocolate ball and roll it out into a rectangle slightly larger than 10 by 15 inches. As you roll the chocolate, be sure to lift it from time to time and dust the surface underneath with a little confectioner's sugar to prevent sticking.

Using a sharp paring knife and a ruler, trim the edges of the chocolate into a neat 10- by 15-inch rectangle. Cut the sheet in half crosswise to obtain two 7½- by 10-inch sheets. Stack the sheets, cover tightly with plastic wrap, and set aside at room temperature.

Roll and cut the remaining ball of chocolate in the same fashion, for a total of 4 sheets of molding chocolate.

SHAPE THE SUSHI LOGS: Place a sheet of molding chocolate on the work surface with a longer side toward you. Place a white truffle log on the bottom of the chocolate sheet. Place a dark truffle log right next to the white one, then press them lightly together to make them adhere. Roll up the molding chocolate as tightly as you can without squeezing the truffle inside. Gently press the seam to seal. Wrap the chocolate roll in plastic wrap and refrigerate.

Repeat with the remaining truffles and molding chocolate sheets to make 3 more rolls. Cover and refrigerate until firm.

TO SERVE: Generously dust the logs with cocoa powder. Using a sharp knife, cut with a sawing motion into ¾-inch "sushi."

appendix

Chicken Broth

Chicken broth is the most versatile of all stock. It can be substituted for beef, veal, and other meat stocks, even fish and vegetable broths. Once you have a good broth you are almost guaranteed great soups and sauces. Although chicken broth is normally made with chicken bones, I like to make mine with chicken wings, which are inexpensive but very flavorful and give the stock extra body. To obtain a clear broth, do not disturb it in any way as it cooks.

YIELD: About 3½ quarts

SPECIAL EQUIPMENT: An 8- to 10-quart soup pot; a 5-quart soup pot

6 pounds chicken wings
4 medium turnips, peeled and quartered
2 medium carrots, peeled and quartered
2 large onions, peeled and halved
1 stalk celery, washed and cut into large chunks
1 medium leek, trimmed, quartered, and washed
8 large garlic cloves, crushed and peeled
3 bay leaves
1 tablespoon black peppercorns
½ bunch fresh thyme or 1 tablespoon dried thyme leaves, crumbled
1½ tablespoons salt
Stems from 1 bunch fresh parsley

Rinse the chicken wings well under cold running water.

Place the wings and 4½ quarts of water in a deep stockpot and bring to a boil over high heat. Boil, skimming off all the foam as it comes to the surface, for about 5 minutes. Add all the remaining ingredients and bring back to a boil. Reduce the heat to moderately low to maintain the liquid at a steady simmer. Partially cover the pot and simmer gently until all the ingredients have sacrificed their flavors to the stock, about 2½ hours. Do not disturb the broth as it simmers. When the broth is ready, the wings should be cooked through and almost falling apart.

Remove the pot from the heat and let cool. Carefully strain the liquid through a strainer or colander lined with a double layer of dampened cheesecloth into a clean 5-quart soup pot. You should have about 16 cups (4 quarts) stock. Discard the solids. Taste the broth for strength. If its flavor is weak, boil it over high heat to concentrate its strength, about 10 to 15 more minutes.

If the broth is to be used immediately, degrease it by skimming all the fat off the surface with a ladle, using a circular motion. If the broth is not to be used immediately, let it cool completely without degreasing it. Tightly covered, the stock can be stored for up to 5 days in the refrigerator. Remove the layer of fat that has congealed on top before using.

For longer storage, chicken stock can be frozen for up to 2 months. Transfer the broth to smaller nonreactive containers (e.g., plastic, glass, or stainless steel). It is helpful to use containers of different sizes, as recipes may call for varying amounts of stock. It is also a good idea to freeze some broth in ice cube trays for the purpose of adding small amounts to certain dishes. When the cubes are solid, they can be transferred to plastic bags and stored in the freezer. Once the broth has been thawed, use it immediately. Do not refrigerate or refreeze.

Beef Broth

A good beef stock is the basis for numerous soups, sauces, and stews. It can be made in large quantities and frozen for future use. This is one of those things that take time to prepare, but it is not complicated. Don't bother peeling the vegetables. The peels will give a rich color to the stock. Once the broth is cooked, the beef brisket can be used for other things, such as sandwiches or a beef hash.

YIELD: About 3 quarts

SPECIAL EQUIPMENT: An 8- to 10-quart soup pot; a 4-quart bowl

5 pounds beef bones, preferably marrow and knuckle bones, sawed into 2-inch pieces (have the butcher do this)
5 pounds lean brisket or chuck
8 whole cloves
4 bay leaves
2 large onions (unpeeled), halved
4 medium parsnips, quartered
2 medium carrots, quartered
1 large head garlic, halved crosswise
1 stalk celery, cut into large chunks
1 small bunch fresh parsley
1 tablespoon black peppercorns
1½ tablespoons salt

Rinse the bones and place them into a deep stockpot. Add water to cover and bring to a rolling boil over high heat. Boil vigorously, skimming off all of the foam as it comes to the surface, for about 5 minutes. Drain the bones, discarding the liquid. Rinse the bones and the stockpot.

Place the bones back in the stockpot and add 4 quarts of water. Bring to a boil over high heat, then reduce the heat to moderately low to maintain the liquid at a steady simmer. Cook, uncovered, until the bones have sacrificed their flavors to the stock, about 3 hours. Keep an eye on the stock; as the liquid boils away, add just enough fresh water to keep the bones covered.

Use a large slotted spoon to remove all the bones from the pot; discard. Add the meat and 2 quarts of water to the pot. If the meat isn't quite covered with liquid, add up to 2 cups more water. Bring to a boil over high heat, and boil, skimming off all the foam as it comes to the surface, for about 5 minutes. Use 2 cloves to pin a bay leaf to the flat surface of each onion half. Add the studded onions and all the remaining ingredients and bring back to the boil. Reduce the heat to moderately low to maintain the liquid at a steady simmer. Partially cover the pot and simmer gently until all the ingredients have sacrificed their flavors to the stock, about 2 hours. Do not disturb the broth as it cooks. Keep an eye on the stock; as the stock boils away, add just enough water to keep the meat covered.

Remove the meat from the pot and reserve it for another use. Remove the pot from the heat and let cool, undisturbed. Carefully strain the liquid through a strainer or colander lined with a double layer of dampened cheesecloth into a clean 4-quart bowl or container. Discard the solids. You should have about 11 to 12 cups of stock.

If the broth is to be used immediately, degrease it by skimming all the fat off the surface with a ladle, using a circular motion. If the broth is not to be used immediately, let it cool completely without degreasing it. Tightly covered, the stock can be stored for up to 5 days in the refrigerator. Remove the layer of fat that has congealed on top before using.

For longer storage, beef stock can be frozen for up to 2 months. Transfer the broth to smaller nonreactive containers (e.g., plastic, glass, or stainless steel). It is helpful to use containers of different sizes, as recipes may call for varying amounts of stock. It is also a good idea to freeze some broth in ice cube trays for the purpose of adding small amounts to certain dishes. When the cubes are solid, they can be transferred to plastic bags and stored in the freezer. Once the stock has been thawed, use it immediately. Do not refrigerate or refreeze.

Crème Fraîche

This thickened soured cream is reminiscent of the French specialty made from raw cream allowed to mature naturally. Crème fraîche is great as a substitute for sour cream in cooking because it is less likely to curdle when added to hot mixtures. For a refreshing dessert, serve it chilled over sliced fruits. Crème fraîche should be prepared at least two days before using. Covered and refrigerated, it will keep for up to a month.

YIELD: About 2 cups

1 cup heavy cream
2 tablespoons buttermilk
⅔ cup sour cream

Place the heavy cream in a small saucepan over moderately low heat. Heat just until the cream reaches a temperature between 110°F and 115°F. Remove the pan from the heat, and whisk in the buttermilk and sour cream. Pour the mixture into a glass jar, cover, and let the mixture stand in a warm place (about 75°F) for about 18 to 20 hours, or until the cream is thickened.

Refrigerate the crème fraîche. Use it within 1 month. If some liquid collects in the bottom of the jar, don't stir it back into the cream. The thicker the cream stays, the better it is.

INDEX

ABOUT THE AUTHOR

Nicole Routhier was born in Saigon to a Vietnamese mother and a French father. At a very young age she developed a great interest in cooking from her mother, who owned a restaurant in Laos. As a teenager, Ms. Routhier lived in France and Belgium, where she became versed in European styles of food preparation. Currently she is a professional chef and teacher in New York City. Her first book, *The Foods of Vietnam*, won the IACP best book of the year award (1989).